AMERICAN GUIDE SERIES

CONNECTICUT

A GUIDE TO ITS ROADS, LORE, AND PEOPLE

Written by Workers of the Federal Writers' Project of the Works Progress Administration for the State of Connecticut

SPONSORED BY WILBUR L. CROSS, GOVERNOR OF CONNECTICUT

Illustrated

D1481516

HOUGHTON MIFFLIN COMPANY - BOSTON

The Riverside Press Cambridge

Republished 1973
SOMERSET PUBLISHERS — a Division of Scholarly Press, Inc.
22929 Industrial Drive East, St. Clair Shores, Michigan 48080

348899

Library of Congress Cataloging in Publication Data

Shepard, Odell, 1884-1967.
   Connecticut, past and present.

   Reprint of the 1st ed. published by Knopf, New York,
London.
   1. Connecticut—History.   2.   Connecticut—
Description and travel.   I.   Title.
F94.S48   1973   974.6   72-84464
ISBN 0-403-02159-6

F
100
.F45
1973

PREFACE

THIS book is the result of the collaboration of many hands and many minds, and it would perhaps be strange to expect it to lie quietly between covers and compose a picture of its subject. Indeed, it would be a brave man who would sit down, alone or with company, and attempt a portrait of this State. Present-day Connecticut is too diversified and restless to yield an easy likeness. Besides, a guidebook should not be overambitious. At best it can hope to provide a few thumbnail sketches, some directions to help the visitor, and a modicum of more or less relevant information to enlarge his understanding of what he will see. It must be forever pointing and turning from one thing to the next. The section, *Notations on the Use of the Book*, will explain the method of assembling this material. In the end, it must properly be left to the visitor to shape his own impressions into an individual whole.

A hundred years ago this would have been a vastly simpler process. In 1836 John Warner Barber was driving from town to town in his horse and buggy, gathering material for his 'Historical Collections,' 'relating to the History and Antiquities of Every Town in Connecticut with Geographical Descriptions,' and making a 'general collection of interesting facts, traditions, biographical sketches, anecdotes, etc.' The prospectus-like title of his book is a promise of variety amply justified by the contents, but the modern reader or imitator is more impressed by the appealing unity of the subject. Barber was fortunate in the time at which he wrote. Connecticut was nearing the end of its formative period. The eighteenth-century pattern persisted, the industrial revolution was only about to begin.

As he went about among the 136 towns, his engravings reveal more tellingly than any camera the pleasing sameness of his view. Sometimes we find him seated on Round Hill taking a northwest view of Farmington, or looking down on the south view of Tariffville with its flourishing carpet factory, while he discusses local affairs with a villager. When the smoke of commerce rises over some of the larger cities, it comes from steamboats along the river front or in the harbor, rather than from factory chimneys. The centers of the towns show the courthouse, a school, perhaps a jail, and always the church or churches, for Barber was traveling just after the finest period of church-building. The buildings, somewhat sparsely grouped even in the centers of population, are delineated with a certain homely veracity, a little pinched in their perspective, and the elongated steeples of the churches rise toward Heaven rather higher than a modern eye allows.

It is significant in the history of this State and even for the Connecticut of today that for a period of about sixty years, from 1780 to 1840, the homogeneous population remained comparatively static. While the other New England States increased from two to nine times, Connecticut could not quite achieve a fifty per cent gain in numbers. Never was Connecticut more independent nor its towns more sturdily conservative than during this first half century and more of the Republic. Hartford and New Haven, the two capitals, did not unduly dominate in 1800; they were merely two of the six towns with a population of over 5000. The largest, Stonington, had 5437 inhabitants; four towns had 4000 or more; there were fifteen over 3000; the other eighty-three were closely ranged, with three exceptions, between one and three thousand. Under the Constitution of 1818, this equality of the towns was perpetuated and local particularism maintained.

Constant emigration threatened to overbalance immigration and a high birth-rate. In this way, the more heady and adventurous elements were continually drawn off from the body politic and a conservative, stable base remained. The glacial soil of Connecticut, unimproved by fertilizers and new techniques of farming, was unfitted to support a large population. It was necessary to call upon Yankee ingenuity. This was first applied in commerce, in shipping, in shrewd marketing and hard bargaining. By the middle of the eighteenth century, the Yankee Pedlar had made his appearance; in the period 1780 to 1840 he flourished. The Sam Slicks went forth with their tinware and their wooden nutmegs, and a market was created along the Atlantic Seaboard and over the Appalachians to Detroit, St. Louis, even New Orleans. Small fortunes accumulated to furnish fresh capital, and the invention of the manufacturer was called upon to match the skill of the salesmen.

Long before the close of this period, the Yankee inventors had outstripped the Yankee pedlars. From the time the Patent Office opened in 1790, Connecticut inventors have led those of other States in number of patents in proportion to population. Hats, combs, cigars, seeds, clocks, silk thread, plows, axes, carpets, pins, kettles, brass pipe, tacks, hooks and eyes, vulcanized rubber, shaving soap, friction matches, spoons, engine lathes, threaded bolts, furniture, firearms: in all these fields and more, important patents gave Connecticut inventors and manufacturers a leading position. Every town had its local industry and the way was prepared for the transition from handicraft to mass production. Inventors in near-by towns would perfect the same invention: Simeon North of Berlin and Eli Whitney of New Haven can share the credit for introducing the system of interchangeable parts and standardized production into the manufacture of firearms. The seeds of the industrial revolution were scattered far and wide through the State and the Nation.

It was also the period of Noah Webster, of Timothy Dwight, of the Hartford Wits, of Oliver Wolcott, the moderator. When the Hartford Wits looked across the border into Rhode Island or Massachusetts, they were perturbed: 'There Chaos, Anarch old, asserts his sway,' they told the inhabitants of Connecticut. Timothy Dwight became President of Yale and drew the students back down the sawdust trail to the old-time Congregationalism. 'Pope Dwight,' they called him, 'a walking repository of the venerable Connecticut *status quo.*' Noah Webster, who helped the country achieve a measure of linguistic independence and whose spelling became more and more American, was a stout Federalist and defender of the established order. Even the moderate Oliver Wolcott, who presided at the making of the liberalizing Constitution of 1818, was no great radical of post-Jeffersonian days.

Looked back upon, it is an age of almost paradoxical contrast, with its conservatism politically and socially, and the radical changes preparing in its factories and workshops, a strange mixture of the past and future working together in a harmonious present, which seemed likely to prolong itself indefinitely. The visitor in search of a portrait of Connecticut might well keep in mind these years of growth and stability when the balance shifted slowly from a long colonial age of agriculture and commerce toward the industrial age of railroads, immigration, and mass production. Then, for a protracted period, the pattern of Connecticut living was stamped deep into the character of its people and its civilization. Successive waves of immigration have altered it surprisingly little. Perhaps this civilization, an epitome of many deeply rooted American characteristics, may be able to assimilate new elements and still maintain its finest qualities as a tradition and a guide to future generations. '*Qui transtulit sustinet.*'

It remains to express our indebtedness to the citizens of Connecticut who have contributed materially to this work; so large is their number that we can thank only a few of our benefactors. We are especially indebted to Mr. Edgar L. Heermance, whose 'Connecticut Guide' was our predecessor and inspiration, and who graciously allowed us the use of his files containing valuable field notes and historical information. The librarians of the Yale University Library, the New Haven Public Library, the Hartford Public Library, and Miss Scofield of the New Haven Colony Historical Society have generously given us their trained assistance.

We have received valuable aid and criticism from Mr. Norbert Lacy, and Dr. Nelson Burr of the Historical Records Survey; Professor Leonard Labaree, and Mr. Gerald M. Capers of Yale University; Professor George Matthew Dutcher of Wesleyan University; Mr. J. Frederick Kelly, and Mr. George Dudley Seymour of New Haven; Mr. A. Everett Austin of the Avery Memorial, Hartford; Mr. John Phillips of the Yale Gallery of Fine Arts; Mr. William L. Warren of the American Index of Design; Mr. Edward H. Rogers, Principal of the Devon High School; Mr. Arthur W. Brockway, ornithologist, of Hadlyme; Mr. John J. Stevens, Principal of the Ansonia High School; Mr. Goodrich K. Murphy, assistant to passenger traffic manager, of the New York, New Haven and Hartford Railroad; and Mr. Joseph Tone, State Commissioner of Labor.

Professor C. R. Longwell of Yale University has contributed the essay on *Geology*. Mr. Wayland Wells Williams, State Director of the Federal Art Project, has helped us in innumerable ways, besides contributing the essay on *Connecticut Art*, and much of the material on Yale University.

Mr. Samuel R. Chamberlain has kindly allowed us to use several photographs from his notable Connecticut series; the Scovill Manufacturing Company, the American Brass Company, the Chase Brass and Copper Company, Inc., the Pratt and Whitney Company, the Sikorsky Aviation Corporation, the Ætna Life Insurance Company, the Travelers' Insurance Company, and the New York, New Haven and Hartford Railroad have contributed photographs.

In administering and carrying out this Project we have had the constant co-operation of Miss Mary M. Hughart, State Director of Women's and Professional Projects, and Administrators Vincent J. Sullivan, Robert A. Hurley, and Matthew A. Daly. We owe a special debt of gratitude to Senator Daly, in whose administration this book was begun, for his friendly advice and counsel.

Finally, we are under great obligations to His Excellency, the Governor of this State, Wilbur L. Cross, for his distinguished sponsorship and foreword, and to Mr. Philip Hewes, the Governor's Executive Secretary, who gave freely of his time to offer most useful criticism.

This volume was prepared under the editorial direction of Mr. Joseph Gaer, Editor-in-Chief of the New England Guides and Chief Field Supervisor of the Federal Writers' Project.

JOHN B. DERBY, *State Director*

CONTENTS

I. CONNECTICUT: THE GENERAL BACKGROUND

II. MAIN STREET AND VILLAGE GREEN

(City and Town Descriptions and City Tours)

III. HIGH ROADS AND LOW ROADS (TOURS)

(Mile-by-Mile Description of the State's Highways)

ILLUSTRATIONS AND MAPS

MAPS

NOTATIONS ON THE USE
OF THE BOOK

General Information on the State contains practical information for the State as a whole; the introduction to each city and tour description also contains specific information of a practical sort.

The *Essay Section* of the *Guide* is designed to give a brief survey of the State's natural setting, history, and social, economic, and cultural development. Limitations of space forbid elaborately detailed treatments of these subjects, but a classified bibliography is included in the book. A great many persons, places, and events mentioned in the essays are treated at some length in the city and tour descriptions; these are found by reference to the index. The *State Guide* is not only a practical travel book; it will also serve as a valuable reference work.

The *Guide* is built on a framework of Tour Descriptions, written in general to follow the principal highways from south to north and from west to east, though they are easily followed in the reverse direction.

As a matter of convenience, lengthy descriptions of cities and towns are removed from the tour sections of the book and separately grouped in alphabetical order.

Each tour description contains cross-references to other tours crossing or branching from the route described; it also contains cross-references to all descriptions of cities and towns removed from the tour descriptions.

Readers can find the descriptions of important routes by examining the tour index or the tour key map. As far as possible, each tour description follows a single main route; descriptions of minor routes branching from, or crossing, the main routes are in smaller type. The newer and better highway usually carries the 'Alternate' highway number, such as US 6A, while the older route retains its original number.

Cumulative mileage is used on main and side tours, the mileage being counted from the beginning of each main tour or, on side tours, from the junction with the main route; mileage is started afresh on side routes branching from side routes. The mileage notations are at best relative, since totals depend to some extent on the manner in which cars are driven — whether they cut around other cars, round curves on the inside or outside of the road, and so forth. Then, too, the totals will in the future vary from those in the book because of road building in which curves will be eliminated and routes will by-pass cities and villages formerly on the routes.

Inter-State routes are described from and to the State Lines; in the *Index to Tours* and in the tour headings the names of the nearest out-of-State cities of importance on the routes are listed in parentheses so that travelers may readily identify the routes.

Descriptions of points of interest in the larger towns and cities are numbered and arranged in the order in which they can conveniently be visited.

Points of interest in cities, towns, and villages have been indexed separately rather than under the names of such communities, because many persons know the name of a point of interest, but are doubtful as to the name of the community in which it is situated.

GENERAL INFORMATION

Railroads: New York, New Haven & Hartford (N.Y., N.H. & H.), Central Vermont (C.V.), Central New England (C.N.E.).

Highways: Six Federal highways; State police highway patrol with occasional inspection of operator licenses and registration. State highways cleared and sanded during winter. Gasoline filling stations numerous on all main highways. Federal gas tax 1¢, State gas tax 3¢ (total tax 4¢).

Bus Lines: New England Transportation Co.; Greyhound Lines (national coverage); Short Lines (Springfield, Portland, New York, Waterbury, Worcester, and Boston); Arrow Line (New Haven, Hartford, Pittsfield, Mass., Albany, N.Y., Montreal, Canada); Blue Way Lines (Portland, Me., and Boston to New York, via Springfield and Worcester); National Trailways System; and several smaller lines.

Airlines: American Airlines Inc. (between Newark, N.J., and Boston, Mass.) stop at Hartford (*see Transportation Map*).

Waterways: Summer day excursions, Bridgeport to New York. Ferries from New London, Bridgeport, and Stamford to Long Island (*see General Information under those cities*).

Traffic Regulations: Motorists from States that do not require operator licenses must take out a Connecticut operator's license except when driving a vehicle registered in their own jurisdiction.

Speed: Maximum speed on Federal and State highways is indicated on roadside signs. In general, the rate of speed should at all times be 'reasonable,' with regard to the width, traffic, and use of the highways, intersections, and weather conditions. At no time is a maximum of more than 50 miles per hour permitted. White center lines are painted at all dangerous curves and hills. Drivers must keep to the right of these lines, and refrain from passing on stretches so marked, or at any intersection. Stops must be made not less than 10 feet behind trolley cars stopping to take on or let off passengers. On wide streets it is permissible to pass a stopped trolley at a distance of 10 feet or more. Hand signals required. No parking allowed within 10 feet of any fire hydrant, within 50 feet of any vehicle already parked on the opposite side of the highway, or with right-hand wheels more than 1 foot from curb.

Lights: Make full stop before entering or crossing 'through ways' indicated by STOP signs. Slowing down and shifting gears are not sufficient; make complete stop. No right turns on red lights, except where indicated.

Report at once all accidents involving any personal injury, or any property damage in excess of $25.

Specific traffic regulations noted in General Information of large cities. Reciprocal privileges extended visitors in regard to licenses and registration.

Reflectors, for safeguard when taillight fails, required on all visiting cars after September 1, 1937.

Accommodations: Tourist accommodations of every type are available in practically any part of the State. Inns, hotels, tourist houses, and cabins will be found within short distances on any main highway, rates ranging from 75¢ up. Trailer stops are not yet numerous, but are provided by many cabin owners. State-regulated tourist and trailer camps are maintained at Hammonasset Beach State Park (*see MADISON, Tour* 1), and at Rocky Neck State Park (*see EAST LYME, Tour* 1F).

Climate and Equipment: Summer travelers to Connecticut should be prepared for moderately warm weather, with infrequent hot and muggy days; nights are generally cool. Winter visitors should be prepared for sub-freezing to near zero weather, occasional snow storms and dangerous ice storms which make driving hazardous until the highway crews sand the roadways.

Poisonous Plants and Reptiles: Poison ivy, or three-leafed mercury, is common throughout the State, growing on stone walls, roadside trees, banks, and over old barns and buildings. After the first frost its leaves turn a deep scarlet, inviting the uninformed to pick it and become miserable within a few hours. Poison sumac is not as common, but is perhaps more irritating; this shrub is also found throughout the State but seldom beside the State highways.

Rattlesnakes are plentiful around Kent, Canaan Mountain, Glastonbury, and in sections of Salem. All these 'snake dens,' however, are off the beaten track, usually far from the highway, and are dangerous only to the hiker through rocky woodland or mountain area. Snake dens along hiking trails are marked, and there is usually a glass jar handy containing first aid treatment for snake bites. Copperheads are found in the swampy lowlands of Connecticut, and are dangerous because they strike without warning. It is therefore advisable to wear boots when walking through swamplands in the copperhead country.

Plant Regulations: Laurel, the Connecticut State Flower, which blossoms in woods and along the highways of the State during the month of June, must not be picked under penalty of the law.

Information Bureaus: State of Connecticut Publicity Commission, State Capitol, Hartford. Connecticut Chamber of Commerce, Dept. SN 35, 410 Asylum St., Hartford, Conn.

RECREATIONAL FACILITIES

Beaches and Camping Grounds: Three State parks (Sherwood Island, Hammonasset Beach, and Rocky Neck) bordering Long Island Sound provide clean, safe, properly protected bathing facilities. Camping grounds are open to the public, space is set aside for trailer parking, and the mosquito menace is reduced to the minimum. Pavilions and bathhouses are open during the summer and early autumn.

Inland waters also offer recreational opportunities. Lake Candlewood is the State's largest inland body of water, but Waramaug, Twin Lakes, or any one of the several larger lakes afford equally fine facilities for fishing, boating, or skating in season. Almost every one of the 169 towns has at least one good spot for the enjoyment of water or ice sports.

Fishing: Fishermen find ample opportunity for their sport in the 7619 miles of rivers and streams, or in the thousand lakes and ponds covering a total area of 43,597 acres. The 245 miles of shore line on Long Island Sound and the Atlantic Ocean are dotted with boat liveries, where qualified skippers personally conduct fishing parties or rent boats to the saltwater angler. Commercial swordfishermen often take paying guests, usually from the Stonington docks, to enjoy a sport as exciting as whaling.

Hunting: Shooting alongshore and on the Connecticut River is excellent. Migratory wildfowl pay their autumn call after a summer of fattening in the rice beds of northern lakes. Upland game birds have suffered from the encroachment of industrial and residential areas into their natural cover; but pheasants have partially replaced the native ruffed grouse and quail. Better control of shooting promises a gradual improvement in this sport. No eastern State offers better rabbit hunting; raccoons still frequent the heavy timber and swamplands; and squirrels are abundant, except when the nut crop fails and they are forced to migrate to other areas. Deer are protected in Connecticut, and have become so plentiful that the farmers often secure special permits for their destruction to save crops and young orchards.

Fish and Game Laws: (Digest) Licenses required of persons 16 years old and over. Issued by Town Clerks or by State Board of Fisheries and Game. Hunting license, resident $3.35; non-resident $10.35. Fishing license, resident $3.35; non-resident $5.35 minimum (residents of a State having a non-resident fee in excess of $5.35 are charged the same fee in Connecticut). Combination hunting and fishing licenses, residents $5.35; non-residents $14.35. For regulations and permits, write State Board of Fisheries and Game, State Office Building, Hartford, Conn., or apply to patrolmen on streams.

Boating: Yachtsmen will find safe anchorage and good service in numerous harbors, or quiet waters in the lee of green islands on Long Island Sound.

Motorboat enthusiasts can cross the State from the Sound to the Massachusetts State Line, via the Connecticut River, with only one short trip through locks at the Enfield Rapids. Canoe trips are possible on any one of Connecticut's three larger rivers. Trains take sportsfolk from the metropolitan area to Falls Village where, after assembling their portable craft, they embark on the Housatonic to enjoy the European sport of 'faltbootpaddeln' over a 17-mile course strewn with rapids and boulders.

Hiking: Hiking trails are well marked and never far from civilization. The great Appalachian Trail crosses the State, and many feeder trails, or short trails of local importance, thread their way through woodland and hill-country of entrancing beauty. Trail maps can be secured (for 25¢) from the Connecticut Forest & Park Association, 215 Church St., New Haven.

Riding: Riding has grown in popularity in Connecticut and many excellent stables rent saddle horses and riding togs. Although all of the main highways are hard-surfaced, there are many hundreds of miles of gravel or dirt roads where motor traffic is light and where riders can explore the back-country in perfect comfort and safety. Private property rights are carefully respected in this State, and wire fencing is the rule; but almost any farmer allows a rider to cross pastureland or other terrain not actually under a crop, if the request is properly made and if gates or barways are closed to prevent stock from roaming.

Hunt Clubs and Horse Shows: Hunt clubs are few and exclusive in Connecticut. The best pack of hounds in the State is at Watertown, but hunts at Durham, Fairfield, and Norfolk attract riders in season. As farm folk do not approve of fox hunting, most hunters either own or lease their own acreage. Horse shows of local importance are held at many widely separated points in the State. Harness racing is a feature at Danbury Fair (first week in October), and a few local tracks have their quota of lovers of 'silks and sulkies.' No running races are held within the State, but flat races and the occasional rather easy steeplechase of the amateur huntsfolk are staged in season. Four troops of National Guard cavalry, polo at Yale, Farmington Polo Association, and at Avon Old Farms, and an annual indoor horse show at the New Haven Arena complete the more serious side of the mounted sports card in Connecticut.

Climbing: Mountain climbing is not a popular pastime in the State, although the sheer cliffs of the Hanging Hills and the slightly easier slopes of Mt. Carmel tempt an occasional devotee of the Alpine art. The highest land in Connecticut is in the extreme northwestern corner, where Bear Mountain pierces the blue at 2355 ft. and Gridley Mountain rises to 2200 ft.

Bicycling: Cyclists pedal over many back roads, and the railroad encourages this sport by operating cycle trains from New York City to the Canaan Hills. Regulations covering the operation of cycles on the highways are concerned with the proper lighting of vehicles and the use of reflectors on the rear.

Winter Sports: Snow trains cross the State on their way from the larger cities to the Berkshires and the northern New England hills. Skating and hockey are favorite sports in every town. Bobsledding increases in popularity with the construction of better runs, but tobogganing is not practiced. Ski runs are many; the better clubs are in Litchfield County, where the snow falls earliest and stays longest.

Golfing: Golfers can always find a course within convenient reach.

Tennis: Tennis courts have been built in practically all municipal parks throughout the State.

CALENDAR OF ANNUAL EVENTS

(nfd — no fixed date)

March	nfd	New Haven	Paint and Clay Club art exhibit.
March	nfd	Hartford	Exhibit of work by Connecticut artists.
March	Easter Sunday	New London	Sunrise Service in Coast Guard Academy Bowl, 7 A.M.
		New Haven	Sunrise Service, East Rock Park.
	Easter Monday	New Haven	Egg Hunt, East Rock Park and Edgewood Park.
	Easter Week	New Haven	Easter Flower Show, East Rock Park Cineraria Show, Pardee Gardens, East Rock Park.
March	nfd	New Britain	Ukrainian Festival in memory of the Ukrainian bard, Taras Shevchenko; concert and folk dances presented in native costumes.
April	nfd	Hartford	Antique Exposition; exhibits and lectures.
April	nfd	Hartford	Spelling Bee (local finals), Bushnell Park.
May	1	Storrs	Connecticut State College May Day Exercises; pageant.
May	1	Willimantic	State Teachers' College May Day Exercises; pageant.
May	nfd	New Haven	Powder House Day; pageant based on historical episode.
May	2d wk	New Haven	Annual Iris Show, East Rock Park.
May	nfd	Hartford	Flower Mart and Show, Old State House.
May	2d or 3d Saturday	Derby	Blackwell Cup or Carnegie Cup Crew Race on Housatonic River.
May	nfd	Middlefield	Apple Blossom Festival, Lyman Orchards.
May	nfd	Farmington	Peach Blossom Time, Tunxis Orchards.
May	30	New Haven	Skeet Shooting; five-man team championship.
May	31	Hartford	Russians celebrate their national holiday with athletic events, folk dances, and songs, in Charter Oak Park.

June	mid-month	Winsted	Laurel Week.
June	mid-month	Hartford	Flower Show, Old State House. Rose Week, Elizabeth Park.
June	2d or 3d wk	New Haven	Yale University Commencement. Rose Show, Pardee Rose Gardens, East Rock Park (continuing through summer).
		New London	Yale-Harvard Freshman, Combination, and Junior Varsity Crew Races, A.M. Yale-Harvard Baseball Game, Mercer Field, P.M. Yale-Harvard Varsity Crew Race, 7 P.M. Graduation exercises of Coast Guard Academy. Graduation exercises of Connecticut College for Women.
June	15 to 20	Middletown	Wesleyan Commencement exercises; band concert and college sing.
June	nfd	Stratford	Skeet Shooting; Great Eastern States and National Telegraphic Championship, Remington Gun Club, at Lordship.
June	last wk	Greenwich	Dog Show, Greenwich Kennel Club.
June	29	Greenwich	Annual golf championship matches, Greenwich Country Club.
June	nfd	Lyme	Art exhibit begins, lasting through summer.
July		Falls Village	Subscription concerts every Sunday, under auspices Jacques Gordon Musical Foundation, Music Mountain.
July	2	Fairfield	Horse Show.
July	4	Greenwich	Scottish Games Association.
Aug.	1st Friday	East Hampton	Old Home Day Celebration; 3-day event; pageant, concerts, drum corps exhibition, parade.
Aug.	2d Saturday	Litchfield	Horse Show; fancy riding, jumping.
Aug.	nfd	Hartford	Lawn Bowling Tournament, Elizabeth Park.
Aug.	3d wk	Hartford	Gladiola Show, Old State House.
Aug.	nfd	Old Lyme	Art exhibition.
Aug.	nfd	Durham	Middlesex County 4-H Club Fair.
Aug.	nfd	West Goshen	Litchfield County 4-H Club Fair.

Aug.	nfd	Wolcott	New Haven County 4–H Club Fair.
Aug.	nfd	Long Island Sound	New York Yacht Club Cruise.
Aug.	21, 22	North Stonington	New London County 4–H Club Fair.
Aug.	latter part	Lyme	Hamburg Fair.
Sept.	nfd	West Avon	Hartford County 4–H Club Fair, Cherry Park.
Sept.	nfd	Goshen	Goshen Fair.
Sept.	nfd	Haddam Neck	Haddam Neck Fair.
Sept.	nfd	South Woodstock	Woodstock Fair.
Sept.	nfd	Old Saybrook	Horse Fair.
Sept.	(3 days before and including Labor Day)	Willimantic	Elks County Fair.
Sept.	nfd	Wethersfield	Horse Show.
Sept.	nfd	Greenwich	Horse Show.
Sept.	nfd	Brooklyn	Brooklyn Fair.
Sept.	nfd	Guilford	Guilford Fair.
Sept.	nfd	Hartford	Hartford County Food Exhibit, State Armory.
Oct.	1st wk	Danbury	Danbury Fair.
Oct.	1st wk	Harwinton	Harwinton Fair.
Oct.	2d wk	Durham	Durham Fair.
Oct.	nfd	Riverton	Riverton Fair.
Oct.	nfd	Stafford	Stafford Fair.
Oct.	27	New London	Navy Day celebration at U.S. Submarine Base.
Nov.	6	Hartford	Swedish population celebrates national holiday with songs and dances.
Nov.	nfd	New Haven	Chrysanthemum Show, East Rock Park.
Dec.	2d wk	Hartford	Connecticut Vegetable Growers' Meeting.
Dec.	nfd	Hartford	Pomological Show, Women's Club, Broad St.
Dec.	24	Hartford	Community sing, Prospect St.

I. CONNECTICUT: THE GENERAL BACKGROUND

GENERAL DESCRIPTION

CONNECTICUT, the 'Nutmeg State,' is one of the thirteen original States. From east to west it extends about ninety-five miles, from north to south about sixty miles. Its area of 4965 square miles could be contained in Texas fifty-three times; only two States, Rhode Island and Delaware, are smaller in size. It is bounded on the north by Massachusetts, on the east by Rhode Island, on the south by Long Island Sound, and on the west by New York. In 1936 the population was approximately 1,725,000.

The coastline of the State is typical of New England, rock-bound and rugged, with numerous sandy beaches and occasional 'salt meadows.' In general, the landscape is mildly rolling near Long Island Sound; toward the north, and especially toward the northwest, the slopes become more pronounced. The point of highest altitude is Bear Mountain, in the extreme northwest corner of the State, with an elevation of 2355 feet. There are two distinct series of hills, usually roughly designated as the eastern and western highlands, between which lies the central lowland interrupted by the traprock ridges of New Haven and Hartford Counties. The Berkshire Hills, extending south from Massachusetts and Vermont to the city of Danbury, provide most interesting scenery. Both the Norfolk and Litchfield Hills, famed in song and story, attract swarms of summer tourists, artists, and vacationists; many of these visitors have purchased secluded hill farms and return each summer.

Connecticut is rich in interesting and romantic place names, such as Dublin Street, Jangling Plains, Dark Entry, Cow Shandy, Dodgingtown, Padanaram, and the Abrigador. Many of the names of towns or topographical features are of English, Biblical, or Indian origin. What names could retain more of the flavor of old England than Greenwich, Cheshire, Durham, Cornwall, Avon, and Wallingford — to cite but a few? What terms are more redolent of the Old Testament than Canaan, Hebron, Goshen, Bethany, Lebanon, and Zoar? The Indian names, which are legion, have a delightfully primitive quality: Yantic, Cos Cob, Quassapaug, Naugatuck, Quinnipiac, Wequetequock. The very name of the State itself harks back to the earlier form 'Quinatucquet,' meaning 'upon the long river.'

Connecticut's scenic advantages have but recently been recognized as a tourist attraction. Forest-clad hills, kept green during the summer by abundant rainfall, lakes scattered over the State, and miles of breeze-swept bathing beaches along the Sound provide a variety of recreational facilities. Excellent highways make travel to these points easy. A well-kept and well-marked system of hiking trails and bridle paths invites the hiker and the rider to venture into country not reached by motor roads. In Connecticut the enthusiast may enjoy some of the wildest and most rugged scenery in the East. The gorge of the Mianus River on the Connecticut-New York State Line is considered one of the most primitive spots within a short distance of New York City. North of Old Lyme, the Devil's Hop Yard, now accessible to motorists, is marked by piney depths, massive granite boulders, and splashing streams. Near-by is the ghost town of Millington Green, a relic of the days when lumbering was carried on extensively. The panorama from the mesa-like Hanging Hills of Meriden is one of great beauty.

In contrast to the rough back country is the quiet neatness of the village green in each small community, adorned by its Congregational church and magnificent elms. Especially beautiful are the greens at Sharon, Woodstock, Tolland, Pomfret, and Windham. Those interested in well-proportioned churches of the Colonial period will delight in the handsome edifices of Canterbury, Killingworth, Litchfield, Lebanon, and Brooklyn. Towns unrivaled in the beauty of their elm-shaded main streets are Ridgefield, Lyme, Roxbury, Colebrook, Madison, and Litchfield. The usual country house is well painted and built far enough from the highway to insure a certain degree of privacy and dignity. White paint is spread with a lavish brush; green trim and blinds are popular. Occasionally a red-brick or yellow Colonial house varies this rural color scheme of white and green.

The country landscape, with its broad fields of different crops, offers varied shadings of green. Waving corn, hillside orchards, acres of shade-grown tobacco under netting that appears from a distance like a vast sea, meet the eye of the traveler and leave the impression of a land of plenty, a land that is kind to its people. The dairying section of Connecticut — and much of the land is devoted to dairying — furnishes the contrast of red barns, white farm houses, tall silos, and orderly fence rows against a background of alfalfa and timothy fields, with pasture land dotted with black and white Holstein or yellow and white Guernsey cattle. Connecticut is proud of her farms, and eighty-three per cent of the farmers are landowners. Very few farmhouses are left unpainted, although the older barns, usually with native pine, hemlock, or chestnut siding, are often weathered to a soft gray. Old rail fencing can still be seen in the back country, and the many walls of field stone are proof that a Connecticut farmer has to work for what he gets.

The winter scene in Connecticut is especially beautiful. The rolling character of the country lends itself readily to all manner of winter sports. Ski jumps of national importance are found at Norfolk and Colebrook River, where many meets are held. Professional ski jumpers and ski runners congregate at Salisbury, Norfolk, and Winsted, where competition is keen. The tourist is surprised to find winter sports' centers easily accessible over roads that have been cleared of snow and properly sanded. Connecticut offers many of the facilities of Banff and Lake Placid within easy driving distance of many of the large eastern cities.

Residents of New York City do not commonly realize that over the New Haven Railroad the distance from their city's limits to the Connecticut State Line is but twelve miles, and that at another point Connecticut comes within seven miles of the Hudson River. To such an extent does a corner of New England thrust itself into the metropolitan area! With the extension of the Hutchinson River Parkway in Westchester and the completion of the Merritt Parkway in Connecticut, a hitherto untapped region of beautifully wooded hills and rocky dells will be accessible to the motorist.

Connecticut is dotted with inns of various sorts. Hotels and garage service are generally excellent. Many rustic eating places border the highways in the back country. Here a barn has been equipped as a studio and lunch room; there an ancient house serves a light snack in the atmosphere of another day. Artists sketch along the country roads, and operate tourist houses for a supplementary income. In season, a system of State-inspected roadside markets cater to passers-by. The traveler along the Boston Post Road, with its gasoline stations and wayside restaurants, gets but a few glimpses of charming coastal villages and sequestered inland hamlets set among the hills; but let him wander off the beaten paths and he will discover a countryside much as it was in the pre-Revolutionary days.

Quiet country towns with close-clipped lawns and stately shade trees, picturesque islands offshore, sunrise over the hills of Cornwall, sunset over still pastures, the roar of Kent Falls and the silence of the Cathedral Pines — all these await the traveler who cares to venture away from the larger cities. Few States have more to offer in natural beauty, in contentment, and in peace.

Connecticut occupies approximately one-half the southern portion of the New England peneplain. The surface of the State has the characteristics of a gently undulating upland, with the Connecticut Valley lowland separating this upland into two nearly equal divisions. From the northern shore of Long Island Sound the land rises at the rate of twenty feet a mile to a general elevation of one thousand feet at the northern boundary; in the northwestern section of the State there are a few points where the altitude exceeds two thousand feet. As a contrast, the lowland attains a height of only one hundred feet at the northern border. The total area of this lowland is about six hundred square miles. Along the Massachusetts boundary, the lowland is about fifteen miles in width, and at New Haven, where it dips into the Sound, it narrows to a mere five miles. Such a condition is the result of a weak bed of rock eroding after the general upland surface had been elevated subsequent to its formation near sealevel. Within this bedrock was enough harder traprock to resist erosion; hence such features as the Hanging Hills of Meriden and the ridges in the vicinity of New Haven. These ridges are characterized by deep notches and high points that equal in elevation the upland levels east and west of the lowland region.

At East Haddam, where the Fall Line intersects the lower gorge of the Connecticut River, one hundred and forty-five earthquake epicenters were located by the French seismologist, F. de Montessus. More recent research indicates that the greatest intensity of disturbance occurs on a line rather than at a given point. The village of Moodus in East Haddam lies at the intersection of many converging seismotectonic lines. Scientific investigation has thus accounted for the mysterious and dreadful 'Moodus Noises,' early interpreted by the Indians as the rumblings of evil spirits, and by Cotton Mather as the voice of an angry God.

The western upland is decidedly more rugged than the one east of the valley; here several isolated peaks terminate the line of the Green Mountains and Berkshire ranges. With few exceptions, the highlands are broken by deep and narrow valleys running in a southern and southeastern direction. The ridges are heavily forested, and provide a pleasant contrast to the fertile fields in the river valleys.

The Connecticut River drains only the northern portion of the lowland. Southeasterly from Middletown the river has carved for itself a narrow valley in the eastern upland. The Housatonic and Naugatuck Rivers drain the western highland; and the Thames system — composed chiefly of the Yantic, Shetucket, and Quinebaug Rivers — drains the eastern area. On the Connecticut River, navigation extends to Hartford, on the Housatonic to Derby, and on the Thames to Norwich. Oil tankers, coal barges, and pleasure craft make up most of the traffic on these rivers. The depression of small valleys along the shore has created a number of good harbors.

The lakes, waterfalls, and pot-holes, so common over the State, owe their origin to glacial action. There are more than a thousand lakes, with a total area of some 44,000 acres. Among the natural lakes are Waramaug, Bantam, Pocotopaug, Gardner, and Twin Lakes. Artificial lakes include Lake Zoar and Candlewood Lake, the latter being by far the largest body of water in Connecticut.

The State's coastal plain, extending along Long Island Sound, is well developed commercially and residentially. Seaside resorts, State parks, and bathing beaches line the shore, with some intervening marshland. There are several good harbors, the most important of which is at New London, where the United States Government has a submarine base and a Coast Guard Academy. Shipping was once of great importance, but it is now relatively negligible except for coastwise traffic.

NATURAL RESOURCES AND CONSERVATION

Minerals: There are few States where the rocks and minerals are so well exposed for observation as in Connecticut. Minerals occur in great diversity of genetic types, but their commercial exploitation has not been substantially profitable.

The garnet and iron mines of Roxbury, the nickel mines of Litchfield, and the iron mines of Salisbury have long since ceased production. Copper mining at Granby, Bristol, and Cheshire was attempted even as late as World War days, but the workings are now idle. Roxbury granite is only locally important, Portland brownstone went out of fashion shortly after the last dust-ruffle brushed the sidewalk, but the traprock quarries are always busy supplying stone for highway and construction work. The lime kilns of the State are rusty wraiths of their former selves, the breakwater stone quarries are idle, and the last silica mill has been torn down; but the Strickland quarries in Portland produce material for a well-known commercial scouring agent, a garnet mine is active in Tolland County, and a prospector blasts hopefully for platinum in the rough hillsides of Sherman.

Soils: The soils of Connecticut furnish a livelihood for many farmers and dairymen. No State in the Union has better markets so close to the fields where crops are grown, and few other States are so free from problems of drought, soil depletion, and erosion. Early in the history of Connecticut, Yankee farmers learned the rudiments of 'side-hill farming'; modern guidance by an ever-vigilant State agricultural service has perpetuated the fertility and encouraged the wise utilization of the soil, and the State has made the most of this rather limited resource.

Water-Power and Watersheds: The streams of the State provided early mills with an abundance of water-power. As industry expanded, the rivers became ever more important to the growth of the State and its economic self-sufficiency. Water-power used directly at the site is still important, and an abundance of electrical energy is generated from the rivers that plunge over the Fall Line on their race to the sea. Only one of the State's 169 towns (Union) is without electrical service, and no hydroelectric power is 'imported.'

Scarcely a single community in Connecticut suffers for lack of a pure, soft, potable water supply. Watersheds are usually controlled by municipalities, but numerous privately owned water companies also function satisfactorily. The watersheds are vigilantly protected and conserved. Pine plantings around reservoirs are seen in almost every section of the State. Notices warning the passer-by of the dangers of fire and pollution are posted, and all watersheds are patrolled. Pollution is slowly being eradicated on streams not used for public water supply, and industry is conscious of the necessity for better and more sanitary disposal of waste material. Only the Naugatuck River shows any marked degree of pollution, and State authorities are now (1937) actively concerned with the purification of this one offensive stream among Connecticut waterways.

Flood Control: The State is alive to the necessity of long-term planning for eliminating the menace of floods such as have twice swept the State during the past nine years. Losses in soil have not been severe, but the economic waste through lost time on production and the damage to industrial equipment is so costly as to create a major problem. Connecticut's interest and position in the matter of flood control are of course largely influenced by the attitude and action of the States to the north. The General Assembly in 1937 ratified an interstate compact on flood control calling for the construction of dams on streams tributary to the Connecticut River in the States of New Hampshire, Vermont, and Massachusetts.

Forests: With an occasional exception, such as the conservation work of the Shaker Colony at Enfield, where a pine grove was planted under the direction of Elder Omar Pease in 1866, the preservation and renewal of Connecticut's forests have been grossly neglected by past generations.

The chestnut, fastest growing of the State's timber trees, for many years supplied most of the wood cut for commercial use. But the chestnut blight destroyed chestnut trees, and the 'peckerwood' sawmill operator moved on to a new stand. Timber production dropped from the record figures of 168,371,000 board feet, cut by 420 mills, in 1909, to only 20,525,000 board feet, cut by 85 mills, in 1930. Seventy-five per cent of the recent cut has been in hardwoods, and the average annual output for thirty years has been slightly under eighty million feet. Cordwood for lime kilns and brass mills took most of the remaining timber, and every farm woodlot kept a family in fuel. Forests were depleted, and new plantings were scattered and thin.

Before State control and the work of the Civilian Conservation Corps, about 27,000 acres of forest, on a yearly average, were devastated by fire. A similar loss was formerly suffered from the ravages of insects and ice-storm damage. But in 1932, owing largely to the patrol work of trained fire crews, only 7000 acres were burned over.

In 1937, 1,789,000 acres in Connecticut, or 56% of the State's total area, consist of forest land. This is an estimated increase of some 300,000 acres in the past fifteen years. Further increases are probable. The State owns about 75,000 acres, and is planning additional purchases; municipal water boards and companies own 100,000 acres; and the remainder is privately owned and controlled. Although plantings are increasing, the softwood supply in Connecticut plantations totals only about 23,000 acres.

PLANT AND ANIMAL LIFE

SHRUBS

MOUNTAIN LAUREL (*Kalmia latifolia*), the State Flower, is as typical of the rocky Connecticut hillsides as the rhododendron is of the Appalachians. Protected by law, this shrub, which furnishes a dark evergreen cover, grows profusely in the woodlands and has been planted in shady highway gardens along the roadsides. The Laurel Festival is an annual three-day event in Winsted in honor of the beautiful pink and white blossom.

The shelving pink or white dogwood blossoms are almost as common as laurel and present a magnificent display in June. Especially noteworthy growths are in Hubbard Park in Meriden, in the rocky glens of Greenwich, on the King's Highway in the eastern hills of Wolcott, and on Greenfield Hill. The pink azalea, locally named 'honeysuckle,' blossoming in pinks shading to red, is found almost everywhere. Clusters of white wild cherry blossoms appear early in the spring. The bark of this tree is used as a cough mixture, but its wilted leaves are poisonous to horses and cattle.

Pasturelands abound with three shrubs: the sweetfern, the bayberry, and sheep-laurel. The latter is poisonous to sheep and cattle. The bayberry fruit has a wax content that has been used since Colonial days in the making of scented candles. Sweetfern has a delightful odor and taste. Its dried leaves are often smoked by youngsters. Juniper bushes, spreading evergreen branches along the ground, produce berries valued as flavoring in gin.

Huckleberry and blueberry bushes of both high and low varieties bear edible berries of commercial value. The Ivy Mountain area of Goshen is especially productive as berry country. Several kinds of blackberries are conspicuous in June for their wands of white blossoms, and ripen somewhat later than the low bush blueberries. Occasional patches of wild raspberries survive in the State. The black raspberry or thimbleberry is widely distributed. Pokeberries, which abound, though not edible, are used as dye for homespun. Cranberries are native to Connecticut; their present-day commercial production here is negligible, but many good natural bogs exist, notably one to the east of the Cheshire–Waterbury road and one near Twin Lakes.

At the edge of the Appalachian hardwood belt where it merges into the northern evergreen forest cover, watered by bountiful rainfall, Connecticut borrows some plant life from each of these two types of cover.

WILD FLOWERS

As soon as the snow melts from the Connecticut countryside, a trip into the deep woods and a climb into the hill country are rewarded with the discovery of trailing arbutus, which sometimes blooms beneath the snow. Blue and white violets cover the lowlands, and the cool woods shelter the hepatica and the yellow dogtooth violet. The starry-flowered bloodroot is another conspicuous spring plant in suitable situations in wood and shady glen. The Indian turnip, or jack-in-the-pulpit, in marshy places, is ever ready to 'preach' for the youngsters who pinch the strange bloom with inquisitive fingers. Cowslips, deserving a much fairer name, spread a yellow glow along quiet swamp pools. Country people prize the leaves of this plant as 'greens,' cooking it as they do the dandelion, milkweed, and dock. In May or June, meadows are alternately white with daisies or yellow with buttercups. Wild geraniums lend a touch of lavender against the varied greens and, later, the lupine, in favored locations, covers sandy banks and sterile fields with a wash of blue.

In midsummer, the wild rose blooms. A trip into the deep woods is rewarded with the discovery of some one of the more delicate orchids. The Pyrola and the Indian pipe cannot be found by the roadside, but reward the botanist who wanders far afield. Evening primroses, vetches, clovers, mustard plant, vervains and composites are a part of the pattern, and even the hated wild carrot, or Queen Anne's Lace, is a weed of beauty. Later, at the brook's edge, the scarlet cardinal flower raises its gaudy spire as the trout play below its roots.

The Connecticut countryside often appears at its best in autumn. The gaudy scarlets of the woodlands merge with the yellow of the golden-rod and the browns of ground vegetation. Ivy, climbing around trees and stone walls, adds a flaming red equaled only by the sumach. Swamp sumach, distinguished by very green and shiny leaves, is poisonous, but the upland staghorn type, with great spikes of turkey-red berries in autumn, is not only harmless but has medicinal properties. The three-leaved poison ivy, often called mercury, should be avoided, but the five-leaved Virginia creeper (a cousin of the grape) is harmless.

MEDICINAL PLANTS

Among the often-missed, delicate blossoms to be found between wheel tracks of old wood roads, are a large variety of herbs, including penny-royal, and lobelia, whose medicinal properties are valued by the well-informed 'herb-doctor,' homeopath, and country housewife. Partridge-berry, a tiny woodland vine found creeping beneath the running or Princess Pine, produces a brew which was believed to lessen the dangers of childbirth for pioneer women and their dusky predecessors.

Witch-hazel, a shrub blooming in October with a delicate yellow flower, furnishes a lotion, concocted at home in the early days, which is now manufactured at several distilleries in the State. The root of the aromatic sassafras, found along the edges of woods and in fence corners, is used both as a flavoring and as a cure for throat ailments. Black birch, a tree which blossoms in the form of a tassel, is valued for the preparation known as 'oil of birch,' used as a substitute for wintergreen.

Old charcoal pits provide ideal soil conditions for rank growths of poke-berry and mullen. Mullen tea is locally believed to be effective in treating fever and reducing bruises. Thoroughwort, or boneset, with a white blossom, and skullcap with a blue one, are other common and useful Connecticut medicinal plants.

NATIVE TREES

The deciduous woodlands of Connecticut vary from the soft maple and pepperidge in the swamps to the oak, ash, birch, hickory, poplar, yellow poplar, sycamore, beech, hard maple, and butternut of the ridge. North-ward, the woodland changes from hardwood second growth to a pre-dominance of evergreens, ranging from seedling plantings to the towering white pines of Cornwall. Spruce and balsam are not plentiful but hem-lock and white pine are abundant and readily re-seed and flourish. Beautiful stands of hemlock are numerous, notably at Sandy Hook, along the Mianus and Shepaug Rivers, at Cornwall, Canaan, New London, Hartland, and Goshen. Red pine, which has proved resistant to rust and blister, covers many municipal watersheds. Tamarack, or eastern larch, which is still plentiful, furnished the early settlers with ideal wood for snowshoe frames, ship timbers, ladders, and fence posts. Tamarack gum was regarded as superior to spruce gum as a balm for wounds.

The hop-hornbeam and ironwood (or blue beech) are both common, and their wood is used for whipstocks and tool handles. Black walnut and hickory are fast disappearing in commercial quantities. The elm and sugar maple are favorite shade trees in all Connecticut villages. Willow, one of the first trees to show leaves in the spring, supplies material for basket splints, and its charcoal a base for gunpowder. Recently, the persimmon has been grown as far north as Rockville. Catalpa, horse chestnut, and locust are introduced species in the State, and are becoming naturalized in various places.

ANIMAL AND BIRD LIFE

The smaller mammalia all adjust themselves to conditions in this industrial region, and in recent years, as more land is returned to forest cover through State, municipal, or Federal purchases, they seem to multiply and thrive. On rural highways skunks dispute the right-of-way with many a midnight motorist. Woodchucks sit erect in clover fields beside the road, solemnly surveying the passing traffic. Even the white-tailed deer, dazed by the glare of approaching headlights, often stands rigid in the center of the less frequented roads. Foxes, both red and gray, prey on country henroosts in the rural sections or lead deep-voiced foxhounds a merry chase through moonlit woodland and over frozen stubble.

Fur-bearing animals are plentiful enough in the State to furnish a fur crop valued at from $80,000 to $100,000 per annum. Country lads trap muskrats, mink and an occasional otter. On the highway above the Hamburg Cove a dealer in raw furs swings a sign from a cedar pole and 'trades' for pelts with all the sagacity of the native Yankee. Catalogue houses regularly stuff country mail boxes with price lists of raw furs, and rural mail carriers obtain additional income by running trap lines, usually of Connecticut-made steel traps.

In the Canaan Mountain region and the wild country near Winsted

a few cow moose are said to be at large. Near Colebrook, the horn of
a bull.moose was found in 1936. Undoubtedly, these animals escaped
from captivity. Canada lynx very rarely wander in from 'up north' to
furnish sport for the more highly skilled rural hunters. Bobcats or Bay
lynx, now scarce, furnish an average of about twenty pelts a year in
Connecticut, but are not hunted seriously. Cottontail rabbits are so
plentiful as to be classified as pests. The snowshoe rabbit or varying hare
is not uncommon in Litchfield County and occurs throughout the northern
uplands. The European hare is an introduced species which has become
widely though sparingly established.

BIRD LIFE IN CONNECTICUT

Among the New England States, Connecticut is unique in possessing
within its borders three faunal life zones: upper austral, transition, and
Canadian. Typical of the upper austral birds which breed regularly in
Connecticut are: clapper rail, fish crow, orchard oriole, hooded warbler,
worm-eating warbler, Louisiana water thrush, seaside sparrow; and
representative of the Canadian Zone in the high hills of the northwestern
part of the State, as regular summer residents, are: the brown creeper,
black-throated blue warbler, northern water thrush, junco, and white-
throated sparrow, with such spasmodic breeding species as sapsucker, saw-
whet owl, and golden-crowned kinglet. The vast majority of the breeding
birds are typical of the transition zone which covers most of southern New
England. Connecticut is particularly fortunate in lying well within the
edge of the great eastern fly-way for migrants which pass each spring and
fall up and down the Hudson, Housatonic, and Connecticut River Valleys.
These two facts, in conjunction with the maritime situation along the
route of the shore bird and waterfowl migration, account for the rich and
varied bird life of the State.

Among the game birds, the fresh-water ducks are the most important,
but, with the exception of the local black ducks and the protected wood
ducks, are rapidly becoming scarcer, owing largely to continued over-
shooting. Second in importance is probably the ruffed grouse, which
continues to hold its own, particularly in protected woodlands, despite
the ravages of obscure and supposedly exotic diseases. The bob-white or
quail are now protected and in consequence are slowly but surely regaining
their insecure foothold as a characteristic bird of orchard, pasture, and

thicket. A very marked increase in numbers has occurred in 1937. The ring-necked pheasant has thrived as an introduced game bird, and offers good sport to local gunners.

Some authorities, including authors of several official bulletins of the U.S. Department of Agriculture, decry the reduction in the numbers of predatory hawks and owls, slaughtered by the representatives of the State Department of Fish and Game. They argue that the balance of nature has been upset and that much economic loss has been sustained from the over-abundance of rodents, rabbits, snakes, and other vermin. These views are not shared by some of the agriculturists and rural taxpayers, nor by some of the practical conservationists in charge of the forests and wild life of Connecticut.

Control: Six or seven hundred predatory hawks are annually destroyed. Crows furnish a yearly bag totaling 3500, and about 150 great horned owls are killed as State foresters and game protectors clear the cover for the protection of game birds.

Fish wardens captured and donated to the poor over 51,000 pounds of snapping turtles during the year 1936–37. Over 2300 watersnakes were destroyed by the same agency. Trappers are licensed to destroy fox, lynx, bobcat, and other predatory beasts.

Caution: The only wild life in Connecticut to be avoided are skunks, copperheads (in the swampy lands), and rattlesnakes (in a few isolated hill regions). Skunks never invite trouble and only their curiosity and independence cause them to be ranked as undesirable. It is advisable to give the skunk more than half of the road.

GEOLOGY

SURFACE FORMS

TO ANYONE driving a car over ridge and vale in northwestern Connecticut, or climbing laboriously to the high summit of Bear Mountain, the chief characteristic of the topography seems to be irregularity. Nevertheless the surface of the State, viewed as a whole, may be described as an old plain, gently tilted from northwest to southeast and more or less dissected by streams. The truth of this statement is demonstrated by study of a relief model made of plaster or clay and showing all landscape features in proper scale. A sheet of cardboard laid on such a model is not held up by a few scattered high points; it rests rather snugly on many broad areas that are nearly flat or gently rolling, and slopes gradually from the northern boundary to the shore of Long Island Sound. It is evident that if the stream valleys on the model were filled, the cardboard would then fit the top of the model rather accurately. In other words, the ruggedness of the upper Housatonic Valley and similar areas is chiefly due, not to scattered peaks and ridges that rise to exceptional height, but to numerous steep-walled valleys cut below a surface that originally was remarkably even.

The part of the State that would require the largest amount of fill to raise it to the level of the ideal plain is the wide lowland belt bordering the Connecticut River in the vicinity of Hartford, and extending generally southward to New Haven Harbor. This belt includes much of the best farming land of the State. The soil is predominantly reddish in color, in agreement with the bedrock beneath, which consists largely of red-tinted sandstone and shale. On the other hand, the higher ground on each side of the low belt is underlain by granite and similar rocks that are much more resistant than the sandstone and the shale. Within the low belt itself are steep-sided ridges, such as Mount Carmel, Pistapaug Mountain, and the Hanging Hills of Meriden. These ridges are on dark basaltic rock, as hard and resistant as granite. It seems, then, that there is a general relation between the topography of the State and the character of the bedrock. The north-south belt of low country mentioned above is called the Central Lowland; the higher areas east and west of it are known respectively as the Eastern and Western Highlands.

BEDROCK

The rocks that underlie the surface of Connecticut may be divided into two general groups according to age and structure. The Central Lowland, which extends from north to south entirely across the State and nearly across Massachusetts, is floored with reddish sandstone and shale in which are included sheets and dikes of dark basalt and related igneous rocks. A small detached area in Southbury is underlain by rocks of the same kind. The sandstone and shale have been eroded to form the lowland, whereas the more resistant igneous masses are responsible for the numerous bold ridges that diversify the scenery of the low belt. All of the bedrock within this belt was formed during the Triassic period of earth history. The strata of shale and sandstone were laid down as layers of mud, sand, and gravel, partly in the channels and on the flood plains of ancient streams and partly on the floors of shallow lakes. Strange extinct reptiles known as *dinosaurs* inhabited the region in large numbers; thousands of their footprints, perfectly preserved when the old muds hardened into rock, are to be seen in museums as well as in their original positions in old quarries. Three times during the Triassic period great floods of molten lava poured over the land and formed sheets of black basalt, which in turn were buried by thick layers of mud and sand. In a final great mountain-making upheaval, all of the Triassic deposits were broken and tilted toward the east. During succeeding ages the upturned edges of the mountain blocks have been eroded, and now a complete section of the beveled strata, nearly three miles in total thickness, can be seen by traversing the lowland belt from west to east. Comparison of the Triassic rocks in Connecticut, New York, and New Jersey suggests that these rocks originally covered a much larger area than at present.

Rocks much older than the Triassic underlie the Eastern and Western Highlands. These older rocks are here grouped together, although actually they form a complicated assemblage, containing many rock types and units that differ greatly in age. Some of these rock units originated on the floors of ancient seas. For example, in the western part of the State there are extensive belts of marine limestone. The layers of limestone and shale, once nearly horizontal, were folded and contorted by mountain-making forces, and in many places they are now vertical or even overturned. In connection with the mountain-making, great masses of molten rock welled up, cutting across and partially engulfing the folded strata. This molten material solidified to make coarse-grained granite, a type of rock that is formed thousands of feet below the earth's surface. Since the granite is now exposed over large areas, as at Stony Creek, Stonington, and Thomaston, we know that erosion has carried away vast quantities of rock, completely removing an old mountain system.

When the tremendous forces were compressing and folding the rock strata and the granite bodies were being formed, the combination of pressure and heat changed or *metamorphosed* much of the older rock. Limestone became marble; shale changed to slate, or in part to a rock composed largely of mica and known as mica *schist*. Garnets, some of large size, developed in parts of this metamorphic rock. Many other peculiar minerals were formed in the old mountain zone. Bodies of very coarse-grained granite, called *pegmatite*, yield dozens of mineral species, including some that are radioactive. By analysis of radioactive minerals found in quarries in the town of Portland, it has been determined that the pegmatite in that vicinity was formed 280,000,000 years ago.

In brief outline, the story recorded in the bedrock of Connecticut is as follows: the land was covered by ancient seas, and strata made of the old marine deposits were later folded to form high mountains. Erosion during long ages wore the mountains down and exposed the granite in their cores. Part of the land then began to sink slowly, and into the basin thus formed streams swept gravel, sand, and finer débris derived from the granite and older rocks. Dinosaurs left their footprints and bones in these deposits before the latter were hardened into rock. Great flows of lava poured over the land. Again there was mountain-making movement, which broke and tilted the new-made sandstones and lavas, making ranges similar to those in the present Great Basin of Nevada and Utah. Long-continued erosion then planed down these ranges until a wide region, including much of New England, was reduced to a plain near sea level.

In this long history of erosion, undoubtedly the areas on weak bedrock were worn down rather rapidly, whereas the resistant rocks stubbornly withstood the attacking forces for long ages. However, the weakest rocks cannot be cut below sea level by the running water of streams, and given time enough even the most resistant bedrock is brought down to the same critical level. Thus it was that the surface of our State became a monotonous plain, or near-plain, on which large rivers meandered widely.

The next event was slow and nearly uniform uplift of northern New England, tilting the old plain gently toward the Atlantic. Streams began to flow more swiftly and to cut downward. Again the weak bedrock yielded readily to the attack of erosion, and permitted some belts to be reduced to low elevation before the areas of resistant rock showed any appreciable effect. This selective wearing away may be compared to an etching process used in engraving. A plate of metal is covered with wax, which is then cut away with an engraver's tool until the desired pattern is produced. Acid applied to the plate attacks the bare metal, but cannot touch the areas protected by wax. In this way the surface, originally smooth, is etched into relief.

GLACIATION

The present surface of Connecticut represents natural etching that has partially destroyed the old tilted plain, which is still identified by numerous remnants. However, another modifying influence was required to shape the landscape as we now see it. This second agent was the moving ice cap of the Ice Age. The cause of this widespread glaciation is still largely a mystery; but an abundance of evidence demonstrates the existence of the ice sheet, both on this continent and in northern Europe. Over all of Connecticut the sheet was thick enough to bury the highest hills and to move slowly under its own weight. Soil and loose stones were moved along, blocks of bedrock were pried loose and added to the mass of moving débris, and the entire bedrock surface was polished, scratched, and gouged by the relentless grinding mill. Much of the original mantle of Connecticut was moved as far south as Long Island. During hundreds of thousands of years the ice sheet waxed and waned. At last the climate became more temperate, and the gigantic cap began to waste by melting from the top and from the front. Gradually all of Connecticut was set free. But for a long time floods of water poured across the State from the ice remnants farther north. Large temporary lakes were formed where stagnant ice dammed the old stream valleys. Water escaping from these lakes poured over cliffs as falls, and with the aid of hard pebbles as grinding tools, wore circular pot-holes, as deep as wells, into the solid rock. The wasting ice dropped its load of débris, and thus Connecticut, which had lost much of its original cover, inherited soil and boulders brought from Massachusetts and even from Vermont and New Hampshire. Scattered glacial boulders that obviously have strayed far from their original source are common features in all parts of the State.

Contrary to common opinion, the ice sheet did not erode deeply into bedrock and fashion the topography anew. It is clear that the ridges and valleys we now see were formed by running water long before the Ice Age. The moving ice used its energy chiefly in moving soil cover and dumping it haphazardly, thus modifying the older topography more largely by deposition than by erosion. Large piles of this glacial débris form the elongate *drumlins* near Storrs and elsewhere in the State. In the last stages of the glacial history, when the rotting ice was transected by long crevices, running water filled many of these elongate depressions with sand and gravel. When the surrounding ice melted away, these deposits remained as long narrow ridges. Elsewhere isolated masses of ice were partially buried in gravelly deposits, and later melted to leave the undrained depressions known as *kettles*.

The haphazard shifting of débris by the glacier ice resulted in many changes of the older drainage. The Farmington River flowed south in preglacial times and emptied into New Haven Harbor. After the ice disappeared, the old channel was left filled with glacial deposits in the vicinity of Plainville, and the river found it necessary to seek out a new route to the north, through an old gap at Tariffville, and finally into the Connecticut River at Windsor. Dumping of glacial débris obstructed many smaller stream valleys to create the lakes and swamps that are so common in all parts of the State.

The Connecticut shoreline is made ragged by many deep bays and inlets, and rocky islands are numerous offshore. The lower parts of the large stream valleys are 'drowned' to form estuaries, and in the Connecticut River the tides reach as far inland as Hartford. All of these features suggest recent sinking of the coastal belt; but at least a part of the real cause is actual rise of sea level due to return into the sea of vast quantities of water that were locked up in the great ice sheets during the Ice Age.

All of the numerous effects of glaciation form conspicuous features in the Connecticut landscape of today; but these effects are merely a veneer superposed on older features of the bedrock. Glaciation occurred only yesterday, from the geologic point of view. It is barely ten thousand years since the last of the glacier ice wasted away; but millions of years have elapsed since the Connecticut and Housatonic rivers began to cut their present valleys, and the old plain that was partly destroyed by the valley cutting was formed tens of millions of years ago. In the bedrock itself we see evidence of great changes in still earlier times, including the uplift of lofty mountains beneath which lay the granite now so widely exposed. Like human civilizations, landscapes come and go, each built on the ruins of another.

THE INDIANS OF
CONNECTICUT

ETHNOLOGISTS distinguish four main groups among the aborigines of Connecticut: the Nipmuck, the Pequot-Mohegan, the Sequin or 'River Indians,' and the Matabesec or Wappinger Confederacy. The first of these, the Nipmuck, occupied the northeastern corner of the State and part of Massachusetts. They had no ruler of their own, and were subject to one or another of the neighboring tribes. The Pequot and Mohegan, although politically distinct, were linguistically and otherwise closely related tribes, and actually formed a single people. They established themselves in the southeastern section of Connecticut after an invasion before 1600. The 'River Indians,' who consisted of a group, or league, of tribes under one chief, called the central part of the present state their own; while the Matabesecs, who were forced to share their territory with the Mohicans of eastern New York, occupied its western part.

Both the 'River Indians' and the Matabesecs were broken up into a number of localized tribes, the former being subdivided into the Tunxis, Poquonnuc, Podunk, Wangunk, Machimoodus, Hammonasset, and Quinnipiac, while the latter counted among their tribes the Pootatuck, Wepawaug, Uncowa, and Siwanoy. All of the Connecticut tribes were frequently invaded by the powerful Mohawks, who kept them under complete domination for long periods at different times.

The first contact between the whites and the Indians of Connecticut was probably made around the year 1614 by Dutch traders. Shortly after, in 1633, the Dutch established themselves in what is now Hartford, and in the next few years the influx of English settlers from Massachusetts began.

It was not long before the Connecticut settlers became involved in a life-and-death struggle with the Pequots, the most virile of the tribes. The first outrage on the Indians' part was the murder of Captains Stone and Norton on their way up the Connecticut River to trade.

The killing of the adventurer, John Oldham, off Block Island in 1636 led to ill-advised reprisals by a force from Massachusetts under Captain Endicott. The Pequots, enraged by the burning of some of their houses and corn, attempted to form an offensive alliance with the Narragansetts of Rhode Island. Had they been successful, the white settlers might well have been annihilated. Through the fall and winter of 1636–37, a series of attacks at Saybrook, Wethersfield, and other settlements kept the whites in a constant state of alarm.

On May 1, 1637, the General Court of Hartford decided to take the field against the Pequots. Ninety men were levied — forty-two from Hartford, thirty from Windsor, and eighteen from Wethersfield, and Captain John Mason was put in charge of the expedition. Ten days later Mason's party, with seventy Mohegan allies, sailed down the Connecticut River to Saybrook, where they joined Captain Underhill with twenty men from Massachusetts.

As the Pequots were in possession of two strongly fortified encampments and had a force of nearly five hundred warriors, the undertaking was a formidable one. The original plan to attack from the western or Thames River side, where the movements of the whites would have been under the constant observation of the Indians, was wisely abandoned. The main body of troops was sent over to Narragansett Bay to attack from the east. On the morning of May 24, the long overland march began for the little band of seventy-seven Englishmen with a small army of Indian observers, sixty Mohegans and four hundred Narragansetts. This retinue was more of a hindrance than a help, and might easily have constituted a potential menace, if the attack were not successful. On the morning of the 26th, an hour before dawn, the English advanced on the chief fort at Pequot Hill, West Mystic. It consisted of a circular area of several acres, surrounded by a twelve-foot palisade and containing some seventy wigwams. The surprise was successful; both entrances were taken and the work of slaughter began. It was a slow and confused business. Mason, therefore, decided to fire the encampment. Aided by a rising wind, the flames swept the fort; those who ran out were shot down, the Mohegans and Narragansetts lending a hand in this work. The destruction of the main body of the Pequots was complete, with a loss to the English of only two killed and twenty wounded. The other Pequots at Fort Hill made a sally, but were driven off. It was the most decisive battle ever fought on Connecticut soil, although one more action was needed to bring the war to an end. In a swamp fight at Fairfield on July 13, 1637, Mason overtook and destroyed the fleeing remnants of the Pequots, leaving one hundred and eighty captives to the whites and a few fugitives among the New York tribes. On September 21, 1637, a treaty of friendship was concluded between the English on one side, and Uncas of the Mohegans and Miantonomo of the Narragansetts on the other.

A period of peace followed, which lasted for nearly forty years, with growing tension as the settlers took over more and more of the Indians' hunting grounds. The fate intended for the Indians was clear, but before submitting to the white men's depredations, the original owners of the land rallied under Philip of the Wampanoags, a tribe of Rhode Island and Massachusetts. Intelligent, brave, made desperate by the injustice of the invaders, this Indian champion of a lost cause, abandoning all hope of peace, attempted to unite all the Indians of New England in a general conspiracy. His plans were revealed to the English by a Christian Indian, who was promptly murdered by Philip's henchmen. The execution of these murderers was the signal for the outbreak of what became known as King Philip's War. In June, 1675, Philip attacked Swansea, near Mount Hope, Rhode Island, killing nine and wounding seven of the inhabitants.

This time the Narragansetts, although still reluctant, were forced to participate on the side of King Philip. The colonists, aware of the seriousness of the situation, mobilized an army of one thousand men. On December 18, 1675, the Connecticut forces, consisting of three hundred Englishmen and one hundred and fifty Pequot and Mohegan Indians, under the command of Major Treat, joined those of Massachusetts and Plymouth. In combination, they made a desperate attack upon the Indian fort at Mount Hope; and after suffering heavy losses, they succeeded in completely subduing the Indian tribes.

Many of the survivors of the sorely defeated people moved out of New England northward or southward, others re-established themselves in New York State, while still others settled down in small groups in their original territory at the sufferance of the colonists. Thus a small number of Paugussets, Uncowas, and Pootatucks finally found a home several miles from Kent on the Housatonic River, where a reservation, called Schaghticoke, consisting of about four hundred acres and harboring a dozen half-breeds, is still maintained. Another band of Pequots settled near Stonington, where seventeen descendants are maintained at present as State wards. Still another group, of which nine members survive, were allowed by Governor Winthrop to settle near Ledyard. This settlement is known as the Ledyard Pequot Reservation, and comprises one hundred and twenty-nine acres of rough land. Aside from these few State wards, thirty-one descendants of the Mohegan tribe are living as members of the community in the town of Montville. They are concentrated in the section known as Mohegan, where they still observe on certain occasions some of their native customs — although they have long been Christianized, and maintain a church of their own, the Mohegan Congregational Church. The rest are scattered in towns and villages throughout the State. Altogether, only one hundred and sixty-two Indians survive today in Connecticut.

As to the original number of Indians in the State there is a lack of agreement among the authorities. While some put the number as high as from 12,000 to 15,000, others assert that no more than from 4000 to 5000 aborigines occupied the territory. At any rate, the first of these estimates is undoubtedly highly exaggerated.

COLLECTIONS OF INDIAN MATERIAL IN CONNECTICUT

Public displays of relics relating to the Indians of Connecticut are on view at the following institutions: Bruce Memorial, Greenwich; Pequot Library, Southport; Barnum Museum, Bridgeport; Hagaman Library, East Haven; Blackstone Library, Branford; Stratford Historical Society, Stratford; New London Historical Society, New London; Peabody Museum, New Haven; Old Stone House, Guilford; Norwich Free Academy, Norwich; Wesleyan University, Middletown; Litchfield Public Library, Litchfield; Mattatuck Society, Waterbury; Newgate Prison, Granby; Athenaeum, Hartford. Some of the more notable private collections belong to the following: Dr. F. H. Williams, Bristol; Crandall's Poultry Farm, Poquonock Midway, near Groton; Norris L. Bull, 1565 Boulevard, West Hartford; Edward H. Rogers, 340 Bridgeport Avenue, Devon; Joseph Lamb, 29 Park Place, New Britain; W. Shirley Fulton, 170 Hillside Avenue, Waterbury; Duffield B. Peck, Clinton; Elliott R. Bronson, Winchester Center; C. C. Coffin, Milford; Lyent Russell, 154 Hemingway Street, East Haven; Mathew Spiess, Center Street, Manchester; William Fenton, Westport.

HISTORY

THE settlement of the Connecticut Valley in the 1630's was the beginning of the westward movement of the English colonists in the New World. When news of the fertility of the Connecticut Valley reached Massachusetts, many land-hungry groups who had grown restive under the restrictive Massachusetts laws began to migrate westward.

A Dutch navigator, Adriaen Block, was probably the first to observe the possibilities of the region, when he sailed along the coast and up the Connecticut River, which he discovered in the year 1614 and called the Varsche River. Nearly twenty years passed, however, before the Dutch established a trading post and fort near the future site of Hartford (June, 1633). By this time the Indians had reported the existence of a fertile country with valuable trading possibilities to the Plymouth colonists, and Edward Winslow made an exploratory visit to the Connecticut Valley in the summer of 1632. Next year a Plymouth expedition sailed up the Connecticut, past Dutch Point, to the mouth of the Farmington River. There, on September 26, 1633, they established a post at Mattaneaug (Windsor). In the same year, John Oldham of Watertown and three others explored the Connecticut Valley, and 'discovered many very desirable places upon the same river, fit to receive many hundred inhabitants.' This report accomplished what the persuasions of Winslow and Bradford had not effected, and stimulated the first permanent settlement from the Bay towns of Watertown, Dorchester, and New Town (Cambridge).

In 1634, a large party from Watertown, with Oldham among them, settled at Pyquag (Wethersfield). They claimed that they were the first settlers to plant a crop in the valley. In the summer of 1635, emigrants from Dorchester settled in Windsor, erected a building, and thereby gave present historians of Windsor an opportunity to argue that this town was the first. But the severity of the winter was such that most of the 'inhabitants' were driven down the Connecticut River to the new military post at Saybrook, where they took ship to their homes in Dorchester.

In October, 1635, the first general migration took place, when fifty persons from New Town (Cambridge) under the leadership of John

Steel moved across Massachusetts with all their household goods and settled at Suckiaug (Hartford) close by the Dutch trading post. The Reverend Thomas Hooker and his congregation trekked westward in the following spring. The prime motive of these migrations was land hunger, as the constant arrival of newcomers from England taxed the resources of the early towns of Massachusetts Bay. To economic causes were added the rivalries of strong-willed men, such as Hooker and John Cotton, and a dislike of some of the autocratic and theocratic features of the government of Massachusetts. These colonists from Watertown, Dorchester, and Cambridge, who were settled in Wethersfield, Windsor, and Hartford, soon absorbed the small number of Plymouth people and kept the Dutch confined to their trading post, which was finally abandoned in 1654. In 1638, the Fundamental Orders, drafted under the inspiration of Hooker's sermon of May 31 and largely the work of Roger Ludlow, were drawn up, and in January, 1639, they were adopted by the three towns. Under this document, sometimes called the first practical constitution, the towns formed 'one publike State or Commonwealth.' Already (April 26, 1636) a general court had been held, in which Steel and Ludlow took part; and it now became the supreme authority, with deputies from the towns acting in concert. It is not without significance that Thomas Hooker was John Pym's brother-in-law. To Pym, Hampden, and other reformers in the mother country, the main organ of political power was the House of Commons. So here in Connecticut, the Governor was merely a presiding officer, and the courts were creations of the legislature by which their judgments could be set aside. Until the Constitution of 1818 replaced the Fundamental Orders and the Charter of 1662, the legislative body continued to dominate the executive and the judicial. It is worthy of note that the preamble presumed a close relation between Church and State, and that in 1659 the general court imposed a property qualification for suffrage. There was a distinct aristocratic element in this democracy.

In 1635, a second settlement, Saybrook, was established at the mouth of the Connecticut River by order of an English company of lords and gentlemen, among whom were Lord Say and Sele and Lord Brooke for whom the Colony was named. John Winthrop, Jr., son of the Governor of Massachusetts, was in charge of this enterprise, his chief aids being Colonel George Fenwick and Captain Lion Gardiner. The Saybrook group possessed a deed of conveyance from its patron, the Earl of Warwick, under date of March 19, 1632; but Warwick never received a patent to support the large claims later made by the Connecticut Colony to lands from Narragansett Bay westward to the Pacific Ocean. As the other Puritan lords and gentlemen became involved in the Cromwell Revolution, the settlement did not thrive at first and was important only as a fort and trading post. After several years of negotiation, Fenwick sold his rights to the Connecticut Colony in 1644. There is no evidence that he had any authorization from the company to convey the property, nor did Warwick's original deed carry jurisdictional rights. At any rate, the separate existence of Saybrook Colony came to an end in 1644, and Connecticut succeeded to a doubly doubtful title.

The third settlement was made in 1638 at Quinnipiac (New Haven) by colonists of the English merchant class, under the Reverend John Davenport and Theophilus Eaton. Land was acquired by purchase from Momauguin, chief of the local Indians, and the lack of a patent or charter vexed the Colony from its inception until its absorption by Connecticut in 1665. After living for a year under a plantation covenant, the colonists organized a civil government in June 1639. 'Seven pillars' were chosen, chief of whom was Theophilus Eaton, the elected magistrate. It was stipulated that all free burgesses should be church members, a restriction which proved increasingly irksome to the settlers. Internal dissatisfaction with the 'judicial laws of God as they were declared by Moses' became an acute problem. These 'Blue Laws,' as they were called by the Tory historian, Samuel Peters, in his 'General History of Connecticut' (1781), were Mosaic only in capital cases, and in general closely resembled the Cotton Code of Massachusetts. They contrasted unfavorably, however, with the wider freedom of the Connecticut Colony, particularly in the matter of franchise.

In 1643, New Haven was extended as a colony to include Milford (1639), Guilford (1639), and Stamford (1641); Branford (1644) and Southhold, Long Island (1640), later came under its jurisdiction. Two attempts to settle a subordinate colony in Delaware were opposed by the Swedes and the Dutch, and ended in failure. Although the Colony was founded to promote the peculiarly Puritan combination of piety and commercialism, its commercial enterprises did not thrive, and its piety was over-zealous and repressive. Its shipping activity was short-lived, and was featured by the loss at sea of the 'Wonder-working Providence' with several leading citizens on board. This ship set sail for England in January, 1646, and was never heard of again. Only as a 'phantom ship' did it appear miraculously in the clouds before the sight of the grieved New Haveners. In general, the colonists were forced to depend for a living on agriculture, in a coastal region less well adapted to agricultural pursuits than the fertile Connecticut Valley.

HOMES OF PATRIOT AND MERCHANT PRINCE

CONNECTICUT was primarily a farming community where the struggle for life was not easy. But a few families rose to prominence through trade, bringing the wares of the great world to the remote country villages. It was these families, in the main, who supported the Revolution, sometimes at the loss of their fortunes.

The earliest house of the Huntington family in Norwich is the narrow gambrel, much added to later, built by Joshua Huntington about 1719. The earliest house of the Trumbulls was built by Governor John Trumbull the first, in 1740. In the same year, Oliver Ellsworth's father, David, built the Ellsworth House in Windsor, one of the first to make the central hall popular. A little later, in 1753, the merchant prince of Wethersfield, Joseph Webb, built the house that was to become memorable as the meeting place of Washington and Rochambeau, where the campaign of Yorktown was planned. All these, and such houses as the manses in Suffield and Woodbury, 1742 and c. 1750, developed many interior elegances not found in the ordinary house. The Smith Mansion in Sharon is akin to the Van Cortlandt Mansion in New York.

After the Revolution, large fortunes began to be made in commerce between the more prosperous rural centers and the outer world. These were reflected in the Morris Mansion of New Haven, practically a house of 1780, the Stanton House and Store in Clinton (both now open to the public), and such later houses as the Julius Deming House in Litchfield (1793) and the Noble House in New Milford. These later showed a more definite architectural purpose, which culminated in the Greek Revival, as illustrated in Winsted, in Colebrook, and very notably in a number of houses in Farmington. The tranquil village of Windham shows the contrast between the simple little type of store upon which many of these country fortunes were based, and a mansion of the later Greek Revival.

JABEZ HUNTINGTON HOUSE, NORWICH

GOVERNOR TRUMBULL HOUSE, LEBANON

WEBB HOUSE, WETHERSFIELD

OLIVER ELLSWORTH HOUSE, WINDS

BE HOUSE, WOODBURY

GAY MANSE, SUFFIELD

WEST FRONT OF THE GOVERNOR SMITH MANSION, SHARON

RIS HOUSE, NEW HAVEN

STANTON HOUSE, CLINTON

MAJOR TIMOTHY COWLES HOUSE, FARMINGTON

NOBLE HOUSE, NEW MILF

ING HOUSE, LITCHFIELD

ROCKWELL HOUSE, WINSTED

OLD STORE, WINDHAM

PERKINS HOUSE, WINDI

Both New Haven and Connecticut had bought land from the Indians but neither possessed a title valid under English law. The Say and Sele group, though it had a deed of conveyance from Warwick, was similarly insecure in its right, since there was no evidence that the original Warwick patent had been executed, and the deed would not have survived close legal scrutiny. Connecticut recognized the insecurity of its position, for it had bought whatever rights Colonel Fenwick possessed, in 1644, but upon his return to England he failed to get the patent confirmed or renewed. Consequently, when Charles II was restored to the throne in 1660, the Colony fully realized how precarious the situation was.

It took little persuasion, therefore, on the part of Winthrop, who had been elected Governor in 1657 and re-elected in 1659, to induce his brethren to send him to England to see what could be done. The story of his negotiations is vague, but he somehow succeeded in obtaining a royal charter which placed the King's approval on the system of government already in existence, with a few minor modifications. The boundaries set forth in the charter, furthermore, extended from Massachusetts to the Sound, and from Narragansett Bay to the Pacific. Whether or not the royal authorities or Winthrop intended to destroy the independence of New Haven, the fact remained that by royal grant the New Haven colony had been incorporated into Connecticut. Naturally, the Colony immediately voiced a loud protest, and surrendered in 1664 only because it was faced with the greater evil of being included in the area granted to the Duke of York.

Thus, so early, Connecticut reached its full proportions, which it succeeded more or less in holding by constant vigilance and dexterity over a period of a century. Connecticut twice resisted Sir Edmund Andros — once in 1675, when he was acting as emissary for the claims of New York and attempted to land a force at Saybrook; and again in October, 1687, when the charter whose surrender he demanded was snatched from under his nose and hidden in the famous Charter Oak at Hartford. In the face of such efforts of Crown officials to regulate Colonial affairs, only Connecticut and Rhode Island retained their corporate existence; and Rhode Island, because of its dependence on foreign trade and its prominent position in the English mercantile system, was actually far less autonomous than Connecticut. Pennsylvania and Maryland, though they were still in the possession of the heirs of the original proprietors at the time of the Revolution, suffered from proprietary restrictions. After 1689 the status of Massachusetts became that of a semi-royal province, and Connecticut alone of the Puritan commonwealths carried on the Puritan experiment.

This amazing degree of autonomy was not solely the result of skillful policy and the work of able men; it was due more to the self-sufficient nature of the Colony. Only North Carolina traded less with the outside world. In Colonial Connecticut, agriculture was the main occupation; and there was no staple crop, such as tobacco in Virginia, to induce English regulation. The Crown exercised little control over Connecticut because there were few occasions for such control. The Colony, realizing the strength of its position and the support its policy would receive from a Parliament that was becoming more and more determined to limit the royal prerogative, trod warily, and deliberately refrained from giving royal officials an opportunity for punitive measures.

During the century between the granting of the charter and the Revolution, Connecticut played its part in the larger events of the New World. It hanged a few witches about the middle of the seventeenth century, and joined its neighbors in King Philip's War of the 1670's, though it suffered far less in that struggle than Maine, Massachusetts Bay, and Plymouth. From 1687 to 1689, as part of the Dominion of New England, it was subjected to the harsh rule of Andros. Within a few years, however, government was resumed on its former basis with the approval of Crown lawyers, who ruled that the charter was still valid. The Colony participated in the Colonial wars: in 1690, Fitz-John Winthrop led an unsuccessful expedition against Montreal, and twenty years later three hundred Connecticut militiamen were among the troops that captured Port Royal during Queen Anne's War. It was well represented in the force that took Louisburg in 1745; and during the French and Indian War it wavered, like its neighbors, between co-operation and obstruction.

In the seventeenth and eighteenth centuries, boundary disputes with adjoining Colonies were incessant. Encouraged by the charter of 1662, the Connecticut Colony attempted to take Westchester and the western towns of Long Island from New York. In 1664, the royal grant to the Duke of York conflicted with the Connecticut charter by assigning all land up the Connecticut River to New York. As previously noted, this claim was decisive in persuading New Haven to choose a union with Connecticut. The most serious controversy occurred over land claimed by Connecticut in the Wyoming Valley of Pennsylvania. Here war actually broke out between rival settlers just before the Revolution, causing a bitter dispute that was not adjudicated until 1782. Similar boundary disputes with Rhode Island and Massachusetts were frequent, but after years of wrangling were ended in compromise.

In 1708, the General Court, which had occupied itself with ecclesiastical affairs, summoned delegates to a synod to be held at Saybrook. At this convention, the conflict between the strict Congregationalists, who held that each church body was a unit with full powers of administration and discipline, and the moderate 'Presbyterians,' who favored centralization, was settled by a compromise. The Saybrook Platform, adopted by the twelve clergymen and four laymen who composed the convention, provided for biennial meetings of the ministers of each county in consociations to consider matters of common interest and exercise a certain control over the ministry. This form of polity has been called 'modified Presbyterianism'; and, in fact, the terms 'Presbyterian' and 'Congregational' were used indiscriminately until the middle of the eighteenth century. The platform resulted in a permanent establishment that tempered the excesses of the 'Great Awakening' of 1740 and remained in force until the adoption of the Constitution of 1818. A toleration act was added by the General Court, and further exceptions were made for the Episcopalians in 1727 and the Baptists and Quakers in 1729, enabling them to pay their ecclesiastical taxes to their own denominations.

Connecticut produced many men of talent and strong character, but the same isolation that preserved its freedom also fostered a pronounced provincialism. Each town lived unto itself and looked to its own concerns, and this self-sufficiency developed into an intense particularism that did not welcome outside influences. The Colony was poor, for there was little foreign trade to bring in hard money; and colonists given, as Roger Wolcott once said, to 'detraction and censoriousness' were far too strong-minded for co-operation. The rugged soil they tilled made thrift and self-reliance their outstanding virtues — and, in the eyes of the inhabitants of other Colonies who dealt with them, their chief faults.

In the circumstances, it is not surprising that conservatism became characteristic of the commonwealth. Few men were rich and few were poor; few owned very large or very small estates. Averseness to change, of which vestiges still remain, became almost a second religion with the political and social leaders. To their minds, democracy would have been as great a calamity as a royal governor; and the government, though autonomous, was popular only in the sense that elections were held. Beneath an outwardly popular form prevailed a system that was aristocratic and paternalistic, and the governorship was held for long periods by one man.

Connecticut, like Massachusetts, was an unwilling member of the British colonial system. Because of its tradition of self-government, a fear of interference, aroused by the new imperialistic policy of the mother country after 1763, led most of its 198,000 inhabitants to support the revolt in 1775. During the Stamp Act controversy, the General Court instructed its London agent to insist on the 'exclusive right of the colonists to levy their own taxes.' Immediately after the battle of Lexington, six regiments were mobilized — in fact, preparations for war had been under way for more than a year.

The more important military operations that took place in Connecticut during the Revolution were the skirmishes at Stonington in 1775, Danbury in 1777, New Haven in 1779, and New London in 1781. Undoubtedly the Colony's most brilliant military figure was Benedict Arnold, although Ethan Allen, a colorful natural leader, has a strong claim to the title. The Connecticut militia participated in the early expedition against Canada. The outstanding civil figures during the war were Jonathan Trumbull, the only Colonial Governor who was not deposed during the Revolution, Oliver Wolcott, and Silas Deane, the first agent of the Continental Congress in France.

From 1775 to 1818, Connecticut moved slowly away from its extreme conservatism. There the war had not been a social revolution because no back-country bloc had existed; but in the period that immediately followed, a definite trend towards liberalism can be seen. Religious dissent became acute because of the increase of Episcopalians, Baptists, and Methodists, who, by supporting the Toleration Party, helped to secure the Constitution of 1818 that disestablished the Congregational Church.

Conservatism, however, was merely modified. Frightened lest Shays' Rebellion should spread southward, the State lent its support to the Constitutional Convention of 1787 and hastily ratified the resulting document, which protected and favored the rights of property. Although the religious dissenters joined the Democratic-Republican Party in hope of ejecting the Congregationalists from their privileged position, this party was born late and made slow progress. Connecticut looked askance at the election of Jefferson, whom it considered tainted with the skepticism of the French Revolutions. His embargoes infuriated the State; and during the War of 1812, Connecticut refused the War Department the use of its militia.

The movement for a Federalist convention, launched by Massachusetts to consider some united action and possible secession, found favor in anti-administration Connecticut, and delegates were sent to the Hartford Convention of December, 1814. Delegates from Massachusetts, Rhode Island, and Connecticut expressed opposition to the war, which was injuring the commercial interests of New England, and strongly denounced the policy of the administration, particularly in respect to forcible drafts. The general aim seems to have been to obtain certain reforms in the direction of State rights; but as the sessions were held in secret, false reports were circulated that the convention plotted a dissolution of the Union. The coming of an early peace rendered superfluous the acts of the convention, and its chief result was to bring considerable odium to the New England Federalists.

The political revolution of 1818 was the product of basic economic changes that were occurring in the State and in the Nation during the two-score years after the Declaration of Independence. Banks were unknown in Connecticut as late as 1792, but by the year of the Hartford Convention ten State banks had been organized, with a capital of more than three million dollars. The wars of the Napoleonic period encouraged a brisk carrying trade which brought prosperity to the towns along the Sound and the Connecticut River; and when Jefferson's embargoes cut this commerce off in its infancy, the State, like the rest of New England, was forced into manufacturing. Gristmills, textile mills, and factories of various sorts sprang up everywhere.

Nineteenth and twentieth century Connecticut presents a striking contrast to the Colonial commonwealth. Within fifty years a homogeneous agricultural State became a highly complex, heterogeneous, industrial society which retained certain of its earlier spiritual characteristics. This transformation was the direct result of the development of the Industrial Revolution, of the constant migration of settlers to the West, and (in the later period) of heavy immigration from Europe.

Connecticut was the product of the first expansion of New England; it became in turn the source of incessant migrations. In the late seventeenth century, New Jersey was the popular destination, and in the eighteenth century, the Berkshires, Vermont, New Hampshire, up-State New York, and Pennsylvania. Two large land companies, the Delaware and the Susquehanna, were formed in the State. After the Revolution, migration was directed toward northern New England, Pennsylvania, New York, and the Western Reserve in Ohio, an area that Connecticut excepted from the cession of its holdings in the Northwest Territory to the Federal Government in 1787. Throughout the early nineteenth century, this movement continued unabated, reaching the upper and lower Mississippi Valley, central Texas, and even the Pacific coast.

It is difficult to estimate the actual number of emigrants, but it is safe to say that today many more of the descendants of Connecticut colonists live in the Middle West than in the State of their ancestors. In a gazetteer published in 1819, Pease and Niles estimated that the emigrants and their descendants numbered more than 700,000, while fewer than 300,000 remained. From 1789 to 1889, thirty-four men born in Connecticut served in the United States Senate as representatives from fourteen other States, and 187 in the House from twenty-two other States. It is significant that, though the United States as a whole showed a population increase of about thirty-three per cent in every decade between 1800 and 1840, Connecticut had an increase of only four or five per cent in each of those decades.

Towards the middle of the nineteenth century this emigration dwindled, and immigration from Europe began — at first from the North, later from central and southern countries. As early as 1870, twenty-eight per cent of the State's population was foreign-born; and in the first three decades of the twentieth century, the foreign-born population of Hartford and New Haven has varied between twenty-five and thirty per cent. If native whites born of foreign or mixed parentage are counted as foreigners, then today considerably more than half of the residents of Connecticut are foreign.

This movement of population accompanied and accelerated a definite trend toward modern industrialism. The glacial soil of Connecticut, outside of the narrow river valleys, has never been fertile; and when babies came as regularly as the seasons, the population tended to reach such proportions that the soil could not support it. Confronted with the alternative of migration or starvation, most of the youth chose to migrate. Some, however, preferred to risk starvation rather than to leave their homes; and since complete dependence upon agriculture was no longer possible, the more ingenious turned to manufacturing.

Although it possessed numerous small factories, Connecticut was largely agricultural before 1840. In 1820, cloth was still spun in the home, and the 'cities' were little more than country towns. Each community possessed enough artisans to be self-sufficient, and the State specialized in supplying its neighbors with foodstuffs. Natural resources were scanty, and capital was scarce; but with a supply of labor to be had at less than a dollar a day, the money and the raw materials necessary to industry could be found outside. By the middle of the century, textiles were the leading manufactured product, though clocks, locks, tools, hats, gin, firearms, tinware, and dozens of 'notions' such as mouse-traps and combs were being turned out in large quantities. Yet the outstanding characteristic of Connecticut industry in this era was not so much the excellence of its craftsmanship as the skill with which goods were marketed. The 'Yankee Pedlar' became well known throughout the nation.

With the construction of railroads in the forties and fifties, Connecticut became a predominantly industrial State. The continued influx of European immigrants insured a constant supply of cheap labor. Almost every town in the State has specialized in the manufacture of some particular product. It must suffice to point out that between 1860 and 1929, the value of the industrial output of Connecticut increased from $82,000,000 to $1,472,000,000, though in national rank the State dropped from fifth to thirteenth place.

If Connecticut, at present, does not lead the Nation in manufacturing, it does lead in insurance, for Hartford is the insurance center of the United States. Fire and marine insurance companies appeared before 1800. The first of such companies was the Mutual Assurance Company of the City of Norwich, incorporated in 1795; but perhaps the best known was the Hartford Fire Insurance Company, organized in 1810. Other corporations were soon formed for the same purpose; and about the middle of the century, life insurance was first written. In 1930, the policies of Connecticut life insurance companies represented a total of $10,000,000,-000, and the company assets amounted to $1,650,000,000.

Despite a century of immigration, Connecticut retains to an amazing degree its traditional characteristics. The masses derived from recent immigration will become inevitably a paramount influence, and are now rapidly gaining political and social predominance. Their progress to political power has been delayed by a striking survival from the particularism of the Colonial era — the law allowing many towns, regardless of size, two representatives in the lower house of the legislature. The rural communities have remained, generally speaking, the stronghold of the older stock. Still it cannot be denied that Thomas Hooker, or even the liberal Oliver Wolcott, who became Governor in 1817, would be surprised at the transformation of Connecticut. Could they return they would find, instead of their rural commonwealth, a complex and highly industrialized society; instead of a homogeneous people, a melting-pot composed of many European nationalities; and instead of a strongly Protestant community, a society where Catholics, Protestants, Jews, and free-thinkers intermingle.

GOVERNMENT

CONNECTICUT, the 'Constitution State,' still operates under one of the oldest of State constitutions, adopted in 1818. Long before 1818, however, Connecticut was governed by a basic organic law established by her own citizens. In 1639, the river towns of Windsor, Hartford, and Wethersfield adopted a set of laws known as the Fundamental Orders. These have often been called 'the earliest written constitution in history,' although present-day scholarly opinion inclines to the view that they were not a constitution at all but merely a set of statutes. At any rate, they did set up a system of government providing for semi-annual general assemblies of deputies to be sent from the towns, and for the election of magistrates and a governor. They also laid down rules for conducting the assemblies and elections, and for defining the powers of all officials.

These laws remained in effect until 1662. In that year, Governor John Winthrop, Jr., obtained from King Charles II a charter on which Connecticut based her government for one hundred and fifty-six years. This astonishing document granted the Colony practically full self-government at a time when England's policy was very definitely moving in the direction of complete royal control over the Colonies. Just how Winthrop managed to get this liberal charter signed has never been fully explained; but it proved so satisfactory that, when the Colonies separated from England during the Revolutionary War, and all the other States except Rhode Island adopted new constitutions, Connecticut chose to continue under its old charter, only slightly amended, until 1818. This charter, which was similar to that of a private joint-stock trading company, provided that men of sufficient property and reputation should choose a governor, deputy governor, council, and house of representatives. The house elected the other executive officials and the judges.

In 1818, Connecticut adopted the constitution under which it still operates. This document began with a declaration of rights; it went on to separate the government's powers into three departments, legislative, executive, and judicial; and it then defined the powers and duties of each department. Moreover, the constitution greatly extended the franchise (although universal white manhood suffrage was not in force until 1845), disestablished the Congregational church, and furthered the cause of education by confirming the Charter of Yale College and perpetuating the school fund. More than forty amendments to this constitution have been passed in the last one hundred and twenty years, but it has never been thoroughly revised, as other State constitutions have been. In 1902, a convention to revise the constitution was called; but after long debate the convention made only a few relatively slight changes, and even these were decisively defeated when submitted to the people for ratification.

The legislature is still the most important of the three departments of government. Like that of the Federal Government and of nearly all the States, it is bicameral in form, with a senate of 35 members and a house of representatives of 267. Members of both branches are elected for two years, and meet in regular session in odd-numbered years only, although the governor may call a special session in case of emergency. The regular session begins in January and must, according to the constitution, adjourn early in June. The assembly may pass laws on any subject not forbidden by the Federal or State Constitutions, and the restrictions are slight in comparison with those in other States. The procedure in passing legislation shows the influence of leisurely pre-Colonial English Parliaments, since every bill must be read three times before each house and must also be considered in committee before it can become a law. Connecticut long held staunchly to the usual New England system of submitting bills to a joint committee of both houses; but in 1937, because the two houses, controlled by different political parties, were unable to agree as to the proper representation on such a committee, this time-honored custom was abandoned.

Two points regarding the legislative department deserve special mention, as indicating the power and peculiarity of that body in Connecticut. The first is that, while the governor may veto any act of the general assembly, the latter may revalidate the law by a mere majority vote of both houses. This leaves the assembly practically supreme in the field of legislation, the usual American check of the executive veto being quite shadowy. In this matter, as in so many others, Connecticut's dislike of change is leaving her outside the current trend of American government.

The other noteworthy feature is the system of representation in the general assembly. Like the Federal Government, Connecticut has a small senate and a large house. But unlike the Federal Government, the senate is elected from districts based on population, while election districts for the house are geographical. In both branches the representation is unequal. According to the State constitution, all senatorial districts should contain approximately the same number of people; actually the number varies from 20,000 to 90,000. By a division that shows suspicious signs of gerry-mander in favor of the country as against the city, the average senatorial district, in 1924, in the four urban counties (Hartford, New Haven, Fair-field, and New London) had 43,584 people, while that in the four rural counties (Litchfield, Tolland, Windham, and Middlesex) had only 25,480. This inequality was even greater in 1937. But this balance in favor of the rural regions in the senate pales into insignificance when compared to that in the house of representatives. Representation is based on the towns, as it has been as far back as 1662. Those that have more than 5000 inhabi-tants or were incorporated before 1818 (99 in all) send two representatives; all the others (69) send one. Of course, the towns vary greatly in size, yet Hartford with a population of 164,000 chooses two representatives and so does Union with a population of only 196! Well over half of the State's population lives in the seven cities of Hartford, New Haven, Bridgeport, Waterbury, New Britain, Stamford, and Meriden; yet these cities elect only 14 of the 267 representatives. In 1924, one sixth of the people, those living in the most sparsely settled regions, elected more than two-thirds of the house. When it is realized that adoption of a constitutional amend-ment requires a two-thirds majority of each house and that ordinary legis-lation has to pass both houses, the power of the country districts of Con-necticut becomes clear. Small wonder that the government is conservative and cautious.

And yet Connecticut is well and honestly governed, although its govern-ment can hardly be called democratic. The representatives from the rural districts, many of whom are solid farmers and business men, compare favorably with the city politicians in the adjoining seats. Legislative ab-surdities, such as the Standard Time Laws of the 1920's which required all public clocks to exhibit eastern standard time while most of the citizens lived by daylight saving time, are rare. Extreme anti-city legislation is prevented by the number of urban members of the senate. One result of the overwhelming power of the rural regions in the house of representa-tives has been to keep the Republican Party in power there even after such a Democratic landslide as that of November 1936.

Of the executive officials, the governor is of course the foremost. He is chosen by the people at the regular State election held in November in even years, and holds office for two years. He wields legislative and judi-cial as well as executive powers. He may grant temporary reprieves after convictions for all crimes except impeachment. He suggests legislation in his messages on the state of the government, and he may use his political power with his party, which usually has majority control in at least one of the houses of the assembly, to push through the measures he desires. He may postpone legislation by vetoing it; and, if he has public opinion behind him or the legislative body is closely divided on the bill, his veto is likely to be sustained. As the State's chief executive, he appoints the judges of the higher courts, most of the commissions which administer the government, and the directors of the State's humane and penal institutions. Some of the appointments require the consent of the Senate, some of both houses, and others are direct.

Connecticut's governors have usually been men of probity and ability. Especially was this true of the period before the constitution of 1818, when such men as John Winthrop, Gurdon Saltonstall, Roger Wolcott, Jonathan Trumbull, and Oliver Wolcott, to mention only a few, held office for long periods. When Connecticut finally adopted a constitution that put into effect the ideas of the Revolutionary fathers, who feared a strong executive and saw in the legislature the guardian of American liberties, the governor's power was considerably diminished and he became more of a figurehead. His power has remained comparatively slight, despite the growth of State business resulting from the great increase in population and industry. There is need for a strong executive, who not only will have the power to manage well but will also concentrate in his person the responsibility for such management. Only in this way can the electorate exercise the control required of them in a democratic system of government. Other States, which preceded Connecticut by a generation in cutting down the governor's power, have increased that power in recent years; but this State, as usual, has preferred the old ways. From time to time, however, efforts have been made to lengthen the governor's term and increase his veto power, and of late there has been a strong drive toward these ends.

As in other States, the day-to-day business of running the government is in the hands of a considerable number of executive officers. Some of these, notably the secretary of state, treasurer, comptroller, and attorney general, are elected by the people. Others, many of whose positions are of equal importance with those of the elected officials, are appointed by the governor, usually with the consent of the senate. Examples in this group are the commissioner of finance and control, bank commissioner, commissioner of health, highway commissioner, insurance commissioner, commissioner of labor and factory inspection, commissioner of motor vehicles, state police commissioner, commissioner of welfare, tax commissioner, commissioner of public works, and the members of the public utilities commission. Apparently the chief reason why the first group of officials is elected is that they were important in the nineteenth century when the constitution was set up, while the functions of the second group have developed gradually during the last thirty years.

The officials mentioned above are only a few of the many who carry on the multifarious activities of the State government today. They number nearly a hundred in all. (A complete list may be found in the 'State Register and Manual' published annually at Hartford by the Secretary of State.) The various administrative bodies have grown up in a rather helter-skelter fashion, especially since the World War, and now represent a conglomerate of overlapping organizations. A thorough reorganization is needed, such as has already been carried through in other States comparable to Connecticut in population and economic activity. Such a reorganization has long been in the minds of Connecticut officials, and the general assembly of 1937 made some progress in this direction.

Like all English Colonies, Connecticut had courts from its beginning, and the present court system is a growth and adaptation of the English system brought to America in the seventeenth century. Throughout the Colonial period, the general assembly, or general court as it was called until 1662, was the highest judicial as well as legislative body. Before 1640 a smaller tribunal to decide petty disputes had been set up — the particular court. This lasted until 1665 when, with the institution of counties, county courts were created, and a court of assistants was appointed to take over a large part of the judicial work of the general assembly. The office of justice of the peace, instituted in 1669, was not fully defined until 1702; it is still important as the petty tribunal of the smaller towns. Before 1700, there was a probate court in each county. In 1711, the superior courts, one for each county, replaced the central court of assistants. Shortly after the Revolutionary War, the general assembly relinquished its judicial powers, and the supreme court of errors started on its long and honorable career in 1784.

The supreme court of errors, consisting of a chief justice and four associate judges, is today the State's highest judicial tribunal. Solely a court of appeal, it reviews cases brought up to it after trial in an inferior court. However, it is closely integrated with the superior court, since its judges are also members of that court. The superior court, the key agency in the State's judicial system, is the highest court actually to try cases. Its jurisdiction includes all matters not specifically delegated to the inferior courts, and it hears appeals from those courts. It holds sessions in each of the eight counties. About 1870, the amount of business before the court in the more populous counties became so excessive that new judicial bodies, called courts of common pleas, were created to take over the less important cases. Below these county courts are the probate courts, which today number about 115; the town, borough, and city courts, 68 in number; and the justices of the peace.

Court procedure is relatively simple, and has been so since the last quarter of the nineteenth century. As in other parts of the government, startling innovations have been few, but the courts are keeping abreast of modern methods. For instance, a bench of three judges may be substituted for a jury trial at the option of an accused person, even in a homicide case. The larger cities have juvenile courts for the young, legal aid bureaus for the poor, and small claims courts where cases involving small amounts of money are handled cheaply and speedily. There is a strong movement in the State today to abolish town courts, most of which try few cases and operate on the fines they collect, and to replace them with district courts, each covering several towns and having a full-time and well-paid judge.

A word must be said about local government. The eight counties are chiefly judicial districts, with no legislative and only minor executive functions. In this, the county in Connecticut resembles that of other northeastern States and contrasts strongly with the South and West, where counties dominate the field of local government. Below the counties are towns, cities, and boroughs, of which the towns are the oldest and historically the most important. One hundred and sixty-nine in number, geographically they cover every inch of the State. Where no borough or city exists, the town government is the sole instrument for carrying on local affairs. Even where a city or borough has been superimposed, the town remains a living unit of government, for it is only as residents of a town that Connecticut's citizens vote for members of the State's house of representatives. In the smaller towns, the town meeting, at which all adults may speak and vote, presents an unusual example of a pure democracy, wherein the people, and not their representatives, make laws to govern themselves, in addition to choosing all the town officials. In populous districts this system has proved impractical, and boroughs (23) and cities (21) have been incorporated. Where these exist, their officials have taken over most of the work of the town officers; but the latter continue to be elected, giving to Connecticut local government the aspect of a bewildering palimpsest of efficient modern political machinery, necessary in teeming industrial communities, imposed upon the simple democratic forms of a quieter and less populous age.

It is clear that the most important characteristic of Connecticut's government is its conservatism. With its roots well grounded in the seventeenth and eighteenth centuries, its main outline has varied very little from that fixed by the constitution of 1818. However, many features have changed, as the forty amendments to the constitution indicate. But there has been no complete revision and, in the field of government as it was known to the nineteenth century, no innovations such as the initiative, referendum, and recall of elected officials. Legislation, too, has been along well-established lines; it is significant that no Connecticut statute has ever been declared unconstitutional by the United States Supreme Court. There are indications, such as the present movement to reorganize the executive departments, that Connecticut may some day make her entire governmental structure up-to-date.

THE RACIAL MAKE-UP OF CONNECTICUT

CONNECTICUT'S population, like that of Massachusetts and Rhode Island, is composed largely of people either born abroad or born in this country of foreign or 'mixed' parentage. According to the United States Census figures of 1930, only 34.1 per cent of the State's present population is of native parentage, and this small percentage includes many persons only one generation removed from foreign origin. Rhode Island is the only State in the Union with a smaller proportionate population of descendants from native-born parents.

Connecticut's Colonial population was almost entirely of English origin. Although the white population of the State increased rapidly from 1640 to 1650, during the following years up to 1790 the rate of increase dropped to only an estimated 17 per cent. By the end of the eighteenth century, immigration barely filled the gap left by the great tide of migration which carried Connecticut families westward to new lands. Entire towns were depopulated. The Yankee was restless. He sought more fertile fields. Behind him were left the older folk or the commercially inclined — the inventor with his back-yard factory. Infant industries were hampered by lack of enough hands or power to manufacture the goods needed by a new and vigorous civilization.

The development of water-power, harbors, and navigable rivers encouraged growing industry. Isolation resulting from the embargo during the War of 1812 forced Connecticut to turn to the production of goods formerly imported, and Yankee ingenuity harnessed the streams and equipped little factories, beginning the activity that has molded this Commonwealth into an industrial State. By 1840, the new order had so far succeeded that there was a shortage of labor to do the work contracted for. Industrialists turned to Europe for the labor they required, and Europeans were attracted to America as the land of promise.

Among the earliest groups to arrive were the Irish, who formed the larger portion of the 'old immigration' and were numerically important even during the Colonial era. The Irish helped fight our early wars, shoulder to shoulder with the natives. They bought lands here, made the tinware for our first Yankee 'pedlars,' and worked in woods and fields as well as in factories.

Although the main immigration of Irish to Connecticut occurred after the potato famine of 1846–47, Irish laborers were busy here during the early nineteenth century, building roads, canals, bridges, and dams. With the development of railroad transportation after 1830, Irish laborers were in great demand, and Connecticut — like New York, New Jersey, Pennsylvania, Massachusetts, and Rhode Island — became one of the chief centers of Irish concentration.

Some 70,000 foreign-born Irish were in Connecticut in 1870; most of their descendants are included in the native stock. American-born Irish of the first and second generation now number 151,893. Most of the Irish in the State are two or three generations removed from foreign-born parents; they have been assimilated in Connecticut economic life, and are well represented in all professions and occupations.

English immigrants of the period from 1830 to 1840 were usually of the skilled or semi-skilled laboring class. They were largely absorbed by the developing Connecticut brass industry.

The first German settlers in the State, stragglers from the Hessian reinforcements of the British army in the Revolution, were few in number. Not until the period of 1880-1910, long after these pioneers had settled in New York and the Middle West, did German immigrants come to Connecticut in large numbers. Unlike most of the other ethnic groups, the Germans do not form compact colonies, but are well-distributed in every section of the cities and suburbs. The Connecticut Germans are also engaged in many occupations. Of the 76,281 Germans in the State, 52,816 are American-born.

Canadians, including both the French and natives of the Maritime Provinces, began arriving in Connecticut at a very early date. They numbered only 3145 foreign-born in 1860. The Canadian immigrants soon outstripped both the English and the German newcomers. By 1930, the foreign-born Canadians numbered 38,566; and the combined groups, including those of foreign or 'mixed' parentage, numbered 97,105. The French Canadians (67,130) are concentrated mainly in the northeastern part of Connecticut, where they are chiefly employed in the textile mills. The English-Canadians settle in the larger cities, particularly in Hartford, and are engaged in various occupations.

The year 1870 marked the arrival of considerable numbers of Scandinavians. In the present-day Scandinavian group, 41,374 are Swedes, including the native-born of foreign or 'mixed' parentage. The Danes total 6124, and the Norwegians number 3898. Most of the Scandinavians in urban communities are employed as mechanics, machinists, tool-makers, and woodworkers, and those in the rural districts work chiefly as gardeners, florists, and farmers.

The arrival of Italian immigrants in any considerable number dates from the 1870's, when a group of about 100 settled in New Haven. A hardware manufacturer employed many of them, while the others worked as railroad section hands and truck gardeners. Within two years the Italian population of New Haven numbered 200; in 1880 it had increased to 500, and by 1889 more than 2000 Italians resided in the city. By 1907, the hardware concern that first brought these people to Connecticut employed nearly 3000 Italians, and a near-by rubber plant had about 1000 on its payroll.

The peak of Italian immigration came during the years from 1900 to 1916, when the Italian population of Connecticut increased to 60,000. These people now make up the State's largest foreign group, leading the 'new immigration' from the countries of southern Europe. Today, there are 227,262 Italians in the State, with the metropolitan area of New Haven alone claiming 55,000 inhabitants of Italian descent.

Although invariably living in separate compact colonies, the Italian group has made a place for itself in commercial, industrial, and agricultural Connecticut. American-born Italians of the second generation quickly shake off the influence of the mother country, are eager to be considered Americans, and are inclined toward active participation in political as well as commercial life.

The Poles are numerically one of the most important ethnic groups in Connecticut. Their heaviest immigration came in 1907, and their concentration, usually in group settlements, is notable in cities such as New Britain and Bridgeport. The 1930 census lists 133,813 Poles in the State. They are well distributed in both agriculture and industry, and have a larger proportion of farmers than most of the other eminent groups.

Of the other Slavic groups, only the Lithuanians (30,690) and Czechoslovakians (32,491) are numerically important. The Lithuanians are heavily concentrated in the brass industries of Waterbury, and the Czechoslovakians are employed in considerable numbers in Bridgeport factories, which also employ large numbers of Magyars. These latter people, numbering 23,175 in Connecticut, usually are skilled and semi-skilled workers.

Jews have been resident in Connecticut since Colonial days. Even at the time of the Revolutionary War they had a part in commerce and finance, and early replaced the Yankee 'pedlar' as purveyors of goods. Figures on the Jewish population are at best inaccurate, as the Jews come from many countries, and data listed under 'country of origin' are confusing. Estimates place the total number of Connecticut Jews at 91,538, with Hartford and New Haven ranking second only to Atlantic City and New York in the proportionate size of their Jewish population. Connecticut is one of the very few States that has a Jewish farming population, with possibly about 1000 families engaged in agriculture. The majority of the Jews engaged in industry and trade are concentrated in the larger cities.

As early as 1774, there were 6562 Negroes in the State. But the present-day Negro population are not descendants of these eighteenth-century Connecticut slaves. Most of them have come from the Southern States in a steady migration lasting from about 1870 until after the World War. By 1910 there were 15,174, and in 1930, 29,354 Negroes in the State. They are employed chiefly in the unskilled labor and service occupations.

Various other ethnic groups of lesser numerical importance, including Greeks, Scotch, Finns, Ukrainians, French, Austrians, Armenians, and Swiss, make their individual contributions to the cosmopolitan pattern of Connecticut life.

The State has, within little more than a half century, been transformed from the habitat of a fairly homogeneous people to the workshop of a heterogeneous population.

TABLE I

RACIAL COMPOSITION OF THE POPULATION OF CONNECTICUT IN 1790 AS INDICATED BY NAMES OF HEADS OF FAMILIES

(According to the Federal Census Bureau, *A Century of Population Growth*)

NATIONALITY	NUMBER	PER CENT OF TOTAL
TOTAL................	232,236	100
English...............	223,437	96.2
Scotch................	6,425	2.8
Irish.................	1,589	0.7
French...............	512	0.2
Dutch................	258	0.1
Hebrew...............	5 } Less	
German...............	4 } than 1%.	
All Others............	6 }	

TABLE II

NUMERICAL GROWTH OF THE LARGEST FOREIGN-BORN WHITE STOCKS IN
CONNECTICUT, ACCORDING TO COUNTRY OF ORIGIN BY DECADES: 1860–1930

(Based on the Census Reports of the United States)

COUNTRY OF ORIGIN	1860	1870	1880	1890	1900	1910	1920	1930
England.........	8875	12992	15453	20572	21569	22422	22708c	22062
Scotland.........	2546	3238	4157	5992	6175	6750	7487	10013
Ireland..........	55445	70630	70638	77880	70994	58458	45464	38418
Sweden..........	42	323	2086	10021	16164	18208	17697	18453
Germany.........	8525	12443	15627	28176	31892	31127	22614	23465
Poland [1].........	73	83	225	1504	10698		46623	49267
Czechoslovakia [2]..		95	125	177	493		6558	12220
Austria..........	172	154	287	1187	5330	23642	12699	6306
Hungary.........		30	76	1146	5692	13855	13222	9836
Russia...........	46	34	65	3027	11404	54121	38719	25769
Lithuania [3].......							11662	13247
Greece..........	6	4	1	5	121	1074	3851	3337
Italy............	61	117	879	5285	19105	56954	80322	87123
Canada and Newfoundland [4]...	3145	10840	16444	21231	27045	26898	24967	38566

[1] The 1910 figures for Poland are included in those for Russia, Germany, and Austria.

[2] Up to 1900 inclusively figures given are of those coming from Bohemia; figures for 1910 are included in those for Austria.

[3] Since Lithuania did not achieve an independent status until after the end of the World War, figures prior to 1920 are lacking.

[4] It can be estimated that about two-thirds of those coming from Canada after 1870 were French-Canadians.

TRANSPORTATION

HIGHWAYS

THE tourist entering Connecticut today finds hard-surfaced highways leading to every section of the State. Early travelers were not so fortunate. Letters written in 1780 by a European visitor, Count Chastellux, mention the highways through Litchfield as being more for 'the roebuck than for laden horses and conveyances'; and in another place, 'you mount four or five miles, continually bounding from one large stone to another, which cross the road and give it a resemblance to stairs.' In 1716, the inhabitants of Hartford complained that 'the Collegiate School of Connecticut' (later Yale College) should not be situated in New Haven because it was 'so remote' and the transportation by water was so uncertain. They also recorded that there was 'but little communication between the colonies' (meaning the towns of Hartford, New London, and New Haven).

Not until well into the eighteenth century was there much travel in New England. Those who passed through Connecticut found the State peculiarly backward. The Yankee individualist stayed at home, and thought other people should do the same. In a pamphlet issued in 1935, Miss Isabel S. Mitchell summarizes the situation thus: 'Bad roads discouraged intercourse, lack of intercourse increased isolation, isolation developed independence and a lack of co-operation, which in turn caused the roads to suffer.' The stagecoach era began in the eighteenth century, and reached its height after 1840. The first regular line of stages, established in 1783 between Hartford, Boston, and New Haven, met with spirited opposition. It is recorded that 'when Levi Somers proposed the scheme to a friend of his in Boston, the latter ridiculed him as a visionary, saying "The time may come when the public will support a stage between Hartford and Boston, but not in your day or mine."'

Beginning late in the eighteenth century, private corporations were chartered to construct and maintain specific roads, given a franchise for collecting tolls, and often allowed to raise funds by lottery to finance construction. The first toll road in the State was the Mohegan Road, following the course of an old Indian trail, between Norwich and New London. In May, 1792, an act was passed by the legislature establishing a toll-gate (the second authorized, but the first to be completed, in America), and appointing a board of commissioners to maintain this highway, which was not owned by a corporation, but was really one of the earliest State roads in America. Toll collections were continued on this highway until 1849, when the New London, Willimantic and Palmer Railroad opened its line parallel to the Mohegan Road. The third toll-gate in the United States was established on the Greenwich Road in 1792. An October session of the General Assembly in 1797 granted a franchise to the Boston Turnpike Company over roads 'from Hartford, through East Hartford, Bolton, Coventry, Mansfield, Ashford, Pomfret, and Thompson to the Massachusetts Line.' This route became known as 'the middle turnpike.' It was on this road that a famous old Connecticut tavern, Woodbridge's in Manchester, stood. In every case, the toll roads granted exemption to churchgoers, funeral attendants, members of the militia, and people going to the mills.

Between 1795 and 1853, one hundred and twenty-one of these toll-road or turnpike franchises were granted. A charter for a turnpike to Bristol was granted in 1801 and revoked in 1810. The Talcott Mountain Turnpike Company was chartered in May, 1798, to construct and maintain a road from Hartford through Farmington to New Hartford. Other important pikes were built by the Greenwoods Company and the Hartford and New Haven Turnpike Company. These corporations failed to satisfy the public, and about 1850 they began to relinquish their franchises. Governmental action then became imperative.

The year 1895 saw the abandonment of the franchise for the Derby Turnpike, the last of the old pikes. A new era in road-building started in that year with the creation of a State commission to assume responsibility for Connecticut highways. Through routes were designed as trunk lines, and provisions made for their maintenance in 1908. 'Feeder roads' became known as State Aid roads. Since 1931, the dirt or third-class roads have been in another classification, and a yearly grant of $17,500 is made by the State to each of the 169 towns, to be expended on dirt roads of their selection, under supervision of the State highway engineers.

A significant date in the annals of road construction is 1858, when Eli Whitney Blake of New Haven invented the stone crusher that made possible the economical construction of highways on a large scale. There were scarcely a dozen miles of macadam roads in all New England as late as 1851, but today there are more than five thousand miles of hard-surfaced highways in Connecticut alone.

The landscaping of highways and the establishment of more than 125 shaded roadside parks are conspicuous developments in Connecticut. Clay banks are sodded, or planted with iris and rambler roses; and tri-angular plots at main intersections bloom with flowering shrubs. Rag-weed along the highways is cut, in deference to hay-fever sufferers. Woodland areas close to waterfalls and roadside brooks have been con-verted into small State parks, and equipped with tables and other facili-ties for picnicking.

Winter road conditions in Connecticut are usually very good. Strate-gically stationed highway crews turn out with plows and sand trucks at the first sign of snow or sleet. Experimental highway lighting is being tried in several sections, but no permanent installations have been made as yet (1938).

RAILROADS

The introduction of railroad transportation into Connecticut met with considerable opposition. Connecticut rivers offered easy access to the back country; Long Island Sound furnished coastwise transportation facilities; and the owners of the turnpike system were active in obstructing competition. The typical Yankee dread of change and satisfaction with 'things as they are' may also have had some bearing on popular reluctance to adopt the new and faster mode of transport.

In 1832, a charter was finally granted to the New York and Stonington Railroad, after prolonged debate in the General Assembly, during which a memorial was prepared stating that a railroad would 'produce more harm than good, and may result in great injury and injustice to private property. A railroad is a monopoly in a peculiar sense.' This memorial was signed by Roger Sherman, Simeon Baldwin, William Bristol, and J. Wood, all 'overseers of turnpike stock.'

The next charter, granted later in 1832, was to the Boston, Norwich and Worcester Railroad to operate between Norwich and Worcester. This route tapped the rich industrial region to the north, and eliminated the hazardous sea route around Point Judith, connecting both Boston and Worcester with the sheltered water route along Long Island Sound through the Thames River at Norwich. Practically all the early railroads ran north and south, connecting the back country with the seaports. It was not thought possible to build a coastwise rail line at this time, because of the numerous rivers to be bridged.

The Hartford and New Haven Railroad opened a line to Meriden in 1838. Later, in 1839, this was extended to Hartford, connecting with a Springfield, Massachusetts, line that brought this railroad into direct competition with the Norwich and Stonington lines for New York to Boston traffic. When this charter was granted, the people of Newington presented a petition stating that they were a 'peaceable, orderly people' and begging that their quiet might not be disturbed by 'steam cars and an influx of strangers.'

The Housatonic Railroad was chartered in 1836 to connect western Massachusetts with Long Island Sound and to form a connection between New York and Albany by way of Bridgeport. Until 1848, this was Bridgeport's only railroad. The line along the old Farmington Canal, chartered in 1846, was opened between New Haven and Plainville in 1848, and extended to Northampton, Massachusetts, in 1855.

The first east-and-west railroad line in the State was the New York and New Haven Railroad, chartered in 1844 and opened late in 1848. This line absorbed the Hartford and New Haven Railroad in 1872. Consolidation and refinancing marked the history of Connecticut railroads for several decades after the Civil War. Trolley lines, steamship lines, and even hotels were absorbed by the railway financiers. Attempts were made to operate independent lines, but the great New Haven system managed to absorb most of them.

Electric power was in use on the New Britain to Hartford branch of this road as early as 1901; the main line was electrified as far as Stamford in 1907, and to New Haven in 1914. The 'Comet,' first stream-lined train on the New Haven system, made its initial run between Providence and Boston on June 5, 1935. A second stream-lined train now operates between Bridgeport and Hartford.

Early in 1937, the New Haven system petitioned the Interstate Commerce Commission for permission to abandon many miles of non-productive track throughout the State. Among the lines slated for abandonment are the Litchfield branch, with one hundred forty-seven curves between Hawleyville and Litchfield, a distance of about twenty-five miles, over which only the 'K–1 type' of engines can run.

The only railroad other than the New Haven operating in Connecticut today is the Central Vermont, a subsidiary of the Canadian National System.

CANALS

An occasional crumbling stone arch, or a stretch of over-grown ditch filled with stagnant water, now the home of muskrats and herons, is all that remains of the former canal system which Connecticut hoped might compete with the great Erie Canal.

On January 29, 1822, citizens from seventeen towns met to discuss the building of the Farmington Canal. In May of the same year a charter was granted to the Farmington Canal Company, as part of a grand project that was expected eventually to connect the St. Lawrence River with Long Island Sound. Work was started near the Massachusetts border on July 4, 1825. Three years later the canal was opened from New Haven to Cheshire. Progress was thenceforth rapid, and in 1829 the canal was operated to Westfield, Massachusetts, bringing some benefits in reduced fuel costs to communities along the route. But continuous landslides raised the cost of maintenance so high that a loss was sustained each year. In 1846, the stockholders refused to subscribe for more stock; and in 1847, operations were finally suspended. The only dividend ever paid to the stockholders of this company was derived from the sale of hay along the right of way. Many of the stockholders were New Yorkers, and they petitioned the legislature for permission to build a railroad to replace the canal. This petition was granted, and a line of steel later traversed the same lowlands where the lazy canal boats once crept along with their cargoes.

Canals have never prospered in Connecticut, but the largest failure was that of the Farmington venture. The Blackstone and Middlesex canals were relatively short lived, and did not pay. The Windsor Locks Canal, completed in 1828, was in a somewhat different category, because it was built to take river traffic around the rapids and to provide water power. This canal, with its crude hand-operated gates and locks, is still open to traffic.

Failure was swift and conclusive for the Quinebaug Canal of 1824, the Saugatuck and New Milford ditch of 1829, and the Sharon Canal venture of 1826. Connecticut financiers and engineers decided that the Nutmeg State was too hilly and rough to make any canal project a paying venture.

BUS LINES

In Connecticut, as elsewhere, the rapid development of improved highways has been accompanied in recent years by a no less rapid development of bus transportation. Some fifty companies, covering nearly 2250 route miles, now operate within the State; and all of the larger eastern interstate lines cross through its territory. Although about 350 miles of street railway remain (1937), bus service has made heavy inroads upon this form of transportation. Railroad-owned buses shuttle back and forth across country where the steam lines have ceased to be remunerative; and large fleets of school buses take youngsters to and from the consolidated schools that have recently replaced many of the old district schools in the State.

AVIATION

The new era in transportation marked by the conquest of the air was recognized by Connecticut as early as 1911, when the State adopted the first code of laws in the country governing the registration, numbering, and use of aircraft, and the licensing of pilots. In 1936, there were 21 aviation fields, 765 licensed pilots, and 322 registered air-craft within the State. The only strictly commercial airport is Rentschler Field at East Hartford; here an airline operating between Newark and Boston, on a schedule of three trips daily each way in summer and two in winter, picks up approximately 450 passengers and 2700 pounds of mail and express each month. The State's air routes are well marked with both directional markers and beacons.

INDUSTRY AND COMMERCE

SHIPPING AND SHIPBUILDING

THE early settlers of Connecticut, concentrated in compact settlements for protection from unfriendly Indians, soon discovered that it was not possible to live by agricultural pursuits alone. Although practicing an economy which at first was almost wholly self-sufficient, there were still a few necessities that had to be imported; and as living conditions gradually became less primitive, there was an increasing demand for other imports. Most important of all, as they established themselves more firmly, they required an outside market for their surplus crops, livestock, hides, etc., and for such early manufactures as bricks and forest products.

Thus it was that, within a relatively short time after the first colonization, many of the settlers became shipbuilders, mariners, and traders. Onions from Wethersfield, tobacco from Windsor, oak staves from the back country, cattle and hides from the rich pasture lands, were shipped in home-built sloops, often of only ten or twelve tons, down the rivers to the sea and the West Indies. The first voyages were blind ventures into the unknown from which many ships never returned. The 'Great Shippe' which sailed out of New Haven in 1646, laden with produce to recoup the fortunes of the settlers, became one of these ghost ships.

These hardy sailor-farmers often had more difficulty in getting out of the rivers than they later experienced in reaching the West Indies. They were often delayed by flood tides rising against the current, shoal water, or a changing channel that put the little sloops aground before their sails could fill with an offshore breeze to carry them away to Caribbean ports.

A bit of old Connecticut can still be found in Paramaribo, Dutch Guiana, where most of the buildings were erected by Connecticut traders. The traveler is puzzled by the incongruity of fireless houses equipped with brick chimneys, heavy green-painted shutters, and cupolas perched atop steeply pitched shingled roofs. He wonders at the doors in true New England Colonial style, with fan-lights and wooden pilasters. The Town

Hall at Paramaribo was built of brick brought from Connecticut by Captain Joshua Green of Glastonbury.

The record of one ship, the 'Neptune,' which sailed from New Haven in 1797 for China, is representative of the success that attended many Connecticut shipping ventures. The 'Neptune,' commanded by Captain Townsend, carried a general cargo and $500 in gold coin. In the West Indies, her master traded for rum and sugar; at Rio, he bartered for fustic, indigo, sandalwood, and other Brazilian products. Around the Falkland Islands and Tierra del Fuego, the crew of the 'Neptune' spent some time in sealing. Rounding the Horn, they sailed for the South Seas, where they carried on a brisk exchange of calico and other cotton cloth, brass wire, and old iron for dividivi (the pods, used for tanning and dyeing, of a native tree), pearls, and pearl shell. Finally reaching the coast of China, Captain Townsend bartered sealskins and the remainder of his original cargo for teas, silks, lacquerwork, porcelain, sandalwood, and ivory. After two and a half years, the 'Neptune' returned to New Haven on July 11, 1799, with a cargo valued at $250,000 and the original stake of $500 in gold intact.

Shipbuilding at Derby, on the Housatonic River, dates from 1657. Thereafter this port, at the head of tidewater, rapidly became the shipping center for products of the surrounding inland districts. In addition, the Derby Fishing Company carried on an extensive trade with the West Indies and Mediterranean countries. Not until the building of highways and railroads deflected commerce from the Housatonic Valley to the better ports of New Haven and Bridgeport did Derby lose its importance in shipping.

The port of New Haven, although hampered by the slow development of communications with the back country, still managed to build up, after 1763, a thriving trade with the West Indies, Newfoundland, and the neighboring ports along the Atlantic coast. By 1800, trade flourished with China, the Pacific, the East Indies, and the South Seas, and an average of one hundred ships cleared New Haven Harbor annually. In 1802, Long Wharf was built, and a sealing fleet operated out of New Haven. At the opening of the War of 1812, the port had six hundred registered seamen, engaged in privateering or in regular service. The loss of foreign trade through the war and the preceding Embargo Act, the opening of the Farmington Canal in 1828, and the building of the Hartford and New Haven Railroad in 1833–38 gave such an impetus to industrial development that manufacturing rapidly became the chief interest of the city.

Bridgeport was a center of privateering activities during the Revolution, and acquired a portion of Derby's trade when the highway from Newtown was built in 1798–1801.

The first shipbuilding in New London dates from the John Colt venture in 1664. New London was sending ships to all oceans by 1819, and its skippers were in great demand at other ports. At the peak of activity, about 1846, the New London whaling fleet consisted of seventy-one ships, the last survivor of which came to port in 1909. Captain Stevens Rogers of New London was master of the 'Savannah,' the first steamship to cross the Atlantic. The present shipyards at Essex, Noank, and Groton, all that remains of this formerly important industry, continue to enjoy a brisk trade. Submarines are built at Groton, pleasure craft at Essex, and the Noank yards are busy on various classes and tonnage.

Mystic and Stonington were especially active in shipping and shipbuilding. The former was noted for its clipper ships, the latter for its whaling fleet. Toward the close of the clipper-ship era, Mystic took the lead in this type of construction, producing a vessel that combined large cargo space with speed. In 1860, the modified clipper ship 'Andrew Jackson,' Captain John E. Williams commanding, established a record of eighty-nine days and four hours from New York to San Francisco, breaking by nine hours the record made by the 'Flying Cloud' in 1851. The 'Andrew Jackson' was built by Irons and Grinnell in 1854. The yachts built in Mystic by D. O. Richmond in 1870–80 held all records until the ballast-keel type was designed. Stonington interests controlled nineteen whalers between 1830 and 1850. '

Practically all of the Connecticut River towns served as early commercial and shipping outlets for 'back-country' produce and manufactures. Middletown developed into an important shipbuilding and commercial center, carrying on a thriving trade with the Orient; Rocky Hill, Wethersfield, and Windsor became warehouse and shipping centers. At Wethersfield was built the first ship in the State, the 'Tryall,' in 1649. A canal around the rapids at Windsor Locks brought some commerce to that town in 1829. A warehouse was established about 1636 at Warehouse Point. The old Gildersleeve Shipyard at Portland, where an occasional barge is still built, was once one of the most active on the river; a schooner of ninety tons came off the ways there as early as 1741, and during the Revolution a number of war vessels were turned out, including the 900-ton 'Bourbon.' Ships for the New York and Galveston Line, established in 1863, were built in Portland. East Haddam was an important center of shipping and shipbuilding. Sloops were built on the Salmon

River at Leesville. Thomas Childs, a Middle Haddam shipbuilder, is said to have laid down 237 vessels. Essex was such an important ship-building center that it was raided by the British during the War of 1812. Old Saybrook, at the mouth of the Connecticut River, was an important port for coasting vessels and for the trans-shipment of goods from smaller river boats to seagoing ships. More than sixty skippers and their crews from Old Lyme sailed clipper ships to China and the Far East, and later manned packet ships to Liverpool and Havre.

Rumors of slave trade in connection with these early voyages were numerous; whenever a skipper was suspiciously overdue from the West Indies, gossips would speculate on the possibility of profit in a cargo of 'black ivory.' Undoubtedly, many Connecticut fortunes were thus founded in those early days.

Today, Connecticut's freighting traffic is handled almost entirely by rail and by truck. A few boats still carry cargoes to New York from New London, New Haven, and Bridgeport; an occasional tug wheezes up the Connecticut River with one or two coal barges, or a tanker whistles for the opening of the draw at East Haddam. But the romantic era of the merchantman, the privateer, the clipper ship, and the whaler has long since passed. Old sailors pour gasoline into the tanks of their modern fishing boats, and dream of more adventurous days.

MANUFACTURING

While Connecticut's ships were exporting staple provisions to many other States and foreign countries, thousands of discontented farmers were migrating to the West, for, despite the fertility of the Connecticut Valley, large areas of the State were rock-ribbed and untillable. As early as 1840, the density of population was sixty-four persons to the square mile, equaling the 1930 distribution in Kentucky or North Carolina. Many of those who remained were forced to find more profitable sources of income. The pressure of necessity, aided by an abundance of swift streams providing water-power, developed the industrial ingenuity and resource-fulness that thenceforth characterized the Connecticut Yankee. Home industries that at first supplied merely local markets began to lay the foundations for Connecticut's transition to an industrial State.

A small water-power mill began operations in New London as early as 1650, and one at Derby in 1679. Bog iron was worked at Lake Saltonstall, East Haven, in 1665. Nails were made and exported before 1716. An effort was made to introduce silk-culture into the Colony in 1732, and a silk factory was opened at Mansfield in 1759. London hatters were complaining as early as 1732 of the competition of Connecticut hats. In 1737, a Simsbury blacksmith produced the first copper coins made in the Colonies, using copper mined at East Granby. The paper mills of Norwich date from 1768, and those of East Hartford from 1776. Brass was being worked at Waterbury in 1749, and the first tinware made in this country was produced at Berlin in 1740.

As soon as the small industries had supplied local markets, some of the manufacturers — as, for example, the Pattison brothers of Berlin, makers of tinware — set out on foot, with packs upon their backs, to seek a market in outlying districts. Within a few years, scores of peddlers employed by numerous small manufacturers had made their way as far west as Lake Erie and St. Louis, and south to New Orleans. Coastal blockades during the Revolution and War of 1812 stimulated local manufacture. The peddler whose original pack had been confined to tin goods was soon recognized as a vendor of Yankee 'notions' — buttons, pins, hats, combs, brass kettles, and clocks. Almost every important present-day Connecticut industry received its original impetus from the Yankee peddler, who supplied ever-extending markets as he followed the tide of migration westward.

Hartford claims the first woolen mill in New England, established in 1788. A noteworthy improvement of native wool is credited to General David Humphreys, who very early in the nineteenth century imported one hundred merino sheep and developed a superior strain on his farms in Watertown. In 1806, Humphreys built a complete factory town — nucleus of the present-day Seymour — where he established a school and an apprentice system, and produced paper, woolens, tools, and metal goods.

The first successful cotton mill in the State was built by Samuel Pitkin and Company at Hilliardsville (in Manchester), in 1794. Cotton mills established at Vernon in 1804 were followed by mills at Pomfret in 1806 and at Jewett City in 1810. As late as 1810, it was estimated that two-thirds of all the cloth made in the country was of household manufacture.

Since the opening of the Patent Office in 1790, Connecticut has received more patents in proportion to its population than any other State in the Union. This inventiveness and skill in mechanical design has greatly furthered the success of Connecticut industries. The advantage

INDUSTRY

YANKEE ingenuity has been the mainspring of Connecticut industry ever since pioneer Connecticut farmers first launched little ten-ton sloops and sailed off over uncharted seas, seeking a market in the West Indies for surplus crops and food products. The infant industries originally furnished goods for home consumption, but when that market was supplied, turned to the production of varied merchandise for the 'Yankee Pedlar' trade. Buttons and the smaller metal specialties formed a great part of the stock of these itinerant merchants. Wherever they went they discovered demands for new articles, and when they returned for fresh stock, their crude drawings and patterns furnished fresh stimulus to the little streamside industrial plants. No matter what the demand, the factory seldom failed to furnish the desired article, even though it were first necessary to devise hand-made tools. This leadership in the working of metals, in skill and design, has been responsible for the success of Connecticut's industrial plants, which today lead the country in the production of precision tools and scientific recording instruments as well as in a score of other lines of manufacturing. All kinds of brass articles are made in Connecticut, totaling 30 per cent of the country's output.

The movement of goods to and from markets by railroads has played an essential part in the development of Connecticut industry, dependent as it is on distant raw materials and nation-wide custom, and today new air trails are blazed to far places by planes, propellers, and motors of Yankee manufacture.

BURNISHING BRASS, SCOVILL MANUFACTURING COMPANY, WATERBURY

PRATT AND WHITNEY, AIRCRAFT MANUFACTURERS, EAST HARTFORD

ASSEMBLY DEPARTMENT OF THE PROPELLER DIVISION, UNITED AIRCRAFT
CORPORATION, EAST HARTFORD

FINAL ASSEMBLY DEPARTMENT, SIKORSKY AIRCRAFT, STRATFORD

EXPERIMENTAL DEPARTMENT, SIKORSKY AIRCRAFT

INSPECTING POLISHED COPPER SHEETS, AMERICAN BRASS COMPANY, ANSO

FORGING HOT BRASS, SCOVILL MANUFACTURING COMPANY, WATERBURY

CASTING SHOP, AMERICAN BRASS COMPANY, WATERBURY

WITHDRAWING A HEATED COPPER BILLET FROM THE FURNACE, AMERICAN
BRASS COMPANY, WATERBURY

LINE-UP OF LOCOMOTIVES, NEW HAVEN RAILROAD, CEDAR HILL

STEAM POWER, STREAMLINED TRAIN, NEW HAVEN RAILRO

attained by the early Connecticut craftsmen in the working of metals has grown, until today the State leads the country in the production of precision tools and scientific recording instruments, as well as in a score of other manufactures.

Eli Whitney's invention of the cotton gin in 1792 was a milestone of accomplishment for Yankee mills and southern agriculture. Whitney's introduction of quantity production methods in his firearms factory in Hamden also had a far-reaching effect upon industry throughout the Nation. His production of interchangeable parts, and his system of specialized labor, each worker having but one operation to perform, gave Connecticut industry an early advantage. Upon this system has been built the carefully planned high-speed production and the assembly line of modern industry. Whitney worked closely with Simeon North (see below) in inaugurating these modern production methods.

In the brass industry, Connecticut took an early lead, starting in 1749. Brass buttons were manufactured in 1802 by Abel Porter at Waterbury. Rolled sheet-brass, drawn brass wire, brass pins, rods, spun brass shapes, shellwork and eyelets, all were developed as the industry grew and the Connecticut brassmakers attained greater skill. Connecticut produces thirty per cent of the brass manufactured in the United States (1937), and leads all other States in this field. Britannia ware was introduced by Charles and Hiram Yale in 1815. The world's largest factory engaged in the production of silverware is situated in Meriden, and the State as a whole ranks fourth in this manufacture.

The discovery of the process for vulcanizing rubber, in 1839, by Charles Goodyear of Naugatuck, brought a thriving industry to Connecticut and was an important contributing factor in the development of modern motor transportation, electric power distribution, and industrial efficiency.

Clockmaking in Connecticut is noteworthy as an example of the development from household or one-man manufacturing into an important industry, which now leads all other States in the value of production. Connecticut clocks were first produced by individual craftsmen and distributed by peddlers, who soon made the sundial and the 'time stake' obsolete throughout the original Colonies.

Benjamin Cheney produced wooden clocks about 1745, in a small back-yard shop at East Hartford. Thomas Harland of Norwich made a few clocks, in connection with other mechanical devices, about 1773. Daniel Burnap, an apprentice to Harland, established his own shop at East Windsor about 1780, and first advertised 'brass wheeled clocks' on March 14, 1791. Gideon Roberts was making wooden-movement clocks in 1790 at his Bristol shop. These makers were all limited to a very small output, and they were often their own peddlers. Eli Terry was constructing clocks by hand in 1793. In 1807, he purchased an old mill in Plymouth, and equipped it with machinery, producing in 1808, the first five hundred machine-made clocks manufactured in America. Joseph Ives, who entered the field in 1811, was a clockmaker of exceptional inventive ability; in 1832, he placed on the market clocks with brass works, and later patented and produced clocks with a cantilever spring. In 1812, Seth Thomas started operations in the Thomaston plant which still bears his name. The quality clocks of Sessions and New Haven are likewise time recorders that today find world-wide markets. The first cheap watch, the once-famous Waterbury, with its seemingly endless spring, was also a Connecticut product; the Ingersoll and Ingraham watches of today are made in this State.

With Simeon North's introduction of the system of interchangeable parts for firearms in 1813, this industry developed rapidly in Connecticut, until the names of North, Whitney, Sharps, Spencer, Winchester, Colt, Remington, Savage, Parker, Ballard, and Marlin had become famous in this country and abroad. The State now leads all others in the production of firearms and ammunition.

The first actual use of a submarine for war purposes is credited to David Bushnell, a Connecticut designer, who made an unsuccessful attempt in 1776 to sink the British warship 'Eagle' off New York. Simon Lake of Milford did considerable early research work on submarines, and is credited with the perfection of the first even-keel submarine, in 1894. Groton shipyards are now (1937) at work on submarines for the United States Navy.

Astonishing growth has been attained in the aircraft industry. Plants in East Hartford and Stratford have kept ahead of the field, and operate on schedules that keep the test pilots busy. Government orders continue to come in; and constant improvement in motors and propellers, together with a supply of especially skilled labor, promise well for the continued growth and expansion of the industry. Fighting ships, cargo and transport planes, either built complete in Connecticut or powered by Connecticut motors, now duplicate the feats of the old Connecticut clipper ships in breaking speed records to the far corners of the world.

Two once-thriving Connecticut industries have experienced difficulty in adapting themselves to changed conditions. Cutlery manufacture, formerly of importance, has practically ceased because of foreign competition;

and the cotton and silk mills have suffered greatly from low-wage southern competition. A shift in manufacture to rayon goods has not solved the textile industry's problem. Some smaller mills have been taken over by garment manufacturers from other States, but the change is usually unsatisfactory to labor and the community alike. Woolen mills occasionally enjoy short-lived prosperity when new blood or new backing is obtained. The plush mills at Seymour, using the Tingue process, operate with outside capital. Mohair mills in Shelton enjoy spasmodic activity which fluctuates with the demands of the motor industry, but the Montville mills have closed. The smaller mills that specialize on a single product are more successful in weathering the storm; but as a whole, the textile industry in Connecticut has fallen upon evil days.

Connecticut ranks first among the States in the production of commodities as varied as typewriters and felt hats. Danbury is 'the hat center of the world,' and Fairfield County produces thirty-eight per cent of the American output in this field. About one-half the hooks and eyes, pins, needles, and snap fasteners produced in this country are manufactured in Connecticut.

The period of the State's greatest development in manufacturing began soon after the War of 1812. During the years from 1850 to 1900, the population of the State increased 145 per cent, but the average number of wage-earners employed in manufacturing establishments increased 248.3 per cent. Wage-earners so employed in 1850 constituted 13.7 per cent of the State's total population, and 19.5 per cent in 1900. The decade of greatest relative development was that of 1909–19, including the war years, when factory output increased 184 per cent. New factory construction in 1923 and 1924 was valued at $16,807,775. In 1937, more than 60 per cent of Connecticut's population depended upon some three hundred manufacturing establishments for a livelihood.

MINING AND QUARRYING

Nearly every known mineral has been found in Connecticut, and the exploitation of its mineral wealth dates back to Colonial days, when Governor Winthrop and others seized lands and mineral rights. Yet there had been little commercial mining in the State, especially of the more precious minerals. Some rocks of the western highlands are believed to be of the Pre-Cambrian age; gold has been discovered and actually mined; garnets are taken from a carefully guarded working in Tolland County today, but the quantity is unknown except to the owner of the mine.

Portland quarries still produce feldspar in marketable amounts. Roxbury granite from Mine Hill, of excellent quality and available in unlimited quantities, is now used for residential and public buildings. The lime quarries of western Connecticut yield a fine quality of building lime, and the output of agricultural lime more than suffices for local needs. Brick clays are of frequent occurrence. Traprock quarries are worked more extensively than any others, because of the demand created by highway construction and the excellent quality of the stone.

Commercially unimportant production of mica is carried on in backyard mines in Middlesex County. Bismuth mines in Monroe are worked by hand and by crude mechanical processes. Silica is available almost everywhere in the State; and no iron ore is of better quality than the limonite, or brown hematite, once produced by the now flooded Ore Hill pits. Near New Haven, in the dense brush of a hillside pasture lot, a crude windlass marks the spot where a hard-working Italian secures a yield of about three dollars a day from his private gold mine. The discovery of coal at Southbury caused some excitement when drilling crews came in to prospect for oil between Poverty Hollow and Bates Rock, but the small deposits were never exploited.

At Mine Hill in Roxbury a vertical vein of siderite, six to eight feet thick and of undetermined length, was prospected at various times from 1724 on. A great plant for the smelting of ore was constructed, 'lease hounds' operated unrestrained, a German goldsmith was engaged to develop what was supposed to be the silver content of the ore, and tales of the wondrous wealth of the hill beside the Shepaug River spread abroad. The ore was a spathic and ferrous carbonate with an iron content running to 57 or 60 per cent, but the gas content made pre-heats necessary and caused many explosions in the furnaces. Dank drifts reach into the heart of the hill, furnaces and stacks stand gaunt and neglected, and the Columbia School of Mines utilizes the site as a field practice area. Equally promising at one time were the garnet mines of Roxbury, where tons of crystals were mined and ground for abrasive purposes by local labor. Silica paints and wood fillers were once exported from the State, but the stone has no commercial value today; the mines are water-filled, and the last mill has been burned or abandoned.

Brownstone from Portland quarries changed the complexion of New

York, when stone boats plied from the riverside workings to the city where brownstone fronts were popularized. A well-known scouring powder is still produced in a country mill with Connecticut stone furnishing the base; but Winthrop's cobalt mines are now disused, and his 'tall tales' of gold in purest form are discredited.

FISHERIES

Connecticut's commercial fisheries have long suffered from stream and harbor pollution, but this hazard is gradually being eliminated by a vigilant State Water Commission and State Health Department. Restocking is now carried on with considerable success, and the return of shad to the Connecticut River is especially notable.

Commercial interests and the State Shellfish Commission have devoted much attention to the cultivation of oysters and lobsters. The Commission has helped to develop these natural resources by establishing an efficient lobster hatchery at Noank, regulating the harvesting of shellfish, fixing closed areas, eliminating pests, licensing vessels, and taxing oyster acreage to support these regulatory activities.

Scallop fisheries on the Niantic River, swordfishing out of Mystic and Stonington, flounder fishing offshore, and the harvesting of soft or long clams are important marine industries. The shad fisheries of the Connecticut River make a valued contribution to the part-time income of rivermen, who haul nets in season and secure other employment when the 'run' is over. With excellent markets at their very door, Connecticut fishermen probably could dispose of many times their present annual catch without exporting any part of it.

Oyster farming is an important activity in Connecticut. A yield of as much as a thousand dollars an acre has been recorded from the underseas gardens in which the oysters are planted, cultivated, and harvested. Seed oysters bring about eighty cents a bushel in the shell, but good seasons are considerably less frequent than poor ones. The last really good 'catch' in Connecticut waters was in 1931. Local experience determines the best location for the beds, which are kept clean for the fattening process. Oysters are left on the fattening beds for a year or more, to eliminate all copper coloring or pollution resulting from the absorption of industrial wastes. Connecticut oyster beds in 1934 covered an area of 47,826 acres.

LABOR

WITH the emergence of an industrial wage-earning class at the close of the eighteenth century, labor organization became possible. The opening of small factories around New Haven, Hartford, and New London created a great demand for skilled and unskilled labor, a demand that was met somewhat by the use of skilled artisans. Until 1810, however, manufacturing was greatly hampered by the high cost of labor, for unskilled workers found the cheap western lands a more attractive goal.

The skilled workers were at this time in their heyday. Their social status was high and their political influence greater than their numbers justified. At the same time, ample opportunity was allowed them to enter the ranks of the employing class. The higher educational level of the artisans was evidenced by the fact that in 1793 they established a technical and literary library in New Haven.

In 1807, the General Society of Mechanics of New Haven was organized with a membership of ninety-five. Its objectives were 'To relieve such of the members as are reduced to a state of suffering: to assist young mechanics by loans and to promote the mechanical arts.' By 1811, the loan fund of the society amounted to more than $450.

After 1815, industry developed more rapidly than did the available supply of labor. Yet, despite the growing shortage of workers, a form of economic feudalism prevailed, since employers still continued the tradition of the indentured apprentice. However, the shortage was met somewhat by the increased employment of women and children. The 'sun to sun' system of labor, practiced by farmers, was transferred to the growing factories, and approved by public opinion, for Connecticut tradition had invested 'industrious habits' with the sacredness of a moral, if not a religious, precept.

By 1830, the shortage of labor was somewhat alleviated by the growing tide of immigration from Europe. Unskilled labor became more plentiful, resulting in a drop in wages. In 1831, $3 a week for men and $2 for women were considered fair wages, from which $1.25 was deducted for company board. Children were paid from fifty cents to one dollar a week, according to their age and degree of skill. These wages were based upon a working day of from fourteen to sixteen hours in summer, and from ten to twelve hours during the winter months.

The main complaint voiced by the skilled workers at this time had to do with their lack of economic and political equality. Their independence was submerged under a general wave of 'shop discipline,' and their political interests were merged with those of their employers. Socially, too, they no longer occupied the position that had been theirs in the closing years of the eighteenth century.

It was due to these dissatisfactions on the part of skilled labor that the first industrial union in this country, the New England Association of Farmers, Mechanics and Other Workingmen, was organized in Lyme in 1830. New Haven, Hartford, and New London were the centers for this new political and industrial union in Connecticut. In New London, in 1831, three candidates of the Association were elected to the State legislature, and its entire slate of town officers was elected to office. Due to lack of support from the unskilled workers, the Association went out of existence in 1834.

The first important strike in Connecticut took place in the latter part of 1833, when weavers employed by the Thompsonville Carpet Manufacturing Company quit work to enforce a demand for higher wages. In retaliation, the company brought suit against the strike leaders, charging them with conspiracy to ruin the business — the first such suit in the United States. Three separate trials took place, the last occurring in 1836 when a verdict was rendered for the defendants after the jury had been instructed that it was legal to combine to raise wages but unlawful to conspire to ruin an employer's business.

Although the ten-hour day had been established in New York by 1830, mechanics and laborers in Connecticut still worked from dawn to dusk. The first strike in connection with the ten-hour day took place in Hartford in 1835. Although unsuccessful, it was the forerunner of many such efforts to shorten the working day for Connecticut labor. In 1835, the cordwainers of New Haven organized a union to obtain shorter hours and increased pay.

The fifties brought the first of the modern protective trade unions to Connecticut. In 1852, the first typographical union in Connecticut was started in New Haven; and in 1853, the Hat Makers' Association was organized in Danbury to strengthen the apprentice system, much abused by the employers of that day. The cigar makers of New Haven had developed an effective union by 1853, and two years later a convention was held at Hartford to plan an organization for the cigar makers of New York, Connecticut, and Massachusetts.

The manufacturing boom of the reconstruction period following the

Civil War greatly stimulated the growth of labor unions. Among the groups that organized during this period were the Iron Molders of Bridgeport, and in New Haven the Bricklayers and Plasterers, the Locomotive Engineers, and the Stone Masons. In 1867, labor votes made possible the election of James E. English to the governorship of Connecticut. For their political aid, the unions were promised an eight-hour day; a law to that effect was subsequently passed by the legislature, but with the provision that it was not obligatory upon employers if the latter had made other arrangements with their employees. Needless to say, the law was unenforceable. With the depression of 1873, labor organization in Connecticut declined, and further unionization was not attempted until the Knights of Labor came into the field in 1878.

In 1874, a consumers' co-operative, the Sovereigns of Labor, made a bid for labor support. In 1875, the organization claimed that it had 1200 members in New Haven, 1000 in Hartford, 500 in Meriden, and 500 in Bridgeport and Middletown. Organized and led by employers and politicians, it made arrangements with merchants whereby discounts were given to members. Soon, as the result of protests that inferior products were given with the discounts, the organization opened its own stores, employing a business firm in Hartford to act as its commission agents in purchasing products directly from grangers and manufacturers. By 1876, little remained of the Sovereigns of Labor.

The first local assembly of the Knights of Labor was organized at New Britain in 1878. Unlike the later American Federation of Labor, the Knights of Labor did not confine its membership entirely to employees. Labor was organized on a basis of regional assemblies, rather than by separate industrial unions. In 1885, some 6000 persons were enrolled in ten assemblies in New Haven, and the entire State membership was nearly 12,000. The New Haven Trades Council was closely affiliated with the Knights of Labor during this period, as were many of the other Central Labor Unions in Connecticut.

Many of the labor and factory laws now appearing on the Connecticut statute-books were first introduced by the various assemblies of the Knights of Labor. Largely to their efforts are due the rehabilitation of the Bureau of Labor Statistics, and the enactment of laws limiting the working hours of women and children to sixty per week, prohibiting employment in factories of children under fourteen years of age, and providing for inspection and proper safeguards in factories.

Wages were so low in the early seventies that the Connecticut Bureau of Labor Statistics reported in 1875 that the children in working-class families were contributing from one-fourth to one-third of the family income, while children under fourteen supplied about one-sixth of the family weekly earnings. Without the wage increases of the eighties, the prohibition of child labor would have been an economic calamity to most of the working-class families of Connecticut.

The long working day of the preceding decades was much curtailed during the eighties. The ten-hour day became an accomplished fact for most of skilled labor, while in some trades an eight-hour day was established. In 1886, the cabinetmakers, printers, piano-makers, tailors, and carpenters had a sixty-hour week. The cigarmakers had a forty-six-hour week, although two years previously their hours had ranged from ten to fourteen a day. The painters were on a fifty-two-hour week, while the telegraphers worked nine hours if employed during the day or forty-five hours a week if employed at night. Baking and barbering were the only two organized trades in which working hours of more than sixty hours a week prevailed.

The Knights of Labor had its greatest growth in Connecticut between the years 1881 and 1886. In a militant attempt to expand its growing membership, it introduced the boycott as a strike weapon. In 1885, the boycott was used against four leading hat manufacturers of South Norwalk and Danbury who refused to arbitrate a strike. At the Crofut and Knapp factory in South Norwalk, in the same year, dynamite was used for the first time in Connecticut in connection with a strike. The Derby Silver and the Southington Cutlery strikes of 1886 revealed the weak organization of the Connecticut Knights of Labor and its lack of competent leadership. With the decline of the national organization after 1886, the field was left open for the growth of the craft union.

The Connecticut Federation of Labor was organized at Hartford on March 9, 1887, by various labor groups from New Haven, Hartford, Meriden, Danbury, and Waterbury. Unlike the Knights of Labor, it made a clear-cut distinction between employer and employee, its plan of organization was on the basis of trade or craft unions, and it made its appeal to the skilled rather than the unskilled workers. An immediate improvement in standards of wages, hours, and conditions was its objective.

During the later eighties, the Connecticut Federation of Labor succeeded in organizing an average of seven locals annually; and throughout the severe depression of 1893–97, nine locals were being organized yearly. With the turn of the century, labor organization increased at an even more rapid rate. In 1900, there were 14,000 members of labor unions in Connecticut; in 1902, the number had increased to 32,000, or 10 per cent of

the total number of wage-earners in the State. By 1905, however, the resistance of employers to the unionization of their shops had become an
almost insurmountable obstacle for labor organizers.

From 1881 to 1905, during the rise of the craft union in Connecticut,
930 strikes were called in 2111 factories. In more than half of these cases,
the strikes were unsuccessful, due to the fact that labor's right to bargain
collectively was not recognized either by employers or by public opinion.
Although the bloodshed and violence that marked many labor difficulties
elsewhere were largely absent, labor history was made in one of these
conflicts and its later legal developments — the famous Danbury Hatters' Case.

In 1902, attempts were made to unionize the hat-making establishment
of D. E. Loewe in Danbury, against the owner's insistence upon an open
shop. After a long-drawn-out strike, marked by a refusal of the company
to deal with the strike leaders, the union officials requested union men and
labor sympathizers throughout the country to boycott the products of the
company. In 1903, with its business at a standstill because of the boycott,
the company brought suit for damages against the officers of the American
Federation of Labor and the United Hatters of North America, as well as
a large number of individual members of both organizations, alleging an
unlawful conspiracy on the part of the defendants to ruin their business.
In 1908, the United States Supreme Court handed down a decision in
favor of the company, stating in its majority opinion that a boycott by
labor unions against a producer doing an interstate commerce business
violated the Sherman Anti-Trust Law of 1890. Damages of nearly
$300,000 were levied against 186 members of the Hatters' Union, the de-
cision being affirmed by the Supreme Court in 1915. The American Federation of Labor replied with a campaign against the use of the Sherman
Act in labor disputes; and in the Clayton Act of 1914, labor organizations
were specifically exempted from the provisions of the anti-trust laws.

During the years from 1905 to 1917, while trade-union membership
more than doubled in the country as a whole, Connecticut labor bodies
were mainly occupied with holding whatever members they did have.
Membership began to decline after 1906, and after the final decision in the
Danbury Hatters' Case, the open-shop movement received great support
and impetus in Connecticut.

The World War did little to aid the growth of unionism in Connecticut.
The great proportion and heterogeneous character of unskilled labor employed in Connecticut industry hampered, rather than aided, such
growth, both during the war and after. In manufacturing and labor

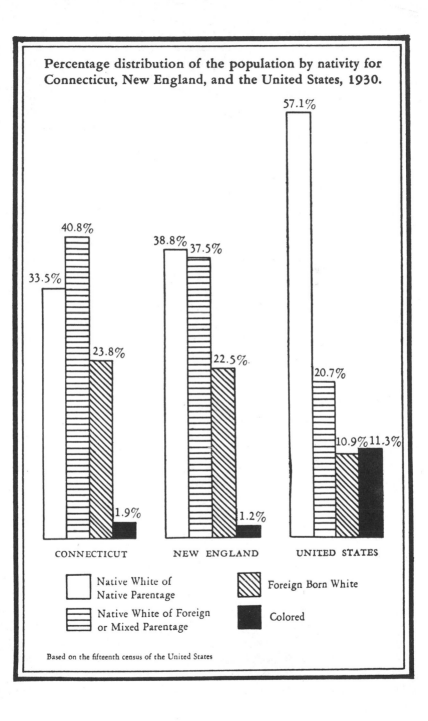

Percentage distribution of the population by nativity for Connecticut, New England, and the United States, 1930.

57.1%

40.8%

38.8% 37.5%

33.5%

23.8% 22.5%

20.7%

10.9% 11.3%

1.9% 1.2%

CONNECTICUT   NEW ENGLAND   UNITED STATES

Native White of Native Parentage

Foreign Born White

Native White of Foreign or Mixed Parentage

Colored

Based on the fifteenth census of the United States

circles, Connecticut was considered one of the foremost 'open shop' States in the industrial North.

The so-called 'American Plan' of company unionism came early to Connecticut, and during the period from 1922 to 1929 it displaced many of the old and established craft unions within the State. Not until 1934 did labor begin to regain something of its former strength. Even then, the percentage of unionized workers was no greater than it had been in 1904, for labor organization could not keep pace with the growth of industry.

The Amalgamated Clothing Workers and the International Ladies Garment Workers' Union were the only two labor bodies to benefit from the application of the labor provisions of the National Recovery Administration to Connecticut industry. Public opinion had been much aroused by the influx of sweatshops into Connecticut, caused in great part by the higher labor costs in New York City; and when data appeared showing the abuses engaged in by these 'fly-by-night' enterprises, church and civic organizations united to prevent a reversion to the labor conditions of a century ago by encouraging the unionization of workers in these plants. The reaction of the public against the sweatshop system was so overwhelming that shop after shop was compelled to treat with its employees through the unions. In this case, Connecticut opinion tacitly recognized labor's right to organize.

The history of labor in Connecticut during the past hundred years has been a series of attempts on the part of bodies of workmen to achieve some form of economic and social status commensurate with their contribution to industrial life. As the history of colonial Connecticut was one in which the middle class of free-holders and independent artisans demanded further rights for themselves as a class, so the history of industrial Connecticut can be said to be a record of the attempts of wage-earners to gain broader interpretations of their rights as citizens and members of an emerging and numerically powerful group.

AGRICULTURE

ORIGINALLY so important agriculturally as to be designated the 'Provision State' by General Washington during the Revolution, Connecticut has seen its agriculture gradually supplanted by industrial activity. Nevertheless, the farm crops today are valued at about $40,000,000 in an average year. Total crop acreage for 1936 was 427,200 acres, as compared with 424,000 in 1935.

Agriculture was the State's leading occupation until the middle of the nineteenth century, when industry became of prime importance. In 1930 only 29 per cent of the population was classified as rural. A farm census of 1935, the first accurate census of this type ever made in Connecticut, lists 34,853 farms, valued roughly at $230,000,000. Although 75 per cent of the land surface of the State is included in farms, only 7 per cent of this portion is actually under cultivation. Recently there has been a trend toward subsistence, or part-time, farming. The Resettlement Administration is now (1936) retiring 11,000 acres of submarginal land through purchase, and it is expected that these lands will be returned to forest under State lease on the standard Resettlement ninety-nine-year contract.

News of the fertility of the Connecticut Valley, reported by the John Oldham expedition from Watertown, Massachusetts, in 1633, stimulated early English colonization in this section. The first settlers found it possible to produce bumper crops along the alluvial bottomlands without much effort. Wethersfield colonists planted rye as soon as they arrived, and later became famous as the largest onion producers of the State, exporting more than 1,000,000 bunches annually. Onions sent to West Indian ports were always strung or bunched. The natural grasslands of the Hartford and Glastonbury meadows furnished ample forage for what little livestock the colonists brought with them. Tobacco was grown at the Windsor plantations very early in the life of the Colony, and the first American cigars — known as 'Long Nines' — were made by Mrs. Prout of South Windsor, in 1801. Cattle were raised with such success that they became an export commodity only a little later than tobacco, onions, and oak staves.

Tobacco is the outstanding cash crop in the Connecticut Valley today.

For more than a century some of the best wrapper leaf in the world has been produced here. Connecticut shade-grown tobacco is the nation's highest priced cigar leaf. 'Connecticut broadleaf' is universally known, and commands a premium price. The sorting, stripping, and curing of tobacco leaf furnishes employment for many persons in season. In 1936, the Connecticut tobacco crop was 21,429,000 pounds, raised from 14,500 acres.

The usual rotation crops on tobacco soils are potatoes and corn. A very high yield of corn is obtained, and the potato yield is occasionally in excess of 600 bushels to the acre. The local markets easily absorb all potatoes and corn raised in the State, and the short haul to market enables the local grower to meet outside competition without loss. Potato plantings in 1936 covered 16,700 acres and yielded 2,839,000 bushels. Many varieties of corn are raised; some is fed out as green fodder, some used as ensilage, and some is allowed to mature for grain. The State produces much sweet corn for immediate consumption, but very little is commercially canned.

The soils of Connecticut are favorable to a considerable diversification of agriculture. The loams of the central valley, ideal for raising the better grades of wrapper-leaf tobacco, are adapted also to potato growing. The sweet potato is now being successfully grown in the older tobacco soils, and State experiment stations are encouraging farmers to expand their acreage on this new crop. Truck crops are easily raised in the lighter sandy loams, and with some success in the heavier soils. A natural grass soil is found in the valleys and on the hilltops of Litchfield County, where the Charlton loam, a common hilltop type of soil in New England, holds a greater moisture content in dry seasons than is found in the more sandy loams. A plentiful supply of lime for agricultural purposes is available within easy hauling distance throughout the State. Vegetables are successfully grown in the tobacco soils, berries thrive on the sandy loams, and celery is raised successfully on the heavier soils. Windham County raises more Brussels sprouts than any other county in the country, with the exception of one in California.

Dairying is important on 80 per cent of all farms operating commercially, and there are 120,000 dairy animals in the State. Connecticut is now declared to be a 'modified accredited State' by the Bureau of Animal Industry, thus becoming the thirty-ninth such State in the Union. Poultry raising is rapidly increasing. About 2,500,000 chickens produce approximately 22,500,000 dozen eggs annually. Turkeys of excellent quality are successfully raised. Fruit orchards are recovering from the damage suffered during the severe winters of 1933–35; and a yearly crop of apples, peaches, and pears valued at about $3,000,000 is harvested.

The Farm Bureau and the county agents are occasionally helpful to the small farmer, but more active among the larger agriculturists. Egg and berry auctions are held at key points throughout the State; a State-inspected and regulated system of roadside markets caters to the traveling public; and 'Connecticut fancy turkeys,' advertised on billboards during the winter holidays, are carefully graded and sold under a co-operative marketing scheme.

Eleven hundred poultry producers own and control the Connecticut Farmers' Co-operative Auction Association, a non-profit organization that holds egg and poultry auctions at West Hartford. Similar auctions are held at Willimantic, Manchester, and Hamden. These organizations are producer co-operatives, but Connecticut also has combination producer-consumer and straight consumer 'co-ops' that function well. The great Eastern States Co-operative has many members in Connecticut; the United Farmers Co-operative Association has at least one branch in the State, made up almost entirely of Finnish farmers; the Quinebaug Valley Fruit Growers Association, Inc., functions with a limited membership in northeastern Connecticut; and Italian fruit growers have formed a co-operative in the Glastonbury area.

The most unusual organization of its kind is the so-called 'Father Dunn Co-op' in Ashford, one of the few co-operatives in the country founded and operated by a priest. This organization of poorer farmers in the submarginal eastern highlands of the State now owns a store and a fleet of trucks. Throughout the depression it functioned without difficulty.

The Connecticut Milk Administration is making progress with milk control and the regulation of marketing in the State. Assisted by two deputies and five inspectors, the Milk Administrator has done much for improved conditions in classification and retailing, but the producer still seeks relief from the unusually low prices paid for his product. Retailers are licensed, their books are opened to the inspectors, efforts are made to insure prompt payment to producers, and price wars are infrequent.

Connecticut State College at Storrs carries on an efficient and helpful work for the farmer. Experiment stations at Storrs and New Haven issue frequent bulletins; and a tobacco substation at Windsor offers advice on that crop. A cow-testing association helps to keep its member herds free from 'boarders' and to attain a higher efficiency in butterfat output. A State market bulletin is issued thrice weekly, offering information regarding the produce market at six points within the State, printing advertising for the individual farmer, and keeping the rural communities supplied with news of interest.

The Farm Bureau and the county agents are not especially helpful to the small farmer, but are active among the larger agriculturists. The Grange has one hundred and forty-one local and eleven Pomona units, in addition to the State organization. Some five thousand women are engaged in home-making projects, and more than five thousand boys and girls participate in 4–H Club activities. Agricultural and grange fairs continue to be popular, thirty-seven of these being held in 1936. There are also five 4–H Club County Fairs, to which youthful exhibitors bring their prize stock just as it is ready to show at the Eastern States Exposition in Springfield, Massachusetts.

Connecticut farmers have to contend with many difficulties. Living costs are inevitably high in a State that is predominantly industrial. Taxes continue to mount with the increased valuation of acreage as residential sections expand into the country; and the area of tillable land is usually small in comparison to the total taxable area of individual farms. The average farm is so small that the use of highly developed farm machinery is impracticable. The water and power companies' purchase of large and sometimes fertile areas of cultivated land restricts normal farm expansion. Despite these unfavorable conditions, however, the natural advantages of a temperate climate and adequate rainfall, the accessibility to good markets by means of excellent highways, and the co-operation afforded the farmer by various State bureaus and marketing organizations are factors which seem to assure a successful future to Connecticut agriculture.

EDUCATION

IN THE field of education, Connecticut's record is a long and distinguished one. The Puritan preachers early encouraged learning with the object of offsetting 'the chief project of that old deluder, Sathan, to keepe men from the knowledge of the scriptures.' The church and school stood side by side, and the minister often assumed the duties of schoolmaster. The schoolhouses were rudely constructed one-room buildings, equipped with rough wooden benches and desks, ink made of tea and iron filings, and few if any books.

One of the first public school systems in the history of education was founded in Connecticut shortly after the establishment of free public schools in New Haven (1642) and Hartford (1643), a system that for many years was unsurpassed in its uniform application to all classes. A general code enacted in 1650 ordered the establishment of elementary schools, for the teaching of reading and writing, in all townships of fifty families or more; and of Latin grammar schools, for the preparation of those more gifted students who might wish to enter the college at Cambridge, in towns of 100 families or more. Penalties were imposed upon parents who neglected the education of their children, and the towns reserved the right to remove boys from the homes of such parents and to apprentice them to masters who would train and educate them. Towns employing a schoolmaster might provide for his salary by levying a town tax on property, by tuition fees from those who attended, or by any other means agreeable to an individual township. Although the State fixed the minimum requirements for provision and attendance, it neither supported the schools nor maintained any direct control, tending to shift the entire responsibility to local supervision.

In 1671, the State ordered the four county towns of New Haven, Hartford, New London, and Fairfield to establish grammar schools, under penalty of a fine of ten pounds. In the following year, the General Court granted 600 acres of land in these counties for educational purposes. In 1690, these grammar schools were made free, and the State contributed thirty pounds towards the salary of the master of each school. In 1795, Connecticut contracted for the sale of 3,000,000 acres of land in northern Ohio, which had been assigned to the Colony by the original charter from

King Charles II and was known as the Western Reserve. The income from the proceeds of this sale was set aside for educational purposes, and became known as the 'school fund.' Administered under the supervision of the State Treasury, the fund up to July 1, 1931, had earned $13,620,-372.42, all of which was used for the support of common schools in Connecticut.

In the latter half of the eighteenth century, public education was neglected because of the more pressing problems of war and reconstruction. At the turn of the century and during the early decades of the nineteenth century, a growing demand for broader education led to the establishment of privately owned academies offering a wider curriculum and drawing students from a more extensive area than did the public schools.

The system of public high schools was initiated as a result of the work of Henry Barnard, who devoted his life to the furtherance of education. In 1838, he originated a bill in the State legislature providing for State supervision of the common schools. A Board of Commissioners was promptly created, with Barnard as secretary; and for the first time, annual reports on school conditions were required. To relieve the congestion discovered in the ungraded schools, Barnard suggested a higher school, and before long the system of public high schools was well under way. In addition to his services to the State, Barnard was the first United States Commissioner of Education, and from 1855 to 1893 he edited the *American Journal of Education*.

Secondary education is now provided in Connecticut by 137 high schools, junior high schools, and trade schools, with an enrollment of about 100,000 pupils. Public, private, and parochial elementary schools number 1,286, with more than 390,000 pupils registered. State funds ensure modern educational methods and trained teachers for the rural districts, and transportation to and from school for children living in remote sections. Within the last fifteen years, consolidation of grades and districts has resulted in the elimination of 600 one-room buildings.

Connecticut maintains eleven trade schools, all established since 1907. The founding of these schools was begun under the administration of Charles G. Hine, who served on the State Board of Education for more than 37 years. Hine also helped to establish the library extension service and the system of rural education. By State law, every town with a population of 10,000 or more must establish and maintain evening schools for the instruction, in elementary subjects, of persons over fourteen years of age. Perhaps the most important ruling of the State Board of Education in recent years was made in 1922, when it was decreed that only graduates

Education 77

of approved normal schools, or those of equal professional training, would be certified for teachers' positions in elementary schools. There are normal schools at New Britain, New Haven, Danbury, and Willimantic.

In addition to the support given the public schools, the State maintains an industrial school for boys at Meriden, a similar school for girls at Long Lane Farm, Middletown, and a school for imbeciles and defectives at Mansfield.

The education of Indians and Negroes began at an early date in Connecticut. Moor's Indian Charity School was established at Columbia in 1735 by the Reverend Eleazar Wheelock, who instructed the aborigines in religion and the English language, training them to be sent forth as missionaries among their own race. Funds for the development of the school were sought abroad, and the King of England and Lord Dartmouth were among the contributors. The school was removed in 1769 to Hanover, New Hampshire, 'to increase its usefulness,' and has since become known as Dartmouth College.

The first effort towards education for Negroes was made in 1832 by Miss Prudence Crandall, a Quakeress of Canterbury, who accepted a young Negro girl into her school. The other pupils promptly quit the place, and the courageous young woman replied by turning her school into an institution exclusively for 'young ladies and little misses of color.' As a result, race feeling ran so high that in 1833 the Connecticut 'Black Law' was rushed through the legislature. This made it illegal to establish schools exclusively for the instruction of Negroes without the permission of local authorities.

About the middle of the nineteenth century, free public schools supplanted the privately owned academies, which had grown to be more or less aristocratic institutions charging high tuition rates. Many of these academies, however, continue to function as preparatory schools, and have been attended by famous men from all over the country. One of the oldest of these is Bacon Academy, established at Colchester in 1803, and now serving as the free high school for that town. The Cheshire Academy in Cheshire is on the site of the Cheshire Episcopal Academy, which numbered among its student body the elder J. P. Morgan, Admiral A. A. Foote of the United States Navy, and Gideon Welles, Secretary of the Navy during the Civil War. Other preparatory schools of note are the Taft School in Watertown, Choate School in Wallingford, Hotchkiss in Lakeville, Kent at Kent, Pomfret at Pomfret, and Avon Old Farms at Avon. Among the nationally known girls' boarding schools are Miss Porter's School at Farmington, the Ethel Walker School in Simsbury, the Westover School in Middlebury, and Rosemary Hall in Greenwich.

It was the original intention of the settlers to found a college in each of the New England Colonies. To this end, in 1648, the General Court, assembled in New Haven, gave power to a committee to choose a site 'most commodious for a college.' Massachusetts, however, objected that 'the whole population of New England was scarcely sufficient to support one institution of this nature [Harvard], and the establishment of a second would, in the end, be a sacrifice of both.' Thus the plans of John Davenport of New Haven came to nothing, notwithstanding the fact that in 1655 more than £540 had been subscribed for the new college. Half a century later, under the leadership of the Reverend James Pierpont, ten clergymen met in the house of the Reverend Samuel Russell at Branford and made the famous gift of books for 'the founding of a College in this colony.' A month later, on October 16, 1701, the General Assembly in New Haven passed 'An act for liberty to erect a Collegiate School' where youth might 'be fitted for Publick employment both in Church and Civil State.' The founders chose the Reverend Abraham Pierson of Killingworth (now Clinton) as rector and Saybrook as the site. During Pierson's lifetime the scholars met in Killingworth, and only after his death in 1707 were classes held in Saybrook. From there the college was moved in 1716 to its present situation in New Haven. At the commencement exercises in 1718, the name of Yale was given to the new college, in recognition of timely pecuniary assistance (in the sum of £562 12s.) received from Elihu Yale, a London capitalist of American birth, who had amassed a large fortune as governor of the English trading post in Madras.

Yale's subsequent growth has been steady and at times startling. In 1846, its library was housed for the first time in a separate building, and in the next year a course of advanced studies was instituted from which the Graduate School developed. Yale was the first institution of higher learning in America to grant, as it did in 1861, the degree of Doctor of Philosophy; and in 1869, the Yale School of Fine Arts was founded, the first of its kind in any such institution. Under the guidance of such outstanding presidents as Ezra Stiles (1776–95), the two Timothy Dwights (1795–1817, and 1886–99), Theodore Woolsey (1846–71), and Arthur Twining Hadley (1899–1921), the college reached its second centenary and became a university of eleven schools, with more than five thousand students, nearly a thousand faculty members, and an endowment approximating one hundred million dollars. The depression found Yale in the midst of the most extensive building program ever undertaken by any university. One result of this extraordinary outburst of construction has been to divide the undergraduate body into smaller colleges, nine in number, where the benefits of the Oxford-Cambridge system of education can in some measure be obtained.

Other notable institutions of higher learning within the State include Trinity College, established at Hartford in 1823, under the auspices of the Episcopal Church; Wesleyan University, founded by Methodists in 1831 at Middletown; and Connecticut College for Women, opened in 1915 at New London. The Hartford Theological School (Congregational) was chartered in 1834. The Berkeley Divinity School (Episcopalian), now situated in New Haven, was founded at Middletown in 1854.

One of the oldest agricultural schools in America was opened in 1845 by Dr. Samuel Gold and his son, T. G. Gold, at Cream Hill, Cornwall. The State College was established at Mansfield in 1881 by Charles and Augustus Storrs, who provided land, buildings, and an endowment fund. It was also financed from the proceeds of the sale of government lands allotted to Connecticut. First known as Storrs Agricultural College, it was later called the Connecticut Agricultural College, and finally Connecticut State College. Classified as a Federal Land Grant College, it offers wide facilities for studies and practical work in agriculture and home economics.

ARCHITECTURE

I

TODAY, the well-informed traveler is as much interested in the architecture of a country as he is in the manners and customs of its people. For in essence one is a reflection of the other. Whether in Bali, Gizeh, Nürnberg, Normandy, or our own Connecticut, the structures reared by a people are the most public and often the most permanent expression of its social life — the translation of habits of life and modes of thought into wood and stone.

Such of the early architecture of Connecticut as still remains is a fascinating and partly open book to those who drive through the State's villages and along its country roads, and who know something of its history. It is not alone churches and houses and barns that appear — but the drama of a frontier, of English-born people struggling with the soil and with the rigid molds of their ancestors' standards, and gradually achieving greater sophistication, freedom, graciousness, charm, and variety, while at the same time manifesting a provincial yearning for cosmopolitanism.

This development is traceable more clearly, perhaps, in Windsor than in any other Connecticut town. One of the very earliest domestic buildings in the State is the ell of the Fyler House in that town — a little house which in its primitive simplicity typifies the utter plainness of the first permanent homes of the settlers. A more imposing example of the second type developed can be seen in what remains of the old Deacon Moore House, with its framed overhang, pendant drops, gable brackets, and rare crossed summer beams within. This is representative of one of the most persistent characteristics of all our early architecture, the harking back to old precedents. The first colonists left England scarcely a quarter century after the age of Elizabeth had passed, and they built Elizabethan houses here. Yet it must be remembered that every house was a compromise, a translation of Old World ideas into frontier terms. A new stereotype arose, derived partly from English precedents and partly from the need of building hastily with materials that were strange to the builders — a style quite distinct, and yet in some ways akin to the Georgian. Parson William Russell's home on Broad Street Green may serve as the typical example, a large eighteenth-century house with central chimney, capacious yet simple, with its own sparing type of ornamentation — a really American product.

As prosperity brought greater financial ease and sufficient means for expansion, many builders erected the central-hall type of house with a chimney at each side. One of the earliest of this type is 'Elmwood,' which David Ellsworth built in 1740. It is interesting to note that in a second house built ten years later, Ellsworth reverted to the established form, with central chimney, but with greater freedom in the employment of decoration.

The loftier wing that Oliver Ellsworth added to his father's comfortable farmhouse reveals the lawyer who had become acquainted with Georgian elegance and had brought back to his home town something of an international experience. In 1807, the house built by Oliver for his son Martin shows the freedom, and yet the outward austerity, of the new republican era which was adapting and formalizing new elements, drawn frankly now from Renaissance motifs, in wood. Its gable end to the street is asymmetrical yet formal, self-conscious yet stately; but it breaks away from the time-honored arrangement with a small square hall at the front, inconspicuous stairs at the left, and a dignified drawing-room at the right. The regularity of the orders on the exterior gives little indication of the freedom of arrangement within. Precedents were being broken, giving way to new tendencies which in time became formalized in new traditions, such as characterized the progress of the nineteenth century.

The same developments translated into the language of brick can be followed at Windsor, notably in the Chaffee, Nathaniel Hayden, and Halsey houses. Every town in Connecticut contains its own particular version of this same history — luxurious and expansive when it reflects an early industrial and shipping prosperity, as in Norwich; or plain and bare, when the living was sparse and frugal, as in many of the hill towns. Connecticut, on the whole, was handicapped by its stony, unproductive fields, and could show little to compare with the relative luxury of Massachusetts and Rhode Island. Here the struggle for existence — spiritual as well as economic — produced a simple and sturdy indigenous mode of building less influenced by foreign precedent than any other Colonial architecture. Connecticut is pre-eminently the home, for example, of the salt-box type of house, the most distinctively American of any of our Colonial forms.

The very earliest abodes have, of course, not survived. They were compromises with the crudest necessity, and were not expected to last.

A pit was dug into a bank or elsewhere and lined with upright planks, or with stone, to a height somewhat above the surface of the ground; then it was covered with logs chinked with clay, or with poles upon which bark or thatch was laid. Reproductions may be seen in the Pioneer Village in Salem, Massachusetts, a permanent exhibit; and one was constructed in Waterbury for the Tercentenary of 1935. Such rude 'dug-outs' have always been built under pressure — by the soldiers at Valley Forge, as sand and cyclone shelters on the western plains, and on the western front in the Great War. In their early form, they were an expression, not of some past tradition, but of the struggle with drastic necessity. Nor were they, as might at first appear, wholly apart from the main current of architectural development. The dug-out form of cellar was later used in many houses; several homes in Chester and the charming Woodbridge Tavern (about 1750) in Old Mystic were designedly built into hillsides for warmth and protection.

An account of the erection, by John Talcott in 1636, of one of the earliest houses in Hartford shows that it followed the usual rule, said to be invariable in Rhode Island, that seventeenth-century houses were built with their fronts to the south — probably with a view to facing the sun as much as possible. There were some exceptions: the Henry Whitfield House (1640), an English manor house of stone in Guilford, faced west, as did the Whitman House in Farmington; while the Comfort Starr House in Guilford and the Williams House in Wethersfield faced east. But, as a rule, especially in the outlying districts, the earliest houses faced south, whatever the location of the road. This arrangement was generally abandoned in the eighteenth century.

The Talcott House mentioned above is interesting from another point of view. It represents two stages of construction. In the first stage, it was simply a single large room with an end chimney, and perhaps with an attic above. Not every house got beyond this stage, and presumably a number of the earliest houses were of this simple plan. The early ell of the Fyler House in Windsor illustrates this type of construction.

In the second stage another room was added on the other side of the great chimney. Often a second story was added, making a tall narrow house, two stories high, but one room deep, with the chimney occupying most of the space between the two ground-floor rooms. The small hall, or 'porch' as it was called, in front of the chimney provided an entrance to the rooms on either side, and allowed a cramped winding stair to the apartment above. Cottages of this sort, but only one story in height, are frequently found in all sections of New England and derive from all periods. The popular home and garden magazines sentimentally term them 'Cape Cod cottages,' although the type reached perfection in certain parts of Connecticut, as around Clinton. Examples of the early type in its two-story proportions are excessively rare; the best is the Williams House (1680) on Broad Street in Wethersfield.

With the third stage, architectural progress really begins. Even from the earliest period — 1635 to 1675 — most houses now appear to have had at some time a later addition at the rear. The latter was often a necessity arising from the pressure of overcrowded families when the elder son married. The family had then to give up part of the room in the old house, or else go to the expense of building another, as the son would naturally stay and work the farm which he was eventually to inherit. An additional reason for enlarging the house in the early days was the greater security provided in being all together. The addition was a lean-to at the rear which had the appearance of an old-time salt-box, such as commonly hung on the kitchen wall. This addition may often be recognized by the fact that the lean-to rafters were spliced on at the upper plate at the back, giving a broken but graceful curve to the long rearward slope of the roof. It provided one long room, with two small rooms at either end; the long room, or new kitchen, had access to the rear side of the chimney. In some regions, such as Rocky Hill, many houses were never finished in the second story, the children and servants being obliged to make shift in one big unfinished room.

The salt-box addition, though by no means confined to Connecticut, was more characteristic of this State than of its neighbors. Some of the finest examples are in eastern Massachusetts, but on the whole it is a Connecticut Valley feature, not ranging far east of that valley, but traceable in narrowing territory up its stream into the edges of New Hampshire. A regional distribution such as this can be traced in other forms as well. It has never been studied, and remains one of the adventures that beckon the traveler.

Once developed, the salt-box became, in many localities, the prevailing form of construction for a century. Houses began to be built in that shape from preference, with what may be termed an integral lean-to, the rafters running right through from roof-tree to plate. Most salt-boxes that we see today have this uncompromising straight roof-line. The integral salt-box dates from approximately 1700 to about the time of the Revolutionary War, when the provincial period was over; and it is typical of what may be called the fourth stage in the development of the Colonial house.

In the fifth stage, the logical next step came rapidly with growing ease and independence — the raising of the entire frame to create a two-story house with four rooms in each story, and a broad peak or gable roof above. This was done, for instance, with the General David Humphreys House in Ansonia. It is the typical house of the eighteenth century, still built around a broad central chimney, with cramped stair and 'porch' between the chimney and the front door. The Elisha Williams House (1716) at Rocky Hill is among the earliest and best of those built complete at one time. One- or two-story ells were added at will, or perhaps a small lean-to — as in the Trumbull House (1740) at Lebanon. Most of the 'Colonial' houses in Connecticut villages are of this form, which was followed throughout the eighteenth century and even later.

There was little more that increasing prosperity could do in the matter of style and arrangement, except what may be taken as the last of the stereotyped styles — the sixth stage. In this, for additional warmth and convenience, the house was built around two chimneys, one between the front and back rooms on each side, and the hall ran straight through the house. Perhaps the earliest example of this style is Oliver Ellsworth's house, 'Elmwood,' built by his father, David Ellsworth, in 1740. The hesitation in adopting the central hall, with its added graciousness, is amusingly illustrated by the way the stairs in this house are hidden away in a recess. This was a local peculiarity, as was in other localities the 'central hall' that did not continue all the way back through the house. Stereotyped forms of building were, like the characters of their builders, rather unyielding in the old days.

From this time on, progress was in the general direction of greater freedom in design and embellishment, and Colonial architecture was no longer a direct and frank expression of the character and struggles of the builders. When a medium is too easily mastered, when it becomes simply the expression of individual taste, when mere facility supplants creative effort, decadence sets in.

But it must not be thought that because these stereotyped forms changed with difficulty they were the only forms the architectural language permitted. From the very beginning there were exceptions, due to the fact that aristocratic elements had come over with the English settlers, elements that were to become alien in our essentially democratic body politic, but which were predominant for a while because of their greater cultural and social prominence. Such exceptions are the manor houses of Haynes (built before 1646) and Wyllys (1636) in Hartford, and the 'grate houses' of Eaton and Davenport and Allerton in New Haven.

These houses were built around a central court, or in the form of a cross or an ell; and Eaton's house had twenty-one rooms, with furnishings comparable to those of a manor house in England. Representing as they did a temporary phase of aristocratic leadership in a new country, rather than the permanent democratic organization of our society, it was natural that these houses should have been the least permanent type in early American architecture, a type of which scarcely a survivor remains.

In the Connecticut Colony, around Hartford, the adherence to the 'framed overhang' of Elizabethan England was most pronounced. In a house with framed overhang, the second-story girts and walls of the front are projected a short distance (commonly from eighteen to twenty-four inches) beyond the ground-floor posts and walls, usually with a lesser 'overhang' at the sides, and none at all at the rear. The overhanging second story is still found in Farmington and Windsor, with steep gables, brackets, and carved pendants or drops reminiscent of English homes. The type seems to have been characteristic only of the northern colony, and of the earliest period. Six examples are all that remain today, the best preserved specimen being the Whitman House (about 1660) at Farmington. It is often repeated that the overhang was designed for defense against the Indians, but both its geographical and its period limitations indicate that it is an Elizabethan feature instead.

A Kentish and Sussex type of hewn overhang, rare in England, became the most prevalent type in New Haven, and in a modified form was widely used throughout Connecticut. It consisted in carrying out the ground-floor corner posts into brackets, upon which the second story projected a few inches. The same construction was frequently followed in the gable ends — whence the name 'gable overhang.' A house overhanging on both the second and third stories is said to have a double overhang; this modified type appeared until well after 1800.

Structurally, the seventeenth-century house was often framed in the manner of English half-timber work of various types, but was covered with clapboards or shingles. The roof, modeled on English lines and covered with either shingles or thatch, was pitched very steep to shed water. As time went on, up to the middle of the nineteenth century, the roof became progressively flatter. The earliest houses had the steepest roofs. The gambrel roof, common in Rhode Island, is prevalent in the southeastern part and the Connecticut Valley, and in some western parts of Connecticut. This type, of which the roof of Connecticut Hall (1752) on the Yale campus is a notable example, was often adopted for brick houses. No other roof is capable of such subtle grace and charm as the gambrel.

Another type experimented with early in the eighteenth century was the hip roof. At first, a single big chimney sticks up like a thumb in the middle; later on, two chimneys flank a ridge-pole. This type is always an interesting variation, but of awkward arrangement within.

Interior construction can be only briefly touched upon here, though it is the interior upon which one must depend most in judging the age of a house. In the seventeenth century, of course, construction was of the most heavy and often primitive type. There was no attempt to disguise the functional aspect, and little was added by way of interior embellishment. Corner posts partly projected into the room, displaying a flare toward the top to form a better support for the horizontal members which were framed and pegged into them. Sometimes this flare grew evenly from the base; sometimes it was carved out in 'knees.' Summer beams and supporting joists carried the weight of floors above. These summer beams were ordinarily parallel with the main line of the house; they were beaded in the eastern towns, and chamfered in the Valley and western parts of the State — in which case the joists were likely to be beaded. Chamfering or beveling reached its height in the accuracy and delicacy of the 'lamb's tongue' scrolls and other 'stops' at the end of the bevel, in the region around Guilford. In the earliest and crudest houses, the bevel was irregular and sometimes ran into the side wall. The Deacon Moore House (about 1660) in Windsor has the very unusual feature of cross-summers, beautifully chamfered.

As the eighteenth century wore on, and especially as the trend increased toward plastered and then papered walls, it became the tendency to box in the posts and summers, and then to cover the frame entirely. This, of course, often happened later to earlier work, as if its frankness of construction were something to keep hidden. On the other hand, many well-meaning amateurs uncover the 'beams' of a ceiling in the mistaken notion that the exposed frame was typical of all periods. The thin and bare uncovered rafters of an early nineteenth-century house look even more out of place than do the heavy corner posts and summers of two centuries earlier clothed in a useless casing.

The misguided enthusiasm of a good many local historians is responsible for markers with seventeenth-century dates on houses whose light construction betrays much later origin to anyone really acquainted with early architecture. Seventeenth-century work, good or bad, is rare and should always be treated with reverence. It was the most frank and fearless work of our ancestors.

The interior walls were practically always finished with wood in the earliest days. The boards used for this work were of two types — beaded and featheredge. They are found in a hard pine no longer grown on these shores, in soft pine, whitewood, chestnut, or butternut. The earlier floors were usually of oak; a few much later floors of maple are found in the northwest section of the State. Paint, in the seventeenth century, was unknown and unnecessary. There is no rarer or more beautiful sight than a wall of unpainted featheredge (as in the Graves House in Madison), which has softened and grown rich in patina through the years.

Featheredge is the board from which paneling developed. It always remained in use in the hinder parts of the house. One edge of the board was so beveled that it fitted like a tongue into the groove of the next board; at the top of the groove, a half-round or bead was inserted. This made an interesting and varied wall surface, especially when the boards ran, as they customarily did, horizontally on the two outer sides of the room and vertically on the inner sides.

The typical 'raised panel' or eighteenth-century paneling simply fitted this edge into patterns. The first panels, appearing around 1690 to 1710, were large and very regularly spaced. As time went on, the panel arrangement of fireplace wall-ends was made more delicate and varied. The study of eighteenth-century paneled fireplace walls is one of endless fascination and variety, because with them artistic design entered home building.

At the end of the eighteenth century, the beaded edge was elaborated and the early bold contours of the paneling were flattened. Then the raising of the panel dropped out entirely: it became a sunken instead of a raised panel. In a general way, featheredge was characteristic of the seventeenth century, raised panels of the eighteenth, and sunken panels of the nineteenth. The Greek Revival period, though it had its new graces of dignity and proportion, simplified doors and panels into a new and self-conscious severity, and finally paneling went out of fashion.

Windows were a necessity, as well as a luxury and a point of embellishment. In the seventeenth century, they were always of the casement variety brought from England, with diamond-shaped panes set in lead. They were characteristically narrow, and high under the eaves or girts, with plain frames projecting from the house. They were sometimes irregularly spaced, and set where convenient. An original casement is occasionally found in some inside partition or tucked away in an attic — as in the Lee House at East Lyme and the Fiske-Wildman House at Guilford. The typical eighteenth-century window was at first of six, eight, nine, and finally of twelve panes of six- by eight-inch glass. These

were held in muntins seven-eighths of an inch or more wide. Later these
muntins were narrôwed, and the panes of glass used were larger. Even
the average 'restored' house of the eighteenth century usually has nineteenth-century windows. These can be identified because their muntins,
or subdivisions, are deep and narrow rather than wide and flat.

Paint was an innovation of the eighteenth century. The earliest color
known was an earthy 'Indian red.' Then a gray-green in varying shades
began to be used, and later on a widening variety. Today we seldom have
any idea of how colorful and cheerful an eighteenth-century house was.
The colors were bright and frank and lively — a 'break-away' from the
rich gloom of aging unpainted panels. White was probably not much
used in this country before 1800. The outer walls, when painted at all,
were red or yellow or gray. Toward the end of the century, imported
wall papers came into use; the earliest known in New England is the
paper put on the side hall of the magnificent Lee Mansion at Marble-
head in 1768.

II

One feature of our architectural inheritance that is not sufficiently appreciated is the contribution to town planning made by the Connecticut
'village Green.' While by no means confined to this State, it was here,
as nowhere else, almost the rule in small villages as well as large. Cows
were at one time given pasturage on the 'Commons' or 'Green' belonging
to the whole community. The church, the school, and the principal homes
of the colonists, the stocks, the pound, and later the general store were
clustered about it. Many of these old Greens still exist today, practically
untouched — as in Wolcott, Windham, and Woodstock, for example.
Where there was not a Green, there was a broad and definitely recognized
'four corners.'

As a general rule, it was the community centralized most definitely
around a Green that developed the strongest communal life. New
Haven Green, with its four churches, its college, and its municipal buildings, is the perfect example of one that has developed into a civic center,
from which radiate in orderly progression the main streets of the town.
The debt that modern city planning owes to the foresight of earlier generations in this respect is one that will be appreciated more and more as time
goes by.

Outstanding in the early community was the one public building as
important to the inhabitants as their own homes — the church. This

CONNECTICUT'S ARCHI-
TECTURAL HERITAGE

NO EXAMPLE of the one-room, end-chimney house, which was the earliest sort of permanent dwelling of the colonists, now remains unaltered, but several have been incorporated into buildings of later types. Such a one is the Hempstead House at New London.

The second type consisted of two rooms, both upstairs and down, with a central chimney. The Older Williams House, Wethersfield (1680), is an example. A third type has the added lean-to across the back, as in the Acadian House in Guilford (c. 1670). From this developed the 'salt-box' which is particularly characteristic of Connecticut. The Stone House in Guilford, though one end of it is probably the earliest construction in the State, is a direct descendant of the English manor house, a type that was never a frequent visitor to our shores.

In various communities, different methods of building reflected the parts of England from which the settlers came. Around Hartford, the framed overhang with pendant drops was a survival of mediaeval England. The hewn overhang was more common farther south. The Whitman House (c. 1660), Farmington, and the Hollister House (1675), Glastonbury, illustrate these variations.

In the eighteenth century, public buildings began to assume a greater importance. They form a closer link than houses do with the contemporary architecture of England. The churches are a chief part of Connecticut's architectural heritage, and none among them has more of its original atmosphere than old Trinity Church in Brooklyn (1771). At the end of the century, gentlemen architects had begun to make a profession of what had previously been left to master builders. The first to achieve a name in New England was Charles Bulfinch of Boston, designer of the old State House in Hartford (1796), as well as of the State House of Massachusetts. In the nineteenth century, a wider range of architectural forms were adapted to American use, among them the Gothic. The old building of Linonian and Brothers Library at Yale (1846), now remodeled for use as a chapel, was designed by Henry Austin. In contrast with it is the modern Gothic of the Harkness Quadrangle, one of the most ambitious Gothic buildings in America.

TFIELD STONE HOUSE, GUILFORD

JUDGMENT ROOM, THOMAS LEE HOUSE, EAST LYME

ACADIAN HOUSE, GUILFORD

ONS HOUSE, GREENWICH

GRAVE HOUSE, MADISON

FRAMED OVERHANG, WHITMAN HOUSE, FARMINGTON

HEWN OVERHANG, HOLLISTER HOUSE, GLASTONBU

INTERIOR, TRINITY CHURCH, BROOKLYN

INTERIOR, HOUSE OF REPRESENTATIVES, OLD STATE HOUSE

GAMBREL ROOFS, PLAINFIELD

CROSBY TAVERN, THOMPS

INTERIOR OF DWIGHT CHAPEL, YALE UNIVERSITY

LINONIA COURT, YALE UNIVERSITY

was the center of social as well as of religious life. Although often not erected until several years after a settlement had been founded, it was the first public building, and the most important. The colonist made no separation of Sundays and weekdays, of church and home. But the church, once erected, did symbolize to him the one influence to which his independence bowed.

The first church edifices were seldom more than large houses in appearance. The earliest now standing in Connecticut, the disused meeting-house of the Long Society of Preston (1726), still looks like a dwelling house temporarily closed, though it does stand a bit incongruously among gravestones. It was largely renovated in 1819, but the interior is essentially that of an eighteenth-century meeting-house, with its entrance in the middle of one long side, a high pulpit opposite, and box pews around the sides and filling the central floor. The earliest churches after this one — Salem Town Hall (1749), Abington (1753), and Hampton (1754) — have been so modernized as to have little antiquarian value. The brick Congregational Church (1761) of Wethersfield is still a noble structure, reminding one of the old brick churches of Holland, and preserving not only a rarely beautiful spire but the general outlines of its period. Then follow three which were built in 1771 and which remain the best examples we have of the eighteenth century — the Congregational Church of Farmington, and the two old churches in Brooklyn. The Farmington church, except for a later portico, is essentially unchanged; as is Trinity, the towerless little Episcopal church in the grove at Brooklyn. The Congregational Church at Brooklyn, now a community center, has a handsome exterior, but there is little of interest within. The old Stone Church (1774) of East Haven is another of which the same can be said.

The tower, an embellishment attempted only by the State church, the Congregational, was always offset during this period. It stood at one end, practically a separate structure, and contained a subordinate portico, repeated perhaps, but without the steeple, at the other end. With the arrival of the classic influence about the turn of the century, the tower began to be drawn into the nave (as in Bloomfield and Canterbury, each 1804), and finally was centered directly over the front façade of the main building. Then a projecting portico, smaller than the façade, was often built out in front, enclosing the tower and protruding beyond it. The lines of the lower portico pediment repeat those of the front gable. The two Congregational churches on the Green in New Haven exemplify this. At the same time, the open and rather stiff tower of the earlier period began to come under the influence of English design. The books of James Gibb and Sir Christopher Wren had come over (Peter Harrison, who died in New Haven, left a considerable architectural library). Towers now began to have octagonal as well as square stages, and to be given a degree of embellishment never before seen in New England. The golden age of church architecture here came not in the strictly 'Colonial' period, but in the years from 1810 to 1825. In this short period most of the churches were built to which the traveler turns with keenest interest. And in this connection, it is of note that the churches of theocratic Connecticut surpass those of any other New England State.

Ithiel Town had designed Center Church (1812–14) at New Haven largely from English plans. It is generally conceded to be drawn to some extent from St. Martin's in the Fields, which again was influenced largely by Wren's fifty-three London churches. Like most English-derived churches, it combined an imposingly classical front and a handsome well-organized interior with very weakly designed sides and rear end. The United Church (1813–15) to the north of it, by David Hoadley, was more American in conception, in fact a more consistent whole, with a more graceful and spontaneous tower, but with a poor interior. Hoadley soon became the popular church architect of Connecticut, and the most potent influence of the period. Killingworth (1817), the two churches in Avon (1817, 1818), the two churches in Woodbury (1814, 1819), and the First Church of Milford (1823) all followed his style; and Avon and Milford were actually built by him. The First Church in Milford was taken as the perfect flower of the period (as in many ways it is), and was copied directly in Cheshire (1826), Southington (1828), and Litchfield (1829). Very slight differences in detail can be noticed, each version being refined to the last degree. The Litchfield structure, which was once used as a motion-picture theater, may well be taken as the ultimate and most worked-over masterpiece among our churches.

At first Roman and then earlier Greek elements began to hold sway, and to be copied with more and more scholarly accuracy. Two of the outstanding pure 'classical revival' churches remaining are Cornwall (1841) and the Baptist church (1841), now converted to Catholicism, in Old Lyme. But after a pedantic period, more and more freedom set in — a 'renaissance,' when classical forms were easily adapted in any way that the imagination of the day might dictate. A counter impulse came in when the Episcopal churches, conscious of their own Gothic tradition, sought to adhere to that tradition. Trinity Church (1814–15), on the New Haven Green, by Ithiel Town (perhaps assisted by Hoadley), was the earliest example of Gothic in Connecticut. Straightforward, but still obviously an immigrant, the style is far more convincing within than without. Lancet windows began to appear even in wooden buildings. The Gothic influence can be traced in St. Peter's (1825) at Hebron, in Kent (1826), in Riverton (1829), and in that little gem at Barkhamsted Hollow (1816) which the Episcopalians shared with the Universalists, and which now seems doomed to destruction by a water development. A last flare of the Gothic spirit even invades the classical in the eclectic tower of Bristol (1832). Both styles were to draw apart again, and after a period of disuse to come to real fruition in a later day.

III

With the dawn of the nineteenth century, industry and trade were thriving, and consequently houses tended to become larger and better appointed. By 1820, for instance, the story-and-a-half cottage that had been the typical home in many communities began to disappear, and another type was taking its place — the two-and-a-half-story house, with a gable end to the road and a doorway in one corner. Among the wealthier classes, the central-chimney house with the stairs in a tiny square hall in front of the chimney was giving way to the central-hall type with a long flight of stairs and two chimneys. The new measure of ease and refinement found expression in a new delicacy of detail. 'Architecture,' based now on definite Georgian precedents in England, and detail, influenced by the over-delicate classic refinements of the Adam brothers, were now the vogue.

During the early part of the nineteenth century, the professionally trained architect became an established figure, and greatly influenced the trend of building activity by the creation of such outstanding major buildings as the Old State House (1796) at Hartford, by Charles Bulfinch; Center Church (1812–14), New Haven, by Ithiel Town; and the North Church (1814–15) on New Haven Green, by David Hoadley. The work of these men had its influence on many of the churches and houses built throughout the State. 'Architecture' had become established as such, and buildings were being 'designed' rather than developed from their immediate environment under the competent hands of country craftsmen. Though the work of the early nineteenth-century architects had gained over that of the eighteenth and seventeenth centuries in the matter of studied design and the scale and elegance of detail, a certain sophistication had taken the place of the naïveté that charms one in the work of the earlier builders.

That the outstanding excellence of early nineteenth-century architecture was not logically carried on to the evolution of a distinctive type of American architecture is one of the calamities in American cultural development. The cause of the decline in architectural taste is a matter that is open to debate. But a decline there was, which continued through several decades, reaching its lowest level in the orgy of jigsawed and turned woodwork of the sixties and seventies.

This decline, however, was gradual, for a style that made its appearance about 1820 and was prominent until about 1850 had possibilities of being a continuation of the architectural development so well begun. Known as the 'Greek Revival,' it drew its inspiration from the architecture of classical antiquity. Its first manifestations were in the form of minor details of Greek ornament used in buildings that, in mass and general scale and detail, were purely Colonial — i.e., in the tradition that was current before the Revolution. An interesting example of its beginnings is the Congregational Church at Guilford, built in 1829, a building which in mass is traditional Colonial but which bears an imaginative adaptation of the 'Greek fret' ornament around the entrance doors and some Greek decoration at the corners of one of the stages of the steeple.

As the movement progressed, the buildings and their details became heavier and larger, and the refined delicacy that had characterized the preceding Federal period largely disappeared. Moldings, columns, and ornamental details were copied directly from Greek examples — until, when the period had reached its height, public buildings and even residences assumed the form of colonnaded Greek temples. In most cases, however, the general plan and mass of the houses still retained their earlier character, and the Greek influence was felt more in the type of molding or the incorporation of a two-column entrance porch in the Greek manner. So popular was this vogue that many owners of eighteenth-century houses had the old entrance motives replaced by new ones of Greek design, thereby often injuring the original character of the house. Outstanding examples of the Greek Revival in Connecticut are the row of high colonnaded houses on Huntington Street in New London; the Congregational Church (1838) at Madison; Plymouth Church (1834) at Milford; the Westville Congregational Church (1838) at New Haven; the Second Congregational Church at Derby; and a small house on the north side of Route 80 in North Branford. While this style resulted in many buildings of a certain architectural significance, it cannot be said to have been a progressive improvement on the character of the earlier Colonial. It did not as truly express the functional requirements of contemporary life, but was rather an affected adaptation of an architecture that had reached its highest development in an entirely different climate and civilization. It was not spontaneous — it did not arise directly out of human needs; and it left a weakened architectural impulse that fell prey to the importation of one foreign 'influence' after another.

One of the most interesting, yet also the most artificial and most neglected today, of those importations was nineteenth-century Gothicism. In Victorian England, the Georgian style had had its day; and Englishmen, influenced by the writings of Ruskin, were trying to recapture the spirit and splendor of their natural heritage, the Gothic of the Middle Ages. As the Connecticut colonists had translated the stone forms of the English Georgian into Yankee pine, so again Americans tried to adapt Gothic forms to wood. The development of woodworking machinery, particularly the bandsaw and jigsaw, made it an easy matter to torture wooden boards into uncouth shapes. Throughout the land there sprang up city halls, churches, and houses in the 'Gothic' manner. Houses were built with high peaked gables ornamented with an elaborate system of crockets, cusps, pointed arches, and balustrades — all sawed from inch-thick boards. The sum total was failure. The bandsaw could not translate Gothic into wood. Here and there, however, arose a building whose real picturesqueness of mass induced a feeling of repose and at the same time a certain sense of gaiety. Perhaps the best example of this sort in the State is the Archer Wheeler House, on Golden Hill Street, in Bridgeport.

The outstanding building of this period in Connecticut, and perhaps in the country, is the State Capitol (1872) at Hartford, on its commanding site in Bushnell Park. The composition of the main structure is well studied, and forms, when viewed from a distance, a satisfying base for the high gilded dome. The ornament and decoration, however, are meretricious and meaningless, and miss the true character of Gothic enrichment.

The old Library (1842) on the Yale Campus is a better example of Gothic design. It copies faithfully, and with some relation to material and purpose, an English church in the fifteenth century or 'Perpendicular' style; and though its turrets and finials are excrescences little adapted to our weather, it is a rare and impressive little building. One cannot but be glad that it has lately been transformed into an ecclesiastical edifice, so that the full beauty of its interior proportions can be admired.

As American architects began to study abroad, other imported influences were felt — for example, the brownstone Romanesque, popularized by Richardson (as in the Public Library and railroad station at New London); and the classical renaissance of Italy, so often adopted by McKim (as in the unusual railroad station in Waterbury, with its tower copied from Siena). But these were impulses that usually died with the architect who imported them. As increasingly large sums have been made available for public buildings, architecture has become more and more eclectic and international. Connecticut has had rather more than its share of conspicuous examples of this later trend. Mention can be made only of the newer buildings at Yale, in a freely translated English university Gothic; the incomparable Gothic chapel at Trinity College; and the highly original transcriptions of all the heavy and primitive styles, in the scattered quadrangles of Avon Old Farms, combined in one harmonious whole.

Questions may well be raised as to the future of any American 'style,' based on so many elements. And yet it has become increasingly evident that an indigenous 'Colonial' tradition survives through it all, particularly with reference to domestic architecture. It is with the hope of helping to establish true standards for the appreciation today of its earliest forms that the houses noted in this Guide have been pointed out.

NOTES ON CONNECTICUT ART

I

IF CONNECTICUT'S contribution to the fine arts is less substantial than those of some other northern States, the ultimate reason is to be found in the absence of a conspicuously good harbor along her coast, and the consequent absence of a great metropolis wherein collectors might gather and toward which artists would naturally gravitate. Even with her comparative disadvantages, however, the State has given the world some honorable names and much excellent work.

For the first century and a half the settlers were too busy wresting a living from the soil to think much of the fine arts. During the eighteenth century the usual itinerant portrait painters began to make their journeys to and fro, and left their anonymous works to posterity, stilted and primitive, yet none without a certain naif charm. As a counterpart to these, wall decorators occasionally blossomed forth in an overmantel landscape or figure piece, or perhaps inserted a small mural medallion in an over-all wall decoration. As interest in old houses increases, more and more of these little murals are being uncovered, and tradition frequently associates them with Hessian soldiers. Their primitive, out-of-scale draftsmanship often serves as an advantage rather than a drawback, and the farm-house renovator who finds one beneath several layers of shabby wall paper counts himself fortunate.

The first name of any distinction to be connected with Connecticut is that of Ralph Earl. Though born in Massachusetts, in 1751, he painted most of his portraits in Connecticut, and died there in 1801. Earl might be described as a kind of countrified Copley. He preferred full-length figures on large canvases; his ambition outran his proficiency, but his designs are strong and his figures full of character. Occasionally one finds a child in a portrait group that recalls the whimsical primitiveness which a far-distant and far greater contemporary, Goya, chose to use in his portraits of children.

During the Revolutionary War a disgruntled young ex-officer in the American army lived in London and made copies of old masters in the studio of Benjamin West. This was John Trumbull, born in Lebanon, Connecticut, in 1756, the youngest son of Jonathan Trumbull, governor of the colony and subsequently of the State. John Trumbull also studied in France, and upon his return to America, after the war was over, he had become one of the most talented, as well as versatile, painters of his day. As a portrait painter he was ranked second only to Stuart in his time, and he produced a number of exquisite miniatures. He is seen at his best, however, in the series of small studies for the rotunda in the Capitol at Washington. These eight little canvases, now in the Yale Gallery of Fine Arts, comprising chiefly battle scenes, are full of life, light, and drama, and survive as one of the major treasures of early Republican art. The four full-size panels which he was commissioned to do for the Capitol are less successful; when painting on a large scale Trumbull was apparently affected by a desire for grandiosity, and it is probable that he was further hampered by defective eyesight.

Another portraitist of great ability was Samuel F. B. Morse (1791–1872), associated with Connecticut by his years of study at Yale and the large number of portraits he executed within the State. Morse was well trained in France and England, and his best canvases leave little to be desired. He had simplicity without emptiness, dexterity without virtuosity, style without mannerism, and the characters of his subjects fairly leap from the canvas. When, during the middle forties, he sickened of the smallness of his rewards and turned to electrical experimentation, applied science took a great step forward, but American painting suffered an irreparable loss.

A New Haven painter, Nathaniel Jocelyn (1796–1881), in his early years gave considerable promise. His customary rather somber blacks and reds, and his decorative use of the puffed sleeves and fantastic coiffures of the period, make his earlier portraits a welcome ornament to many a chimney-breast. As his years increased, however, slickness and facility grew on him, and he ended in a rather insipid Victorianism. His pupils, Samuel Lovett Waldo (1783–1861), and Thomas Pritchard Rossiter (1818–71), became two of the most fashionable and successful portrait painters of their time. Rossiter in general loved bright color; his work is less tight and smooth than that of many of his contemporaries, but often shows carelessness. Waldo was the better of the two: his work lacked subtlety and the indefinable last touch that means greatness, but his canvases are often astonishingly good. His name is usually mentioned in connection with that of his partner, William Jewett, who is supposed to have painted in his backgrounds and draperies. With Waldo and

Jocelyn the classic school of Connecticut portraiture — if the foregoing group deserves such a name — ceases, and in subsequent work the great hand of Manet hovers behind almost every brush.

The Hudson River School had few repercussions in Connecticut, but the State contributed one of the most prominent members of the group, John Frederick Kensett, who was born in Cheshire in 1818. Kensett was a leading landscape painter of his day; he had studied and traveled widely in Europe, but he neither lived nor painted considerably in Connecticut. The same may be said of Frederick Edwin Church (1826–1900) of Hartford. Church belonged to the group of landscape painters including Thomas Cole, his master, Bierstadt, and Moran, who went far afield for their subjects and painted them large. They were the pictorial exponents of 'manifest destiny,' and their vast canvases now mostly languish in dark corners of art galleries, awaiting the revival of appreciation which time will inevitably bring.

It remained for an obscure New Haven painter, George Henry Durrie (1820–63), to emerge, after a long period of oblivion, as the first and best interpreter of the Connecticut scene. Durrie was a pupil of Jocelyn and his portraits resemble those of his master. His real field was landscape, the hills and farms that he knew and loved. These he put on canvas with a minuteness of detail probably inspired by Durand. In his best canvases (his work is very uneven), and especially in his winter scenes, Durrie was more than a recorder and became, in flashes, a poet — very much the sort of poet that wrote 'Snowbound.' One can fairly smell the wood smoke in his frosty air, hear the creak of snow under the sledge runners, the barking of distant dogs, and breathe the atmosphere of the old, snug, cheery farm life of the early nineteenth century. Many of Durrie's paintings were used as subjects for Currier and Ives prints, the most famous of these being 'Home for Thanksgiving.' It is a pity that Durrie died in early middle age, for in later life he might well have acquired, as did Inness, the simplicity whose absence kept him from real greatness.

At this point one may digress to mention two engravers who stand at the head of Connecticut's roster in this field. The first was Amos Doolittle (1754–1832), who was born in Cheshire but lived in New Haven. Unschooled as he was, he stands forth as the most interesting American engraver of his time, and his four copper plates of 'The Battle of Lexington,' said to be made from designs by Ralph Earl, are highly prized by collectors. So is his famous 'Display of the United States,' in which the bust of Washington is surrounded by the coats of arms of the thirteen States. John Warner Barber (1798–1885) of East Windsor conceived the idea of making a popular history which could also serve as a guidebook, and illustrating it with copper plate engravings after drawings of his own. In his horse and buggy he covered not only his own State, but almost the entire country, and did more than any other man of his time to familiarize Americans with the history and topography of their native land. His engravings are simple to the verge of crudeness, but they are attractive in their way.

The story of Connecticut sculpture began rather early, in the person of Hezekiah Augur of New Haven (1791–1858). He was the son of a carpenter, and in early life learned to carve in wood. Not content with chair-legs and similar hack-work, which he did very acceptably, he turned to marble, and without instruction or model produced a head of Apollo, using a carving machine designed by Samuel F. B. Morse. His great work, 'Jephthah and his Daughter,' still displayed in the Yale Art School, is sentimental and unsculptural, yet it is done with an irresistible gusto and stands as a not unworthy monument to a man who persisted in aiming high. Washington Allston paid this work the somewhat ambiguous compliment of walking around it for half an hour without uttering a word.

Olin Levi Warner (1844–90) of Suffield, an artist noted for the vigor and sensitiveness of his modeling, produced the statue of Governor Buckingham in the Capitol at Hartford and that of William Lloyd Garrison in Boston. George Edwin Bissell (1839–1920), born in New Preston, took up sculpture when over thirty, and after some years of study in Europe created a number of portrait figures and memorials not only in his own State but in many others.

More distinguished than these was Paul Wayland Bartlett (1865–1925). Born in New Haven but educated in France, he first exhibited in the Salon at the age of 14. The greatest of his many works is the equestrian statue of Lafayette which stands in the Court of the Louvre; a replica is in Capitol Park in Hartford. He is also represented in the Library of Congress, the National Capitol, and the pediment of the New York Stock Exchange. His contemporary, Bela Lyon Pratt (1867–1917), born in Norwich, studied at the Yale Art School, and under Saint-Gaudens, Cox, and Chase in New York. His work is characterized by simplicity and a deep but restrained feeling. He is represented by figures outside the Public Library in Boston, also in the Public Gardens and the State House, as well as by several important memorials scattered through the eastern States, but probably his most appealing works are the 'Spanish War Soldier' at St. Paul's School in Concord, New Hampshire, and his 'Nathan Hale' on the Yale Campus.

Among contemporary sculptors of note living in the State are Robert G. Eberhard, Professor of Sculpture in the Yale School of Fine Arts, Evelyn Longman Batchelder of Windsor, Henry Kreis of Essex, Heinz Warneke of East Haddam, Karl Lang of Noroton, Lewis Gudebrod of Meriden, and A. Phimister Proctor of Wilton.

II

The majority of the artists heretofore mentioned were natives of Connecticut who went forth to work and to make names for themselves elsewhere. In the latter years of the nineteenth century this process was largely reversed, and we find artists who had already won their spurs in other parts settling in Connecticut, either singly or in groups, because it was a delightful place to live and to paint and is not far from New York.

Among the first of those who became Connecticut artists by adoption were the two sons of the Hudson River artist, Robert W. Weir. The elder, John Ferguson Weir (1841–1926), after studying in New York and Europe and painting 'The Forging of the Shaft,' now in the Metropolitan Museum, was in 1869 appointed dean of the recently created School of Fine Arts at Yale, a position he filled until 1913. His reputation as a painter, though overshadowed by that of his brother, is nevertheless high, and his later canvases, thoroughly impressionistic, have much of the light and air and color usually associated with Monet. J. Alden Weir (1852–1919) owned farms in Windham and Branchville. A student of Bastien-Lepage, he started out in the classical manner of nineteenth-century French painting, but became increasingly impressionistic, or 'luministic.' His figure pieces, exceedingly restrained in color and low in value, have a certain fine feeling and nobility which win more praise from artists than from laymen, but his later landscape work is more airy and probably more widely appreciated.

Late in the nineteenth century artists began to assemble in small groups for summer residence in various favorable spots, and the era of the 'art colony' began. The oldest was at Mystic, associated with the names of Charles Harold Davis (1856–1933) and Henry Ranger (1858–1916). Ranger was a popular landscapist during his lifetime, but his work is now rated far below its true merit. Davis, who moved to Mystic in 1890, devoted himself to the Connecticut scene more exclusively than any other painter except George Durrie. It is interesting to compare their styles, the one tight and realistic, the other full of light and air.

Prominent among the group at Old Lyme were Carleton Wiggins and

Eugene Higgins, who might not inappropriately be called the last of the Romantics. Childe Hassam was also an intermittent resident at this place. Similar aggregations of more recent origin have sprung up at Kent, Westport, and Silvermine (in the town of Norwalk). All of these hold annual exhibitions, in some cases in galleries built and operated by the associated artists. These centers and other villages have attracted to the State many of the most prominent artists of the present day, a full list of which would be too long to include, and a partial list would involve invidious distinctions.

Hartford, the second center of population in the State, has produced a group of artists sometimes referred to as 'The Hartford School.' Two of the first to attain national reputations were William Gedney Bunce (1840–1916) and Dwight William Tryon (1849–1925). Both left the State early in their careers, Bunce spending most of his time in Venice, painting his highly subjective and beautifully colored sea-scapes. Tryon did most of his painting near New Bedford. His work, like that of Ranger, Davis, and others among his contemporaries, stands less high at present than during his lifetime, but his accomplishment was genuine, and recognition of it will not die out. Late in the century there was a good deal of artistic activity in Hartford which centered around Charles Noel Flagg and his Connecticut League of Art Students. Flagg came of a family of artists whose members included Washington Allston, George Whiting Flagg, Jared Flagg, and Montague Flagg; he was a friend of Tryon, with whom he had studied abroad, and his League was run somewhat in imitation of the Paris *atelier*. Among the most prominent of his pupils were the sculptor Paul Wayland Bartlett, James Britton, Louis Orr the etcher, Milton Avery, Albertus Jones, and James Goodwin McManus, the last four of whom are still doing admirable work in their various fields.

The State is fairly rich in public collections. The oldest is the Yale Gallery of Fine Arts, which started in 1831 with the purchase by the University of all John Trumbull's works that still remained in his possession. This constituted the first art gallery to be incorporated in an American university. The most important subsequent accretion was the purchase of an extraordinary group of 119 Italian primitive paintings from John Jackson Jarvis in the seventies. The Wadsworth Atheneum in Hartford, founded in 1844, with the subsequent additions of the Morgan Memorial (1910) and the Avery Memorial (1934), forms an important and rapidly increasing collection. In New London is the Lyman Allen Museum and in Norwich the Slater Memorial Museum, the latter perhaps unique in being incorporated with a public school.

Descriptions of these collections occur elsewhere in this volume. At this point it may be relevant to remark that most of them pay but little attention to the work of the artists who were born or flourished in their vicinity. Botticelli's best works are in Florence, Rembrandt's in Holland, Watteau's in Paris, Hogarth's in London, but one may look in vain for Rangers and Davises and Hassams in Norwich or New London, or for Kensetts and Tryons in Hartford. In some cases, indeed, the idea seems to be to make a special effort to concentrate on foreign work. There is in Hartford a small but articulate group of enthusiasts who are ardently interested in contemporary European artists, and have given a fine showing to such members of the post-Picasso group as Tchelitchev, Berman, and Tonny. The best collections of Connecticut furniture, glass, silver, and textiles are to be found in Hartford and New Haven.

The various historical societies also contain many important works of art, and here more attention is paid to local talent. Chief among these societies in size and scope are the New Haven Colony Historical Society, the Connecticut Historical Society in Hartford, and the Mattatuck Historical Society in Waterbury, but many of the smaller ones also possess works of interest and beauty. Among these, with no discrimination against many others, may be mentioned the Winchester Historical Society at Winsted, which, housed in one of the loveliest of early nineteenth-century dwellings, contains a remarkably fine group of primitive portraits.

All the four museums mentioned above foster educational work, either as part of their activities or through organizations closely connected with them. The Yale School of Fine Arts, founded in 1866, is the chief of these, as it is the oldest. It has always been one of the leading art schools in the country, but was particularly successful as a school of painting under the guidance of Professor Edwin Cassius Taylor from 1923 till 1935. In Hartford, the Hartford Art School, run in connection with the Avery Memorial, has largely supplanted the older Connecticut League of Art Students, and is conducted on rather modern principles. The Slater Memorial conducts classes in connection with the Norwich Free Academy, and the Lyman Allen Museum in connection with the adjacent Connecticut College for Women.

An interesting development of recent years has been the employment of artists by the Federal Government under the CWA, FERA, and WPA. By virtue of this, many public institutions have been enriched by works in all mediums by Connecticut artists, and the existence of the fine arts has been brought home to a public previously all too little aware of it.

There are numerous murals from this source in the schools and other public buildings of Hartford, New Haven, and Fairfield County, with a thinner scattering in other parts of the State. Among the best are decorations by James Daugherty in the Greenwich Town Hall, the Stamford High School, and the Holmes School in Darien, and those by John Steuart Curry in the Norwalk High School. One cannot bear to leave this subject without mentioning also two fresco panels, 'Comedy' and 'Tragedy,' in the Bedford Junior High School in Westport, which Curry was enabled to execute by private subscription in 1934. These are a far cry from Trumbull and Morse, but if anyone needs to be convinced that art is not yet dead in the State, let him look at them!

LITERATURE

EARLY Connecticut literature has been aptly described as a 'distinguished blank.' The rigors of survival against hostile Indians and hard winters made the settlers an essentially practical people. Although the New England colonists were of a superior intellectual class, including at one time an Oxford graduate for every 250 persons, daily bread and the salvation of the soul were of first importance. Men whose vigorous intellects might have produced significant literature devoted their energies to the struggle against political oppression and the fear of eternal damnation.

The colonists were militant separatists who felt called upon to justify before the world their self-imposed exile. Their ministerial leaders rose ably to the occasion with consummate theological arguments, and in their weekly sermons provided the chief intellectual and literary advantages accessible to the frontiersmen. The discourses and numerous published tracts of Thomas Hooker, John Davenport, and Henry Whitfield of Connecticut were eagerly read, and played a significant part in guiding public opinion.

In the pioneer days when books were luxuries, almanacs with their varied collections of astronomical data, schedules of court decisions, mileage between taverns, dates of local storms, and interesting predictions, became a household institution. The first almanac with a Connecticut imprint was dated 1709 and written by Daniel Travis. As Thomas Short, the first printer in New London, established his printing press in the spring of 1709, it is probable that this almanac was printed at the 'Sign of the Bible,' Cornhill, Boston. Short's press in New London was the first in Connecticut, and, later sold to Timothy Green, remained the only one for forty-five years. In 1716, Green sold in New London an almanac calculated for the meridian of Boston, written by Daniel Travis and printed by Bartholomew Green of Boston.

The first almanac by a Connecticut author printed in Connecticut, as well as the earliest known to have been printed in the Colony, was Joseph Moss's 'An Almanack ... to the Meridian of Yale,' printed by G. Saltonstall and sold by Timothy Green. In 1753, Roger Sherman, a signer of the Declaration of Independence, wrote an 'Astronomical

Diary,' published by Timothy Green. Many of the early Connecticut almanacs were reprints of Boston's famous 'Ames Almanack,' which was first locally reprinted at New Haven in 1756. In 1761, a Yale 'College Almanak' was written 'By a Student.'

The 'Connecticut Almanack' was first compiled by Clark Elliot, published in New London in 1767, and purchased in 1778 by Nehemiah Strong of Hartford, one of the most prominent of Connecticut almanac authors, whose initial 'Watson's Register' first appeared in 1775. Best known, and celebrated for its almost continuous publication from 1772 to the present day is 'Daboll's Almanac,' first printed by Nathaniel Daboll in New London in 1772 under the name of 'Freebetter's New England Almanack,' and known today as 'The New England Almanac and Farmer's Friend.' Another old almanac that is still published was originated in 1806 by Elisha Middlebrook of Fairfield and published by him until 1860. The 'Beckwith Almanac,' started at New Haven in 1848, and peddled about Connecticut by its author, was published until 1933.

Diaries were among the earliest writings and have preserved in unaffected simplicity detailed accounts of the manners and customs of the colonists. Perhaps the best known Connecticut diary is the one written by Ezra Stiles from 1769 through the period of his presidency of Yale College. A diary kept by Joshua Hempstead (New London, 1711–58), and one by Nathaniel W. Taylor recording his 'Life on a Whaler, or an Antarctic Adventure in the Isle of Desolation,' are preserved in the New London Historical Society collection.

The Journal of William Wheeler (1762–1845), a student at Yale and a resident of Black Rock, Fairfield, records an 'exact and impartial account' of events in that old seaport town. This diary is included in the recently published 'History of Black Rock,' by Cornelia Penfield Lathrop. The Rev. Isaac Bachus of Norwich Town kept a diary from 1748 to 1806, which contains a wealth of information on local and national events. A brief though interesting diary by Mason Fitch Cogswell of Canterbury is devoted to a detailed account of his horseback trip across Connecticut, from November 14 to December 19, 1788, in which he carefully recorded the simple details of life in the homes he visited.

The diary (1797–1803) of Julia Cowles of Farmington, now in print, is an appealing document which vividly presents many phases of the social life of her times, in the record of her girlhood, her reactions to the wickedness of 'modern' life, the tender details of the courting of John Treadwell, son of Governor Treadwell, and of her engagement to him. Despite her lover's pleading, she delayed their marriage because of her failing health, and died while still a young woman.

Roger Wolcott of Windsor (1679–1767), State governor and military leader, found time to write 'Poetical Meditations: Being the Improvement of Some Vacant Hours,' in which his Calvinistic vision saw 'Hell's flashes folding through eternitie.' This was the first book of verse published in Connecticut. And, before the Revolution, there was at least one writer of commanding ability in America, a native of South Windsor — Jonathan Edwards (1703–58). Mystic, metaphysician, and logician, his vivid imagination pictured Hell's torments and the eternally erupting mountains of fire and brimstone, to the prostration of multitudes at the time of the 'Great Awakening.' The very title of his most famous works breathes contempt on the ungodly and looser thinkers: 'A Careful and Strict Enquiry into the Modern Prevailing Notions of that Freedom of Will which is Supposed to be Essential to Moral Agency, Virtue and Vice, Reward and Punishment, Praise and Blame' (1754). For the next hundred years, Connecticut's orthodoxy was noteworthy.

When independence had been won, but divergent doctrines threatened anarchy, a group of distinguished Yale graduates formed a literary society to combat the lawless influences with political satire. This first recognized literary group in the State became celebrated as 'The Hartford Wits,' and included a college president, several foreign ministers and ambassadors, and a judge of the Connecticut Supreme Court. Richard Alsop, Joel Barlow, Timothy Dwight, and the brilliant John Trumbull, who passed the entrance examinations to Yale at the age of seven and entered college five years later, were among the leaders of the group, which also included Lemuel Hopkins, Theodore Dwight, and Col. David Humphrey, aide-de-camp to Washington and author of the earliest biography of Israel Putnam. Jointly they published 'The Anarchiad' (1786), 'The Political Greenhouse' (1799), and 'The Echo' (1807). Joel Barlow, perhaps the group's most distinguished and versatile member, wrote two widely read poems: 'Hasty Pudding,' a realistic portrayal of New England home life; and a ponderous epic, 'The Columbiad,' in which Hesper unfolds to Columbus a retrospective view of the conquest of Mexico, the settlement of North America, and a vision of the future supremacy of America. This latter work, heavy with Latin derivatives, makes laborious reading today, but it was enthusiastically received by the colonists, who even named their coast defense guns 'Columbiad.' John Trumbull's mock-epic, 'M'Fingal,' a Hudibrastic attack on the Tories, ran through thirty editions and earned for Trumbull the title of 'Father of American Burlesque.' Timothy Dwight, president of Yale College for twenty-two years, was the author of a poem of epic proportions, 'The Conquest of Canaan,' dealing with the narrative of Joshua's wars, in which Revolutionary heroes were compared with Biblical characters. His shorter poem, 'Greenfield Hill,' is a delightful description of the Connecticut village with which he was associated for many years. Dr. Elihu H. Smith, physician of Wethersfield and another active member of 'The Hartford Wits,' was the first Connecticut poet to publish a volume of collected verse — 'American Poems, Original and Selected.' Thus, for a few years at the close of the eighteenth century, before the days of the New York and Boston groups, Connecticut could boast of the first literary circle in the new nation. This is the only time in its history when Connecticut can be said to have possessed a literature of its own.

In those days there lived in Connecticut a redoubtable man of letters whose influence was of the most enduring and widespread sort. In the years between the Declaration of Independence and the framing of the Constitution, Noah Webster (1758–1843) brought forth his blue-bound 'American Spelling Book.' Passing through various degrees of spelling reform and Yankee individualism, it appeared throughout a century in unnumbered editions. The success of Webster's first dictionary, published in 1806, led to the compiling of his masterly 'American Dictionary of the English Language' (1828). On this foundation our speech, with the exception of Harvard English and its rival Worcester's Dictionary (1846), has rested.

There was something redoubtable, also, about a Ridgefield minister's son, Samuel Griswold Goodrich (1793–1860), who just before his death declared himself the author of 170 volumes, 116 of them written under the pseudonym of 'Peter Parley.' Inspired by Hannah More, Goodrich purveyed an endless stream of edifying sugar-coated instruction to the young. For him, the shy and fastidious young Nathaniel Hawthorne wrote 'Peter Parley's Universal History' (1837), which sold a million copies, and edited the 'American Magazine of Useful and Entertaining Knowledge'; while in his giftbook annual, 'The Token,' many of Hawthorne's earliest stories appeared.

Fitz-Greene Halleck (1790–1867) of Guilford joined the early New York school of writers, and was co-author with James Rodman Drake of the satiric 'Croaker & Co.' verses. Like many of his contemporaries, he was an imitator of Scott, Byron, and Campbell; his 'Marco Bozzaris' is a spirited Byronesque depiction of the Greek struggle for freedom against the Turks.

One of Noah Webster's assistants was a young botanist-chemist-geologist-poet, whose knowledge of ten languages made him a valuable helper in revising and proof-reading the orthographer's *magnum opus*. Suffering from a persecution complex, James Gates Percival (1795–1856) turned in his versatility from science to poetry and then back again. He was State Geologist of Wisconsin at the time of his death. The sensitive and delicate beauty of his verse missed fame by a narrow margin.

Jared Sparks (1789–1866) of Willington lived to become president of Harvard and to be called the 'American Plutarch.' The country owes him a great debt for his preservation of important documents and letters of Revolutionary times and leaders. His 'Life and Times of George Washington,' bowdlerized but honest, and 'American Biographies' are full of valuable source material. John Fiske (1842–1901), born in Middletown, was a later distinguished Harvard man and eminent historian.

The father of the 'Little Women' was born in Connecticut and began his career as a Yankee peddler and country school teacher. Amos Bronson Alcott (1799–1888) of Wolcott astounded the citizens of Cheshire by his advanced educational methods, the beginning of his greatest contribution to American life and thought. His close association with Concord, Massachusetts, has obscured the fact that the formative years of this 'tedious archangel' were passed in this State.

Several minor poets of Connecticut became more or less prominent in the half century which closed with the Civil War period. John Pierpont (1785–1866) published 'Airs of Palestine,' later visiting the country which his muse had celebrated; he also wrote a number of ardent anti-slavery poems. James Hillhouse (1789–1841) of New Haven was the author of several long Biblical poems and dramas. John G. C. Brainard (1796–1828), born in New London, edited the *Connecticut Union* in Hartford and wrote of the native scene — timidly perhaps, but at times authentically. Henry Howard Brownell's 'Bay Fight,' a stirring description of the battle of Mobile Bay, fired the popular imagination in Civil War times. Brownell (1820–1872), whose war poetry has been collected in a volume called 'Lines of Battle,' was born in Providence, R.I., but spent the greater part of his life in East Hartford. Other poets were known for one or two nationally popular verses. Emma Hart Willard of Berlin (1787–1870), writer of school-books, is remembered for 'Rocked in the Cradle of the Deep.' 'Marching Through Georgia' and that theme song of the temperance movement 'Father, Dear Father, Come Home With Me Now, the Clock in the Steeple Strikes Twelve,' both came from the pen of the talented composer Henry Clay Work.

Most portentous, summing up a whole school of feeling in her obituaries and elegiac verses was Lydia Huntley Sigourney (1791–1865), 'The Sweet Singer of Hartford.' Writing for a sympathetic, even enthusiastic audience, she produced fifty-nine volumes of lachrymose verbosity. The works of this 'American Mrs. Hemans' are now literary curiosities that serve as an excellent index to the taste of a generation to which a cloying sentimentality was endearing and which reveled in polite periphrasis.

Late in the nineteenth century, Mrs. Sigourney found a successor to her popularity in Ella Wheeler Wilcox (1855–1919), who lived for twenty years in a cottage at Short Beach. But sentiment had undergone a startling reversal, and Mrs. Wilcox's philosophy was more cheerful, as expressed in her notable lines, 'Laugh, and the world laughs with you; weep, and you weep alone.' It was also more pungent and outspoken, witness her best-known title, 'Poems of Passion.' The twentieth century was now imminent.

Edmund Clarence Stedman (1833–1908) was born in Hartford, and after leaving college entered the newspaper field, owning and editing at different times the *Norwich Tribune* and the *Mountain County Herald* of Winsted. Then, while still a young man, he left the State, later becoming nationally known as poet, critic, and editor.

Although Lyman Beecher (1775–1863), of New Haven and Litchfield, achieved some fame as a clergyman and writer, at least two of his thirteen children were far more distinguished. These two were Henry Ward Beecher (1813–87) and Harriet Beecher Stowe (1811–96). Both were born at Litchfield, and both left the State with their family at an early age. After the publication of 'Uncle Tom's Cabin' in 1852, Mrs. Stowe came to Hartford, where she had attended school as a girl; and here she built a large home which, along with a later and more permanent residence in Florida, she occupied at intervals until her death. In 'Poganuc People' she has described her early childhood in Connecticut; while the New England scene and character in general are sympathetically portrayed in such other of her later books as 'The Minister's Wooing' and 'Oldtown People.'

Close in spirit to these later books by Mrs. Stowe, as well as to the writings of Mary E. Wilkins and Sarah Orne Jewett, are the New England stories of Rose Terry Cooke (1827–92), of West Hartford. These appeared in *The Atlantic Monthly* for many years, beginning in 1861. Miss Cooke also wrote some poetry of distinction.

The novels, poems, and narratives of outdoor life written by Theodore Winthrop (1828–61) were once popular but are now little read. His western novel, 'John Brent,' anticipated the frontier fiction of Bret Harte. Winthrop was born in New Haven, and studied at Yale. After more than a decade of wanderings outside the State, he was killed at the battle of Great Bethel, early in the Civil War.

More enduring has been the reputation of Donald G. Mitchell (1822–1908), who under the pen-name of 'Ik Marvel' wrote those delicate fantasies, 'The Reveries of a Bachelor' and 'Dream Life,' as well as a number of other books. Mitchell's later years were spent in Virgilian retirement on his estate near New Haven, commemorated in 'My Farm at Edgewood.'

The most lovable as well as the most popular figure in Connecticut's literary annals is Samuel L. Clemens (1835–1910), known the world over as Mark Twain. After wandering through the middle and far West and spending a year abroad, Clemens settled down in Hartford soon after his marriage in 1870, and during his thirty years' residence here he wrote most of the books upon which his fame chiefly rests, including 'Tom Sawyer' and 'Huckleberry Finn.' A number of these books were originally issued by a Hartford house, the American Publishing Company, which also published (in 1900) the first collected edition of his works.

Soon after coming to Hartford, Clemens collaborated with his friend and neighbor, Charles Dudley Warner (1829–1900), in his only piece of contemporary fiction, 'The Gilded Age.' Warner, a brilliant editor and writer, is best remembered for the leisurely charm and keen understanding of human nature embodied in such books as 'Backlog Studies,' 'My Summer in a Garden,' and 'Being a Boy.'

Among the later writers of Connecticut, a prominent place belongs to Charlotte Perkins Gilman (1860–1935), poet, sociologist, and ardent champion of a freer and fuller destiny for women: Mrs. Gilman was born in Hartford, and lived for many years in Norwichtown. Although best known, perhaps, as the biographer of Mark Twain and authorized editor of the latter's posthumous publications, Albert Bigelow Paine (1861–1937) of West Redding wrote a number of stories and sketches characterized by a quiet humor somewhat akin to that in much of Mark Twain's work. Arthur Colton (b. 1868) of Washington is the author of 'The Belted Seas' and 'The Delectable Mountains.' The versatile talents of Lee Wilson Dodd (1879–1933) were chiefly exercised in the fields of fiction and the drama, though he was also an accomplished critic, lecturer, and teacher. Anna Hempstead Branch (1875–1937), whose family dated back to earliest days in New London, is known to poetry lovers through 'The Shoes That Danced' and other books of verse. Odell Shepard, of

Trinity College, has written 'The Harvest of a Quiet Eye' (descriptive of a walking trip in the northern part of Connecticut), two or three volumes of poetry and essays, and a recently published biography of Bronson Alcott.

The influence of Yale University has been notably reflected in American literature since the early nineteenth century. Yale's list of alumni includes many of the country's best known writers, from James Fenimore Cooper to Stephen Vincent Benét, Thornton Wilder, and Sinclair Lewis; and numerous members of its faculty have made important contributions to literature and literary scholarship. Prominent among this latter group in recent years have been Wilbur L. Cross (now governor of Connecticut), author of definitive biographies of Henry Fielding and Laurence Sterne; and William Lyon Phelps, whose published volumes are chiefly popular criticism of modern poetry, fiction and drama. *The Yale Literary Magazine*, edited by undergraduates of the university, dates from 1836 and is now the oldest surviving monthly in this country. *The Yale Review*, which has appeared under its present name since 1892 and under the editorship of Wilbur L. Cross since 1911, is one of the world's most distinguished quarterlies. Finally, in this general connection, a word must be said about the Yale University Press, which has won an enviable reputation in the American publishing field for combining scholarly content with distinguished mechanical form in its output.

Connecticut has provided the setting or background for numerous books of fiction, among them (to mention only a few relatively recent examples) Sinclair Lewis's 'Work of Art,' Edna Ferber's 'American Beauty,' Lee Wilson Dodd's 'The Book of Susan,' J. G. Cozzens's 'The Last Adam,' and Wayland Williams's 'Family.'

CONNECTICUT FIRSTS

1636 First American naval battle (of a sort) is fought off New London.

1639 First constitutional document to set forth the principle that 'the foundation of authority is in the free consent of the people' — the so-called Fundamental Orders of Connecticut — is adopted at Hartford.

1640 First American public election in defiance of the Royal Courts is held at Wethersfield.

1647 First concession or license for off-shore whaling is issued at Hartford.

1662 First American ship in West India trade is 'The Tryall' of Wethersfield.

1670 First survey is made for first turnpike to be completed in America — from Norwich to New London.

1680 First American carding mill is established at Wethersfield.

1724 First American portable house is brought to Windsor from Plymouth.

1727 First copper coins in America are minted by Samuel Higley, a blacksmith of Simsbury. Higley's coins were marked: 'I am good copper. Value me as you will.'

1738 First theological seminary in America is organized by Rev. Joseph Bellamy at Bethlehem.

1740 First American tinware is manufactured by Edward Pattison and his brother in Berlin.

1744 First half-ton of American-made steel is produced by Samuel Higley of Simsbury.

1750 First American hat factory is established at Wethersfield.

1765 First oil mill in New England is built at Leesville.

1769 First type foundry in America is established at New Haven by Abel Buell.

1774 First 'declaration of freedom' from British Crown is adopted by town of Mansfield — 21 months before adoption of the Declaration of Independence.

1775 First American warship, the 'Oliver Cromwell,' 16 guns, is built at Essex.

First Federal prison is established at East Granby.

First pins manufactured in America under bounty are made by Leonard Chester at Wethersfield.

First submarine torpedo boat ever used in naval warfare is invented by Daniel Bushnell of Westbrook; its first action was against the British flagship 'Eagle' in New York Harbor, Sept. 6, 1776.

1779 First British prize, the sloop 'Hero,' is captured by the Wethersfield sloop 'Enterprise.'

1780 First fur hat factory in America is conducted by Zadock Benedict of Danbury.

1782 First law school in America is organized at Litchfield by Judge Tapping Reeve.

1783 First map of the United States engraved in America is produced by Abel Buell in New Haven.

1785 First reports of law cases to be printed in America compiled by Colonel Ephraim Kirby of Litchfield, include the years 1785–88.

1787 First American boat propelled by steam, using paddle-wheels, oars, and screws, is perfected by John Fitch of South Windsor.

1789 First American juvenile publication, 'The Children's Magazine,' is published in Hartford.

1794 First cotton gin is patented by Eli Whitney, a native of Connecticut, and later first manufactured in New Haven.

1796 First American cook book, written by Amelia Simmons, is published in Hartford (republished 1937).

1799 First United States government contract for pistols is awarded to Simeon North of Middletown.

1801 First American cigars, known as 'long nines,' are made by Mrs. Prout of South Windsor.

1802 First commercial ivory combs are made by Julius Pratt of Essex.

First merino sheep in America are imported by Gen. David Humphreys of Derby.

First packaged garden seeds to be sold in America are marketed by the Enfield Shaker Colony.

First standardized interchangeable clock movements are produced by Eli Terry at Plymouth (Todd Hollow).

1803 First tax-supported town library in America is organized at Salisbury.

1806 First American patent for welding iron to steel is taken out by Daniel Pettibone of Roxbury.

First factory town in America is established by Gen. David Humphreys at Seymour.

1809 First United States patent to a woman is issued to Mary Kies of South Killingly for a silk-and-straw weaving machine.

1810 First double-twist augers are made by Walter French of Seymour.

First 'lookout' tower for public use in the United States is built on Talcott Mountain by Dan Wadsworth.

First pineapple cheese is made and patented by Lewis N. Norton of Goshen.

1812 First use of steam power for manufacturing is made in plant of Middletown Woolen Manufacturing Company.

1813 First adoption of standardized production methods is made by Simeon North at his arms factory in Middletown.

First American-made steel fish hooks are produced by Eb Jenks of Colebrook.

First manufacturers' agreement to limit prices and regulate trade practices is made by tin manufacturers of Meriden — 120 years before the N.R.A. (National Recovery Act).

First patent for 'elastic steel-wire teeth for cotton and wool carding' is granted to Eb Jenks of Colebrook:

1814 First 'shelf clock' is patented by Eli Terry of Thomaston.

1816 First fanning mill for separating chaff from grain is patented by Benjamin D. Beecher of Cheshire.

1817 First American school for education of the deaf is founded at Hartford.

1818 First 'knocked-down' furniture is produced by Lambert H. Hitchcock of Riverton, who shipped his famous chairs, etc., in separate parts, to be assembled after delivery.

First successful American milling machine is invented by Eli Whitney, for use in his New Haven gun shops.

1819 First silk thread wound from the cocoon by water-power is produced at Mansfield.

1820 First American plows are manufactured at Wethersfield.

1822 First machine for sawing ivory is invented by John B. Collins of Hartford, and used by the Cheney family at Ivoryton.

1824 First American industrial school is established at Derby by Josiah Holbrook and the Reverend Truman Coe.

1826 First axes commercially manufactured in America are made by the Collins Company of Collinsville.

1828 First American carpet mill is established at Thompsonville.

1829 First double reflecting tin baker is invented by Isaac Dobson of Farmington.

First Fourdrinier paper-making machine in America is produced by Phelps & Stafford of Windham.

1830 First American hoopskirts are made at Derby.

First scroll lathe chuck in America is patented by Simon Fairman of West Stafford.

1831 First discovery of laws of cyclonic storms is made by William Redfield of Cromwell.

First drawn-brass pipe and wire in America are made by Israel Holmes of Waterbury.

First English brass workers are imported by Naugatuck Valley employers and landed in wooden casks from a ship anchored off the coast.

1832 First machine producing pins in one operation is invented by Thomas Ireland Howe of Derby.

1833 First American coffee mill is patented by Amini Clark of Meriden.

First engine lathe in America is built by Aaron Kilbourn of New Haven and Killingworth.

1834 First friction matches in America are made at Coe Town (now Beacon Falls) by Thomas Sanford, who later sold his formula for $10.

First spun-brass kettles in America are made by Israel Coe of Wolcottville (now Torrington).

1835 First 'German silver' spoons in America are made by Robert Wallace of Wallingford.

1836 First American tacks are made in Derby.

First hook and eye fasteners are made by Israel Holmes of Waterbury.

First safety fuse for blasting is made by Ensign Bickford of Granby.

1837 First American paper made of straw is produced by Smith and Bassett of Seymour.

1839 First successful process for vulcanizing rubber is discovered by Charles Goodyear of Naugatuck.

1840 First American shaving soap is made by J. B. Williams of Glastonbury.

First silver-plated spoons in America are made by W. B. Cowles of 'Spoonville,' East Granby.

First machine for threading bolts is invented by Barnes and Rugg of Marion (town of Southington).

1844 First use of nitrous oxide gas as an anesthetic is made by Dr. Horace Wells of Hartford.

1845 First pocket cutlery is produced in this country by Holley Manufacturing Company of Salisbury.

First sewing machine is invented by Elias Howe of New Hartford.

1846 First American table cutlery is manufactured by the Meriden Cutlery Company.

1847 First collegiate agricultural experiment station in America is established by Yale University.

1848 First cylinder lock is invented by Linus Yale of Stamford.

1849 First spool-wound silk thread is produced by Gen. Merritt Heminway of Watertown (silk was previously sold in skeins).

1850 First American 'derby' hat is made at South Norwalk by James Knapp.

1852 First American machine for making wood type is perfected by Edwin Allen of South Windham.

1853 First American trade association, the American Brass Association, is formed by Naugatuck Valley manufacturers.

1854 First spool-wound linen thread in America is made by Willimantic Linen Company.

1856 First commercially successful condensed milk is produced by Gail Borden in Torrington.

1858 First air-tight fruit jar with spring-fastened glass top is patented by W. W. Lyman of Meriden.

First successful stone crusher is invented by Eli Whitney Blake, revolutionizing road-building.

First burners for kerosene oil are manufactured at Meriden.

1860 First American sailing ship to beat the 'Flying Cloud's' record on the New York–San Francisco run is built at Mystic. This ship was the 'Andrew Jackson,' a modified clipper, which made the run in 89 days and 4 hours.

1861 First American degree of Doctor of Philosophy is conferred by Yale University.

First camp for boys in America, the Gunn Camp, is organized at Washington.

1862 First corrugated spring for railway cars is invented by Carlos French of Seymour.

First wheeled horse-rake with lever is patented by Daley and Treat of Morris.

1863 First American accident insurance is issued to James Bolter of Hartford.
      First Civil War monument is erected in Berlin (Kensington Village).

1864 First Fine Arts Department in an American university is opened at Yale.

1866 First American boiler insurance is written in Hartford.
      First commercial center-fire cartridge is developed by Union Metallic
      Cartridge Company at Bridgeport.
      First 'horseless carriage,' steam propelled, is made by Alonzo House of
      Bridgeport.
      First machine-made horseshoe nail is produced at Seymour, under patent
      of Thaddeus Fowler.
      First wire-cutting machine and automatic straightener for pins (revolu-
      tionizing the pin-making industry) are invented by John Adt of Torring-
      ton.

1867 First American-made button hooks are manufactured by Mark Louns-
      bury and Peter Gabriel in Seymour.

1870 First all-metal woodcutting plane is produced at the Stanley Works in
      New Britain.

1876 First automatic turret lathe for cutting screws is made by Christopher
      M. Spencer of Hartford.
      First permanent polish for copper is patented by Thomas James of New
      Haven.

1877 First bicycle factory in America is established at Hartford.

1878 First commercial telephone switchboard is installed at New Haven.

1880 First American hail insurance is written March 24 by Tobacco Growers
      Mutual Insurance Company of North Canaan.
      First American-made mohair plush is produced at Seymour by John H.
      Tingue.

1884 First American braided silk fish-lines are made by Elisha J. Martin of
      Rockville.

1885 First standard measuring machine, accurate to one-hundred-thousandth
      of an inch, is perfected by Pratt & Whitney Company of Hartford.

1886 First American telescopic steel fishing rod is invented by Everett Horton,
      a Bristol mechanic, whose purpose was to develop a rod that could be
      hidden under his coat when he went fishing on the Sabbath.

1888 First electric trolley car in New England makes its first run in Derby.

1891 First American trading stamps are introduced by Sperry and Hutchinson
      of Bridgeport.

1894 First even-keel submarine is developed by Simon Lake of Milford.
      First machine for dipping wooden matches is invented by Ebenezer
      Beecher of New Haven.

1895 First mechanical player-piano is produced by H. K. Wilcox in Meriden.

1898 First American automobile insurance is written in Hartford.

1899 First 'tackling dummy' for football practice is devised by Amos Alonzo
      Stagg at Yale University.

1901 First American automobile legislation ('speed limit, 12 miles per hour,
      8 miles per hour in city') is enacted at Hartford.
      First non-sinkable lifeboat is invented and built by the Holmes Ship-
      building Company on Mystic River.

1909 First successful gun 'silencer' is invented by Hiram Percy Maxim of Hartford.

1910 First steel golf-club shafts in America are made at Bristol.

1912 First use of Diesel engine for submarines is made by New London Ship and Engine Company of Groton.

1920 First acidophilus milk is produced at Fairlea Farms in Orange.

1923 First mercury turbine is operated by the Hartford Electric Light Company.

1936 First accurate aerial map of any State is made of Connecticut — 13 × 18 feet in size, portraying an area of 5004 square miles.

II. MAIN STREET AND VILLAGE GREEN

All Historic Houses mentioned as Points of Interest in the City Tours which follow are private unless otherwise specified.

BRIDGEPORT

City: Alt. 20, pop. 146,716, sett. 1639, incorp. 1836.

Railroad Stations: N.Y., N.H. & H. R.R., cor. Fairfield Ave. (US 1) and Water St.

Airports: Bridgeport Airport, Main St., Stratford, 5 miles east from center of Bridgeport on US 1; 30 min. by motor car. Fare by taxi, $1.50.

Taxis: 30¢ first mile; 10¢ each additional third.

Piers: Ferries to Port Jefferson, L.I., 75¢ one way, and steamer to New York, $1.00 weekdays and $1.50 Sundays and holidays (May 30 to Labor Day), Stratford Ave. Wharf, Water St.

Accommodations: Two hotels in central area.

Information Service: Chamber of Commerce, 2d floor; Connecticut Motor Club, Stratfield Hotel, Main St.; Travellers' Aid, R.R. Station.

Swimming: Municipal Pool, Pleasure Beach Park, fee 10¢ weekdays, 20¢ Sundays and holidays. Public beach at Seaside Park.

Amusement Parks: Pleasure Beach, foot of Seaview Ave.; bathing beach, pool and dance hall; concessions.

BRIDGEPORT spreads over flat country at the mouth of the Pequonnock River on Long Island Sound. The great concentration of industry within a comparatively few years has given the city an appearance of having grown 'without a plan or in spite of one.'

The railroad, elevated on an embankment faced with Roxbury granite, crosses the city, skirting the section where huge manufacturing plants, covering acre after acre, produce munitions and tools, automatic machinery and equipment essential to factories and homes throughout the country. West from the old-fashioned railroad station is the cramped and congested shopping center; but in the outskirts, landscaped residential sections, more than one thousand acres of public parks, and a shore drive of about three miles offer compensations in unusually beautiful vistas of woodland and sea. Many of the streets are lined with stately elms; obsolete trolley tracks in the center of the principal arteries of traffic have been replaced by strips of green lawn that furnish a touch of color and serve as safety zones.

Many races are represented in Bridgeport, a number of whom retain their native customs and religions. Only twenty-five per cent of the population is of full native parentage. Among the heterogeneous foreign group are Italians, Czechs, Hungarians, and Poles, numerically important in the order named.

Although six hundred Pequonnock Indians once lived on a reservation on Golden Hill, in the heart of the city, little of the past is evident in Bridgeport. The Indians bartered most of their land for '30 bushels of Indian corn and 3 pounds worth of blankets,' and in 1842 their remaining eight acres were sold to pay accrued taxes and purchase quarters for them in Trumbull, where their descendants, 'Rising Star' and 'George Sherman,' live on one acre of land.

The community was first settled in 1639 by residents of the older settlements of Fairfield and Stratford, and was known as Newfield, later as Stratfield, until 1800, when the area was extended by the General Assembly and the borough of Bridgeport was incorporated and named for the first drawbridge erected over the Pequonnock River. In 1821, it was incorporated as a town and by 1836 had become a city. Every census from 1800 to 1930 has shown an increase of at least forty per cent. Like so many New England seaport towns, Bridgeport had a lusty whaling trade, but interest in seafaring declined when the opening of the railroad in 1840 brought with it an industrial boom.

Among the earlier manufacturing ventures were the production of hats, pewter ware, carriages, saddlery, furniture, and shirts. In 1856, the Wheeler and Wilson Manufacturing Company, makers of sewing machines, moved here from Watertown, and became the first of the many nationally important industries established in the city. Carriage-making, the most colorful of the nineteenth-century industries, was climaxed in 1894-95 by the building of the first 'horseless carriage,' equipped with hard rubber tires and a self-starter. Unfortunately, the exhaust made the wagon an insufferable hot box, so it was regretfully stored in a shed behind the Armstrong plant where it was made.

In 1902, close on the heels of the last carriage-making industries, the Locomobile Company produced one of the early American automobiles propelled by gasoline, which combined an all-steel frame, sliding-gear transmission, and a vertical cylinder motor at the front beneath a hood, all of which are features of modern automobile design. The company produced a limited quantity of high-quality cars until 1929.

First gramophones in America were produced here by the American Gramophone Co., later the Columbia Phonograph Co., Inc.

Today almost five hundred manufacturing firms, many with a large export trade, produce ammunition and firearms, automatic machinery, nuts, bolts and screws, brass products, brake linings, corsets, chains, electrical and pharmaceutical supplies, hardware, marine cables and engines, machinery, phonograph records, plumbing supplies, rubber goods, sewing machines, scissors, typewriters, steel products, and toys.

Bridgeport does not depend upon any one class of manufactured goods for its prosperity. Probably no city in the United States includes more diversified industries. Although, like other manufacturing cities, it was seriously affected by post-war deflation, statistics show that the value of the city's annual production for the year 1936 exceeded its pre-war rate by 102 per cent. In 1933, the city elected a Socialist mayor and board of aldermen, and has twice since re-elected the Socialist ticket.

TOUR 1

W. from Mill Pond Park on North Ave. (US 1A).

1. The *Pixlee Tavern (private)*, 590 North Ave., SW. of the Park, is a remodeled salt-box house, dating from 1700, now covered with yellow stucco. General Washington is believed to have stopped en route to Cambridge in 1775, thus giving a local habitation to a well-known apocryphal story. It concerns a ruse that he employed to secure his supper at the tavern when he arrived late one night unaccompanied and found every place at the table occupied. The guests failed to recognize the leader of the Continental troops and continued to munch savory fried oysters, increasing the appetite of the hungry general. From his post beside the fireplace, he casually remarked, 'Do any of you gentlemen realize that horses are very fond of oysters?' In the excitement of the lively discussion which followed, one guest offered to wager that 'no horse ever lived that would eat oysters.' Immediately Washington suggested, 'Very well. Why not try them on my horse?' As soon as the excited guests started for the barn, Washington quietly found a place at the table. At the edge of the Park across the street, the *Washington Elm*, named in honor of his visit, is said to be from 250 to 300 years old.

2. *Tom Thumb House (private)*, 956 North Ave. at Main St., is the house most commonly associated with P. T. Barnum's midget attraction, General Tom Thumb (Charles S. Stratton). It is a large square frame dwelling built by the General's father, Sherwood S. Stratton in 1855, but since converted into apartments and shops. To this home, fitted

---

BRIDGEPORT. POINTS OF INTEREST

1. Pixlee Tavern
2. Tom Thumb House
3. Captain Abijah Sterling House
4. Brothwell Beach House
5. Clinton Park
6. Mountain Grove Cemetery
7. Nathaniel Wheeler Fountain
8. United Congregational Church
9. Public Library
10. City Hall
11. Barnum Institute of Science and History
12. Seaside Park
13. Court Marina
14. Fayerweather's Island
15. Site of a Revolutionary Fort
16. Beardsley Park
17. American Fabrics Company
18. Stanley Works
19. John Brooks House
20. General Electric Plant
21. Remington Arms Company
22. Saltex Looms, Inc.
23. Bridgeport Brass Company
24. Singer Manufacturing Company
25. Underwood Elliott Fisher Company
26. Warner Brothers Company
27. Bryant Electric Company
28. Raybestos Division
29. Harvey Hubbell, Inc.
30. Bullard Company

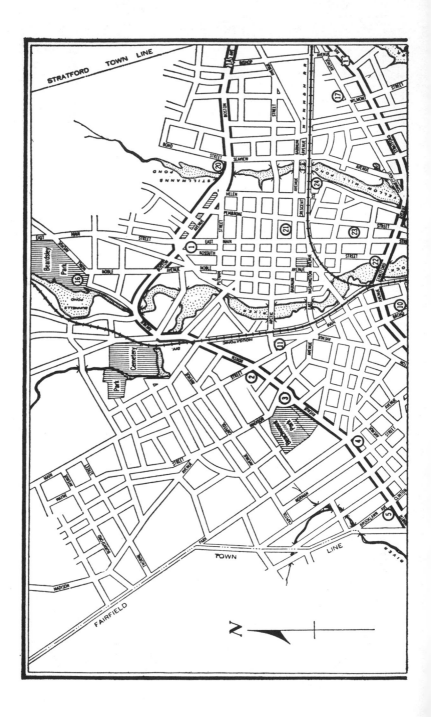

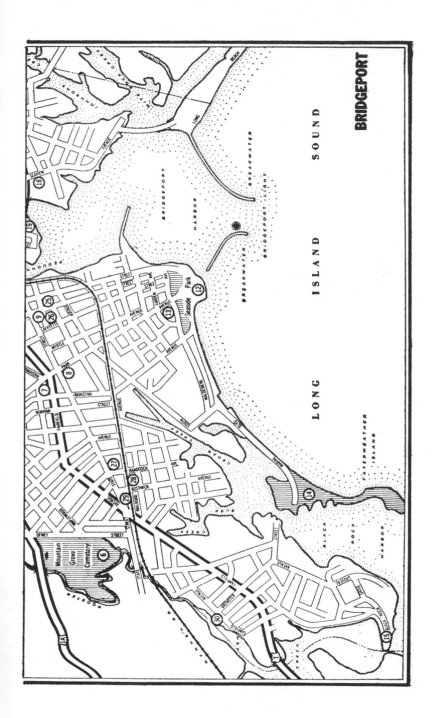

BRIDGEPORT

for his use with miniature furnishings, Tom Thumb brought his tiny bride, Lavinia Bump Warren, after their spectacular wedding in New York, in 1863.

3. The *Captain Abijah Sterling House* (*private*), 1040 North Ave., a salt-box erected about 1760, was the boyhood home of General Tom Thumb.

4. The *Brothwell Beach House* (*private*), SW. cor. North and Park Aves., an early 19th-century building, with a glass fan-light over the front door, leaded in the rare eagle design, was built around, or to replace a tavern erected by Samuel Cable in 1759.

5. *Clinton Park*, cor. North and Brooklawn Aves., was used as a military training ground during the Revolutionary War, and later, during the Civil War. Here a wrestling match took place between Captain John Sherwood and an Indian from Golden Hill who had challenged the white men to a contest. Captain Sherwood, dressed in ordinary citizen's attire, put his hands upon the naked, well-oiled shoulders of the savage, and laid him flat on his back, 'not caring to soften the violence of his fall.'

L. from North Ave. on Dewey St.

6. In *Mountain Grove Cemetery*, Dewey St., 140 acres of landscaped grounds planted with large, stately oaks, are the *Graves of Phineas T. Barnum* (1810–91) and *Tom Thumb*. The former's burial-place, marked by an imposing monument, is directly across from that of Tom Thumb, whose memorial, a 40-foot shaft in Italian marble surmounted by a life-size statue of the famous midget, is simply inscribed 'Charles S. Stratton, Died July 15, 1883, aged 45 years, 6 mos., 11 d.' Buried by his side, in an infant's casket, is the body of his wife, who survived him by more than 30 years, and whose small headstone is marked with the single word 'Wife.'

Near-by, a small, plain stone indicates the *Grave of Fanny J. Crosby* (1820–1915), hymn-writer and poet, who lost her sight when she was six weeks old.

TOUR 2

S. from North Ave. (*US 1A*) *on Park Ave.*

7. The *Nathaniel Wheeler Fountain*, at the intersection of Park and Fairfield Aves., opposite St. John's Episcopal Church, is a memorial designed by Gutzon Borglum to one of Bridgeport's foremost 19th-century industrialists and philanthropists. As organizer of the Wheeler and Wilson Manufacturing Company (*see below*), Wheeler was a pioneer in the development and promotion of the sewing machine.

L. from Park Ave. on State St.

8. The *United Congregational Church* (1926), State St., SW. cor. Park Ave. (R), designed by Allen and Collens, is a striking modern brick version of the early 19th-century church architecture. It is exceptionally broad and has an uncommonly tall and graceful spire. Inside, eclectic influences prevail: the architectural melting pot is seen in the tall Romanesque columns, the Gothic hammer-vault roofing, and the luxurious mahogany pews.

9. In the *Public Library* (*open weekdays* 9–9.30) (1925), SW. cor. State and Broad Sts., a four-story brick and limestone building designed by Frederick J. Dixon, is the *Bishop Room* (*open weekdays*, 9–6), an historical museum. Included among its permanent exhibits of old books, manuscripts, deeds, maps, newspapers, and Connecticut almanacs, are the Americana collections of the Fairfield County and Bridgeport Historical Societies.

10. The *City Hall*, NE. cor. State and Broad Sts., originally a two-story, sandstone building with heavy, fluted Ionic columns in the style of the Greek Revival, erected in 1854–55 and enlarged and remodeled by Joseph W. Northrop in 1905, is historically notable as the scene of an address by President Lincoln on March 10, 1860, an event commemorated by a bronze tablet on the State St. front. Bridgeport newspapers of Civil War days were strenuously antagonistic to the President. The *Bridgeport Farmer* wrote —

> 'Give us a few more months [to end the Civil War], a few hundred thousand more men, a few hundred millions more of money and we will finish up the war,' say Lincoln and his shoddy crew.
>
> Do not be deceived by these fake and plausible stories — the party in power cannot, neither does it intend to bring the war to a conclusion.

R. from State St. on Main St.

11. The *Barnum Institute of Science and History* (*open Mon., Wed., Fri., Sat.*, 2–5, *free*), 805 Main St., occupies the third floor of the mosque-like building of yellow brick erected about 1890 by Barnum. Among the articles exhibited here, those of special interest are an Egyptian mummy, some of the personal effects of Tom Thumb, and collections of old household utensils, army guns and swords, and mounted birds.

Barnum, Bridgeport's most beloved citizen, may be known to the world as the founder of 'The Greatest Show on Earth,' but to this city which became his home, he was an empire-builder and a philanthropist. While the world remembers him as the great showman who packed circus tents with promises of such marvels as 'a cherry-colored cat,' and lived up to the promise, though not to the expectation, by producing an ordinary black pussy, Bridgeport remembers him as a staunch and patriotic citizen. Through his effort many industries established their plants here; when the city needed a harbor, Barnum went to Washington and secured the necessary appropriation for dredging; when the railroad failed to give proper service, Barnum forced improvements; he established parks and an improved water supply, and served the city as both mayor and representative to the Assembly. When Barnum's likeness appeared on the city's centennial half-dollar in 1936, the press of the nation laughed at the idea that the man who has been credited with the phrase, 'Everybody likes to be humbugged,' should be so honored on a United States coin, but Bridgeport has not forgotten that, but for Barnum's efforts, the city might have been little more than a wide place in the road.

Born in Bethel, July 5, 1810, Barnum tried storekeeping with little success. After failure as a lottery agent, Barnum started the *Herald of Freedom*, a weekly newspaper, but was fined and jailed for his outspoken criticism of the contemporary scene.

Barnum drifted to New York with a cattle drover and then on to Philadelphia where he purchased an old Negress, Joyce Heth, who was reputed to be 160 years of age and the former nurse of George Washington. With the Negress as the principal sideshow, Barnum formed a company, writing his own advertising and touring America. When Joyce died in 1836, her age was proved to be only 70, but Barnum's company continued its tour until 1839. The youthful showman again failed, but in 1841 he purchased Scudder's American Museum in New York. His discovery of Charles Stratton, the two-foot son of Bridgeport parents, led to the grand European tour of the dwarf, 'General Tom Thumb,' who was exhibited before Queen Victoria and European royalty. In 1850, Barnum sponsored the American tour of Jenny Lind, giving the 'Swedish Nightingale' a contract that called for a salary of $1000 per night for 150 nights, plus all expenses.

Through an amalgamation of circus, menagerie, and museum of various freaks Barnum formed 'The Greatest Show on Earth' (1871). Military men of many nations copied much of Barnum's technique in handling baggage, materials, men, and animals.

Although Barnum never had a formal education, he wrote several books including 'The Humbugs of the World' (1865), 'Struggles and Triumphs' (1869), and his 'Autobiography' (1854 and later editions). Tales are told of his insistence that 'Barnum' and not 'Webster' should be the authority for the spelling of the names on animal cages. No train passed the winter quarters of his circus in Bridgeport without passengers agape at Barnum's 'Elephantine Agriculture' — a man in Oriental costume mounted on an elephant, plowing a field beside the track.

P. T. Barnum died on April 7, 1891.

12. *Seaside Park*, end of Main St., on the Sound, is a beautiful 210-acre tract, the first land for which was donated to the city in 1865 by P. T. Barnum. Entered through the imposing Perry Memorial Arch and traversed by Marine Boulevard, a scenic roadway extending two and one-half miles along the sea wall, the park provides excellent facilities for bathing, tennis, baseball, and soccer, with a quarter-mile cinder track and a half-mile trotting track. Just beyond the Memorial Arch is a Statue of Elias Howe, Jr., inventor of the sewing machine, who, although born in the town of Spencer, Massachusetts, became during

his residence here, closely associated with the city's industrial and social development.

During the Civil War, Howe recruited a regiment of volunteer infantry (17th Connecticut) and furnished officers' mounts for the outfit. The statue stands on the spot where Howe, with an income of $200,000 annual royalties, slept on a bed of straw as a private soldier.

Although a sewing machine had previously been invented in England, one in France, and one by Hunt of New York, none had been successfully promoted, and Howe, unaware of the earlier inventions, independently developed a lock-stitch machine in 1844. The following year, he obtained his first patent, won a demonstration against five expert seamstresses and exhibited the machine at numerous fairs. British interests advanced capital and Howe went to England to supervise the manufacture of machines, but upon returning to America found that many factories had infringed upon his patents. After considerable litigation, his rights were established in 1854 and other manufacturers compelled to pay royalties to him.

A bronze *Statue of Barnum*, modeled by Thomas Ball and cast by Von Müller in Munich, was unveiled July 4, 1893, here by the seawall, overlooking the Sound.

13. Opposite Seaside Park, in the block between Waldemere Park, Linden, and Park Avenues, is the massive brownstone structure called *Court Marina*, which Barnum erected in 1868–69 as his last residence. This whole region is full of the plethoric houses of the prosperous 80's and 90's, in every conceivable mixture of architectural styles, but set in grounds planted with tall trees and huge rhododendrons.

R. from the end of Main St. on Marine Boulevard.

14. On *Fayerweather's Island*, off the coast at the end of Marine Boulevard, connected with the mainland by a causeway, is the *Old Lighthouse* (*not open*), erected in 1809 and rebuilt in 1823.

Return via Marine Boulevard to the Perry Memorial Arch; L. on Park Ave.; L. from Park Ave. on Fairfield Ave.; L. from Fairfield Ave. on Brewster St.; R. from Brewster St. on Grovers Ave. which becomes Black Rock Drive (no parking allowed).

15. On Black Rock Drive was an early base for whaleboat warfare, and the *Site of a Revolutionary Fort*, erected here in 1776 on a small knoll known as Grovers Hill. The one gun at this fort, which announced to Fairfield the coming of the British in 1779, harassed the enemy continually during the destruction and raid of the town.

In that same year Major-General Silliman, chief of military and safety activities of Fairfield County, and his son were taken prisoner by the enemy. As the Continental forces had no captive of equal rank to exchange for their General, Captains Lockwood and Hawley and a group of 25 volunteers set out in a whaleboat from this harbor one December night. Landing on Long Island, they succeeded in capturing a notorious Tory, Judge Jones, for whose safe return the British relinquished their prisoner, General Silliman.

TOUR 3

E. from Main St. on Congress St. (crossing Pequonnock River); L. from Congress on Noble Ave.

16. *Beardsley Park*, Noble Ave., extending along the western bank of the Pequonnock River, includes 234 acres of rolling, wooded land, through which wind sylvan drives and paths edged with fragrant laurel, kalmia, azalea and holly. Within the park are a lake, a zoo, an 18-hole golf course, a greenhouse, tennis courts, and a reproduction of the *Anne Hathaway Cottage* (*open every day*, 9–5, *free*), set in a formal English garden.

17. *American Fabrics Company* (*open on application at office*), 1069 Connecticut Ave., is 20 times the size of the original plant established in 1910 by Albert Henkels, owner of a lace factory in Langerford, Germany. It was sold to the present owners by the Alien Property Custodian during the World War. Rufflings, woven labels, and many types of laces, such as Cluny, Valenciennes, filet and Spanish, are made here.

18. *Stanley Works* (*open on application at office*), Seaview Ave., producers of electric tools, are the makers of the 'Magic Eye,' a photo-electric cell device combined with a pneumatic mechanism that opens and closes doors without manual aid. Among the best-known installations of the 'Magic Eye' are the doors in the Pennsylvania Station, New York City, and the 500 'roll-up' doors at the Fort Benning barracks, Georgia.

19. The *John Brooks House* (*private*) (1788), at 199 Pembroke St., a frame 'half-house' with a Dutch 'stoop' and little gambrel-roofed ell, is one of the few Bridgeport old houses in almost original condition. It retains its interior paneled walls and corner cupboards.

20. The *General Electric Plant* (*open on application at office*), Boston Ave. at Bond St., has been continually enlarged since the company rented the plant from Remington Arms in 1915 and purchased the property in 1922. It employs 8000 men and women in the production of domestic and industrial electric equipment and supplies. Distribution headquarters for the products of General Electric plants in other cities are maintained here.

West of the electric plant are blocks of neat small brick houses built as a housing development during the days of Bridgeport's rapid growth during the World War. They helped to inaugurate a new movement to provide tasteful, comfortable homes of varied design for the workers who were flocking into the city.

21. The *Remington Arms Company* (*not open*), Barnum Ave., with a

plant covering 60 acres and fields for storage of explosives covering 360 acres, owes much of its prestige to the invention of the central-fire cartridge. The first metallic cartridges were exploded by the pressure of the hammer on a hollow rim in which a small quantity of high explosive, known as a priming mixture, was poured. This method of firing was unsatisfactory as the cartridge case was bent by the crimping and nicking of the hammer. Another method that would permit a second or third use of the original cartridge case was sought. On August 6, 1866, the Union Metallic Cartridge Company of Bridgeport produced a successful central-fire metallic cartridge.

This concern also pioneered in the introduction of the first paper shotgun shells in the United States.

During the World War, about two billion standard 30–'06 rifle cartridges and 1,218,979,300 rounds of other ammunition were produced here.

Established here in 1867 under the name Union Metallic Cartridge Company by the sporting-goods firm of Schuyler, Hartley and Graham of New York, this firm merged with the Remington Arms Company of Ilion, New York, in 1912, and has since been known as the Remington Arms Company, Inc. In 1920, the local plant commenced the production of pocket cutlery and soon became one of the world's largest manufacturers of those products.

In June, 1933, a controlling interest in the plant was purchased by E. I. du Pont de Nemours and Company. Since that time, Remington has purchased the patents and designs of the Parker Gun Company of Meriden. Although frequently associated with military munitions, 98 per cent of the factory's output since the World War has been shotguns and cartridges for the sporting-goods market.

22. *Saltex Looms, Inc.* (*open on application at office*), 217 Kossuth St., now owned by American interests, manufactures seal-plush, velvets and upholstery plushes. This firm was established as the Salts Textile Manufacturing Company, a branch of Sir Titus Salt, Bart. Sons and Company Ltd., of Bradford, England.

23. The *Bridgeport Brass Company* (*open on application at office*), 774 E. Main St., fabricators of brass, was organized in 1865 to make brass clock movements, and later made hoopskirt frames, kerosene parlor lamps and the first successful kerosene bicycle lamp, exhibited at the World's Fair in Chicago, in 1893. An offshoot from clock movements was a spring motor-operated flyfan, forerunner of the modern electric fan; F. R. Wilmot, superintendent, designed a crude micrometer, and the company also made incandescent lamp sockets. Bridgeport Brass Company produced the first copper wire strung between New York and Boston, made many telephonic improvements, features a 'hard-drawn wire,' various alloys of high tensile strength, and was a pioneer in the adaptation of the electric furnace to the brass industry. Duronze, engravers plates, metal bellows for temperature control, galley plates,

tubing, phono-electric trolley wire and sheet brass are among the firm's products.

24. The *Singer Manufacturing Company* (*open on application at office*), 803 E. Washington Ave., now factory No. 10 of the international concern of that name, which produces sewing machines for factory use, was originally the Wheeler and Wilson Manufacturing Company. Organized in 1853 in Watertown, Connecticut, and moved to Bridgeport in 1856, the early company manufactured a machine invented by Allen B. Wilson of Pittsfield, Massachusetts, in 1847. Features of the machine were a curved, eye-pointed needle, a two-pointed shuttle, which made a stitch at each forward and backward motion, and a two-motion 'feed.' The sewing machine which had been previously invented by Howe was hampered by a 'feed' single-motion which did not allow the operator to change the direction of the seam. Wilson's patent of 1850 made it possible for the operator to sew seams of any length at any desired angle. A 'four-motion feed' was patented by Wilson in 1854. Later, to avoid litigation, a stationary bobbin was introduced. The concern was taken over by the Singer Company in 1905. The local plant has not produced machines for household use for the last 25 years.

25. *Underwood Elliott Fisher Company* (*open on application at office*), 575 Broad St., the outgrowth of numerous mergers, produces counting, billing, and adding machines. More than 15,000 machine parts of different design, requiring 150,000 separate operations, are produced here. Among the many accounting machines is one used by automobile finance companies, which figures the number of payments to be made, the number paid, and the balance due.

26. *Warner Brothers Company* (*open on application at office*), 325 Lafayette St., with branches in London, Paris, Hamburg, Brussels, Barcelona, Cape Town, Toronto and Mexico City, has been manufacturing corsets in Bridgeport since 1876. Among the articles of corsetry first made here are: the brassière, the 'corselette,' and the 'two-way stretch' Lastex woven-fabric garments.

27. The *Bryant Electric Company* (*open on application at office*), 1421 State St., the largest single plant in the world devoted exclusively to the production of wiring devices, began in a rented loft-workshop in 1889. More than 3000 wiring devices, including plural plugs and switches of all types, are manufactured here.

28. The *Raybestos Division* of the Raybestos-Manhattan Company, at 1427 Railroad Ave. (*open on application at office*), manufacturers of brake linings and clutch facings, was the firm which contributed a significant development in automobile brake design when it manufactured Raybestos brake lining for the early 'Duplex' brake.

29. *Harvey Hubbell, Inc.* (*open on application at office*), covering two city blocks at Railroad Ave., State St., and Fairfield Ave., producers of wiring devices and machine screws, has to its credit the invention of the pull-socket electric light fixture, the separable attachment plug, the

T-slotted plug, and a toggle switch. Many of the present-day standards in electrical equipment are the result of wiring devices originated in this plant.

30. *Bullard Company* (*open on application at office*), 286 Canfield Ave., produces automatic machinery for an international market. E. P. Bullard, trained at both the Colt Armory and the Pratt and Whitney school of nationally known mechanics, made mechanical history as the advocate of the vertical boring-mill principle of metal working rather than of the horizontal, or lathe method. Starting as an inventor and refiner of the simpler forms, manufacturing a drill press in 1864, Bullard soon branched out into the multiple-spindle lines, and today his Mult-Au-Matics meet all high-speed production needs and are key production units in the factories of the world. Seven of the third generation of the Bullard family continue as executives of the firm.

D A N B U R Y

City: Alt. 375, pop. 22,261, settled 1684, incorporated 1889.

Railroad Station: Danbury Station, White St. for N.Y., N.H. & H. R.R.

Airport: Privately owned; West Wooster St. (US 7). Sightseeing trips on Saturdays and Sundays. Five minutes by taxi from center of city; taxi fare 50¢.

Accommodations: One hotel.

Information Service: Danbury Business Association, 288 Main St.

Annual Events: Danbury Fair, held for one week beginning the first Saturday or Monday in October.

DANBURY, known as 'the Hat City,' is a lively main-street town that has outgrown the main street. Summer residents from Candlewood Lake and workers from the hat factories rub elbows with lanky farm lads and farm women in gingham who bring in eggs and butter to swap for merchandise. Grouped about the county court-house, on irregular building lines, are many small shops, a few brownstone structures, motion-picture houses, and more green-grocer establishments than seem warranted in a town of this size. The city sprawls about the country-side like an overgrown village, seeking room for backyard gardens cultivated by hatters in their spare time. Hat factories radiate from the sites of the water-driven mills of the older generation of hatters, and the residential sections are on sightly elevations which escape the swamp mists.

Founded in 1684 and named for the English town, in 1687, by the 'original

Eight Families' who trekked from Norwalk through Sugar Hollow and over Pandanaram to settle 'Pahquioque,' Danbury was early nicknamed 'Beantown,' because beans grown here were of excellent quality. Local wagons were quickly recognized, as they passed through other villages, by the bag of beans on top of their loads. According to one tradition, the land was purchased from the Indians for one bag of beans. Place names in the town such as Pinchgut, Mashing Tub Swamp, Squabble Hill, Cat-tail Mountain, Monkeytown, and Dodgingtown, intrigue the imagination, but the stories of their origin seem to have died with the early settlers.

By 1784 the community was a half-shire town with Bridgeport; it became a borough in 1822, and was chartered as a city in 1889. At the outbreak of the Revolution the town was an important depot for military supplies and consequently the objective of Tryon's Raid in 1777. The British, who had landed at Westport, burned and looted the town, destroying the church, nineteen houses, twenty-two stores and barns, with all of the military goods. Tory houses, carefully marked, were spared. The townsfolk hid in the surrounding hills and swamps, while the braver spirits shouldered squirrel rifles and shotguns and harassed the raiders. Horse, foot, and guns, the British retreated in good order, fighting an occasional rear-guard action and leaving but few dead and wounded along the way. Reparation for damage to private property was granted Danbury citizens by the distribution of 'Fire Lands' in the Western Reserve.

Zadoc Benedict established the first beaver-hat factory in America here, in 1780, and produced three hats per day. The industry developed rapidly until the city led the entire country in hat production, a position it still maintains today. Fifty-one of the seventy mills in town are engaged in some branch of the hat industry, and many of the others in sidelines connected with it, such as the production of paper boxes.

Hats are made from felts which come from the fur of the Australian rabbit. The hair is sheared from the skins and felted, then the felt is steamed and shaped. Much of Danbury's production is in these rough shapes. Many hats are 'taylor made,' on the Taylor hat machine which turns out a product comparable to the best handmade hat.

The hatters' trade is an unhealthy one, as the workers inhale steam and various chemical fumes from the vats and there is some danger of mercurial poisoning. The craft is highly organized, but increasing mechanization of the industry has resulted in unemployment.

The Danbury Hatters' case made court history. In 1902, the Loewe Hat Shop declared for an open shop, the third such declaration in Danbury history. A strike followed, one of many that have occurred since 1882. The union enforced an effective boycott, and the hatters were cited to appear in court to answer charges that they were violators of the Sherman Act. A judgment of $80,000 was handed down against the union. The case was ultimately carried to the United States Supreme

Court. In the final decision, reached in 1915, the workers lost the verdict and 186 union hatters were forced to auction off their homes to satisfy a court judgment of $300,000 against them. The Loewe firm no longer operates in Danbury.

Danbury has always been a 'sporting town.' Lotteries have been popular since 1791, when funds for a jail to replace the burned structure were raised by lottery. The almshouse was built in 1804 by another lottery, and the transfer of a hotel by lottery was recorded in 1872, an unusual real estate transaction but typical of the sporting spirit of Danbury.

Harness horses, the great animals that cover the mile for 'best two out of three' or 'best three in five' heats, have been bred in Danbury since 1792. Two-year-olds trotted in the little oval of 'Danbury Pleasure Park,' and names like Quartermaster, Blue Bells, Quarterstretch, Sablenut, Villiers, and Onward will long be remembered in the city.

As a partial balance against the influence of trotting horses and lotteries, the Sandemanian Church, an offshoot of the old Presbyterian Church of Scotland, was active in the community. These worshipers opposed lotteries, observed 'love feasts' and declared for a modified community of goods. There is no trace of this sect in the city today.

TOUR 1

N. from West St. on Main St.

1. In the *Danbury Library* (L), 254 Main St., at Library Place, a brick and stone building (1877–79) designed by Lamb and Wheeler, are the files of the *Danbury News* (founded 1865), whose editor, James Montgomery Bailey, 'The Danbury News Man,' Civil War veteran and columnist, brought it a national reputation by his wit and humor, increasing the paper's circulation from 1920 to 30,000 within nine months. The murals (1935) in the Children's Room, depicting scenes from famous stories for children, are the work of the artist and donor, Charles A. Federer of Bethel, Connecticut.

R. from Main St. on White St.; L. from White St. on Holly's Lane which becomes Ellsworth Ave.

2. In *Wooster Cemetery*, Ellsworth Ave., is the grave of General David Wooster, commander of the Danbury forces during the British raid, who died from wounds May 2, 1777. The *Soldiers' and Sailors' Monument* here, dedicated to the unknown heroes of the Civil War, was modeled by Solon Borglum, 1894.

Return via White St. to Main St.; R. on Main St.

3. The *Colonel Joseph Platt Cooke House* (*private*), 342 Main St., which was visited by Washington, Lafayette, and Rochambeau, was built in 1770 and partially burned by the British seven years later. The front

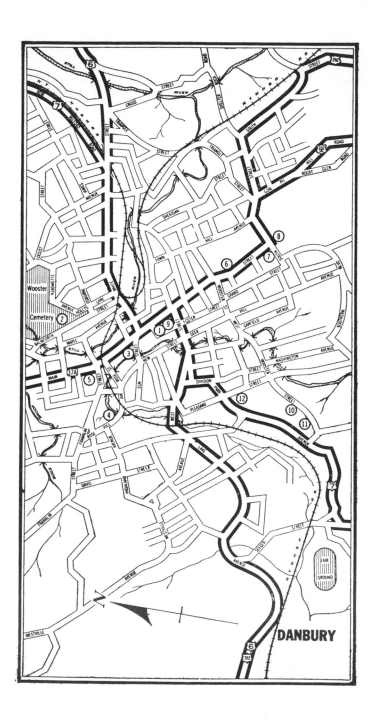
DANBURY

portion, with a wide dentiled cornice and pedimented portico, was added in 1804, and is a handsome though somewhat cramped example of the period which was experimenting in the use of classical motifs.

L. from Main on Rose; R. from Rose on Rose Hill Ave.

4. The *Mallory Hat Company*, covering a city block at Rose Hill Ave. and Franklin St. (*open on application at office*), was established in the Dusty Plain region in 1823 when Ezra Mallory produced two hats per day from local beaver and muskrat fur. The plant's production in 1936 ran to 700 dozens per day, including stiff, soft, straw, and ladies' hat shapes. This concern attracted considerable attention at one time during the era of bare heads by refusing to let a bareheaded salesman interview its purchasing agent.

Return on Franklin to Main; L. on Main.

5. The *Asa Hodge House* (*private*) (about 1695), 384 Main St., a tiny one-and-one-half-story peak-roofed cottage with simple trim, is credited with being the oldest dwelling in Danbury. Unfortunately, the old stone chimney is gone; otherwise the house is in practically original condition.

TOUR 2

S. on Main St. from West St.

6. The *County Courthouse* (*open weekdays* 9–5) (1900), 71 Main St., designed by Warren Briggs, a substantial brick and granite structure with two tall sandstone columns, contains exhibits of costumes, antiques, and war relics. A tablet on a *Boulder* opposite this building marks the spot from which the first shot was fired at the British invaders.

7. At the corner of Main and South Sts. is the *Site of the Early Episcopal Church*, from which Continental military supplies stored there were removed to the streets and burned by the British during their raid on the town in 1777. The church building was untouched because most of its members were ardent loyalists. It was dismantled and moved to the southwest corner of South St. and Mountainville Ave., where it serves as a tenement house.

DANBURY. POINTS OF INTEREST

1. Danbury Library	7. Site of the Early Episcopal Church
2. Wooster Cemetery	8. Milestone
3. Colonel Joseph Platt Cooke House	9. Isaac Ives House
4. Mallory Hat Company	10. Old Town Cemetery
5. Asa Hodge House	11. Old Brookfield Inn
6. County Courthouse	12. Sycamore Tree
	13. Hoyt House

8. *The Taylor's Tavern Milestone* (1789), at the foot of Main St., indicates the distance to Hartford (67 *m.*), and to New York (68 *m.*).

R. from Main on West Main; R. from West Main on Terrace Place; R. from Terrace Place on Chapel Place.

9. The *Isaac Ives House* (*private*) (1780), at 8 Chapel Place, a one-and-a-half-story gambrel-roofed house with a two-and-a-half-story ell, which was moved from Main St. in 1924, has a pedimented portico and an unusual beehive fan-light over the door. Heavy strap hinges run the full width of the door, and the huge lock is original. In this house, a meeting was held, April 8, 1833, to establish a library for mechanics.

TOUR 3

W. from Main St. on West St.; L. on Division; R. on West Wooster St.

10. In *Old Town Cemetery*, West Wooster St., between Winthrop Place and Delta Avenue, the first burial ground of the settlers, is the grave of Robert Sandeman, founder of the Sandemanian Sect (1764).

11. The *Old Brookfield Inn* (*private*), 105 West Wooster St., an exceptionally long, red salt-box house with white trim, has two front doors and a stone chimney. It was probably built in the latter half of the 17th or in the early 18th century. The building was moved here from the Brookfield Iron Works where it served as a tavern. An additional ell has been built at one end, and wide, modern clapboards used on the front. The windows have twenty-four lights.

12. A *Sycamore Tree*, across the street, is believed to be between 300 and 400 years old.

Return on West Wooster to Division St.; L. on Division; L. on Park Ave.

13. The *Hoyt House* (*private*) (1750–60), 16 Park Ave., a steep-roofed, low-ceilinged dwelling, served as a hospital during the Revolution. Human skeletons have been found in the yard, the remains of those who died of a contagious disease and were hastily buried lest others contract the plague. Built on a hillside, one end of the building is one-and-a-half stories high, and the other is two-and-a-half stories. The dwelling has been remodeled, but retains its original steep roof.

OTHER POINTS OF INTEREST

The *Danbury Fair Grounds*, between Park and Lake Aves., is the scene of the Danbury Fair, held the first week in October, which is believed to attract more visitors than any other six fairs in Connecticut and is surpassed by only one in all New England. Exhibitors from throughout the East bring their best cattle, poultry, and stock to Danbury. The racing card is a good one; a day is devoted to dirt-track auto racing. The circus atmosphere of the midway carries over to the infield directly across from the modern grandstand, where, to the disgust of trotting fans, ladies in pink tights swing from the flying trapeze and dancing bears perform.

Fairs were held in Danbury as early as 1821 and the present fair grounds were purchased in 1871. At the Kenosia Trotting Park, on this site, in 1860, in a historic race in which each heat was faster than the one preceding, Flora Temple won from Widow McChree in 2.39, 2.37, 2.33.

The *Frank H. Lee Hat Company* (*open on application at office*), on Shelter Rock Rd. and Power St., covering two city blocks, is among the largest of Danbury's many hat plants and has its origin in the old Glen Factory in Bethel. Moved to Danbury in 1890, this plant is now a leader in the industry, manufacturing soft and stiff hats and hatters' fur.

Points of Interest in Environs:

Lake Candlewood, 6.3 *m.*, State 37 (boating, swimming, picnicking) (*see Side Tour 4A*); Wooster Mt. State Park, 2.9 *m.*, US 7 (*see Tour 4*).

F A I R F I E L D

Town: Alt. 10, pop. 17,218, sett. 1639.

Railroad Station: Foot of Sanford St. for N.Y., N.H. & H. R.R.

Taxis: 15¢ first ¼ m.; 5¢ each additional ¼ m.

Accommodations: One hotel; several inns.

Information Service: Fairfield Historical Society, Post Road; Fairfield Public Library, Post Road; Southport Library, Old Post Road.

Swimming: Fairfield Beach.

FAIRFIELD, an old Colonial town on the King's Highway, has retained many of its early characteristics around the 'Meeting-House Green' and the 'Village Green' that are by-passed by US 1. The King's Highway swung sharply south to serve the older Fairfield; the newer Post Road cuts straight across the township through the modern trading district, avoiding the curves of the rather narrow old thoroughfare marked by Benjamin Franklin when he placed milestones between New York and Boston in 1753.

At the business center on the modern highway, where through traffic is heavy twenty-four hours a day, are small neat shop buildings, a motion-picture theater, a modern brick bank building of Colonial design, and a library. In sharp contrast is the old town center, one block south. There, beneath the shade of towering elms, eighteenth and nineteenth century mansions, set back from the road on wide lawns, border the winding streets about the old white Town House.

Around the edges of the township, especially on the eastern boundary, industry has made use of lands not suited to residential purposes. No industry intrudes into the peaceful village itself, and very few of the local residents find employment in these plants. The total number of employees gainfully employed in factories in Fairfield is well under 3000. The manufacturing area merges with that of the sister community of Bridgeport, where most of the mill employees make their homes. One and two-thirds miles east of the center of the village are four large plants, with some two thousand employees: McKesson and Robbins, chemical plant; Handy and Harmon, smelting and refining of gold and silver; Max Ams Machine Company, can-making machinery; and the Porcupine Company, structural steel. Three quarters of a mile west of the center are two other important plants: the Dupont Fabrikoid Company, producing waterproof automobile cloth; and the United States Aluminum Company, a casting plant.

Originally known to the Indians as Uncoway (corrupted to Unquowa), the fertile fields of this area first came to the attention of Yankee pioneers July 13, 1637, when a band of Connecticut troops under Roger Ludlow pursued the fleeing Pequots from their burned fort in Mystic (*see Tour* 1) to their doom in the Great Swamp Fight (*see Tour* 1). Two years later Ludlow returned with a party of settlers from Windsor, who were later joined by colonists from Watertown and Concord.

The land was twice purchased from the Pequonnock Indians, on May 11, 1639, and on June 24, 1649; a quitclaim deed was obtained from the Sasco Indians, February 11, 1661. Named possibly in a descriptive sense, or for Fairfield in Kent, the settlement soon received a patent. Anticipating the confiscatory methods of Sir Edmund Andros, who claimed all unoccupied lands for the Crown, the territory was divided into lots which ran from the shore inland for about ten miles. As each settler's house occupied the front of a lot, the landholder maintained that the whole was occupied. All measurements were calculated down to the inch, showing an unusual accuracy for that day. A mile of common was reserved in the center of the township, where the village of Greenfield Hill (*see side-trip from Tour* 1) now stands. There 'train bands' were drilled under officers who had fought in all the Indian Wars. Much of the original town has since been annexed by the neighboring towns of Westport, Weston, Redding, Easton, and Bridgeport.

The town had a good harbor at Black Rock, now a part of Bridgeport, and another at Southport (*see Tour* 1A). Much shipping resulted from the agricultural development of the area. The average farmer tilled at least 150 acres of fertile soil, valued in the early nineteenth century at $100 an acre.

During the Revolution Captain Samuel Smedley, a Fairfield youth who became distinguished on the high seas, commanded a privateer at the age of fifteen, and by the end of the Revolution had more prize ships to his credit than any other privateer or naval officer. On April 20, 1777, when returning to port badly damaged with four prizes in tow, his ship, the 'Defense,' sighted the British corvette 'Cyrus.' Though already manning the pumps to keep his ship afloat, and with half his men sick with smallpox, Smedley engaged and captured the 'Cyrus.' When the British commander surrendered he was amazed at the youth of his victor, exclaiming, 'There is little hope of conquering an enemy whose very schoolboys are capable of valor equaling that of trained veterans of naval warfare.'

On July 7, 1779, the village was burned by British raiders under General Tryon. Driving the militiamen back to the hills, the British looted the village and put it to the torch during a severe thunderstorm. About 200 houses were destroyed and the resulting bitterness aided recruiting of the Continental Line. Whaleboat crews conducted reprisals upon the Tories of Long Island, and many Fairfield sailors sought vengeance upon British shipping.

Fairfield early became a center of vigorous intellectual life. Here lived the ancestors of the brilliant Joel Barlow (*see Literature*), who studied law here and was admitted to the Fairfield bar. Dr. Sereno Dwight, president of Hamilton College, and Professor Benjamin Silliman, who has been called 'the Nestor of American Science,' were also residents. Numerous jurists and men prominent in military affairs made their homes in Fairfield and their guests included eminent scholars and statesmen.

TOUR

E. from Unquowa Rd. on New Post Rd.

1. The *Fairfield Memorial Library* (*open* 9–8:30), SE. cor. Unquowa Rd. and New Post Rd., in a two-story brick building with limestone trim, was organized and incorporated in 1876. Memorial Hall, on the second floor, is notable for its panels commemorating early settlers. One wing of the building is devoted to the exhibits of the *Fairfield Historical Society*, which include many rare old books, early town documents, and maps.

2. Surrounded by lilac bushes, the *Isaac Hull House* (*open*), 573 New Post Rd., now a shop, is a weathered gray, two-story, double end-chimneyed house. Under construction by Isaac Hull in 1779, at the time of the burning of the town, it remained but half finished until 1790 when it was completed by the Rev. Andrew Eliot. The interior woodwork is of both the Georgian and post-Colonial type as shown in the raised paneling of the room to the left of the hall and the sunken paneling of the room on the right.

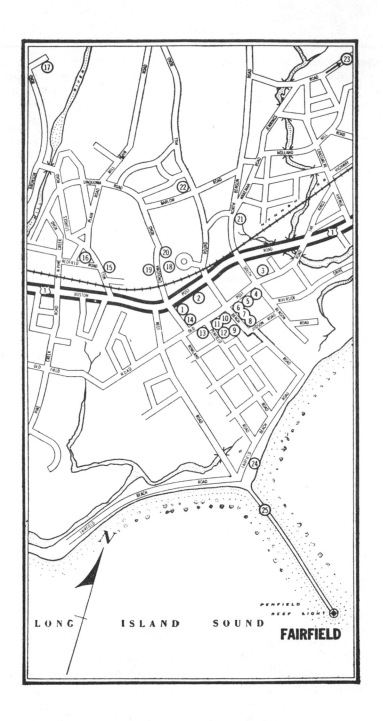

LONG ISLAND SOUND

FAIRFIELD

PENFIELD
REEF LIGHT

R. from New Post Rd. on Benson Rd.

3. *Brigadier General Elijah Abel House (private)* (1780), NE cor. Benson Rd. and Old Post Rd., was operated as a tavern during Civil War days by the Benson family. The old inn sign, which now hangs in the garret, reads, 'Benson House — The Union Must be Preserved.'

R. from Benson Rd. on Old Post Rd.

4. *Jennings Gardens (open 9 to sunset)*, public entrance on Beach Rd., on the grounds of Sunnie Holme, the estate of Miss Annie B. Jennings, have the largest and most beautiful displays of flowering shrubs in the State.

5. *Major William Silliman House (private)*, of 1786–91, 405 Old Post Rd., is a large end-chimneyed structure with wide, flat cornice, bare of mouldings, very narrow clapboarding, and a central entrance covered by a gracefully curved portico supported by slender columns. When a boy, Major Silliman was taken prisoner by the British at Holland Hill.

L. from Old Post Rd. on Beach Rd.

6. *Isaac Tucker House (private)* (1766), 19 Beach Rd., though set on fire when the town was burned, was saved by a Negro servant who had hidden in the attic. It has an asymmetrical plan frequently found in Fairfield, with a corner hall approached now through a later fan-lighted doorway.

7. *Justin Hobart House (private)* (1765), 33 Beach Rd., though remodeled retains much of its original form; it is a square, two-chimney house with dentiled cornice, shutters, and a modern sun-porch and portico. Church meetings and court sessions were held here after the burning of the town, until the meeting house was rebuilt in 1785.

8. *Nathan Bulkeley House (private)*, 37 Beach Rd., is another pre-Revolutionary house built in the prevailing Fairfield mode with two windows on one side of the door and one on the other. The portico is

---

FAIRFIELD. Points of Interest

1. Fairfield Memorial Library
2. Isaac Hull House
3. Brigadier General Elijah Abel House
4. Jennings Gardens
5. Major William Silliman House
6. Isaac Tucker House
7. Justin Hobart House
8. Nathan Bulkeley House
9. Old Burying Ground
10. Town House
11. Sun Tavern
12. Fairfield Academy
13. Thaddeus Burr House
14. Rowland House
15. Milestone
16. Augustus Jennings House
17. David Ogden House
18. Stone Powder House
19. Pulpit Rock
20. Bird Sanctuary
21. 'Uncle Ben' Wakeman House
22. Isaac Jennings House
23. General Gold Selleck Silliman House
24. Fairfield Beach
25. Penfield Reef

19th century. It was the home of Dr. Jeremiah T. Dennison, an early homeopath who was relentlessly persecuted. The house was used as a mess hall by British troops during the occupation.

9. The *Old Burying Ground* (R), Beach Rd., enclosed by a stone wall and entered by a lich-gate, contains gravestones dating from 1687 and the graves of more than 100 Revolutionary soldiers.

Retrace on Beach Rd.; L. from Beach Rd. on the Old Post Rd.

10. The *Town House*, cor. Old Post Rd. and Beach Rd. (L), on the Green, was built in 1794. The central portion, a dignified, hip-roofed, white clapboard structure surmounted by a white belfry, has been restored to the original lines. Restoration in 1937 included the addition of wings at either end to provide office space. At the western end of the Green was formerly a pond in which suspected witches were given 'trial by water.' If they floated they were believed to be guilty, but if they sank they were judged innocent. Here Mercy Disbrow and Elizabeth Clawson were bound and thrown into the water. According to records of the time, 'they buoyed up like a cork.' At the edge of the Green stands the old *Town Sign Post*, still in use.

11. *Sun Tavern* (*private*) on the southern edge of the Green (L), about 400 feet back from Old Post Rd., built by Samuel Penfield in 1780 and maintained as an inn until 1818, is an exceptionally narrow, high gambrel-roofed house with twin chimneys and three original dormers. The fluted pilasters of the entrance doorway lend an air of dignity. Washington's diary says he spent the night here, October 16, 1789. The third floor contains an early ballroom.

12. *Fairfield Academy* (*private*) (1804), Old Post Rd., west of St. Paul's Church, was nationally famous for more than a hundred years. Its simplicity and symmetry are typical of the post-Colonial period when conscious design was beginning to affect building. It is essentially a two-story, peak-roofed building, and has a central gable slightly projecting from the front. Where the two roofs meet is a simple open cupola. The flat-topped entrances in the wings contrast with the pedimented doorway in the projecting section.

13. *Thaddeus Burr House* (*private*) (L). Old Post Rd. between Beach and Penfield Rds., surrounded by lofty elms, is a house whose present appearance belies its age. Built in 1790 to replace the original Burr Homestead, destroyed during the British invasion, it was modeled after the famous Hancock House in Boston, and all of the glass for the windows was the gift of John Hancock. The heavy colonnaded portico of Tuscan order, the front doorway, and the third story were added about 1840. In the garden is a hedge of very old arbor vitae. In the original homestead, John Hancock and Dorothy Quincy were married, August 8, 1775. Dorothy had been a visitor here during the siege of Boston and carried on a gay flirtation with Col. Aaron Burr, much to the discomfort of her fiancé.

R. from Old Post Rd. on Unquowa Rd.

14. *Rowland House*, 570 Old Post Rd. (*private*), with a peak roof and

an entrance at the left corner, built prior to 1769, has unfortunately been considerably remodeled and now has the appearance of a 19th-century house. During the British invasion it was saved by a British officer who had once been entertained in it. Many old and important documents and town records were later discovered in a chest in the attic.

L. from Unquowa on New Post Rd.; R. from New Post Rd. on Mill Plain Rd.

15. The old *Milestone* (R), on Mill Plain Rd., about 1500 feet north of the Post Rd., is one of the stones placed along the old coach routes by Benjamin Franklin in 1753, and is inscribed 'F XX M N H.' (Fairfield. 20 miles to New Haven.)

16. *Augustus Jennings House* (*private*), on Mill Plain Rd. (L), between the Post Rd., and Sturges Rd., built in 1760 and painted white, has a rather interesting exterior, with the northern end shingled, and the southern portion clapboarded, except for the flush boarding which covers the main façade at the first story. The porches and short Doric columns at the entrances are later additions. The dwelling was saved in 1779 by Lucretia Redfield who put out four fires started by the British.

L. from Mill Plain Rd. on Sturges Rd.; R. from Sturges Rd. on Bronson Rd.

17. The *David Ogden House*, Bronson Rd. (R), near the entrance to Oak Lawn Cemetery, was built in 1705. Furnished with antiques and with old-fashioned flower-beds beside it, this house has been restored with unusual skill. Its primitive framing, its L-shaped brick chimney and sparse paneling, and a narrow porch with low turned balusters are its principal features.

18. The *Stone Powder House* of 1812 (*private*), on Unquowa Rd. (L), north from New Post Rd., at the rear of Roger Ludlow High School, is on a plot of land known as 'The Rocks' because of its rugged nature. This storehouse for munitions was doubtless built of stones taken from the home of Dr. Laborie, which had crumbled to ruins. Dr. Laborie, surgeon and preacher, was noted for his missionary work with the Indians.

19. From the rustic pulpit on *Pulpit Rock* (L), Unquowa Rd., diagonally opposite the Roger Ludlow High School, Dr. Samuel Osgood, D.D., preached to audiences gathered in the street and field beyond, during the Civil War. An inscription, 'God, and our Country, 1862,' was cut deep in the rock by a recruit on the eve of his departure for the front. *Waldstein*, Dr. Osgood's home, stands close by amid cedars, on the rocky ledge.

20. The *Bird Sanctuary* (*open Tues., Thurs. and Sun.*, 2–5), on Unquowa Rd. (R), a short distance north of Roger Ludlow High School, covering some 10 acres given by Mrs. Mabel Osgood Wright, is now maintained by the National Audubon Society. Here, in their natural surroundings, birds native to Connecticut are protected and fed throughout the year. A museum contains many stuffed native birds.

21. '*Uncle Ben*' *Wakeman House* (*private*), 546 North Benson Rd., built in 1800, was a rendezvous for a group of early Connecticut peddlers on their journeys through the eastern states. This white clapboarded, peak-

roofed homestead has an unusually fine doorway, recessed about one foot with simple soffit panels and narrow fluted pilasters.

22. *Isaac Jennings House* (*private*), NW. cor. Round Hill and Barlow Rds., is a story-and-a-half gambrel-roofed dwelling (about 1780), with red clapboarded walls and a flaring Dutch hood over the door.

23. *General Gold Selleck Silliman House* (*private*), Jennings Rd., cor. Hunyadi St., 2 blocks west of Black Rock Turnpike, a large, white, central-chimney clapboarded structure, originally shingled, was built in 1756. The modern door, a reproduction, and wide eaves considerably change its appearance. It was from this homestead that General Silliman of Revolutionary War fame was captured by the British and taken to Long Island, and here, that Professor Silliman of Yale (1779–1864), the scientist, was born.

24. *Fairfield Beach*, end of Beach Rd., is one of the safest and most attractive beaches along the shores of Long Island Sound.

25. *Penfield Reef* is a natural breakwater pushing out from Fairfield Beach a mile into the Sound; this narrow, rocky reef has been the scene of many wrecks. During severe storms, the Reef Light is almost submerged by the furious waves.

Point of Interest in Environs:

Greenfield Hill, Timothy Dwight's first Academy, 3.3 *m.* (*see sidetrip off Tour* 1).

FARMINGTON

Town: Alt. 200, pop. 4548, sett. 1640, incorp. 1645.

Accommodations: One inn.

Information Service: Farmington Museum, High St., Barney Memorial Library, School St.

Annual Events: Winter Carnival, held in January or February at the athletic field, Unionville Road, 3 m. from Farmington center; admission 50¢.

FARMINGTON, once a busy trading center, is a residential town of leisurely social life, known for its beautiful tree-shaded streets and stately, well preserved old houses. An aristocrat among towns, it holds itself aloof from the hurry and bustle of the work-a-day world, secure in its background of tradition, culture and wealth.

Often called the 'mother of towns,' because it formerly included land which has been divided into nine other towns, Farmington was settled in

1640 by a party of colonists from Hartford, a year after Captain John Mason had been sent by the three river towns of Hartford, Wethersfield, and Windsor to explore the region then inhabited by the Tunxis Indians. Five years later, the settlement was incorporated and named Farmington, probably for the English Farmington in Gloucester, though the name may have been suggested by the occupation of the settlers.

After the Revolution, the town entered upon a period of industrial activity which continued throughout the eighteenth and early nineteenth centuries. In 1802 and 1803, 15,000 yards of linen were manufactured, and 2500 hats were made by Timothy Root's shop on Hatter's Lane; leather goods were being made in four shops, and muskets and buttons were manufactured. Other industries were operated by clockmakers, silver, gold, and tinsmiths; candlemakers, carriage-builders and cabinet-makers, whose products were shipped to the South and peddled through the States by Yankee peddlers. During this period the Farmington East India Company did a thriving shipping business, and the town became a prosperous mercantile center.

The opening of the Farmington Canal through this section in 1828 brought increased trade and prosperity to the town, which continued until 1848 when the waterway was closed because of landslides. At present, Farmington's commercial activity includes only small local stores and a few wayside tea rooms. Its principal industries are dairying and agriculture.

TOUR

Junction of Main St. and Farmington Ave.

1. The *Rochambeau Monument*, a bronze plaque on a boulder in a small park at the junction of Main St. and Farmington Ave., commemorates the encampment of the French General's troops within the town in 1781.

E. from the Monument on Farmington Ave.

2. The *Elm Tree Inn* (*open*), first block on the north side of Farmington Ave. (L), a brick and frame structure, was erected after the Revolution around a 17th-century house where Philip Lewis started an inn in 1665. The rear ell encloses the original building in which is preserved a large kitchen fireplace. The west end of the house is still covered with beaded clapboards and an interior wall is finished with feather-edged boards.

3. The *Whitman Tavern* (*private*), SW. cor. Farmington Ave. and High St. (R), a yellow, two-and-a-half story, clapboarded house, is a typical example of a sturdy central-chimney dwelling of the 18th century. Built by Captain Judah Woodruff, Farmington's master-builder, in 1786, it served as a shop for journeymen shoemakers from 1812 to 1854, and later housed the village library. In 1791 it was sold to William Whitman, whose descendants own the building.

R. from Farmington Ave. on High St.

4. The *Samuel Whitman House* (*open daily except Monday; adm.* 25¢) (L), now the Farmington Museum, first block on High St., is a carefully restored 17th-century dwelling. One of the oldest frame houses in the State (about 1660), it is easily recognized by its gray-brown, unstained oak clapboards, its 18-inch overhang, and narrow casement windows. They look curious and inadequate to a traveler today, but in the 17th century when glass was at a premium, a house furnished with double or triple casement sash brought from England was luxurious indeed. Two of the four exterior doors are studded.

Exhibits of note are: collections of old deeds and documents; musical instruments used in the church choir; an old hymnal printed in Farmington; old china, including pieces of Lowestoft formerly owned by the Cowles family; and some silver made by Martin Bull of Farmington. A collection of lamps contains a 'courting lamp,' which timed the length of a suitor's visit.

5. The *Judd Homestead* (*private*) (1697), High St. (L), beyond the Samuel Whitman House, is a broad, low, gambrel-roofed house with wide clapboard siding, typical of the late 17th-century frame dwellings.

R. from High St. on Mountain Road; L. from Mountain Road on School St.

6. The *Barney Memorial Library* (*open week-days*) (R), first block on School St., has several interesting exhibits, including a collection of birds' eggs which is one of the finest in the country. Presented by Harry Curtiss Mills, the collection includes more than 8000 eggs of 843 species, among them eggs of the dwarf screech owl, the only known specimens on exhibition in the United States.

Return on School St.; L. on Mountain Road; R. on Main Street to a driveway halfway up the first block; R. on the driveway.

7. The brown shingled *Gleason House* (*private*) (about 1660), behind the dwellings on Main Street, is one of the few houses with a framed overhang still standing in the State. Although the usual drops have been cut off the 18-inch overhang, their bases with gouge carving and two of the original brackets remain.

Return on Main Street; L. on Main Street.

8. *Miss Porter's School* both sides of Main St., at Mountain Road, an exclusive, nationally-known finishing school for girls, was founded in Farmington in 1844 by Miss Sarah Porter, sister of Noah Porter, Jr., eleventh president of Yale, and Samuel Porter, a leader in education for deaf mutes. The main building (about 1828) of the institution, which has an interesting irregularity in the placement of its windows, was erected for a hotel at the time of the opening of the Canal.

9. The *Samuel Deming House* (*private*) (R), next to Miss Porter's School, built in 1768 by Judah Woodruff, has a double overhang and unusual wooden leader heads under a delicate cornice.

10. The *Gad Cowles House* (*private*) (L), on the grounds of Miss Porter's School, opposite the Deming House, dates from 1799. It is the earliest, as well as the largest, of a group of houses which are as typical of 19th-century Farmington dwellings as the framed overhang is of the 17th century. In the tall gable-end facing the street is a Palladian window above an elaborate cornice, supported by tall fluted Ionic pilasters. In one corner of this façade, the delicate detail of a small open porch contrasts with the grand scale of the house. A portico, on the southern wing, with four free-standing columns is the most imposing feature of the building.

11. The *Congregational Church* (1771), Main St. (L), beyond the Cowles house, is one of the few Colonial buildings of which the architect's name is known. He was Captain Judah Woodruff, builder of much that was good in Farmington. The unusually tall steeple of the church, topped with an open-belfry spire, is universally admired as a masterpiece of Georgian-Colonial architecture. The main entrance, placed in the middle of one side in accordance with 18th-century practice, is now obscured by a later Doric portico. The massive scale of the entrance is notable. The impression of great height is due to the narrow graduated clapboarding which materially affects the scale and, in part, to the distance between the first- and second-story windows. It is easy to believe that the Colonial architect, like the Gothic, tried to give his churches a sense of loftiness that houses of the Colonial period lacked. If so, it was a definite spiritual expression that later, more conventionalized generations forgot. The height of rooms increased in their houses, decreased in their churches.

12. A driveway to the right of the church leads to the *Grange Hall*, once the Academy (1816), which is distinguished by a delicate octagonal belfry on the lower ell at the north end.

R. from Main St. on Mill Lane.

13. The *Old Grist Mill*, still grinding corn, at the end of Mill Lane, on the east bank of the Farmington River, was erected by the Cowles family about 1778. At one time owned by the late Winchell Smith, noted playwright, it attracted national attention many years ago when the motion picture 'Way Down East' was filmed here. Hoping to make Connecticut a grain-raising State, Mr. Smith bought expensive harvesting machinery and encouraged the farmers to plant rye, wheat and buckwheat on contract for him; he failed in the marketing of his various ground flours and mixtures and turned to grinding cowfeeds and middlings.

Return on Mill Lane; R. on Main St.

14. The *Major Timothy Cowles House* (*private*) (1815) (L), SE. cor. Main and Church Sts., belongs to the elaborate, Greek Revival group of dwellings beginning with the house of Gad Cowles, which made Farmington famous in the early 19th century. Projecting two-story porticoes of ornate and over-delicate Ionic detail face front, north and south. A Palladian window is almost lost from view over the front door; and a doorway, excellent in

design, is crowded into the angle of the north wing. An over emphasis upon well-executed form, often to the detriment of the whole effect, is characteristic of the Greek Revival.

15. The *Simon Hart House* (*private*) (1804) (L), Main St. just above Colton St., designed in the simplicity of the best early 19th-century architecture, is long and spacious. On the gable end which faces the street is an open Doric portico typical of that period.

16. The *Rev. Noah Porter House* (*private*), SW. cor. Maple and Main Sts., the birthplace of the Porter family, was built of brick in 1808 (without the third story) by the Rev. Noah Porter, who was for 60 years pastor of the Congregational Church. The first meeting of the American Board of Commissioners for Foreign Missions was held here in 1810. Here were born Noah, Samuel, and Sarah Porter (*see above*).

R. from Main St. on Maple St.

17. The *Riverside Cemetery*, one block west on Maple St., on the site of an Indian burying ground, contains a large, brown sandstone monument erected in 1840 in honor of the Tunxis tribe of Indians. Another monument commemorates the Civil War dead. One of the Mendi captives, who died in Farmington while awaiting trial for mutiny, is buried here. The inscription on the stone reads: 'Foone. A native African who was drowned while bathing in the Center Basin August 1841. He was one of the company of slaves under Cinque on board the schooner "Amistad" who asserted their rights and took possession of the vessel after having put the Captain, Mate and others to death, sparing their Masters Ruez, and Mantez.'

Return on Maple St.; R. on Main St.

18. The *General George Cowles House* (*private*) (1803), beyond the Porter Homestead on the west side of Main St., an imposing mansion, has a rather plain brick front relieved only by a recessed arched entrance, unusual in the detail of its downward tapering columns between the door and the side-lights. On the southern façade, which faces Hatter's Lane, is a two-story Ionic portico and a Palladian window in the gable above.

19. Opposite the Cowles House lies the *Old Cemetery* (L), with an entrance in the Egyptian style once much used in Connecticut. The oldest stone dates from 1685.

20. The *Samuel Cowles House* (*private*), SW. cor. Main St. and Meadow Rd., a large gambrel-roofed house with corner quoins, bracketed cornices, and round-headed gable windows of the English Georgian type, is named *Oldgate* from its entrance gate of modified Chinese design. It is not only the most elaborate house in Farmington, but interesting also because it is the first house in the State (1780) that brought into the plain provincial art of the time the influences of the classical renaissance as developed in the English Georgian. It is evidently not the work of a local architect. Woodruff, whose work was contemporary, never attempted a façade like this, which focuses upon a handsome projecting pediment supported

on four Ionic columns.   Above it, pilasters frame a well-designed Palladian window in the second story. Tradition has it that the design was by a British army officer, an architect named William Spratt, who was imprisoned in Farmington for two years. The design of this façade brought Spratt his reputation, and other West Indian merchantmen in Litchfield and East Haddam subsequently employed him. This same motif appears on many other buildings, and sometimes in a debased form was copied in many a village of western Connecticut. The small Dutch-roof ell at the rear was the home (1661) of Farmington's first minister, the Rev. Samuel Hooker, son of the Rev. Thomas Hooker who founded Hartford, and grandfather of the wife of Jonathan Edwards.

21. Another house, contemporary and very simple in contrast with the elegance of Oldgate, but with clear-cut lines and an aspect of serenity, is the *General Solomon Cowles House* (1784), on the next or southwest corner. It is a square house with a hip roof and long piazza.

22. The *Isaac Cowles House* (*private*), built in 1735, on the east side of Main St. (L), facing Meadow Rd., has a double overhang and a well-designed doorway, in which the pilaster caps have been strangely omitted. The very unusual cornice has small carved panels between the brackets.

23. The remains of the *John Cole Homestead* (*private*) (R), west side of Main St. at Tunxis St., have been made into two dwellings. Built in 1661, the structure was the first of the 17th-century houses for which Farmington is famous. Many generations ago the original house was cut in two by two sons who quarreled after the property was bequeathed to them. The southernmost section is on the original stone foundation; its two-foot framed overhang is original. The other half, moved a short distance, has a new overhang built in on the long side facing the road.

GREENWICH

Town: Alt. 60, tax borough pop. 5981, sett. 1640.

Railroad Station: Greenwich Station, Railroad Ave. at Greenwich Ave. for N.Y., N.H. & H. R.R.

Piers: Public Dock, Steamboat Road for Island Beach boats, May 30 to Labor Day (10¢ for residents; 25¢ for non-residents; Sun. and holidays 50¢).

Accommodations: Three hotels.

Information Service: Chamber of Commerce, 34 East Putnam Ave.

Swimming: Byram Park, East Port Chester; Island Beach in the Sound, reached by boat from Public Dock; Milbrook Country Club (*private*).

Bridle Paths: Several miles of marked bridle paths form a network winding through the northern section of the town, passing through some of the finest estates in the vicinity.

Annual Events: The Scottish Games Association holds an athletic and folk dance competition July 4.

GREENWICH, with approximately six miles of coast line along the Sound, is essentially an urban community of the New York metropolitan area with a sophisticated suburban atmosphere, quite unlike the typical Connecticut town. The home of many prominent figures in New York social and financial life, Greenwich is distinguished by its palatial landscaped estates in a natural setting of rolling hills and coves, bays, rivers, and lakes.

Modern shops and large hotels are clustered in the elm-shaded business district. Residential sections stretch southward to the irregular, rock-ridged shore of Long Island Sound, and northward into the hilly countryside. On the outskirts are the districts known as Old Greenwich, site of the original settlement, which has preserved many of its early homesteads; Riverside, where reside many wealthy persons; Milbrook, center of extensive estates about the Milbrook Golf and Country Club; and the residential sections known as Belle Haven, Rock Ridge, and Round Hill.

Settled in 1640 by Daniel Patrick and Robert Feaks, agents of the New Haven Colony, who purchased the land from the Indians for twenty-five coats, the community, named for the English Greenwich, was regarded as of strategic importance, as it represented the most westerly thrust of the English toward the Dutch settlement at New Amsterdam. The Director General of the New Netherlands immediately served notice that the land was rightfully under his jurisdiction. Fearing attack from the Indians, whose friendliness had turned to hostility, and hoping for protection from the Dutch, Captain Patrick signed a treaty at New Amsterdam in April, 1642, wherein the Mianus River between Stamford and Greenwich was agreed upon as the western boundary of Connecticut. Disputes over the boundary continued. In 1650, the Dutch, in a treaty signed at Hartford, ceded Greenwich to Connecticut, but the jurisdiction of territory farther west was disputed for many years.

During the Revolutionary War, the Continental salt works at Greenwich were destroyed, and homes were plundered and burned when the town was attacked by General Tryon and a force of 1200 British and Hessian soldiers. General Putnam and a force of 100 militiamen attempted a defense, but were forced to retreat.

Industry has never been an important factor in the development of the town, although considerable shipping and shipbuilding were carried on in the early nineteenth century, when agricultural products, especially large cargoes of potatoes, were shipped to New York from this port. With the advent of the railroad and subsequent development of farmlands to the west of New York, Greenwich agricultural activities were greatly curtailed.

EARLY CHURCHES OF CONNECTICUT

THE theocratic state was the origin of Connecticut's first government, and the church was always the most important feature of her early architecture.

The oldest churches that remain anywhere near intact are a group from just before the Revolution, in Farmington, Wethersfield, and Brooklyn. Something of the Gothic aspiration for height is to be found in them. The tower is offset, at one end of the building, and after one or two belfry stages, open and closed, terminates in a narrow, tapering spire. The entrance is at the side, opposite the pulpit.

With the movement toward the Classic Revival, church architecture began in the early nineteenth century to borrow more and more of ancient forms. Town's building for Center Church, New Haven (1812–14), was the precursor of the 'golden age' of Connecticut churches. An adapted Renaissance portico now projects from the front of the building, and the steeple rises back of this entrance gable, most of it from within the main edifice of the church. As time went on, the steeple moved backward, as it were, into the church building, and the portico became more and more a separate composition.

David Hoadley did more than any other man to influence this finest period from 1815 to 1830. Four very similar churches culminated in Litchfield (1829) — sometimes considered the perfect example — although Col. Samuel Belcher's church at Old Lyme (1817), now reconstructed, is an artists' favorite. Country churches, as in Killingworth, often achieved more charming results from their very simplicity. Plymouth Church, Milford (1834), represents the later, severer tendency of the Classic Revival. Often this was a careful copying; sometimes, as in the stone Congregational Church at East Granby, a more spontaneous, free rendering brought about an unexpected attractive result.

CONGREGATIONAL CHURCH, FARMINGTON

CONGREGATIONAL CHURCH, WETHERSFIELD

CENTER CHURCH, NEW HAVEN

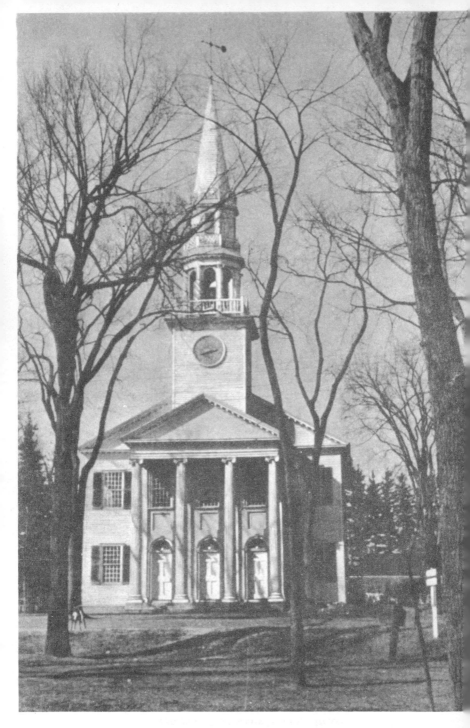

CONGREGATIONAL CHURCH, LITCHFIELD

CONGREGATIONAL CHURCH, OLD LYME

CONGREGATIONAL CHURCH, KILLINGWORTH

PLYMOUTH CHURCH, MILFORD

CONGREGATIONAL CHURCH, EAST GRANBY

Each year on July 4, at the Charles A. Moore estate, is held an international celebration of the Scottish Games Association. Bagpipe bands vie for prizes, and contestants from Scotland, Australia, the United States, and Canada participate in tossing the caber as well as in native dances such as the Highland Fling, sword dance, and foursome reel.

MOTOR TOUR

S. from US 1 on Greenwich Ave. to Steamboat Road.

1. *Bruce Museum (open daily during daylight hours; free)*, in Bruce Park at end of Steamboat Road, a four-story, square, stone house of 1850, with no adornment except an abbreviated French tower, is devoted to exhibits of natural history, art, and history.

Formerly the Bruce estate, the 80 acres and residence were bequeathed to the town by Robert M. Bruce in 1908. The museum is under the direction of Mr. Paul G. Howes, who was formerly with the American Museum of Natural History. Mr. Howes, chief photographer with the scientist William Beebe on the Kalacoon Expedition to British Guiana, collected many of the specimens exhibited.

On the first floor are a herbarium, in which blossoms of shrubs native to Connecticut are reproduced in wax, an art department, and a collection of mammals. Specimens of the wild animals of Connecticut are shown against authentic backgrounds. In addition there are many North American, Australian, and Asiatic specimens.

An ornithological collection occupies the second floor. Here, expertly mounted native birds are classified in four large groups illustrating the four seasons: spring in the woods, summer at the shore, autumn and winter in the woods. An exhibit of birds' nests and eggs has been collected from many parts of the world. An extensive entomological collection, including thousands of local and foreign specimens, is also displayed on the second floor.

A variety of collections occupies the third floor: gems and minerals from various countries; fossils illustrating the history of life on the earth; models showing the evolution of the horse from his tiny ancestor; and extinct reptiles of the Connecticut Valley. A collection of Indian relics includes arrowheads, agricultural implements, and specimens of beadwork and paintings. An American historical collection includes many relics of Colonial days.

At the end of the Point is the *Indian Harbor Yacht Clubhouse*, a large stucco building in Italian style with tile roofs. On the peninsula to the east, the elaborate villa of the late Commodore Elias C. Benedict stands near the site of the headquarters of 'Boss' Tweed's 'Americus Club of New York.' The Tweed estate (1865) stretched from this point to the Post Road.

Return to US 1; *R. on US* 1.

2. The granite *Second Congregational Church* (L), conspicuously placed at the top of the hill, in the center of Greenwich, has a tall, slender broach spire at one corner that towers above the trees and can be seen for miles in all directions.

3. *Christ Episcopal Church* (R), erected in 1908–10, was designed by William Francis Dominick. The three granite buildings of this distinguished Gothic group include the church, with a square, high pinnacled tower and rather flat roof; a cloistered parish house, somewhat recessed from the street; and the rectory, a dwelling of Gothic design.

4. *Putnam Cottage* (*open* 10–5, *Mon., Wed., Fri., Sat.; free*) (1731) (L), 243 East Putnam Ave., is maintained as a museum by the D.A.R. This white homestead with a peaked roof and long, low veranda has undergone several renovations, but retains its original round-ended shingles on the front. According to tradition, it was from this house that Israel Putnam made his daring escape from the British on February 26, 1779. The General, recently arrived at Greenwich to review the Continental troops, was shaving in his room when he saw, in the mirror, the reflection of approaching Redcoats. Outnumbered and totally unprepared, Putnam ordered his men to flee for their lives, and, jumping astride his horse, turned the animal toward the brink of the rocky precipice near-by. The astonished British saw horse and rider disappear over the cliff. Threading his way to right and left, Putnam reached the valley; not one of the dragoons dared to follow him. The Post Road is cut through the rock at about the spot where Putnam made his escape. A small *Bronze Tablet* at the top of the incline, west of the Putnam Cottage, commemorates the adventure.

The house is completely equipped with old furniture and accessories of the 18th and early 19th century. In the parlor is an early spinet, a handsome flat-topped desk, a secretary, an old spinning wheel, and many other objects of interest. In an adjoining room is one of the first Franklin stoves, in the rare, arched style; a pair of old pewter candlemolds, and many other examples of early pewter, including a teapot, plates, bowls, warming pans, etc. There is also on exhibit a chest of drawers made of cherry hewn from a Greenwich tree by a local craftsman in the early 18th century. The bedrooms are furnished with Colonial pieces, including a fine example of an early American cradle.

5. The *High Low House*, Round Hill Road, a composite structure, com-

---

GREENWICH. POINTS OF INTEREST

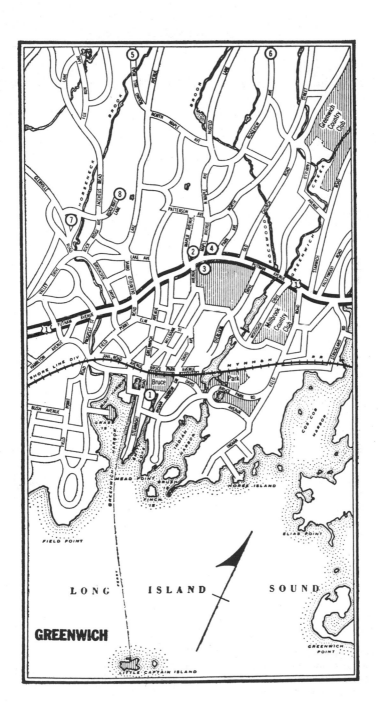

bining a 16th-century English manor house, transported to this country from England in 1911, and a granite Tudor residence, erected in 1905 by I. N. Phelps Stokes, architect and owner, is on private grounds, not open to the public. British supervision of British-American labor assured the sympathetic handling of the 16th-century material. The English dwelling for which the residence is named was erected in Ipswich, Suffolk County, England, about 1507. Built of half timber and brick, with seven sharp gables in its red tiled roof, the old house has a great 12-panel, heavily studded oaken entrance door with a Gothic top and original hardware, a hand-carved header and broad carved lintel. Hand-carved half-columns rise to Gothic brackets; a hand-carved frieze on the second-floor end-overhang, and random brick and timber panels spread to either side of the entrance. The heavy corner posts and brackets are elaborately hand-carved, and weathered rift-grain oak shows wherever the timbering is revealed.

6. The *Milbank Mausoleum*, occupying a commanding position in the Putnam Cemetery, Parsonage Rd., is a scholarly reproduction of an Ionic temple, with columns extending around all sides. From the road below, it appears to be an open colonnade.

7. *Edgewood School*, on Glenville Rd. and Brookside Lane, opened in 1910 on the estate of Mrs. Charles D. Lanier, is a co-educational progressive school with an enrollment of about 200 pupils from 3 to 20 years of age. Conducted on the principle that education to be successful must be interesting from early childhood, the courses in this school seek first to establish an appreciation of intellectual discipline.

The main school building, a spreading structure of granite boulders with a wide covered porch, stands on a 120-acre campus across which Horseneck Brook winds, tumbling in falls and rapids and spreading out in quiet pools.

8. *Rosemary Hall*, at junction Ridgeway and Zaccheus Mead Lane, is a preparatory school for girls founded in Wallingford in 1890 and moved to its present site in 1900. The 25-acre campus includes six school buildings, two hockey fields, two gymnasiums, and a running track. About 200 students are enrolled.

Points of Interest Offshore:

On *Great Captain's Island*, 3 m. out, in Long Island Sound, opposite the entrance to Greenwich Harbor, named for Captain Daniel Patrick, first military commander of the town, is a square stone lighthouse erected by the U.S. Government in the early nineteenth century.

On *Little Captain's Island*, 2 m. out, the town has established a public recreational center. (*Boats, every* 20 *min. from Memorial Day to Labor Day, leave dock at foot of Steamboat Road;* 20-*minute sail; boat fee* 25¢ *round trip; Island Beach, bath-house rental* 50¢.)

Points of Interest in Environs:

Lyon House; Condé Nast Press, Laddin's Rock; Keofferam Lodge, Shore Road; Arcadia (headquarters of National Agassiz Association); Perrot Memorial Library (headquarters Greenwich Historical Society), Old Greenwich (*see Tour* 1).

GROTON

Town: Alt. 60, pop. 10,770, sett. 1649, organized 1705.

Airport: Trumbull Airport, Eastern Point; taxi fare from center of Groton, 75¢ for one or two passengers; time, 15 min. Sightseeing planes, $1 per ride, over harbor. No scheduled service.

Taxis: 50¢ anywhere in village.

Accommodations: One large hotel, open in summer only.

Annual Events: Navy Day Celebration, U.S. Submarine Base, October 26.

GROTON, spreading along the eastern bank of the Thames River opposite New London, clings to the steep slope of Groton Heights, dominated by the granite shaft erected in memory of the militiamen who attempted to withstand two regiments of British regulars in 1781. From the water's edge to the hill crest, the old shipbuilding village of narrow streets and small vine-grown houses seems to have slumbered for years, growing in its sleep and awakening just before the World War to be rediscovered by industry. Although submarines, engines, banjos, thread and castings are produced here, Groton remains a Yankee community with nearly sixty per cent of its population of full native parentage. Village politics, the affairs of the Nation and of the Odd Fellows, the principal organization in town, are discussed in the back room of Groton's leading 'department store.' In summer, a steady stream of sleek motors rolls through the Main Street, en route to Eastern Point, three miles south, an exclusive shore resort.

The countryside around Groton has been drenched with the blood of Indians, patriots, and British invaders. Before the white men came, some of the bloodiest of tribal wars were fought in this hunting ground of the Pequot Indians, who were seldom on friendly terms with the Narragansetts, or later, with the English.

Land in Groton was granted to New London settlers in 1648–49 and, originally known as the 'East Side,' was first occupied in 1649 by Jonathan Brewster, eldest son of Elder William Brewster of the Plymouth Colony, who established a trading post at Brewster's Neck on the Thames River north of the present Groton. Organized in 1705, the town was named for the county seat of the Winthrops in Suffolk, England. The settlement did not develop into a compact little village like most Yankee towns but spread over the broken terrains of 'breezy ridges and sunny valleys' into numerous little streamside communities in the back country and a fringe of shipbuilding and fishing settlements along the shore of the river and Sound. (*See NOANK and WEST MYSTIC, Tour* 1.) The township extends from the Mystic to the Thames Rivers and originally reached from the Sound to the Preston line, until Ledyard (then North Groton) became a separate town in 1836. The town now includes the Borough of Groton, Center Groton, Poquonock Bridge, Noank, and West Mystic. Agriculture was not profitable, but fisheries were. By 1838 some three hundred Groton men and boys were regularly engaged at sea, some fishing off Cuba for the Spanish trade, some in West Indian trade, and others in salvaging operations up and down the coast.

Among the distinguished Groton skippers was Captain Ebenezer Morgan, who returned to New London harbor on September 18, 1865, in his 'Pioneer,' with 1391 pounds of whale oil and 22,650 pounds of bone. The cargo was sold for $151,060, and as the ship and outfit cost only $35,800, a net profit of over 300 per cent was made in the fifteen months' voyage.

Captain James M. Buddington of Groton, commanding the ship 'George and Henry,' in 1855 discovered the abandoned British frigate 'Resolute,' one of the squadron sent out in search of Sir John Franklin. Ice bound in Baffin's Bay, the 'Resolute' was abandoned and drifted 900 miles out into the Atlantic. Captain Buddington brought her safely to New London harbor and received $30,000 for salvage from the United States Government. The English ship was refitted at the Brooklyn Navy Yard and returned to England as a gift from the United States to the Queen.

Captain Joseph Warren Holmes, a Groton skipper, doubled Cape Horn more times than any man afloat, with eighty-three trips to his credit. For pure adventure, little in the annals of the sea surpasses the experience of Captain Ambrose H. Burrows, who sailed from New York, January 24, 1823, commanding the brig 'Frederick' bound for Lima, Peru. At Callao, after a passage of 158 days, he found the city in a state of insurrection. General Bolivar arrived with reinforcements and restored order. Later, on sailing for Quilca, the seaport for Arequipa, capital of Upper Peru, the brig was fired upon and boarded by a crew from a pirate craft, 'Quintanelia,' commanded by an Italian. Short of navigators, the pirates forced Captain Burrows to navigate his own vessel. The skipper asked for the company of his sixteen-year-old son and smuggled his pistols aboard. At pistol point, Captain Burrows took over the ship again, cast the pirates adrift in a longboat, sailed his ship back to Callao, and found the city in the midst of another revolt. Rescued by the U.S. frigate 'Franklin,' Captain Burrows sold his vessel and returned to America on the 'Constitution.'

The wanderlust of John Ledyard, born in Groton in 1751, nephew of the commander at Fort Griswold, is said to have inspired the recurring mystery of 'disappearing freshmen' at Dartmouth College. While a Dartmouth freshman, in 1772, Ledyard fashioned a canoe fifty feet long from a pine tree and paddled down the Connecticut on the first of many voyages which took him to unexplored countries. Arriving at Hartford, young Ledyard shipped before the mast and made a voyage to Gibraltar, the Barbary Coast, and the West Indies. Sailing from London as a corporal of marines under Captain Cook, the Groton youngster was absent for four years on a cruise that took him to Hawaii at its discovery, China, Siberia, and into the Arctic. On his return to America, Ledyard published his journal. In 1786, following Thomas Jefferson's plan for exploration of the Pacific Northwest by way of Siberia, Ledyard traveled on foot from Stockholm, Sweden, to St. Petersburg, Russia, a distance of 1400 miles in seven weeks. He was stopped at Irkutsk and ordered to leave Russia. He returned to London, undaunted in his quest for unknown places. While fitting out an expedition at Cairo, to explore Africa, Ledyard died at the age of thirty-seven.

Shipbuilding was one of the village's important early industries. Large ships were built in Groton yards as early as 1724, and during the Revolution a thirty-six-gun frigate was built in the Poquetanock River at the order of the Continental Congress. In 1812 many privateers were fitted out to run the British blockade. The Eastern Shipbuilding Company established a plant in Groton in 1900 and commenced the construction of two large steamships for the Great Northern Steamship Company, the 'Minnesota' and 'Dakota,' largest merchant vessels of their day, with a displacement of 33,000 tons each.

Groton has had its share of strange cults. Spiritualism held sway under the banner of the First Spiritual and Liberal Society for some years in the early seventeenth century, but gradually died out. The Rogerene Quakers, organized by John Rogers of New London about 1675, were a very strong sect and were so determined in their efforts to make the town of Groton pure that they were occasionally whipped or treated to a coat of tar and feathers by their fellow townsfolks. The only remaining trace of this sect now is in the back country.

TOUR

S. from Post Road (US 1) on Thames St.

1. The *Mother Bailey House (private)* (1782), 108 Thames St., is a two-and-a-half-story frame building with two end chimneys. The entrance porch, supported by Ionic columns, is a later addition. The house owes its fame to an episode of the War of 1812. In June 1813, Commodore Stephen Decatur and his small fleet, pursued by a British squadron, had taken shelter in New London harbor. Fearful of a repetition of

the attack of 1781, terrified inhabitants bundled their household goods into carts and hastened inland. A messenger from the fort, sent through town to collect old rags for gunwadding, was unsuccessful in his quest until he met Mother Bailey (Anna Warner Bailey), who promptly removed her red flannel petticoat and remarked, 'There are plenty more where that came from.' When the petticoat and its story reached the fort, the garrison promptly displayed 'The Martial Petticoat' from a pikestaff planted on the ramparts as a symbol of the devotion of a patriótic lady. After the war, President Andrew Jackson is reported to have visited Mrs. Bailey and presented the iron fence at the west of the house, 'as a token of appreciation.

2. The *Cary Latham House* (*private*), 157 Thames St., called Ferry Tavern, a narrow two-and-a-half-story, peak-roofed structure with a lone chimney, is so small that there are only two rooms within, one above the other. There is little architectural evidence to justify the early date claimed for it (1655).

3. The *Colonel Ebenezer Avery House* (1754), NE. cor. Thames and Latham Sts., with a peak roof and central chimney, was used as a hospital for the wounded in 1781. Although it has been remodeled, this frame dwelling retains the original paneling around the staircase, a fine corner cupboard with a carved rose at the top, and three or four paneled and battened interior doors on the first floor.

L. from Thames on Fort St.

4. *Fort Griswold*, Fort and Thames Sts., commanding the entrance to the Thames, was the site of one of the tragedies of the American Revolution. Here on September 6, 1781, Lieutenant-Colonel William Ledyard hastily assembled 150 militiamen in an attempt to repulse the attack of two regiments of British regulars and the 3d Battalion of New Jersey volunteers, who advanced on Groton after capturing Fort Trumbull, New London. Under the direction of Benedict Arnold, who watched from across the river, the British stormed the fort and killed Colonel Ledyard and most of his brave company. The untrained Colonial riflemen, recruited from near-by farms, sold their lives dearly, accounting for 193 British. Looting, mistreatment of the wounded and prisoners, and the burning of the town followed the slaughter of the defenders. Eighty-five militiamen were killed at the fort and all male members of many families were destroyed; of the Avery family alone, nine men were killed and three wounded.

The General Assembly of May, 1792, offered to those involved in the tragedy, or to the heirs and legal representatives, a half-million acres of land in the Western Reserve, as partial compensation. Ninety-two Groton families benefited by this grant. In May, 1842, title to Fort Griswold was ceded to the U.S. Government. A stone marker, enclosed by an iron fence, marks the spot where Ledyard, the military commander of the district, fell by his own sword which he had trustingly extended to the conquering officer as a token of surrender. Another marker, strangely enough, is a memorial to the Major Montgomery of the British forces, who, while leading the attack over the parapet, was killed by a pike wielded by Gordon Freeman, a Negro servant of Ledyard.

The feeling generated by the massacre has not abated despite the passing years. Commemorative exercises are frequently held on the old battle-ground. For many years Jonathan Brooks of New London (d. 1848) delivered an unsolicited address from the breastworks on the anniversary of the massacre. One year, when only a few people gathered to listen, Mr. Brooks looked out over their heads, cleared his throat, and bellowed, 'Attention, Universe!'

5. *Groton Monument* (*grounds open free;* 15¢ *admission to monument*) (1830), Fort St., was erected under State patronage with funds secured from a lottery. This monument, commemorating the battle of Fort Griswold, is a granite obelisk 22 feet square and 134 feet high. From windows at the top, a view unfolds in all directions, including Watch Hill, Block Island, Gardner's Island, Montauk Point, and the Connecticut coast as far west as the Connecticut River.

At the foot of the monument a little *Monument House* (*open 9–5 during the summer months, free*), built of stone left over from the construction of the shaft, has been furnished by the D.A.R., with relics of the battle and other antiques.

6. *Bill Memorial Library* (*open Tuesdays and Thursdays,* 2–6, *Saturdays,* 2–7) (1890), NW. of the monument, a brownstone building in the roman-tic style of Richardson, has a fine collection of butterflies.

7. The *Joseph Latham House* (*private*) (1717), Monument St., a plain story-and-a-half cottage of four rooms, is called the 'Gore House,' because so many wounded men were quartered here after the battle of Groton Heights.

8. *Electric Boat Company*, Eastern Point Rd., probably the world's largest builder of submarines, operates almost exclusively for the execu-tion of the U.S. Navy contracts. This firm is a successor to the New London Ship and Engine Company which was the first concern to install Diesel engines in submarines (February 14, 1912). On this site were previously located the shipyards of the Eastern Ship Building Company.

Points of Interest in Environs:

United States Submarine Base (*visitors admitted*), Atlantic sub-marine headquarters, 5 *m.* (*see Tour 9A*).
Fort Hill, 4.4 *m.*, West Mystic; Pequot Hill, 5.6 *m.*, US 1 (*see Tour 1*); the Governor Winthrop House, Bluff Rd., 5.7 *m.* (*see Tour 1*).

GUILFORD

Town: Alt. 10, borough pop. 1880, sett. 1639.
Railroad Station: N.Y., N.H. & H. R.R., Whitfield St.
Accommodations: One hotel.
Annual Events: Guilford Fair and exhibit of local agricultural products; held last Wednesday in September from 9 A.M. to 9 P.M.

GUILFORD, named for the town of Guildford in Surrey, England, retains the appearance of a New England village of the early days. More than 150 old houses border its quiet streets, and the wide Green, with its elms and stately Greek Revival church, has a tranquil simplicity characteristic of the town. Situated on the irregular shore of Long Island Sound, the community has attracted many summer residents in recent years.

Founded in 1639, and originally named Menunkatucket, Guilford was settled by a body of Puritans from Kent and Surrey under the leadership of Henry Whitfield and Samuel Desborough. Land extending from the present Branford to Niantic was purchased from the Mohegan Chief, Uncas, under a grant from the British Crown. One of the bloodiest of Indian battles was fought between the fleeing Pequots and the combined English and Mohegan forces at Sachem's Head (*see Side Trip off Tour* 1).

Although Guilford was one of the few shore towns to escape pillaging by the British fleet and General Tryon's troops, the residents, determined to retaliate for the losses suffered by other towns, organized a whaleboat raid, May 29, 1777, on the British provision stores at Sag Harbor, L.I. Rowing from Sachem's Head to the beach at Plum Gut, 200 men, under Lieutenant Colonel Meigs, dragged their whaleboats overland, launched them again on the ocean side, and rowed to a short distance off Sag Harbor. They surprised the British sentry, withstood the fire of a 12-gun schooner, set fire to about 100 tons of hay, 10 transports, wharves, and 1 armed schooner mounting 8 guns, and returned unharmed within 24 hours. In return, the British landed at Guilford in June, but met such spirited opposition that they retired after burning only two houses on Leete's Island.

Guilford is the birthplace of such distinguished men as Abraham Baldwin (1754–1807), member of the Continental Congress, founder of the University of Georgia, and U.S. Senator from Georgia; the Rev. Samuel Johnson, the first president of King's College, now Columbia University (1696–1772), and Fitz-Greene Halleck, the poet (*see Literature*). The town's most picturesque political character, Samuel Hill (1677–1752), is said to have been responsible for the expression 'Running like Sam Hill,' because he ran for office from young manhood. At the time of his death in 1752, he was not only State representative, but also town clerk, probate judge, and clerk of the Proprietors.

Granite quarrying and oyster culture have flourished in the town throughout most of its existence. Quarries opened in 1837 have provided stone for the foundation of the Statue of Liberty, for breakwaters at Block Island, 13 bridges over the Harlem River, New York City, the foundation of the Brooklyn Bridge, the northern half of the Battery wall in New York, and the lighthouse at Lighthouse Point, New Haven.

A leading occupation is the cultivation of roses, carried on at the Pinchbeck greenhouse on State St., said to be the largest single hothouse in the United States. Covered by more than 125,000 square feet of glass, the greenhouse is 1200 feet long, and has produced a record maximum output of 18,000 roses in one day; average production is about 7000 daily.

Schoolroom furniture, canned goods, birch extract, toilet articles, iron, brass and bronze castings are made in Guilford.

TOUR 1

S. from the Boston Post Road on Fair St.

Nine salt-box-type houses on Fair St. give an opportunity to compare the differing lines of this type of dwelling for which Guilford is famous.

1. The *Spencer Homestead* (*private*) (1761), 101 Fair St., retains its original lines, except for the addition of a Greek Revival doorway.

2. The *Stevens House* (*private*) (1726), 77 Fair St., another outstanding example, is built around the chimney of an earlier house (1670), which measures 17 feet × 26 at the base, probably a record size.

3. *Captain Nathaniel Johnson House* (*private*), another salt-box, at 58 Fair St., was built in 1732.

R. from Fair St. on Broad St.

4. *Site of Governor William Leete Homestead*, 6 Broad St., is marked by a later house, an attractive, modernized salt-box dwelling (*private*), built in 1769 by Caleb Stone. Under the garage behind the house is the cellar foundation of the earlier house, where the regicides, Goffe and Whalley, were hidden for ten days and fed by Mr. Leete.

5. *Jared Leete's House* (*private*) (1781), 76 Broad St., was the home of that injudicious drinker of cider and prolific composer of ribald verse. When hunting one day on Moose Hill, he became very thirsty and asked at a farmhouse for a drink of cider. The housewife, who recognized him, at first refused and then agreed to furnish the drink if he would write an epitaph for her. Jared immediately complied with:

> 'Margaret, who died of late,
> Ascended up to heaven's gate.'

The satisfied Margaret brought the cider and he immediately added:

'But Gabriel met her with a club
And drove her down to BEELZEBUB.'

Retrace Broad St.

6. The *Hubbard House* (*private*) (1717), 53 Broad St., with a five-inch overhang at the second-story level, is the largest Colonial house in Guilford. In it the Rev. Bela Hubbard, D.D., was born in 1739. So beloved was he for his faithfulness in attending his congregation through a severe epidemic of yellow fever that he remained an active minister in New Haven throughout the Revolution, despite his pronounced Royalist sympathies.

7. The *Congregational Church* (L), Broad Street, framed through the trees on the Green, was built in 1829 during the decade in which the Greek Revival reached its fullest development, and offers an interesting comparison with the Litchfield Congregational Church, built in the same year. The church is very broad and has an Ionic portico which repeats the lines of the gable. Three arched windows are placed over the three square-topped doors of equal height. These details, although authentically Greek, are somewhat modified by a freer treatment. The rather low steeple has two octagonal stages over the square tower and is surmounted by a conical spire. The architect is unknown, but his skill with classical forms is evident in the design of this building, distinguishing it from the average village church of the time.

R. from Broad St. on Park St.

8. *Smyth House* (*private*) (1820), 55 Park St., where Ralph Dunning Smyth, lawyer, judge, representative, and local historian lived for many years, has an elaborate cornice and a hip-roofed portico, supported by Ionic columns that are typical of the Greek Revival. The large front windows have finely molded heads. According to tradition, Lafayette, who stopped for refreshment on the opposite corner of the Green, remarked of this house — 'C'est gentille.'

GUILFORD.   POINTS OF INTEREST

1. Spencer Homestead
2. Stevens House
3. Captain Nathaniel Johnson House
4. Site of Governor William Leete Homestead
5. Jared Leete's House
6. Hubbard House
7. Congregational Church
8. Smyth House
9. Episcopal Church
10. Whitfield House
11. Lot Benton House
12. Ebenezer Bartlett House
13. Ruth Hart Homestead
14. Hyland or Fiske-Wildman House
15. Levi Hubbard Homestead
16. Caldwell House
17. Ezra Griswold House
18. Acadian House
19. Sabbath Day House
20. Daniel Bowen House
21. Comfort Starr House

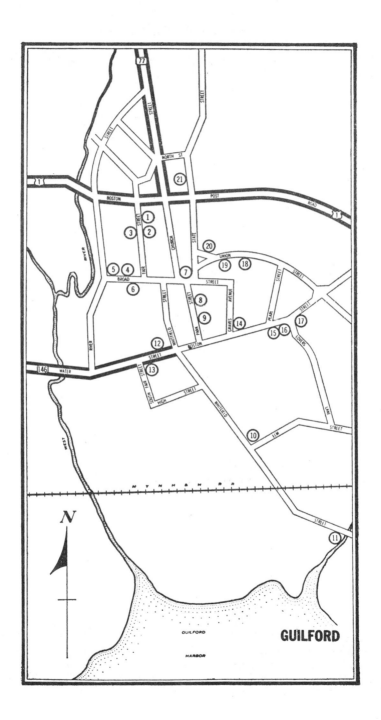

GUILFORD

9. The *Episcopal Church* (L), Park St., between Boston and Broad Sts., a granite building of 1836, is an example of the Gothic Revival, a style popularized in the State by the erection of Trinity Church in New Haven.

R. from Park St. on Boston St.; L. on Whitfield St.

10. *Whitfield House* (*open 9–5 daily; free*), on Whitfield St., is one of the earliest stone houses in America and probably the oldest house in Connecticut. It has been remodeled many times in the last century, and was restored in 1903 and in 1936, so that only about a third of the heavy rear wall, the immense chimney which covers the whole north end of the house, and the line of the foundation remain. The original fortified house was built in 1639–40 by the Rev. Henry Whitfield to serve not only as his home but for all the public uses of the community. The most important house in the town often did have to serve community uses and was, therefore, likely to be a departure from the usual type. In 1936, under a Works Progress Administration project, which was directed by J. Frederick Kelly, an authority on early Connecticut architecture, the house was restored as nearly as possible to its original appearance, even to the odd window which old prints show across the southwest corner. Now maintained by the State as a museum, the building houses a varied collection of antiques and curios.

11. *Lot Benton House* (*private*), on Whitfield St., half a mile south, was erected about 1770 in the center of town where the present Congregational Church stands, but was moved to its present site in 1824, drawn by 35 yoke of oxen. Dr. Lyman Beecher, a ward of Lot Benton, lived in the house occasionally and inherited it.

Retrace Whitfield St.; L. on Water St.

12. *Ebenezer Bartlett House* (*private*), 15 Water St., dating from the second quarter of the 18th century, has a great T-shaped chimney. In this house died the poet Fitz-Greene Halleck (1790–1867).

13. *Ruth Hart Homestead* (*open*) (1780), 68 Water St., a little story-and-a-half Dutch-roofed house, a type rarely found in Guilford, has one very old, many-paned window, with wooden muntins more than an inch wide in the southwest room on the first floor.

Retrace Water St. which becomes Boston St.

14. The *Hyland* or *Fiske-Wildman House* (*open 9–5 during the summer; adm. 25¢*), Boston St. (L), between Graves Ave. and Pearl St., has been restored by the Dorothy Whitfield Historical Society, Inc., and is maintained as a museum. Its date has been the subject of much discussion. Because of the height of its rooms, the best authorities are inclined to believe that it cannot merit the 17th-century date commonly assigned to it. Certainly, with its reconstructed casement windows, it closely resembles the average house of about 1700. The beautifully carved overhang, with its molded chamfer, lambs' tongue, and brackets beneath, is one of the finest examples in Guilford. In this house lived Ebenezer Parmelee, who, in 1727, built one of the first town clocks in America and

installed it in the First Congregational Church on the Green. It served in two succeeding edifices until 1892.

15. *Levi Hubbard Homestead* (*private*) (1761), 311 Boston St., traditionally known as 'Black House,' was the home of Nicholas Loysel, a French refugee, from the Island of Guadeloupe. When Nicholas heard of the execution of Louis XVI, he painted his house black, and traces of the paint remain.

16. The *Caldwell House* (*private*) (1740), southwest corner of Boston St. and Lovers' Lane, was remodeled in the early 19th century, but retains features that link it with the first half of the 18th century. It was originally a central-chimney house, of the 'hewn overhang' type, predominant in the southern portions of Connecticut. The 'hewing out' of the solid corner posts into exterior corbels is plainly visible under the second-story overhang. The excellent portico, the chimneys and windows, are 19th-century; the dormers are 20th-century.

17. On the opposite corner, across Lovers' Lane at 161 Boston St., is the *Ezra Griswold House* (1777), an attractive white salt-box dwelling on a high bank, behind an odd picket fence. Its excellent state of preservation and its charming setting have caused it to be the most photographed house in Connecticut.

L. from Boston St. on Union St.

18. The *Acadian House* (*private*), Union St., between Pearl and Market Place, a sparsely windowed, primitive salt-box dwelling built about 1670 by Joseph Clay, sheltered exiles from Acadia who were put ashore by a British ship after the destruction of Grand Pré in 1755.

On Union St. are two of the tiny, seldom preserved Sabbath Day houses, built by settlers living in distant outlying districts who came into the village on Saturday in order to attend the Sunday services.

19. One *Sabbath Day House* (*private*), at No. 5 Union St., is a story-and-a-half house, with a sharp-peaked roof and a wide cornice, dating from 1730.

20. The *Daniel Bowen House* (*private*), 19 Union St., the other Sabbath Day House, is an exceptionally small dwelling of 1734 with a sharp gambrel at the front and a lean-to at the rear.

Right from Union St. on State St.

21. *Comfort Starr House* (*private*), 138 State St., is one of the oldest frame houses in the State and one of the few remaining homes of the 'Signers' who first settled Guilford. Built by Henry Kingsnorth in 1645–46 and sold to Comfort Starr in 1694, this house retains most of its primitive features, including the five-window front and plain doorway, the stone chimney, the gable overhang, and the awkward roof-line formed by the lean-to added at the rear. The position of this house indicates that in Guilford and the larger communities the usual 17th-century rule of having a house face the south did not always prevail.

Points of Interest in Environs:

Captain Lee House, 0.3 *m.*; Leete Homestead, Leete's Island, 4 *m.*; Sachem's Head, 4.8 *m.* (*see Side Tour from Tour* 1); old churches, North Guilford, 6.5 *m.*; old settlement of Nut Plains, 2.7 *m.*; Thimble Islands, 4.5 *m.* (*see Tour 1F*).

HARTFORD

City: Alt. 40, pop. 164,072, inc. 1784.

Railroad Station: Hartford Station, Union Place and Asylum Ave., for N.Y., N.H. & H. R.R.

Airports: Rentschler Field, 400 Main St., East Hartford, 3¾ m. from center, taxi fare $1.05, time 20 min.; American Airlines, Newark–Boston route, 2 stops each way daily, 3 stops each way on summer schedule, Brainard Field (municipally owned), Aviation Rd. at Maxim Rd., 2 m. S. of center, taxi fare 60¢, time 10 min.; United Airlines, Seaplane Dock.

Taxis: 35¢ first mile, 25¢ each additional mile, $2 per hour, waiting time; $3 per hour, traveling in city; $4 per hour, traveling outside city.

Accommodations: Five hotels.

Information Service: Travelers' Aid, Railroad Station, Union Place; Information Desk, Municipal Bldg., Main St.; Hartford Chamber of Commerce, 805 Main St.; Hartford Better Business Bureau, 190 Trumbull St.; Business & Technical Branch, Hartford Public Library, 730 Main St.; Conn. Motor Club, Heublein Hotel, 180 Wells St.

Boat Landing: Hartford Yacht Club, E. bank of Connecticut River, below Bulkeley Memorial Bridge.

Auditoriums: Horace Bushnell Memorial Hall, 166 Capitol Ave. (3227 seats); Foot Guard Armory, 165 High St. (1500 seats); Avery Memorial Hall, 35 Prospect St.; State Armory, Broad St. and Capitol Ave. (10,000 seats).

Recreation: Tennis courts in city parks, for use after 4 P.M. weekdays or any time Sundays, 5¢ per hour per player, obtain permit at municipal building.

Golf: Keney Park, Barbour St. and Windsor Ave., 25¢ nine holes, $15.00 yearly membership, 18-hole course; Goodwin Park, Maple Ave., 15¢ nine holes, $10.00 yearly membership, 18-hole course.

Swimming: Colt Park Pool; Riverside Park Pool.

Bridle Paths: Keney Park.

Annual Events: Community Sing, Christmas Eve, in front of Hartford Times Bldg., Prospect St.; Rose Week, Elizabeth Park, June, date varies; Conn. State Teachers Association Convention, Bushnell Memorial, 3d Friday in October; Gladiola Show, 3d week in August, Old State House, under auspices of Conn. Gladiola Society; Flower Show, Conn. Horticultural Society, June, Old State

House; Shrine Circus, State Armory, April; Sportsmen's Show, February, State Armory; Home Progress Exposition, March, State Armory; Automobile Show, November, State Armory; Radio Exhibition, October, Foot Guard Armory; Hartford County Food Exhibit, September, State Armory; Conn. Pomological Show, Women's Club, Broad St., December; Transportation Dinner, C. of C., February, Hotel Bond; Lawn Bowling Tournament, August, Elizabeth Park; Opera, at Bushnell Memorial, with nationally known opera companies, twice yearly, either December and February, or January and March.

HARTFORD, the State Capital and the largest city in the State, is a financial-industrial center on the west bank of the Connecticut River. The lofty Travelers' Tower, New England's tallest structure, dominates the serrated skyline, reaching 527 feet into the blue. The gilded dome of the State Capitol, rising above the trees of Bushnell Park, the tower of Trinity Chapel, and the cupola of the Ætna Building also furnish landmarks for aviators. Through the center of the city meanders the narrow, muddy Park River, but the Connecticut River to the east is hidden behind dikes and the railway embankment.

On a gently rolling plain that gradually rises to merge with the foothills of distant mountains, retaining much of the past in the older sections and an almost cosmopolitan sophistication in the modern shopping district, Hartford offers many contrasts. The group of State and county buildings at the crest of the slight rise known as Capitol Hill is one section of national interest. The insurance capitols in the business district, and westward on the edge of the residential area, show a different aspect of Hartford life. To the north, along Main Street, many ultra-modern department stores reflect the prosperity of the city. In a central triangular plot on Main Street is the handsome Old State House. Southward, on the main thoroughfare, the imposing pink granite Morgan Memorial reminds the visitor that Hartford is the birth and burial place of J. Pierpont Morgan and his ancestors. The First, or Center Church building recalls the life of the Reverend Thomas Hooker (1586–1647), its first pastor, who is credited with the liberal ideas embodied in Connecticut's Fundamental Orders of 1639.

Main Street is only forty feet above sea level; Front Street is much lower, and only Capitol Hill and points to the westward are higher than the main thoroughfare. Ever conscious of the flood hazard, the city has built an extensive system of dikes along the lower meadows and around the older factory buildings, and plans have been made for a loftier highway bridge. The better residential sections are farther back from the river.

Hartford has rather distinct foreign residential areas. Front Street, along the river, removed barely enough to escape the ordinary freshets, has an Italian population closely knit and clannish. Windsor Avenue, to the northward, is the quarter where Hartford's Negroes reside. Park Street, to the southwest, is the factory section where Slavs flock together in dingy tenements. On Albany and Blue Hills Avenues, to the northwest, lives most of Hartford's Jewish population, which has enormously increased, until the city has a proportionately larger number of Jews than any other American community except New York or Atlantic City. This growth, the result of an influx between the years 1920 to 1930, is the only noticeable racial trend other than a gradual elimination of the full native parentage group, which has decreased to twenty-eight per cent.

Hartford is the hub of many excellent highways radiating in all directions to the important cities of this and adjacent States. Many of the employees of Hartford's insurance offices and industrial plants are commuters from near-by towns, and highways are crowded during business hours.

Fully twenty-two per cent, or 2700 acres, of the total area of the city is in municipal parks or squares. A city planning commission has functioned in Hartford since 1907, but even before that date careful attention was given to the location of buildings and layout of streets. Approaching the city from any direction, visitors are impressed with the orderliness and width of the main arteries of traffic.

Known chiefly as an insurance center because of the concentration of insurance companies which outnumber those of any other city in the world, Hartford is also an important tobacco and agricultural market. Crops valued at $15,000,000 annually clear through the city. The agricultural influence is also conspicuous during the sessions of the General Assembly when rural gentry from the 169 towns of Connecticut mingle with salesmen in hotel lobbies, or gather in front of shop windows to gaze at the latest styles.

The hotels are crowded during the many conventions, flower, or sports shows held here. Military balls are gay affairs because this is the home city of the 1st Company, Governor's Foot Guard and the ancient Putnam Phalanx. Bearskin shakoes, brilliant uniforms, even the deep drums of Colonial days, are familiar accouterment when the old military organizations pass in review on Inauguration Day.

Hartford has distinct sounds, too. The constant, deep-throated drone of powerful motors and the whir of spinning propellers are forever rising above the street noises. A fleet of army planes roars in from the west for the installation of new motors; a combat ship solos topside, hanging to the highest fleecy cloud; or a 'flying laboratory' grumbles under a test load before attempting to span distant oceans. Motors, ships, variable pitch propellers have all been developed by Hartford manufacturers now serving world markets from their plants just across the broad Connecticut River. The river, ever ready to spread over the lowlands and inundate Hartford's own aviation field, has forced this concentration of the aircraft industry out of the metropolis itself.

The stream has ceased to be important in the commercial life of the city, except for incoming barges, tankers, and coal carriers. Pleasure craft have their anchorage overstream by the left bank, but a hucksters' market operates almost on the river level on Commerce Street, where now rotting steamboat docks were once piled with incoming and outgoing freight.

As a cultural center Hartford has contributed much to the Nation. J. Pierpont Morgan was internationally known as a patron of the arts. Samuel Clemens, Noah Webster, Harriet Beecher Stowe, Charles Dudley Warner, and William Gillette have all claimed Hartford as their home. More than one hundred periodicals were established in the city, among them *The Children's Magazine* (1789), the first juvenile periodical in America. The *Hartford Courant* dates back to 1764, and the *Hartford Times* first went on the street in 1817. Amelia Simmons wrote, and Hudson and Goodwin of Hartford printed, America's first cook book (forty-six pages) in 1796.

The slogan '45 minutes in Havana' was not coined in the Cuban city, but in a Yankee cigar factory here. Tobacco sorting, inspecting, and packing is an important industry, and there is constant competition during the tobacco season between the mechanical industries and the warehouses for the limited supply of female help available after the insurance firms have had their choice. A larger number of female employees is gainfully employed in Hartford than in any other city in Connecticut (23,608). The typewriter plants also furnish employment to many women. Other Hartford industries produce electrical equipment, machinery, precision tools, gold leaf, firearms, printing, screws, castings, tools and dies, coffins, taps, artificial limbs, millwork, forgings, lithography, saddlery, blowers, bedsprings, and pool tables.

Hartford mechanics gave the world the first standard inch when, in 1885, Pratt and Whitney Company perfected a standard measuring machine accurate to one one-hundred-thousandth of an inch. The first pneumatic tires ever built in America came from a Hartford plant in 1894, and Colt's, 'The Arm of Law and Order,' has carried a local trademark to the ends of the earth.

A modern electric generating plant occupies almost the exact spot where the first white men landed in Hartford. In 1633, Jacob van Curler, under orders from the Governor of New Amsterdam (Wouter van Twiller), built a fort and mounted two guns at 'Suckiage.' The Dutch called it 'The House of Hope,' but today the site is known as Dutch Point.

The first permanent settlement was made by the English in 1635 when John Steel and sixty pioneers from Newtowne (Cambridge, Mass.) settled here in October, 1635, followed by the Reverend Thomas Hooker and his company in the spring of 1636. The settlement was named in 1637, from Hartford in England. The General Court of the Bay Colony met to consider the authorization of town governments in the Plantation of Connecticut on October 10, 1639, and laid down definite rulings on April 9, 1640. However, when the colonists discovered that they were no longer within the jurisdiction of Massachusetts, representatives of the river settlements met at Hartford to draw up a plan of government.

Connecticut's Fundamental Orders, said to have been the constitution known to history that created a government, setting forth the radical principle that 'the foundation of authority is in the free consent of the people,' was written in Hartford by Roger Ludlow and adopted here by representatives of the River Towns on January 14, 1639.

Hartford County was organized in 1665, but the city and town were not incorporated until the May session of the General Assembly in 1784, although town meetings and town courts were held and community action taken in the usual manner of the New England town.

The British proved to be better colonizers than the Dutch, and their Windsor, Wethersfield, and Hartford settlements cut off the Dutch trade with the Indians to such an extent that the garrison finally left the fort unoccupied. The Colonial Court met in 1654 and called on Captain John Underhill to occupy the fort in the name of England, a procedure accomplished without firing a shot. The English thereupon posted notices on the doors of 'The House of Hope' and the Dutch were seen no more along the river.

By 1662, the Hartford Colony comprised fourteen towns; it was united with the six New Haven settlements in 1665, and, by decree of the Connecticut General Court, the legislature was ordered to meet in Hartford. For the sake of convenience this agreement was not adhered to, but sessions were held alternately in New Haven and Hartford (both maintaining State Houses) until 1875, when all sessions were held in Hartford.

The charter granted by King Charles II on April 26, 1662, made the Colony independent. The Great Seal was added to the document in May, 1662. John Winthrop, Jr., forwarded it to Connecticut, where it was read to the freemen of Hartford on October 9, 1662. Sir Edmund Andros, appointed Governor of all New England Colonies in 1687, endeavored to induce Connecticut to relinquish its liberal charter. Failing in this, he arrived in Hartford with an armed escort, October 31, 1687, conferred with all officials, read his commission aloud, and formally took office. When Andros demanded the charter, it was brought forth, but the lights were suddenly extinguished and, when the candles were relighted, the charter had vanished. Joseph Wadsworth had secreted the parchment in the hollow of an oak tree on the property of Samuel Wyllys, which thereafter was known as the 'Charter Oak.'

The Andros government lasted only two years and Connecticut returned to its charter form of government. The charter was kept by Wadsworth until May, 1715. About 1817, the wife of one of the keepers of the document is reported to have allowed a neighbor to cut the lining for a bonnet from the history-making parchment. A portion of the charter was saved and can be seen in the rooms of the Connecticut Historical Society in Hartford. The historical duplicate of the original is preserved in a special safe in the Memorial Hall of the State Library. The wood of the Charter Oak has been made into chairs, gavels, and other odd articles now in museums and private collections. A tablet marks the spot where the great tree formerly grew; the name 'Charter Oak' has been freely used on all manner of places and articles, from soft drinks and cigars to a harness-racing track where Grand Circuit horses once pounded down the homestretch, but where poultrymen now auction off eggs. The Harvester made records at Charter Oak Park; Pop Geers drove there against Tommy Murphy and Walter Cox; men and animals as sturdy as the great tree itself fought it out for 'The Charter Oak' or 'The Nutmeg' purses. Hartford should have copyrighted the name. The proceeds would have paid for a forest of oaks.

There is no record of any serious trouble with the Indians in or near Hartford. John Eliot came to preach to the Podunks in 1657, translated the Bible into their language, but made little progress in aboriginal soul-saving. The Indians answered his pleas with: 'No, you have taken away our lands, and now you wish to make us a race of slaves.'

Hartford's fertile meadows produced bumper crops and an early effort was made to control crops and planting. Each landholder was ordered by the town authorities to plant the teaspoonful of flaxseed given him. When John Winthrop, Jr., went to England to secure the charter, his passage was paid with five hundred bushels of wheat and three hundred bushels of peas.

Hartford citizenry took an active part in the Revolutionary War, but there is no record of any outstanding accomplishment by any one individual. The expedition against Fort Ticonderoga was planned in Hartford by Silas Deane, Samuel Holden Parsons, and Colonel Samuel Wyllys, but the capture was accomplished by a lad from Roxbury named Ethan Allen, accompanied by Seth Warner and Remember Baker. The little settlement was already showing signs of becoming a financial and cultural center, concerned more with politics and the social side of war. The city welcomed George Washington in June of 1775 when he was on his way to take command of the Continental Army at Cambridge. Major Thomas Y. Seymour of Hartford convoyed General Burgoyne to Boston after the surrender.

Shipping grew to its zenith in the eighteenth century, and a fleet of vessels plied between Hartford and English, Mediterranean, and West Indian ports. The War of 1812 caused a depression in shipping circles from which the water-borne commerce was never to recover.

Hartford was a center of anti-slavery propaganda and, after the beginning of the Civil War in 1861, its banks lent the Governor of Connecticut half a million dollars to finance the recruiting and equipment of a regiment.

Following the Civil War most of Hartford's history concerns industry and the development of machinery and transportation. As early as 1876, the Hartford Fire Department purchased and operated a steam-propelled fire engine with great success and only minor damage to the nerves of drivers of horse-drawn vehicles. These pieces of fire-fighting equipment remained in service for nearly fifty years and proved an excellent investment for the city.

In 1878, Colonel A. A. Pope built and popularized the Columbia bicycle, which did not differ greatly from the British 'Ordinary' formerly imported by Colonel Pope. The development of the pneumatic tire in 1889, together with the drop-frame machine for lady riders (who were not called 'ladies' after their first ride in public), boomed the business. Pope employed five hundred workers in 1888 and had thirty-eight hundred on his payroll in 1900.

Colonel Pope built and marketed a high-priced vehicle known as the Columbia Electric Phaëton, in 1907. One of these cars is still (1937) in operation in Hartford, driven by a very conservative person who looks with suspicion on the internal combustion motors of the present day. The Pope factory switched from electric-driven cars to gas-propelled vehicles, but the Pope-Hartford motorcar was a short-lived venture in quality automotive history.

In the early 1890's the Whitney Steam Car was seen on the streets of Hartford. F. W. Manross startled the motor world in 1898 when he drove a Winton from Forestville to Hartford, a distance of eighteen miles, in fifty-five minutes. Motors became such a traffic problem in 1901 that the State enforced motor laws, limiting speed to fifteen miles an hour in the open country and to twelve miles within the limits of towns and villages.

The United States Rubber Company built tires in the old Hartford Rubber Works, but closed the plant after the World War, when local labor became too costly. Pipe organs were once an important Hartford product, and the Austin Organ Company has been credited with many important developments in organ manufacturing, such as the 'Austin Universal Air Chest' for the great cathedral instruments such as the Cyrus H. K. Curtis Organ in the Public Ledger Auditorium, Philadelphia, Pennsylvania, often claimed to be the largest organ in the world, having four manuals and two hundred and eighty-three stops.

Aircraft motors were developed by the Pratt and Whitney plant and Hartford forged ahead in that line, hoping to hold its well-earned lead over lesser competitors. The concentration of aircraft manufacturing plants across the stream in East Hartford promises well for the future of the Insurance City as a center of aviation.

The most unusual industry in Hartford today is gold-beating. Marcus Bull started the work prior to 1819, as a pioneer in the gold-beating profession. Dentists patronized him and, in 1866, John M. Ney took over sole control of the business. The company is still doing a modest business, and there are interesting stories about its work. The gold leaf of the dome of the State Capitol (440 square feet of it) was beaten in Hartford by this concern. A Sioux warrior, killed in a Wyoming mail robbery, was found to have all the buttons and metal on his clothing covered with Ney's gold leaf. During the Civil War, the Confederacy was so in need of gold that books with leaves of the Ney product were smuggled in from Havana. Gold leaf takes its name from the fact that it is sold in books.

Insurance was an outgrowth of the banks which grew with early trade and commerce at this river port of entry. Marine insurance was written to cover shipping hazards, but the shifting of commerce to more favorable ports resulted in a trend from marine insurance coverage to fire risks, and, eventually, to the accident, life, and liability fields. Legislation in Connecticut has been favorable to the growth of this business and today forty-four companies have home offices in Hartford, and four hundred and fifty licensed firms or benefit societies are represented here.

The growth of the insurance industry in Hartford dates from February 8, 1794, when a fire insurance policy was issued by the Hartford Fire Insurance Company. The present company of that name was chartered in 1810.

The dramatic manner in which Eliphalet Terry arrived at the scene of the great New York fire, in 1835, and, near the smoldering ruins of some seven hundred buildings, is reported to have mounted a soapbox and assured all of his policy-holders that they would get their money, established public confidence in the firm's integrity. Terry's share of the total $20,000,000 loss was only $64,973.34, but the pay-off was handled in such a dramatic manner that an immediate rush of business came to the Hartford companies. Weathering the Chicago, Boston, Jacksonville, and Baltimore fires successfully, Hartford companies next met a severe test in the San Francisco disaster of 1906 when they paid a total of $15,000,000 in claims.

The first boiler insurance was issued in June, 1866, by the Hartford Steam Boiler Insurance and Inspection Company. The first American automobile insurance was also written in Hartford, February 1, 1898, for a $5000–$10,000 coverage, at a premium of only $11.25.

Travelers, Ætna, Phoenix, Hartford Fire, and Connecticut Mutual are leading companies operating from Hartford, and their claims paid to December 31, 1935, total about six and one-half billion dollars.

TOUR 1

W. from Washington Ave. on Capitol Ave.

1. The *State Capitol* overlooks the city from the landscaped crest of Capitol Hill, with other State buildings standing at a respectful distance to the south, and Bushnell Park sloping down to the business district on the north. The marble and granite structure, designed by Richard Upjohn in 1878, was erected at a cost of $2,532,524.43. The architecture might be considered Gothic from the profusion of crockets, finials, and niches that rise above its somewhat pointed arches to the elongated dome; but it is exuberant and eclectic in spirit, and does not confine itself to the historical precedents of any one style. The mass of the building is dignified and impressive. Two lofty, five-story wings, rising at the east and west façades of the central main building, culminate in the

twelve-sided gilded dome, topped with a winged figure of the 'Genius of Connecticut' by Randolph Rogers. The well-composed exterior is of modified Venetian and French Gothic style with corner towers.

On the first floor are offices, and in the lobbies the battle flags of Connecticut troops in different wars, Lafayette's army cot, the tombstone of Israel Putnam, and a plaster model of the statue on the dome. On the stairway to the House of Representatives, on the mezzanine floor, are copies of the statues around the dome. The second floor contains the offices of Governor, Secretary of State, the legislative halls, and the rooms used for hearings. The presiding officer's chair in the Senate is hand-

---

HARTFORD. POINTS OF INTEREST

1. State Capitol
2. Bushnell Park
3. Equestrian Statue of Lafayette
4. State Office Building
5. State Library and Supreme Court Building
6. Timothy Steele House
7. County Building
8. Bushnell Memorial Hall
9. Phoenix Mutual Life Insurance Company Building
10. Butler McCook Homestead
11. South Congregational Church
12. Charter Oak Memorial
13. Municipal Building
14. Burial Ground
15. First Church of Christ
16. Morgan Memorial Art Galleries
17. Wadsworth Atheneum
18. Avery Memorial Art Museum
19. Hunt Memorial
20. Daniel Wadsworth Barn
21. Hartford Steam Boiler Inspection and Insurance Company Building
22. Travelers' Insurance Company Buildings
23. Site of Oliver Ellsworth House
24. Old State House
25. Hartford Courant Offices
26. Christ Church Cathedral
27. Federal Building, Post Office and U.S. Court House
28. Connecticut Mutual Life Insurance Company Building
29. Hartford Fire Insurance Company Building
30. State Armory
31. Caledonia Insurance Company Building
32. Site of the George Catlin House
33. Ætna Life Insurance Company Building
34. St. Joseph's Cathedral
35. Harriet Beecher Stowe House
36. Charles Dudley Warner House
37. William Gillette House
38. John Hooker House
39. Katherine Hepburn's Birthplace
40. Mark Twain's House and Memorial Library
41. Children's Museum of Hartford
42. Hartford Seminary Foundation
43. Elizabeth Park
44. Hartford School of Music
45. Keney Memorial Tower
46. St. Justin's Roman Catholic Church
47. Connecticut Institute for the Blind
48. Keney Park
49. Fuller Brush Company Building
50. Bulkeley Memorial Bridge
51. Pratt and Whitney Manufacturing Company Plant
52. Pope Park
53. Trinity College
54. Colt's Patent Fire Arms Manufacturing Company Plant
55. Colt Park
56. Goodwin Park
57. Royal Typewriter Company Plant
58. Underwood Elliot Fisher Company Plant

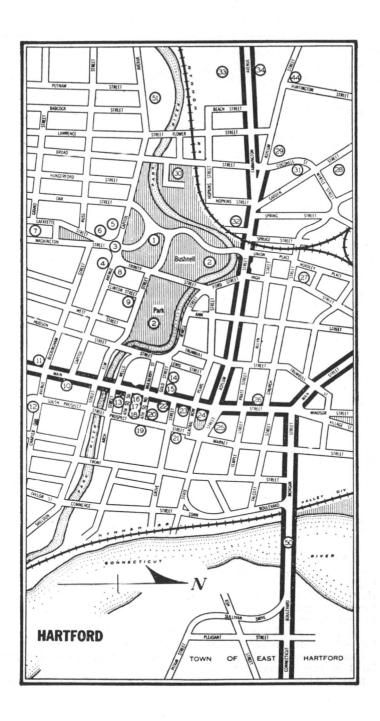

HARTFORD

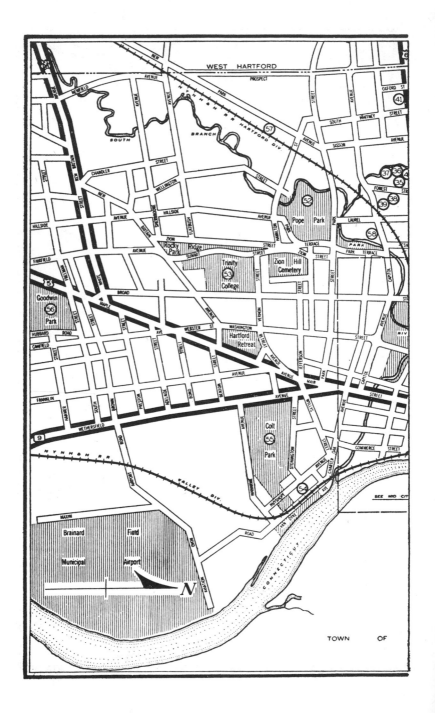

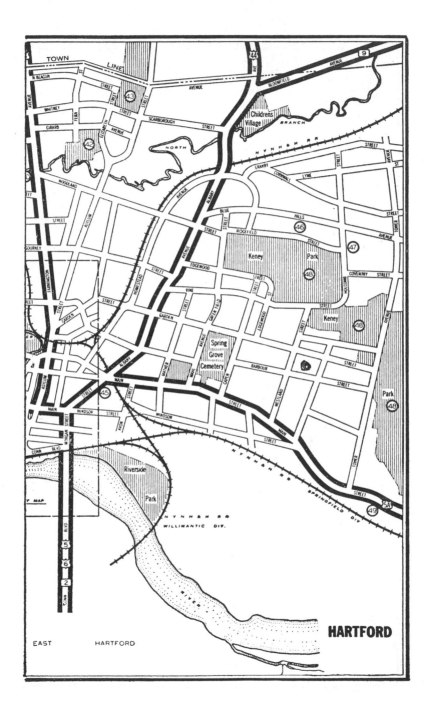

HARTFORD

carved from the Charter Oak. The Attorney General has offices on the third floor, and the fourth floor is devoted to committee rooms. From the *Dome* (*open* 11 *and* 3.30) is a magnificent view of the city and surrounding countryside.

The approach to the Capitol from the east passes the bronze equestrian *Lafayette Statue*, the ugly 13-inch seacoast mortar used at the siege of Petersburg by the 1st Connecticut Heavy Artillery and known as *The Petersburg Express*, a *Statue of Governor Richard D. Hubbard*, and the *Colonel Thomas Knowlton Statue*, erected in honor of the officer in direct command of Connecticut troops at Bunker Hill, the commander of Knowlton's Rangers (*see Tour 3, ASHFORD*).

E. from Capitol Grounds into Bushnell Park.

2. *Bushnell Park* (1853), between the Capitol Grounds, Trinity, Ford, and Asylum Sts. (41.27 acres), was purchased by the city of Hartford in 1853, from Horace Bushnell, for whom the park is named. The Park River, winding along the eastern, northern, and western boundaries, increases the beauty of the tree-lined walks, flower-beds, shrubbery, lily pond, Music Shell, and children's playground. The most pretentious statuary group here is the *Corning Memorial Fountain*, near the north end (Asylum St.) of the park by the river, erected in 1899 by John J. Corning, as a tribute to his father. Designed by Massey Rhind, the fountain has a granite basin and column about which stand the full-sized figures of four Indian maidens and four braves. *The Spanish War Memorial*, at the corner of Trinity and Elm Sts., is the work of the Windsor sculptor, Evelyn Beatrice Longman Batchelder. Its massive central figure of golden bronze represents Columbia with an uplifted torch above bas-relief figures of a soldier and sailor on either side. The *Soldiers' and Sailors' Memorial Arch*, at Trinity St. approach to the Capitol, was designed by Sylvester Bissell in 1885. A medieval arch, 30 feet wide, supported by free-stone round towers at either end, each over 100 feet high and 63 feet in circumference, the structure is enlivened by a terra-cotta frieze representing Civil War soldiers in action. Among other statues in the park are the *Andersonville Prison Boy*, a bronze memorial by Bela Lyon Pratt, to Northern soldiers who died in Southern prisons during the Civil War; the tall bronze *Statue of General Israel Putnam*, just west of Trinity St.; and in the eastern section of the park, a *Statue of Dr. Horace Wells*, the discoverer of the use of nitrous oxide gas as anesthesia; and the *Dahlgren Guns*, taken from the warship 'Hartford.'

S. from Bushnell Park on Trinity St.; R. on Capitol Ave.

3. The *Equestrian Statue of Lafayette*, center of Capitol Ave., at the north end of Washington St., was cast from the plaster model of the original by Paul W. Bartlett, the gift of American school children to the city of Paris.

4. The *State Office Building*, Capitol Ave. (L), between Washington and West Sts., erected in 1930–31, is of modern design. Bronze plaques between the floors are in contrast to the limestone walls; a course :of

heavy dentils lines the cornice below the top floor. J. Henry Miller, Inc. was the architect. The offices of various State departments are housed here.

5. The *State Library and Supreme Court Building*, opposite the Capitol, on Capitol Ave., between Lafayette and Oak Sts., was built in 1910 from designs by Donn Barber. It is of Italian Renaissance design, a style popularized for public buildings by the great expositions, but is here treated with a special vigor and nobility of proportions. An imposing entrance pavilion, with Roman columns, arched doorways, and a heavy superstructure, is flanked with two great sculptural groups over a projecting pair of columns at each end. A long broad flight of steps completes the composition.

The *State Library* (*open weekdays* 9–5), in the east wing of the building, combines the State law, legislative, war, and archives libraries, and is the depository of public records and official publications, and many historical and genealogical collections pertaining to towns, States, the United States, and the British Empire.

The *Connecticut Supreme Court* occupies the west wing in which is Albert Herter's mural, 'Signing of the Colonial Orders.'

Memorial Hall, in the south wing, facing the main entrance, houses some of the State's most cherished relics, among them the Gilbert Stuart 'Portrait of George Washington,' the historical duplicate of the original charter of 1662, signed by Charles II, and complete except for the loss of its green wax seal, portraits of Connecticut governors, the table on which Lincoln signed the Emancipation Proclamation, and the *Mitchelson Collection* of coins and medals.

Return on Capitol Ave.; R. on Lafayette St.

6. The *Timothy Steele House* (*private*), 91 Lafayette St., behind the library and erected in 1715, is the oldest building in Hartford. Its T-shaped chimney rises behind a roof that was originally salt-box.

L. from Lafayette St. on Russ St.; R. on Washington St.

7. *County Building*, 95 Washington St., rising from a low stone terrace, is a limestone building designed in a modified Roman style by Paul P. Cret of Philadelphia, and Smith and Bassette of Hartford. It was completed in 1929. The austerity of the façade, with its flat columns and heavy entablature, is relieved by a bas-relief in the center of the latter, by grilles between the columns, and by four large Roman votive urns. Unlike the usual building of its type, it has only a center entrance to its long hall. *Three Murals* by J. R. L. St. Hubert, a French artist, adorn the main lobby, and the corridor ceilings are decorated with Homeric scenes.

Return on Washington St.; R. on Capitol Ave.

8. *Bushnell Memorial Hall*, 166 Capitol Ave. at Trinity St., a red-brick and limestone building designed by Harvey Corbett, was erected in 1930 by members of the family of Dr. Horace Bushnell, D.D., and contains a

large auditorium (seating capacity 3227). This building has provided Hartford with a perennial topic of discussion. Neither conservative nor modern, its architecture fails to achieve distinction except as a hybrid. The Capitol Ave. façade, taken by itself, is a conservative rendering of old forms, although the Bulfinch-inspired cupola bears little relation to the big foyer building devoted to the many secondary purposes of a community building. The gable end of the building, toward Capitol Ave., with its raised pediment and unevenly spaced Ionic columns, is distinctive, but loses force from the long mass of the auditorium stretching down Trinity St.

The interior of this hall, as large as the Metropolitan Opera House in New York, is a surprise, a bizarre medley of gold leaf and barbaric design. The stage is rimmed in concentric circles of gilt ornament — conventionalized bossed stars caught in a seeming cobweb of cross-lines; and finally, lifted above the center of the auditorium, a zodiacal composition gleams from a field of stars. Torchlike, indirect lighting at the sides makes it all shine in fantastic brilliance, which dims gradually to a sort of moonlight before the curtain goes up. It has a four-manual organ, and complete stage equipment. Metropolitan operas, as well as a series of concerts, are produced here every year. A smaller hall, the Colonial Room, seating 300, is available for chamber music.

L. from Capitol Ave. on Clinton St.

9. *Phoenix Mutual Life Insurance Company Building*, 79 Elm St., at Clinton St. (1917), is a 7-story, dark green ornamental brick structure with inlaid designs of red and blue tile, and a red, Spanish tile roof. Chartered in June, 1851, as the American Temperance Life Insurance Company, insuring only those who totally abstained from alcoholic beverages, the firm in 1861 changed its name and policies, and is reputed to be the first insurance company in this country to have conducted a school for insurance agents.

Return on Clinton St.; L. on Capitol Ave.; L. on Main St.

10. The *Butler McCook Homestead* (*private*), 396 Main St., is a two-and-a-half-story, central-hall, end-chimney house with four yellow, fluted columns at the entrance, built about 1782. Dr. McCook, the present occupant and great-grandson of the builder, has in his possession his doctor-ancestor's record books, antiquated scales, and the old mortar and pestle used for preparing drugs. This is the ancestral home of the 'fighting McCooks,' celebrated in the book of that name.

11. *South Congregational Church*, 307 Main St., at Buckingham St., was organized in 1670 and the present church building, of red brick with wooden trim, was built in 1827. While not of the exquisite proportions of New Haven's churches, it has a restrained Georgian sophistication of spirit that is very pleasing. Three fan-lighted doors in the projecting pediment are separated by composite columns. The steeple rises in several stages, the lowest of brick with clock faces on three sides.

TOWN AND COUNTRY

THE average Connecticut city is an overgrown town with little evidence of planning beyond the central square. Irregular skylines show clusters of stacks, church spires, and an occasional tall building rising above the roof-tops of the more ordinary structures. Shade trees are evident everywhere.

The township is an important political and social subdivision in the State. Every city retains certain town officers and the old town boundaries. In the snug conservatism of the smaller towns, the Yankee 'winds up the world.' The church, a general store, sometimes a pre-Revolutionary inn, the town hall, a Soldiers' Monument, and the village Green form a center from which radiate shady streets lined with comfortable frame dwellings, painted white with green trim. The picket fence is vanishing, but lilac bushes mark the old fence lines. Back-yard gardens bloom from spring until early fall, and the tiger lily and lily-of-the-valley hug the foundation stones of modest houses. The village barn is now a garage, and gayly painted gasoline pumps stand in front of the Post Office. In many of these small towns the socio-economic scheme of things has changed but little since the last century.

NA LIFE INSURANCE COMPANY, HARTFORD

THE STATE CAPITOL, HARTFORD

OLD STATE HOUSE, HARTFORD

OLD ACADEMY, BRANFORD

MENT KILN, WOODBRIDGE

ELY HOMESTEAD, KILLINGWORTH

IN SOUTH BRITAIN

TOWN HALL, SALISI

NEW HAVEN GREEN

HARTFORD SKY LINE

RAILROAD STATION, WATERBURY

OLD IRON FURNACE, ROXBURY

WORLD WAR MEMORIAL, NEW BRITAIN

T'S BRIDGE, WEST CORNWALL

OLD NEWGATE PRISON, EAST GRANBY

STANTON STORE, CLINTON

L. from Main St. on Charter Oak Ave.

12. *Charter Oak Memorial* (1906), at the junction of Charter Oak Ave. and Charter Oak Place, a large granite column, a gift of the Society of Colonial Dames, bears this inscription: 'Near this spot stood the Charter Oak, known in the history of the Colony of Connecticut, as the hiding place of the Charter, October 31, 1687.' The tree was 33 feet in circumference when it was blown down in 1856. Mark Twain mentioned that he had seen 'a walking-stick, dog collar, needle-case, three-legged stool, bootjack, dinner table, tenpin alley, toothpick, and enough Charter Oak to build a plank road from Hartford to Salt Lake City.'

TOUR 2

N. from Arch on Main St.

13. *Municipal Building*, 550 Main St., a four-story stone structure in the French Renaissance style, was designed by Davis and Brooks, local architects, in 1915. Rich and sophisticated, its style more delicate and elaborate toward the upper stories, with its arched windows, Corinthian columns and pilasters, it is an imposing structure.

L. from Main St. on Wells St.; R. on Gold St.

14. *Burial Ground*, Gold St. (L), next to Center Church House, is the oldest cemetery in Hartford, used from 1640 to 1803. One and one-third acres are enclosed by a high, block, iron fence, with two red-brick ports at each side of the gate bearing inscribed tablets. Many of the early governors of Connecticut are buried here.

R. from Gold Street on Main St.

15. *First Church of Christ* (Center Congregational) (1807), 675 Main St., is the oldest ecclesiastical society in the State (1632). The building dates from the early days when experiments in design were being made. The architecture of Hartford, influenced by that of Boston, never quite fitted into the Connecticut style. The unusual features of this building are the squared fronts disguising the pediments and the profusion of urns and classical ornamentation. The steeple, too, is unusually tall and heavy, with four wooden sections surmounting the square brick tower which has clocks in all four faces. It is more elaborate, but not so perfectly proportioned as the churches on the Green at New Haven. Seven of the stained-glass windows came from England. One of them, called the 'Pastor's Window,' was installed in memory of Thomas Hooker, first pastor of the church.

16. *Morgan Memorial* (temporarily closed to the public), 590 Main St., built in 1910 of Tennessee marble from the plans of Benjamin Wistar Morris, was donated to the city by J. Pierpont Morgan as a memorial to his father, a former Hartford merchant. The square Gothic windows of

the first story are in contrast with the Renaissance pilasters, framing medallions in the windowless portion above. A carved head of Minerva in the keystone of the arched entrance and an ornate balustrade around the roof-line are the only conspicuous embellishments.

The Morgan Memorial (1910) is connected, through the Colt Memorial Wing, with the Wadsworth Atheneum. Designed by Benjamin Wistar Morris in rough granite with marble trim to harmonize with the buildings on either side, this memorial in Neo-Classic Italian Renaissance style, now housing paintings and objects of art from the Colt home 'Armsmear' and the *James B. Cone Collection of Firearms*, was provided through the bequest of Mrs. Elizabeth Colt, widow of Colonel Samuel Colt.

Return on Main St.

17. *Wadsworth Atheneum*, 624 Main St., covering one city block, was the first of a group of buildings, including the Colt Memorial Museum, 1910, the Avery Museum, 1934, and the Morgan Memorial, 1910. It was designed in 1842 by Ithiel Town in Gothic Revival style to house a gallery of fine arts, the public library, the Historical Society, and the Hartford Young Men's Institute. The Yale Library had just been done in a collegiate rendering of the style: this structure, somewhat reminiscent of a castle, with its turrets and machicolations, was to be more secular. Funds for the provision of this large Gothic creation of South Glastonbury granite were in the main donated by Daniel Wadsworth and added to by public subscription.

The *Hartford Public Library* (*open weekdays* 9-9) (1844), first floor of the Wadsworth Atheneum, has a collection of more than 208,000 volumes. Among these are about 4000 bound volumes of music, a collection of over 50,000 photographs, engravings, and reproductions, and 10,000 books printed in foreign languages.

The *Watkinson Reference Library* (*open weekdays* 9.30–5.30) (1857), in the east wing, second floor of the Wadsworth Atheneum, contains approximately 118,000 volumes of reference books. Among the priceless and important collections of this library, which was established in connection with the Connecticut Historical Society through the bequest of David Watkinson, a local merchant, are the *Trumbull-Prime Collection* of 1000 rare books including 200 incunabula (printed before 1500), a 58-line German Bible, believed to be the first illustrated Bible, and six copies of the *Nuernberg Chronicle*, printed in 1492, a library of American Linguistics, and the Trumbull Documents on the Indian language.

The *Connecticut Historical Society* (*open weekdays* 9.30–5.30), on the second floor of the Wadsworth Atheneum, is noted for its newspaper files and books on Connecticut history and genealogy. Besides numerous rare maps, manuscripts, and unbound pamphlets, the society has on display a portion of the original Connecticut Charter, Mark Twain's bicycle, Nathan Hale's Diary, two bricks from the Dutch fort on the site of Hartford, and Elder Brewster's sea chest, on which the Mayflower Compact was signed.

R. from Main St. on Atheneum Sq. N.

18. The *Avery Memorial Art Museum* (*open weekdays free*, 10–4, *Oct. — March;* 10–5, *April — Sept.; Sun. and holidays* 2–5), 25 Atheneum Sq. N., is a three-story structure of gleaming Tennessee marble, completed in 1934. Its Prospect St. façade is unadorned, except for four sculptured medallions designed in the conventionalized Greek style, wide fluted pilasters, and a bronze grilled door. Funds for this building, designed by Morris and O'Connor, in the modernistic style, were provided by the late Samuel P. Avery. Benjamin Wistar Morris designed the Morgan Memorial and the State Armory. Built around a central court in which stands a marble statue done by Pietro Francavilla about 1600, the museum is notable for its splendid indirect lighting effects. In rooms to the right of the main entrance are prints and water-colors including the work of such outstanding artists as Cézanne, Sargent, and Picasso; to the left of the entrance are three rooms containing the *Avery Collection* of European and Oriental objects of art. On the second floor is a notable collection of paintings including Copley's portrait of Mrs. Seymour Fort and several by Gilbert Stuart. In the Marine Room near the stairway, are paintings and models of ships. The rest of the second floor is devoted to the *Wallace Nutting Collection of Early American Furniture*, the gift of J. P. Morgan; the *Brainard Collection* of signs from early Connecticut inns; and the *Pitkin Collection* of pottery. In the third-floor galleries hang works by Goya, Tintoretto, Whistler, Veronese, Poussin, Greuze, Bellotto, Canaletto, Guardi, Strozzi, Giordano, Magnasco, Reni, Rosa, Daumier, Tiepolo, Longhi, Piero di Cosimo, Cranach, Largilliere, Murillo, David, and Degas; in addition there is a section reserved for the *Welch Collection* of works by William Gedney Bunce, one of Hartford's foremost artists, and for the *Diaghilew-Lifar Collection* of designs for the Russian Ballet. The auditorium is notable for the skillful suppression of all lines except the horizontal curves of the ceiling.

L. from Atheneum Sq. N., on Prospect St.

19. *Hunt Memorial* (*open free*, 9–5) (1897), 38 Prospect St., opposite Atheneum Sq. N., designed by McKim, Mead and White, is a three-story, red-brick building in modified Georgian style, given by Mrs. E. K. Hunt, in memory of her husband, Dr. Ebenezer K. Hunt, for use by the Hartford Medical Society. The library of the Medical Society is on the second floor and contains more than 17,000 books dealing with medicine and medical problems.

20. The *Daniel Wadsworth Barn*, built in the early 19th century, is at the rear of the Henry A. Perkins House, owned by the Hartford Public Library (*private*) (1843), 43 Prospect St.

21. *Hartford Steam Boiler Inspection and Insurance Company Building*, 56 Prospect St., cor. of Grove and Prospect Sts. was designed by Carl J. Malmfeldt. This three-story limestone building has the flat façade, square, plain windows, and fluted pilasters characteristic of many modern buildings, but with notable references to traditional ornament in the

scroll course between the stories, the diaper panels between the second-
and third-floor windows, and fluted triglyphs and circles beneath a row
of conventional dentils in the Prospect St. cornice.   This company wrote
the first boiler insurance policy in America in the year of its organization,
June, 1866.

L. from Prospect St. on Grove St.

22. *Travelers Insurance Company Buildings* (*tower open free weekdays
9–1.30, 2.30 to sunset*), 26 Grove St., three in number, form a single
architectural unit.   Designed by Donn Barber of New York, the building,
of pink Westerly granite (faced with a light brick on the courtyard side),
is the highest in New England (527 feet), its tower, rising from the 9th
story, topping the structure above the south wing to the height of 34
stories.   It is an architectural focal point in Hartford, a business capitol,
dwarfing even the old legislative capitol on the hill.   On the 17th and
18th stories is a loggia, and above the 20th, a recession in the long face
of the tower brings it into a square.   It is very effective seen from the
broader sides, but suffers from its narrowness seen from the east or west.
Above the pyramidal roof is a metal cupola, the lower portions serving as
an outlet for the smokestack, and the upper portions supporting a finial
with a cluster of metal balls.   The cupola is really a great lantern, 81 feet
high, constructed of copper, and covered with gold leaf.   A beacon here
consists of 36 400-watt projectors and 8 of 200-watt power.   The band
of white light cast skyward is visible for many miles.

A tablet on the wall of the Travelers Building states that here once
stood the Zachary Sanford Tavern, scene of many General Assembly
sessions and of the celebrated Charter hiding episode.   Radio Station
WTIC (*open*), owned by the insurance company, operates from the 6th
floor of this building.

The first American accident policy was written by the Travelers
in 1863.   It offered $1000 protection to James Bolter and covered only
the time he spent walking from the post office to his home.   During 1866
the Travelers offered accident tickets to passengers on train, ship, or
coach; the first aircraft liability and property damage insurance was
issued in 1919.   The company employs 4200 people.

R. from Grove St. on Main St.

23. *Site of Oliver Ellsworth House* (1790), 740 Main St., which was formerly a tavern and for a while the home of the famous jurist (*see WIND-
SOR*).

24. *Old State House* (1796), Main St. at Central Row, contrasts the
epoch-making architecture of the early Republic with such skyscraper
developments as its neighbor, the Travelers Tower.   It was designed by
Charles Bulfinch, the architect of the State House in Boston (1798).
The entrances, on the west toward Main St., and the original main
entrance on the east, are unpretentious doors in the substructure of
high enclosed porticoes.   The dominant feature is the arched windows
over the doors.   The balustrade, added in 1815, ties the whole together,

and the cupola, without which the design would seem unfinished, was added in 1827; the clock was installed in 1848. The wide pane'ed stair-case, with its elaborately turned balusters, rises on either side of the hall, joining in one and turning back on itself. On the landing is the Secretary of State's little office, outfitted by the Daughters of the American Revolution in period furniture and containing the famous, unsupported spiral staircase against the rounded north end. The Senate Chamber, at the south end upstairs, is elaborate with fluted pilasters (a combination of Ionic and Corinthian), and a false balustrade above them around the whole room. Two fireplaces, which look totally inadequate today, once heated the room from the side of the hall. The House of Representatives' Chamber, opposite, contains a paneled gallery sup-ported by fluted Ionic columns over the entrance doorway and the two fireplaces. Downstairs, under this chamber, is the Supreme Court Room. Fluted columns on paneled bases support the ceiling, and corresponding pilasters divide the window spaces on the three outer walls. Only Rhode Island, of the New England States, has an older State House, and nowhere is there a finer example of the civic architecture of the early Federal period.

R. from Main St. on Central Row.

L. from Central Row on American Row; L. on State St.

25. *Hartford Courant Offices*, 64–66 State St. This 5-story, red-brick build-ing houses one of the older daily newspapers in the United States, founded by Thomas Green, on October 29, 1764. The *Hartford Courant* was awarded the N. W. Ayer Cup in 1932, for having the best typographical appearance of any newspaper in the United States.

R. from State St. on Main St.

26. *Christ Church Cathedral* (Episcopal), at 955 Main St., cor. of Church St., is interesting as a Gothic Revival church built at a time (1829) when the Post-Colonial style of church architecture in Connecticut was reaching its peak. It is a dark, ornate building, neither as large nor as early as Trinity Church, New Haven (1814–15). The parish was or-ganized in 1762, and the church was declared a Cathedral in 1919.

L. from Main St. on Church St.

27. *Federal Building, Post Office* and *U.S. Court House* (1931), Church St. between High St., Foot Guard Place, and Hoadley Place, is a long modernistic structure of Indiana limestone. A square, heavy entablature rests on a series of pilasters, with elaborate grille work over the interven-ing windows. The façade would be monotonous if not broken by a long inscription and a central bas-relief of a youth on horseback passing the torch of life to another youth. Surmounting either end are huge bronze eagles with folded wings. Adams, Prentice, and Malmfeldt were the architects.

Church St. becomes Myrtle St.; R. from Myrtle St. on Garden St.

28. *Connecticut Mutual Life Insurance Company Building* (1926), 140 Garden St., cor. Myrtle and Collins Sts., houses the oldest life insurance

company in Connecticut, organized in 1846, and the sixth oldest in the country, noted for having fought against speculative types of insurance for many years.

Return on Garden St.; R. on Cogswell St.; R. on Asylum St.

29. *Hartford Fire Insurance Company Building* (1921), 690 Asylum St., between Summer and Collins Sts., Garden and Cogswell Sts., is one of the oldest insurance companies in the city and State, organized in 1810. Its portico of six columns and flat dome relieve the severity of its mass. It stands on the site of the American School for the Deaf, existent here from 1821 to 1921.

Return on Asylum St.; R. on Broad St.

30. *State Armory* (1909), Broad St. (R), on twelve and a half acres of ground bordering Bushnell Park, is the largest armory in the State, with quarters for thirteen units of the Connecticut National Guard, a divisional headquarters, and an auditorium that seats 10,000. This building stands just west of the Capitol where a railway roundhouse once stood.

Return on Broad St., which becomes Cogswell St.

31. The *Caledonia Insurance Company Building* (1936), Cogswell St., cor. of Garden St., is a branch of the oldest insurance company in Scotland. The structure, designed by Carl J. Malmfeldt, is of modified Georgian design. A bronze bas-relief, representing the company arms in the pediment, and slight flutings around the windows are the only ornamentation. The design of the building recalls the Leominster House in Dublin, which is reputed to have been the basis for the design of the White House in Washington.

R. from Cogswell St. on Garden St.; L. on Asylum St.; R. on Hurlburt St.

32. The *Site of the George Catlin House* (1820), 17 Hurlburt St. Here was the former home of Lydia Huntley Sigourney (Mrs. George Catlin, 1791–1865), Connecticut's famous poetess (*see Literature*), who was allegedly visited by every President in office during her lifetime with the exception of Washington and Polk.

TOUR 3

W. from Asylum St. on Farmington Ave.

33. The *Ætna Life Insurance Company Building*, 151 Farmington Ave., on 28 acres of landscaped grounds, at the geographical center of Hartford, is the most monumental of the city's insurance capitols (1929). It was designed by James Gamble Rogers, in a Georgian style. The building is approached by a semicircular courtyard which leads up to a colonnaded portico. Here the main building, six stories in height, is topped with a lofty cupola. The square cupola is designed with a high Greek pediment, and a New England belfry above it. The plan consists of two main wings

which cross the building like transepts, near the ends, and a larger one at the center, from which rises the tower and cupola. The Colonial lines are especially evident in the eighth floor.

The executive offices on the eighth floor are elaborately finished with teak floors and paneling taken from an old house in Torrington. They open on a roof garden. The hand-carved mahogany table in the directors' room once belonged to Jefferson. The total floor space is 769,000 square feet, so arranged that the building is a unified, though complicated plan, without the usual recourse to a skyscraper solution. The 250-foot belfry is illuminated at night.

34. *St. Joseph's Cathedral*, 150 Farmington Ave., a brownstone edifice, is opposite the Ætna Life Insurance building, and the center of the Roman Catholic Diocese of Connecticut.

L. from Farmington Ave. on Forest St.

35. *Harriet Beecher Stowe House* (*private*) (about 1870), 73 Forest St., a mid-Victorian gray-brick structure entered through a gabled porch, is famous as the home of Harriet Beecher Stowe, author of 'Uncle Tom's Cabin' (*see Literature*), who lived here during the last twenty-three years of her life (1873–96).

36. *Charles Dudley Warner House* (*private*) (1872), 57 Forest St., a red-brick structure with many gables and chimneys, was the home of the former literary editor of *Harper's Magazine*, who was often hailed as 'the greatest literary man of his day' (*see Literature*).

37. *William Gillette House* (*private*) (1830), 49 Forest St., was the home of the former U.S. Senator Francis Gillette and his noted son, the late William Gillette, Shakespearian actor.

38. The *John Hooker House* (*private*) (1857), 34 Forest St., a red-brick structure with yellow wooden trim, was a noted gathering place for literary celebrities during the lifetime of Mrs. Isabella Beecher Hooker, pioneer woman suffragist and the sister of Harriet Beecher Stowe. For several years preceding the erection of the Twain House, now the Mark Twain Memorial Library, Samuel Clemens and his wife boarded here with the Hookers, occupying a western semicircular room, with fireplace and French windows, that has been changed but little.

L. from Forest St. on Hawthorne St.

39. *Katherine Hepburn's Birthplace* (*private*), 133 Hawthorne St., was the home of the motion-picture star, who lived here with her parents until she began her career in the theater.

Return on Hawthorne St.; R. on Forest St.; L. on Farmington Ave.

40. *Mark Twain's House and Memorial Library* (*open weekdays 9–5; free*) (1873), 351 Farmington Ave. This huge, rambling, twenty-room, red and yellow brick structure of Victorian-Gothic architecture was built by Mark Twain who resided here from 1874 to 1879. In 1929 it was acquired by the Mark Twain Library and Memorial Commission and partially restored. The stair hall is rich with quartered oak and inlaid paneled

walls of various woods. In the Memorial Room is a bust of the humorist modeled from life by Louis W. Potter, and a large model of the Mark Twain Memorial; the latter, representing characters from his books flanking the seated figure of Clemens, is to be erected at Hannibal, Missouri, the author's birthplace. Mr. Clemens had the kitchen and servants' quarters built in the front part of his house so that they could look out of the windows 'to see the parade go by.' As he commented, 'It saves time and wear on the rugs.' Unusual features in the Mark Twain House are a Tiffany window over the main fireplace and, in the rear, an addition constructed like a pilot house, which served the elderly author as a reminder that he had, at one time, been a Mississippi River steamboat pilot.

41. The *Children's Museum of Hartford* (*open weekdays* 10-5; *Sun. and holidays* 2-5), 609 Farmington Ave., at Oxford St., maintained by the city, instructs and entertains young people with many fine exhibits, lecture programs, and motion pictures. As floor space is limited, the museum has adopted a system of rotary exhibits, displaying from time to time a variety of collections of minerals, insects, plants, animals, and birds, as well as dolls, stamps, handicraft, and articles from foreign lands. Classes from the primary and grammar schools of the vicinity make regular trips to the museum, which is particularly popular during summer vacations.

Return on Farmington Ave.; L. on Girard St.; R. on Elizabeth St.

42. *Hartford Seminary Foundation* (1926), at 55 Elizabeth St., was organized in 1833 by 36 Congregational ministers at East Windsor, and called the Congregational Ministers College. It received its charter as the Theological Institute of Connecticut in May, 1834, and in 1865 removed to Hartford. The *Hartford School of Religious Education* and the *Kennedy School of Missions* are housed in the Foundation and continue to function as individual units of religious education. Special training is given students seeking to qualify for a missionary career. The 35 acres of landscaped campus contain administrative offices, library, dining-hall, dormitory for women, dormitory for men, furnished apartments for missionary families, and furnished apartments for married students. Parts of the building program were carried out in 1924–25 by Allen and Collens. The buildings, though as yet they seem unrelated, are in sturdy, unassuming Gothic in the Perpendicular style, enlivened by some Elizabethan half-timber work. The design of the tower at the entrance is based upon that of Magdalen College, Oxford.

Case Memorial Library (*open*), Avery Hall, on the campus of the Hartford Seminary, contains 140,890 volumes and 61,062 pamphlets of special interest to students of theology and related subjects. Books in the exceptionally fine Mission Department include, in addition to works on history, philosophy, and religion, the classical literature of the Japanese, Chinese, Arabic, Moslem, Turkish, and Armenian civilizations.

Return on Elizabeth St.; R. on Whitney St.; L. on Asylum St.

43. *Elizabeth Park* (1895), entrance Asylum St., comprises 100 acres, the gift of Charles M. Pond in memory of his wife Elizabeth, for whom it was named. Thousands of people annually visit here during Rose Week in June, to view the 500 varieties of roses in a natural setting of lily ponds, streams, and groves. In hothouses and experimental houses not far from the rose-beds, specialists continually develop more beautiful varieties. National lawn bowling tournaments are held here annually in June; other facilities include the children's playground, picnic groves, tennis courts, and baseball diamond. Most of the park is in West Hartford, but it is owned and cared for by the city of Hartford.

Return on Asylum St.

44. *Hartford School of Music* (1890), 834 Asylum St., reputedly the oldest endowed school of music in Connecticut, is a non-profit corporation providing musical instruction and encouragement to gifted students. Junior and Senior string ensembles are maintained and concerts rendered in both Bushnell and Avery Memorials.

TOUR 4

N. from Pleasant St. on Main St.

45. *Keney Memorial Tower* (1898), cor. of Main and Ely Sts., a French Gothic tower like the Tour St. Jacques in Paris, was built to house a clock and chimes, and to provide 'a monument to a Mother,' by Walter and Henry Keney, Hartford merchants, on the site of their former home. It is said to be the first monument erected to commemorate a woman who had no other claim to greatness than that of being a true and self-sacrificing parent.

L. from Main St. on Albany Ave.; R. on Blue Hills Ave.

46. *St. Justin's Roman Catholic Church,* 256 Blue Hills Ave., attached to a convent, is the most interesting modern church in the city. Erected in 1931, the design of the structure by Whiten and McMann is hard to classify, having Gothic elements, such as its crossing tower and its perpendicular windows, and a Romanesque basilican interior, all treated with a rigorous modern suppression of unnecessary lines. But the perfect proportions, the light and shade concentrated at the altar, and the façade, which might be called a composition of block surfaces, are admirably handled in spite of stylistic inconsistencies.

R. from Blue Hills Ave. on Holcomb St.

47. *Connecticut Institute for the Blind* (*open*) (1911), 260 Holcomb St., at Blue Hills Ave., a three-and-a-half-story red-brick, Georgian-Colonial structure, accommodates 60 blind and partially blind pupils, who receive general elementary education and board. Using the latest aids for the blind, such as guide dogs, the Braille system of writing, and talking

books, every effort is made to make the students as self-supporting as possible.

48. *Keney Park* (1924), entrance at end of Holcomb St., was donated to the city by Henry Keney in August, 1924. This park contains a difficult 18-hole golf course, clubhouse, archery, and lawn bowling grounds, tennis courts, a children's playgound, a refectory, football, baseball, and soccer fields, and bridle paths. Throughout its 694 acres, the scenic drives wind past streams and ponds in acres of natural woodland.

Return on Holcomb St.; R. on Coventry St.; R. on Tower Ave.; L. on Main St.

49. The *Fuller Brush Company Building* (*adm. on application at office*) (1906), 3580 Main St., houses a firm founded in 1906 and incorporated in 1913; this three-story, yellow-brick building occupies more than 160,000 square feet and is the largest brush factory in the world, manufacturing brushes for household use sold on a direct-to-consumer basis. These brushes are sold from door to door by young men, who are as clever salesmen as the original Yankee peddlers.

OTHER POINTS OF INTEREST

50. *Bulkeley Memorial Bridge*, at the end of Morgan St., erected in 1908 at a cost of $1,600,000, spans the Connecticut River between Hartford and East Hartford. Named for Morgan G. Bulkeley, former Mayor of Hartford, Governor of Connecticut, and U.S. Senator, the 9 spans and approaches, 1192 feet long and 83 feet wide, include 100,000 cubic yards of masonry.

51. *Pratt and Whitney Manufacturing Company Plant* (*adm. on application at office*) (1860), 436 Capitol Ave., at Flower St., is noted for its development of standard-length precision gauges and tools. The Sharps rifle was first manufactured on this site by the Sharps Company (1851). Through history-making Civil War and western pioneering days, this early breech-loading arm established an enviable record for accuracy and reliability. Arms machinery orders for export boomed the business in 1873–75, the firm made Hotchkiss guns in 1888, and a one-pounder in 1895. It became a leader in establishing standards, especially of screw threads, and trained many excellent mechanics who became noted in their own right. Among P. & W. 'graduates' who became nationally known were such men as Worcester R. Warner, Ambrose Swazey, E. P. Bullard, F. N. Gardner, and E. C. Henn. The noted 'Wasp' and 'Hornet' aircraft motors were developed by this firm.

52. *Pope Park*, by Park St., was given to the city of Hartford in 1898 by Colonel Albert A. Pope. These 89 acres offer such recreational facilities as a swimming and wading pool, playgrounds, an outdoor gym-

nasium, a baseball diamond, a soccer field, a football field, tennis courts, and a refectory. The pond, used in winter for ice skating, is the scene of a model-yacht regatta every summer. Japanese cherry trees grow here in an abundance.

53. *Trinity College*, between Summit and Vernon Sts., Broad St. and New Britain Ave., a notable classical and scientific institution now secular in character, is an outgrowth of the first Episcopal college established in New England. Incorporated in 1823, it was first known as Washington College, but adopted its present name in 1845. The long range of older buildings, designed in 1874 by William Burgess and centered in a square turreted tower, is now being completed into a quadrangle by the introduction of newer buildings, the Chemistry Laboratory on the south and chapel on the north. A swimming pool and gymnasium building have been added also, down the hill by the athletic fields.

Trinity College Chapel, 1932, designed by Frohman, Robb, and Little, is the most beautiful, as well as most authentic, piece of Gothic architecture in the State. This authenticity applies, not only to the painstaking rendition of the English Perpendicular style, but to the spirit in which the whole was conceived. Throughout its erection, weekday services were held to unite the workmen in a common recognition of the spiritual purpose of their task. Prizes were offered to the workmen for carvings, on any subject they chose, which are now in all parts of the building, from amusing bench ends referring to patriotic or collegiate history to stone carvings of the Angelus or other subject, inset in cloister or porch. The chapel is built as English college chapels usually are, like the choir of a cathedral, the long side benches furnishing seats for the students, while the general congregation sits in the crossing or what remains of the nave. It is from the crossing that the best view of the interior can be obtained. Clustered columns rise about sixty feet to the groined vaulting, and the chancel arch frames the richly mullioned Te Deum window at the east over a simple and dignified altar framed by blue hangings. On the other end, a Rose Window, French rather than English, is dedicated to the Mother of Our Lord. The *Chapel of the Perfect Friendship* runs north from the crossing. But the feature which lingers longest in memory is the tall tower, buttressed by towering corner pinnacles that give it a soaring quality. An outdoor pulpit adds a picturesque touch on the quadrangle side.

54. *Colt's Patent Fire Arms Manufacturing Company Plant* (*adm. on application at office*) (1855), 17 Van Dyke Ave., houses a firm organized in Paterson, N.J., by Samuel Colt in 1836, and removed to Hartford in 1855. Occupying nearly 1,000,000 square feet of floor space in the manufacture of firearms, this plant has been the training school for many of the Nation's industrial leaders. The first successful revolving pistols in the world were manufactured by this company and 'The Arm of Law and Order' is known around the world.

'Colt's Armory' was the training school for Francis A. Pratt and Amos Whitney, founders of Pratt and Whitney. Prof. Charles B. Richards, another Colt's student, became professor of Mechanical Engineering at Sheffield Scientific School of Yale University in 1884 and remained in that capacity for 25 years. George S. Lincoln, milling machine developer, William Mason, George A. Fairfield, C. M. Spencer, and Charles E. Billings were other Colt's students who left their mark in the world of machines. Elisha K. Root, superintendent of Colt's, trained many of these men and received the highest salary paid to any Hartford resident in the year 1865. Root's jigs and fixtures, profile machinery, stock turning, boring and rifling machinery, were used not only in U.S. Government armories, but in foreign lands as well. Transferring from the Collins Company (axe-makers) in 1849, Mr. Root brought forging processes at Colt's to a high efficiency, introducing, among other things, a 4-impression die for drop hammers. Handwork was largely eliminated under Root's management, automatic and semi-automatic machines were installed, and the interchangeable-parts idea of manufacture was carried out to a remarkable degree of efficiency.

The influence of Colt's Armory and of Mr. Root's management and mechanical training on the younger men who worked with him has been notable throughout the machine-tool world. The Weed Sewing Machines, Columbia Bicycles and motorcars, were built by Colt-trained mechanics. The great washing machines that wash and dry dishes in the largest hotels come from Colt's, as do the attachment plugs, cartridge fuses, entrance switches, and molded panels of the electrical system in any household.

55. *Colt Park* (1905), entrance on Wethersfield Ave., a 114-acre park, the gift of Mrs. Elizabeth H. Colt, is a memorial to Samuel Colt, inventor of the Colt firearms. In this park is an enclosed municipal stadium, a quarter-mile running track, swimming pool, baseball, football and soccer fields, bowling greens, tennis courts, and hockey rink. World War Memorial trees planted along the numerous drives create an effect of peace and quiet. A sizable *Memorial to Colt*, designed by Massey Rhind in 1904, stands near Wethersfield Ave. This seated bronze figure represents Colt as a sailor lad, whittling the cylinder for the first Colt revolver model; bas-reliefs on the pedestal depict events in his tour around the world when he and Mrs. Colt were honored by many reigning monarchs of Europe and Asia.

56. *Goodwin Park*, cor. Maple Ave. and South St., comprises 237 acres acquired in 1901. Splendid drives wind around beautiful lakes and through large groves of trees. Recreational facilities include a municipal golf course, clubhouse, playground, tennis courts, a football field, picnic groves, a refectory, and bridle paths.

57. *Royal Typewriter Company Plant* (*adm. on application at office*), 150 New Park Ave. at SE. cor. Francis Court, was established in 1906 by Edward B. Hess, Lewis C. Meyer, and Thomas F. Ryan, in Brooklyn, N.Y., and moved to Hartford in 1908. The second largest typewriter company in the world, it manufactures standard, portable, and noiseless typewriters, which are shipped to all parts of the civilized world. The factory consists of four- and five-story, red-brick structures with small

Norman towers at the corners of the buildings, facing New Park Ave.
The plant has nearly 500,000 square feet of floor space and employs more
than 4500 people (1937).

58. *Underwood Elliot Fisher Company Plant,* SE. cor. Capitol Ave. and
Woodbine St., houses a company organized in 1895 and first located in
New York City. In 1896 the firm moved to Bayonne, N.J., and in 1899
the plant was moved to Hartford, where it occupies the largest typewriter plant in the world, with a floor area of 985,000 square feet. It
employs more than 5000 people and is a leader among Hartford's major
industries.

Points of Interest in Environs:

Birthplace of Noah Webster and the American School for the Deaf,
West Hartford, 5.4 *m.*, US 44 (*see Side Trip off Tour* 3); Pratt and
Whitney Airplane Works, East Hartford, 2.7 *m.*, State 2 (*see Tour*
3*A*).

L I T C H F I E L D

Town: Alt. 960, pop. 3574, sett. 1720, incorp. 1719.

Nearest Airport: Carey Field, Torrington, Torringford Road, 10 *m.* NE. of
Litchfield. Taxi fare, $2.50. Time, 30 min. Passenger service by chartered
plane to and from New York. Sightseeing trips.

Taxis: 50¢ within town limits. $1 within 4 *m.* beyond the town limits.

Traffic Regulations: Speed limit 25 *m.* per hour within town limits. Ample
parking space, no time limit.

Swimming: Sandy Beach, Bantam Lake, 4 *m.* SW. of center on State 109.

Annual Events: Litchfield Horse Show, second Saturday in August. Litchfield
Grange Fair, early September.

LITCHFIELD, on a plateau above the Naugatuck Valley just east of the
Housatonic Valley, is a stately old Connecticut town, with majestic elms
bordering broad roadways, strips of well-kept lawn between sidewalk and
street, and many dignified Colonial homes.

An air of peace and contentment pervades the community. When the
mail comes in, townsfolk gather at the post office; on court days the local
gentry congregate on street corners and speculate on the length of the
term. Natives live to a ripe old age, untroubled by economic maladjust-
ment or crime problems. Just across the Green from the post office is the
county jail, seldom occupied except by some backwoodsman who has been

intemperate; the courthouse is under the same roof. The dog warden usually basks in the sunlight near the harness store or the post office, his golden badge polished bright. The county agent chats with two or three young members of the 4-H Colt Club. Station wagons whisk in from Falcon Flight or Hardscrabble Hill for the day's marketing, and the rural mail carrier pulls away from the curb in his mud-splashed flivver.

The lands, then known as Bantam, that make up the township of Litchfield were bought from the Indians in 1715-16 for fifteen pounds. The town was incorporated in May, 1719, the village in 1818, and the borough of Litchfield was established in 1879.

In 1720-21, the first settlers arrived and named the town Litchfield, after the old cathedral city of *Lichfield* in Staffordshire, England. Newcomers were not permitted to take up a permanent residence until their characters were passed upon by the town fathers. Fears of Indian attack troubled the settlers; palisades were built around five houses to furnish protection in case of raids, and sentries were stationed at the edge of the village. In May, 1722, Captain Jacob Griswold, one of the founders, was attacked and taken captive by the Indians but later escaped and returned to the village. The following August, another inhabitant, Joseph Harris, was captured and scalped by the Indians on a plain just west of the town, which became known as Harris Plain.

Litchfield was an outpost and trading center for the northwest frontier. Agriculture flourished, small mills were built along the streams, and iron was forged into chains and anchors. The first French War passed almost unnoticed, but during the second French War (1755-63), a regiment was raised in Litchfield and near-by towns. At the outbreak of the Revolutionary War, many of Litchfield's reinforcements were sent to Bunker Hill, and Aaron Burr, who had spent the previous year studying law at the home of his brother-in-law, Tapping Reeve, enlisted and served in Arnold's expedition to Quebec. Oliver Wolcott was chosen a member of the Continental Congress, and many other Litchfield citizens took a prominent part in military and governmental activities. The town's protected inland situation and extensive agricultural production made Litchfield a concentration point for army stores and workshops, which became increasingly important after the capture of New York when the northern route through Litchfield was the principal military artery to Boston. Night and day the village resounded with the creak of loaded carts, the pounding of hammers, and the tramp of marching feet. At the close of the war the town made rapid social and educational progress, escaping the somewhat aimless industrial development of many Connecticut factory towns.

Benjamin Hanks, an ingenious maker of clocks and watches, came to Litchfield in 1780, and in 1783 secured a patent on a tower clock automatically wound by air. Hanks built a foundry a 'few rods south of the Court House,' where he carried on a 'Brazier's business' and began the casting of church bells for which he later became famous.

Tapping Reeve (1744-1823) established the first law school in America in Litchfield; after his death, his associates carried on the institution until 1833, when Yale, Harvard, Virginia, Columbia, and other colleges had opened law schools of their own. Most historians date this school from 1784, but Lyman Beecher, in his sermon delivered at the funeral of Reeve, stated that regular lectures were begun here in 1782. According to Simeon E. Baldwin in his 'Great American Lawyers,' these lectures constituted the first law school not only in America but 'in any English speaking country, for the Inns of Court had long ceased to be seats of serious instruction and the "schools" of Oxford and Cambridge were but a form.'

Among the graduates of Reeve's school were one Vice President, five Cabinet Members, seventeen United States Senators, fifty-three members of Congress, five diplomats, three Associate Justices of the United States Supreme Court, four Justices of the United States District or Circuit Court, seven Chief Justices of States, ten State Governors, seven Lieutenant Governors of States, two State Secretaries of State, three State Attorneys, three State Chancellors, four Speakers of the House of Representatives of States, and three college presidents.

Tapping Reeve was among the first to champion an improvement in the legal rights of married women, and imbued his students with a burning desire to defend the oppressed. Many of them returned home to pioneer in legislation that made it possible for married women to transfer their property without permission of their husbands. Many stories are told of Reeve's absent-mindedness. He would walk up North Street, leading a horse that was no longer with him. Holding the bridle rein carefully, the jurist would amble along, absorbed in thought, often reaching the hitching-post and making a knot before he discovered that his horse, having slipped the bridle, was peacefully grazing some blocks behind.

Among the Acadian refugees who came to Litchfield, one found happiness rather than sadness in exile. Sybil Sharway was this young 'Evangeline,' who, in 1764, married Thomas Harrison and lived happily ever after.

Litchfield church circles were once rent asunder by a controversy over a stove. The elder church folk were convinced that the old-fashioned,heatless churches were more conducive to salvation than the superheated edifices in the city. But others were of a different mind. The congregation split into the anti-stove faction and the pro-stovers. One bright September Sabbath, arriving church folk found the leader of the pro-stove group standing over a gleaming wood-burner and rubbing his palms contentedly together. The anti-stove people perspired and mopped their brows in great distress. One indignant lady fainted from the heat and had to be carried to the open air. The sermon over, a bold pro-stove warrior walked over to the cast-iron wonder and placed a hand on the lid. The stove was stone cold.

Much of Litchfield's early affluence was due to the commercial enterprise of Julius Deming, an energetic merchant and shipowner, who moved here

from North Lyme and formed the Litchfield China Company in partner-
ship with Colonel Benjamin Tallmadge and Oliver Wolcott. Their
vessel, the 'Trident,' made China voyages out of New Haven for fourteen
years. The cargoes were freighted overland by ox teams to Litchfield,
headquarters for the traders, who had a string of chain stores in the surrounding towns.

The advent of Connecticut railroads, which were slow in building the
crooked little line, with its one hundred and forty-seven curves within
about twenty-five miles, up the Shepaug River Valley to Litchfield, marked
a transition in the town's history. The Housatonic and Naugatuck lines
diverted industry to the valley towns. Cotton mills, carriage and cabinet
shops, comb and hat shops, even the iron forges, eventually closed, and
the little town dozed while lively new cities boomed. Litchfield was left
sequestered in the quiet back-country, a genuine old New England village, where the population still is 55 per cent of full native parentage. In
recent years Litchfield has become a popular summer resort.

In 1937, Litchfield was faced with the abandonment of all rail facilities, as
the New York, New Haven and Hartford Railroad has petitioned the
State Legislature for permission to abandon the Shepaug Branch. The
town is still paying off the indebtedness it incurred when the railway first
established a station here; an outstanding debt of $50,000 is being retired
at the rate of five thousand dollars per year. Thus Litchfield faces the
misfortune of paying for a railway ten years after service is discontinued.

As Litchfield is a leisurely community, the tourist should enjoy touring
the village on foot. There is little traffic, and all the points of interest in
the community are within easy walking distance.

TOUR 1

W. on East St. from the eastern end of the Green.

1. The *Congregational Church* (R), East St. facing the Green, was built
(1828–29) at the close of the best period of 19th-century architecture. It
closely resembles the Southington Congregational Church, and was probably designed by Levi Newell of that town, but has a far more attractive
setting. It is the last of a series of almost identical edifices that included
the Congregational churches of Milford (1823), designed by Hoadley;
Cheshire (1826), and Southington (1828). It has the same four fluted
Ionic columns in the portico, the same three equal doors (this time with
square panels over their semicircular heads), the same graceful steeple
with two octagonal stages — one open, one closed — each crowned with
a decorative balustrade. The interior, though a modernized reproduction,
is worth seeing for its high barrel-vaulted ceiling, its elaborate candelabra
and mahogany pulpit reached by a double flight of steps. At one time its
beauty was not appreciated, for in 1873 it was replaced by the exotic but

then popular Gothic, and was moved away to serve the baser uses of armory, dance hall and movie house. Reform came at last, however, and private subscription restored the dignified old edifice to its former site and service.

2. *Phelps Tavern*, East St. (R), next but one to the church, built by David Buell and in continuous service, 1787–1937, is the most impressive example of an early tavern in the State. In its unusual height, three and a half stories, and in its pretentious piazzas that run up to the wide overhanging flare of the roof, it reflects the importance of Litchfield as a shire town. It was erected only five years after a tavern of more ordinary proportions was built in the town.

3. The *Old Curiosity Shop*, East St. (R), close to the tavern, one of the few early shops still in existence, was built in 1781 as an apothecary shop by Dr. Reuben Smith, a pioneer in the use of smallpox inoculation; with its gable end to the street and two low windows flanking the entrance, sheltered under a hood that stretches across the front, it is an unusual relic.

4. The *Collins House* (1782), next door, on East St., with an end chimney and a double overhang, was originally an inn managed by John Collins, who kept the establishment with the approval of his father, Timothy Collins, Litchfield's first parson, until his hostelry was displaced by the Phelps Tavern.

R. from East St. on North St.

5 and 6. The *Corner House* (*private*) (1792), NE. cor. East and North Sts., was essentially a town house built for Charles Butler in the style now associated with the early 19th century. It is replete with quoins and bracketed cornices, has its doorways pressed close into the very corners of the house, and experiments with fan-light and quadrant windows in the gable. The two-story columns on the porch in the ell are a favorite feature in Litchfield. Directly across the street (L), at the cor. of West and North Sts., is the brick *Litchfield County Jail* (1811). In front of the jail is the *Whipping Post Elm*, 12 feet in circumference. The sheriff once lashed lawbreakers in the shade of this great tree, but today it looks down on more modern corrective measures. Prisoners from the jail clip the grass, or rake leaves, suffering only from the confinement incident to the normally light sentences handed down by the judge of the County Court.

7. The old brick *Bank Building* (L), next north on North St., with a shallow two-story portico and stately colonnade, was built in 1815 as a branch of the Phoenix Bank in Hartford.

8. The *Benjamin Tallmadge House* (*private*) (1775), next door on North St., was built in 1775 and bought in 1782 by Colonel Tallmadge, Chief of the Intelligence Service and a friend of Nathan Hale. He identified Major André after his capture. The tall gambrel-roofed house is flanked by two lower wings, with two-story columns, a mode that became popular in Litchfield and Farmington. Its 'captain's walk' is a feature which the merchant prince borrowed from dwellings near the sea.

9. *The Lindens (private)*, opposite on North St. (1790–93), is the most pretentious old house in Litchfield. Designed by William Spratt, a London architect who served in the British Army and was the designer of the Samuel Cowles House in Farmington, this large house was decorated with material brought from England by the owner, Julius Deming, a merchant prince and shipowner. The cornices and window heads have elaborate moldings, brackets, and dentils. Above the colonnaded entrance portico is an excellently proportioned Palladian window. The lines of the hip roof repeat the lines of the pediment over the entrance, and four tall chimneys give a strong accent to the design, which is Spratt's best. The south colonnade and the rear ell are later additions.

10. *Sheldon's Tavern (private)* (1760), opposite on North St., easily recognized as Spratt's work, has an imposing hip roof which Spratt added some time after 1790, when the house was sold to Senator Uriah Tracy. Spratt also introduced the projecting entrance, without pilasters, fanlight or quoins, characteristic of his work. The tavern, originally operated here by Samuel Sheldon, is mentioned in Washington's diary, which tells of his spending a night here.

11. *Miss Pierce's Academy*, opened in 1792, the first institution in America for the higher education of women, once stood on the plainly marked *Site* (L), north of the Sheldon Tavern. During the 40 years of its existence this school was attended by 3000 young women.

12. The *Lynde Lord House (private)* (1771), SW. cor. North and Prospect Sts. (L), is a stately example of an early twin-chimney, gambrel-roofed homestead.

13. On the corner of North and Prospect Sts. (L), is a covered well and a large elm tree marking the *Site of the Reverend Lyman Beecher Homestead*, which has been moved to Norfolk Road, where it is the main building of the Spring Hill School, a co-educational institution for younger children. In this building, erected in 1775 and now drastically remodeled, were born the Rev. Henry Ward Beecher (1813–87) and his sister, Harriet Beecher Stowe (1811–96), author of 'Uncle Tom's Cabin.' The Rev. Lyman Beecher (1775–1863), their father, came to Litchfield in 1810 as pastor of the Congregational Church, serving the parish for 16 years.

L. from North St. on Prospect.

14. Around the corner (L), on the south side of Prospect St., is the *Quincy Memorial (not open)*, built in 1904, a large reproduction of an old house, left by Miss Mary Quincy to the Society for the Preservation of New England Antiquities. Here are preserved collections of family heirlooms and old laces.

FOOT TOUR 2

South from the Green on South St.

15. At the corner of East and South Sts. (L), facing the Green, is the two-story, red-brick structure that houses the *Wolcott* and *Litchfield Circulating Libraries* (*open weekdays* 10–12.30, 2.30–6). In the eastern wing, owned by the Historical Society, is a collection of portraits and Indian relics.

16. The *Tapping Reeve House* (*open weekdays* 10–12, 2–5; *Sundays and holidays* 2–5; *June* 1–*Nov.* 1; *adm.* 25¢) (1773), South St. (R), is the former home of Judge Reeve, whose wife, Sally, was the sister of Aaron Burr. This hip-roofed dwelling has an excellent interior furnished by the Litchfield Historical Society. The ventilators under the roof and the doors are features added much later. Next to the dwelling stands the tiny *Law School* (1784) on its original site. It looks like an early district school.

17. The *Older Oliver Wolcott House* (*private*), (1753–54), South St., opp. Wolcott Ave. and the Law School, has a porticoed ell, the earliest of this Litchfield type. It differs little from the typical house of the period except for the pediments over the windows. In the garden of this house, the leaden statue of George III, torn from its pedestal in Bowling Green, New York, by enraged patriots and smuggled to Litchfield in an oxcart, was melted and molded into 42,088 bullets by the ladies of the Wolcott family and their patriotic friends.

18. The *Ephraim Kirby House* (*private*) (1773), South St. (L), is directly below the Older Oliver Wolcott House. The wings of this imposing structure are supported by two-story columns. These wings and the numerous Palladian windows in the gables were probably later additions. Colonel Kirby compiled the first reports of law cases ever printed in America, covering the years 1785–88; these served as a model on which Connecticut and Massachusetts based subsequent reports.

19. The *Second Oliver Wolcott House* (*private*), SW. cor. South and Wolcott Sts., built in 1799 by Elijah Wadsworth, was soon sold to Oliver Wolcott, Jr., who succeeded Alexander Hamilton as Secretary of the Treasury in 1795. Wolcott was the first president of the Bank of America and Governor of Connecticut for ten years (1817–27). This house, one of the few private houses equipped with a ballroom, has been so altered as to lose its original simple lines.

R. from South on High St.

20. The *Birthplace of Ethan Allen* (*private*), High St. (L), a small gambrel-roofed house, is reputed to be the oldest house in the village.

Ethan Allen, a lieutenant colonel in the Colonial service, was born in Litchfield on January 10, 1737. His parents moved to Cornwall and later to Vermont, and Ethan, a young firebrand and opportunist, took an active part in Vermont's opposition to New York State rule. One hundred and fifty pounds were offered for his apprehension as an outlaw, but Allen's men, 'The Green Mountain Boys,' took good care of their leader. The intrepid soldier was authorized and paid by the General Assembly of Connecticut to raise a regiment of rangers and to proceed against Ticonderoga. Two hundred and thirty Connecticut Yankees accompanied him on the expedition, more than were raised by Benedict Arnold in Massachusetts; the Green Mountain Boys refused to acknowledge the 'foreign' Arnold as their leader and Allen took the command. Ethan Allen forced his way through the gates of the fortress at the head of his troops on May 10, 1775, formed his patrol on the parade grounds, routed out the commanding officer while that gentleman was still in his nightclothes, and demanded surrender of the post 'In the name of the Continental Congress, by God!' The British capitulated, surrendering 49 prisoners and valuable stores to the Green Mountain Boys without a fight. Crown Point fell the same day, and the mastery of all Lake Champlain passed to the Americans. Allen had unusual ideas about religion, believing that men's souls after death entered the bodies of beasts, fishes, reptiles, and birds. His own choice for a future life was a large white horse. Allen published works ridiculing the doctrine of Moses and the Prophets, the State of New York, and the British Army. Vermont has made him a popular hero; an army post there is named for him, a highway in Connecticut bears his name, and the exploits of his men are the subject of many folk tales throughout New England. He died February 13, 1789, in Colchester, after a fall from his horse, and was buried in Burlington, Vt.

MERIDEN

City: Alt. 190, pop. 38,481, sett. 1661, incorp. 1867.

Railroad Station: Meriden Station, State St. near East Main St. for N.Y., N.H., & H. R.R.

Airport: Municipal Airport, Evansville Ave., between Main St. and Cheshire Rd.; 2½ *m.* from city; taxi fare approximately 75¢, time 10 min. Sightseeing trips offered by Stinson Aircab Service; $1.50 for 5 min. No scheduled service.

Accommodations: Two hotels.

Recreation: Swimming: Baldwin's Pond Municipal Pool and Beach, junction North Wall St., Britannia St., and Westfield Rd.; free parking and showers, 10¢ locker fee for adults; Dossin Park Beach, NW. corner Cheshire and Oregon Rds.; free parking and showers, 15¢ locker fee for adults; Y.M.C.A., 110 West Main St., fee 25¢; St. Rose's Community House, 24–26 Center St., fee 25¢.

Stadia: St. Stanislaus Stadium, SW. corner Gale Ave. and Harrison St.; Insilco Field, West Main St.; Washington Park off Liberty St.; Columbus Park, foot of Lewis Ave.; baseball, football, and track events held at all four stadia, admission from 25¢ to 40¢.

Information Service: Meriden Chamber of Commerce, 7 Colony St.; 110 West Main St.; Y.M.C.A., 32 Crown St.; Curtis Library, corner East Main and Pleasant Sts.

MERIDEN, seat of an extensive silver-plating industry, lies in the central Connecticut Valley. Flanked by the Hanging Hills on the west and the scenic Mt. Beseck range on the east, it has one of the most attractive natural settings of any city in the State.

Numerous large public parks with shady drives winding past woodland lakes are quiet oases amid the industrial activity of the city. The business district, in which are concentrated six of the plants of the International Silver Company, said to be the largest manufacturers of silverware in the world, is typical of most industrial communities. In addition to the silver factories, about 75 other plants are engaged in the production of such diversified products as ball bearings, electric lamps, fixtures and household appliances, automotive accessories, and thermos bottles.

In 1661, Jonathan Gilbert of Hartford was granted a farm of 350 acres in this district by the General Court. Edward Higbee, who was put in charge of the estate, 'was the first white man to take up his abode in Meriden,' which was named for Gilbert's birthplace, Meriden Farm, in the English county of Surrey.

The history of Meriden is closely identified with the development of the silver industry which was an outgrowth of a small pewter shop. As early as 1794, Samuel Yale, who had worked with the craftsman, Thomas Danforth of Rocky Hill, commenced to produce pewter buttons. Numerous button and tin shops soon followed. The manufacture of Britannia ware was introduced here in 1808 by Ashbel Griswold. Griswold first used a mixture of tin and lead that was little more than pewter. Teapots were cast in two parts, and soldered together; spouts and handles were cast separately and soldered in place. Each article was then put on a lathe, turned and polished. Other small plants sprang up and by 1852 were so numerous that many of them combined to organize the Meriden Britannia Company. Shortly afterward, improved machinery made possible the rolling and pressing of metal by means of dies and forms. A new alloy of tin, antimony, and copper produced a more durable metal, which retained a more pronounced luster.

The first mechanical piano-player in the world was the *Angelus,* manufactured by H. K. Wilcox in Meriden in 1895. The former Angelus plant is now a subsidiary of General Electric, producing molded plastics for electrical equipment.

Although about 68 per cent of Meriden's population is either foreign-born or of foreign or mixed parentage, the newcomers have been quickly assimilated and there are no areas distinctly typical of any one nationality.

Several prominent literary and musical figures have been residents of Meriden. Rosa and Carmella Ponselle, of the Metropolitan Opera Company, spent their childhood here and received their first training in music from a local teacher. Gerhart Hauptmann, German dramatist, wrote his poetic drama, 'The Sunken Bell,' while living in the city, and is said to have derived his inspiration from Meriden's Hanging Hills (*see Tour* 2 *Alt.*). Ella Wheeler Wilcox was a resident for many years.

POINTS OF INTEREST

N. from East Main St. on State St.

1. At 48 State St. is the main office of the *International Silver Company* (*admission on application at office*), largest manufacturers of silver and silver-plated ware in the world, normally employing about 3000 people. Six of the firm's 14 plants are in Meriden. In 1857, the Britannia Company bought the Rogers Plant in Hartford, which had been producing silver-plated ware since 1847, and the Rogers Brothers took over supervision of local production. In 1898, the Meriden Britannia Company merged with several independent concerns to form the International Silver Company.

Return on State St. to East Main; L. on E. Main.

2. The *Eli Birdsey House* (*private*), SE. cor. E. Main and Broad Sts., with a two-story colonnaded portico, is a pretentious dwelling dating from 1830.

At the junction of E. Main and Broad Sts. is the northern end of *Broad Street Memorial Boulevard* which parallels the long Green, once a training ground for Revolutionary soldiers.

3. The *Center Congregational Church* (1831), SW. cor. E. Main and Broad Sts., is a white clapboarded structure with a portico of six fluted Doric columns. The three large front doorways have eight-panel doors; on each side of the building are six windows with molded window heads. Above the portico gable rises a tower in three stages with a clock in the first stage. The upper two stages are reminiscent of Hoadley's United Church in New Haven. The open work of earlier church steeples has been replaced with louvres flanked by classic columns supporting cornices worked out in considerable detail. Above the upper stage, which is octagonal, is a drum with wreath ornament and a small dome.

MERIDEN. POINTS OF INTEREST

1. International Silver Company
2. Eli Birdsey House
3. Center Congregational Church
4. Baptist Church
5. Benjamin Curtis House
6. Ephraim Berry House
7. Site of the First Meeting-House
8. Plumb House
9. James Hough House
10. Moses Andrews Homestead

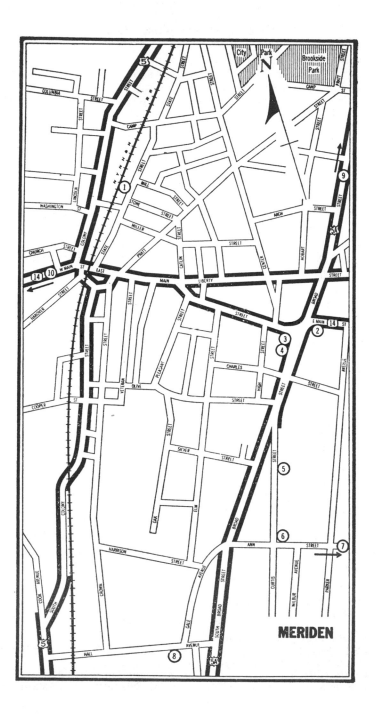

MERIDEN

R. from E. Main St. on Broad St.

4. The *Baptist Church* (1847), next door to the Congregational Church, is severely plain except for the ornamental balustrade around its octagonal spire. Four smooth Doric columns support the wide portico. The serenity of the front is due partly to the smooth boarding of the portico, unbroken except for the single door. When ground was first broken for this building, the Congregational Society resorted to an injunction to prevent the erection of the Baptist Church. According to the records, the Congregationalists had 'no objection to the Baptists as Christian people, as good neighbors and as worthy citizens,' but the Reverend Mr. Miller, pastor of the Baptist Church, had 'a peculiarly sharp ringing voice' that the Congregationalists feared might disturb their society in meeting.

L. from Broad on Curtis St.

5. The *Benjamin Curtis House* (*private*), 75 Curtis St. (1795, possibly earlier), is a white clapboarded, peak-roofed dwelling with a double overhang, which has been little changed through the years.

6. The *Ephraim Berry House* (*private*), sometimes known as the Aaron Higby House, recently moved to Curtis|St., at the corner of Ann, is a stone-chimneyed, white salt-box dwelling with a double overhang, built by Ephraim Berry in 1743.

L. from Curtis St. on Ann St.

7. At the end of Ann St. on Buckwheat Hill is the *Site of the First Meeting-House* and the original burying ground, where stands a monument erected by the town in 1857 in honor of the first settlers.

Return on Ann St.; L. from Ann on Gale Ave.

8. The *Plumb House* (*private*) (before 1733), SW. cor. Hall and Gale Aves., a story-and-a-half cottage with but two windows downstairs and three dormers, is one of the city's oldest buildings.

Other Points of Interest:

9. The *James Hough House* (*private*), Westfield Rd., 0.6 *m.* east of Broad St. via Britannia St., a peak-roofed, clapboarded house with but five windows on the front, was built before 1740 when the first transfer of the building was recorded. The heavy brownstone chimney, which is about 12 feet square at the base, gives an impression of sturdy simplicity.

10. The *Moses Andrews Homestead* (*private*) (1760), 425 W. Main St., is a brick-chimneyed salt-box house of the later type, with a double overhang and an unusually long straight rear roof. This building, now used by the Meriden Board of Education, was in 1789 the first Episcopal place of worship in Meriden.

Points of Interest in Environs:

Hubbard Park, including West Peak and Castle Craig, 1.8 *m.* (*see Tour 2 Alt.*); Goffe House, oldest in town, 1.3 *m.*, US 5 (*see Tour 7*).

MIDDLETOWN

City: Alt. 50, pop. 24,554.

Railroad Station: N.Y., N.H. & H. R.R. Station on Gilshenan Ave., at eastern end of Rapallo St.

Piers: Public Dock, College St. at Water St.; Middletown Yacht Club, reciprocal pleasure craft privileges, 100 yds. upstream from Public Dock.

Accommodations: Four small hotels.

Information Service: Chamber of Commerce, Central National Bank Bldg., Main St.

Swimming: Pameachea Pond and Y.M.C.A., Crescent St.

Annual Events: Wesleyan University Commencement, 3d week in June. Apple Blossom Festival, Middlefield (*see Side Trip off Tour 2 Alt.*).

MIDDLETOWN, shopping center of Middlesex County, the home of Wesleyan University, once an important West Indies shipping port, if often compared with the newer cities of the mid-West because of its exceptionally wide main street and spaciously arranged business and residential districts.

From the main street, which runs parallel with the Connecticut River, about 45 feet above its banks, elm-shaded avenues climb a gradual hill to an altitude of 190 feet, from which the University and stately residences overlook the winding river. From 1750 to 1800 Middletown was rated the wealthiest town in Connecticut; evidence of its prosperity is the large number of bank buildings, usually constructed of solid Connecticut brownstone, along the main thoroughfare.

Settled by Puritans from the colonies of Hartford and Wethersfield in 1650, the town was first known as Mattabeset, and in 1653 was named Middletown because of the settlement's location midway between Hartford and Saybrook. The early settlement was divided into sections by a small tributary stream, later known as the Little River. The northern section, which remained part of Middletown until it was incorporated as the town of Cromwell in 1851, was known until that time as the 'Upper Houses,' as distinguished from the southern section, now Middletown, known as the 'Lower Houses.' Both lumber and farm products were shipped to the West Indies at an early date, and maritime trade became one of the principal industries of the colony.

Here Colonel Return Jonathan Meigs recruited a company for Revolutionary War service, which fought at Bunker Hill and was cited for bravery by Washington. Simeon North, the first official pistol-maker of the United States Government (contract 1799), established his arms factory here during the Revolution and is said to have introduced the principle of line assembly and interchangeable parts in 1813.

Yankee peddlers carried Middletown elastic webbing, first produced here in 1841, and at least one present-day manufacturing plant owes its prosperity to this line of rubber goods. Rubber footwear was an early product and still is manufactured here by the Goodyear Rubber Company. Marine hardware has been forged and cast in Middletown since 1847; metal pumps, silks, and silverware all bear a Middletown trademark; and Remington Noiseless Typewriters are produced here.

Among the distinguished native sons were Commodore Thomas Mac-Donough, hero of the battle of Lake Champlain during the War of 1812; Captain Partridge, who founded here a military academy, later moved to Norwich, Vermont; Richard Alsop (1761–1815), one of the 'Hartford Wits'; Henry Clay Work (1832–84), author of the spirited Civil War song 'Marching Through Georgia,' and the ballad 'Father, Dear Father, Come Home with Me Now,' which became the theme song of 'Ten Nights in a Bar-Room'; Reginald DeKoven (see Music), composer of 'Robin Hood' and famed for his 'Oh! Promise Me.'

TOUR 1

E. from Main St. on Washington.

1. The brick mansion of *Benjamin Williams (private)* (1791–95), 27 Washington St. (R), is a house of distinction stranded in mediocre surroundings. The flaring stone lintels over the windows, the large 7 × 9 panes of glass (a novelty when the house was built), the delicate cornice, and the group of three dormers in the hip roof, two with triangular and one with a curved pediment as in Rhode Island work, all give the house a touch of the stateliness and taste of the best Georgian design. But the wide, flat-arched, open-pediment portico is distinctively of Connecticut, an early and beautiful example of what is sometimes called 'the Connecticut porch.'

Return on Washington St.; L. from Washington on High St.

2. The *Russell House (private)* (1828), 350 High St., a dignified, massive, brownstone structure fronted by a portico of fluted Corinthian columns,

---

MIDDLETOWN. Points of Interest

1. Benjamin Williams' Brick Mansion
2. Russell House
3. Gothic House
4. Alsop or Dana House
5. Wesleyan University
6. Middlesex County Historical Society
7. Benjamin Henshaw House
8. Randolph Pease House
9. Joseph Hall House
10. Samuel Mather House
11. Union Green
12. Site of the Home of Colonel Meigs
13. Henry Clay Work Park
14. Wilcox, Crittenden and Company
15. Riverside Cemetery

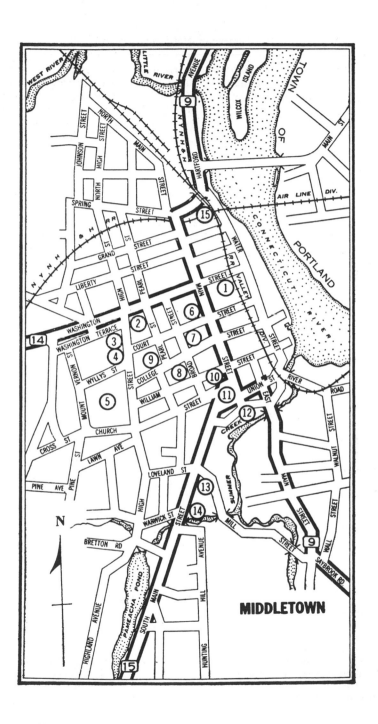

was designed by David Hoadley. Surrounded by spacious lawns and large shade trees, this outstanding example of the Greek Revival represents not only a later phase of the luxury of Middletown's day of prosperity, but the very peak of the tendency to translate old forms (in this case, that of a Roman temple) to any use, ecclesiastical or domestic. The property was presented by the Russells to Wesleyan University in 1936.

3 and 4. Along the other side of High St. the expanding eclecticism of 19th-century architecture may be traced. A dark Victorian *Gothic House* of the 1870's, opposite, has an air of rather studied romance, with elaborate grapevine designs in the verge boards and oriel windows. The famous *Alsop* or *Dana House* (1843), at 30 High St., runs to the other extreme and is Mediterranean, if not Italian, in feeling. It has a delicate iron grille outlined against its broad flat surfaces. In the middle of the century the use of grilles was a favorite method of relieving the heavy ugliness of the square, flat-roofed and cupolaed houses. The interior was painted in muresco by imported Italian artists.

R. from High St. on Wyllys St.

5. The elm-shaded campus of *Wesleyan University*, with its old brownstone and modern brick buildings, extends from Wyllys St. to Lawn Ave. Founded here in 1831 by the Methodist Conference, the college has continuously been non-sectarian, operating under a charter which forbade a religious test.

L. from Wyllys St. on High St.

South College (W), High St., was the building originally occupied by Captain Partridge's Military Academy, which was moved to Norwich, Vermont in 1829. It is a three-and-a-half-story brownstone edifice, the earliest in the college, and has a square militaristic tower, surmounted rather awkwardly by an octagonal belfry which looks like that of a church. Previously a dormitory, South College now houses the administrative offices. Chimes in the tower, presented by the Class of '63 in 1918, play each weekday evening at twilight.

In the *Chapel*, High St., are commemorative windows in honor of Wesleyan men who were killed in the Civil War and of seven former presidents of the college.

Rich Hall, formerly the library, has been remodeled into a little theater, where college assembly is held.

Judd Hall, now occupied by the College Museum (*open daily* 9–5), the Departments of Music, Geology, and Psychology, is named for the donor, Orange Judd, '47.

In the entrance hallway are slabs bearing dinosaur footprints, which were found in Connecticut. The two upper stories are devoted to the museum. On the second floor are located mineralogical, paleontological, archeological, and ethnographic exhibits. The mineral collection includes a comprehensive exhibit of specimens found in this vicinity; numerous fossils of plants, animals, and fish representative of the different geological ages were collected in the Connecticut Valley and in Wyoming by S. Ward Loper, a former curator. The ethnological section contains exhibits of Chinese life and customs, Egyptian, Mexican, and Indian relics, and pottery from Peru.

R. from High on Church St.

Beyond Scott Hall, the physics laboratory, is *Olin Library*, erected in 1928 largely through a gift of Mrs. Stephen Henry Olin. Its most prominent external feature is the rather overwhelming renaissance colonnade at the entrance. The architect was Henry Bacon, designer of the Lincoln Memorial at Washington, D.C. Memorial Hall, finished in Italian marble with mosaic floor, contains busts of President Stephen Olin and Acting President Stephen H. Olin, in whose memory the building was erected. Three *Davison Art Rooms* within this building provide exhibition rooms for paintings, etchings, and prints. In the *Gribbel Room* are exhibited first editions and other rare books. The *Hallock Room* is devoted to Americana, and the *Henry Bacon Room*, furnished like the original study of the famous architect, contains his books, furniture, pictures, and scrapbooks.

In the *Wesleyan Memorabilia Room* is the Olin Collection of coins and medals, the Rogers Collection of autographs, the Governor Winthrop chair (1629), and a collection of 5000 maps.

TOUR 2

S. from Washington on Main St.

6. The *Middlesex County Historical Society* (*open 3 to 5, 1st and 3d Fri. each month*), NW. cor. of Main and Court Sts., has a valuable collection of early Americana.

R. from Main on College St.

7. The *Benjamin Henshaw House* (*private*), NE. cor. College and Broad Sts., of brick, with a wide gambrel roof, shows through its modern stucco walls the details of a stately house of about 1785. The little gambrel ell on Broad St. dates from 1756.

8. The *Randolph Pease House* (1817), SW. cor. College and Broad Sts., is now a Christian Science church. The ecclesiastical windows are modern. Originally it was a simpler and smaller forerunner of the Russell House, with four Ionic columns instead of the eight Corinthian columns of the latter.

9. The *Joseph Hall House* (1765), College St. (R), between High and Pearl Sts., has a steep gambrel roof and an early porch with free standing columns. The clapboards, graduated from narrow at the bottom to broad at the top, increase the impression of height, as does the new stone foundation to which the house has been moved.

Return on College St. to Main St.; R. on Main St.

10. The *Samuel Mather House* (*private*) (1810), at 151 Main St., is a spacious brick example of the style of the early 19th century. The well-designed, arched open porch, covering the fan-light, and the picket fence with ornamental posts add much to the picture.

11. *Union Green,* Main St. at Pleasant St., is a small community park with a Civil War Soldiers' Monument.

Main St. becomes South Main; R. from South Main on Crescent St.

12. At 64 Crescent St. is the *Site of the Home of Colonel Meigs,* hero of the Quebec and Sag Harbor campaigns in the Revolutionary War, and later Governor of the Northwest Territory. The building was torn down in 1936.

Return on Crescent St. to South Main St.; L. on South Main.

13. *Henry Clay Work Park,* South Main at Mill St., has a bust of the composer of 'Marching Through Georgia,' for whom it was named.

14. *Wilcox, Crittenden and Company* (*open; apply at main office*), 8 South Main St., annually produces about $600,000 worth of marine and industrial hardware. The plant has preserved in the wall of one of the buildings a fragment of the Thomas Miller Gristmill, dating from 1655.

15. *Riverside Cemetery,* on the south side (R) of St. John's Square, which dates from 1689, was the site of the first meeting-house in the Middletown settlement. A boulder here commemorates the founding of the town. Near the marker is the grave of Commodore Thomas MacDonough, victor in the Battle of Lake Champlain, September 11, 1814.

Points of Interest in Environs:

Dinosaur tracks in sandstone quarries, Portland, 0.7 *m.* (*see Tour 2 Alt.*).

MILFORD

Town: Alt. 10, pop. 12,660, sett. 1639.

Railroad Station: Milford Station, High St. and Railroad Ave., for N.Y., N.H. & H. R.R.

Accommodations: Two hotels, 20 inns at the beach resorts, open in summer only.

Information Service: Chamber of Commerce, 1 River St.

Recreation: Swimming: Gulf Beach (municipal), off River St., no bath-houses, admission free; Tower Beach (municipal), near Trumbull Beach, no bath-

houses, admission free; Walnut, Laurel, and Silver Beaches, bath-house facilities, small fee.
Amusement Park: Walnut Beach, southeast of center.
Theater: Plymouth Playhouse, West Main St., summer theater.

MILFORD, just off the busy traffic of the Boston Post Road, is a pleasant residential community around a long, narrow, elm-shaded Green. The little Wepawaug River flows through the village between wide land-scaped banks to tumble in a waterfall over a dam into the shallow, unnavigable bay where clam diggers work at low tide. Oyster fisheries, the staple industry of the community, line the edge of the village on Long Island Sound. In summer, the narrow, shaded streets are crowded with summer vacationists from near-by beach resorts.

Oysters and clams have been important Milford products since the earliest days of the settlement. The Connecticut Oyster Farms Company of Milford owns 7400 acres of undersea oyster beds, and many other large oyster firms operate here. The shellfish are planted, cultivated, and harvested like any other crop. Efforts are being made by State authorities to eliminate the hazard of pollution by cleaning the tributary streams that empty into the Sound.

Other present-day industries include the growing of vegetable and field seeds, and the manufacture of brass fittings, locks, rivet machinery, elastic fabrics, screw machine products, tools, and metal specialties.

The original township, named for the town in Pembroke, England, was founded in 1639 by the Rev. Peter Prudden, who purchased the district, known to the Indians as Wepowage, for 6 coats, 10 blankets, 12 hatchets, 12 hoes, 24 knives, 12 small mirrors, and a kettle. Later, five other cities or towns were cut from this area. Controlled like the parent New Haven Colony by the 'Seven Pillars,' who derived both name and authority from the text: 'Wisdom hath builded her house, she hath hewn out her seven pillars,' Milford was a rigid 'Church State' in which only church members had suffrage. Indeed, Milford's admission to suffrage of six non-members barred her from admission to the New Haven Jurisdiction until it was agreed in 1644 that none of the six might hold office. In 1666, two years after the New Haven Colony was absorbed by the Connecticut Colony, Robert Treat of Milford, later Governor of Connecticut, led many of his churchmen southward where they helped to found Newark, N.J.

The rather self-righteous religious feeling of the early settlers is manifested in this perhaps apocryphal resolution which, the story goes, was passed by the colonists in 1640:

Voted: That the earth is the Lord's, and the fullness thereof.
Voted: That the earth is given to the Saints.
Voted: That we are the Saints.

Palisades enclosed a plot about a mile square. The Indians were numerous and inclined toward hostility, but there is no record of any white man in the settlement ever having been killed by them.

Milford is the home of Simon Lake, inventor of the even-keel submarine torpedo boat, in 1894. In 1897, he made his trial run in the open sea with the 'Argonaut,' the first submarine to be successfully operated by an internal combustion engine. Mr. Lake has served as consulting engineer for the United States Government and foreign powers. In recent years, he has devoted his efforts to the perfection and promotion of salvaging devices for the recovery of sunken cargoes.

TOUR

E. from the Boston Post Road on Broad St.

1. The *Stockade House* (*private*) (R), Broad St. west of the Green, so-called because it is supposed to have been the first dwelling built outside the stockade, is easily identified by its recently truncated gables, reminiscent of an old German farmhouse. Any or all of the dates, 1659, 1690, or 1700, given this house may be correct as they probably refer to the date of the original building and of substantial additions; the builder was Ensign George Clark. Its fine unpainted paneling dates from about 1740, its door from about 1840, and examination of the wooden-pegged shingles on the outside walls shows them to be very old.

2. *Milford Green*, between Broad and Golden Hill Streets, stretching east and west for about one-half mile, is said to have been replotted and cut to the shape and dimensions of the hull of the ship, 'Great Eastern,' which laid Cyrus W. Field's first Atlantic cable. The original Green was laid out many years earlier.

R. from Broad St. on High St.

3. *Eels-Stow House*, 32–34 High St., now owned by the Milford Historical Society (*open May to Nov., weekdays*, 10–5; *Sun.*, 2–5, 7–9; *free*), is a 17th-century house which has had many alterations, including the large ell built in 1880 on the south end. Its most unusual features appear to date from a remodeling about 1720, when the house seems to have been enlarged to the south. The end chimney was then replaced by the present

---

MILFORD. POINTS OF INTEREST

1. Stockade House
2. Milford Green
3. Eels-Stow House
4. Colonel Stephen Ford House
5. Gunn House
6. Clark Tavern
7. Town Hall
8. First Congregational Church

9. Plymouth Church
10. Samuel Durant Homestead
11. Thomas Buckingham House
12. Old Burying Ground
13. Memorial Bridge
14. Fowler Memorial
15. The Gulf
16. Indian Shell Heap

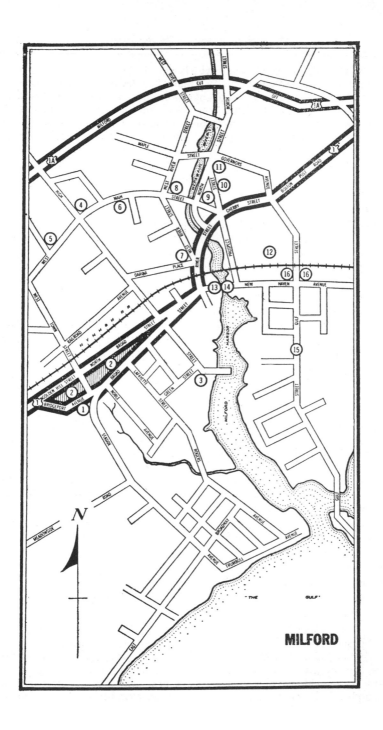

MILFORD

hallway and 'dog-legged' stairs which double back on the handrail, a feature not found elsewhere in this country. The 'coved' cornice under the front eaves is a restoration of a type of cornice that was not uncommon. After 1754 this dwelling was the home of Capt. Stephen Stow, whose heroic service as a volunteer nurse to 46 Revolutionary War prisoners, the victims of smallpox, cost him his life. The soldiers, among a group of 200 set ashore by a British prison ship on New Year's Eve, 1777, were cared for at the homes of settlers until the next day when the Town Hall was converted into a hospital. All of the victims and Stow were buried in a common grave.

Return on High St.

4. The *Colonel Stephen Ford House (private)*, 51 W. Main St., NE. cor. of High and W. Main Sts., an impressive old house marked with a 17th-century date but probably built in the ornate era of the 18th century, about 1765, has a huge chimney which might have been part of an earlier house.

L. from High on W. Main St.

5. The narrow, steeply roofed little *Gunn House*, NE. cor. of W. Main and Gunn Sts., now a grain store, is a 17th-century building. Inside can be seen the heavy 'knees' of the carved corner posts, the low ceilings and summer beams used in the earliest Connecticut houses.

Return on W. Main; R. from W. Main on W. River St.

6. The *Clark Tavern (private)*, 46 W. River St., is reputed to have been erected for the second minister, Roger Newton, in 1660, but was so drastically remodeled between 1815 and 1875 that only a little of the interior justifies the assumption of an earlier date. Washington stopped here for supper in 1789 when the building was kept as a tavern by Andrew Clark. A story of his visit relates that when Washington was served with the milk and bread he had ordered for his meal, he objected to the pewter spoon and asked for a silver one. When told that the tavern did not afford silver spoons, he handed a shilling to an attendant and directed that he 'go to the minister's and borrow one.'

7. The *Town Hall*, junction of River and W. River Sts., on landscaped grounds by a millpond and falls of the Wepawaug River, is a long, low, modern brick and marble building with a colonnaded rotunda, topped with a dome.

Return on W. River to W. Main; R. on W. Main St.

The charm of Milford centers about its two Congregational churches, which stand on either bank of the Wepawaug River.

8. The *First Congregational Church* (1823), W. River St. (L), said to have been designed by David Hoadley, is an example of the best period of Connecticut church architecture. The design was copied in numerous churches: in Cheshire (1826), by Levi Newell, in Southington (1828), and in Litchfield (1829). It has a graceful Ionic portico projecting from the body of the church and shielding three round-headed doors of ap-

proximately even height, and a belfry in two octagonal stages — one closed, and one open, under the spire. The interior has a finely proportioned gallery and domed ceiling.

9. *Plymouth Church* (1834), W. Main St., on the opposite bank, is a monumental structure in the heavier Doric of the developed Greek Revival style. Its heavy domed cupola and fluted columns are in contrast with the delicate detail of First Church. The parishes of these two churches are now united, and Plymouth Church serves the community as a summer playhouse.

L. from W. Main on North St.

10. *Samuel Durant Homestead (private)* (about 1725), 10 North St., behind Plymouth Church, attracts attention by its odd roof, straight in the rear, and sloping in a steep but Dutch curve at the front to cover a piazza. The small houses on the outskirts of Milford were built in this fashion, a peculiarity which seems to have been purely local.

11. *Thomas Buckingham House (private)*, 27 North St., has a traditional date of 1640. If so, it rivals the Fyler House in Windsor and the Stone House in Guilford as the earliest house in the State. As the building stands, however, it is almost a mid-eighteenth-century house, with many restorations in harmony with an earlier date.

Return on North St.; L. from North St. on Cherry; R. from Cherry on Prospect.

12. *Old Burying Ground*, Prospect St., just north of the R.R. underpass (L), is one of the oldest cemeteries in the State, in use since 1675. It contains the graves of Jonathan Law, governor of Connecticut from 1742-51; Robert Treat, commander of the Connecticut troops during King Philip's War, deputy-governor and governor of the State for thirty-two years, and founder of Newark, N.J.; and the Rev. Samuel Andrew who, besides serving as pastor of the church for 50 years, was rector of Yale College from 1707 until 1719. A monument to Captain Stephen Stow marks the common grave where he and his smallpox patients are buried.

R. from Prospect St. on New Haven Ave.

13. *Memorial Bridge*, spanning the Wepawaug River, was opened in 1889 (replacing Fowler's Bridge on the same site) to commemorate the 250th anniversary of the founding of Milford.

14. The *Fowler Memorial*, at the eastern end of the bridge (R), housing the Milford Post of the American Legion, stands on the site of the first mill in the New Haven Colony, erected in 1640 by William Fowler. In this mill the regicides Goffe and Whalley were concealed for two days before they fled to Judge's Cave. One of the original millstones forms a seat on the bridge.

Return on New Haven Ave.; R. on Gulf St.

On Gulf St. are a number of old houses with Dutch gambrel roofs in front and straight, sloping roofs behind, typical of Milford architecture.

15. *The Gulf*, on a bay on Long Island Sound, at the end of Gulf St., is one of the most popular bathing beaches in the vicinity. Extending eastward and westward from the Gulf are several other good beaches. Offshore due south of Milford and connected with the mainland by a narrow sand bar, Charles Island was the site of the summer palace of Anasantawae, the Indian sachem who sold this area to the white men. Here, tradition says, Captain Kidd once buried a vast treasure, although many efforts to discover it have failed. The fact that records show that the famous pirate actually visited the town twice, boldly striding through the village streets despite the price on his head, has stimulated many treasure hunters. The most nearly successful, according to legend, were two men who uncovered an ironclad chest on the Island but were frightened away by the ghostly apparition of a headless body, swathed in flames, which came rushing upon them from the heavens. Next day the searchers returned but found no trace of chest, hole, or spades.

16. An *Indian Shell Heap*, on both sides of Gulf St., north of New Haven Ave., is the largest in Connecticut. Covering 24 acres, this tremendous heap of shells testifies to the many aboriginal dinners eaten here. The rows of oystermen's huts thatched with seaweed that lined the shore at this point in the 19th century have fallen to ruins and disappeared.

NEW BRITAIN

City: Alt. 200, pop. 68,128, sett. 1686, incorp. 1870.

Railroad Station: Station on Church St. for N.Y., N.H. & H. R.R.
Airports: (see HARTFORD).

Accommodations: One modern hotel.

Information Service: N.Y., N.H. & H. R.R. Station; Chamber of Commerce, 300 Main St.; Burritt Hotel, West Main at Washington St.

Annual Events: Rose Week, Walnut Hill Park, in July. All Souls' Day Observance by Polish population, last Sunday in October, procession to cemetery with lighted candles. Ukrainian Festival, held in March.

NEW BRITAIN is known as the 'Hardware City' because it produces almost half the State's output of builders' hardware. In the shallow basin surrounded by a factory belt, the center of the city is frequently overshadowed by the smoky haze of industry. The railroad swings through the main part of the town, creating many grade crossings, especially in the factory district. In the center of the city a small central Green struggles for existence, dividing traffic on either side through rather narrow streets where parking space is limited. The outer residential districts have been greatly beautified by the establishment of a fine park system which has been steadily improved through the years.

First settled in 1686 by an overflow of Berlin colonists who drifted northward into the area now known as the Stanley Quarter, New Britain has been called 'the daughter of Berlin and the grand-daughter of Farmington.' Later settlers went further south and formed the Great Swamp Settlement. In 1754 the district became the New Britain parish of Farmington. In 1785 the town of Berlin was incorporated and in 1850 the town of New Britain was organized from a section of Berlin. Part of the town became the city of New Britain in 1870, and in April 1905 the town and city were consolidated.

The city's industrial development received its first impetus about 1800 when James North and Joseph Shipman started the manufacture of sleigh bells. Yankee peddlers marketed the bells and created a demand for other articles of light hardware. Locks, tools, saddlery hardware, cutlery and light metal articles were produced by numerous small shops for the peddler trade, but the lack of adequate water power delayed the growth of factories until about 1832, when steam power was introduced 'in the Stanley Lock factory.'

Most of the products of the first half-century of manufacturing in New Britain are no longer made, but from the early industries have been formed great corporations and combines, whose products in international commerce have familiarized nearly all the civilized world with the name of the city. After the panic of 1837 many of the small concerns were consolidated and the organization of many large factories between 1839 and 1850 laid the foundation for the city's present-day industry.

Among the large present-day companies organized at that time were the Stanley Works, steel and hardware; P. and F. Corbin, and Russell and Erwin, builders' hardware; Stanley Rule and Level Co., carpenters' tools; North and Judd, saddlery and automobile hardware; Landers, Frary and Clark, household utensils; and the New Britain Machine Company, automatic machinery. Such varied articles as electric ranges and wood planes, sheet steel and wood rules, carpenters' levels and ball bearings, cabinet locks and washing machines, lathes, chucks and paper goods are turned out in quantity by New Britain factories. A large number of the concerns now in business not only trace their beginnings to the first enterprises, but draw their executive personnel from the families of the founders, and in many cases, derive their names from the same source.

Nils Nelson and Charles K. Hamilton of New Britain were pioneers in early aviation ventures. Nelson designed a four cylinder, thirty horse power motor in 1910 and on June 13th of the same year, Charles K. Hamilton (sponsored by Curtis-Wright), demonstrated the commercial possibilities of the heavier-than-air machine by flying the first air mail from New York to Philadelphia, winning a prize of $10,000 for this first cross-country flight.

About the middle of the 19th century, New Britain factories began to attract foreign labor. In 1852 the population was only 5212; by 1870 it had increased to 9480 and in 1900 was 28,202. Today fully 48 per cent of its population is of foreign or mixed parentage, representing many racial groups.

Early immigrants were the English and the Irish; the Germans followed, and at the beginning of the 20th century a Slav migration created a distinct change in the population. Many of the newcomers are said to have purchased passage not to a port of entry, as was the custom, but directly to New Britain; here they had little difficulty in obtaining employment before they had even the most elementary command of the English language. As a result, New Britain is a city of many communities with a diversity of interests and customs, assimilating, rather than being assimilated by, the native stock. So pronounced is this condition that travelers have humorously said that the visitor to New Britain 'needs a passport.'

A picturesque celebration, the Ukrainian Festival, is held every March in New Britain in honor of the great Ukrainian bard, Taras Shevchenko (1814–61). Shevchenko's plays, or plays dealing with his life, are presented in Ukrainian. The most significant feature of the celebration is a concert of Ukrainian music, the lyrics for which were written by Shevchenko. The members of the chorus in their peasant costumes create a colorful scene reminiscent of their native land.

Another Ukrainian custom, the annual Easter dinner, which has been observed for centuries in Europe on the Sunday following Easter Sunday, was celebrated for the first time in New Britain in 1936. Ukrainian folk dances and century-old games followed the dinner.

TOUR 1

E. from Main on E. Main; L. from E. Main on Elm St.

1. *Smalley Park*, Stanley, Smalley, and Elm Sts., is the site of the first meeting-house in the settlement and served as a drill ground for Continental soldiers.

NEW BRITAIN. Points of Interest

1. Smalley Park
2. Fairview Cemetery
3. Teachers College of Connecticut
4. John Clark House
5. New Britain Institute Museum
6. Walnut Hill Park
7. Franklin Square Park
8. Willow Brook Park
9. Hungerford Park
10. Remains of the Hart Gristmill Dam
11. Deacon Elijah Hart II House

NEW BRITAIN

R. from Elm on Smalley St.

2. *Fairview Cemetery* (L), on Smalley St. between Gladden and East Sts., contains many graves dating from Revolutionary times. Some of the older monuments have been restored so that inscriptions are legible.

Return on Smalley St.; R. from Smalley on Stanley.

3. *Teachers College of Connecticut* (R), Stanley St. between Francis and Wells Sts., which occupies a group of modern Georgian buildings (1924–28), designed by Gilbert and Betelle of Newark, New Jersey, on 25 acres of landscaped grounds, was established in New Britain in 1850, the first normal school in the State. Henry Barnard of Hartford, who served as the first principal, later became the first U.S. Commissioner of Education.

4. The *John Clark House* (*private*) (1745), on North Stanley St. (L), a two-and-a-half-story white clapboarded salt-box dwelling with a double overhang has a well-designed doorway with fluted pilasters. The porch and ell have been added to the original structure built in 1745.

TOUR 2

W. from Main on West Main St.; R. on High St.

5. The *New Britain Institute Museum* (*open weekdays* 3.30 *to* 5.30), 8 High St., built in 1901 and designed by William S. Brooks, shares with the public library a spacious two-story granite building fronted by a limestone Doric portico. The Museum, housed in the upper story, contains many historical, natural history and art exhibits. Included among them is a copy of the Bible printed in Hartford in 1829 by Hudson and Goodwin; a collection of skulls of small animals; a miniature of Elihu Burritt; a seal used on public documents in the reign of George III; part of the wing of the N.C.-4, first airplane to cross the Atlantic Ocean; and various relics of the Revolutionary and Civil War. In 1908, a collection of minerals and a collection of mounted birds were presented to the museum by the late James Shepard and Eugene Schmidt.

Included in the permanent exhibit is a collection of paintings by American artists which includes the works of Walter Nettleton, Charles Noel Flagg, George Innes, Robert Bolling Brandagee, Gardner Symons, Frederick J. Waugh, William Gedney, William Sartain, Alexander H. Wynant and Childe Hassam.

Return on High St. to West Main; R. on West Main; L. on Park Place.

6. *Walnut Hill Park*, the first of New Britain's parks, includes 90 acres of rolling terrain in which the principal attractions are rose gardens, a rock garden, and a tropical fish pool. Facilities are also provided for tennis and baseball. At the highest point in the park stands the 97-foot *World War Memorial*, a massive shaft of limestone surmounted by stone

eagles, designed by H. Van Buren Magonigle and dedicated in 1928. The shaft, reflected in a fountain-fed wading pool, lighted by floodlights at night, is visible for many miles.

TOUR 3

S. from West Main on Main St. which becomes South Main.

7. *Franklin Square Park* (R), on S. Main at its junction with Glen St., is a small landscaped plot on which stands a granite memorial monument to New Britain's most famous son, Elihu Burritt (1810–79), the 'Learned Blacksmith' and 'Apostle of Universal Brotherhood.' At the age of 15, Burritt apprenticed himself to a blacksmith and, while at the anvil he studied Greek and Hebrew. At the age of thirty he had a working knowledge of nearly fifty languages. In 1846 he went to England to promote interest in the 'League of Universal Brotherhood.' Through his effort, peace conferences were held at Brussels, Paris, Frankfort and London. Burritt was Consular Agent for the United States at Birmingham, England, from 1865 to 1869. In 1870, Elihu Burritt returned to America to spend his declining years in New Britain.

R. from S. Main on Mill St.

8. *Willow Brook Park* (L) is the entire length of Main St., and covers 93 acres. At the eastern entrance is a Spanish-American War Memorial (1927) designed by Perry and Bishop, a miniature reproduction of Morro Castle at Havana. Near the northeastern corner of the park is a public swimming pool.

9. *Hungerford Park*, adjoining Willow Brook Park to the south, is a former private estate, bequeathed to the city. This park's facilities include an archery field and seven miles of bridle paths.

L. on Mill St.; R. on Pond St.

10. Beside the road at the curve where Mill St. becomes Pond St., are (L) the stone *Remains of the Hart Gristmill Dam*, one of the city's earliest enterprises.

Pond St. becomes Kensington Ave.

11. The *Deacon Elijah Hart II House* (*private*) at 63 Kensington Ave., is composed of two early salt-box houses. The northern end dates from 1757 and the southern end from 1787.

Other Points of Interest:

The *Deacon John Osgood House* (*private*), 5 Osgood Ave., erected in 1780, is the ell of the two-and-a-half-story main building which dates from 1812. The most interesting feature of the house is the stairway to the attic of the ell in which each step is a solid triangular block of wood.

NEW HAVEN

City: Alt. 30, pop. 162,655, sett. 1638, inc. 1784.

Railroad Station: Union Station, Union Ave. and West Water St. for N.Y., N.H. & H. R.R.

Airport: Burr St., East Haven, near Townsend Ave., 3¾ *m.* from city, taxi fare, $1.50; time, 20 min.

Piers: Municipal docks, New Haven Harbor, Water St. Bridge, 1½ *m.* from central Green, commercial. City Point Yacht Club, Hallock Ave., and New Haven Yacht Club, Morris Cove; reciprocal pleasure craft privileges.

Taxis: Standard rate, 20¢ first ⅓ *m.*, 10¢ each additional ⅓, one to five passengers.

Accommodations: Four first-class hotels.

Information Service: Chamber of Commerce, 152 Temple St.; AAA Conn. Motor Club, 34 Whitney Ave.; N.H. Public Library, Elm and Temple Sts. For information pertaining to Yale University, Secretary's office, Woodbridge Hall, Wall St.

Theaters: Shubert Theater, 71 College St., openings and road companies.

Athletic Fields: Edgewood Park, entrance Chapel St. or Whalley Ave.; Beaver Park, Goffe St.; East Rock Park, State St.; Lighthouse Point Park, southeastern section of the city, via Water St., Forbes and Townsend Aves., 4 *m.* from center; Yale Bowl, Derby Ave.

Swimming: Lighthouse Point Park, end of Lighthouse Rd., southeastern section of city, bathhouse charge 25¢ except Thurs. (*free*); Clinton Park, Middletown Ave.; Nathan Hale Park, Townsend Ave.; children at Beaver Park, Goffe St.

Golf: Municipal Golf Course, Clifton St., extreme eastern section of city, nonresidents weekdays only.

Tennis: Beaver Park, Goffe St.; East Rock Park, Orange St.; Clinton Park, Peck St. near Middletown Ave.; Nathan Hale Park, Townsend Ave.; Kimberly Playgrounds, Kimberly Ave.

Lawn Bowling: West Rock Park, near Whalley Ave.

Archery: Edgewood Park, Whalley Ave.; East Rock Park, State St.

Annual Events: Yale University Commencement, June, semi-public; Powder House Day, Monday nearest April 24, on Green, colorful historical pageant based on Revolutionary episode. Flower shows, spring and summer, Pardee Gardens and Greenhouses, East Rock Park, State St.

Museums: Peabody Museum of Natural History, open weekdays, March to October, 9–5; Nov. to Feb., 9–4.30; Sun. and holidays, 2–4.30, admission free. Gallery of Fine Arts, Chapel St. at High, open daily, 2–5, admission free. New Haven Colony Historical Society, 114 Whitney Ave., open daily 9–5, admission free.

NEW HAVEN is an industrial city distinguished as the home of Yale University and celebrated for its elm-lined streets. On a broad but very shallow harbor, at the confluence of the Quinnipiac, Mill, and West Rivers, New Haven is flanked by the red profiles of East and West Rocks.

The outstanding feature of the downtown area is the broad sixteen-acre Green, its trinity of churches standing in stately dignity with university buildings forming a western background. Facing the other three sides of the Green are substantial office, public, and commercial buildings, well-kept shops and department stores. To the north and west of the Green are the principal residential districts and most of the university buildings; to the south and east are business and commercial buildings and a more congested dwelling area broken by small parks and squares. New Haven's shore front is largely given over to business structures, tank farms, and wharves. To the southeast there is considerable beach development at Nathan Hale Park, Morris Cove, and Lighthouse Point, with its municipal bathhouses. The harbor entrance is protected by three strips of breakwater with attendant lights. The harbor and its approaches are difficult to navigate except at high tide.

The waterfront is only moderately active. Oil and coal come in by boat, but there is little outgoing freight. A lumber schooner from the north discharges fragrant spruce and pine, or a blunt-nosed tramp steamer opens hatches and slings western fir to the dock. A barge loads scrap iron, and a nitrate boat gradually shows a red waterline as clamshell dippers transfer its load to a waiting string of gondolas on the siding. A seamen's bethel stands on Water Street where sailors, between voyages, can look toward the sea. A pork-packing plant on Long Wharf Road sometimes offends the passer-by with odors hardly less unpleasant than those formerly rising from the holds of the town's sealing ships, in from Patagonia, where in the early nineteenth century they sun-dried sealskins on a tract of land called 'the New Haven Green.'

New Haven is perhaps best known as a cultural center, but industry has been important here since early days. The Winchester rifle, Sargent locks and hardware, New Haven clocks, pork products, toys, and fiber boxes bear New Haven trademarks.

The city is an important produce market. Commission houses grouped about the public market, in the area around the railroad station, do business totaling about $6,000,000 annually. These markets are open at night and transact a brisk business from 2 A.M. to midday, hucksters bidding for produce, marketmen buying their stock, and the out-of-town merchants and peddlers obtaining loads for distribution in outlying towns. Heavy industry is not important, but all forms of light manufacturing and service industries prosper and offer excellent facilities to expanding markets. The production of seed oysters is a business worth about $2,500,000 annually. The New York, New Haven and Hartford Railroad has its headquarters in the city, and rail service is excellent.

The population includes many ethnic groups. The first and second generation Italians number 41,858, giving New Haven probably a larger proportion of these people than is found in any other American city. The Irish number 18,351 in the first and second generations, and there are at least as many of the third and fourth generations. New Haven is the home of nearly 30,000 Jews, engaged largely in business and industry. Other groups, though they include many races, are numerically less important.

Week ends are gay in the autumn when all roads lead to the Yale Bowl and out-of-State cars outnumber local vehicles. Hucksters offer 'winning colors' to the throng, parking lots bustle with activity, and a worried local traffic squad shuttles back and forth trying to relieve congestion at busy intersections as the football crowds pour in and out of town.

Discovered in 1614 by Adriaen Block, who called it 'Rodeberg,' meaning 'Red Mount Place,' New Haven was not settled by white men until April 10, 1638, when the Reverend John Davenport, a Puritan minister of London, and Theophilus Eaton, a prominent merchant of his congregation, led a band of pioneers to this port from Boston. Shortly after the Davenport party arrived in Boston on June 26, 1637, Colonial troops, returning from their pursuit of the Pequot Indians (*see WEST MYSTIC and FAIRFIELD, Tour* 1), brought news of an excellent harbor in the district of the Quinnipiac Indians' hunting grounds. Eaton and his party of scouts investigated, found that the harbor possessed the trading possibilities desired by the colonists, and the following April the settlement was established. At first called Quinnipiac, the name was changed in August, 1640, to New Haven, for the English seaport in Sussex.

The initial land purchase included not only the site of the present city, but the districts now known as North Haven, Wallingford, Cheshire, Hamden, Bethany, Woodbridge, and Orange, for which the Indians were paid 23 coats, 12 spoons, 24 knives, 12 hatchets, scissors, some hoes and porringers. To Montowese, the sachem, was given 'a particular coat.'

The colonists had ambitious plans for their city and laid out the Colony in nine squares. The central square was set aside as a common green for a daytime market and a night pasture for stock, and about this green they built their homes.

Shortly after their arrival the settlers gathered to adopt a *Plantation Covenant*, binding themselves by signature to be governed solely by the laws of Moses. This code of authority sufficed for a year, when more permanent laws seemed necessary and a civil government was organized, amenable in all things to the dictates of the church.

On June 4, 1639, a meeting of 111 men was held in 'Newman's Barn,' and a constitution was adopted that ignored allegiance to the King, all English statutes of common law, and trial by jury. The 'Word of God' was to be the absolute rule. 'Seven Pillars' — from Proverbs 9:1, 'Wisdom hath builded her house; she hath hewn out her seven pillars' — were elected to head the church and State government. On October 25, 1639, the 'Seven Pillars' met with nine other citizens and elected Theophilus Eaton the first Governor of New Haven Colony. Until the actual union of the Colony with Connecticut in 1664, only members of the church were allowed to vote, and the New Haven government remained largely the crystallized thought of the Reverend John Davenport. Twelve church members elected the 'Seven Pillars' and the resultant rulings of this small select group limited the growth of the Colony during its early days. This theocracy, based on the strict laws of the Old Testament, provided the foundation for the Blue Laws of New Haven. The Reverend Samuel Peters, in his work. 'A History of Connecticut,' exaggerated the Blue Laws, but they did include 'Capital Lawes' providing a death penalty for any child over sixteen who was found guilty of cursing or striking his natural parents; a death penalty for an incorrigible son; a law forbidding smoking except in a room in a private house; another law declaring smoking illegal except on a journey five miles away from home, which made it impossible for most servants to smoke; and many other laws fully as unreasonable. Quakers were punished by branding, whipping, and banishment from the Colony. Fines were freely imposed on anyone bringing in heretics and on those who consorted with Quakers or owned a Quaker book. Baptists were no more popular than the Quakers, but they were not treated as roughly.

In 1643, Guilford, Milford, and Stamford were admitted to the Colony; in 1651, Southold, L.I., where land, purchased by Connecticut residents, was settled by a congregation from Hingham, England, and in 1656, Branford also were admitted. Thereafter followed many disputes with these confederate settlements because of their failure to enforce the fundamental article of the New Haven Constitution, that only members of the church might vote.

The boundaries of the Colony of Connecticut, as stated in the Charter of 1662, included all lands held by the New Haven Colony. New Haven vigorously objected and some outlying communities even took up arms with the avowed intention of retaining their independence from the river plantations. Meanwhile, the Duke of York held grants to the eastward that caused considerable worry, as New York was under the rule of the 'Royalists, Romanists, and Stuarts,' more unattractive to New Haven colonists than the Connecticut government. After prolonged negotiations Davenport's Colony submitted and, on December 13, 1664, became a part of the more liberal and democratic Connecticut Colony. The founder complained that the Colony's independence had been 'miserably lost.'

The church held grimly to its privileges. Preachers asked for and received authority to levy a town head tax on all citizens without regard for church affiliation. The 'Halfway Covenant,' giving the citizenry church privileges in return for their support of the institution, was adopted in 1677.

The first of the city's elms were planted in 1686 when members of James Pierpont's congregation gathered to present gifts and to furnish t' house of their pastor. One poor man, William Cooper, brought as donation two elm saplings, which he planted before the minister's The two inner rows of elms on the east and west sides of the Gree planted by the Reverend David Austin, member of the family founded Austin, Tex., and other elms on the Green were planted by James Hillhouse in 1787, when he obtained subscriptions from the towns-folk to beautify the Green.

New Haven shared with Hartford the honor of being the joint capital of the State from 1701 to 1875. The first State House was erected on the Green in 1717-19; a second in 1763-64, and a third in 1829-31.

In 1641, Captain George Lamberton, New Haven skipper, in an effort to stimulate the fur trade, purchased Indian lands in Delaware. No sooner had he built his trading post than the Dutch and Swedes ordered him to leave and burned his establishment.

Pinched by the failure of their efforts in Delaware, and hoping to recoup their fortunes, the New Haven traders in 1647 fitted out 'The Great Shippe' for a commercial voyage to England. The finest products of craftsmen and farms were loaded on board, but, by the time the ship was ready to sail, it was January, thick ice had formed on the river, and to the dismay of the superstitious sailors, she was towed stern-first to open water through a path cut in the ice. As she swung before the wind, a light fog obscured her canvas and carried the voice of the Reverend Mr. Davenport in muffled, portentous tones to the crew as he prayed, 'Lord, if it be Thy pleasure to bury these, our friends, in the bottom of the sea, take them; they are Thine; save them.'

Day after day, through the hard winter and the spring, anxious eyes searched the seaward horizon. Other ships arrived, raising false hopes, but none brought news or had heard of 'The Great Shippe.' Then, on one bright June day, a joyous cry echoed along the waterfront. With every sail set, 'The Great Shippe' was running into port. As hurrying feet echoed along every street, a hush of awe crept over the waiting throng. The squarerigger was sailing free, *into* the wind! Not a man appeared on deck save a solitary figure at the bow who, with sword up-raised, pointed unwaveringly toward the sea. Suddenly the maintop snapped, hung an instant entangled in the shrouds, then masts and spars were blown away. The hull, still making straight for shore, shivered and plunged beneath the surface, enveloped in an enshrouding mist. When the cloud lifted, no sign of wreckage floated upon the quiet waters.

Not until the beginning of the nineteenth century did New Haven be-come an important commercial port, when more than one hundred ships were regularly sailing on coastwise, West Indian, and Oriental routes. Ships arriving from England often brought bricks as ballast, and these bricks, bearing a London imprint, were found as late as 1860, when the Atwater House was demolished. Nine years after the founding of the Colony, shoes were being exported, and beef was shipped the following ar. Branded biscuits were shipped to the West Indies and to Virginia, ir weight and quality regulated by law.

64, the brig 'Derby of Derby' arrived at New Haven with twenty f coal and thirty-eight Irish servants. Shortly afterward the ad-ent of 'A Parcel of Irish Servants, both Men and Women, just imported from Dublin in the brig Derby, and to be sold cheap,' was broadcast by one Israel Boardman of Stamford.

From 1783 until 1786, the steps of the old State House were the scene of annual auctions of paupers. These unfortunates were sold to persons who would keep them at the lowest rates. Children were still indentured in the 1700's, and the laws of the Colony always favored the master, not the servant.

New Haven has a fine reputation for furnishing men, arms, and financial support in all the country's wars. A volunteer artillery company was formed as early as 1645. In 1654, fifty men were furnished for an expedition against the Dutch in Manhattan, and in 1656, general reviews were held six times a year on the Green. Two to three hundred militia attended and the clergy frequently complained about horseplay in the military pews near the doors of the churches. A colorful event still celebrated by the city was Benedict Arnold's demand for the keys to the Powder House on the occasion of the receipt of news of the Lexington Alarm. The community failed to celebrate the signing of the Declaration of Independence, but later made amends by celebrating the defeat of Cornwallis in 1781. In that year, three hundred horse, and a like number of foot troops, under Lauzun, encamped on the Green.

The period of public improvement started in 1820, and a business boom was anticipated when work began on the Farmington Canal. People flocked to the offices to beg the company to accept their money. The eventual failure of the canal (*see Tour* 6) cost New Haven investors more than one million dollars.

The Log Cabin and Hard Cider campaign awoke the echoes of the stately Green in 1840. The Maine Law (liquor control), in 1854, precipitated violent partisanship. March of 1856 found anti-slavery speakers spreading their arms in dramatic appeal for aid for 'bleeding Kansas.' The Kansas Rifles were organized; Henry Ward Beecher delivered a farewell address at the North Church, and twenty-seven rifles were pledged the adventurers from the pulpit. When Lincoln was elected in 1860, cannon roared from the Green.

TOUR 1

CENTRAL NEW HAVEN

The *Green* with its three churches forms a spacious and distinctive civic center surrounded by public, university, and commercial buildings. Originally a swampland where Indians cut their alder arrows and settlers pastured their cattle, buried their dead, and gathered to trade, the Green has been administered by a Proprietors' Committee since the ground was received as a town common soon after the settlement of the Colony in 1638.

In 1639, the first meeting-house was built, followed by the erection of a watch-house (1640), a schoolhouse before 1648, the town jail before 1660, the State House and County Courthouse (1718), all of them long since removed. Here, too, were the stocks, the *Old Sign Post*, which survives (at a Church St. entrance), and the whipping post, at which stern-faced Elder Malbone publicly flogged his daughter Martha for having attended a house-warming with a young gentleman of her acquaintance. Gradually the rough wooden buildings were replaced by brick structures, trees were planted in orderly rows, the park was enclosed by a fence, and the Green of today evolved, with its triumvirate of churches, memorial flagstaff, and marble corner drinking-fountain modeled after the Choragic monument of Lysicrates in Athens.

NE. from Chapel St. on Temple St.

1. *Trinity Episcopal Church*, south on the Green, designed in 1814 by Ithiel Town, possibly with the assistance of David Hoadley, is the first real attempt here at Gothic Revival, expressed in seam-faced traprock with brownstone trim. Its original tower was square and short, with corner buttresses ending in finials. Although the exterior is unconvincing and somber, the interior, with its shapely clustered columns, has much of Town's taste for good proportions. The successful design of this church gave a great impetus to the Gothic Revival in America. Town, a native of Thompson, Conn., came to New Haven in 1810.

2. *Center Church* (1812–14) on the Green, the fourth edifice of the Congregational Society, was also designed by Town. His work, extending over 34 years, represents the full development of the Classic Renaissance. In designing this church he was undoubtedly inspired by St. Martin's-in-the-Fields, Trafalgar Square, London, one of the most notable works of James Gibbs. But Town, though a scholarly classicist, was by no means a copyist: hence Center Church is a masterly translation from the Georgian stone edifice to New England terms of brick and wood. The steeple, entirely of wood, achieving a lightness and delicacy that is lacking in the more solid stone tower of London, was constructed on the ground inside the brick tower, and raised to its present position by a system of windlasses.

The beautifully proportioned interior, with a gallery on three sides supported by fluted Ionic columns, has a segmental vaulted ceiling enriched with delicate plaster ornament. Behind the pulpit, a great arched Tiffany window portrays Davenport delivering his first sermon beneath the oak tree that stood near the settlers' landing place; at the base, seven columns and a seven-branched candlestick symbolize the 'seven pillars' chosen to form the Colony's church and civil government. On the walls of the church are tablets commemorating distinguished ministers of this church: John Davenport and his assistant, William Hooke, who returned to England to serve as Cromwell's chaplain; James Pierpont, one of the founders of Yale College; and Leonard Bacon, an ardent abolitionist, whose writings against slavery influenced Lincoln. A memorial tablet to Theophilus Eaton is on the exterior wall at the rear of the church, near his burial place.

The Crypt, beneath Center Church, is a part of the original burying ground that was used from the time of the first settlement (1638) until 1815. In 1821, that part of the burial plot lying outside the church walls was leveled off and the monuments removed to Grove Street Cemetery. Covered with a cement floor in 1879, the crypt contains 139 stones, the oldest of which, marking the grave of Mrs. Sarah Trowbridge, dates from 1687. Also buried here are the Reverend James Pierpont and his three wives; the first Mrs. Benedict Arnold, who died while her husband was yet a patriot; and Jared Ingersoll, a member of the Continental Congress who, before the Revolution, served for a time as stampmaster, but resigned when his efforts to enforce the act were unsuccessful.

The *Dixwell Monument*, at the rear of Center Church, enclosed by an iron railing, marks the grave of John Dixwell, one of the regicides, who lived for many years in this city under the name of James Davids. The rectangular granite stone, engraved with the important events of Dixwell's career, was erected by his descendants in 1847. Two tablets on the rear wall of the church commemorate the other regicides — General Edward Whalley, Cromwell's cousin, and General William Goffe — who also found refuge in this city.

3. *United Church* (1813–15), on the Green, formerly called North Church, is the work of Connecticut's Yankee genius, David Hoadley, a much more prolific and imaginative architect than Town, who designed Center Church. It is much more typical of the local early 19th-century ecclesiastical architecture than that church. Its projecting portico framed with pilasters, its three identical arched entrances, its central steeple set back from the façade and built up in three stages, and its many-paned windows in the two separate stories are characteristic of the Georgian Colonial. The repressed delicacy of its general design stands up well beside the masterly proportion and more resourceful technique of the cosmopolitan Center Church. The interior, with its fine paneling and French-made glass chandelier dating from the time of the building's erection, contains tablets to David Hoadley; Roger Sherman, American statesman, signer of the Declaration of Independence and first mayor of New Haven; Governor Simeon E. Baldwin, Simeon Baldwin, and Governor Roger Sherman Baldwin, eminent jurists.

It was in this church that Henry Ward Beecher delivered a sermon in 1855 to 80 men of Captain Line's anti-slavery band who were leaving to join John Brown in Kansas. With funds donated by the congregation, Beecher provided the entire company with Bibles and Sharps rifles.

4. At the SE. cor. of Church and Court Sts. stands the *United States Post Office*, a classical marble structure erected in 1923. Authentically designed by James Gamble Rogers, and beautifully proportioned in every detail, it is, however, overlarge for its style.

5. The *City Hall* (1871), 169 Church St., of brownstone, designed by

NEW HAVEN. Points of Interest

1. Trinity Episcopal Church
2. Center Church
3. United Church
4. United States Post Office
5. City Hall
6. Union and New Haven Trust Company Building
7. John Cook House
8. Bishop Homestead
9. County Courthouse
10. Ives Memorial Library
11. Governor Ingersoll House
12. Pierpont House
13. Bushnell House
14. Tory Tavern
15. First Methodist Church
16. Elizabethan Club
17. Southern New England Telephone Company Building
18. Bacon Homestead
19. Bowditch House
20. Weir House
21. Silliman Homestead
22. New Haven Colony Historical Society Building
23. Ithiel Town Homestead
24. Dana House
25. Home of Noah Porter
26. President's House of Yale University
27. Professor James M. Hoppin House
28. Sachem's Wood
29. Grove St. Cemetery
30. Site of First Settlers' Landing
31. Site of Roger Sherman's Homestead
32. Christ Church
33. Elisha Hull, or Bennett House
34. Old Campus
35. Memorial Quadrangle
36. Jonathan Edwards College
37. Weir Hall
38. Hall of Skull and Bones
39. Gallery of Fine Arts
40. Briton Hadden Memorial Building
41. Wolf's Head Hall
42. University Theater
43. Delta Kappa Epsilon Fraternity House
44. Pierson College
45. Davenport College
46. Yale Record Building
47. Trumbull College
48. Berkeley College
49. Calhoun College
50. William L. Harkness Hall
51. Sprague Memorial Hall
52. Sterling Memorial Library
53. Sterling Law Buildings
54. Hall of Graduate Studies
55. Mory's
56. University Heating Plant
57. Payne Whitney Gymnasium
58. Ray Tomkins House
59. Hewitt Quadrangle
60. Scroll and Key House
61. 'Sheff Campus'
62. Timothy Dwight College
63. Sterling Memorial Tower
64. Berkeley Divinity School
65. Osborn Laboratories
66. Peabody Museum
67. Sage Hall
68. Sloane Physics Laboratory
69. Sterling Chemical Laboratory
70. Farnam Memorial Garden
71. Marsh Hall
72. Sterling Divinity Quadrangle
73. University Observatory
74. Connecticut Agricultural Experiment Station
75. Albertus Magnus College
76. East Rock Park
77. Punderson Homestead
78. Arnold College for Hygiene and Physical Education
79. Monitor Square
80. Yale Bowl
81. Hopkins Grammar School
82. Edgewood
83. Edgewood Park
84. West Rock Park
85. Institute of Human Relations and the Sterling Hall of Medicine
86. New Haven Hospital
87. Defenders' Monument
88. A. C. Gilbert Company Plant
89. National Folding Box Company Plant
90. New Haven Clock Company Plant
91. Sargent and Company Plant
92. Winchester Repeating Arms Company Plant

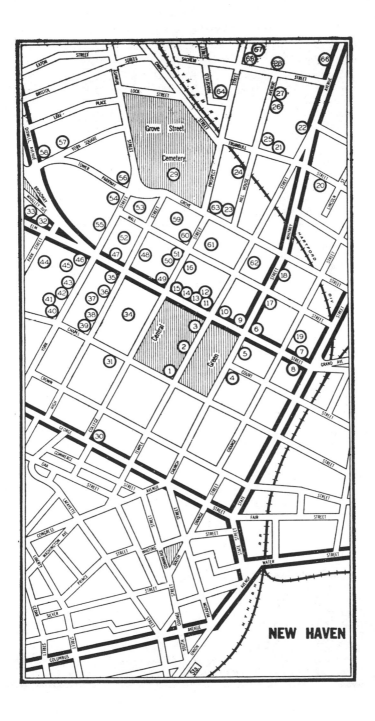

NEW HAVEN

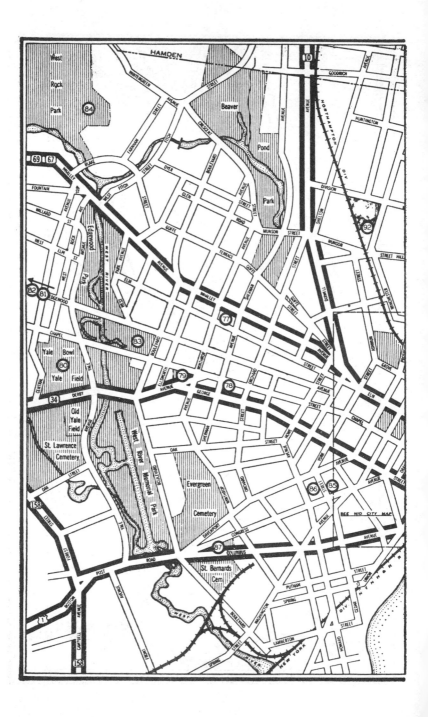

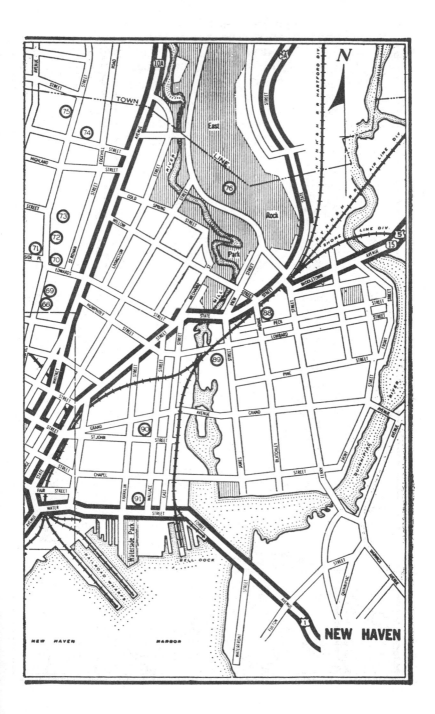

NEW HAVEN

Henry Austin, was erected in the era when the Venetian-Gothic style was thought to lend dignity to any public building.

6. The *Union and New Haven Trust Company Building*, NE. cor. Church and Elm Sts., designed by Cross and Cross (1926–28), is one of the city's modern skyscrapers. Of modified Georgian-Colonial style, the edifice is constructed of red brick with white trim. The façade is cut at an angle at the street intersection, and its 12 stories are topped with a tower of excellent proportion.

R. from Church St. on Elm St.

7. The *John Cook House (open)*, 35 Elm St., a large square brick mansion occupied by the Visiting Nurses' Association, was built in 1807 on the site of the former home of Governor Theophilus Eaton, whose high-tempered, non-conformist wife, Anne, was expelled from the church and eventually returned to England. This house, painted dull brown, with stone quoins and lintels, was probably remodeled by David Hoadley for Captain James Goodrich, when a pretentious ballroom with vaulted ceiling and two fine Adam fireplaces were added on the third floor.

8. The *Bishop Homestead*, 32 Elm St., almost opposite the Cook House, was built in 1815 on land which was the garden plot of the Rev. John Davenport. Its simple triple window, a modification of the traditional Palladian motif, and a fan-light over its pillared façade repeat on a large scale the leaded fan-light of the entrance. The building is now used as a store.

Return on Elm St.

9. The *County Courthouse* (1912), NW. cor. Elm and Church Sts., is a massive marble structure designed by Allen and Williams, and modeled after St. George's Hall (1838–54) in Liverpool. While somewhat ungainly, chiefly because of its bulk, the austerity and impressiveness of its general design are well suited to the dignity of the law.

10. The *Ives Memorial Library (open 9–9 weekdays)*, NE. cor. Elm and Temple Sts., constructed of brick and marble and designed in the early 20th-century Neo-Classic style, was first occupied in 1911. The work of Cass Gilbert, it was planned to mediate between the simple Georgian-Colonial architecture of the three old churches on the Green and the Neo-Classic style found in the newer public buildings.

11. The *Governor Ingersoll House*, built in 1830, NW. cor. Temple and Elm Sts., the home of the *Yale University Press*, is a spacious hip-roofed building, of impressive height. Its massive simplicity and recessed door-way flanked by plain Doric columns are characteristic of the Greek Revival period.

12. *Pierpont House (private club)*, 149 Elm St., with a central brick chimney, was built by the Rev. John Pierpont in 1767 and is now used by the *Yale Faculty Club*. Its only exterior ornamentation is in the molded window caps, and in the restored doorway with its cross-paneled double doors, a feature long hidden by a closed-in porch. Inside, there are

rooms of excellent raised paneling, restored to 18th-century coloring, and a shallow but wide 'porch' or stair hall.

13. The *Bushnell House* (1800), 155 Elm St., once the home of Eli Whitney Blake, the inventor of the stone crusher, is an excellent example of the Federal style that developed in the 19th century. A central-hall house with three end chimneys, it has a well-designed, open-pediment porch, covering a narrow, round-headed door with plain tracery and without side-lights. Above is an austere Palladian window which breaks through the main cornice and is framed by a small gabled pediment. *The Graduates' Club* now occupies the building.

14. *Tory Tavern*, 175 Elm St., built by Nicholas Callahan just before the Revolution, a small building with a later two-story porch, was such a notorious meeting-place for Tories that it was confiscated by the town in 1781. It is now used as a clubhouse by the *Elihu Club*, an undergraduate society.

15. The *First Methodist Church* (1854), NE. cor. Elm and College Sts., an impressive, though rather stereotyped example of the Greek Revival, has a colonnaded porch reached by a flight of steps on three sides. The square-shaped interior has a domed ceiling supported by huge green stone columns.

R. from Elm on College St.

16. The *Elizabethan Club* (*private*) (about 1815), 123 College St., is another of the houses set end to the street that used the early Classic Revival motif in a more elaborate and delicate form than in later periods. A Palladian window is elevated to a place in the front gable. The club, a meeting-place for literary-minded undergraduates and graduates, houses one of the finest collections of Elizabethan literature in the world. Alexander Smith Cochran, B.A., 1896, was the founder (1911) and benefactor.

R. from College on Wall St.

17. The *Southern New England Telephone Company Building*, SE. cor. of Church and Wall Sts., is the administrative headquarters for this pioneer communication service. Designed by R. W. Foote and Douglas Orr, and built in 1937, this 17-story limestone and steel office building makes use of simple modern lines. The first commercial telephone switchboard in America was installed in New Haven on January 28, 1878. Within less than threescore years the service has developed to a fully automatic exchange with a remarkable record for efficiency and financial stability.

L. from Wall on Church St.

18. The *Bacon Homestead* (*private*), 247 Church St., thought to have been built by Joshua Chandler in 1760, formerly stood at the corner of Church and Court Sts. Originally used as a coffee-house, frequented in Revolutionary days by ardent patriots, it was moved in 1820 to its present location by Dr. Leonard Bacon, pastor of the Center Church,

who occupied it until his death in 1881. It is a central-hall dwelling with four end chimneys. The porch with an alcove over it was Dr. Bacon's addition, and the building in general has the character of a house of his period.

Return on Church St.; L. on Wall St.; R. on Orange St.

19. The *Bowditch House* (*open*) (about 1815), 275 Orange St., where Eli Whitney, the inventor of the cotton gin, died in 1825, is the work of David Hoadley. In the front room, which now serves as an art store, is a fine mantel flanked by arched recesses.

L. from Orange St. on Trumbull St.

20. The *Weir House* (*private*), 58 Trumbull St., built by James Kingsley about 1810, has had two former locations — Temple St. at the corner of Trumbull, and Hillhouse Ave., where it once served as a select girls' school. The open portico shelters a doorway whose pilasters are ornamented with a design of rings, resembling wooden bull's-eyes, and the window caps are designed with an entablature with a trio of plain blocks supporting a molded top. Within, there is a variety of beautiful mantels.

21. The *Silliman Homestead* (*private*), 87 Trumbull St., was the first house to be built on Hillhouse Ave., and was later moved to its present site. It was bought in 1809 by the elder Professor Benjamin Silliman, a chemist who was the founder of the first Collegiate Agricultural Experiment Station in the country at Yale in 1847. Lafayette, on his last visit to America, was a guest of 'Madame' Trumbull, widow of the second Governor Jonathan Trumbull, and mother of Silliman's wife. Colonel John Trumbull (1756–1843), noted artist, also lived in this house during his later years.

R. from Trumbull St. on Whitney Ave.

22. The *New Haven Colony Historical Society Building* (*open daily* 9–5; *adm. free*), 114 Whitney Ave., a handsome structure designed in Georgian-Colonial style by J. F. and H. S. Kelly (1930), contains many relics of the early days, including a snuffbox owned by John Dixwell; the apothecary sign, mortar, and daybook of Benedict Arnold; Webster's writing-desk; sidearms used by General Andrew Jackson at the battle of New Orleans; and Eli Whitney's original model of the cotton gin. Especially noteworthy are exhibits of pewter plate and old blue-and-white Staffordshire ware, collections of prints and early American portraits, and the society's fine historical and genealogical library.

Return on Whitney Ave.; R. on Grove St.; R. on Hillhouse Ave.

Hillhouse Avenue was laid out in 1792 by Senator James Hillhouse, whose desire to improve and beautify the city led to the planting of trees throughout the community, winning for it the name of 'Elm City.' Although less impressive than in the 19th century when it was sometimes called the most beautiful street in America, its former splendor is recalled by the spaciousness of the wide, elm-arched thoroughfare, with its imposing town houses, examples of the decadent period of the Greek Revival.

23. The *Ithiel Town Homestead* (*private*), 4 Hillhouse Ave., was the residence of the eminent architect who, after his success with churches, was in great demand for planning the more impressive type of house. It was remodeled by Joseph Earl Sheffield, benefactor of the Sheffield Scientific School at Yale, who added the towers and wings at the time when the Italian villa style in architecture began to appeal to romantic taste.

24. The *Dana House* (*private*), 24 Hillhouse Ave., built in 1849 in the Egyptian manner, with an extremely flat roof and wide overhang, was for 40 years the home of the well-known geologist and mineralogist, Professor James Dwight Dana (1813–95).

25. The *Home of Noah Porter*, 31 Hillhouse Ave., a plain wooden dwelling of 1826, later remodeled with a mansard roof, was originally built on another street. Porter (1811–92), a philosopher, editor, and educator, was president of Yale University.

26. *President's House of Yale University* (*private*), 43 Hillhouse Ave., a remodeled, half-medieval brick dwelling, was erected by Henry Farnam, an engineer associated with Sheffield in the building of the Farmington Canal in 1828 (*see Tour* 6). This canal cut diagonally across Hillhouse Ave.

27. At the *Professor James M. Hoppin House* (*private*) (1862), 47 Hillhouse Ave., many distinguished men and women have been entertained, including Phillips Brooks, Lady Fitzmaurice, and Von Herkomer. It was the President's House during the Angell régime, 1921–37.

28. *Sachem's Wood* (*private*) (1829), facing the Avenue from the hilltop, is a somber brown homestead built by James A. Hillhouse, poet. His father, Senator James Hillhouse, called 'the Sachem' by his fellow members in Congress because of his resemblance to an Indian, spent his declining years in this house with his daughter, Mary Lucas, who, as a child, frequently visited President and Mrs. Washington in Philadelphia.

Return on Hillhouse Ave.; R. on Grove St.

29. *Grove St. Cemetery* (1796), Grove St., entrance opposite High St., the first burial ground in the country to be laid out in family lots, and containing the graves of many illustrious dead, is entered through an impressive Egyptian pylon gateway (1845–48), designed in brownstone by Henry Austin (1804–91), an apprentice of Ithiel Town. Attached to this gate is the old bell from the first cemetery on the Green, which was formerly rung during burial services. The large golden butterfly on the front of the caretaker's building is the Egyptian symbol of immortality.

The grave of Jehudi Ashmun (1794–1828), first Colonial agent to Liberia, is left of the entrance; beyond is that of Benjamin Silliman (1779–1864), chemist. On Cedar Ave. are buried James D. Dana (1813–95), geologist, General David Humphreys (1752–1818), Revolutionary diplomat, industrialist, and the first man to introduce merino sheep in

Jedediah Morse (1761–1826), American geographer; Theodore Winthrop (1828–61), novelist, and one of the first officers killed in action in the Civil War; Noah Porter (1811–92), eleventh president of Yale; the Rev. Lyman Beecher (1775–1863), reformer and father of Harriet Beecher Stowe and Henry Ward Beecher; Eli Whitney (1765–1825), and Noah Webster (1758–1843), compiler of the first American dictionary. Paralleling Cedar Ave. is Locust Ave. with the graves of Timothy Dwight, 2d (1829–1916), one-time president of Yale; Elias Loomis (1811–89), mathematician; Arthur T. Hadley (1856–1930), another Yale president; and Josiah Willard Gibbs (1839–1903), founder of the science of physical chemistry.

In the northwest corner of the cemetery on Sycamore Ave. are buried Chauncey Jerome (1793–1868), pioneer clockmaker, and Charles Goodyear (1800–60), inventor of vulcanized rubber. Lining the walls of this section are 400 brownstone markers that were removed from the burial ground on the Green.

On Ivy Path, bordering the northern wall of the cemetery, are monuments to President Theodore D. Woolsey (1801–89), and General Alfred Howe Terry (1829–90), the hero of Fort Fisher.

South on Linden Ave. are the graves of Eli Whitney Blake (1795–1886), inventor; Edward E. Salisbury (1814–1901), orientalist; and William Dwight Whitney (1827–94), linguist; and the poetically inscribed stone of Governor Theophilus Eaton, whose body lies in the crypt on the Green. On Maple Ave. are buried three Yale presidents, Ezra Stiles (1727–95); Timothy Dwight (1752–1817); and Jeremiah Day (1773–1867); Admiral Andrew H. Foote (1806–63); Senator James Hillhouse (1753–1832); Roger Sherman (1721–93).

On Cypress Ave. are the graves of two Yale presidents, Thomas Clap (1703–67), and Naphtali Daggett (1727–80), who died as a result of injuries received at the hands of a British officer during the English invasion of New Haven.

Return on Grove St.; R. on College St.

30. The *Site of First Settlers' Landing*, cor. College and George Sts., is marked by the *First Settlers' Tablet*. Stepping from their heavily burdened little vessel which had forced its way with some difficulty up a narrow inlet, long since filled in, these pioneers knelt beneath a mighty oak, while the Rev. John Davenport preached on 'The Temptations in the Wilderness.'

Return on College St.; L. on Chapel St.

1. The *Site of Roger Sherman's Homestead*, 1032 Chapel St., has a ʻarker on the wall of a brick building to indicate the home which Sherman occupied from 1761 until his death in 1793. Sherman was the only to sign all four fundamental documents on which the United Government is based: the Articles of Association in 1774; the ʻion of Independence, 1776; the Articles of Confederation in 1778; ʻederal Constitution of 1787.

R. from Chapel St. on High St.; R. on Elm St.; R. on Broadway.

32. *Christ Church* (1895), conspicuously situated at the triangular inter-section of Broadway and Elm St., is more nearly designed in the old English tradition of Gothic than more recent forms that have raised their towers in neighboring college yards. The simple, tall, brownstone tower with four large pinnacles is modeled after that of Magdalen College, Oxford. The interior of the church is of brick, in a rather severe Perpendicular style, relieved by the delicate tracery of the rood screen and altar. Henry Vaughn was the architect.

33. The *Elisha Hull*, or *Bennett House* (*private*), 86 Broadway, a buff-colored clapboard dwelling, is one of the few homes designed by Hoadley (about 1812) that survive in the city. The fan-light above the door is surrounded by a pattern of interwoven circles peculiar to New Haven architecture, and the high flat window heads have a delicate diamond design.

TOUR 2

YALE UNIVERSITY

A college in New Haven Colony was one of John Davenport's ambitions, but his hopes were not fulfilled during his lifetime, as Harvard's facilities were sufficient to supply the needs for higher education in the New England Colonies. By the end of the seventeenth century, however, it became clear that there was room for another college, and in 1701 several Connecticut clergymen, all Harvard graduates, met at the house of the Rev. Samuel Russell, in Branford, to consider the founding of a 'collegiate school.' According to tradition each of them laid some books on a table with the words, 'I give these books for the founding of a college in this colony.' Whether this be true or not, in 1702 the college, officially located at Saybrook, began its existence with one student in the house of the Rev. Abraham Pierson, its first rector, in Killingworth, now Clinton. On Pierson's death, in 1707, the classes were moved to Saybrook, and in 1716 the college was transferred to New Haven. About the same time, Elihu Yale (1648–1721), born in Massachusetts, later a merchant prince of the East India Company, and Governor of Madras, was persuaded to contribute a gift of merchandise later sold for £562, in gratitude for which the institution was named in his honor.

Early in the nineteenth century, professional schools were organized in connection with the college, but the title 'Yale University' was not offi-cially adopted until 1887. There are (1938) ten professional and graduate schools, in addition to the original Yale College. In 1933, the college, together with the other undergraduate units of the Sheffield Scientific School, and the School of Engineering, reorganized in so far as their residential system was concerned, into nine colleges of about one hundred and eighty students each. This was made possible chiefly through a gift of Edward S. Harkness, class of 1897, who gave an endowment to Harvard for the same purpose. Although superficially similar to the colleges at Oxford and Cambridge, the Yale colleges are substantially different, being merely residential units under centralized control, without individual endowments. Each college has its separate dining-hall, common rooms, and library, and also a rapidly growing set of traditions.

Since its beginning, Yale has been notable for the scientific scholarship of its faculty. Benjamin Silliman in chemistry, James Dwight Dana in geology, Willard Gibbs in physical chemistry, Othniel Marsh in paleontology, William Graham Sumner in sociology, and Ross Granville Harrison in zoology have made contributions of major importance in their various fields. A remarkable number of Yale men have become the first presidents of other colleges and universities. Among them are Jonathan Dickinson (Princeton), Samuel Johnson (King's College, now Columbia), Eleazer Wheelock (Dartmouth), Ebenezer Fitch (Williams), John H. Lathrop (Missouri and Wisconsin), Henry Durant (California), Daniel Coit Gilman (Johns Hopkins), William P. Johnson (Tulane), Andrew D. White (Cornell), and William R. Harper (Chicago).

Other distinguished graduates include Jonathan Edwards, 1720, theologian; Samuel Seabury, 1738, first bishop of the American Episcopal Church; David Humphreys, 1771, Washington's aide and subsequently minister to Spain; Nathan Hale, 1773, the patriot martyr; David Bushnell, 1775, inventor of the torpedo; Noah Webster, 1778, lexicographer; Joel Barlow (1754–1812), poet and diplomat; James Kent, 1781, jurist, author of *Kent's Commentaries*; Eli Whitney, 1792, inventor of the cotton gin; John C. Calhoun, 1804, Vice-President of the United States; James Fenimore Cooper, expelled, 1805, novelist; S. F. B. Morse, 1810, artist and inventor of the telegraph; William M. Evarts, 1837, Secretary of State; Samuel J. Tilden, 1837, who lost the Presidency of the United States to Rutherford Hayes, in a contested election; Morrison R. Waite, 1837, Chief Justice of the United States; William H. Taft, 1878, President, and later Chief Justice of the United States.

Campus Tour
   Guide Service, June — Sept., Phelps Gateway, College St., bet. Chapel and Elm, free. Weekdays 10.30, 1.30 and 3; Sun. 1.30 and 3. Sept.— June; guides furnished at the Bureau of Appointments, 144 Grove St.

N. from Chapel St. on College St.

34. The *Old Campus*, bounded by Chapel, High, Elm, and College Sts. (entrance on College St., Phelps Gateway), has been the nucleus of Yale life since the college was moved from Saybrook in 1716. Here can be seen examples of the four chief architectural periods through which the University has passed — the 18th century, the Victorian age, the first era of the so-called 'collegiate Gothic' of the 1890's and early 1900's, and the great building period of 1919–35, chiefly Gothic, and dominated by the personality of James Gamble Rogers. More than two centuries of constant use, and its fine trees, rather than architectural merit, have

given the Campus an air of distinction. *Connecticut Hall* (1752), near the southeast corner, is the oldest of extant Yale buildings, and sole remnant of the Old Brick Row, which formerly extended from Chapel to Elm Sts. Unfortunately, those buildings had to be destroyed in order to utilize the square on which they stood. Nathan Hale, class of 1773, roomed in Connecticut Hall, though his room has not been identified. A *Statue of Hale*, by Bela Lyon Pratt, stands in front of the building. Just south of Connecticut Hall, formerly stood Mother Yale, the first and for many years the only Yale building in New Haven, erected in 1717. The other brick building of Georgian-Colonial design is *Edward McClellan Hall*, erected in 1925. On the west side of the Campus is the second oldest Yale building, built in 1842 and now the headquarters of the University Y.M.C.A., *Dwight Hall*. The middle section of the building, now *Dwight Memorial Chapel*, with a fine west window, was originally the University Library; the wings to north and south housed the collection of the two debating societies, Linonia and Brothers in Unity. South of this are *Linsly* and *Chittenden Halls*, later additions to the old library, now used as recitation halls. Chittenden is the sole remaining example at Yale of the Richardsonian Romanesque style of architecture of the late 19th century. South of Chittenden, on the corner of Chapel and High Sts., is *Street Hall* (1866), the original home of the School of Fine Arts, the first art school in the world to be incorporated as part of a university. It is still used for this purpose. *Durfee Hall* (1871), and *Battell Chapel* (1876), on the north side of the Campus, and *Farnam* (1869), and *Lawrance* (1886) *Halls*, on the east, all designed by Russell Sturgis, Jr., represent the mid-Victorian Gothic. *Phelps* (1895), and *Welch* (1892) *Halls* on the east side, and *Vanderbilt Hall* (1893), on the south, were all built during the first period of collegiate Gothic. *Bingham Hall*, on the southeast corner, and *Wright Hall*, on the northwest, both in collegiate Gothic, were built in 1928 and 1911 respectively.

Exit from Campus on Elm St.; L. on High St.

35. The *Memorial Quadrangle*, Elm, High and York Sts., was designed by James Gamble Rogers, and built in 1917–21 as the gift of Mrs. Stephen V. Harkness. This structure, now divided into *Branford* and *Saybrook Colleges*, marked an era in American collegiate architecture. Its most original features are the warm yellowish, naturally weathered sandstone of which it is composed, and its many charming decorative details, reminiscent of Yale history and Yale men. The passageways, or slypes, are named in honor of early benefactors of the college, and the entries for prominent graduates. *Harkness Tower*, on High St., 221 feet in height, built in memory of Charles W. Harkness, class of 1883, is the most conspicuous feature of the group, and perhaps the most distinguished structure in the University. It is a 'crown' tower, showing the influence of such European Gothic models as St. Botolph's in Boston (Lincolnshire), and the 'Tour de Beurre' of Rouen Cathedral, with the difference that the octagonal crown is extended to two stories and the whole unified into a coherent mass. On the ground floor of the tower is

a lofty room with a fine window and fan-vaulting. Carvings around the top of the wainscot portray the history of many incidents and customs of the University. *Branford Court* (entrance at the south), now a part of Branford College, is the largest and most beautiful of the seven quadrangles enclosed by the structure. *Wrexham Tower*, a copy of that at Wrexham in Wales, under which Elihu Yale lies buried, rises above the small Wrexham Court, now a part of Saybrook College (entrance on Elm St.). A stone from the original Wrexham Tower is built into the wall over the doorway.

36. *Jonathan Edwards College*, 70 High St., is named for the eminent 18th-century divine. A bronze statue of a slave boy holding a sundial (1708), that once belonged to Elihu Yale, stands in the west end of the court.

37. Beyond Jonathan Edwards College, on High St., is the entrance to *Weir Hall*, a building of eccentric charm, with its romantic stairway and a grass court raised 30 feet above the surrounding level. This is now the home of the department of architecture of the Art School. It was built of stones from Alumni Hall, a Gothic building of the 1850's, and sold to Yale University by the alumnus who designed it.

38. Next, beyond, is the *Hall of Skull and Bones*, the oldest of the college senior societies.

R. from High St. on Chapel St.

39. The *Gallery of Fine Arts* (1928) (*open daily* 2-5), cor. Chapel and High Sts., entrance on Chapel St., connected with Street Hall by an arched bridge over High St., was designed by Egerton Swartout in a style reminiscent of the Italian medieval period, and built of sandstone. The main entrance and the basement windows are covered with intricate wrought-iron grilles, and the façade, as yet unfinished, is broken by five large arched windows that light the gallery. In the first-floor lobby, a tablet marks the place beneath which the first distinguished Connecticut artist, Colonel John Trumbull (1756-1843), is buried beside his wife. To the left of the entrance is *The Sculpture Hall*, exhibiting fine examples of Babylonian, Assyrian and French Romanesque statuary; the *Elihu Yale Tapestries*, woven in London in the late 17th or early 18th century by John Vanderbank in the 'Indian manner,' which is a variation of the popular chinoiserie style; and a hall for temporary exhibits of art. Adjoining the main hall is the assembly room, hung with tapestries and paintings, where public lectures are held during the academic year. On the second, or mezzanine floor, are the administrative offices, classrooms, and photograph and lantern slide collections. Here among reproductions of medieval sculpture and metal work, is the original group, *Jephthah and his Daughter* (1853), one of the earliest pieces of American sculpture in marble, by Hezekiah Augur, who began life as a wood carver (*see ART*). The third floor contains Flemish confessionals from a Ghent museum, carved in the 17th-century Baroque style; exhibits of early American glass; and the *Mabel Brady Garvan Collection* of American silver (1650-1825), the most representative and finest collection of its

EDUCATION

CONNECTICUT has had a distinguished record in the field of education from the days of Edward Hopkins and John Davenport, when Oxford and Cambridge scholars helped to lay the first foundations of sound learning, to the present time, when Yale University has made New Haven a city of towers and colleges. Bred in a tradition of service to 'Publicke State,' Nathan Hale found the path short that led him from a country schoolmastership to a martyred hero's death. Figures such as Bronson Alcott with his radical theories of child education, Prudence Crandall with her school for negro girls, the solid Emma Willard, and the fertile Henry Barnard are part of this long and progressive history.

One of the first public school systems in the world was established in Connecticut only eleven years after the first white settlement. From the sale of her lands in the Western Reserve the State drew funds to support these schools. The nineteenth century academies have become public high schools housed in buildings of modern design or developed into the many private preparatory schools, some of them nationally known.

The graduates of Connecticut institutions of higher learning have contributed abundantly to American education.

HAN HALE SCHOOL, NEW LONDON

AVON OLD FARMS SCHOOL POST OFFICE

BULLET HILL SCHOOL, SOUTHBURY

ANSONIA HIGH SCHO

DAVENPORT COURT AND PIERSON TOWER, YALE UNIVERSITY

PAYNE WHITNEY GYMNASIUM, YALE UNIVERSITY

HARKNESS TOWER, YALE UNIVERSITY

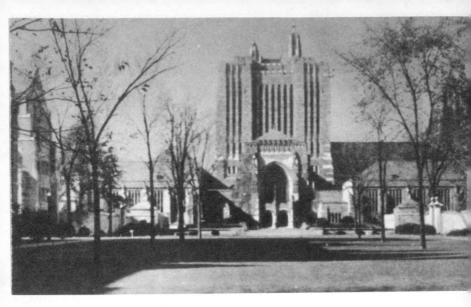

STERLING MEMORIAL LIBRARY, YALE UNIVERSITY

CONNECTICUT HALL, YALE UNIVERS

TRINITY COLLEGE CHAPEL, HARTFORD

COAST GUARD ACADEMY, NEW LONDON

STERLING DIVINITY QUADRANGLE, YALE UNIVERS

kind. Among the silversmiths whose work is represented are: Hull and Sanderson, Jeremiah Dummer, John Coney, Edward Winslow, John Dixwell, Peter Van Dyck, Jacob Boelen, Philip Syng, and Joseph Richardson. The especially noteworthy *Jarves Collection* of Italian primitives includes important paintings by Pollaiuolo, Piero di Cosimo, Sassetta, and Titian. In the smaller rooms off the main gallery are exhibits of ancient and Oriental art; a reconstruction of a Christian chapel of the third century, A.D., with original frescoes from Dura-Europos; and prints, paintings, and drawings of the Renaissance and modern periods. East of the stairway is the *American Room*, with choice pieces of early American furniture by Thomas Affleck, John Goddard, Samuel McIntyre, and Duncan Phyfe, and hung with Colonial and early Republican portraits — the work of such artists as John Singleton Copley, Charles Willson Peale, Gilbert Stuart, Thomas Sully, Ralph Earl, and Samuel F. B. Morse. Off this are two paneled rooms from the *Rose House* of North Branford (1710), and above them a bedroom and sitting-room from the *Joel Clark House* in East Granby (1737). In the *Trumbull Room*, beyond these, are canvasses and miniatures largely from the Revolutionary period, by Colonel John Trumbull, son of Governor Jonathan Trumbull, artist and patriot, friend and aide to Washington. It was with these works and the gift portrait of George I as a nucleus, that the Trumbull Gallery, the first collegiate art gallery in America, was established in 1831. Recent acquisitions include the *Hobart Moore Collection* of textiles, chiefly from the Near and Far East, and a collection of paintings and drawings by Edwin Austen Abbey.

R. from Chapel St. on York St.

40. *Briton Hadden Memorial Building* (1932), York St., between Chapel and Elm Sts., houses the *Yale Daily News*, the oldest college daily in the country. Briton Hadden, B.A., 1920, a *News* editor, was co-founder of *Time* and *Fortune* magazines.

41. Surrounded by a high stone wall, *Wolf's Head Hall*, York St., housing a senior society, stands beside Briton Hadden Memorial Building. It was designed by Bertram Goodhue in 1925. There are several fraternity buildings in the Tudor style behind it.

42. Next beyond, *University Theater (open during college session)*, on York St., the seat of the Department of Drama of the Art School, was built (1926) when Professor George Pierce Baker came to Yale from Harvard. Students engage in the various phases of dramatic production, from playwriting and directing to stage lighting, scene, and costume designing. Major plays are produced about once each month in the upper theater, which has a remarkable mechanical and electrical equipment. In the experimental theater, downstairs, an average of three student-plays are produced each week.

43. *Delta Kappa Epsilon Fraternity House*, York St., adjoins the University Theater.

L. from York on a passageway beside Delta Kappa Epsilon House.

44. *Pierson College*, Park St., between Elm and Chapel Sts., entered under a fine Colonial clock tower, is built of brick in the Georgian style At the south end of the quadrangle are the dormitories humorously named 'slave quarters,' a group of low buildings surrounding a small paved court, with attractive doorways and ironwork.

Return to York St.; L. on York St.

45. *Davenport College*, York St., between Chapel and Elm Sts., has a stone Tudor-Gothic front masking interior courts of brick Georgian-Colonial architecture.

46. The *Yale Record Building*, York St., is the home of the college humorous publication, the *Yale Record*.

R. from York St. on Elm.

47. *Trumbull College*, Elm St. between York and High Sts. (L), has an impressive court backed by the mass of the University Library.

48. The southern half of *Berkeley College*, NE. cor. Elm and High Sts. This building has been divided into two sections in order to permit an unobstructed view of the Sterling Memorial Library. It was named after the philosopher, George Berkeley, Bishop of Cloyne, who was an early benefactor of Yale.

49. *Calhoun College*, NW. cor. Elm and College Sts., was designed by John Russell Pope and named for John C. Calhoun, class of 1804 and Vice-President of the United States.

L. from Elm on College St.

In the middle of the block between Elm and Wall Sts., the *Cross Campus* affords a fine vista from College St. It passes between Calhoun College (L) and William L. Harkness Hall (R), reaches an axis at Blount Ave., and then passes between the southern and northern halves of Berkeley College, which are joined by an underground passage, to the main entrance of Sterling Memorial Library on High St. At the Cross Campus, the work of the landscape architect of the university, Beatrix Farrand, appears to advantage.

50. *William L. Harkness Hall* (1927), on College St., between Elm and Wall Sts., is a recitation building, designed by William Adams Delano.

51. *Sprague Memorial Hall* (1917), SW. cor. College and Wall Sts., of which Coolidge and Shattuck were the architects, is the main building of the School of Music. Its handsome auditorium, with excellent acoustics, seats 728 and is used for chamber music and small orchestral concerts.

L. from College on Wall St.; L. on High St.

52. The *Sterling Memorial Library*, High, Wall, and York Sts., was completed in 1931 from designs by James Gamble Rogers. It is the chief memorial to John W. Sterling, B.A., 1864, who left a large endowment to Yale for building and other purposes. The main exterior feature is the impressive *Stack Tower*, rising 14 stories above street level, best seen from

York St. The interior is a model of good planning. The *Reserve Book Room,* and *Linonia and Brothers*, an open-shelf room for general reading, stand to the left and right of the main entrance respectively. Beyond the former, to the south is the *Yale Memorabilia Room*, and on the second floor in this part is an interesting collection of the books of the library as it existed according to a catalogue of 1742, arranged, so far as possible, in their original shelf distribution. In this room also are preserved the front doors of the Samuel Russell House in Branford in which the founders of Yale met in 1701. The impressive, nave-like entrance hall, with sculptures in relief showing the history of the library, leads past the catalogue on the left and an exhibition space on the right, directly to the delivery desk. Over this is a mural painting, 'Alma Mater,' by Eugene F. Savage, N.A. At the left of the desk is the long *Reading Room*, its fine proportions impaired by unfortunate lighting fixtures. To the right of the desk is the periodical reading room and a glazed cloister, used for temporary exhibitions, with a view into an attractive court on the right. The tympani of the eastern windows of this court have carved on them colophons and signatures of great printers and engravers from all lands. Down the cloistered passage is the *Rare Book Room* with ample working space for special students. At the east end, in an elaborately vaulted, shrine-like room, is a copy of a Gutenberg Bible of about 1460.

Return on High St.; L. on Wall.

53. The *Sterling Law Buildings*, facing the library on Wall St., were designed by James Gamble Rogers and completed in 1931. On the top floor of the east portion along High St., is the Law Library, a high, dignified room with traceried windows and a polychromed ceiling. An interesting view of gables, chimneys, and roofs is obtained from the cloister in the main court, or from the windows above it.

54. *Hall of Graduate Studies*, at end of Wall St., on York St., also designed by Rogers, was completed in 1932. There are two courts and a high tower of brick and limestone.

L. from Wall on York St.

55. *Mory's*, 306 York St., occupies a small white house. Originally a bar and chop-house on the corner of Temple and Center Sts., under the proprietorship of one Moriarty, it was so popular among Yale undergraduates of many generations that on the destruction of the old building in 1912, the whole interior, with all its furnishings and decorations, was moved to a similar house on the present site, and the management incorporated as a club.

L. from York St. on Tower Parkway.

56. The *University Heating Plant* (1917), Day and Klauder, architects, NW. cor. York St. and Tower Parkway, is an interesting example of modernized Gothic with two handsome tall chimneys.

57. *Payne Whitney Gymnasium* (*open during college year*), on York Sq., facing Tower Parkway, was completed in 1932 from designs by John Russell Pope. The central tower contains rowing tanks, a trophy room,

a practice swimming pool 50 meters long, and many rooms for exercise and indoor sports. The north wing contains the main amphitheater, and the south wing, the exhibition swimming pool; on the floor above are squash and handball courts. The *Francis P. Garvan Collection* of sporting prints is distributed among the rooms and corridors.

L. from Tower Parkway on York Sq.

58. *Ray Tompkins House*, NW. cor. York Sq. and Broadway, completed 1932, is of Briar Hill sandstone in Gothic style. John Russell Pope was the architect. In it are the offices and headquarters of Yale athletic departments and quarters for visiting teams.

Return on York Sq.; R. on Tower Parkway, which becomes Grove St.

59. *Hewitt Quadrangle*, SW. cor. Grove and College Sts., consists of the *University Dining-Hall, Memorial Hall, Woolsey Hall,* and *Woodbridge Hall*. They were all erected in 1901 to commemorate the 200th anniversary of Yale's founding, and all except Woodbridge Hall were designed by Carrère and Hastings. The *Colonnade* on the south side of the Dining-Hall, with a stone cenotaph, was added in 1928 in memory of Yale men who died in the World War. The long interior, finished in brick and sandstone, has a handsome open timber roof decorated in polychrome. Memorial Hall, on the corner of College and Grove Sts., with a baroque dome, forms the main entrance for the Dining-Hall and Woolsey Hall. On the ground floor are marble tablets, upon which are inscribed the names of all Yale graduates who have fallen in six wars. On the second floor is a circular reception room; in the hall outside are pictures and autographs of eminent Yale men, collected and presented by the Rev. Anson Phelps Stokes, a former secretary of the University. On the third floor (*open Sun. aft., or by permission*) is a collection of early keyboard and stringed instruments of the 17th and 18th centuries, presented by the late Morris Steinert of New Haven. An addition to the collection is a *Piano* that belonged to Beethoven. *Woolsey Hall* is an auditorium seating about 2800; it contains the *Newberry Memorial Organ*, one of the largest in the country. *Woodbridge Hall*, Wall St., between High and College Sts., is a small building somewhat reminiscent of the Senate House at Cambridge, England. It contains the offices of the president, secretary, and treasurer of the University, and a meeting room for the corporation, its governing body.

R. from Grove on College St.

60. *Scroll and Key House*, NW. cor. College and Wall Sts., designed in the Moorish style, is occupied by the senior society of that name.

61. The '*Sheff Campus*,' College St. (L), between Grove and Wall Sts., is occupied by buildings designed by Charles C. Haight between 1904 and 1913. It is expected that this group, when completed, will be incorporated as Silliman College, the only unfinished unit of the college plan.

L. from College on Wall St.; L. on Temple St.

62. *Timothy Dwight College* (1935), Temple St. between Wall and Grove

Sts., is a brick Georgian-Colonial structure with a graceful clock tower, named for two men of the same name, grandfather and grandson, who were both presidents of Yale.

L. from Temple on Grove St.

63. The *Sterling Memorial Tower*, NE. cor. Grove and College Sts., for which Clarence C. Zantzinger was the architect, was completed in 1932. It forms a unit with *Sheffield Hall*, in which are the administration offices of the Sheffield Scientific School, and with *Strathcona Hall*, built from a bequest of the late Lord Strathcona, containing a lecture-hall and classrooms for the study of transportation. An *Inscribed Stone*, from Mt. Sir Donald in the Selkirk Mountains of British Columbia, named for Lord Strathcona, formerly Sir Donald Smith, is built into the exterior of the east wall.

R. on Prospect St.

64. *Berkeley Divinity School* (Episcopal), Prospect and Sachem Sts., is affiliated with Yale University. The school was located in Middletown from its founding in 1854 until 1928.

65. *Osborn Memorial Laboratories* (1914), NE. cor. Prospect and Sachem Sts., devoted to zoology and botany, have a pleasant vista through the archway. Charles C. Haight was the architect.

R. from Prospect on Sachem St.

66. *Peabody Museum* (*open daily* 9–4.30; *free*), NW. cor. Sachem St. and Whitney Ave., designed in 1925 by Charles Z. Klauder and built of brick and artificial sandstone in the French Gothic style, is one of the most notable natural history museums in the world. A small mineralogical exhibit was assembled more than a century ago by Benjamin Silliman; to this were added the fossil and meteorite collections of Othniel C. Marsh, Yale's first professor of paleontology. The museum, which originally stood at the corner of Elm and High Sts., was formally established in 1866 through the gift of George Peabody, a London banker and the uncle of Marsh, whose interest in the institution was stimulated by the enthusiasm of his nephew. The present building is three stories high with a 93-foot tower and an octagonal entrance hall that rises two stories to a stone-vaulted roof, modeled after the Château Coucy in France. On the first floor of the museum the exhibits are chronologically arranged, showing the progress of life from its earliest forms to man. Directly in front of the entrance hall, where a pendulum swings back and forth throughout the day indicating the earth's rotation from west to east, is the *Hall of Invertebrates*, with fossil exhibits arranged in two series — geologic and biologic. The first, occupying cases 5–15, beginning at the left of the entrance, includes specimens that inhabited the earth during the five major geologic eras, while the second, cases 16–43, classifies these animals according to their structural development. Here, also, will be found several habitat cases, and in case 47, on the right, a panel depicting the Tree of Life, in which man's development is traced as it is believed to have occurred.

In the *Great Hall* are exhibits of the earliest vertebrates — fishes, am-phibians, reptiles, and birds — and one of the most complete dinosaur collections in the country, gathered by Professor Marsh, the first man to discover the bones of these prehistoric reptiles in America. Standing in the center of the hall is a huge brontosaurus that weighed more than 35 tons in the flesh, and was 70 feet long and 15 feet high at the hips. In habitat cases along the walls, other dinosaur types have been reproduced in their natural settings. In the *First Hall of Mammals*, adjacent to the Great Hall, exhibits illustrate the next step in the development of the vertebrate series, including the warm-blooded mammals, which from the standpoint of intelligence far surpassed the reptilian species. Of special interest is the skeleton of the early ground sloth (case 8), with patches of hide and hair still clinging to it, found in a New Mexican cave after thousands of years of burial; at the eastern end of the hall are speci-mens showing the evolution of the horse, perhaps the most important of Professor Marsh's paleontological discoveries. In the *Second Hall of Mammals*, the carnivora, represented chiefly by archaic and contemporary game and sea animals, are outstanding. The *Hall of Man* traces the story of man's physical development from the apes, and in case 2, compares the human embryo with those of other animals. Here also, is shown man's cultural progress as demonstrated by the products he has fashioned with his hands.

The third floor of the museum includes the *Hall of Meteorites*, with 300 'chips of other worlds,' the largest of which is a specimen found in Texas weighing 1635 pounds; the *Hall of Minerals*, containing an extensive collection, one of the most unusual features of which is the ultra-violet exhibit showing unsuspected colors in ordinary stones; the *Halls of Economic Zoology* and *Local Zoology*, pertaining chiefly to contemporary animals indigenous to southern New England; and the *Hall of Anthro-pology*, containing exhibits illustrating man's cultural development.

Return on Sachem St.; R. on Prospect St.

67. *Sage Hall*, Prospect St. (R), between Sachem and Edward Sts., de-signed by William Adams Delano (1923), a four-story brownstone build-ing in Tudor style, is the home of the *School of Forestry*.

68. *Sloane Physics Laboratory*, Prospect St. (R), designed by Charles C. Haight (1912), is of Longmeadow brownstone, in collegiate Gothic style.

69. The *Sterling Chemical Laboratory* (1922), Prospect St. (R), was designed by William Adams Delano, incorporating the Gothic forms used in Cambridge University.

70. The *Farnam Memorial Garden*, NE. cor. Prospect and Edward Sts., formerly the property of William Whitman Farnam, treasurer of Yale, was donated to the University by his widow in 1930.

71. *Marsh Hall*, Prospect St. (L), just beyond Hillside Place, is the former home of Othniel C. Marsh, an early authority on paleontology and collector of much of the material now in the Peabody Museum. The grounds, laid out chiefly by Marsh himself, are kept as a *Botanical Garden*

and contain many rare trees and shrubs, as well as a collection of irises, native American plants, and a rock garden.

72. The *Sterling Divinity Quadrangle*, Prospect St. (R), between Edward and Canner Sts., completed in 1932, was designed by William Adams Delano. In plan it is reminiscent of Jefferson's for the University of Virginia, at Charlottesville, with symmetrically placed buildings connected by colonnades leading up to an important central mass; but the general effect, as well as many details, is quite different. The two small octagonal buildings fronting on Prospect St. are a porter's lodge and a guest house. The eight gabled buildings beyond these contain living quarters and offices; each unit is named for a prominent Yale divine. Beyond these the vista broadens out into a quadrangle; at the right are the libraries and at the left an auditorium; in the center, flanked by wings containing classrooms and administrative offices, is *Marquand Chapel*, with its rather severe but beautifully proportioned lantern tower. The interior is a modified reproduction of an old New England meetinghouse without galleries. Back of the chapel is another quadrangle, with a large common room, refectory, gymnasium, and squash courts. The Divinity School, which is inter-denominational, has about 220 students; the quadrangle accommodates about 170.

73. *University Observatory* (R), Prospect St., has in its buildings several telescopes, a heliometer, and an astronomical camera.

TOUR 3

E. from Prospect St. on Huntington St.

74. *Connecticut Agricultural Experiment Station*, 123 Huntington St., the first State-supported agricultural experiment station in America, was established at Middletown in 1875, and removed to New Haven in 1877. It is devoted to research on plant breeding, pest control, and soil chemistry.

Return on Huntington St.; R. on Prospect St.

75. *Albertus Magnus College*, 700 Prospect St., offers courses in liberal arts and science, and a pre-medical course leading to a Bachelor of Arts degree. It is a Roman Catholic college for women, founded in 1925 by the Sisters of Saint Dominic, of Saint Mary of the Springs, East Columbus, Ohio. New Haven was selected because there was no other Catholic college for women in this section, and because of the unusual educational facilities available.

The college property includes 21 acres with 4 buildings, formerly private estates: *Rosary Hall*, containing a temporary chapel, library, dining-room, recitation rooms, and offices; *Imelda Hall*, the residence hall; *Walsh Hall*, with fully equipped modern laboratories for chemistry and biology; and the *Students' Building*, containing a cafeteria, auditorium, scenery rooms, dressing-rooms, and showers. There are tennis courts and a hockey field on the property. Plans have been drawn for a chapel in the Georgian-Colonial style to be dedicated to Saint Thomas Aquinas. In 1937 the enrollment was 143.

OTHER POINTS OF INTEREST

76. *East Rock Park*, 1.5 *m.* NE. of the Green, end of Orange St., containing 446 acres of woodland, landscaped gardens, and expansive fields, with 8½ *m.* of drives and bridle paths, affords the best outlook over the city. A wide panorama discloses magnificent views of New Haven, its commodious harbor, and the residential and business districts. At the foot of the abrupt precipice, Mill River meanders in its serpentine course, forming ox-bows and little islands. At the summit (accessible by car) stands the 112-foot granite *Soldiers' and Sailors' Monument* (1887), visible for many miles.

There are many romantic legends about this rock, including that of Seth Turner, said to have owned the property early in the 19th century. Disappointed in love, he built here a stone house, where he lived as a hermit, tending his walled-in garden and caring for his goats and sheep. Since he rarely spoke with anyone, the townspeople concocted many fantastic tales about him. But his real story remains untold, as he froze to death in his hut during the winter of 1823. In 1855, Milton J. Steward is reported to have purchased the top of the rock, where he built a house, and, believing that a second flood was imminent, began work on a 40-foot steamboat, an amazing contraption built without regard to the practical necessities of navigation. Later, when the city bought the summit, this vessel (no longer extant) was filled with earth and utilized as a mammoth flower pot.

The *Pardee Rose Garden*, near State St., presents in spring an impressive scene of multi-colored and fragrant blooms. Within the grounds are also *Blake Field, Rice Field*, and *College Woods*, all well equipped for various forms of recreation, including tennis, football, baseball, basket and volley ball, boccie, quoits, and horseshoe pitching; and an archery field, the only municipally owned full-sized range in Connecticut.

Indian Head Peak, a wild section at the eastern end of East Rock Park (footpaths only), was used by the Quinnipiac Indians as a signal point. At the top of the rock there are several cement emplacements, used in the World War for anti-aircraft guns.

77. The *Punderson Homestead (private)*, 338 Whalley Ave., a Dutch-roofed dwelling, was erected in 1787 by descendants of one of the first settlers in New Haven, but has been somewhat remodeled by the addition of a narrow piazza across the entire front, and a large central dormer window. The heavy, five-panel double doors, however, are original.

78. *Arnold College for Hygiene and Physical Education*, 1466 Chapel St., is a co-educational institution offering a four-year course in physical culture, supplemented by summer work at the college camp at Silver Sands.

79. In *Monitor Square*, at the junction of Chapel St., Derby and Winthrop Aves., a small triangle of greensward, enclosed with an iron and stone fence identical to that which surrounds the Green, is a *Monument to Cornelius Scranton Bushnell* commemorating a former citizen of New Haven who was chiefly responsible for the successful construction of the 'Monitor' from plans devised by John Ericsson. The ship is pictured in bas-relief above the inscription. The memorial, designed by Charles A. Platt, architect, and Herbert Adams, sculptor, represents a large bronze eagle, wings outspread in a gesture of defiance, surmounting a globe of the same metal supported by four dolphins, emblematic of the sea.

80. The *Yale Bowl* (*open*) (1914), Derby Ave., between Yale and Central Aves., an amphitheater covering 25 acres of ground and seating about 71,000, is approached through the imposing *Walter Camp Memorial Gateway* (1928), erected in memory of the dean of modern American football, with funds donated by alumni of Yale and 593 other colleges and schools. Designed by Charles A. Ferry, the Bowl has 30 entrances, only one of which, portal 10, is kept open for visitors. Surrounding it are the Yale tennis courts, baseball diamond, practice football fields, polo grounds, track field, and cross-country track course.

The *Charles E. Coxe Memorial Gymnasium*, adjacent to the Bowl, a brick building with marble trim, erected in 1928, provides facilities for indoor athletics.

The *Lapham Field House*, cor. Derby and Tryon Aves., an athletic clubhouse containing lockers, showers, and dressing-rooms for 2000, was built in the Georgian-Colonial style of red brick with marble trim in 1924, the gift of Henry T. Lapham, an alumnus.

81. The *Hopkins Grammar School*, 986 Forest Rd., a preparatory school, is a development of the third oldest school in the country, founded in 1660 with funds provided by Governor Edward Hopkins.

82. *Edgewood* (*private*), Forest Rd. (L), opposite end of Edgewood Ave., was the home of Donald G. (Ik Marvel) Mitchell, author, whose descendants still possess it.

83. *Edgewood Park*, Chapel St., between Boulevard and Yale Ave., includes 121 acres of heavily wooded slopes, rolling meadowlands, winding paths and drives bordered with fragrant flowers, ornamental shrubbery, and sparkling lagoons. On the upper terrace are colorful flower beds, a playground with sandboxes and doll-houses, and another with swings, teeters, and merry-go-rounds for older children. Excellent facilities for football, baseball, soccer, soft ball, and archery are provided on the lower terrace.

84. *West Rock Park*, Blake St., an attractive public park, affords an extensive view from the summit. In it is *Judges' Cave*, the hiding place of

the regicides, Whalley and Goffe, who, after signing the death warrant of Charles I, were forced to flee from England. Landing in Boston on July 27, 1660, they remained there until the following year when, fearing apprehension, they fled to New Haven, arriving on March 7, 1661. They lived unmolested until news reached the city of the proclamation issued by Charles II, ordering their arrest and deportation to England. They fled to Milford, but returned on March 27, and were for a while concealed at the home of the Rev. John Davenport, whose sermon, 'Hide the outcast, betray not him that wandereth,' aroused sympathy for the condemned men. Whalley and Goffe, however, realizing they would involve Davenport with the British authorities if they continued to accept the safety of his home, were about to forfeit their liberty when West Rock was suggested as a shelter. A tablet there is inscribed: 'Resistance to Tyrants is Obedience to God.' Frightened from the sanctuary by wild animals, the regicides escaped to Milford, where they remained for two years, returning again to New Haven in 1664 before taking up permanent residence in Hadley, Mass.

Near the beginning of the Summit Drive is the entrance to Baldwin Parkway which extends for more than six miles to Bethany Gap. The parkway winds to the north over the forested top of the West Rock ridge and affords superb views of New Haven and the surrounding country. When the Merritt Highway is completed, it is expected that this parkway will form a main approach to New Haven.

85. The *Institute of Human Relations*, and the *Sterling Hall of Medicine*, Cedar St. at Davenport Ave., designed by Grosvenor Atterbury, 1930, and Day and Klauder, 1923, respectively, occupy two sections of a large brick and limestone building, three to five stories high, and extending along two sides of a city block. Established in 1929 by gifts from the Rockefeller Foundation and the General Education Board, the Institute of Human Relations is administered jointly by the University and the New Haven Hospital, and promotes cooperative research in the social sciences. It has facilities for the study of psychiatry, mental hygiene, psychology, anthropology, and has a clinic of child development.

86. The *New Haven Hospital*, 789 Howard Ave., organized in 1826, was one of the first in the country (1873) to establish a school of nursing, which has become the Yale School of Nursing. Conducted in conjunction with the Yale School of Medicine, the hospital is the only one in the State conducting diagnostic ambulatory clinics for general service. With the Yale School of Medicine, it maintains the New Haven Dispensary, where approximately 50,000 persons are cared for annually.

87. *Defenders' Monument* (1911), at the junction of Davenport, Congress, and Columbus Aves., honors the citizens and Yale students who joined in repulsing the British invaders in 1779. Designed by James E. Kelley, this monument consists of three bronze Colonial figures: a student, farmer, and merchant, defenders of their homeland.

88. *A. C. Gilbert Company Plant* (*adm. on application at office*), Blatchley

Ave., between Peck and State Sts., manufactures Erector Toys as its best-known product.

89. *National Folding Box Company Plant* (*adm. on application at office*), Alton and James Sts., engaged in the production of folding paper boxes and lithographing, employs several hundred persons.

90. *New Haven Clock Company Plant* (*adm. on application at office*), 133 Hamilton St., is a leading producer of clocks and watches. Thomas Nash, Colonial gunsmith and clockmaker, handled all the Colony's time-keeping problems in 1638, but Chauncey Jerome (1783–1868), the Henry Ford of the clockmaking industry, brought his designs for brass-wheeled clocks to New Haven and developed the industry now known as the New Haven Clock Company in 1845. Jerome's use of standard metal parts for clocks was an innovation, and his initial success with a cheap, one-day, all-metal clock brought many changes to the industry. The New Haven Clock Company took its name in 1853 and has remained in business since that date.

91. *Sargent and Company Plant* (*adm. on application at office*), Water and Wallace Sts., occupies approximately four city blocks. This hardware plant was started in 1813 at Leominster, Mass., moved to New Britain, Conn., in 1840, and to New Haven in 1864. Joseph Denney Sargent founded the business, which was eventually incorporated by Joseph Bradford Sargent. The plant has more than 30 acres of floor space, manufactures builders' and casket hardware, employs about 2000, and is credited with introducing Italian labor into New Haven industry.

92. *Winchester Repeating Arms Company Plant* (*adm. on application at office*), 275 Winchester Ave., manufactures firearms and ammunition, sporting goods, cutlery, and tubing. In 1638, Thomas Nash was the only gunsmith in New Haven Colony. Nash 'mended' clocks and repaired fowling pieces in his backyard shop. In 1798, Eli Whitney secured an order from the government for 10,000 rifles, set up a system of inter-changeable parts in his armory, and invented a milling machine and gauges for the standardization of manufacturing. This Whitney Arms Company was the forerunner of the Winchester Repeating Arms Company, organized by Oliver Winchester in 1866, removed to Bridgeport, and returned to New Haven in 1871, where it has remained.

Points of Interest in Environs:

Eli Whitney Gun Shop and Barn, Whitney Ave., Hamden, **1.6** *m.* (*see Tour* 6); Lighthouse Point and Morris House (Colonial museum), Lighthouse Road (*see Tour* 1).

NEW LONDON

Town: Alt. 40, pop. 29,640, sett. 1646, incorp. 1784.

Railroad Station: Union Station, foot of State St., for N.Y., N.H. & H. R.R. and Central Vermont R.R.

Accommodations: Two hotels.

Information Services: Chamber of Commerce, 12 Meridian St.

Airport: Trumbull Airport, Eastern Point, Groton; no scheduled service.

Piers: Passenger steamers dock at foot of State St. Trips to: Block Island, July 1 to Labor Day, $2 Round trip, automobile rate $5 to $7. Fisher's Island, N.Y. (from Ferguson's Wharf) 50¢ and $1 one way; automobile rate $2.50. Runs year round. Montauk Point, Long Island, July 1 to Labor Day. Round trip $1.75; automobile rate $5; round trip $9. Orient and Greenport, Long Island, May to October. Round trip $1.75; automobile rate $5; round trip $9. Public Landing, foot of State St.

Recreation: One legitimate theater.

Swimming: Green Harbor Beach, Pequot Ave. (for children); Butler Beach; Indoor pool, Y.M.C.A., Meridian and Church Sts., 25¢ fee; Ocean Beach, Long Island Sound (State 213 from city); Riverside Park, Crystal Ave.

Skating: Caulkins Park, Riverview Ave.; Bates' Wood (fireplaces).

Golf: New London Country Club, 9 holes, fee $1.

Annual Events: Yale-Harvard Boat Race Day, Friday of Commencement week, June. Includes freshmen, combination, and junior varsity crew races in forenoon. Yale-Harvard baseball game at Mercer Field in afternoon and the Varsity Race (Yale-Harvard) at 7 P.M. Graduation exercises of both the Coast Academy and Connecticut College, annually in June. Easter Sunday, 7 A.M. Sunrise Service in Coast Guard Academy Bowl, usually attended by 3000 or 4000 people.

NEW LONDON, at the mouth of the Thames River where a drowned valley forms one of the deepest harbors on the Atlantic coast, is a beautiful city that stretches three miles along the river, to Long Island Sound. Up rolling hills to the northwest, the narrow crooked streets are gay with the uniforms of Coast Artillerymen from the island coast defense posts outside the harbor, and sailors and officers from the submarine base, the Coast Guard Academy just up the river, and the Coast Guard Base 4 at Fort Trumbull.

Rendezvous of privateers during the Revolution, home port of a mighty fleet of whaling vessels in the nineteenth century, headquarters of minelayers, submarine chasers and submarines during the World War and of the Coast Guard's swift 'rum-chasers' in the prohibition era, New London offers much of historic and maritime interest.

The annual Yale-Harvard Boat Races are held over a four-mile course north of the Thames River bridge each June. Yachts and schooners, cabin cruisers and speed boats, flying code flags and college banners, come from many ports to line the course and herald with a gathering *crescendo* of whistles the progress of the slim racing shells.

Industry in New London has never intruded on the residential area. The mills are either on an unattractive section of the waterfront or in secluded parts of the town. The chief products are silk, machinery, printing presses and garments.

The second smallest township in the State (only 3452 acres), New London was settled in 1646 by John Winthrop, the younger, who had previously established a residence on Fisher's Island. By 1648 there were more than forty families in the area, known to the Indians as 'Nameaug,' but to the white settlers as 'Pequot.' In the belief that the city would become a great commercial center, the settlement was named New London, in March, 1658, and the river, formerly 'Monhegin,' was called the Thames. The town was incorporated in 1784.

Whaling dates from the sailing of the 'Rising Sun,' on May 20, 1784. When the ships which sailed to the Brazil banks returned in 1785 with more than three hundred barrels of whale oil, the *New London Gazette* enthusiastically exhorted, 'Now my horse jockeys, beat your horses and cattle into spears, lances, harpoons and whaling gear, and let us all strike out; many spouts ahead! Whale plenty, you have them for the catching.' For the next hundred years most able-bodied New London men and boys went down to the sea in ships. In 1864, New London's whaling fleet was only one ship less than New Bedford's, with seventy-two ships and barks, one brig and six schooners, representing an invested capital of $2,500,000.

Many local fortunes were founded by the sturdy captains who sailed to the Arctic and Antarctic. The profits on successful voyages were high. One voyage of the 'Pioneer,' the first steam whaler afloat, commanded by Captain Ebenezer Morgan, which left New London, June 4, 1864, and returned September 18, 1865, yielded $151,000 net. The 'MacClellan' of New London is credited with having captured the largest right whale recorded, which gave 362 barrels of oil and 40,000 pounds of bone. In 1850, over $1,000,000 worth of whale oil and bone passed through the New London customs. The last whaler to make this port was the schooner 'Margaret,' in 1909, commanded by Captain James Buddington.

Captain Dudley Saltonstall of New London was the first to unfurl the Stripes, the first national flag of the Colonies, on the high seas, December 3, 1775, when with a fleet of four vessels outfitted at New London, he stormed and captured New Providence, Nassau, B.W.I.

The first commission ever granted to an officer in the U. S. Marine Corps was granted to Samuel Nicholas of New London on November 28, 1775.

More privateers sailed from New London during the Revolutionary War, than from any other port in New England. They wrought such havoc to British shipping that the town was burned and the port blockaded by the English in an attempt to curb their activities. Among the three hundred prizes were the 'Lively Lass' of London, with a cargo valued at $125,000, and the 'Hannah,' worth $400,000.

The 'Spy,' a tiny schooner engaged in privateering in English waters, sailed undetected through the English fleet anchored in the Channel, as the British never suspected that so small a ship could be an enemy vessel from across the ocean. Another New London vessel, captained by Ebenezer Dayton and Jason Chester, sailed across Long Island Sound to Long Island. The crew disembarked and traveled overland, towing their boat on wheels to Southampton. Launching the schooner, they set sail for Fire Island where they captured five British ships.

On September 6, 1781, the town was attacked by a British force led by Benedict Arnold. When two warning guns were fired from Fort Trumbull, the British fleet, evidently apprised of the signal, fired a third. As three guns were the local signal for a celebration, the militia was not assembled in time and Fort Trumbull fell almost without a struggle. The town was burned and the British crossed the river to attack Groton Heights (*see GROTON*).

Thomas Short of New London established the first printing press in Connecticut here in 1709. His successor, Timothy Green, specialized in almanacs, and in 1753 published an 'Astronomical Diary' written by Roger Sherman, a signer of the Declaration of Independence. When Green died in 1793, Nathan Daboll carried on the work with his series entitled, 'The New England Almanac and Farmer's Friend.' This almanac is still published.

The *Munsey Magazine* was printed in New London in a plant established by Frank Munsey in the annex of the present Mohican Hotel. When a change in laws made it necessary to imprint the location of the printing plant of a magazine, Munsey turned the plant into a hotel.

Eugene O'Neill once wrote a daily column in the *New London Telegraph*, a morning paper that has since been discontinued; and Richard Mansfield II, son of the famous Shakesperian actor who lived in 'The Whaling City,' produced a volume of poetry here.

TOUR 1

N. from Water St. on State St.

1. The *Parade*, a small square at the foot of State St., was long the center of village activities. Just beyond it were the wharves where townsfolk greeted the whalers returning from their long voyages. In 1691, during the Indian Wars, the Parade was fortified with six six-pounder guns from Saybrook. In the tavern which once faced the parade, Nathan Hale made an impassioned speech on the day news came from Lexington. Shortly afterward he closed his schoolhouse on the hill and left to join Knowlton's Rangers.

On the Parade, S. of the Soldiers' and Sailors' Monument, a *Memorial to Whalemen of New London*, designed by P. Leroy Harwood and executed by Gorham and Co., was dedicated September 4, 1937.
On a circular stone base, flanked on either side by capstans to which it is connected by anchor chains, the Memorial is an authentic whaleman's try-pot (kettle used on board ship in trying the oil from the blubber), surmounted by a tripod of bronze replicas of two types of harpoons and a lance, or killing iron. Hanging from the center of the tripod is a reproduction of a whaleman's lantern. On one of the two bronze plaques at the sides of the try-kettle, is inscribed the whalemen's slogan, 'A dead whale or a stove boat.'
2. The *Union Bank*, NW. cor. Main and State Sts., established in 1792, shares with the Hartford Bank, founded in the same year, the honor of being the first bank in Connecticut.

R. from State on Main St.

3. The *Captain Stevens Rogers House*, 294 Main St., which has been converted into a tenement and stores, was the home of one of the two commanders of the 'S. S. Savannah,' the first steamship to cross the Atlantic (Savannah to Liverpool, 1819). Captain Stevens Rogers, a sailing master, was engaged to take charge if the steam power should fail. His brother-in-law, Moses Rogers, also of New London, was the steamship captain. The initial trip of the 'Savannah,' a full-rigged ship of 350 tons, equipped with an 80–90 horse-power engine, was made without cargo to test the practicability of steam power in ocean navigation. The ship reached Liverpool in 22 days, 14 by steam and 8 under sail, the sail being used to conserve fuel against a possible emergency. Before returning to this country, the 'Savannah' visited Stockholm and St. Petersburg, where she was inspected by the King of Sweden and the Emperor of Russia. The logbook of this voyage is in the National Museum, Washington, D.C.

R. from Main on Mill St.

4. *Old Town Mill* (*open daily* 9–5), in a rocky glen shielded by a grove

NEW LONDON. Points of Interest

1. The Parade
2. Union Bank
3. Captain Stevens Rogers House
4. Old Town Mill
5. Lyman Allyn Museum
6. U.S. Coast Guard Academy
7. Connecticut College
8. Connecticut Arboretum
9. Whaling Museum
10. County Courthouse
11. Public Library
12. Jedediah Huntington House
13. Coit Houses
14. St. James Episcopal Church
15. Site of the First New London Pound
16. Statue of John Winthrop, Jr.
17. Nathan Hale School
18. Shaw Mansion
19. Shepherd's Tent
20. Huguenot House
21. Hempstead House
22. Fort Trumbull
23. Old Powder House
24. Gardiner's Cemetery
25. Ocean Beach
26. New London Light

T H A M E S

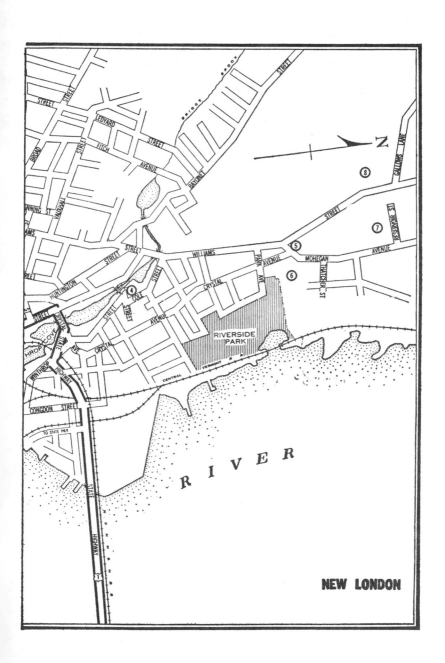

NEW LONDON

of elms from the shops and homes of a closely built-up section, is a low gambrel-roofed gristmill established by John Winthrop in 1650 and rebuilt in 1742. Its overshot wheel, churning the waters of Jordan's Brook, is a replica of the original. The beveled weather-boarding at the west end is probably original. Inside, the flared corner posts, the beams, and the gears and grinders of the mill itself remain. Winthrop's home once stood beyond the mill (L) on the Knoll occupied by the Winthrop School, a public grade school.

Return on Mill St. to Main St.; R. on Main which becomes Williams St.; R. on Mohegan Ave.

5. *Lyman Allyn Museum (open weekdays except Mon. 10–5; Sun. 2–5)*, 100 Mohegan Ave., a memorial to an old whaling captain, designed by Charles A. Platt, of New York, and built of Connecticut granite trimmed with Vermont marble in a modern adaptation of the Greek style, is beautifully situated on landscaped terraced grounds. Permanent exhibits include the Miner Collections of American and European furniture, pottery, ironwork, pewter, and textiles; the Benjamin collections of Mediterranean antiques; and small collections of drawings, sculpture, and Chinese pottery.

6. *U.S. Coast Guard Academy (open weekdays, 1 to sunset, guides furnished upon application to the sentry at the gate)*, Mohegan and Park Aves., covering 45 acres on the Thames River, is the $2,500,000 'Annapolis' of the Coast Guard Service, appointments to which are made on a competitive basis. The 15 buildings include barracks, infirmary, observatory, gymnasium, and an armory which houses the Perham collection of small arms and weapons of historical value. A battalion review is held at 3.30 P.M. every Thursday in April, May, October, and November. On the riverfront is the Academy's seaplane landing with a ramp, wharf, and boat sheds. Floating equipment includes cruising cutters, surf and whale boats, eight-oared shells, sailing sloops, schooners, and patrol boats.

The first school for training officers for the Coast Guard (then the Revenue Cutter) Service was established July 31, 1876, aboard the schooner 'Dobbin,' based at New Bedford. In 1900 the school was transferred ashore to Arundel Cove, Maryland, and in 1910 was moved to Fort Trumbull, at New London. The present quarters were completed and occupied in September, 1932.

7. *Connecticut College*, Mohegan Ave. (State 32), on a spacious hilltop campus of 352 acres with an extensive view of the harbor and Long Island Sound, is a women's college of liberal arts and sciences. At the entrance is the Washington Memorial Gateway, a gift of the D.A.R. in 1932. The ivy-covered buildings of native granite are arranged in quadrangle formation between Mohegan Ave. and Williams St., but the campus slopes from Mohegan Ave. to the river on the east, and west, beyond Mohegan Ave., through a rocky wilderness. Opened in 1915, with an original endowment of $1,000,000 presented by Morton F. Plant, the college has a student body of 689, representing 27 states and four foreign countries,

and a faculty of 67. East of the campus the Caroline A. Black Botanic Garden includes an iris collection, rock garden, and pool.

8. *Connecticut Arboretum* (*open daily*), Connecticut College campus, Mohegan Ave., opposite the Washington Memorial entrance, is a 70-acre tract maintained by the college, which contains about 300 varieties of trees and shrubs native to Connecticut. Open to the public, it is used as a recreation spot by the college students. Wide, grassy steps, flanked on either side by laurel bushes and red cedars, lead down the hillside to an amphitheater by a tiny lake and a bird sanctuary.

A well-marked trail leads from the Arboretum into *Bolles Wood*. This ancient hemlock forest, practically untouched since Indian days, includes trees which are probably 450 years old. The remarkable preservation of the forest is due to the care of the Bolles family, in whose possession it remained from Colonial days until presented to the college by Anna Hempstead Branch, the poetess. Most of the oldest trees stand near a small clearing at the top of a ravine strewn with great boulders. Carved on one tree is a copy of the deed to this land by Chief Owanoco of the Mohegans to the first of the Bolles family. The original deed is now in the possession of Connecticut College.

TOUR 2

W. from Main St. on State St.

9. *Whaling Museum*, in *Mariner's Savings Bank* (L) (*open during banking hours, adm. free*), at 224 State St., a modern red-brick and white marble structure, was founded in 1876 by men associated with the whaling industry. It houses more than 200 whaling relics, large mural paintings, and whaling prints of exceptional merit.

10. The *County Courthouse* (*open during business hours*), at the head of State St., of Georgian design, was built in 1784, and renovated in 1909. Its size is accentuated by its hill-crest location. It is almost more a Rhode Island building than one of Connecticut design, with its high, rather peaked, flaring, gambrel roof, its free use of quoins, and the marking off of wooden clapboards to look like stone. In its time few courthouses aspired to such architectural dignity, but New London was then a seaport second only to Newport and Providence on the southern New England coast. The two stories are horizontally distinct, a Rhode Island characteristic, even to the difference in the corner pilasters. The rather flat, central pediment frames, in the second story, a debased Palladian window with rounded tops in all three sections. A small, neat cupola tops the whole.

11. The *Public Library* (*open* 9–9), SE. cor. State and Huntington Sts., is a small, but typical example of the work of Richardson, the Boston architect who exerted a great influence on American architecture in the last quarter

of the 19th century. His buildings were, like this one, essentially massive and heavy with Romanesque detail, built of sandstone of two contrasting colors, with ordinarily an entrance doorway framed in a semicircular arch. For contrast, the railroad station at the foot of State St., a more conventional product of his office, may be compared with it.

R. from State St. on Huntington St.

12. The *Jedediah Huntington House* (*private*) NW. cor. Huntington and Broad Sts., an imposing, hip-roofed, brick structure painted white, on a wide triangular lawn, was built by Huntington in 1790 when he came from Norwich to become Collector of Customs. A two-story colonnade of free-standing square columns covers both the southern and eastern sides.

13. The *Coit Houses* (*private*), Nos. 105, 111, 115, and 119 Huntington St. (R), are four large, almost identical homesteads with two-story porticoes, built about 1830 in the Greek Revival style. They are locally known as 'Whale Oil Row' because their builders were leaders in that industry. The first house (No. 105) has wings, which the others do not, and wider cornices and corner boards, as if afterthought had decided to free it in part from the family uniform. It is probably the latest, as its detail is simpler and heavier. The doorways of all four vary considerably.

14. *St. James Episcopal Church*, SE. cor. Huntington and Federal Sts., is a brownstone building of Gothic feeling, with a high spire and heavy buttresses. It is the second successor of the church of which the Right Rev. Samuel Seabury, the first Episcopal bishop in America, was rector. His body is buried in the chancel.

15. The *Site of the First New London Pound* at Huntington St. and Bulkeley Place is occupied by the Bulkeley School.

16. The *Statue of John Winthrop, Jr.*, opposite, on Bulkeley Sq., facing Huntington St., a memorial to the founder of New London, who served his Colony as Governor for 18 years, was designed by Bela Lyon Pratt, a descendant (*see Art*). On April 23, 1662, Winthrop secured Connecticut's charter from Charles II. The form of government established by this charter was the fundamental law of Connecticut for 156 years. Known as the Father of American Chemistry, Winthrop spent much energy and money in trying to develop the mineral resources of the State, and promoted the settlement of many remote areas.

17. *Nathan Hale School* (1774) (*open weekdays; Tues., and Thurs. free; other days 10¢*) is in a corner of '*Ye Ancientest Burying Ground*,' Huntington and Richard Sts. The school, moved to its present site and restored in 1901, is the building in which the Revolutionary hero taught from March, 1774, to June, 1775. Tradition says that on the high ground nearby, where the tomb of Jonathan Brooks stands, Benedict Arnold sat on horseback and watched the destruction of the city by the British in 1781. The burial ground, laid out in 1653, contains graves of the ancestors of many persons prominent in the life of this country.

TOUR 3

S. from State on Bank St.

18. The *Shaw Mansion* (*open daily* 10–12, 2–4; *adm.* 25¢; *free on Wed.*) (1756), 287 Bank St., cor. Blinman St., is a stone building with almost a full story basement under its long porch. The granite for its construction was quarried from a ledge on the site by 35 Acadian refugees, quartered at that time in New London. The house was remodeled about 1840, when the porches, the long balustrade along the roof, and the marble mantels within, were added. Shaw's son, Nathaniel, in charge of naval affairs for Congress during the Revolution, used his home as naval headquarters for outfitting privateers. The house was also a hospital for prisoners of war, from one of whom Mrs. Shaw contracted a fever which ended her life. When it was fired by the British in 1781, vinegar, stored in the attic, extinguished the flames. The room in which Washington spent the night, in 1776, remains intact. The mansion, maintained by the New London Historical Society, has been restored and furnished. In the old-fashioned gardens at the rear is an authentic 18th-century summer house.

R. from Bank St. on Blinman St.; R. on Truman St.

19. The *Shepherd's Tent* (*private*), 77 Truman St., is a steep-roofed little dwelling. Dated 1739 by some authorities, the building served as the meeting place and theological seminary of the disciples of the Rev. John Davenport and the Rev. George Whitefield. Here on March 6, 1743, Davenport preached the frenzied sermon in which he exhorted the congregation to burn their most precious possessions as a demonstration of their freedom from worldly covetousness. After the service, the zealous church people hastened home and then to the Parade, where they kindled a fire and heaped upon it not only their treasured satin cardinals, calashes, silk stockings, and silver buckles, but all their religious tracts and sermons.

20. The ivy-covered, broad shouldered *Huguenot House* (*open as a teahouse*), 75 Truman St., at the junction of Jay, Hempstead, and Truman Sts., was built, it is said, in 1751, of split granite quarried on the grounds by Huguenot refugees. With narrow chimneys at either end, the moderately pitched gambrel roof is pierced by two dormers and a hatchway door. The builder, Nathaniel Hempstead, was a descendant of Sir Robert Hempstead, who was granted a large estate by King James I.

L. from Truman St. on Hempstead St.; R. on Hempstead Court.

21. The *Hempstead House* (1678, c. 1710), directly behind the Huguenot House at 11 Hempstead Street, is undoubtedly New London's oldest dwelling. In it the development of the 17th-century house can be traced with unusual clearness. The first section built was the west end, a one-room, end-chimneyed structure with a single summer beam running

from front to back. Later, a room with two summer beams was built on the other side of the chimney and at that time or later, a lean-to was built across the rear. A curious feature is that, in the oldest part, the sills extend into the room, as do the rude corner posts, the end girts, and the summer beams. In its position facing south, its two-foot overhanging cornice, its heavy framing, and primitive lines, the house still shows its early date, despite the later shingles and the new brick chimney-top that shows behind the ridge. The house was once a station in the Underground Railway. Joshua Hempstead wrote his often quoted 'Diary' in this house, which was occupied by a descendant, Anna Hempstead Branch, a distinguished poetess.

The Hempstead House will be opened to the public by the Antiquarian and Landmarks Society, Inc. The New London County Historical Society and the Hempstead Family Association will each nominate a member of the Society's Committee on Ancient Structures which will have charge of this landmark.

TOUR 4

S. from Bank St. on Howard St.; L. from Howard on Walback St.; L. on East St.

22. *Fort Trumbull (open on application to sentry at gate)*, East St., on the grounds of U.S. Coast Guard, Base 4, is a low fortification of millstone granite, which occupies the site of two earlier garrisons on an isthmus jutting into the Thames River. The building, long since outmoded and considered obsolete for coast defense, serves as Coast Guard patrol headquarters for this district.

23. The *Old Powder House* (1775), near-by, 'stands like a sepulchre on which the old forts lie entombed.' Powder was stored here during Revolutionary days.

R. from East St. on Trumbull St.; L. on Pequot Ave.; R. on Plant St.; L. on Ocean Ave.

24. In *Gardiner's Cemetery*, Ocean Ave. at Gardiner's Lane, is the grave of Richard Mansfield (1857–1907), famous Shakespearian actor.

25. *Ocean Beach*, at the foot of Ocean Ave., one of the finest white sand beaches on the Sound, affords excellent bathing, with lifeguards in attendance and the usual amusement concessions.

Return on Ocean Ave.; R. from Ocean on Mott which becomes Pequot Ave.

26. The *New London Light (not open)*, on Pequot Ave., a white, flat-sided masonry lighthouse, 89 feet high, was the first on the Connecticut coast and one of the oldest in the country. The original structure of 1760 was rebuilt in 1801 from the proceeds of a public lottery. The old oil lamp

and the foghorn have long since been replaced with an automatic light and reflector, though the beacon's value has become negligible since the construction of the brick *Southwest Ledge Light*, erected on a bare ledge, outside the harbor, commemorated by F. Hopkinson Smith in his 'Master Diver' immortalizing Tom Scott of New London. Scott headed a wrecking company that was later absorbed by the Merritt, Chapman & Scott Corporation.

Points of Interest in Environs:

U.S. Submarine Base, Groton, 6.4 *m.* (*see Tour 1G*).

NORWALK

Town: Alt. 60, pop. 36,019, sett. 1649, incorp. 1893.

Railroad Stations: Norwalk Station, Railroad Ave., and East Norwalk Station, East Ave., bet. Point and Winfield Sts., for N.Y., N.H. & H. R.R.

Taxi: Flat rate 50¢ within central zone; 25¢ each additional ½ *m.*

Steamship Pier: Water St. Excursion boat runs between Bell Island and New York during summer months; rates on weekdays $1 round trip; 75¢ one way; Sundays and holidays $1.25 round trip; $1 one way.

Accommodations: One hotel.

Recreation: Studio Playhouse in Norwalk Library; Theater-in-the-Woods, legitimate productions during summer.

Swimming: Y.M.C.A.; fee 30¢.

Amusement Parks: Roton Point, 2 *m.* south of South Norwalk center; Calf Pasture Point, East Norwalk.

Information Service: Chamber of Commerce, Frost Building, US 1.

NORWALK (Ind.: *Norwaake*, or *Naramake*) is an industrial city, spreading across both sides of the island-fringed harbor of the Norwalk River. Manufactures include such diversified products as Dobbs Hats, Cash Woven Name Tapes, Norwalk Tires, Binner Corsets, and Church Expansion Bolts. Oyster culture has been a leading industry of the town since the friendly Indians showed the first settlers the natural beds off the Norwalk shores. A Norwalk oysterman, Captain Peter Decker, was the first in the industry to introduce steam power in oyster dredging (1874). This local industry once shipped three-fourths of the trans-Atlantic oyster export in addition to an extensive domestic supply (1870–90). Handicapped for many years by the careless depletion of the natural beds, the pollution of waters, and differences between State and town authorities, it is rapidly regaining its former status, and in the year 1936–37 had its most productive season in recent years.

The consolidated city of Norwalk covers the entire territory of the town of Norwalk, including the former cities of Norwalk and South Norwalk, originally known as Old Well because of the spring which supplied water to West Indian trading ships, and the communities of Rowayton, East Norwalk, West Norwalk, Cranbury, Winnepaug, Silvermine and Broad River.

To the north, in the gently rolling rural districts and along the shady banks of Silvermine Brook, is a widespread settlement of artists, sculptors and writers. Along the fine beaches of the southern coast are numerous summer colonies.

Settled in 1649 by colonists from Hartford under the leadership of Roger Ludlow and incorporated as a town in 1651, Norwalk is one of the two towns in the State having Indian names. Many evidences of an earlier Indian habitation (probably of the Mohawk tribe) have been found west of the harbor on Wilson Point. During the Revolutionary War, Norwalk was harassed by the depredations of British raiders. Rowayton offered a sheltered landing place for marauders who, working with Tory sympathizers living within the town, crossed from Long Island to steal cattle, grain and vegetables for their troops. On the eve of July 11, 1779, 26 British vessels, carrying a land force of 2500 men, disembarked on Calf Pasture Beach. The patriots, scarcely more than 400 in number, were no match for the Redcoats who took possession of the town and fired both the Congregational and Episcopal churches, 80 dwellings, 87 barns, 22 storehouses, 17 shops, 4 mills, 5 vessels, and all the stores of wheat, hay, and grain.

Norwalk's development as an industrial center dates from before the Revolution, when the manufacture of clocks, watches, shingle nails and paper was started between 1767 and 1773. A few years later, probably as early as 1780, a pottery kiln, the first of several which produced the stoneware pottery for which Norwalk became famous, was erected at Old Well. Among collectors' pieces are examples of red, yellow, brown and black ware, all of simple design with the exception of the early pie plates, now museum pieces, which were distinguished by their Oriental decoration, showing the influence of the China trade on home industry.

TOUR 1

E. from the center on US 1 (Westport Ave.).

1. The *Town House (private)*, atop the hill (R), a one-story brick building erected in 1835, is now a D.A.R. Chapter House.

2. Beyond the Town House stands a *Monument* commemorating the burning of Norwalk by General William Tryon.

3. The *Norwalk Green*, at the circular traffic intersection, was the starting-point of a little band of Norwalk families who left in 1820 to take up 'Fire Lands' in Ohio. Homesteads were granted by the General Assembly in 1792 as a recompense for the destruction of their homes and supplies in the burning of Norwalk by the British, during the Revolution, but not until 28 years later was the migration organized. On a chill November day, as the wagon train of prairie schooners wound down Barkmill Hill, the cheers of those who were left behind merged into the chant of the doxology. Those who watched remained standing on the Green for a long time after the wagons had disappeared, some talking of the dangers that awaited the expedition, others still trying to decide whether or not they too should have gone. The colonists were evidently well satisfied with their Ohio homesteads, for none ever returned. Their new settlement prospered and was named Norwalk, Ohio.

R. from US 1 on East Ave.

4. The old *Governor Fitch House (private)*, 173 East Ave., the ell of which dates from 1754 and the main house from 35 years later, stands behind spreading lilac bushes. Thomas Fitch was governor of Connecticut, 1754–66.

R. from East Ave. on Hendricks Ave.

5. *Site of the Yankee Doodle House* (R), Hendricks Ave., only the cellar of which remains, was once the home of Colonel Thomas Fitch, whose shabbily dressed troops, which he led from here to the French and Indian War, inspired a British army surgeon, Dr. Shuckburgh, to write the derisive 'Yankee Doodle.' According to local tradition, Elizabeth Fitch, on leaving the house to bid good-bye to her brother was dismayed by the ill-assorted costumes of the 'cavalry.' Exclaiming, 'You must have uniforms of some kind,' she ran into the chicken yard, and returning with a handful of feathers announced, 'Soldiers should wear plumes,' and directed each rider to put a feather in his cap. When Shuckburgh saw Fitch's men arriving at Fort Cralo, Rensselaer, New York he is reputed to have exclaimed, 'Now stab my vitals, they're macaronis!' sarcastically applying the slang of the day for fop, or dandy, and proceeded to write the song, which instantly caught popular fancy.

Return to East Ave.; R. on East Ave.

6. The *Old Red School House*, 185 East Ave., now a private residence, stands behind a low stone wall, sheltered by a towering elm. Believed to have been built in 1700, although its arched ceiling is certainly of later date, it was one of six buildings on the route of Tryon's march which escaped destruction when the town was burned.

7. The *Hales-Fitch House (private)*, 195 East Ave., was set on fire but saved. The ell of this gambrel-roofed house, with two chimneys strangely placed near the rear corners, is said to have originally been a house built, facing south, by Thomas Hales in 1652.

L. from East Ave. on Gregory Blvd.

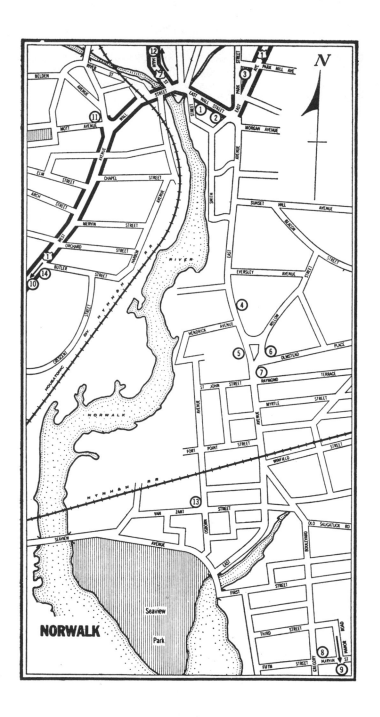

NORWALK

8. At the intersection of Gregory Blvd. and Fifth St. is a granite *Memorial to Roger Ludlow*, deputy governor of the Connecticut Colony, who in 1640 purchased Norwalk by a treaty with the Indians for the price of '8 fathams of wampum, 6 coats, 10 hatchets, 10 hoes, 10 knives, 10 scizers, 10 juse harps, 10 fathams tobacco, 3 kettles (3 hands about), and 10 looking glasses.'

L. from Gregory Blvd. on Ludlow Parkway.

9. *Calf Pasture Point*, at the end of the Parkway, once used by the Indians as a pasture ground, is developed as an attractive city park, from which there are splendid views of the Sound and the Norwalk Islands.

Here, among the reefs offshore, 'Rock Scorpions,' Continental whaleboat crews, retaliating against the depredations of Tory 'Sand Spaniards' of Long Island, plotted their raids and secreted their boats. At *Cedar Hammock Island*, Nathan Hale, who had stealthily made his way by the Old Shell Path to Wilson Point, embarked on the sloop 'Schuyler' on the courageous mission from which he never returned. Near-by on the *Fort Molly Rocks* stand the ruins of a Civil War fort. Tradition persists that on *Pilot Island*, at the entrance to the western channel, Captain Joseph Merrill found pirate gold after three successive dreams that revealed its location; among the aged residents are several who insist that they heard him tell the story and saw him spend Spanish coins. In the group beyond the eastern channel, *Goose Island*, entirely stripped of vegetation, is reputed to owe its dreary waste to the zeal of treasure hunters; in 1895 the island became an experiment station for the Carnegie Institute, which used a species of rat to develop a serum for yellow fever. On *Ram Island*, the Mormons established an unsuccessful settlement in 1842. *Chimons Island*, largest of the group (63 acres), was formerly the site of an extensive summer colony; here three meteorites lie where they fell: one on the hotel porch, one in the garden, and one near the sea wall. *Sheffield Island* has an ancient lighthouse tower rising steeple-like above an old stone house; it was sold by the Government in 1914 when Green's Reef Lighthouse was erected, and is, like the other islands, privately owned. Jesuit priests from other sections of New England spend their summers at the *Retreat* on *Manresa Island*, formerly named for John H. Keyser, a member of the Boss Tweed Ring of New York, who owned it from 1859 to 1887.

NORWALK. POINTS OF INTEREST

1. Town House
2. Monument
3. Norwalk Green
4. Governor Fitch
5. Site of the Yankee Doodle House
6. Old Red School House
7. Hales-Fitch House
8. Memorial to Roger Ludlow
9. Calf Pasture Point
10. Flax Hill Memorial
11. Studio Playhouse
12. Theater in the Woods
13. Crofut and Knapp
14. Matthews Estate

TOUR 2

S. from US 1 on West Ave.; R. from West Ave. on Flax Hill Road.

10. *Flax Hill Memorial*, Flax Hill Road, rear Bayview Ave., marks the site of the Battle of the Rocks (July 12, 1779) where the colonists took cover behind boulders while attempting to stop the British march. The memorial is a boulder in which is embedded a British cannonball.

Return via Flax Hill Road and West Ave. to Belden Ave.; L. on Belden Ave.

11. The *Studio Playhouse*, in the basement of the Norwalk Library, Belden and Mott Aves., first sponsored as an FERA Project and then taken over by the WPA (1936), won the respect of metropolitan critics as a 'little theater' under the direction of Cleveland Bronner. Truly a little theater (the lobby will accommodate only four persons), every available inch of the playhouse is utilized. The professional, dramatic, and artistic groups of the community have aided in assembling remarkably effective settings and stage equipment at a minimum cost.

12. At the *Theater in the Woods*, Oakwood Ave., the Norwalk Civic Opera Company presents operettas with casts of Metropolitan Opera stars during the summer months.

13. *Crofut and Knapp*, Van Zant St., East Norwalk, are successors of the firm of James Knapp who produced the first derby hat ever made, in South Norwalk in 1850. The early beaver hats were made on square blocks. The price was usually about seven dollars and they were expected to last a lifetime. However, the square corners often wore through. Knapp experimented with an oval block and finally produced the first derby hat, founding one of Connecticut's important industries.

14. Opposite the Armory, on the corner of US 1 and West Ave., is the *Mathews Estate (private)*, covering 32 acres, with a great stone mansion of Italian marble, erected by LeGrand Lockwood at a cost of $1,200,000, in 1864. After the death of Lockwood, who lost his fortune on the Wall Street 'Black Friday' of September 24, 1869, the property was sold to Charles O. Mathews of New York and is still owned by his family.

Points of Interest in Environs:

Buttery's Mill, Silvermine Road, oldest sawmill still operating in the United States (1688) (*see Tour* 4).

NORWICH

City: Alt. 100, pop. 23,021, incorp. 1784.

Railroad Stations: North Main St. (opp. No. 291) for New York, New Haven & Hartford Railroad; West Main St. at North Thames St. for Central Vermont Railroad.

Taxis: 35¢ anywhere within city limits, one to four passengers; $2 per hour for shoppers; $3 per hour sightseeing anywhere.

Accommodations: Two hotels.

Information Service: Chamber of Commerce, Main St.

Swimming Pool: Y.M.C.A., 25¢.

Camping Facilities: Fort Shantok, 3 *m.* from Norwich on Route 32.

NORWICH, a busy industrial city at the junction of the Yantic and Shetucket Rivers which merge to flow into the drowned valley known as the Thames River, is on terraced hillsides at the head of navigation on that stream. In the crowded downtown section the narrow, crooked streets, always climbing a hill or detouring around one, are lined with commercial buildings dating from many different periods, and on the river front factory buildings crowd close to the old wharves. Many of the streets are paved with cobblestones, slick with ice in winter, reflecting the heat in summer, scarred with calk marks made by generations of draft horses that have clawed for a toe-hold as they hauled heavy drays from the docks. The hillside residential section of impressive nineteenth-century mansions on elm-shaded streets to the northwest, and Norwich Town, site of the original settlement, where fragrant old-fashioned gardens surround mellowed old homes, justify the city's traditional sobriquet, 'The Rose of New England.' Across the Shetucket, a broad granite cliff overlooks the city, and behind it to the north and east are ever-rising terraces of sparsely wooded country.

Mrs. Lydia H. Sigourney, prolific writer (*see Literature*), who lived in Norwich, described the view from the east, 'like a citadel, guarded by parapets of rock, and embosomed in an amphitheatre of hills whose summits mark the horizon with a waving line of forest green.'

But there was little except natural beauty to inspire the pioneers who first tried to wrest a livelihood from the stony soil in colonial times. The Mohegans and the Narragansetts battled desperately for this territory. To Thomas Leffingwell, an ensign from Saybrook, who brought aid to Uncas, chief of the Mohegans, when he was besieged by the Narragansetts in his Thames River fortress in 1645 (*see Tour* 9), Uncas gave a deed to the 'Nine Mile Square' on which Norwich was founded. This deed did not convey lands to the south between New London township and Norwich, and the intervening three-mile no-man's land was a source of constant difficulty for lawyers, settlers and surveyors for many years. A later deed, June 6th, 1659, conveyed practically the same lands to Leffingwell, John Mason, the Reverend James Fitch and others. In the spring of 1660, the Reverend James Fitch led a portion of his congregation from Saybrook into the Norwich lands. Three or four persons joined them from New London, and others came from Plymouth and Marshfield, Mass. The town was incorporated in 1784. Early Indian reservations in the vicinity totaled four or five thousand acres.

The area was infested with rattlesnakes, and land was of such little value that the Reverend Gurdon Saltonstall of New London, in 1697, received a grant of land to the west of the settlement for preaching an election sermon in Hartford. An early Norwich Pied Piper used a violin to charm rattlesnakes and is reported to have come into town from Waweekus Hill with assorted snakes, varmints, and goats trailing him. Many settlers raised goats because those animals could resist rattlesnakes and subsist on the rocky pastureland. In 1722 one flock of fifty-four goats was impounded for straying into town and held until their owner paid for his carelessness in not repairing fences.

Acadians, driven from their homes in Nova Scotia, swarmed into the impoverished little settlement in such numbers during 1755 that they became an early social problem. Conversely, Norwich residents seeking fertile land, after the peace of 1763, migrated to Nova Scotia, where they founded the towns of Dublin, Horton, Falmouth, and Amherst. One hundred and thirty-seven sailed together in one group. Other discouraged Norwich farmers settled in Delaware. In 1767, two hundred and forty Acadians were corralled by a Norwich skipper, loaded onto a boat, and put ashore at Quebec. Norwich, N.Y., and Chelsea, N.H., drew their early settlers from Norwich, Conn., and many other widely scattered settlements in the Midwest became the homes of pioneers who despaired of making a living on the Thames. Those who remained were troubled by religious as well as economic and social problems. The Rogerenes, a Quaker sect, caused much agitation in the early eighteenth century. In July, 1726, six of them were arrested for traveling on Sunday, tried and committed to prison.

Following the success of New London boat yards, Norwich turned to shipbuilding and in 1760 had seven ships making regular trading voyages to the West Indies. A road, laid out before 1700 by order of the General Assembly, connected New London with Norwich, but the river was for many generations the chief route of communication.

Mediterranean Lane probably was named by an early skipper. In the late eighteenth century the Landing became the business section of the settlement. By 1795, forty-two ships were regularly clearing from the port, usually for the West Indies, with cargoes of horses, oak staves and produce, Many Norwich skippers later turned to whaling and some to slave-trading.

An unusual custom observed in the old city was the election of an

African governor. The affair was conducted with considerable pomp and circumstance, parades were held and the 'reigning' monarch assumed a patriarchal attitude toward his people. Among the best-known African monarchs were 'Boston' Trowtrow (about 1772), and Sam Hun'tin, who held the Negro governorship for more years than his master and namesake, Samuel Huntington, who was actually governor of the State (1786–96).

Early industry did not attain any importance until 1772 when a Bean Hill blacksmith, Edmund Darrow, produced from barrel hooping the first cut nails in America. Richard Collier, a former Boston brazier, made warming pans about this time, and Noah Hidden manufactured combs in 1773. Ships knees and cordwood were cut and shipped to the New York market. Thomas Harland arrived from London in 1773, established a business of watch and clock making, and trained a number of Connecticut clockmakers who later established their own mills. Harland, a man of considerable genius, made Norwich's first fire engine. Before 1750, Dr. Daniel Lathrop opened an apothecary shop, believed to have been the first in the State, which was patronized by country doctors from as far away as Waterbury. Joseph Lathrop successfully spun cotton in 1790.

During the Revolutionary War, cannon were manufactured by Elijah Backus, who welded together pieces of iron and made a fieldpiece that is reported to have stood up under the weak charges used in that day.

The War of 1812, with its blockade of the New England ports, left its mark on the community. Norwich men fought at the Battle of Bridgewater (Lundy's Lane), July 25th, 1814, and her skippers ran the blockade of the Thames on dark, stormy nights. Social affairs were enlivened by the presence of men from the blockaded American ships who made merry at dances, 'tripe' suppers, and 'turtle entertainments.'

One of the most interesting legends of Norwick and a favorite story of Aaron Cleveland, great-grandfather of Grover Cleveland, concerns the freshet of March, 1823. The sudden rise of water washed away the Methodist Chapel, which, with lights still burning, is reported to have sailed serenely down the river and past astonished skippers on Long Island Sound. The elder Cleveland was a noted politician, speaker, writer, Congregational minister and abolitionist.

In 1842 Ethan Allen and Charles Thurber set up a pistol shop at *The Falls*. Smith and Wesson, who later moved to New Haven, established a pistol and rifle factory here in 1853, and patented a 'volcanic repeating pistol' in 1854, and Christopher C. Brand made possible an important advance in the efficiency of whaling by his combination 'whaling gun and bomb lance' patented in 1852.

During the Civil War three full volunteer companies were raised in Norwich, and the demand for supplies brought a boom to trade and manufacturing interests. Joseph D. Mowry took a contract to produce thirty thousand Springfield rifles in 1862, and the tanneries had more leather orders for military knapsacks, boots, belts, cockades, whip lashes, snappers, cartridge-boxes, and drumheads than they could fill. Apprentice boys were sent from shop to shop in search of 'stirrup oil,' 'limbering oils,' and 'green lampblack.' The Norwich Arms Company was formed and filled many Government orders.

The Adams Express ¡Company was an out growth of personal package delivery services between Boston and New York, originated by Alvin Adams of Norwich in 1840, and by Fred Harnden, a conductor on the Boston and Worcester Railroad in 1839. Adams and Harnden consolidated and formed the Adams Express Company in 1854.

Today, Norwich produces thermos bottles, velvets, woolens, awnings, clothing, table cutlery, silks, leather goods, shoes, and metal products. Its industry has spread far beyond the city limits into many of the surrounding mill towns.

Norwich has been the home of many prominent persons, including the ancestors of Presidents Fillmore, Grant, Hayes, Garfield, and Cleveland. Donald G. Mitchell ('Ik Marvel') (*see Literature*), and Daniel Coit Gilman, president of Johns Hopkins University, were born in Norwich.

TOUR 1

W. from Park St. on Main St.

1. *Buckingham Memorial* (*private*), 307 Main St., was the home of William A. Buckingham, Civil War Governor of Connecticut from 1858 to 1866. On receipt of news from Fort Sumter on April 13, 1861, Governor Buckingham, confronted with the fact that he had no power to order militia to leave the State, called for a regiment of volunteers. When the

---

NORWICH. POINTS OF INTEREST

1. Buckingham Memorial
2. Nathaniel Backus House
3. Glebe House
4. General Rockwell House
5. Slater Memorial
6. Boulder
7. Joseph Teel House
8. Uncas Monument
9. Uncas Ravine
10. Site of the Birthplace of Benedict Arnold
11. Reynolds House
12. Leffingwell Inn
13. Thomas Harland House
14. Dr. Daniel Lathrop House
15. Gov. Samuel Huntington House
16. Jedediah Huntington House
17. Joshua Huntington House
18. Old Burial Ground
19. Site of the First Meeting-House
20. Simon Huntington House
21. Andre Richards House
22. Dr. Daniel Lathrop School
23. Joseph Carpenter Store
24. Norwichtown Congregational Church
25. Eleazer Lord Tavern
26. Diah Manning House
27. Post Gager Burying Ground
28. Adams Tavern

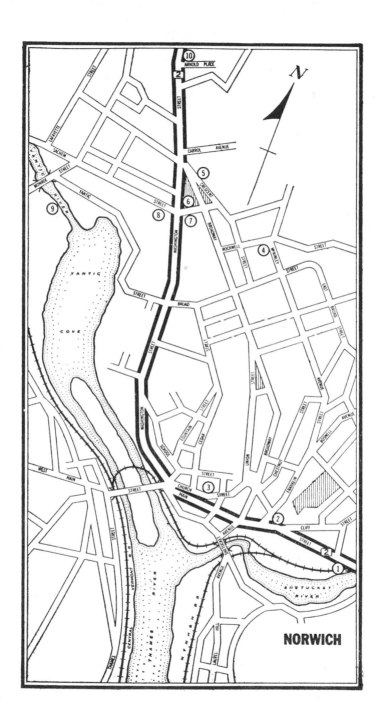

NORWICH

First Connecticut Regiment reached Washington, May 13, it was so well equipped that its teams were borrowed by the Government, and General Scott is said to have exclaimed, 'Thank God, we have one regiment ready to take the field! Colonel Tyler is prepared not only for a battle but for a campaign.' For many years this house was used as headquarters by the Grand Army of the Republic, but the last Norwich member of that organization died in 1937.

R. from Main St. on Broadway.

2. The *Nathaniel Backus House* (*private*), 49 Broadway, between taller buildings in a commercial district where it was long used as a store, is a two-and-a-half-story peak-roofed frame structure with two end-chimneys on the south; it appears to date from about 1825–30. Its most notable feature is a square doorway richly embellished with pineapple and acanthus leaf carving, a decoration typical of Norwich doorways of 1825.

L. from Broadway on Church St.

3. The *Glebe House* (*private*), 62 Church St., was built (1748) by the Rev. John Tyler, rector of Christ Episcopal Church for fifty-four years and one of the clergymen who met at Woodbury in 1783 to elect the Right Rev. Samuel Seabury, D.D., the first Bishop of an Episcopal Diocese in America. During the Revolution, services were held in this house. It later became the residence of William Tyler Olcott, the astronomer, who founded the Society of Variable Star Observers. The building is a two-and-a-half-story dwelling, quite plain except for an elaborate wide cornice with very heavy dentils. The wooden observatory with a revolving hexagonal tower, perched behind the roof, was added by Olcott.

Return on Church St. to Broadway; L. on Broadway; R. on Rockwell St.

4. The *General Rockwell House* (*open* 3–5.30, *June to Oct., adm. free*), 42 Rockwell St., a two-story stone dwelling surrounded by heavy porches, with a mansard roof and two wide, thin chimneys, was built by Major Joseph Perkins, a member of the Committee of Safety in 1814. It was later occupied by Brigadier General Alfred Perkins Rockwell, who served at James Island, Fort Darling, and Fort Fisher during the Civil War. It is maintained as a museum by the Daughters of the American Revolution.

Return on Rockwell St. to Broadway; R. on Broadway.

5. The *Slater Memorial* (*open weekdays* 8.30–5; *Sun.* 2–4, *free*), Broadway at Chelsea Parade, is a stone building of Romanesque design, on the grounds of the Norwich Free Academy.

The Norwich Free Academy, endowed and chartered in 1854, with the status of a private school, is the public high school of the city of Norwich. The *Memorial*, center of the aesthetic interests of the city, was erected by William Slater in honor of his father, John Slater, early cotton manufacturer, and presented to the Academy in 1885.

On the main floor to the right of the entrance is the *Peck Library*, founded in 1859 by Mrs. Harriet Peck Williams in honor of her father, Captain

Bela Peck of the Continental Army. The library departments of Art, Education, General Literature, and History are well equipped and many additions have been made to the rare books of the original collection.

On the first gallery is an extensive exhibit of plaster casts of Classic and Renaissance sculpture, Greek coins, and Renaissance metal work.

On the second gallery is the notable *Vanderpoel Collection* of Oriental wood-carvings, textiles, stencils and art, recognized as one of the best private collections of Japanese art in America. This collection was presented to the Academy by Mrs. John Vanderpoel of New York City in 1936.

In the basement, at the foot of the main staircase, is the *Edmond Indian Collection*, which includes 5400 arrow heads from 23 states, 250 spear-points, 500 stone implements, ceremonial articles, pipes, beadwork, and pottery. Other Indian exhibits include a Mound Builders' idol from Tennessee, Aztec pottery, jasper and copper flakes and implements, and a number of prehistoric relics from Labrador and Europe.

Annexed to the Slater Memorial is the *Converse Art Gallery (adm. as above)*. The lower floor is devoted to the Art Department of the Academy. The large gallery on the upper floor is reserved for the many temporary art exhibitions held during the year.

In connection with the museums, the Academy conducts a system of traveling exhibits that are loaned to the grammar schools of the adjacent rural area.

6. On Chelsea Parade, a small triangular green at the junction of Broadway and Washington St., are a number of monuments, including a modest *Boulder* to gallant Captain Samuel Chester Reid, hero of the naval battle of Fayal and designer of the present American flag. Reid originated the idea of having thirteen stripes, alternate red and white, with a blue union containing a star for every State. His design was approved and a resolution of thanks passed by both houses of Congress on April 4, 1818. Previously the number of stars in the flag had equaled the number of stripes.

Reid was the son of a British naval officer who was captured by the Continentals during the Revolution. The elder Reid fell in love with a New London girl, but she refused to marry him until he resigned his commission in the British Navy. The younger Reid entered the U.S. Navy and commanded the U.S.S. 'General Armstrong,' September 26, 1814, at Fayal, Azore Islands, where he engaged three British ships, 'Carnation,' 'Plantagenet,' and 'Rota' bringing infantry reinforcements to the British command at New Orleans. Although beaten, with his ship a shambles at the end of a twenty-four-hour battle, Reid refused to surrender, blew up his ship, and with his remaining men escaped ashore. The British ships were so severely damaged that they had to refit and delayed so long that the American forces were able to assemble, fight, and win the decisive battle at New Orleans. Upon Captain Reid's return to this country, he was honored by many States for his gallant conduct.

L. from Broadway on Chelsea Parade, S.

7. The *Joseph Teel House* (*private*) (1789), on Chelsea Parade South between Washington St. and Broadway, set back among shaded lawns, is an imposing three-story brick house, with four tall chimneys buttressing the corners and a heavy balustrade around the edge of the hip roof, an excellent example of the early Federal period. Painted white with green shutters and used as the parsonage of the historic Park Congregational Church, the building was originally built as an inn, *At the Sign of General Washington.*

Chelsea Parade S. becomes Sachem St.

8. The *Uncas Monument* (L), cor. Sachem and Washington Sts., in a small plot enclosed by a chain fence, was formerly maintained by the red men as a royal burying ground for the graves of Mohegan sachems and their offspring. In 1833, President Jackson laid the cornerstone of the monument, a straight shaft of granite finally erected in 1842 by descendants of the white settlers whom Uncas befriended (*see Tour* 9). Near-by are the smaller gravestones of other Indian rulers, and a boulder marks the grave of Mamohet who died in England.

L. from Sachem St. on Grosvenor Place.

9. *Uncas Ravine*, at the corner of Grosvenor Place and Yantic Ave., has an impressive natural beauty despite the encroachment of near-by industrial plants. Through the narrow gorge, between steep cliffs, known as Indian Leap, the Yantic River rushes southward to tumble over the Yantic Falls where it meets the tidewater of the Thames.

Return on Grosvenor Place and Sachem St. to Washington St.; L. on Washinton St.

10. The *Site of the Birthplace of Benedict Arnold* (1741–1801), Revolutionary War general and American traitor, at NE. cor. Washington St. and Arnold Place, is indicated by a wooden marker.

TOUR 2

N. from Sachem on Washington St.

11. The *Reynolds House* (*private*), 328 Washington St., a two-and-a-half-story grayish-brown salt-box house, bears a shield with the date 1659, marking the traditional date of its construction by John Reynolds, one of the first settlers. It is probable that a single-room, end-chimney house of that time is incorporated in the present dwelling which has suffered many additions and modernizations. The location of the chimney behind the ridge indicates an early date.

12. The *Leffingwell Inn* (*private*), 344 Washington St., is an added lean-to salt-box house, with a long ell to the south which gives it the appearance of a hip-roofed structure. The oldest section was built by Stephen Backus,

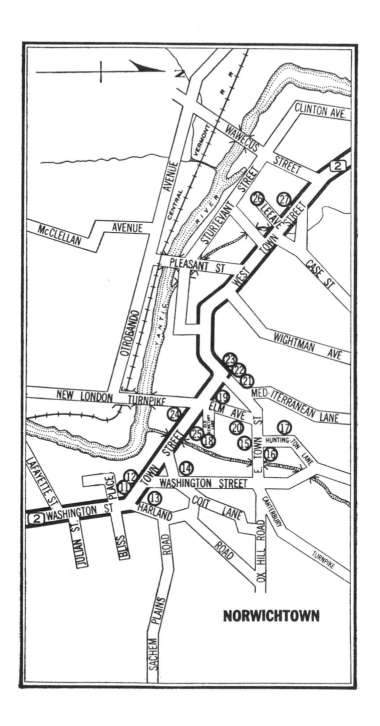

NORWICHTOWN

probably in 1666; it was sold in 1701 to Sergeant Thomas Leffingwell, who added most of the present structure when he was appointed 'Ensign' and given permission to keep a 'publique house.' This section has a chimney back of the ridgepole; in the interior is some exceptional raised paneling. The northeast room is known as the Washington Room because the General dined there. According to tradition, slaves were auctioned off at the north door. This house was later occupied by Christopher Leffingwell, who engaged in many early enterprises including the establishment of a paper mill, a fulling mill and dye house, grist, chocolate and pottery mills. He probably added the southernmost part of the ell, and embellished the house with its richest features.

13. The *Thomas Harland House* (*private*) (1779), at 357 Washington Ave., was the home of Thomas Harland, early Connecticut clockmaker to whom Daniel Burnap (*see Industry*) was apprenticed. Harland learned his trade in England and came to Boston in 1773 in the ship from which the tea was thrown overboard in the Boston Tea Party. He settled in Norwich where he had a shop until 1807 and made 'spring, musical and plain clocks,' with brass works and a 40-inch pendulum that swung every second. The cases were about 6 ft. high. Sometimes the clocks were hung up, without cases, and were called wag-on-the-wall clocks. The house has been frequently remodeled.

14. The *Dr. Daniel Lathrop House* (*private*) (1745), 380 Washington St., a big, four-chimneyed, gambrel-roofed house with a completely modernized interior, was the home of one of the Lathrop Brothers, who were among the earliest druggists in the State and amassed a fortune importing drugs. This house was the childhood home of Lydia Huntley Sigourney, the poetess. It was also the home of Daniel Coit Gilman (1831–1908), president of the University of California, of Johns Hopkins University (1875–1901), and of Carnegie Institute (1901–04).

L. from Washington on East Town St.

15. *Gov. Samuel Huntington House* (*private*), 34 East Town St., was built in 1783–85 by that statesman, who signed the Declaration of Independence, served his State as member of Congress, Chief Justice of Connecticut, and Governor. He was President of Congress through three years of the Revolution. The large white clapboarded structure has been extensively modernized. Only the central dwelling with the corner pilasters is original.

16. *Jedediah Huntington House* (*private*) (1765), 23 East Town St., is a broad two-and-a-half-story white clapboarded house with an unusually flat gambrel roof, two chimneys back of the ridgepole, a wide cornice and heavy gable overhang. Now masked by an added porch, the projecting central panel, which includes the doorway, is a feature frequently found in dwellings built in the eastern part of the State in succeeding decades. Huntington, who later moved to New London to become Collector of Port, entertained both Washington and Lafayette here.

R. from East Town St. on Huntington Lane.

17. The *Joshua Huntington House* (*private*) (1719 or earlier), 16 Huntington Lane, a two-and-a-half-story, central-chimney, clapboarded house with a long gambrel-roofed ell, is one of the three remaining structures built by a founder of the town. The huge stone chimney and part of the framing are probably all that is left of an original one-room house built by John Bradford, son of the Plymouth governor. In 1691 the house was purchased from the Bradfords by Simon Huntington, whose son Joshua built the gambrel-roofed section in 1719. The heavy, plain box cornice, the attic overhang, and the pediments over the end windows are all primitive features of the 1719 addition. The broad rear ell along Huntington Lane was built by Joshua's son, General Jabez Huntington, a wealthy West Indian trader and officer, who came into possession of the property in 1745, and at that time installed much of the fine interior paneling.

Some of the shutters have heart-shaped openings, and the double door on the ell is studded with nails in diamond patterns. The interior hardware is notable, and a few of the doors have wooden locks. Leaden sash weights from this old house were cast into bullets to be used against the British during the Revolution.

Return on Huntington Lane to East Town St.; R. on East Town St.; L. on Cemetery Lane.

18. *Old Burial Ground*, end of Cemetery Lane, entered through the Hubbard Gates inscribed with the names of Revolutionary soldiers buried within, dates from 1699 and contains the brick tomb of Governor Huntington and a memorial boulder marking the graves of 20 French soldiers who died in Norwich during the War of Independence.

Return on Cemetery Lane to East Town St.; L. on East Town St.

19. *Site of the First Meeting-House* (1660), on Norwichtown Green, East Town and Elm ·Ave., was used as a training ground for Continental troops. At the southern end stood the old Court House where the Mutual Assurance Company of the City of Norwich, the first insurance company incorporated in the State, was established in 1795. This company issued local policies on a mutual basis for dwelling houses within a risk limited to $1000.

L. from East Town St. on Elm Ave.

20. *Simon Huntington House* (*private*), 2 Elm Ave., was a tavern in 1706 and was probably built before 1700, but was rebuilt and enlarged in 1782–83. It is now a long, red house with a double overhang, handsome double raised-panel doors and excellent paneling within.

21. The *André Richards House* (*private*), 8 Elm Ave., was built in 1737, probably around the 'great room and lean-to' dwelling of Madame Sarah Knight, a tavern keeper long remembered for her sprightly journal which recounts the story of her journey alone on horseback from Boston to New York in 1704. Enlarged and rebuilt, the house was bought in 1757 by Joseph Peck, who operated it as a tavern that was a gathering place for

both drovers and notables. The present structure has few distinctive features other than a recessed interior overmantel such as is found in other early Norwich houses. On the grounds stands a great elm tree beneath which the early tavern keeper built a large arbor, reached by a plank gallery that extended from a second-story window of the house.

Return on Elm Ave., to East Town St.; L. on East Town St.

22. *Dr. Daniel Lathrop School (private)* (1783), East Town St. (R), between Mediterranean Lane and Town St., with a gambrel roof and small wooden belfry, is one of the earliest brick schoolhouses still standing in the State. The school was named for Doctor Lathrop because of his efforts in fostering its erection.

23. The *Joseph Carpenter Store (open Wed. and Sat. afternoons, during the summer, free)*, East Town St. next to the school, a small gambrel-roofed structure recently restored by private subscription, was built in 1772 as a silversmith shop, and the upper end was used by Joseph's brother, Gardner, as a general store. The shutters are original.

24. *Norwichtown Congregational Church* (1801), East Town St. (R), opposite the head of Town St., representing the period when the huge barn-like structures of the 18th century were becoming more ornate, has a square two-story tower and a projecting portico which repeats the rather flat lines of the roof and the corner quoins of the main building. The chief ornaments of the façade are one square, and two round-topped beaded doors on the first floor, and one round, and two square-topped beaded windows on the second. The building was remodeled in 1845 and at later intervals. Brooding over the rear church lawn are *Meeting-House Rocks*. Atop this mass of stone once loomed the second meeting house whose tower served as a lookout against Indian raids.

L. from East Town St. on Town St.

25. *Eleazar Lord Tavern (private)* (about 1760–73, date uncertain), 86 Town St., standing four-square with the points of the compass, is a plain clapboarded structure that from all outward appearances might have a date as late as 1870. New sash, doors, and a hooded entrance have been added to this old tavern, which, according to tradition, was built in forty days. As the court house stood on the opposite corner until 1833, the inn was formerly the gathering place of lawyers who were attending court sessions. The ell of the inn served as a postoffice from 1836 to 1907.

26. The *Diah Manning House (private)*, 85 Town St., a little gambrel-roofed house built in 1750, was the home of the boyish drum major of Washington's bodyguard. Manning was detailed to serve breakfast to Major André on the day the British spy was executed.

Return on Town St. to East Town; L. on East Town St. which becomes West Town St.; L. on Lee Ave.

27. *Post Gager Burying Ground*, end of Lee Ave., is an oblong plot purchased by the town in 1661 for a common burial ground. Here are buried many of the town's early leaders. The John Mason Monument was

erected in 1872 as a memorial to Captain Mason, leader of colonial troops in the Pequot War (*see WEST MYSTIC, Tour* 1).

Return on Lee Ave. to West Town St.; L. on West Town St.

28. *Adams Tavern* (*private*), 112 West Town St., a small gambrel-roofed house on a high brick foundation, was built as a hat shop by Aaron Cleveland, religious and political leader, great-grandfather of President Grover Cleveland. The early date claimed for the hat shop, 1647, twelve years before the founding of the town, is not confirmed by any of the architectural features. From the light framing to the slope of the roof, the construction indicates that it was erected about 1780.

Points of Interest in Environs:

Miantonomo Memorial, 3.6 *m.* (*see Tour* 9).

OLD LYME

Town: Alt. 10, pop. 1313, sett. 1665.

Accommodations: Several hotels and inns. Both American and European plans. Cabins, with electricity, on US 1, $1 per person.

Information Service: Chamber of Commerce, Main St.

Annual Events: Exhibits of arts and crafts during the late summer, adm. free, Old Lyme Guild. Exhibits of water colors and etchings, June; paintings and sculpture, end of July through first week in September — 9–5, adm. 50¢, Lyme Art Gallery.

OLD LYME, an elm-shaded village steeped in seafaring tradition, peacefully dozes beneath the white spire of the Congregational Church. Here 'a sea captain once lived in every house.' In dignified old dwellings their descendants treasure teak-wood chests, Paisley shawls, ivory images and exquisite tapestries collected in the Orient. The variety of Old Lyme's landscape, combining shady streets with stretches of marsh land and tranquil meadows with a rugged shore line on Long Island Sound, has attracted many artists. Today there are no industries in Old Lyme. The permanent residents are largely elderly people of modest incomes, content to live with their memories, although numbers of summer residents bring life and gaiety to the community.

The town of Old Lyme, once known as Black Hall (*see Tour 1C*), was named for Lyme Regis in Dorsetshire, England, the port from which Matthew Griswold, the first settler, sailed for America. The town of Lyme was set off from Saybrook in 1665 and the present Old Lyme was incorporated from Lyme as South Lyme, a separate town in 1855. The present name was adopted in 1857. Many tales are told of the pranks of the eight sprightly Griswold daughters, who were known as 'The Black Hall boys.' Phoebe took special delight in embarrassing her husband, the parson. One day she removed a leaf from his Bible and was delighted by the embarrassment of minister and congregation when he read 'and the wicked shall flourish like a green bay' and turning to the opposite page, added — 'mare.' A Griswold son was one of the champions who took part in the wrestling match which determined the town line (*see Tour* 1C).

Among the early industries, fishing, shipping, shipbuilding, and the manufacture of salt, in which Lyme had a state monopoly, were important. Graceful clipper ships slid down the ways on the Lieutenant River to set sail for the Pacific and return with rich cargoes and fabulous tales of foreign ports. Here were born two governors, Roger and Matthew Griswold; a Chief Justice of Connecticut, Henry Matson Waite; a Chief Justice of the United States (1874–88), the Hon. Morrison R. Waite; an American Minister to Austria, Charles Johnson McCurdy; a Justice of the United States Circuit Court, Judge Walter C. Noyes; and many lawyers who have gained distinction throughout the country.

TOUR

S. from Boston Post Road on Neck Rd. which becomes Ferry Rd.

1. The *Green*, a triangular plot at the junction of Lyme St., Shore Rd., and Ferry Lane, has been the center of town life since the first settlement. Here stood the old whipping-post and stocks, and here on March 16, 1774, Lyme had its own little 'Tea Party' when a traveling peddler was found to have sacks of tea on the back of his donkey and the townsfolk burned his wares on the Green. On this spot in July, 1778, the Stars and Stripes waved beside the white *fleur-de-lys* of France over the brilliant uniforms and *tricornes* of Lafayette's men.

2. The *Congregational Church*, SW. cor. Ferry Rd. and Lyme St., is recognized as one of the most perfect early 19th-century churches in New England. The present structure is a copy of the original church, built 1816–17, by Colonel Samuel Belcher, who, according to tradition, followed plans of a Christopher Wren church in London; the actual contract, however, seems to disprove this. The church, burned on the night of July 3, 1907, was reproduced as faithfully as possible in the present building which was dedicated June 19, 1910, when the principal address was made by Woodrow Wilson, then president of Princeton University. Above the Ionic portico, which has a rich and delicate cornice, the white steeple rises with a square clock-tower, one closed stage, and one octagonal stage to the slender spire. The general lines of the building have been reproduced in Saint Mary of the Lake, chapel of the Catholic Training School

at Area, Ill. The church has frequently served as a subject for the paintings of Childe Hassam and other artists.

3. The *John McCurdy House (private)*, NE. cor. Lyme St. and Shore Rd., shows, in its pedimented windows and the fine arch pediment above the doorway, that it was a house of much distinction, though it has been considerably changed in appearance by the addition of a new roof and numerous ells. Like some other Old Lyme houses, it has a projecting closed porch. The paneled entrance doors are flanked by fluted pilasters which are topped with delicately carved rosettes, characteristic of the Connecticut Valley from 1740 to 1770. The interior walls are handsomely paneled. John McCurdy, the merchant who bought it in 1753, entertained Washington here in 1776, and Lafayette in 1778.

R. from Lyme St. on Shore Rd.

4. The *Ludington House (private)*, Shore Rd. (R), a large, modern dwelling with a rounded porch entrance, stands on the *Site of the Old Parsons Tavern*, the birthplace of General Samuel Holden Parsons, a Revolutionary leader. In the garden is a large rock from which George Whitefield, noted 18th-century evangelist, preached a sermon at the time of the 'Great Awakening.'

5. *Duck River Cemetery*, Shore Rd. (L), one of the oldest burying grounds in the State, contains the graves of many men who were prominent in the early life of the settlement, including five veterans of King Philip's War.

Return on Shore Rd.; R. on Lyme St.

6. The *Samuel Mather House (private)*, Lyme St., now the Congregational Parsonage, built about 1790, is a dignified, gambrel-roofed house, with two chimneys and little exterior ornament except the corner pilasters and a perfectly proportioned front doorway. The door is framed by fluted pilasters and a heavily moulded entablature. The width of the clapboard siding is graduated.

7. *Boxwood Manor* (R), Lyme St., operated as a hotel, a massive square three-story structure of brick and clapboard, was built in 1848 for Richard Sill Griswold, a prominent shipping merchant of New York and Lyme. The original homestead, two stories in height and constructed of brick, has had many additions, including an elaborate porch across the front, and numerous ells.

8. The *Captain Daniel Chadwick House* (1830) *(private)*, Lyme St., was built for the 'Admiral of the steampacket fleet.' The façade is adorned with heavy pilasters which rise to the balustraded roof. At the entrance, a small flat-roofed porch is supported by Tuscan columns; narrow sidelights flank the door. The frame dwelling is unaltered with the exception of two second-story front rooms, added in 1905.

9. The *Moses Noyes II House (private)* (L), cor. Lyme St. and Beckwith Lane, probably built about 1712, is a plain white dwelling which might easily be overlooked. Although some of its distinguishing features have been altered, it is one of the oldest and most interesting houses in town.

The present structure illustrates in brief the history of Colonial architecture. Built at the time when it was the custom to panel every room in feather-edge boarding, the house was evidently 'modernized' in the days of the richest 18th-century paneling (about 1750), and when moved in 1816 from its original location on the site of the present William Noyes house, acquired a new door, new roof, chimney, and windows.

10. The *Captain John Sill House* (1818) (*private*), Lyme St., is a square yellow frame structure with white trim, its doorway now somewhat obscured by a later piazza. As originally designed by Belcher, a flight of steps led up to the door. The quoins at the corners and the wide balustrade around the roof show what an effect of dignity and simplicity Belcher could achieve without the use of columns. In a closet hidden within a cupboard the Captain was believed to have concealed smuggled silks and satins. He was removed to New Haven and placed under bond not to leave that town. But, according to tradition, Captain Sill often sped by night on horseback to Saybrook, thirty-six miles distant, where a cousin rowed him across the river to his young wife who was waiting on the opposite shore.

11. The *Avery House* (*private*), Lyme St., believed to date from 1726, is a small gambrel-roofed structure sometimes known as the Deming House. Recently, when the fireplace in the north room was repaired, a sampler was discovered which was embroidered in the center with a Magna Charta and bore the words 'King' and 'Constitution.'

OTHER POINTS OF INTEREST

12. At the *Lyme Art Gallery*, Boston Post Road, are exhibited the canvases of the many artists who have a colony here.

13. *Peck Tavern*, in the fork made by the Post Road and Sill Lane, is headquarters of the Old Lyme Guild. The main part, built before 1675, is one of the town's earliest buildings. The projecting closed porch is characteristic of Old Lyme architecture and that of Massachusetts. Many of its features are later additions, for example, the old taproom and a second-floor ballroom with a partition that hooks up to the ceiling. In this building John McCurdy opened his first modest store, then the only one on the Boston Post Road between New London and Guilford.

14. The *William Noyes House* (1817) (*private*), Post Road, known locally and to many artists as 'Miss Florence's,' was the headquarters of the art colony to which Miss Florence Griswold was patron saint from the time Henry W. Ranger first came to board in 1900 until her death in December, 1937. Soon afterward Willard Metcalf, then unknown, went to Miss Florence's 'because he was poor and had heard of the four vegetables she was famed for serving with each meal.' Metcalf painted the exterior of the Griswold house in the moonlight, called it 'May Night,' and entered the canvas in the annual competition in 1907 at the Corcoran Gallery, Washington, where it was awarded a $2500 first prize.

This impressive early 19th-century house, designed by Colonel Belcher, has a handsome two-story, colonnaded portico on the front, its two middle columns being widely spaced to permit a view of the fan-lighted door. Under the central pediment a plain window with side-lights is substituted for the usual Palladian window. Within are fine fireplaces with mantels of native pine. Many of the panels have been painted by artists who have boarded here, including Walter Griffin, Paul Dessar, Chauncey Ryder, Carleton Wiggin, and William S. Robinson.

15. *Almon Bacon House* (1817), Ferry Rd., an inn, is a large, rambling brick structure, with many white frame additions and a two-story Tuscan portico with fluted columns at the doorway. It was built by a partner of Cornelius Vanderbilt, who operated it as a Ferry Tavern in connection with the company's Hartford–New York steamship line.

16. *Judge Matthew Griswold House* (*private*), Black Hall Rd. (off State 156), built in 1798, the earliest of the Griswold houses in the vicinity, is plain, except for an elaborately carved doorway and cross-panel doors. This house, still in the possession of the Griswold heirs, was built by the son of Matthew the fourth, and his cousin-wife Ursula, daughter of Governor Wolcott. In this house, built on the site of his grandfather John Griswold's homestead, erected in 1713, Judge Griswold taught law to a group of young men, many of whom became prominent jurists.

17. The *Colonel Charles Griswold House* (*private*), Black Hall Rd., adjoining Judge Griswold's House, is a brick structure with an end entrance and four chimneys. It was built in 1822 by a son of Governor Roger Griswold

Points of Interest in Environs:

Hadlyme Landing, 4.7 *m.* (*see Tour* 1D); Bride's Brook, 8.6 *m.* (*see Tour* 1F).

OLD SAYBROOK

Town: Alt. 5, pop. 1643, sett. 1635, incorp. 1854.
Railroad Station: N.Y., N.H. & H. R.R. station just north of US 1 at center.
Taxis: 10¢ within village limits.
Accommodations: Several small hotels and inns.

OLD SAYBROOK, at the mouth of the Connecticut River, the fourth oldest town in the State, is a quiet, elm-shaded village that has changed but little in the last century. Summer colonies have sprung up at Fenwick and Cornfield Point, and along the broken shoreline of Long Island Sound, but the little coastal town retains its air of simplicity.

The Connecticut River flows past the eastern edge of the township and numerous tidal inlets reach long fingers into the salt marshes. Residents rent small boats during the duck-hunting season. In summer, sailing craft keel to the lee rail in a spanking breeze, jockeying for position at the start of a race, or cruise about trolling for bluefish. Along the waterfront, lobstermen are busy with their traps and bait, and in the spring the teeming activity during the run of shad recalls the early importance of Saybrook's fisheries, when thousands of shad were caught daily, salted down and shipped inland.

Saybrook Point was first occupied by white men in 1623 when 'two families and six men' were sent by the Dutch of Manhattan Island to take possession of lands at the mouth of the river. Evidently they were soon frightened away by the unfriendly Indians, as there was no evidence of the settlement in 1633 when a party from a Dutch ship landed here, named the point 'Kievet's Hook,' because of the cries of the sandpipers, and affixed the coat of arms of the States General to a tree. Wishing to eliminate the danger of Dutch occupation, the English granted a patent to Lord Say and Sele, and Lord Brooke, who commissioned John Winthrop, Jr., as agent and governor of the 'River Connecticut, the harbors and places adjoining these unto.'

Arriving at Boston in October, 1635, Winthrop immediately dispatched a party of men, who reached Saybrook November 9. Winthrop arrived shortly afterward and named the settlement Saybrook. Lion Gardiner, an engineer formerly in the employ of the Prince of Orange, came several months later. The Dutch shield was torn from the crotch of the tree and in its place was carved a grinning face. The English had barely thrown up earthworks and mounted their guns when a Dutch fleet sailed into the harbor. The little fort broke out the Union Jack and manned its guns, and the Dutch withdrew without firing a shot.

The settlement was originally planned as a baronial center of landed estates for the few aristocratic sympathizers of Oliver Cromwell who were expected to seek refuge here. According to Macaulay, Hampden and Cromwell had actually boarded a ship in the Thames to embark for this country, but were not permitted to sail. Colonel George Fenwick was the only Puritan aristocrat to settle here. He served as governor of Saybrook from 1639 to 1644, and after the death of his wife, Lady Boteler, returned to England.

The band of defenders had to endure the privations of bitter winters and the terrors of marauding Indians. During the Pequot War the colony lost nine men and nearly all of its cattle, buildings and corn. When Captain Gardiner's contract expired, he moved to the island in the Sound which now bears his name.

In 1675, Governor Andros of New York attempted to take possession of Saybrook. Hoisting the King's flag over his ship, he demanded the fort's surrender. Captain Thomas Bull, then in command, promptly raised His Majesty's colors over the fort, and Andros, not daring to fire on a British flag, was persuaded to settle the matter at a conference with the General Court.

Saybrook was the original site of Yale College, which was established here as The Collegiate School in 1701. Although some of the early classes were held at the home of the Rev. Abraham Pierson, the first rector, in Killingworth (now Clinton), Saybrook was the official site of the college. Here the first commencement was held September 13, 1702, when the master of arts degree was conferred upon five graduates of Harvard. On April 4, 1716, the trustees met to consider complaints of Hartford and Wethersfield students as to the 'insufficiency of instruction and inconveniences of the place,' but after a debate of several days, 'the trustees were no better agreed than the students,' and 'leave was given to the students to go to such places of instruction as they pleased.' A smallpox epidemic soon scattered the student body, some going with their tutors to Wethersfield, others to Hartford. On October 17, 1716, the trustees voted to move the college to New Haven. But Saybrook did not part with the institution without a struggle. Delegates sent to move the books found the house in which they were stored fortified and guarded by townsmen. Aid was called and an entrance forced, but while the delegates gathered up the books, their horses were freed and their carts damaged. Even when new wagons were obtained and the procession set out for New Haven, the way was beset, for the men of Saybrook had taken the planking from the larger bridges and had entirely removed the smaller ones.

In 1708, a council of twelve ministers and four laymen met here to draw up the Saybrook Platform, a general plan of church government and discipline under which the Congregational Churches of the State were united. The articles drawn up were approved by the Legislature in 1709 and were a legally recognized standard until 1784. Printed by the New London Press in 1710, the Platform was the first volume to be published in Connecticut.

Washington passed through the town April 9, 1776; local troops marched away July 7, 1776; and on August 11 of the same year, the fort at the point was strengthened and a saltpeter works was established. On August 30, 1777, records show that nearly threescore ships passed the settlement, and it was believed that most of them were British. One patriot allowed his son, a lad of 15, to substitute for another man during the defense of Fort Griswold (see GROTON), for the price of one barrel of cider. In the fall, after the lad was killed, the cider was delivered as per agreement.

The first resort development here was recorded in 1870 when a company was formed to build cottages and hotels at Lynde's Farm, or Light House Point. The temperature at this point has seldom been known to rise above 84 degrees, and sea breezes blow from three points of the compass. This early development set a new standard for seaside resorts by restricting building specifications and prohibiting amusement concessions.

MOTOR TOUR

S. from the junction of US 1 and US 1A, on Main St. (US 1).

1. In the *Elisha Hart House* (*private*), Main St., a gambrel-roofed dwelling of 1783, the seven beautiful and talented Hart daughters entertained distinguished guests, including Washington Irving, Fitz-Greene Halleck, and the South American patriot, Bolivar. One of the Hart daughters married Commodore Isaac Hull, commander of the frigate 'Constitution' in the capture of the 'Guerrière,' and her sister married his nephew, Commodore Joseph Hull. Another Hart daughter fell in love with Bolivar during his visit here, but the marriage was prevented by the objections of her father.

2. *Ye Old Saybrook Inn* (1800), at the corner of Main St. and the Old Boston Post Rd. (R), has a low hip roof surrounded by a simple balustrade over an elaborate cornice of Greek detail. The building was erected by Major Richard William Hart, a son of General William Hart, who was one of the company that purchased lands of the Western Reserve from the State of Connecticut in 1795. Later, while the house was owned by Captain Morgan, a famous shipmaster, many distinguished guests were entertained here, including Charles Dickens, in 1867–68, who depicted his friend Captain Morgan as Captain Jorgen in 'A Message from the Sea.'

R. from Main Street on the Old Boston Post Rd.

3. The *Acton Library* (*open daily*), Old Post Rd., near Main St., a two-story modern structure, houses in the upper floor a small museum in which are displayed relics of the early Saybrook settlement and several rare books.

Return to Main St.; R. on Main St.

4. *Pratt Tavern* (R), Main St., a large central-hall building of fine proportions, with a three-inch overhang at the second floor and gables, was built in 1785 and visited by Lafayette and other dignitaries in 1824. The handsome front door of many small raised panels is somewhat obscured by a square portico added in 1840. The most attractive feature of the house is its two-and-a-half-story gambrel-roofed ell, which contains on the second floor an unpainted ballroom in its original condition.

5. On the *Drugstore* (R), Main St., a tablet advises the passer-by that 'In this shop Lafayette made a purchase in 1824.'

6. The *General William Hart House* (*private*), Main St. (L), erected in 1767, a dwelling of gracious proportions, with end chimneys and a later open pedimented Doric porch, is distinguished by its beaded clapboards and fine cornice. The nine windows on the front have the original sash of 12 lights each.

7. The plain white *Congregational Church*, Main St. (L), built in 1839, is of heavy construction. Its small, square two-stage tower rises above

a portico with four impressive Tuscan columns. On the church a plaque is inscribed, 'This church was organized in the Great Hall of the Fort in the summer of 1646.'

8. Beside the road (L) is an *Old Mill Stone*, Main St., removed from the gristmill which operated at Saybrook Point. According to tradition the stone was brought from Holland about 1638.

L. from Main St. on North Cove Rd.

9. The *William Tully House* (*private*), North Cove Rd. (L), sometimes called the Captain John Chauncey Whittlesey House (1750), a two-and-a-half-story house with its original huge off-center chimney, has an exceptionally well-designed front doorway flanked by narrow pilasters which are topped with the carved English rose. The side lights and top-lights are narrow, and at the center of the top-lights is an odd sash, shaped like two hearts lying on their sides. Here, on August 8, 1774, occurred William Tully's skirmish with Tories, which has been roguishly referred to as 'the most successful battle of Revolutionary times.' Tully had been left in charge of contraband goods seized from a Middletown vessel that attempted to run out of the river to trade with the British. When eight Tories forced an entrance, Tully aimed his flintlock and fired. The ball passed through the first man, but the second man in line dropped dead. As the first man reached for a chest of tea, he too fell dead. The rest of the raiding party fled in terror. Tully was credited with a victory in which the British sustained 25 per cent casualties while the local force was unscathed.

10. The *Black Horse Tavern* (*private*) (L), built about 1720 for John Burrows, long enjoyed a profitable business when steamboat passengers landed at the wharf in its back yard to transfer to the Connecticut Valley Railway. Although the building has been remodeled, the old parlor retains its two old summer beams and burnt oystershell plaster. The fireplace has some plain, though excellent, wide paneling.

11. The large brick, two-and-a-half-story *George Dickinson House* (*private*) (L), built in 1790, with pilasters at the center which seem to divide it into two sections, has two doors, an elaborate one to the east with heavy cross panels and a brass knocker, and a plain door to the west.

Return on North Cove Rd. to Main St.; L. on Main St.

12. An arbor-sheltered *Boulder* (R) bears a bronze plate marked '*The First Site of Yale College*,' but recent research seems to indicate that the original college building stood on the site of the William Willard House, 400 feet away on Willard Ave.

13. In Cypress Cemetery (R), surrounded by an iron fence, is the *Tomb of Lady Alice Boteler Fenwick*, wife of Colonel George Fenwick, the only titled person to brave the dangers of the Indian-harassed settlement, who died shortly after the birth of her daughter in November, 1645. Among the many old graves in this cemetery is that of Ellen Gold, whose three husbands were Continental officers killed during the Revolutionary War.

A widow three times, she was awarded three pensions for the services of her husbands.

14. Opposite the cemetery on the site of the old fort, the *Statue of Lion Gardiner*, in cuirass and helmet, straight and stalwart, symbolizes the personality of the builder and commander of the fort which once dominated the harbor and the river mouth.

15. The Causeway, from the end of Main St., extends across South Cove, connecting Saybrook Point and the Cape of Fenwick, at the eastern extremity of which stands the white, flat-sided masonry *Lighthouse of Lynde Point* (*private*), built in 1839 to replace an early wooden structure.

16. Beyond, at the far end of a breakwater, may be seen another, the *Jetty* or *Saybrook Lighthouse* (*private*), built in 1866 and more favorably placed than the Lynde tower for the guidance of ships at the river mouth. There is excellent snapper bluefishing in the waters offshore during August and September.

Points of Interest in Environs:

> The Sill House, in the ell of which David Bushnell, inventor of the submarine torpedo (1777), carried on his experiments — State 9A (*see Tour* 8); site of old Ferry Landing in continuous use from 1662–1911 (*see Tour* 1).

S T A M F O R D

City: Alt. 20, pop. 46,346, sett. 1641, inc. 1893.

Railroad Station: 521 Atlantic St. for N.Y., N.H. & H. R.R.
Taxis: 15¢ for first one-quarter mile; 5¢ each additional quarter mile within town limits; flat hourly rate.

Accommodations: One principal hotel; tourist accommodations at private homes.

Information Service: Chamber of Commerce, 417 Main St., Stamford Historical Society, 16 Fourth St.; Town Clerk's Office, Town Hall; Ferguson Library, Broad and Bedford Sts.; Stamford Guide, weekly pamphlet obtainable at leading stores, the library, and post-office.

Recreation: Woodside Park, reached via Summer St., baseball facilities.
Swimming: Cummings Park on the Sound, reached via Elm St., admission free.
Golf: Cummings Park, admission free; Five Ridges Country Club, fee $1.50; Hubbard Heights Golf Club, fee $1.50.
Tennis: Cummings Park, admission free; Five Ridges Country Club, 50¢ per hour.

Annual Events: Annual regatta, end of July; Vineyard Haven sailing race over Labor Day week-end.

STAMFORD, a manufacturing center on a wide bay crossed by two tidal inlets, is a city of contrasts. There are many landscaped estates in the residential section of Stamford's hills. The workers' dwellings are scattered through many sections of the city. In an effort to improve housing conditions among the workers, an appropriation of $800,000 has been made for a Federal Housing Project, the only one in Connecticut. Neither railway nor highway offers an approach that does the city justice. The central square is clean but congested and the better shops are often on the side streets. Traffic is too heavy for the narrow streets and parking is a problem. The factory district is well hidden behind the railroad embankment. Long Island Sound crowds in along an indented shoreline where there is considerable salt marsh and a few good sandy beaches: the Rippowam River meanders across country to split the township and eventually to join with the water of the Sound.

Stamford is closely linked to New York City with excellent express service by rail on a forty-eight and fifty-three minute schedule. The New York State Line is only eleven miles away and 104 passenger trains daily carry large numbers of commuters to New York and back.

The outlying sections of Stamford have interesting place names. At Turn of River, which is north of the business center, the Rippowam flows past many small estates and pleasant homes. In 1825 an English metal worker, William Lecon, was associated with a local mechanic named Davenport in the operation of what is claimed to be America's first wire factory. Their mill workers, who lived at Turn of River, made a reputation as gay, carefree folks, spending the Sabbath drinking and singing rather than in proper worship, and earned the name of 'Sodom' for their little community. Bangall Road took its name from the noise made by a pioneer tin shop. Strawberry Hill now produces no strawberries, but there are beautiful homes there and flower gardens that do not hide behind fences.

Glenbrook, called New Hope in Colonial times, is an attractive residential section to the northeast, occupied chiefly by commuters whose business interests are in New York. The hilly section through which Courtland Ave. runs was the common pasture land, known as 'Cow's Delight' until 1750 when the land was parcelled and sold. The Charles H. Phillips Chemical Company has operated in Glenbrook for several generations.

High Ridge, close to the New York Line on the north, is one of Stamford's most exclusive sections, claiming as residents such well-known persons as Dr. Robert T. Morris, surgeon; Deems Taylor, composer; Heywood Broun, author; and Peggy Wood, actress. To the east of High Ridge is Long Ridge, formerly the site of a large shoe industry, now known for its extensive estates and magnificent scenery.

Captain Nathaniel Turner, agent for the New Haven Colony, explored this Rippowam area in 1640, purchased land from Ponus, Sachem of the

Siwanoys, and sold out to twenty-eight pioneers from Wethersfield who took possession in 1641. By 1642 the newcomers had named the place Stamford, for the English town in Lincolnshire, and soon afterwards furnished the nucleus of a settlement across the Sound at Hempstead, Long Island. Stamford was in the New Haven Colony until two years before the latter was merged with Connecticut. Stamford submitted to the jurisdiction of Connecticut in October, 1662.

The railroad came to Stamford in 1848. The city was incorporated in 1893. Business improved as transportation facilities advanced and commuters discovered the little city on the Rippowam. Industry expanded as Stamford builders' hardware, electric hoists, ball bearings, postage meters, rubber goods, brass, druggists' supplies, oil burners, cocoa, paints, bronze powders, machinery, lacquers, stoves, boats, and garments found a world-wide market.

There are many historic and noteworthy points of interest in the city, although most of Stamford's older houses lie on the outskirts.

TOUR 1

1. *Atlantic Square*, in the heart of the business district, formerly the site of the first meeting-house and the whipping-post, stocks, and pillory is now an attractive parkway, planted with shade trees. Opposite is the gray stone *Town Hall*, built in 1907, and designed by Mellon and Josselyn.

E. on Main St. to Elm; R. on Elm St.

2. *Cummings Park*, at the end of Elm St. on the Sound, was named for the U.S. Attorney-General, Homer S. Cummings, a resident of Stamford. In the park are a *Children's Museum of Natural History* (*open Tues., Wed., Thurs., Fri., Sat., 10–4, free*), a small harbor known as Halloween Basin, and the Halloween Yacht Club. To the west and east of Cummings Park stretch several fine public beaches.

R. from Elm St. on Leonard St. to McGee Ave. which becomes Shippan Ave.

STAMFORD. Points of Interest

1. Atlantic Square
2. Cummings Park
3. Low and Heywood School
4. Shippan Point
5. Washington Building
6. Site of Abraham Davenport's Homestead
7. Site of the Stage House
8. Frederick Webb House
9. Ferguson Library
10. Barnum House
11. Davenport House
12. Ingersoll or Block House
13. John Brush Farmhouse
14. Yale and Towne Manufacturing Company

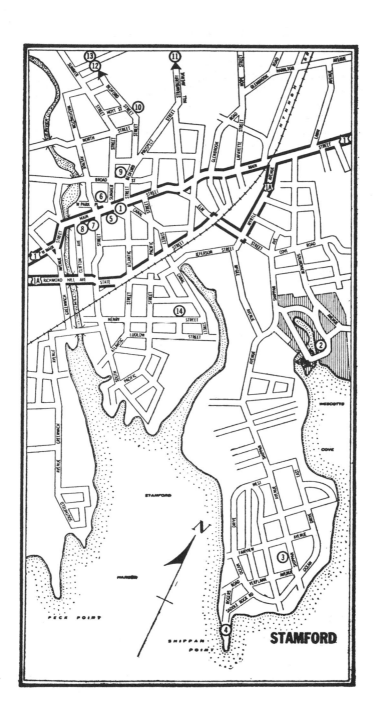

STAMFORD

3. The *Low and Heywood School* (L), 873 Shippan Ave., boarding-school for girls, was founded in 1855 by Miss Catherine Aiken. The late Georges Clemenceau, one-time Premier of France, taught French and philosophy here, and married one of his pupils, Mary Plumly.

4. *Shippan Point*, jutting into the Sound at the foot of Shippan Ave., is Stamford's most exclusive residential section. First used by the colonists as a common pasture ground for horses, it was developed as a pleasure resort in the summer of 1845. During the Revolution, American troops under the command of Colonel Tallmadge encamped here.

TOUR 2

W. on Main St. from Atlantic Square.

5. The *Washington Building* (L) cor. Main and Bank Sts., stands on the *Site of Webb's Tavern*, where, one morning in October, 1789, General Washington, according to an entry in his diary, stopped for breakfast. Mrs. Washington, too, is said to have stopped here for refreshment in 1775 when on her way to Massachusetts to join her husband.

6. At the northwest corner of Main and Summer Sts. (R) is the *Site of Abraham Davenport's Homestead*, now occupied by a hotel. Abraham Davenport, grandson of the Rev. John Davenport, founder of the New Haven Colony, was for many years a member of the State Legislature. A man of remarkable character and integrity, his strong sense of duty is extolled in a legend of Connecticut's 'Dark Day' — May 19, 1780. At that time the Legislature was in session at Hartford, and the members, noting with fear the increasing darkness, thought that Judgment Day had come. In the House of Representatives, a motion for adjournment was made and carried, but when the same motion came before the Council and Davenport was asked for his opinion, he replied: 'I am against adjournment. The Day of Judgment is either approaching or it is not. If it is not, there is no cause for adjournment; if it is, I choose to be found doing my duty. I wish therefore that candles may be brought.'

7. At the southeast corner of Main and Relay Place (L) is the *Site of the Stage House*, a hotel built in the first decade of the 19th century, which remained in business for almost 100 years. Relay Place derived its name from the fact that in the days of stagecoach travel it was one of several stops between Boston and New York regularly used for the relaying or changing of horses.

8. The *Frederick Webb House* (*private*), SE. cor. Main and Clinton Sts., almost hidden behind a gas station (L), is one of the two 18th-century dwellings in town. The salt-box roof has a curious flare both back and front.

OTHER POINTS OF INTEREST

9. The *Ferguson Library* (*open weekdays* 9–9; *Sunday and holidays* 2.30–6), cor. Bedford and Broad Sts. (L), a handsome modern Colonial building. in red brick, has frequent exhibitions of paintings, sculpture, and sketches.

10. The *Barnum House* (*private*), 913 Bedford St., a salt-box dwelling with stone chimney and sash dating from the mid-eighteenth century, is smaller than the Webb House and probably older.

11. The *Davenport House* (1775), 4.5 *m*. north on Davenport Ridge Road, a low, one-and-one-half-story cottage with three dormer windows, stands on a hilltop, surrounded by trees and shrubbery, in a superb rural estate setting. The stone chimney is well forward of the ridge, an indication of a comparatively late date.

12. The *Ingersoll* or *Block House* (*private*), Farens Road, 0.5 *m*. west of Riverbank Road, encircled by a stone wall, is built of large blocks of gray stone 20 inches thick, with arched red brick caps over the doorway and windows. The brick, differing from any made in this country at the time, is believed to have been part of a consignment from Swansea, England. Although usually given a date of 1721, it has many features, such as the two end chimneys, the corner hall, the high space between windows and cornice, the fan-light and block-like laying of the stone, which indicate a later date. The ell was built in 1821.

At the rear are the ruins of an old stone workshop where, according to legend, fleeing Continental soldiers were sheltered after the battle of White Plains. Here Simon Ingersoll invented the friction clutch, spring scale, and steam-driven wagon. This steam-wagon, a forerunner of the automobile, was demonstrated on the streets of Stamford in 1858.

13. The *John Brush Farmhouse* (*private*), on East Middle Patent Road, by a millpond, is sheltered by tall lilac bushes and an arbor vitae over 200 years old. Though much of the detail seems later, the frame, central-chimney house is said to have been erected in 1770.

14. *Yale and Towne Manufacturing Company*, 200 Henry St., manufactures Yale locks, electric hoists, and builders' hardware. The first revolving crane built in this country was made in Stamford in 1833 by the two inventors, Yale and Towne. Linus Yale made the first cylinder lock in the world at Stamford in 1848, revolutionizing an industry which dates back to the Egyptians and laying the foundation for a branch of the hardware business in which the United States leads the entire world. Yale's invention made the heavy keys of older locks unnecessary, as it separated the key mechanism from the lock by adapting the old Egyptian principles to modern use, making it unnecessary for the key to pass through

the door. The Yale lock made it possible to use as many as 32,768 different keys in one lock mechanism.

Point of Interest in Environs:

Mianus Gorge on State 104, 8.5 *m.* (*see Tour* 1).

STONINGTON

Town: Alt. 5, borough pop. 2006, sett. 1649, incorp. 1801.

Railroad Station: N.Y., N.H. & H. R.R., on Water St.

Accommodations: Six inns.

Recreation: Swimming in season on three public beaches, two boating clubs, one golf course.

STONINGTON is a quiet old town of modest, shady streets on a narrow, rocky point. It lies so close to the eastern State boundary that Dr. Dwight once wrote in his 'Travels in New England and New York' (1825), 'Stonington and all its vicinity suffers in religion from the nearness of Rhode Island.' Off the Boston Post Road, quite by itself on a long point that juts out into the ocean with magnificent marine views, the community has an atmosphere of old whaling days. Dreamy seaside lanes, large white houses where former sea captains came at last to a safe anchorage, a white Congregational church, and row on row of elms that cast long shadows under sun and moonlight — all are typical of Stonington. Some houses have a 'captain's walk' around the chimney, from which shipowners and anxious wives watched for the glint of sails, hull down on the horizon. Fishing gear and lobster traps are piled on the docks at the end of the side streets; and activity offshore during the summer months brings back something of the old seafaring past. The fishing fleet comes in with bluefish, swordfish, and haddock; summer residents cruise in power boats or set sail on schooner and yawl; and clam-diggers swarm on the flats at low tide.

The point of land on which the community stands, called by the Indians *Pawcatuck* and *Mistack*, was occupied by Narragansett Indians before the arrival of William Chesebrough and a group of colonists from Plymouth in 1649. Ownership of the territory was disputed for several years by Massachusetts and Connecticut. Massachusetts named the settlement Souther Towne in 1658. Connecticut renamed it Stonington in 1666, after the agreement of 1662 under which the town again came within the boundaries of the Nutmeg State. The name is descriptive, for there are many stones in the area and little profitable agricultural acreage.

Although the scene of considerable Indian warfare, there were few white casualties in the early fights around Stonington. On April 9, 1676, during King Philip's War, Canonchet was captured on the Pawcatuck River and sentenced to die. When advised of his fate the chief said: 'I like it well that I should die before my heart is softened and I say things unworthy of myself.' Thereupon this son of Miantonomo was carried to Stonington and executed by Indians who were friendly to the white men.

Little remains of the early shipbuilding that made Stonington a center of such importance in the Colony of Connecticut that the village was popularly known as a 'Nursery for Seamen.' Masters from the little town sailed the Seven Seas with merchant vessels, opening up new markets for the infant industries of the colony; and whalers with a Stonington registry searched uncharted oceans, returning with heavy cargoes of oil and whalebone to lay the foundations of many fortunes. One of the first whaling franchises ever granted in America was issued to a Mr. Whiting for the waters between Stonington and Montauk Point in 1647. Stonington became an important port of entry, as more and more ships cleared from the harbor that was protected by a breakwater for which the Federal government expended $34,766 in 1828–34. Shipbuilding continued until after the Civil War, but declined with the introduction of steamships.

Captain Edmund Fanning of Stonington served as a midshipman under John Paul Jones. When he was but eighteen years of age, he discovered the Fanning Islands, on June 15, 1798. These islands are now of great importance on the trans-Pacific route of the Connecticut-built Sikorsky Clipper ships. Captain Fanning's brother, Nathaniel, was maintopman of Jones' 'Bonhomme Richard,' and took part in the fight with the 'Serapis.' In 1820, Nathaniel B. Palmer, commanding the sloop 'Hero,' sailed for the Antarctic Ocean with a squadron of whalers; in 1821, the twenty-one-year-old sea captain discovered the Antarctic Continent, and an archipelago has been named 'Palmerland' in his honor.

During the Revolutionary War and the War of 1812, the town was twice attacked from the sea. The first British attack, made by a foraging party landed by H.M.S. 'Rose,' August 30, 1775, was met by local militia who, with one casualty, repulsed the invaders. From August 9 to 12, 1814, the village was bombarded by a British fleet made up of H.M. ships 'Ramillies,' 'Terror,' 'Pactolus,' 'Despatch,' and 'Nimrod,' under the command of Admiral Nelson's favorite officer, Captain Thomas Masterman Hardy, who had been one of the heroes of the battle of Trafalgar. Mounting a total of 140 guns, the attacking fleet engaged without success a shore battery of only two cannon, a six-pounder and an eighteen-pounder, manned by the Connecticut militia. Cannon balls from the King's navy, which fell harmlessly in the fields and woods about the town, are among Stonington's most valued relics. The British casualties totaled ninety-four, and the ship 'Despatch' was badly damaged. The militia reported only three men wounded. Abandoning the attempt to take the town, the British sailed away, and Stonington has chanted through the years, 'It cost the King ten thousand pounds to have a dash at Stonington.'

Present-day Stonington has an involved government peculiar to some Connecticut towns, consisting of a borough within the township, with two separate taxing units and two sets of municipal officials administering civil affairs. The borough was the first incorporated in the State (May, 1801).

The industry of the community is varied. One factory produces fine silk-throwing machinery, one mill makes velvet, and another produces various forms of rubber molds.

TOUR

SW. from Broad on Elm St.

1. The *Dudley Palmer House*, built in 1765, 14 Elm St., a white clapboarded, two-and-a-half-story, peak-roofed house, with a brick central chimney, has a delicately designed cornice with capped corner boards. The heavy paneled front door is flanked by fluted pilasters and topped with a transom of five square lights. The owner, Dr. J. H. Weeks, who is an authority on local history, has collected many relics of whaling days and uses a part of his home for a *Whaling Museum (open weekdays, free)*.

2. The *Congregational Church* (1829), SE. cor. Main and Elm Sts., represents one of the last stages of the architectural development known as the Greek Revival. In contrast with an 18th-century church its tower is low and set within the main building. It is built of two square stories, each framed with pilasters, and the horizontal lines are the heaviest and most prominent. The portico is shallow but heavy. The windows extend the whole two stories and are filled with stained glass. Each part may be correctly worked out as a single unit, but a building of this period always lacks grace.

L. from Elm St. on Main St.

3. The *Captain Lodowick Niles House* (*not open*), 68 Main St., a substantial two-and-a-half-story clapboarded dwelling built early in the 19th

---

STONINGTON.   Points of Interest

1. Dudley Palmer House
2. Congregational Church
3. Captain Lodowick Niles House
4. Eells House
5. Colonel Joseph Smith Homestead
6. Samuel Denison House
7. Doctor Lord's Hall
8. Amos Palmer House
9. Colonel Oliver Smith House
10. Old Stone Customhouse
11. Stone Bank
12. Old Breakwater
13. Elkanah Cobb House
14. Old Stone Lighthouse
15. Amos Sheffield House
16. Peleg Brown House
17. Polly Breed House

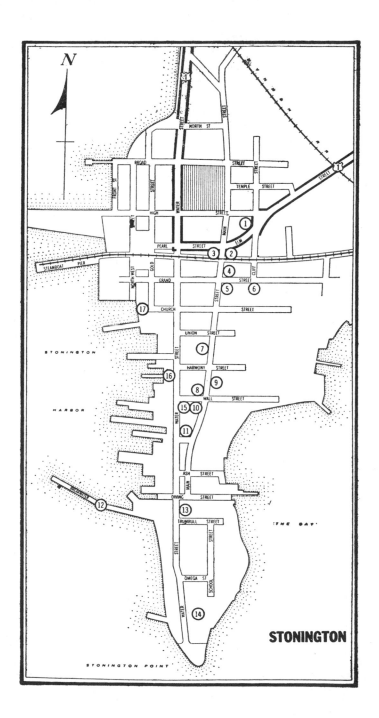

STONINGTON

century, has an elaborate Doric portico enlivened with carved wreaths in the entablature, a successful adaptation of the style used in ecclesiastical architecture.

4 and 5. On the corner of Main and Grand Sts. (L), are two well-preserved white houses. The *Eells House*, built in 1785, NE. corner, is a simple two-and-a-half-story clapboard dwelling with a well-designed doorway of later date. The transom is delicately ornamented with leaded grill work and is surmounted by a heavy cap. The *Colonel Joseph Smith Homestead*, SE. cor., is a hip-roofed, square house. Its fan-lighted door is set in a slightly projecting pediment that breaks through the roof and shelters a similar fan-light above the cornice line. The Longfellow house in Cambridge, Massachusetts, has the same design. Colonel Smith built the house about 1800, adding to it over a period of years; he is credited with being the designer-builder of several other Stonington houses.

In a fence post at the corner is embedded a cannon ball fired by the British warship 'Terror,' August 10, 1812.

Left from Main on Grand St.

6. The *Samuel Denison House* (*not open*) (L), on Grand St., across from Cliff St., is an ornate two-and-a-half-story hip-roofed dwelling built prior to 1811, distinguished by its 'captain's walk' around the large central chimney.

Return on Grand St. to Main St.

7. *Doctor Lord's Hall* (*not open*) (R), 34 Main St., a long, two-story building with three front entrances of very simple design, was used as a schoolhouse and also as a meeting place during a revival period when dancing was prohibited in the community. It may be only a coincidence that the hall stands near the corner of Harmony St.

8. The *Amos Palmer House* (*not open*), built in 1787, NW. cor. Main and Wall Sts., a very high house with a huge gable breaking the roof, and two circular flights of steps, was severely damaged by the British bombardment of 1814. Repaired and remodeled, it was the boyhood home of James Abbott McNeill Whistler (born at Lowell, Massachusetts, in 1834). Whistler's father was an engineer of repute, builder of the Providence to Stonington railway line, and owner of a horse-drawn vehicle in which he took the family to church over the twin rails of the road he built.

9. The *Colonel Oliver Smith House* (*private*), 25 Main St. (L), was erected in 1761 by Colonel Smith, a shipbuilder of local fame. It is a small, unspoiled story-and-a-half gambrel-roofed dwelling with two small dormer windows and an exceptionally large chimney, recently retopped.

10. The *Old Stone Customhouse* (*private*), 16 Main St. (R), a small building of split stone on a high stone foundation, has a Doric portico and a roof of rather flat pitch. Built in 1823 as Stonington's first bank, it was taken over by the Government in 1842 when the harbor became a port of entry. In 1895, the port of entry was transferred to New London.

R. from Main St. on Cannon Square.

11. Facing Cannon Square, the southern center of the borough, where are placed two of the guns used in defense of Stonington during the British attack of 1814, is the solid little *Stone Bank* (1850), the first National Bank. A heavier version of the customhouse, the structure is built of dressed granite, with free-standing Doric columns, long windows, and triglyphs in the entablature.

Left from Cannon Square on Water St.

12. Extending 740 feet into Stonington Harbor, from behind the Atwood Machine Company plant (manufacturers of silk-throwing machinery), is (R) the *Old Breakwater*, built by the Government, 1828–34, of riprap stone with a coursed stone top. Old stone posts, where whalers and sealers tied their craft, are still standing. Fully 100,000 sealskins were unloaded here during a good year.

13. The one-and-a-half-story *Elkanah Cobb House*, which was built in 1760, close to the sidewalk, at 35 Water St., now a store, is one of the more attractive of the smaller gambrel-roofed seamen's cottages that stood in the direct line of the British bombardment. The unusual windows have nine lights in the bottom sash and six in the top.

14. The *Old Stone Lighthouse* (*open; no fee*) (L), at the end of Water St., now a museum and tearoom, is a squat, granite building once painted white, with an octagonal tower topped with a windowed hood from which the light shone. The heavy window caps and diamond-paned casement windows give a hint of unexpected Tudor influence.

Among the historic maritime exhibits is the figurehead of the 'Great Republic,' the largest ship of the mid-nineteenth century, and one of the first to be rigged as a four-masted barque. Built in Boston by Donald McKay in 1853, her registered tonnage was 4555. She caught fire and had to be scuttled while loading for her maiden voyage, and never went to sea as originally designed. Under modified rigging, she was a failure commercially, but did good work as a troop ship in both the Crimean and American Civil Wars. As the 'Denmark' out of Liverpool, she foundered in the North Atlantic in 1872.

Other exhibits include a Liverpool pitcher made in celebration of 'The Gallant Defense of Stonington,' several pieces of old pewter, spinning and weaving implements and equipment, nautical instruments, old books, bank notes, bedspreads, fabrics, portraits, and documents.

Return N. on Water St.

15. The *Amos Sheffield House* (*not open*), 73 Water St., corner of Wall, a severe white clapboarded dwelling, built prior to 1783, stands close to the sidewalk on a high brick basement that served Aunt Honor States as a store for the sale of dry goods, light groceries and fruit. The building has been kept in excellent repair and is little changed. The doorway, reached by a double flight of stone steps flanked by a delicately hand-wrought iron rail, is designed in excellent proportions and ornamented with fluted pilasters, a five-light transom, and a heavily molded cap. Fluted

pilasters, carried up through the second story at the corners of the building, and a deep, elaborate, molded cornice give this house a dignity its otherwise plain exterior lacks.

Other Points of Interest.

16. *Peleg Brown House* (*open, no fee*), built in 1798, 94 Water St., a long, two-and-a-half-story clapboarded dwelling with two entrance doors, topped with simple three-pane transoms, is the birthplace of Captain Nathaniel Palmer (1799–1877), the discoverer of Palmerland in the Antarctic. This old house contains the log books of the skipper, mementos of his life and accounts of his voyage.

17. The early 18th-century *Polly Breed House* (*not open*), at the west end of Church St., is probably the oldest house in the borough. A long, low one-and-a-half-story gambrel-roofed cottage, on a stone foundation, is typical of the homes of seamen found in the outlying parts of the town.

The stately houses of a later generation of sea captains and shipowners stand facing Wadawanuck Park, which lies between Water and Main Sts., in the northern part of the village.

Point of Interest in Environs:

Wequetequock Cemetery, with old wolf stones, 2.9 *m.* (*see Tour* 1).

W A T E R B U R Y

City: Alt. 280, pop. 99,902, sett. 1674, incorp. 1853.

Railroad Station: Union Station, Meadow St. for the N.Y., N.H. & H. R.R.

Accommodations: One first-class hotel.

Information Service: Chamber of Commerce, 7 Field St.

Swimming: Municipal Pools, free at Hamilton Park, 1334 E. Main St.; Chase Park, Chase Park Ave.; Public Pools, 25¢ fee at Boys' Club, 22 Cottage Place, and Y.M.C.A., 136 W. Main St.

WATERBURY, the center of the brass industry in the United States, lies in the valleys of the Naugatuck and Mad Rivers, and on the somewhat abrupt, brown hills that rise from the streamsides. Black iron and yellow firebrick stacks tower above the casting shops and rolling mills, throwing off saffron-yellow and greenish clouds of smoke. The railway follows the river, with spurs running into the side valleys, where the flat cars and gondolas, like strings of square beads, are switched to the brass shops. In spite of the fact that the speckled-brown and granite-gray hillsides have been stripped of all except third-growth saplings to provide 'muffle wood' for the annealing and heat treatment of brass, exposed ledge outcroppings of granite prevent erosion.

Waterbury is a Yankee industrial town that has grown without a city plan. Office buildings of an imposing character were built along Grand Street by the brass companies before their mergers with western copper. A great fire in 1902 burned the entire business section of the city, but the rebuilding was done with little idea of plan.

Known by the Indians as Mattatuck, meaning 'badly wooded region,' Waterbury was settled as a part of Farmington in May 1674, incorporated and named, May 1686, from the 'abundant waters.' The township was so rugged and sterile that, after a four-day survey, scouts made the report, 'our apprehensions are that it may accommodate but 30 families.' Rough estimates place the initial population at 150. There was no increase in the population for 35 years, and not until 1840 was there any appreciable growth. It was chartered as a city in 1853, and the town and city were combined in 1901.

Waterbury's entire industrial development has been built around the brass industry. The early braziers bought scrap brass, bronze, copper and zinc, melted their own metal, rolled it in the crude iron rolls of the day, and often blanked out brass buttons by footpower or even hammered them out by hand. Early button shops flourished in 1790, and in 1802 James Harrison built a water wheel and applied the power thus developed to the manufacture of clocks. By 1814 there were four clock shops in the community. Despite a heavy migration from Waterbury to the western lands between 1810 and 1820, many new shops sprang up, and the production of Yankee notions was added to that of clocks, brass, pewter, bone and ivory buttons. The community furnished much of the stock for Yankee peddlers.

If a new finish was needed, if a new pin or a new fastener was marketable, Waterbury mechanics found a way to produce it. Imported hooks and eyes sold for $1.50 per gross in 1810, but by 1836 the Waterbury mills produced them for 40 cents. Competition was keen but there was a margin of profit of about 47 cents per pound during the golden years of the brass business.

The brass industry owes much to imported English labor. James Croft, a British subject, was hired by Leavenworth, Hayden & Scovill in 1820 to produce the striking orange tint that Americans then favored on their brass buttons. Heavier rolls were imported from England in 1823, and an expert British mechanic came to Waterbury to assist the Yankee millmen in copying them. A variety of better finishes became possible after electro-plating was developed in 1837. In 1842 the brass masters discovered the right mixtures and annealing methods and made still further advances in their craft. Wire-forming experts turned to the manufacture of pins in 1842, and created a market for the overproduction of brass wire that was first drawn by Israel Holmes in 1831. Holmes also produced brazed tubing that was shipped to the New York Gas Company in 1836.

The disks for U.S. nickels are blanked by Waterbury mills, and coins for many South American countries are produced here. Cartridge brass forms a large percentage of Waterbury's tonnage whenever war brews anywhere in the world. Shell cases of assorted sizes, time fuses, even the hydraulic speed gears that turn battleship turrets are made behind carefully guarded gates. A quarter-million pounds of copper and copper alloys were shipped from Waterbury mills for the great Boulder Dam power plant. The American Brass Company which owns and controls exclusive patent rights for the construction of hollow and ventilated busses from rectangular copper bars, channels or angle shapes, originated many new processes and mixtures, advancing the science of metallurgy as applied to nonferrous metals.

The production of dollar watches furnishes employment for the wives and daughters of Waterbury brass workers. Formerly a department of a brass mill, but made a separate unit on March 27, 1857, the Waterbury Clock Company designed, tooled-up, and manufactured the first successful cheap timepiece. Robert H. Ingersoll contracted for the entire output of the plant in 1892, advertised his wares, and was successful in marketing about 5,000,000 Yankee watches per year until his death in 1922.

A State law authorizing the formation of stock companies in Connecticut was passed in 1837, enabling the pioneer industrialists to expand and perfect the capital structure of their organizations.

The American Brass Association, formed in February 1853 to control the output of brass in the Naugatuck Valley, became the first trade association in America. The first large consolidation came in 1899 with the formation of the American Brass Company. In 1917 the company started the assembly of fabricating units in other regions, and in 1922 the Anaconda Copper Company, buying into the American Brass Company, completed the first of the 'mine to consumer' outfits. The second such combination came in 1929, when the Chase Companies, Inc., outgrowth of the enterprise and genius for organization of A. S. Chase, joined with the Kennecott Copper Company. But Waterbury still keeps her independent brass mills; the Scovill Company combinations, the Somers Brass and Waterbury Rolling Mills retain their independence and their position in the industry.

Only 26 per cent of Waterbury's population is of full native parentage. A variety of racial types can be seen in a poor district called 'The Dogs' Nest,' in the 'Catherine Lane' area, or in Brooklyn, just across the bridge.

TOUR

N. from the Green on North Main St.; L. from N. Main on Cooke St.

1. The *Cooke Homestead*, NE. cor. of Cooke and Grove Sts., a tiny white gabled house with green trim, is Waterbury's only remaining 'old house'

(*private*). Some of its timbers are from the original 1741 structure, but it has been altered and enlarged until there is no evidence of its age other than the roof lines of the older one-and-a-half-story portion of the dwelling.

2. *Fulton Park*, Cooke St., is a fine expanse of grassy lawns, flowering shrubs and flower gardens, especially noteworthy for its rock garden, beautiful with sedums, Alpines, and dwarf evergreens. Tennis courts, baseball diamonds, swimming pools, and children's playgrounds are among the facilities provided.

Return on Cooke and North Main Sts. to the Green; R. from North Main St. on West Main St.

3. The long central *Green*, W. Main and N. Main Sts., once a frog pond, is shaded by tall elm trees. On the SE. corner, the *Town Sign Post* reminds strangers that town government is still of major importance in Connecticut. At the western end is a very elaborate *Civil War Memorial* (1885), by George E. Bissell, surrounded by cannon, a typical monument of the era. At the eastern end of the Green is a large *Memorial Fountain* (1885), presented by Caroline J. Welton (born, Waterbury, 1842), an organizer of the Connecticut Humane Society. Topping the fountain's many basins for horses and dogs is a great bronze figure of 'Knight,' who is affectionately remembered as 'Carrie Welton's Hoss.' The sculptor is unknown, and the fountain is a simple memorial to a lover of animals.

4. The *Church of the Immaculate Conception* (1928) facing the Green from the NW. corner of W. Main and Prospect Sts., is an ornate, white marble structure of monumental proportions designed in the manner of a Renaissance basilica. It is the work of Maginnis and Walsh. The dim interior is impressive in its simplicity. The rounded apse centers attention on the baldachino covering the altar.

L. around the Green.

5. *St. John's Episcopal Church* W. end of the Green, designed by Richard Upjohn, was destroyed by fire December 24th, 1868. It was rebuilt of granite in 1870, and is a consistent, though not an outstanding, example of the middle Victorian Gothic period.

6. Facing the south side of the Green is the *Mattatuck Historical Society* (*open weekdays* 10–5; *free*), 119 W. Main St. In the room to the right of the entrance is exhibited a collection of clothing and furniture of the Victorian period. The room to the left of the entrance is devoted to temporary exhibits. In the rear, is the main exhibition hall that includes the *Pritchard Alcove*, furnished as an early American kitchen-living room; an *Industrial Loft*, a reconstructed Colonial attic with crude tools used in home industries; and varied collections of pottery, platters, pitchers, old guns, kits and instruments used by early doctors and dentists. The second floor is devoted to the genealogical library, offices of the Society, and a larger hall for temporary exhibits and lectures. A *Children's Museum* in the basement includes Indian relics, a collection of antique dolls, and geological exhibits.

Return to SE. corner of Green; L. from the Green on Leavenworth St.; L. from Leavenworth on Grand.

7. The brick and limestone *Chase Brass & Copper Company Office Building* (L), cor. Grand and Leavenworth Sts., an entire city block wide, was designed by Cass Gilbert and erected in 1917. This four-story building, with wings extending to the streets at both ends, is designed with more restraint than the City Hall opposite.

8. The *Municipal Building* (1914), W. side of Grand St., also designed by Cass Gilbert's office, is of the combined marble and brick, so often associated with Gilbert's work. The three-story structure, with a formal garden and fountain at the front, is topped with a delicate belfry. The lower story of white marble, laid in rusticated courses, has windows with square heads set in shallow surface arches. The second and third stories are of red brick with white marble Corinthian pilasters which extend from the second floor level to the cornice. The Chase Infirmary, the Waterbury Bank, and Waterbury Club are also from Cass Gilbert plans, making Waterbury an unusual monument to one of the greatest of American architects.

9. On the grounds of the *Silas Bronson Library*, 267 Grand St., a balanced, conventional brownstone structure, is a bronze *Statue of Benjamin Franklin*, by Paul W. Bartlett (*see Art*).

10. The *Railroad Station*, at the end of Grand St. on Meadow, facing Library Park, was the work of McKim, Mead & White. Its slender clock tower is an adaptation of the Torre del Mangia in Siena. President C. W. Mellon of the New Haven Railroad traveled in Italy, the story goes, noticed the tower, and decided to put it on the next depot he built.

R. from Grand on Meadow St.; L. from Meadow on Freight St.

11. Beyond the rolling and wire mills of the American Brass Company, on Freight St., across the Naugatuck via the concrete bridge, is the *Pilgrim Memorial* designed by Herman MacNeil, a carving of Pilgrim figures on granite.

Straight ahead from the foot of the Memorial on Chase Parkway.

12. The *Settlers Village* (*no longer open*), behind a sturdy stockade on

---

WATERBURY.   POINTS OF INTEREST

1. Cooke Homestead
2. Fulton Park
3. Green
4. Church of the Immaculate Conception
5. St. John's Episcopal Church
6. Mattatuck Historical Society
7. Chase Brass & Copper Company Office Building
8. Municipal Building
9. Silas Bronson Library
10. Railroad Station
11. Pilgrim Memorial
12. Settlers Village
13. Town Plot
14. Hamilton Park

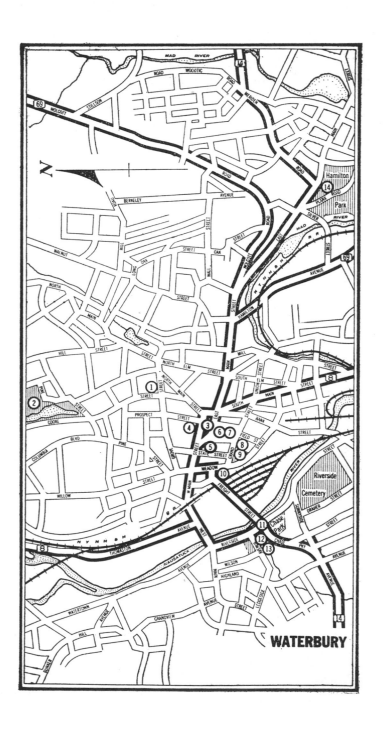

Chase Parkway, was erected in 1935 by the city with the help of Federal funds, in observance of the Connecticut Tercentenary. To the left of the entrance are buildings representing early Colonial dwellings, with a typical early Town Hall in the center. In the Town Hall is an industrial exhibit.

The *International Group* of houses, including dwellings planned by the Irish, Italian, Polish, French, Lithuanian, and Russian residents of the Brass City, are reproductions of the types of homes in the countries from which these groups have migrated.

13. The *Town Plot*, Chase Parkway at Sunnyside Ave., at the top of the bluff west of the river, was the site of the first settlement. A tablet on a roadside boulder commemorates the event. The best view of the city as a whole may be obtained from this point.

14. *Hamilton Park*, at East Main and Silver Sts., is the largest in the Waterbury municipal park system. Many fine drives, a zoo, a dance hall, swimming pools, nature trails, and sports fields offer facilities for recreation. At the extreme eastern end of the park is an old *Waterwheel* dating from 1845 that formerly furnished power for an early brass mill.

Points of Interest in Environs:

Mattatuck State Forest, Jack's Cave, Indian Heaven (*see Tour* 5).

WETHERSFIELD

Town: Alt. 40, pop. 7512, sett. 1634.

Airport: Brainard Field, Hartford, 6 m. from Wethersfield for American Airlines.

Accommodations: Tourist homes in the center, and cabins on the Berlin Turnpike.

Boating: On Wethersfield Cove.

Annual Events: Horse Show, September, Griswold Road; Flower Show, middle of June, 371 Wolcott Hill Road; Grange Fair, last week in September, Grange Hall, Hartford Ave.

WETHERSFIELD, a suburb of Hartford on a plain along the west bank of the Connecticut River flanked by partly wooded western ridges, is one of the State's earliest settlements. The shady main street, with a Common at the north end of the village and a central Green nearer the southern limits of the community, is a typical Yankee thoroughfare. Large elms border the Green and older streets; the bank occupies a Colonial mansion; the general store furnishes very nearly everything man requires; seed warehouses are modestly set back from the road, and a chain store shoulders close to the sidewalk in the only block of modern buildings in the business section.

Across the fields is the river. Occasionally a bright oil barge passes, seemingly afloat on the grass itself. A passenger steamer formerly passed the town twice daily. Residents used to set their watches by the clumsy old river boat and relied upon the frantic toots of the captain's whistle to warn them of fire at an isolated farm, or of river boatmen in distress. Today, pleasure craft and freight carriers dock not far from the wharves where West India sailors loaded their vessels with staves, fish, onions, and salt beef.

The newer buildings in Wethersfield are grouped to the west of the older plains sections of the town and on the western hills. The village is a community of home-owners with few tenant houses. Fully fifty-four per cent of the population is of native parentage and only seventeen per cent is foreign-born. Suburban residents have fitted gracefully into the life of the older community, and the social pattern of the town remains practically unchanged.

In 1634, John Oldham, an adventurer of Watertown, Mass., who had explored the region during the previous year, settled here with a following of ten men. Later they were joined by additional colonists from Watertown, Mass., many of whom came by boat. On this colonization, Wethersfield bases its claim to the honor of being the first English settlement in Connecticut, because it was the only one of the 'Three River Towns' (Hartford, Windsor, and Wethersfield) which was originally founded as a permanent settlement rather than as a trading post.

Here, as recorded in Irving's 'Knickerbocker's History of New York,' the colonists 'extended their plantations of onions,' for which the town is noted, 'under the very noses of Fort Goed Hoop, insomuch that the honest Dutchmen could not look toward that quarter without tears in their eyes.' In 1637 the village was given its present name in memory of the English birthplace of many of the settlers. The Indian name for the area was *Pyquag*.

Although the Podunk Indians were friendly, the Pequots, determined to recover their traditional hunting grounds, kept the settlers in continual fear of raiding parties. In April, 1637, the Wethersfield Massacre, in which six men and three women were killed and two girls taken captive, precipitated the Pequot War.

Wethersfield witnessed the first demonstration of the American people for independence, when, on April 11, 1640, the citizens held a public election in defiance of the Royal Courts. The town was fined five pounds for its indiscretion and refused to pay. Later, during the Stamp Act Controversy, Jared Ingersoll, a newly appointed collector, was surrounded on the Broad Street Green and forced to march, under escort of the Sons of Liberty, to the General Assembly at Hartford to resign his office.

When the witchcraft hysteria swept through New England in the middle of the seventeenth century, Mary Johnson of Wethersfield was hanged after her confession of 'familiarity with the devil,' and John Carrington and his wife were convicted of witchcraft and hanged.

The rapid growth and early prosperity of the town was fostered by its shipping activities. The 'Tryall,' first Connecticut-built ship, launched here in 1649, led the way for Connecticut's great merchant fleet of river vessels. Trade with the West Indies and other ports was begun here in 1648. Exports included furs, hides, bricks, onions, fish, and salt beef. At the height of the export trade, more than one million bunches of onions were shipped annually. At one time there were as many as six warehouses in the village, one of which, built between 1661–91 is still standing. A carding and fulling mill, said to be the first established in New England, was built by Jacob Griswold in 1680 at Griswoldville, Wethersfield, and was operated until 1839. A plow factory established in 1820 for many years shipped one thousand plows annually to Carolina planters.

The importance of Wethersfield as a center of commerce and industry declined when shipping activity was attracted to coastal ports, and came to an end about 1880. Of the early industries, only market gardening and two large seed concerns, operated since the days of the town's merchant marine trade, survive.

TOUR 1

E. from Main St. on Marsh St.

1. The *Congregational Church*, NE. cor. Main and Marsh Sts. (1761), like the Old South Church in Boston, is an 18th-century church of brick. Although its interior was, unfortunately, remodeled in 1882 and the tall stained-glass windows and ugly main entrance added, the building has retained much of its exterior beauty in the diamond patterned brickwork, like that of some old church in Holland, and in its open belfry and slender spire. The two pairs of cross-panel doors in the tower are among the best of a type popular in the Connecticut Valley.

2. In the *Burial Place*, Marsh St., behind the church, are the graves of many of the early settlers. The oldest stone, that of Leonard Chester, crudely engraved with his family coat of arms, is dated 1648. An Indian, interred in a sitting position, facing east, was uncovered here in 1832, confirming a previous belief that the Indians also used this plot as a graveyard.

A *Boulder*, on a small triangular plot at the junction of Marsh, Ferry and Broad Sts., was placed here in memory of Richard Smith, Jr., the first licensed ferryman who operated the little boat that plied across the Connecticut River from the foot of Ferry St. (Wethersfield) to Silver Lane in the town of Hockanum. The ferry was operated by Smith and his descendants from 1674–1762.

R. from Marsh St. on Broad St.

3. The *Older Williams House (private)* (1680), 249 Broad St., on an elm-shaded lot where the road narrows at the end of the Green, is one of the best preserved 17th-century dwellings in the State. This structure is the best existing example of the transition in New England's Colonial architecture from the original end-chimney, single-room house to the central-chimney house, by the addition of a second room on the other side of the chimney. Usually these houses, two-stories high but one room deep, were completed by the addition of a lean-to at the rear, and converted into 'salt-boxes.' The huge chimney back of the ridge, its two-foot overhang at cornice and gable-end, and its original, unpainted condition, make it a stark and impressive reminder of its period.

4. *Broad Street Green*, at the south end of the village, was the center of the residential section of the old town. The original Wethersfield Common is now under water, having been inundated many years ago as a result of the shifting channel of the Connecticut River. This Green, which served as a training ground for colonial militia, is surrounded by many plantings of elm and maple that have grown to immense size.

5 and 6. The *Skaats House (private)*, 138 Broad St., a wide-roofed wooden building with one window to the left of the door and two to the right, is half of a large tavern built by the Chester family before 1750. The other half, its windows arranged in the opposite way, stands across the Green at 25 Garden St.

7. The *Wethersfield Elm* (L), on the east side of the Green, is the largest elm in America, 102 feet high, 41 feet in circumference, with a spread of 146 feet. According to an old diary this tree was planted about 1758.

Continue around the Green to Garden St.; L. on Garden St.

8. The *Michael Griswold House (private)* (1730), 116 Garden St., is an unaltered example of a salt-box house of the 'integral' type, in which the rear rafters extending from the roof-tree are in one piece. The unusual, raised panels of the double front doors are old, but are a type used a century after the house was built. This dwelling is now owned by the family of the builder.

R. from Garden St. on Main St.

9. The *Ashbel Wright House (private)* (1787), 133 Main St., became in 1824 the 'commodious academy' of the Rev. Joseph Emerson who moved here from Saugus, Massachusetts. Mary Lyon, founder of Mt. Holyoke College, was one of the first pupils to attend this 'Female Seminary,' which attracted nearly 100 pupils — a large number in the days when higher education for women was deemed unnecessary.

10. *The Academy* (1801–04), 150 Main St., typical of the public schools built by the more prosperous towns in the early Federal period, is a long plain brick building, with little ornament but the bell-shaped cupola at the center of the roof, the stone lintels over the windows, and fan-light over the simple door. This building, in which the Rev. Mr. Emerson

conducted many of his classes, became a public school in 1839, and now serves as the Town Hall and Library.

11. The *Historical Society*, 196 Main St. (*small fee*), occupies four rooms in the *Welles School*, where it maintains an exhibition of records and antiquities.

12. The *Silas Deane House* (*private*), 203 Main St. (L), is set rather inconspicuously behind lilacs close to the sidewalk and half disguised by a long modern porch across the front. It was built by Silas Deane, a wealthy merchant, in 1764, after his marriage to the widow of Joseph Webb, who lived in the big house next door. She was used to a house of much elegance, and this house, though smaller, was in its spacious and informal rooms one of the most gracious homes of the northern Colonies. Its unusual corner hallway has an elaborate staircase with balusters of three different turnings on each tread. The six paneled interior walls are equally rich and varied; and the entrance doorway is handsomely proportioned. Washington spent the night here, June 29, 1775.

Deane, known as the 'Father of the American Navy,' because of his efforts in developing the naval strength of the Colonies, was the first American diplomat and commercial agent. In 1774–76 he was sent to France to secure military supplies and French support. While still abroad in the service of his country, he was charged with embezzlement of Government funds. Broken in health and courage, Deane died in 1798, when, completely exonerated, he was about to return to his homeland.

13. Next door is the *Webb House* or Hospitality Hall (*open weekdays* 10–5; *adm.* 25¢; *children* 10¢) (1752), 211 Main St. (L), now the headquarters of the Connecticut Society of the Colonial Dames. A tall, imposing house with a steep gambrel roof, the impression of height is increased by the graduation of its clapboards, which are very narrow at the bottom. A narrow, pedimented porch — one of the earliest — shelters the Dutch door. Inside, the central hall, with a floor painted in a pattern of blocks, runs through to a colonial garden. The north parlor, with arched cross-

---

WETHERSFIELD.   Points of Interest

1. Congregational Church	13. Webb House
2. Burial Place	14. Henry Deming House
3. Older Williams House	15. Simeon Belden House
4. Broad Street Green	16. Sergeant John Latimer Homestead
5. and 6. Skaats House	17. The Warehouse
7. Wethersfield Elm	18. Titus Buck Place
8. Michael Griswold House	19. Standish Park and Athletic Field
9. Ashbel Wright House	20. Wethersfield State Prison
10. The Academy	21. Lemuel Deming House
11. Historical Society	22. Jonathan Deming House
12. Silas Deane House	23. Ichabod Welles House

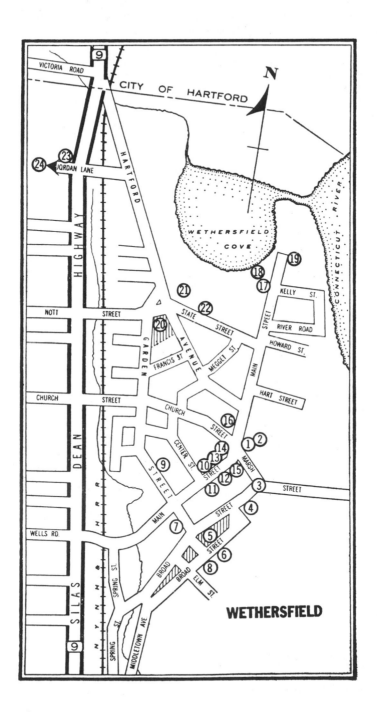

panel doors flanking the fireplace, is one of the most beautiful 18th-century rooms in the State. The south parlor, though supplied by Wallace Nutting with later paneling from a Rhode Island house, is interesting as the Council Chamber where, in May 1781, Washington, Rochambeau, and De Ternay held their historic four-day conference to plan the Yorktown campaign. Upstairs, Washington's bedchamber is preserved with the original wallpaper.

14. The *Henry Deming House* (1790), opposite, now the Wethersfield Bank, contrasts with the earlier simplicity of the Webb house. The Tudor rose, so often used over pilasters in Connecticut Valley houses between 1740 and 1770, appears in the abbreviated Palladian window over the door. The window heads are each elaborated with a dentil course over a half-round member, a mode that was prevalent after the Revolutionary War.

15. The *Simeon Belden House* (*private*) (1767), 251 Main St., is a gambrel-roofed house with well-preserved detail, including narrow clapboards and a broken-pediment doorway that ranks among the best in the town.

16. The *Sergeant John Latimer Homestead* (*private*), 580 Main St., a steep, narrow gambrel-roofed house, which was later enlarged into a rather awkward salt-box, has been in the Latimer family since its erection in 1690. Like those around it, this house suffered greatly in the flood of 1936, which revealed that the outer walls were built of rough vertical planking, two inches thick, but finished with a feather-edge on the inside, a unique piece of 17th-century workmanship.

17. *The Warehouse* (*open*), at the end of N. Main St., on the edge of Wethersfield cove behind the Latimer House, a plain, broad gambrel-roofed house, built of 15-inch sheathing, is the last of six similar structures erected at the bend of the river prior to 1691, when Wethersfield was a 'Port of Exchange between the Interior and the Old World.'

18. The *Titus Buck Place* (*private*) (1767), 583 Main St., opposite the Latimer House, is a typical mid-18th-century house, with a central brick chimney, and an old ell with exceptionally narrow clapboards. Here Sophia Woodhouse Welles made fine leghorn bonnets from grasses she found growing on the Common. A bonnet of red top and spear grass made by Mrs. Welles was awarded a prize of 20 guineas at the Society of Arts in London when exhibited there in 1820, and was patented in this country in 1821. These Wethersfield hats were much admired by Mrs. John Quincy Adams, who ordered several.

TOUR 2

NW. from Main St. on Hartford Ave.

19. *Standish Park* and *Athletic Field*, Hartford Ave., Nott, Garden, and Francis Sts. In the northeast corner of the grounds, near the highway,

is a sandstone seat made of a stone slab more than 21 feet in length, bearing the imprint of a dinosaur's foot. This stone was originally used as a doorstep at the store owned and operated by Silas Deane, Revolutionary diplomat, and later served as the stepping-stone to the old Post Office on Main St.

R. from Hartford Ave. on State St.

20. The *Wethersfield State Prison*, State St. (L), operated on the Auburn plan of penology, was opened in 1827 when 127 prisoners were marched here from Newgate in East Granby. The prison buildings stand well back from the street and are surrounded by well-kept lawns.

Within the Prison Chapel is a fresco painted by Miss Genevieve Cowles. Her interest in the prisoners was aroused when she visited the penitentiary in search of a model for panel designs on each side of the altar in the chapel of Christ Church, New Haven. Her design is based on the chant:

> 'O Key of David and Scepter of the House of Israel, Thou that openest and no man shutteth, and shuttest and no man openeth; come and loose the prisoners from the prison house and him that sitteth in the darkness and the shadow of death.'

A life prisoner volunteered to be the model. During her many visits to the prison, Miss Cowles came to know many of the prisoners and to take a deep interest in their problems. Desiring to bring solace and inspiration to them, she offered to paint a fresco for the chapel and asked the inmates to choose the subject. After much interested discussion they decided upon the 'Sea of Galilee.' Miss Cowles spent several months in the Holy Land preparing for this work.

On the prison grounds stands the hip-roofed *Solomon Welles House* (1774), 220 Hartford Ave. Completely changed from its original appearance by the addition of dormers and a porch, it serves as the Warden's home. Near-by is the site of the home of Governor Thomas Welles, who wrote the first State Constitution.

21. The *Lemuel Deming House* (*private*) (1750), at 74 State St., somewhat modernized, was erected on the site of the first hat factory in New England (1724), where Captain Deming turned out hat shapes of beaver, coon, otter, and other skins.

Return to Hartford Ave.; L. from Hartford Ave. on Jordan Lane.

22. The *Jonathan Deming House* (*private*), NW. cor. Jordan Lane and Silas Deane Highway, is a restored salt-box. With five narrow windows, a projecting hood over the door, and added lean-to, this old farmhouse is known to have been erected before 1733. The slight flare of its eaves adds to its piquant character.

23. The *Ichabod Welles House* (*private*), cor. Jordan Lane and Ridge Rd., on the site of the Wyllys Welles House of 1684, dates from 1715. The chimney, 16 × 18 feet at the base, a record size, may be a relic of the earlier dwelling. The fine paneling throughout dates from the early 18th

century. Of greater interest, however, is the *Barn* at the rear of the house. Primitive in construction, this building probably dates back to the time of the original homestead. Its roof is gambrel on one side and cut on the other to form a two-story front; and its corner posts, crude and heavy, support the girts by means of natural tree-branches which serve as brackets.

W I N D S O R

Town: Alt. 60, pop. 8290, sett. 1633.
Railroad Station: N.Y., N.H. & H. R.R. Station at 11 Central Ave.
Airports: See HARTFORD.
Accommodations: Hotel.
Information Service: Custodian of the Walter Fyler House, 96 Palisado Ave., will supply information on places of historical interest.
Amusements: Trotting races at Sage Park (western part of town) for one week in season.
Boating: Boats for use on the Connecticut River can be rented from the Loomis Institute boat-house, or from the Hartford Y.M.C.A. The Camp Rainbow Committee rents boats on the Farmington River.

WINDSOR, stretching along a river plain on the western bank of the Connecticut River, was one of Connecticut's three earliest settlements. Still a village of considerable charm, the old community is traversed by heavy traffic and, influenced by the extending metropolitan area of Hartford, has the appearance of a suburb of that city. The new Americans, who now till the loams of the river plain, erect stands at the roadside for the sale of farm and garden produce. Northward, the town tapers off to scattered farms and a few orchards beside the road.

Windsor has been a tobacco town since 1640. Normally three thousand acres are devoted to tobacco cultivation. The State maintains an Experiment Station here to aid tobacco-growers, and a large sorting plant is operated under Lorillard management. Some tomatoes and squash are also produced for canning in a local plant. The barns are small, unlike the larger structures of the dairying countryside to the west. Green carpets of seed rye cover the tobacco-fields that are frequently close to the center of this village. Away from the road many tobacco sheds with their red paint or weathered gray unpainted sidings seem to merge into the backdrop of distant hills. When the 'vents' are open and the leaf is curing, the sheds look like many-legged prehistoric animals, standing in the rear of the fields as if guarding the fertile acreage.

The center of Windsor conforms to the New England pattern of houses clustering around a Green. South of the Farmington River is Broad Street Green, the business center of modern Windsor; and north of the river is the church and Palisado Green. Along the streets that join above Broad Street Green, forming a sprawling Y — Poquonock Road, the left branch; Windsor Avenue, Broad Street and Palisado Avenue (US 5A), the stem and right branch — are numerous old houses, surrounded by unfenced lawns that stretch down to the street and are shaded by venerable elms and maples (the Windsor Historical Society has marked old buildings with placards, giving dates and names of original owners). Windsor is remarkable for the variety of its architecture, which includes examples from the simplicity of the seventeenth century to the diversity of the nineteenth, as well as handsome twentieth-century buildings.

On September 26, 1633, Captain William Holmes and a small band of men from the Plymouth Colony, who had brought with them the frame of a house ready to raise, sailed up the river and established a trading post at the mouth of the Tunxis (Farmington) River, on land previously bought from the Indian tribe who had lived there until driven out by the Pequots. Previously, the Dutch, led by Adriaen Block, had discovered and claimed this valley of the Long River (Quinatucquet) and, when 'messages of friendly kindness and good neighborhood were passing between New Amsterdam and Plymouth,' commended this region to the English as a 'fine place for both plantation and trade.' In response to an invitation from the local Indian chief, Governor Winslow and a group of men investigated the territory, claiming it in the name of England. When Holmes sailed up the river, he was hailed by the commander of the Dutch fort on the present site of Hartford, who ordered, 'Strike your colors or we will fire.' Holmes replied, 'I have the commission of the governor of Plymouth to go up the river and I shall go.' Later the Dutch sent a force of seventy men from Fort Amsterdam to drive the newcomers away, but found the English post so well fortified that they withdrew. In June and November of 1635, Holmes was joined by English Puritans from John Warham's parish in Dorchester, who were displeased by the political restrictions in Massachusetts. This group settled on the great meadow north of the Farmington River. A second group of colonists, who came from England under the sponsorship of Sir Richard Saltonstall and led by Stiles, settled further upstream in the vicinity of the present Ellsworth home. These settlers called the Dorchester group 'pious bandits' because they settled on the best lands. The new settlement, at first called Matianuck, then Dorchester, was named Windsor in 1637 after the Berkshire residence of the English sovereigns.

The original town of Windsor comprised what is now the towns of Windsor, Windsor Locks, Granby, East Granby, Simsbury, the southerly part of Suffield, and part of Bloomfield on the west bank of the Connecticut River, and East Windsor, South Windsor, Ellington, and the northern part of Vernon on the east side of the river.

Nature was not kind to the little colony. The first winter saw the river frozen tight by mid-November and snow so deep that the pioneers despaired of ever getting through to Plymouth Colony to secure rations and aid. The 'Rebecca,' a sixty-ton rescue ship from Boston, narrowly escaped being ice-bound, but finally succeeded in reaching Saybrook, where it picked up seventy Windsor colonists, who returned to Massachusetts. Those who remained here throughout the winter to care for livestock at the Palisado suffered severely. Many tales of fortitude are told in Windsor regarding the early herdsmen and soldiers who kept the feeble embers of colonization aglow when there seemed little likelihood that the settlement would ever succeed. Yankee grit was developed, perhaps, behind the crude stockade which stood on the land now Palisado Green.

Although the local Indians befriended the settlers, the little town was in constant fear of Pequot raids. Finally, after the Pequots attacked Wethersfield in April, 1637, the colonists organized a band of ninety men under the leadership of Captain John Mason of Windsor who swooped down on the Pequots and burned them in their Mystic encampment (*see Tour* 1, *MYSTIC*). Thereafter the community was comparatively untroubled until King Philip's War in 1676, when the palisades of Windsor gave refuge to the fleeing farmers of Simsbury.

Communications were established between the right and left banks of the river in 1639; John Bissell operated a ferry in 1648. A school was provided for in 1647, and a church was raised the same year; the school to the south of the Farmington River was not built until 1674. In 1760, Benjamin Franklin's newly established mail coach line went through the village on the Philadelphia–Boston run that took six days, for a record-breaking, average daily travel of about fifty miles. At the mouth of the Farmington River, in a meadow beyond Island Road, a boulder marks the site of the old Plymouth Trading Post. Between the river and the road, a dirt lane leads eastward opposite 546 Palisado Avenue to the site of the old Bissell Ferry and Stoughton's Fort. Both are on private property.

Sergeant Daniel Bissell was cited by General Washington, May 9, 1783, and became one of the three Connecticut men to receive the Purple Heart. Charged with desertion while he was serving with Benedict Arnold's regiment and gathering valuable information, Bissell became a Colonial hero immediately on his return to the American lines. Only three Purple Hearts were awarded during the Revolutionary War and all of these went to Connecticut soldiers.

Christopher Miner Spencer, inventor of the Spencer repeating rifle, the piece that Confederate soldiers said, 'the Yanks loaded on Sunday for the rest of the week,' conducted a factory where the P. Lorillard and Company now maintains a warehouse for the sorting, storage, and packing of wrapper-leaf tobacco. Harvard (water-struck) brick has been exported from Windsor for nearly a century. This face brick has been extensively used in many Yale University buildings in New Haven.

Many citizens of Windsor have attained prominence. Roger Ludlow of Windsor, who shares with Thomas Hooker the honor of framing the Fundamental Orders of Connecticut (January 14, 1639); Oliver Ellsworth, appointed Chief Justice of the Supreme Court by Washington and sent in 1799 as Envoy Extraordinary to Paris where he successfully negotiated a treaty with Napoleon; Roger Wolcott, Governor of Connecticut, 1751–54; John W. Barber (1798–1885), historian; and the poet Edward Rowland Sill (1841–87), known as 'The American Shelley.'

Windsor today is an interesting example of suburbanization. The Hartford residential area overlaps the town line, Lithuanian and Polish farmers have come to work in the tobacco-fields, and Danish truck farmers operate their own vegetable farms. The descendants of the original settlers have, in many cases, moved farther back into the surrounding country.

TOUR 1

1. On Broad Street Green, beside the World War Memorial, stands Windsor's *Constitutional Oak*, presented by General Joseph R. Hawley to the Windsor delegate to the convention which revised the constitution of the State in 1818.

2 and 3. Two of the houses on Broad Street Green present the contrast of the two prevailing types found frequently throughout Windsor. The *Dr. Alexander Wolcott House* (*private*), facing the Green on the north, built in 1745 by a son of Governor Roger Wolcott, is the typical simple, white, peak-roofed, central-chimney house of the eighteenth century, while the brick *James Loomis House* (*private*) (1822), on the west side of Broad Street Green, its gable end to the road, and its door in one corner, is duplicated many times on Windsor Avenue to the south.

R. from Broad St. Green on Elm St.

4. The *John Moore House* (*private*), 35 Elm St., built in 1664, though it might now pass for a modern building, is the oldest house in town. It is one of six in the State that show the framed overhang of the Hartford Colony. Under the piazza roof are two of the original 'drops' or pendants beneath the overhang.

Return to Broad Street Green; R. on Broad St.

5. At the southern end of Broad Street Green is the *Oliver Mather House* (1777), now the Public Library (*open weekdays* 9–5), a white house with graduated clapboards, which was remodeled about 1840 with a heavy balustrade across the front of the house and over the square hip-roofed entrance porch. These alterations have wholly changed the character of the house.

L. from Broad St. on Island Rd.

6. The *Loomis Institute*, at the south end of Island Rd., an endowed

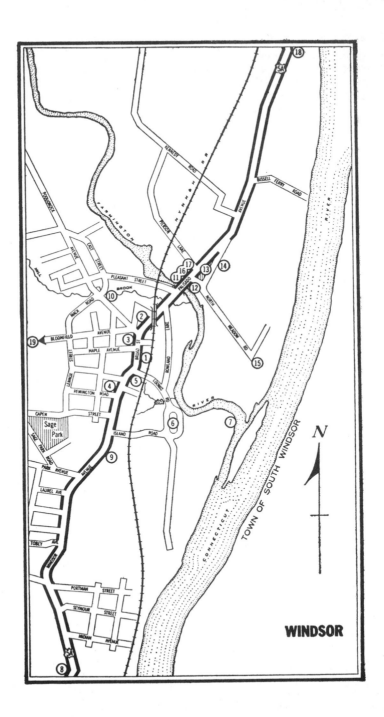

WINDSOR

school for boys, occupies a group of modern buildings on the 'Island.' Northeast of the main buildings stands the old *Joseph Loomis House* (*private*) in excellent condition. In digging for the Institute buildings, remains were found of a dugout cabin, the earliest type of refuge made by the settlers. Records show that Joseph Loomis took up his claim here in 1639 and died in 1658. Whether he built the dugout — the only one which has remained to modern times — or even the salt-box ell of the house, is a matter of conjecture. But tradition states that this was his house, built before 1652, and that the main part of the house was erected in 1688-90. These dates seem early for some of the features, which may have been added later. The 18th century has left its mark on the house, in its paneling, the molded window heads, the slight flare to its roof lines, and the cased framing within. The most curious feature of the building is the window sash, two and one-half panes in height. The foundations of both parts are of cut stone, unusual in Windsor, and transported probably from Portland, but both of the chimneys are of brick throughout, which has been made in Windsor since Colonial times. On the school grounds is the *Studio of Mrs. Evelyn Beatrice Longman Batchelder*, sculptress.

7. Near the river, south of the school, a *Boulder* marks the spot where the colonists, under the leadership of Captain Holmes, first settled.

Return on Island Rd. to Windsor Ave. (Broad St.); L. on Windsor Ave.

8. The *Captain Thomas Allyn Homestead* (*private*), 573 Windsor Ave., is curious in that it is of brick, originally built in salt-box form, as an examination of its end walls clearly indicates. Though assigned by tradition a 17th-century date (1670), it bears a resemblance to the Day House (1758) of West Springfield, Massachusetts, which is also a brick salt-box; the earlier date is now accepted by authorities to be a transposition of figures for 1760. The end chimneys, the central hall, and the paneling inside all point to this later date.

9. Hidden in the brush at the entrance to the Clayton P. Chamberlain Estate, 1228 Windsor Ave., is a *Monument* erected (1907) by the Hartford Dental Society to Dr. Horace C. Hayden of Windsor (1769-1844), who

WINDSOR. POINTS OF INTEREST

1. Constitutional Oak
2. Dr. Alexander Wolcott House
3. James Loomis House
4. John Moore House
5. Oliver Mather House
6. Loomis Institute
7. Boulder
8. Captain Thomas Allyn Homestead
9. Monument
10. Warham Gristmill
11. First Congregational Church of Windsor
12. Lieutenant Walter Fyler House
13. Monument to Original Settlers
14. Hezekiah Chaffee House
15. Eighteenth-Century Houses
16. Rev. William Russell House
17. Martin Ellsworth House
18. Elmwood
19. Tobacco and Vegetable Field Sub-Station

established the first dental school in America (at Johns Hopkins University, Baltimore, Maryland, February 1, 1840), and founded the American Society of Dental Surgeons (1840). The monument is a square, brick pillar, 12 feet high, topped by an illuminated glass globe. A bronze tablet on the face records memorable events in Dr. Hayden's career.

TOUR 2

NW. from Broad Street Green on Poquonock Ave.

10. The *Warham Gristmill* (*open*), corner Poquonock Ave. and East St., the earliest mill in the State, was the gift of the town to its minister, the Rev. John Warham, in 1640. Although the exterior was remodeled in the early 19th century, the original frame with its old beams and heavy rafters still remains. Here are many of the old grist stones used by the mill in grinding corn for almost 300 years.

Return to Broad St.; L. from Broad on Palisado Ave.

11. The *First Congregational Church of Windsor* (1794) stands (L) just past the north bank of the Farmington River. Despite the very heavy Greek Revival Doric portico and square tower, added in 1844, it still retains much of its 18th-century appearance in its corner quoins, and the large key blocks over the round-headed windows. One of the windows still has the 35-paned sash. Inside are the old box pews.

Behind the church is the *Palisado Cemetery*, containing the graves of such eminent Windsor citizens as Oliver Ellsworth (*see Elmwood*); the Rev. John Warham, leader of a group of early settlers; Roger Wolcott, Governor of Connecticut; and the Rev. Ephraim Hait, who died September 4, 1644; his tombstone is thought to be the oldest in the State.

12. The *Lieutenant Walter Fyler House* (*open Mondays and Thursdays, 1–5, May to October; at other times by appointment; adm. free*), 96 Palisado Ave. at the foot of the Green, is now the property of the Windsor Historical Society. The story-and-a-half ell toward Palisado Avenue is perhaps the oldest frame building in the State, since records show that Lieutenant Fyler had built here in 1640. The original dwelling was of the one-room, end-chimney type and faced south. The chimney on the end toward the street was removed, probably at the time the larger, gambrel-roofed section was built in 1772–73. The new brick chimney built at the intersection of the two structures affords diagonal fireplaces in some of the rooms. These and the sliding shutters, and fluted pilasters with rosettes lend to the interior a touch of the romantic that was characteristic of the height of 18th-century architecture. The long added ell to the south is a still later addition. A Colonial garden has been planted on the grounds.

13. Around Palisado Green, the center of the old settlement, are a

number of interesting buildings and monuments, including the *Ship Monument to Original Settlers* (1930), designed by Mrs. Evelyn Beatrice Longman Batchelder, and the *Grant Memorial Tablet* to a keeper of early town records. The *Site of the Matthew Grant Homestead*, where an ancestor of General U. S. Grant once lived, is marked, as is the *James Hooker House* (*private*), built in 1772; in the latter Edward Rowland Sill (1841–87), Connecticut poet, educator, and one-time professor of English at the University of California, was born. It is now a part of the Chaffee School, the girls' department of the Loomis Institute.

14. The *Hezekiah Chaffee House*, built in 1759, 108 Palisado Ave., occupied by the Chaffee School, is one of the oldest brick houses in the State.

R. from Palisado Green on Meadow Rd.

15. On Meadow Rd., which winds down to the river, are a number of *Eighteenth-Century Houses* (*private*) with a wide variety of roofs and doorways. The last house on Meadow Rd. is the 18th-century cottage of *Captain Samuel Cross*, the ferryman.

Return to Palisado Avenue; R. on Palisado Ave.

16. The *Rev. William Russell House* (*private*) (1753) across the Green, at 101 Palisado Ave., has a beautiful doorway, the best in Windsor. It reflects the rather Jacobean formality of the mid-eighteenth century with its rusticated setting of imitation stone, its elaborate entablature, and the fluted pilasters topped by rosettes which were popular in the Connecticut Valley from 1740 to the Revolution.

17. Next, north, stands the *Martin Ellsworth House* at No. 115, built by Oliver Ellsworth in 1807 for his son, which represents the conflicting tendencies which characterized early 19th-century architecture. Detail was much more carefully studied, and the general composition of the broad gable facing the street has more sophistication and dignity, but there is also greater informality within the rigid framework.

18. *Elmwood* (*open Sundays and Mondays, 9–5; May–Nov., adm. 25¢*) (1740), 778 Palisado Ave., the home of Oliver Ellsworth, minister to France and third Chief Justice of the United States Supreme Court. In the front yard is a wooden stump which is all that remains of the famous '*Old Hunting Tree*' beneath which Indian chiefs held their councils. Two of the 13 elms planted by the great jurist to commemorate the adoption of the Federal Constitution stand near the road. The house is now owned by the Daughters of the American Revolution.

The house itself is interesting as one of the earliest in Connecticut to have two chimneys and a central hall. It had so long been the practice to cramp the stairway of a house into a narrow space that despite the central hall, the stairs in this house were not even visible, but were hidden away behind a partition. Builders did not immediately discover how effective a feature the stair could be made. The colonnaded addition to the plain country farmhouse was added when Ellsworth returned to his native village from the courts of Europe. The woodwork of the spacious, lofty drawing room is mahogany-grained. Yet with all the splendor of this elaborately paneled room, it is worthy of note that the old Chief Justice slept in a room unheated by any fireplace. His room had wallpaper imported from France in 1802.

Among the interesting exhibits are the Shepherd Lad tapestry presented to Ellsworth by Napoleon at the time Ellsworth negotiated a treaty with France. Upstairs is a rare musical instrument, brought from France by the envoy, which plays tunes with the tone of a piano, though turned by a hand crank.

19. The *Tobacco* and *Vegetable Field Sub-Station* of the Connecticut Agricultural Experiment Station, at Cook Hill, puts scientific methods to work in the field for the commercial agriculturist, and offers facilities to all growers in the vicinity. On a 15-acre plot, the plant of the Station, which is the only tobacco experiment station in New England and one of four or five of its kind in America, includes a laboratory, greenhouse, warehouse and tobacco barns.

Organized in 1922, after experiments dating back to 1880, this station conducts tests to determine the best methods of curing tobacco in storage, tests to eliminate or control tobacco diseases, and to determine the chemical content of the soils best suited to tobacco culture. A disease study unit offers advice on pre-treatment of tobacco seed-beds to eliminate 'Wild Fire' and other destructive tobacco diseases. The lysimeter equipment measures the seepage of plant elements through various types of soils, and provides accurate information for soil conservation through fertilization, crop rotation, liming, and the planting of cover crops. A field soil testing unit extends this service; Windsor bulletins circulate in Russia, Japan, and Australia as well as throughout the United States. Visitors from Europe and Africa have studied the experiments at this station.

Windsor fertilizer experiments have been especially helpful to growers of cigar-leaf tobacco. The quality of cigar leaf is governed largely by the magnesium content of the soil. Black ash indicates magnesium deficiency; white, flaky ash shows too high a magnesium content. With the aid of the Experiment Station, Windsor growers have been able to control the quality of their cigar tobacco within very close limits and are able to command good prices for a uniform leaf.

The Windsor Station encourages diversified farming and rotation of crops and develops species best suited to climatic and soil conditions in the Connecticut Valley.

Potatoes are a popular rotation crop on all tobacco soils, and the Windsor Experiment Station is encouraging sweet potato culture, too. New vegetables are developed in the Plant Breeding Department under Dr. Lawrence C. Curtis, the originator of an improved sweet pepper plant, known as the 'Windsor-A,' which is now rated among the highest producers grown in Connecticut soils. Trial plots at this station are also used in the development of disease-resistant varieties of vegetables, sweet corn and tomatoes.

III. HIGH ROADS AND LOW ROADS

All Historic Houses mentioned in the following Tours as Points of Interest are private unless otherwise specified.

TOUR 1: *From* NEW YORK LINE (*New York City*) *to* RHODE ISLAND LINE (*Westerly*), 117.1 *m.*, US 1 and US 1*A*.

Via (*sec. a*) Greenwich, Stamford, Norwalk, Bridgeport, New Haven; (*sec. b*) New Haven, Guilford, Old Saybrook, New London, Groton, Stonington.
N.Y., N.H. & H. R.R. parallels the route.
Four-lane concrete highway over large part of route.
Excellent accommodations of all types at frequent intervals.

Sec. a. GREENWICH to NEW HAVEN, 47.8 *m.*

THE first post rider on the American continent was dispatched over this route, from New York to Boston, in 1673, following the old Pequot Path, then only a blazed trail through the wilderness. Later, post and coach routes traveled via Hartford. As described by Madam Knight, who made the trip on horseback in 1704: 'The Rodes all along this way are very bad, Incumbred with Rocks and mountainos passages, which were very disagreeable to my tired carcass; .... in going over a Bridge under which the River Run very swift, my hors stumbled, and very narrowly 'scaped falling over into the water; which extreemly frightened mee. But through God's Goodness I met with no harm, ———.' Near Stamford, she passed 'thro' many and great difficulties, as Bridges which were exceeding high and very tottering and of vast Length, steep and Rocky Hills and precipices (Buggbears to a fearful female travailer.)'

Over this route in December, 1773, Paul Revere, spurring his foam-flecked horse, dashed on his way to Philadelphia with confidential news of the Boston Tea Party. When the half-frozen horseman paused at Guilford to 'bait' his horse, the astonished natives gaped wide-eyed at the streaks of war paint on his face.

Today, this highway, the 'Roaring Road,' varied in width and surface, is the only direct route across southern Connecticut from border to border; it is a section of the chief vehicular highway through the North Atlantic States, and the most heavily traveled road between New York and the cities of the New England seaboard. Although this route parallels the shore, numerous by-passes short-cut past picturesque coastal villages and permit but occasional views of Long Island Sound. A number of short side tours and the longer alternative routes of Tour 1A (west of the Connecticut River), and Tour 1F (east of the river), lead to old settlements along the shore and inland, rich in scenic charm and in relics of Colonial life and historic events.

US 1 crosses the State Line from New York State into Connecticut, 26.6 miles east of Columbus Circle, and 21.5 miles from the George Washington Bridge.

Beyond the Connecticut bank of the Byram River (New York–Connecticut boundary) — the shortened 'Buy Rum' River of the Indians who traded there — is (R) the weathered *Thomas Lyon House* (1670), now headquarters of the local Lions Club. Originally on the other side of the highway, it faced south as did many 17th-century dwellings. It is an added-lean-to salt-box dwelling covered with long, round-headed shingles, which form an unusual scalloped pattern. Inside, instead of the feather-edge sheathing found throughout most of New England, there is beaded-edge board, which the Dutch preferred.

GREENWICH (town pop. 33,112) (*see GREENWICH*), 2 *m.*

At 2.4 *m.* US 1 descends *Put's Hill* (*see GREENWICH*).

At 2.5 *m.* (L) is *Boxwood* (*private*), a large house of 1799 built by Ebenezer Mead. Although considerably remodeled, it is noted for its two magnificent old box trees, flanking the door, which have grown as high as the modern piazza, added across the front of the house.

COS COB (Town of Greenwich), 4 *m.*, bears the name of an Indian chief and is noted for its production of fine marine motors.

On the plains immediately to the right of US 1, by the millpond, is a large *Burial Mound*, and the *Site of the Indian Village of Petuquapaen.* Here the Dutch and the English united to annihilate the Siwanoy tribe which had resisted the encroachments of the white settlers upon the Indians' best hunting ground. According to a contemporary account, 'the Lord having endued the colonists with extraordinary strength,' not a man, woman or child of the several hundred inhabitants escaped the fire set to their wigwams on a bitter February night in 1644, 'nor was any outcry whatsoever heard.' Public thanksgiving and general rejoicing was the order of the day when this news reached New Amsterdam.

To the right, conspicuously situated on the west shore of Cos Cob Harbor, is the Power-House which furnishes electricity for the main line of the New Haven Railroad.

> Right from Cos Cob on Strickland Rd. to the junction with River Rd., 0.3 *m.* Here (R), almost concealed from the roadway by an old lilac hedge, is the *Holley House*, which was built in the mid-eighteenth century by Captain Justus Bosch, a Dutchman. Its high ceilings, profuse paneling and lack of summer beams preclude any likelihood of an earlier date usually claimed, which is based chiefly on the age of the stone chimney resting on an arch in the cellar. The original windows and beaded clapboards have been retained.

At 4.3 *m.* is the junction with Orchard St.

> Left on this street is the *Obadiah Timpany House* (*private*), 33 Orchard St., 0.1 *m.*, a salt-box dwelling built in 1700. Although the house is covered with modern shingles, a portion of the rear wall is exposed showing what appear to be the original shingles of cedar, weathered and worn but retaining the strong odor of the wood. Stone steps, hand-hewn from solid rock, lead from the front hall into the cellar.

At MIANUS (Town of Greenwich), 4.8 *m.*, named for Chief Mayannos, the highway crosses the river below a dam impounding the raised waters of old *Dumpling Pond* (L).

When the British raided this section in 1779, some of the soldiers tarried at the gristmill, then a century old, about 1.5 *m.* upstream from the present bridge. They invited themselves to a meal of dumplings which the miller's wife chanced to be making; she told them to wait a few minutes until the food was cooked. Taking advantage of a lapse in their attention, she threw the dumplings into the millpond, an act that is commemorated in the name.

At 5.7 *m.*, on SE. corner of US 1 and Sound Beach Ave., is the *Adams House*, a tiny salt-box dwelling which dates from 1721. Unusual interior decorative features are the small heart-shaped openings in panels over some of the doorways.

> Right on Sound Beach Ave., through the section known as Old Greenwich. The *Peck Homestead* (*private*) (1703), 0.1 *m.*, 44 Sound Beach Ave., with a modern porch and six columns at the front, is a two-story salt-box house originally built without the use of plaster; it has the same openings in the panels above the doors as are found in the Adams House.
>
> The *Perrot Library* (*open 2–5, 2d and 4th Tuesdays*), at 0.5 *m.*, is headquarters of the Greenwich Historical Society. It has a varied exhibit of antiques.
>
> The *First Congregational Church*, on Sound Beach Ave. (L), 0.6 *m.*, is one of the square-towered little buildings that were built of rough hewn stone, about 1890, and called Gothic because of their battlemented parapets and wooden-mullioned windows shaped like those in stone in English Perpendicular work.
>
> At 0.7 *m.* is the junction with Webb Ave. Left on this road is *Arcadia* (*open daily*), headquarters of the National Agassiz Association, an organization devoted to nature study. Several acres, with a 480-foot road frontage, are devoted to a display of wild flowers. One of the largest apiaries in the country is conducted for educational purposes. A section, known as 'Little Japan' is planted with Japanese cherry trees. On the grounds is a small observatory equipped with a 6-inch Alvan Clarke telescope.
>
> Farther south on Sound Beach Ave., at 1.4 *m.*, is the *Quintard House* (*private*), NW. corner of Sound Beach and Quintard Aves., said to be the oldest house in Old Greenwich (about 1700). On well-kept grounds in a setting of trees and shrubs, this one-and-a-half-story house with a one-story lean-to has been somewhat remodeled but retains the old red shingles on one end.
>
> At 1.8 *m.* is the junction with Shore Road. Right on this road, 1.2 *m.*, is the *Keofferam Lodge* (about 1735), at the NW. corner of Shore and Hawthorne Rds., a central-hall-type house with two chimneys, named for the Dutchman who first purchased this land from the Indians. If the date assigned to the house is correct, the structure is one of the first of the type erected.

At 6.3 *m.* is the *Condé Nast Press*, a fine example of a modern industrial plant in landscaped surroundings. Here are published *House Beautiful* and *Vogue*.

At 6.4 *m.* (R), midway between the railroad and the Post Road, along the Greenwich-Stamford town line, is *Laddin's Rock*, in a private estate. According to local legend, Indians attacked the home of an old Dutch settler, Cornelius Labden, who was forced to see his family scalped. Escaping, he leaped on his horse and galloped through the hemlocks toward the brink of the cliff crying, 'Come on, ye foul fiends; I go to join your victims.' In the rush of pursuit, the Indians blindly rode their horses over the rock and all went crashing to their deaths at the jagged base.

During the Revolution this entire district was preyed upon by lawless bands of bushwhackers called 'skinners,' who owed allegiance to neither side.

STAMFORD (city pop. 46,346) (*see STAMFORD*), 7.6 *m.* Throughout this area a large proportion of the residents are commuters to New York. At Stamford is a junction with State 104.

> Left from Stamford on State 104, 8.3 *m.*, to a junction with a cross-country path that leads (L), 0.2 *m.*, to the precipitous gorge of the Mianus River on the New York Line. Within the twilight shade of primeval hemlocks the narrow river swirls through dark pools and tumbles over shoals strewn with boulders of pink quartz, forming one of the wildest spots near New York City.

The traveler soon becomes aware of the importance of the Connecticut township. Signs indicate town lines, but the town center is often many miles away.

Just east of the Stamford-Darien town line, on the north side of the highway, stands Darien's oldest house, built in 1680, the *Weed Homestead*, or 'House Under The Hill.' Its huge stone chimney back of the ridge, the wide cornice overhang, and the break in the back line of the roof, all bespeak its 17th-century origin. The house is open as an antique shop, and inside can be seen the 'gunstock' corner posts, the huge summer beams, and the stone chimney front exposed on the stairs.

NOROTON, 10.6 *m.*, a village in the western part of the town of Darien, is called for Chief Rooaton, whose name is also preserved in the nearby localities of Rowayton and Roton Point. At Noroton is a *Soldiers' Home.* Beside the road is a military cemetery where the solid, uniform headstones, stretching away on a battalion front, mark the graves of Connecticut men who have served their country in all of the Nation's wars.

> Right from Noroton on Ring's End Rd. to Swift's Lane (L), 0.3 *m.*, where a miniature *Colonial Village* (*private*), a collection of small buildings of that period moved from various New England towns, is plainly visible from the roadway. At the end of Ring's End Rd., 0.5 *m.*, on the waterfront, are the *Old General Store* and *Custom House*, both erected in 1737.

DARIEN (town pop. 6951), 12.2 *m.*, is a residential town within the metropolitan district of New York City, where local constabulary are especially efficient. To the south, winding lanes go down to the shores of Long Island Sound; north of the main road the wooded countryside is dotted with homes. Separated from Stamford in 1820, formerly the parish of Middlesex, this town was named for the Isthmus of Darien. The highway is narrow on this older 'bottleneck' section of the Post Road, and the work of the old turnpike builders has had to contend with the ever-increasing flow of traffic. Darien was the scene of Tory raids, the worst on July 22, 1781, when the Rev. Dr. Mather and 50 prisoners were spirited away from the parish.

At Darien is the junction with State 136 (*see Tour 1A*).

> Left from Darien on State 29 is NEW CANAAN (town pop. 5456), 5.1 *m.*, a community of carefully tended country estates and polo fields. This town is exclusively a residential community, situated on high ridges, which in many places command views of the Sound.
>
> > 1. Left from New Canaan on Mead St. (one block) is the *New Canaan Bird Sanctuary* in *Mead Memorial Park*, one of the first established in the United States.

Left from New Canaan on Railroad Ave.; right on Weed St.; left on Wahackme Rd. to its termination in Ponus Rd., and right on that highway, is *Ponus Monument*, 1.3 *m.*, erected in honor of Chief Ponus, to mark the old Indian trail which led to the Hudson River.

NORWALK (town pop. 36,019) (*see NORWALK*), 16.3 *m.*

At Norwalk is the junction with US 7 (*see Tour* 4).

Right from Norwalk at the traffic rotary on a side road is SOUTH NORWALK, 1.2 *m.* (*see Tour* 1*A*), where the manufacturing enterprises of the town are concentrated.

WESTPORT (town pop. 6073), 19.9 *m.*, is chiefly a residential community; a number of artists and literary folk have established studios and permanent homes along the seashore and about the countryside.

Separated from Fairfield, Norwalk, and Weston in May, 1835, this town was formerly known as Saugatuck. As early as 1645, Thomas Newton, smuggler, put out from this port to trade with the hated Dutch; he was jailed in 1650 when his activities were reported by Dame Goody Johnson, but escaped and lived happily on his ill-gotten wealth. The town was twice invaded by loyalists during the Revolution; and during Tryon's Raid, April 25, 1777, seventeen green militiamen actually fired one volley at 2,500 British regulars before taking to their heels.

'Pedlar' ships operated from Westport and developed a 'commission trade' as romantic as that of the Mississippi steamboat era. The wharves are now crumbling and only pleasure boats use the harbor.

Among Westport residents are Van Wyck Brooks, author; Lillian Wald, founder of the Henry St. settlement; Rollin Kirby, cartoonist, William McFee, author; and Rose O'Neil, originator of the Kewpie doll.

At the brow of the hill west of Westport stands the *Bedford High School* (L), gift of E. T. Bedford, a native son. Here in the high school are murals, painted by John Steuart Curry, a prize winner in the Carnegie International Exhibit of 1933, whose work is also represented at the Metropolitan Museum, New York. The Curry murals here depict 'Tragedy' and 'Comedy' and include such recognizable figures as Little Eva, Uncle Tom, Charlie Chaplin, Sherwood Anderson, Theodore Dreiser, Eugene O'Neill, Mickey Mouse, Will Rogers, Hamlet, a Kewpie doll, and Mr. and Mrs. Curry.

On the hill which US 1 climbs from the center is the well-proportioned *Congregational Church* (R), built in 1830, shining white behind tall spruces.

Left from Westport on State 57, through rough hill country is WESTON (town pop. 670), 5 *m.* From this high ground are fine views of the surrounding countryside, especially from the lawn of the *Congregational Church* (1830), 0.2 *m.* (R), from State 57, at the cross road, a simple, well-proportioned structure of the Federal period, with small window panes now turning violet with age. At the entrance to a residence across the way are old gas lamp posts that once lighted the New York street corners. The street names can still be discerned.

At 5.7 *m.* State 57 intersects State 53.

Left on State 53 to the intersection with a side road, 7.7 *m.*

Right on this side road, 0.4 *m.*, is *Music Hill*, a natural amphitheater, seating 3000 people, where concerts are given throughout the summer months under the direction of Nikolai Sokoloff of the New York Symphony Orchestra. On Mr. Sokoloff's property, near-by, concerts are also presented at *The Barn*.

State 53 joins US 202 at Grassy Plain (*see Side Trip off Tour* 4).

At 23.7 *m.* (R), just east of the Westport–Fairfield town line among some willows, is a granite monument marking the *Site of the Great Swamp Fight* which ended the Pequot War in July, 1637, when the survivors of Mason's West Mystic attack on that hostile tribe were either killed or sold into slavery. Subsequently, this fertile territory was settled in comparative peace.

At 24.7 *m.* is the junction with Bronson Rd., where US 1 crosses the railroad on a concrete overpass.

Left on Bronson Rd., which turns north through an underpass to the colonial settlement of GREENFIELD HILL (Town of Fairfield), 3.3 *m.*, site of the Academy conducted by the Rev. Timothy Dwight from 1786 until 1795, when he became president of Yale College. Grouped about the old Green are numerous old houses and taverns, and near-by is the *Hubbell House* (1751), on the west side of Hillside Rd., where Dr. Dwight held his first classes before the erection of the Academy building, now gone. In spring the village streets are beautiful with pink and white dogwood and there are extensive marine views from the hilltops.

On Bronson Rd. (R) is the *Old Greenfield Cemetery*, now filled to capacity and no longer in use. Here are buried 98 Revolutionary soldiers and the two earliest Greenfield preachers, the Rev. John Goodsell (d. 1763) and the Rev. Seth Pomeroy (d. 1770).

From Greenfield Hill came Abraham Baldwin, recorded in history as 'The Savior of Georgia' and honored with a State holiday. The monument to Mr. Baldwin in the Old Greenfield Cemetery bears the inscription: 'Abraham Baldwin lies buried at Washington. His memory needs no marble. His country is his monument, her constitution his greatest work. He died a Senator in Congress, March 4, 1807, aged fifty-two.'

The gambrel-roofed house at the southern end of the Green, the *Rev. Seth Pomeroy House*, was built in 1757. The *Dr. Rufus Blakeman House* of 1822 has a wide, open portico, a delicate diamond pattern on the cornice and, within, a circular staircase. The *Squire Samuel Bradley Jr. House* (1750), just around the corner on Old Academy Rd., has a handsome portico and shallow windows beneath the cornice. On Hillside Rd. straight ahead from the Green, is the *Rev. Richard Varick Dey House* (about 1823) with a Dutch roof sloping over long porches, and the *Zalmon Bradley House* (about 1750), with a porch which, unlike those of the Dey House, is a later addition.

Across the road from the church was a store, kept continuously for about 200 years until 1925. This store was the customhouse for the Fairfield District for many years. Whenever a ship arrived in Black Rock Harbor (then a part of Fairfield) it was necessary for the master to make the four-mile trip uphill to Greenfield to have his papers put in order.

For nearly 100 years, until 1796, all the little schools in the outlying districts of Fairfield were under the control of the citizens of Greenfield Hill. Eight scattered, widely separated, one-room schools, some of them heated by fireplaces and taught by spinsters who believed implicitly in the efficacy of the birch rod, made up the primary educational facilities of the older settlement. School meetings were violent affairs, attended by everyone in the township and, sometimes, in the case of a tie vote, men ran from house to house, routing out the hired men to vote and break the tie.

Old sailormen returned to Greenfield Hill to raise chickens and plant a flower garden in the back yard of their snug harbor. Privateersmen, whaleboat warriors, the 'rock scorpions' of the shore who preyed on all passing vessels during the Revolution, finally cast anchor in the fastnesses of this beautiful hill country to bask in the sunshine and live on in memory forever, because old sailors, like old soldiers, never die — they fade away.

At 24.9 *m.* (R), is the intersection with a dirt road (*see Tour 1A*).

FAIRFIELD (town pop. 17,218) (*see FAIRFIELD*), 25.8 *m.*

The outskirts of Fairfield merge into those of Bridgeport.

BRIDGEPORT (city pop. 146,716) (*see BRIDGEPORT*), 30.5 *m.,* foremost industrial city of the State.

At Bridgeport is the junction with State 58 (*see Tour 1B*).

US 1A by-passes the center of the city as well as that of Stratford, but US 1 leaving Bridgeport on the newest of the many bridges which gave the city its name, proceeds to the town of Stratford.

STRATFORD (town pop. 19,212), 33.8 *m.,* a town with many well-preserved old houses, now principally a residential suburb of Bridgeport, also has considerable manufacturing. Settled in 1639, and named for 'Stratford-on-Avon,' the town's early activities were confined to shipbuilding and oyster fisheries.

US 1 enters Stratford on Stratford Ave. and turns left onto Main St.

Proceeding north on Main St. this route passes (R) the conspicuous *David Judson House* (*open daily, adm.* 25¢) (1723) now owned by the Stratford Historical Society, which has in the doorway the earliest bull's-eye glass in the State. In the cellar is a great cooking fireplace with two Dutch ovens; the oak beam which forms the cellar lintel is 18 inches square. The paneling upstairs is a notable example of the early use of fluted pilasters.

On Elm St. one block right of Main St. and parallel with it, are many well-preserved old houses dating from the 18th century and earlier.

Here in Stratford the Rev. Samuel Johnson founded the first Episcopal Church in Connecticut (1723–43). Atop the present *Christ Church* (R), is a weathercock from the spire of the original building, which still bears the bullet holes of British marksmen under Colonel Frazier who, when quartered here in 1757–58, amused themselves by using the chanticleer as a target.

Right on Main St. to the *Sikorsky Airplane Plant* (L), 1.1 *m.,* where amphibian airships are made. From Stratford come the huge Sikorsky trans-Pacific Clipper ships 'Frisco to China!' now spanning the western ocean on a seven-day schedule. Few people outside of the Sikorsky plant in Stratford have heard of Pointe Noire or Dakar, towns on the African West Coast. Today, although 3000 miles apart, these outposts are linked together by a fleet of Hornet-powered Sikorsky amphibians carrying mail, passengers and express. The *Bridgeport Airport* opposite (R), purchased by that city in 1937, was formerly Mollison Airport named for the British fliers who crashed here in 1935, after having successfully flown across the Atlantic. Across the most extensive salt meadows in Connecticut, is the solitary old *Lighthouse* (1822) at *Stratford Point*, 3.3 *m.* Off in Long Island Sound, 6.5 miles due south, is the famous *Stratford Shoals Lighthouse*.

On a knoll behind the church is the *Oldest Episcopal Burying Ground* in the State, laid out in 1723.

Main St. northward becomes State 8 (*see Tour* 5).

US 1 turns right at Stratford and rejoins US 1 Alt. at 34.8 *m.*

The *Washington Bridge*, 35 *m.*, carries US 1 over the Housatonic River into New Haven County. This point on the river was the site of the ferry which started operations in 1650 under Moses Wheeler, who was born in England in 1598 and died in Stratford in 1698, said to be the first white centenarian in the country. South of the bridge was the scene, in 1649, of the cross-river swim of a Milford man who escaped from a public lashing imposed for breaking the Blue Laws forbidding a man to kiss his wife on the Sabbath. He was later rejoined by his family in Stratford, where he became a leading citizen.

East of the bridge is the village of DEVON (Town of Milford), 35.7 *m.*, a residential community with beaches and cottages on the shore to the South.

At 37.2 *m.* is the western junction with US 1 Alt., the Milford by-pass.

Right on the old road; US 1 leads to the business section of MILFORD (town pop. 14,870) (*see MILFORD*), 0.5 *m.*, a historic village. At the village center is the junction with State 122.

Right on State 122; this route passes sandy flats where shore birds may be seen feeding. From the tiny bays and coves along this shore oystermen put to sea to harvest a crop from submerged lands that have been productive since the first actual cultivation of shellfish in 1845. There are records of these oyster-beds having produced profits in excess of $1000 an acre in one year. Indians came here to feast and dry the shellfish. The industry today flourishes and the oyster fleet is seen offshore almost any day during the season.

Crossing *Oyster River*, 2.1 *m.*, which might, like Powder River, be described as being 'a mile wide and an inch deep,' State 122 follows the coast line to WOOD-MONT, 3.6 *m.*, a summer colony.

Leaving Woodmont, the road passes a succession of beaches (R), and rows of summer cottages (L) en route to *Savin Rock*, 6.1 *m.*, 'the Coney Island of Connecticut,' a widely known amusement resort. A plaque near a concession marks the spot where Tryon's Redcoats disembarked in 1779.

Leaving the shore, State 122 turns left to West Haven.

WEST HAVEN (town pop. 25,808), 8 *m.* The business center is concentrated on the east side of the large Green which was presented to the town by Shubael Painter in 1711. West Haven was the home of General Tom Thumb, celebrated midget, and was the scene of a raid by the British on July 5, 1779, when General Tryon brought 3000 Redcoats ashore, pillaged the church, burned documents, and looted the town. Facing the Green on the south is *Christ Episcopal Church* (1909), designed by Cram, Goodhue, and Ferguson, one of the finest Gothic churches in Connecticut. It is in restrained Perpendicular style with a short, square tower and cloister. Right on Main St., opposite the High School, stands the *Painter*, or *Peter Mallory House* which is dated 1695, but is possibly of even earlier construction. This large salt-box house, with narrow windows and a huge chimney, shaded by giant maple trees, stands on the very edge of the sidewalk. It is an example of the larger 17th-century houses, and has the unbalanced window arrangement common to this region.

On Elm St., just east of Campbell Ave., stands the *Ward Heitman House*, a very old (1684) salt-box house with a central-chimney and an added lean-to. It has the old stair but later mantels and paneling.

State 122 rejoins US 1 at 9.8 *m.*, 2 miles west of New Haven at the foot of Allingtown Hill.

At 38.8 *m.* is the western junction with US 1A.

At 41.2 *m.* is the junction with State 152.

> Left on State 152 past the extensive *Fairlea Farms* (R), where acidophilus milk was first developed, and traversing fertile farming country to the center of ORANGE (town pop. 1530), 1.7 *m.*, overshadowed by its white *Congregational Church* (1810). The *Racebrook Country Club*, off Derby Rd., one of the outstanding golf courses in Connecticut, is the only country club in the State with two 18-hole golf courses.

At 45.8 *m.* at the top of Allingtown Hill is the junction with Prudden St.

> Left on Prudden St., one block, is a small triangular Green (L), with a *Monument to William Campbell*, a British adjutant, who, among other acts of mercy, saved the life of the local pastor who had broken a leg while fleeing from the Redcoats when they invaded the town on July 5, 1779. That same day the officer was mortally wounded.

At 46 *m.* is the junction with State 122 (*see above*).

NEW HAVEN (town pop. 162,655), 47.8 *m.*, a university community (*see NEW HAVEN*). At New Haven are the junctions with State 10 and 10A (*see Tour 6*), US 5 (*see Tour 7*), State 15 (*see Tour 7A*) and State 67 (*see Tour 1C*).

Sec. b. NEW HAVEN to RHODE ISLAND LINE (Westerly), 69.3 *m.*

US 1, in NEW HAVEN, follows Water St. E. and crosses the northern cove of New Haven Harbor on Bridge St., at 1 *m.*

The *Old Stone House*, 153 Forbes Ave., 1.5 *m.*, now the parsonage of the Forbes Ave. Church, was built in 1767, but retains little of its original appearance. An eastern wing, a new portico, and triple windows at the main entrance have been added.

At 1.9 *m.* is the junction with Woodward Ave.

> Right on Woodward Ave. to *Fort Hale Park*, 1.8 *m.*, with spacious, hilly, wooded grounds and a public bathing beach. The park includes 51 acres of smooth tree-sheltered lawns, bold rock bluffs, and sandy beaches. Named for the martyred Continental spy, this park was the site of a fort twice destroyed by the British (1779 and 1781), but rebuilt in 1809 and so re-equipped that it successfully kept off the enemy during the War of 1812. Enlarged on several later occasions, the fort was permanently dismantled during the latter half of the 19th century and turned over to the city for use as a public park.
>
> *Morris Cove*, 2.4 *m.*, is one of the better, less crowded shore resorts. Here (L), at 325 Lighthouse Rd., is the *Morris House* (*open May–October 1, weekdays 10–5, Sundays 2–5, free*), a conspicuous clapboard and stone structure (1670, 1767, and 1780). Most of the present dwelling dates from the rebuilding in 1780 on the ruins of a 17th-century house burned by the British July 5, 1779. The stone wall and chimney nearest the street are all that is left of the earlier house, which was probably a two-chimney structure. The kitchen wing, known to have been built in 1767, survived the fire. The lean-to toward the street contains an earlier kitchen on the ground floor and a ballroom added about 1800.
>
> *Lighthouse Point*, at 3.4 *m.*, is a popular municipal park and beach resort for those who seek a safe, clean beach with ample parking space and the usual forms of shore amusements. The *Old Lighthouse* (*admittance on application to park supt.*), Lighthouse Point Park, Lighthouse Rd., a tall octagonal structure, was erected in 1840–45 on the site of an earlier lighthouse, built in 1804. The present building, 90 feet high, was constructed of East Haven sandstone, painted white, and lined with North Haven bricks. A spiral staircase of granite leads to the large circular light,

visible over a radius of ten miles. Government operation of the light was discontinued in 1877 when the offshore light on the breakwater at New Haven was completed. Since that time the older building has served as a signal station of the United States Weather Bureau.

At 3.3 *m.* is the junction with State 142.

Right on State 142, 1.3 *m.* to the junction with a side road.

Right on this road, 1.1 *m.* to *Momauguin*, a beach resort.

Farther east on State 142, beyond several beaches lined with summer cottages, is *Short Beach*, 2 *m.*

EAST HAVEN (town pop. 7815), 3.4 *m.*, includes comparatively level agricultural land devoted to truck gardening to the north, and numerous residential colonies and summer resorts along the shore of Long Island Sound to the south. The town is now receiving the overflow from many of New Haven's expanding activities.

At the NE. cor. of Main and High Streets is East Haven's *Old Stone Congregational Church* (1774). It was built of local dark red sandstone, laid with shell lime mortar, from designs by George Lancraft, one of the few pre-Revolutionary architects known by name. The present interior (entered through the tower at the west end, and not, as originally through the side) dates from 1850, and the present spire from 1858.

Right from the center on Thompson St. is New Haven's municipal airport, opened in 1931, which has a field capacity of 200 ships, a hangar, and modern equipment.

Facing the Green, at 298 Hemingway Ave., is the *Stephen Thompson House*, which dates from 1760, with its stone end-walls and overhanging eaves. The *Abraham Chidsey House*, standing on the north side of the Green, is a Dutch-roofed structure of one-and-a-half stories. It is the earliest (1750) and the best preserved old house in the town.

Right on Hemingway Ave., four blocks, is the central-chimney *Elnathan Street House*, which is a splendidly preserved example of early 19th-century construction, with an entrance porch in the Greek Revival style said to have been built at the time of the original structure (1810).

At 57 Main St. stands a house that was built in 1694, so remodeled as to be scarcely recognizable as a colonial structure, but interesting nevertheless because the stone end-walls and first story are parts of the structure which tradition says was the *John Winthrop Forge*. This building was continuously in use as a blacksmith shop until 1920.

US 1 descends a hill to *Lake Saltonstall*, at 4 *m.* Here, on the Beaver River (L), stands an old *Mill* with hewn timbering, on the site of the first iron mill in Connecticut (third in America), though undoubtedly it is not the original building; bog ore was refined here. A clause in the deed, making it mandatory for the owner to grind corn or any grain brought to him by a property owner of East Haven, might prove embarrassing to the present owner as only one millstone now remains.

Mr. Saltonstall was a choleric gentleman who was often on unfriendly terms with his neighbors. The old fellow was put in his place one day when attempting to ferry over Stony River after bargaining with the ferrywoman, Deborah Chidsey. Dame Chidsey, dissatisfied with his terms, stranded her craft in midstream, stepped over the side, gathered her skirts high and waded ashore, flapping her arms like an excited gander. Saltonstall was especially dressed for a trip to New Haven and demanded immediate relief, but Dame Chidsey advised him to wait for a tide or wade ashore. Saltonstall sat sunburned and fuming, until the moon, calling the waters home, at length released him.

At 5.6 *m.* is the junction with US 1 Alt. which bears left, by-passing the center of Branford.

US 1, no longer than the cut-off, passes through the center of Branford.

BRANFORD (town pop. 7022), 6.7 *m.*, named for Brentford in the English county of Middlesex, is a pleasant residential town, formerly a busy center of shipping. Here is the site of an important salt works, the product of which was used in the preservation of meat for the Revolutionary army.

At 112 West Main Street is the salt-box *House of Nathaniel Harrison*; this dwelling was built in 1690 when very simple paneling was just coming into use. The original clapboards can still be seen in the lean-to attic.

On a knoll overlooking a small green is the *James Blackstone Memorial Library*, a marble building of 1896, which, if pretentious, is an uncommonly fine library for so small a town.

Beyond, grouped around the *Green*, a large triangular plot (R), are the town's public buildings, churches and monuments.

On the south side of the Green stands the little old *Branford Academy* building of 1820, which is topped with a cupola. It is occupied by the local historical society. On the SE. corner is a small commemorative tablet near the *Site of the Reverend Samuel Russell House*, where in 1701 ten clergymen met and donated books for the founding of the Collegiate School, later Yale College.

In this township, where the ministerial house lot was on 'Pig Lane,' the citizens felled the fluted pillars of the old Meeting-House and cut them up for well curbings. These peculiar well curbings can still be found in the farming country around Branford.

In the eastern section of the town are many fine old houses, among which one of the best is the *Samuel Frisbie House*, on East Main St. (US 1), a red, two-story, clapboarded structure (R), unaltered since it was built, in 1792.

> Right from Branford on State 143, which traverses the pleasant residential section of *Indian Neck* and passes through the attractive summer colony of PINE ORCHARD, at 3.3 *m.* The harbor here, at which some of the finest yachts and sailing craft on the Sound are anchored, is noted for its clear waters, its pink granite breakwater, and its narrow sandy beach broken by smoothly worn rocks.
> From this point, *Rogers' Island* to the east and the *Blackstone Rocks* scattered to the south are seen to the best advantage; the wide view of ships, sea, sand and rocks, is not often surpassed.

A nine-hole golf course extends north of the bay, giving the resort a verdant background, and shaded streets about the vicinity are lined with estates and landscaped gardens.

Eastward, State 143 follows a winding roadway which climbs and descends gentle slopes, with pine woods to the left and marshland dotted with large boulders to the right. Right from State 143 on State 146, at 6.5 *m.*

State 146 enters the *Stony Creek District* of Branford, at 7.3 *m.*, one of the oldest fishing villages of the vicinity, now primarily a summer resort with the *Stony Creek Playhouse*, where professionals entertain during the summer season.

Offshore, like a section of the Maine coast drifted into Long Island Sound, is the rocky, green-crowned archipelago of the *Thimble Islands.* Passenger launches plying between the scores of large and small islands afford delightful marine views and opportunities to visit the larger islands, occupied by summer colonies and hotels. On *Money Island*, Captain Kidd is traditionally believed to have buried treasure.

At 9 *m.* is the intersection with a dirt road.

> Right on this dirt road to *Hoadley Point*, 1 *m.*, where from the top of an old granite quarry, a fine view is obtained of the Thimble Islands, scattered to the west.

State 146 continues over the swampy district known as *Leete's Island*, at 9.5 *m.*, the scene of a spirited encounter between the Guilford Militia and the British who landed here in 1777. The settlement, now chiefly an artists' summer colony, has moved slightly west from its original location to more solid and rugged ground overlooking *Island Bay.*

At 10.7 *m.* (at the railroad underpass), is the junction with a dirt road.

> Right on the dirt road to *Sachem's Head*, 2 *m.*, on a rocky promontory of historical interest. Here a bloody battle of the Pequot War was fought in 1637. Tradition says that the head of an Indian, slain in combat, was placed by Uncas in the fork of a tree where the skull remained for many years, giving the point its present name. The ledge-lined harbor rimmed with well-kept estates affords a protected anchorage for a large yachting fleet; the yacht club is built on the outermost promontory.

From here this route follows a meandering course along the irregular coast line to the Guilford Green, 13.5 *m.*, where it rejoins US 1.

At 7.6 *m.* US 1 Alt., by-passing Branford, rejoins US 1 (*see above*).

At 7.8 *m.* US 1 crosses the Branford River which empties into Branford Harbor, 2 miles to the south.

On a hillside, at 10.1 *m.*, is the large, red *Edward Frisbie Homestead* (R), now known as the Hearthstone Tea Room, marked 1685, although its architecture suggests that the present structure is mid-eighteenth century, possibly built about the chimney of an earlier house. The interior is well preserved and interesting, with an unusually large stone slab hearth. Beyond, US 1 swings north around *Moose Hill* (alt. 260), affording a fine view of the countryside.

US 1 now crosses the upper section of the village of Guilford. At 15 *m.* is the junction with State St.

> Right on State St. into the village.

> GUILFORD (town pop. 3117) (*see GUILFORD*), 0.3 *m.*, is an early Colonial village which has preserved the most varied collection of authentic early houses in New England.

Left from Guilford on State St. to the intersection of North St., 0.2 *m*. Here at 1 North St. stands the *Home of Samuel Lee*, Captain of the Coast Guards in Revolutionary days. During Captain Lee's absence, Tories often raided the house in search of contraband articles which had been seized by the Coast Guard, but they were always outwitted by the Captain's wife, Alice. It was she who fired a cannon in the yard to warn the colonists who were working in their northern fields when the British landed at Leete's Island, in 1777. Northward on State St., which becomes Nut Plains Rd., is the delightful sequestered village of NUT PLAINS, 2.7 *m*., where hickory and walnut trees shade the quiet main street. Here lived General Andrew Ward, Revolutionary hero who covered Washington's retreat by keeping the campfires at Trenton burning, thus successfully deceiving the British until the Continental army had safely withdrawn. Among the ten grandchildren in General Ward's household was the studious Roxana who tied her French textbook to the spinning wheel, so that she might study as she worked. She became Mrs. Lyman Beecher, mother of Henry Ward Beecher, noted clergyman, and Harriet Beecher Stowe, author of 'Uncle Tom's Cabin.'

At 3 *m*. (L), stand two *Hall Houses* (1740), the frames of both of which were raised on the same day. One, in a dilapidated condition, boasts an 'ell'-plan chimney. The other, built by a brother on adjoining property, is in excellent condition, although it has never been painted. Most of the interior woodwork is original and, as the timbering is exposed, offers a good opportunity to study early framing.

At 15.2 *m*. is an unusually large single-unit greenhouse (L), 1200 feet long, which is devoted exclusively to the cultivation of roses.

At 17.1 *m*. is a highway picnic area, *Clearview Rest* (R).

At 18.3 *m*. is apparently the 17th-century salt-box *William Shelley House* built in 1730, with a sweeping roofline and T-shaped chimney. The frame of an old casement is still to be seen in the lean-to attic.

MADISON (town pop. 1918), 20.2 *m*., a village by the sea, incorporated in May, 1826, contains many old landmarks grouped about a long, dignified central Green. Here lived Cornelius Scranton Bushnell, builder of Civil War battle craft and financial sponsor of Ericsson's 'Monitor.' Early industries were fishing, shipbuilding, and the burning of charcoal.

Overlooking the Green from the west is the stately *Congregational Church* (1838), whose gilded, cylindrical spire, thrusting above the trees, guided returning seamen straight to Madison Harbor. The six fluted Doric columns of the portico uphold a high entablature decorated with triglyphs, and the pilasters on the side of the building have birds' beak capitals. The whole structure shows a freedom and imagination seldom found in Greek Revival work.

A series of houses along the south side of the Green illustrates the development of domestic architecture in the 18th and 19th centuries. The *Gilbert Dudley House*, on the SW. corner of Wharf Rd., is a salt-box house (1740), with a peculiar double featheredged siding and lamb's tongue stops on its chamfered summer beams, typical of the 17th century; but here in Madison such details persisted later than in most communities.

The *Colonel J. S. Wilcox House*, standing next west, representative of the other end of the architectural scale, was erected in 1830. Its features include the 'waffle-course' of augur holes in the cornice and the mid-nineteenth-century iron grill on the veranda.

The *Graves House*, located east of the Green (L), a weather-worn shingled salt-box dwelling (1675), is the best preserved 17th-century house in Connecticut. In the house are still to be found family records that give a complete contemporary account of the building of the dwelling and of the court that John Grave, as magistrate, held here. The large southeast room, where court was held, is still known as the Judgment Chamber. Many of the rooms are sheathed in featheredged boarding that has never been painted and has aged to a soft brown.

The *Nathaniel Allis House*, now the headquarters of the Madison Historical Society (*open weekdays 2–6, June–Oct.; adm. 25¢*), was built in 1739; it is a long low building at the center, much remodeled. The interior is maintained as an old dwelling of its period, with each room appropriately furnished.

Many Madison houses include one of Connecticut's usual domestic features, the cat-hole. The Yankee, always thrifty, deplored the necessity for holding doors open on cold wintry nights for the house cat to go out and in. Some early craftsman cut a round opening in the lower panel or rail of the door, fitted a swinging cover over it and solved the problem by teaching the family tabby to push her own door open. Some cat-holes have a little peak-roofed portico to protect them from the weather.

> Left from the Green on Scotland Rd., 1.5 *m.* to *Duck Hole*, at Four Corners, near a bridge over the Hammonasset River where an old milldam in a sylvan setting offers the visitor a quiet resting-place.

Beyond Madison at a large traffic rotary, 22.4 *m.*, is the junction with a firm dirt road.

> Right on this road is *Hammonasset State Park*, a tract of 954 acres with bathing, boating, and camping facilities for more than one and a half million visitors annually. The sandy beach, extending 5 miles along the shore, is the largest public beach in Connecticut.

Beyond the entrance to Hammonasset State Park, US 1 proceeds past many restaurants and hotels where 'shore dinners' are a specialty. Occasional water scenes and rural landscapes offer diversified scenery. Long Island, 25 miles distant, may be seen across the Sound where pleasure craft spread white sails, coastwise steamers ply between New York and New England ports, and tugs with strings of barges fling plumes of smoke across the sky.

At 23.9 *m.* is the junction with Swaintown Rd.

> Left on Swaintown Rd., at its intersection with Cow Hill Rd., 1.4 *m.*, is a *Little Red Schoolhouse*, an example of the early New England school. This one-room building, erected in 1800, has windows fitted with batten shutters.
>
> Left on Cow Hill Rd., at 1.5 *m.*, is the *Stevens Farm*, cultivated since 1675 by nine generations of the Stevens family. The salt-box homestead, with exposed timbers in some of the rooms, was built in 1699. Among the many heirlooms preserved by the family, is a copy of the original grant to the property received by John Stevens from King Charles II of England, as well as rifles used by members of the family in the Revolutionary and Civil Wars, and in hunting forays on Roast Meat Hill to the west.

CLINTON (town pop. 1574), 24.1 *m.*, a clean, quiet village, one-half mile inland from its harbor, was once busy with shipping and shipbuilding, but is now disturbed only by the unhurried arrival and departure of pleasure boats and trawlers. The manufacture of Pond's Extract from native witch hazel cut in back-country brush lots and sometimes distilled in backwoods stills, is the town's chief industry. This most populous portion of the old town of Killingworth was incorporated as a separate town in May, 1838, and named for Governor De Witt Clinton of New York. On the small triangular Green (L) is a cannon used by Gideon Kelsey in his single-handed defense of the local coast line against the British invasion in 1812.

In the center of the Green, opposite the church, is a *Monument* commemorating the early years of the Collegiate School, later Yale, 1701–07 (*see below*). Across the way is a *Milestone* (R), one of many placed along the highways by Benjamin Franklin. *Stanton House* (L), built in 1789, is a Colonial museum (*open weekdays 2–5, adm. free*). Within is displayed an excellent collection of old china and furniture. The paneled walls on either side of the hall are hinged, and may be raised to hooks in the ceiling, making the front of the house one large room. The original wall paper, a handsome French product, covers two walls of the southwest room. The *Adam Stanton Store*, in the ell with a long veranda, has been restored to its early condition, with its original counter, shelves, and drawers, still bearing the printed labels of their contents. The accountant's desk and ledgers occupy their place by a rear window. Behind this house is the *Old Well* used by the Rev. Abraham Pierson, first rector of the Collegiate School. The famed clergyman's homestead formerly stood on this site, and the first Yale students attended classes in it until the opening of the college in Saybrook. At 95 E. Main St. is the *Wright Homestead*, which was built in 1807, birthplace of General Horatio G. Wright, commander at the battle of Winchester, whose skillful rallying of his panic-stricken troops made possible Sheridan's Ride, the subject of the poem by that name. Fort Wright on Fisher's Island was named for him. At 101 Main St. is another *Wright House*; this dwelling, built in 1819, has a fan-light and cornices of unusual delicacy. A side trip down the garden-bordered Waterside Lane, lined with fishermen's tiny cottages, some of great age, leads to a sleepy little hamlet, presided over by the *Farnham House* (1800).

At 25.1 *m.* is the junction with the western end of State 145.

> Right on State 145 to the summer colony at *Kelsey Point*, and *Grove Beach*, a mile long stretch of sand which forms one of the finest bathing beaches in the State. This road rejoins US 1 at 2.6 *m.*

At 26.5 *m.* is the eastern junction with State 145 (*see above*).

US 1 passes a fine State-maintained picnic area (L), at 26.9 *m.*, and crosses Patchogue and Menunketesuck Rivers just north of their confluence at Menunketesuck Point, where sand bars across the marshy district made it possible to ford the streams before the building of bridges.

WESTBROOK (town pop. 1037, inc. May, 1840), 28.7 *m.*, is the birthplace of David Bushnell, torpedo and submarine inventor. In the western part of Westbrook (R), is the *David Bushnell House* (*adm.* 35¢), the home of Bushnell's uncle, where the inventor often visited while a youth. This story-and-a-half red cottage, erected in 1678–79, has been restored, and is now maintained as a museum. Among the exhibits are parts of Bushnell's original 'turtle' submarine.

At 28.9 *m.* is the intersection with a dirt road.

> Right on this road to the shore of Long Island Sound, 0.4 *m.*; a short distance off-shore is *Salt Island*, affording an anchorage for fishing schooners and other small craft. Accessible on foot by sand flats at low tide, this islet was formerly the site of extensive salt and fish-oil works.

At 30.4 *m.*, just east of the Old Saybrook town line, is (L) the *Elisha Bushnell House* which, built in 1678–79, has been recently restored. It is now a salt-box house, with irregular window arrangement and rooms less than seven feet high. Originally a one-room central-chimney house, it is believed to be the only house in New England, with the exception of the Fairbanks House in Dedham, Mass., that still shows the old wattle-and-daub construction.

At 31.9 *m.* is the junction with US 1 Alt., which by-passes Old Saybrook. US 1 following the old Post Road, bears right to the center of Old Saybrook.

OLD SAYBROOK (town pop. 1643) (*see OLD SAYBROOK*), 33 *m.*, is a coastal village at the mouth of the Connecticut River, and one of the oldest towns in the State.

At 33.2 *m.*, US 1 Alt. rejoins the main route. At 33.8 *m.* is the junction with State 9 (*see Tour* 8). At 35.1 *m.* is the junction with State 9 Alt. (*see Tour* 8), and at 35.8 *m.* (middle of bridge), US 1 crosses the Connecticut River. Good views of the broad stream unfold at this point. The *Ferryhouse* on the site of the old landing, which handled all cross-river traffic here from 1662 to 1911, stands below the eastern approach to the present highway bridge.

At 36.3 *m.* is the junction with State 86 (*see Tour* 1E), and State 156 (*see Tour* 1F).

At a rotary, 37 *m.*, US 1 turns abruptly left avoiding the elm-shaded center of Old Lyme (*see OLD LYME*).

On the outskirts of Old Lyme, the highway passes the beautiful *Mile of Roses* (R), planted by Judge W. E. Noyes, along a stone wall of his estate. The house, built by Dr. Richard Noyes in 1814, has an unusually broad open pediment porch of graceful lines and fine detail.

Traversing fertile valley farm lands, US 1 passes through the hamlet of LAYSVILLE (Town of Old Lyme), 39.6 *m.*, once the center of a small woolen industry.

The Stone Ranch Military Reservation (L), 41.9 *m.*, bordering US 1 intermittently for about 2 miles, was formerly the property of Fred Stone, the comedian, and was outfitted by him as an example of a typical western ranch. Now State-owned, it is maintained as a Civilian Conservation Corps camp and public shooting ground. *Pataganset Lake* (L), 43.9 *m.*, has an unusual number of aquatic plants.

EAST LYME (town pop. 2575, inc. May, 1839), 45.2 *m.*, a rural village. On the side roads of this district are many well-preserved homesteads of early settlers.

At East Lyme is the *Colonial Inn (open)*, built at the height of the Greek Revival, and at the rear of the small Baptist church is the *Justin Beckwith House (private)* (1785), with an elaborate façade exemplifying the beginning of the Greek Revival.

East, US 1 takes a somewhat winding course keeping well inland, except for two glimpses of the upper reaches of the salt inlet known as the Niantic River.

At the northeast corner of the junction with State 161, at the village center, stands the remodeled *Calkins Tavern*, of about 1700, where both Washington and Lafayette stopped.

At 50.3 *m.* is the junction with State 156 (*see Tour 1F*), the shore route between Old Lyme and New London.

NEW LONDON (town pop. 29,640), 52.3 *m.*, a historic maritime town (*see NEW LONDON*). At New London is the junction with State 85 (*see Tour 3A*) and State 32 (*see Tour 9*).

At New London US 1 crosses the Thames River on a steel bridge that is sufficiently high to afford a view straight down New London harbor (R), one of the deepest on the Atlantic coast with more than three miles of navigable water frequented by seagoing vessels of many types. The view (L) up the tidal course of the Thames River extends about 2 miles over a part of the course of the annual Yale–Harvard crew races. On the west bank are the modern brick buildings of the U.S. *Coast Guard Academy (see NEW LONDON)*, and on the hilltop farther north, the campus and native granite buildings of *Connecticut College (see NEW LONDON)*. On the east bank is the Atlantic Base of U.S. Submarines (*see Tour 1G*).

US 1A, the new road, by-passes the main street (R) of GROTON (town pop. 10,770) (*see GROTON*), 53.7 *m.*, reached by turning right at the eastern end of the bridge). At Groton is the junction with State 12 (*see Tour 1G*) and State 84 (*see Tour 1H*).

This route follows US 1 Alt., a new cutoff and at 54 *m.* intersects with State 84 (*see Tour 1H*). The road ascends to a hilltop at 54.6 *m.* from which a wide view extends over the countryside southward to Long Island Sound.

At 55.3 *m.* US 1 Alt. rejoins US 1. At the intersection is a dignified shaft in Avery Memorial Park (R), marking the *Site of the 'Hive of the Averys,'* the homestead which from 1656 to 1894 was occupied by seven generations of the descendants of Captain James Avery. The shaft, topped by a bust of the original settler in Puritan costume, was a gift of the late John D. Rockefeller, a descendant, and was designed by the sculptor, Bela Lyon Pratt, another descendant. The old homestead, destroyed by fire on July 20, 1894, had been enlarged by the addition of the former

Blinman Church of New London to the older structure in 1686. From the Hive many mariners, soldiers, and substantial citizens went forth to make America. At home, the Averys were farmers and civic leaders. An old well-sweep with an oaken bucket stands invitingly beside the tall memorial shaft.

At the head of the small salt inlet of Poquonock River is the hamlet of POQUONOCK BRIDGE (Ind.: 'cleared land') (Town of Groton), 56.4 *m.*

At the Poquonock Bridge is a junction with a side road.

> Right on this road, 3 *m.*, is the *Governor Winthrop House*, Bluff Point, set among rocks at the top of a hill. The interesting features of this peak-roofed frame dwelling built about 1700 are an underground exit, tunneled about three hundred feet from the cellar to the barn, and a large brick chimney, arched in the basement, where it forms a room-like space paved with a stone floor, reputedly built as a shelter for women and children during Indian raids. The staircase to the second floor is encased in featheredged boards and has a high hand rail without spindles.

At 58.1 *m.* (L) is *Fort Hill* where Pequot reinforcements encamped when Mason burned their stronghold at Pequot Hill. The remnant of the tribe was pursued by Mason to Fairfield and there perished in the Great Swamp Fight.

East of Fort Hill, the highway runs inland crossing low hills which, several miles to the south, level into peninsulas, notably cottage-covered *Groton Long Point* and *Eastern Point* with its wealthy summer colony.

At WEST MYSTIC (Town of Groton), 59.6 *m.*, the 'Galena' (1862), first ironclad warship laid down in the country, was built by the Maxon Fish Co. The 'Monitor,' widely known because of its spectacular battle with the 'Merrimac,' was designed while the 'Galena' was under construction and was truly a floating battery rather than a ship adapted to sea duty.

> Left from West Mystic on Elm St. is *Pequot Hill*, 0.9 *m.*, on which the *Mason Monument* marks the spot where Captain John Mason with a force of 77 men burned a Pequot fort in 1637.
>
> Early reports of the Pequot War describe the main fort of the Indians as a long palisade, with two entrances, enclosing the wigwams of the tribe. Captain John Mason, with a force of some 90 men from Hartford, Windsor, and Wethersfield, made his celebrated attack on this stronghold in 1637, following Pequot depredations on the outskirts of river and coastal towns. Mason was assisted by about 400 friendly Indian allies under Sachem Uncas. The combined forces of Mason and Uncas swooped down on the warlike Pequots about daybreak, and set fire to the stockade. Some 600 or 700 Pequots were burned alive; only 7 were taken captive and about 7 escaped. The returning Colonial soldiers were each given a bonus of several acres of land, Captain Mason became a hero, and the Boston divine, Cotton Mather wrote: 'The greatness and the violence of the fire, the flashing and roaring of the arms, the shrieks and yells of men, women and children within the fort, and the shouting of Indians without, just at the dawning of the morning, exhibited a grand and awful scene. It was a fearful sight to see them frying in the fire, and the streams of blood quenching the same, horrible was the stink and scent thereof; but the victory seemed a sweet sacrifice, and they gave the praise thereof to God.'
>
> Right from West Mystic, State 215 runs along the shore of Mystic Harbor past numerous old houses and new summer homes to NOANK (Ind.: 'point of the land'), 2.5 *m.*, home of sword-fishermen, lobstermen, and boat-builders. Their gear-laden wharves and motley craft fringe the water front, and their dwellings

cluster on the hillside of the seagirt point, where the old lighthouse beacon has guided home generations of seafarers.

US 1 crosses the Mystic River to Mystic.

MYSTIC (Town of Stonington, pop. 9019), 59.8 *m.*, is an old maritime community of trim white houses on the green-fringed irregular Mystic Harbor, the tidal outlet of the Mystic River. For generations Mystic was the home of daring mariners and fishermen and was feared by the British during the Revolution as 'a cursed little hornet's nest.' The village teemed with shipbuilding activity during the 1849 gold rush days. Then the Mystic River echoed with the pounding of hammers 'knocking away the shores and spurs,' as the graceful hulls of swift clipper ships slid down the ways to make world records on their thrilling runs around the Horn to California. Here was built in 1860 the 'Andrew Jackson,' a modified clipper combining cargo space with speed, which hung up a record of 89 days, 4 hours, breaking by 9 hours the record of the famous 'Flying Cloud' (1851) (89 days, 13 hours). In succeeding passages the 'Andrew Jackson' made the best average time of any ship sailing to San Francisco.

Left from Mystic on State 169, a short distance, is the *Marine Historical Museum* (*adm. on application to curator*), an old wooden mill building (L), which houses one of the finest collections of clipper-ship models in America, in addition to old figureheads and paraphernalia of whaling and sailing days.

On the museum grounds is the hull of the famous small sailboat 'Annie,' designed by D. O. Richmond, which defeated all-comers in the sandbagger class from 1870 to 1880. Its designer was one of the most successful yacht builders of the era preceding ballast keel construction.

At 60.9 *m.* is the intersection with a paved side road.

Right on this road to *Mason's Island*, 0.8 *m.*, which commands an impressive view of Fisher's Island. Mason's Island, edged with rocky ledges and sandy beaches, was presented to Captain John Mason of Windsor in appreciation of his victory over the Pequots. It is now occupied by summer homes. Though the island is accessible by a private road over a causeway, sightseers are not welcome.

From the bridge crossing the long and narrow Quiambog Cove, 62.3 *m.*, is an excellent view (R) of Fisher's Island, three miles offshore, one of the numerous islands northeast of Long Island, which are part of New York State. Crossing a broad neck of land that terminates in LORD'S POINT, a summer colony on the Sound, the highway parallels the northern shore of Stonington Harbor and skirts, at 64.6 *m.*, the northern end of the village of STONINGTON (borough pop. 2025) (*see STONINGTON*). The greater part of the quiet old whaling port is on a peninsula, undisturbed by the rush of traffic. To reach the town center turn right on East St.

WEQUETEQUOCK (Town of Stonington), 66.8 *m.*, on the long salt inlet known as Wequetequock River, was named from the Indian word describing the district.

Right from Wequetequock, at an irregular crossroad, opposite the small 19th-century meeting-house, on a dirt road that leads across Wequetequock Cove and branches sharply right past an old graveyard, 0.2 *m.*, the earliest in the town of Stonington; here are 'wolf stones,' heavy slabs of rude stone which, according to tradition were laid over graves in primitive settlements as protection against the bold and numerous wolves which then ravaged the countryside. The oldest stone is dated 1690.

At 69.3 *m.* US 1 crosses the Rhode Island Line at the Pawcatuck River which separates the village of PAWCATUCK (Town of Stonington) from Westerly, Rhode Island (*see Tour 1J*).

T O U R   1 A :   *From* DARIEN *to* FAIRFIELD, 17 *m.*, State 136, West Way and Harbor Rds.

Via South Norwalk, Saugatuck.

Macadam-surfaced highway.

Limited accommodations.

STATE 136 follows the shore with frequent views of Long Island Sound, picturesque harbors, and sail-dotted inlets.

Leaving US 1 (*see Tour 1*) at the railway underpass in DARIEN, State 136 passes in the block of stores (R), at 0.1 *m.*, an old-fashioned country hardware store, formerly the original parish edifice unsuccessfully fired by the British during the Revolution. To the south, at 0.6 *m.*, is the residential district of TOKENEKE (Town of Darien).

Crossing Five-Mile River, State 136 passes through Rowayton.

ROWAYTON (Town of Norwalk), 1.9 *m.*, is an old landing place on the Five-Mile River which basks sleepily in daydreams of the past when ships ran alongside the rock ledge at full tide to load and unload their cargoes.

At 2.3 *m.* is the intersection with a macadamized road.

Right on this road to *Roton Point Beach* and *Amusement Resort*, 0.4 *m.*

Past the peninsulas of Roton Point and Wilson Point, State 136 veers left across a railway siding at 3.3 *m.* and beneath a railway overpass at 4.1 *m.* to SOUTH NORWALK, 5.5 *m.*, the manufacturing center of Norwalk (*see NORWALK*).

Across the Norwalk River at EAST NORWALK (Town of Norwalk), 7 *m.*, is the junction with Ludlow Parkway.

Right on Ludlow Parkway to *Calf-Pasture Point*, 1.3 *m.*, once used as a pasture ground by the Indians, but now developed into an attractive city park. Offshore are numerous large islands famed in legendary tales of pirate gold, privateers, British raids, and smuggling. On Cedar Hammock Island, Nathan Hale stealthily lingered as he waited to be picked up by the sloop 'Schuyler' which carried him on his fateful mission to Long Island to obtain British military information for General Washington.

Proceeding right beneath a railroad underpass, at 8.3 *m.*, this route follows the Saugatuck River for two blocks past a settlement of fishermen and lobstermen to the old shipping port of SAUGATUCK, 9.3 *m.* State 136 crosses the Saugatuck River to the junction with Compo Rd., at 10.6 *m.*

At the junction is the statue of a *Minuteman* which commemorates the heroism of the defenders of Compo Hill (L), where Westport patriots attempted to halt Tryon's retreat from Danbury.

> Right on Compo Road to *Compo Beach*, where, on the point, two cannon presented by the United States Government mark the spot where Tryon landed a force of 2000 British to raid the Continental stores at Danbury. 'The House on the Pond' (L) is the home of Lillian D. Wald, founder of the Henry Street Settlement, New York City. Passing the Compo Yacht Basin, the side road rejoins State 136.

Skirting the landscaped *Estate of Arnold V. Schlaet*, State 136 turns sharp left, then right, and after circling inland comes to a junction with a paved road, at 13.3 *m.* (sharp right on a curve).

> Right on this road to *Sherwood Island State Park*, 0.8 *m.*, where a sandy beach and adjacent acreage are equipped with free dressing-rooms, parking space, tables and benches for picnickers.

At 13.5 *m.* is the intersection with a side road.

> Left on this road for a short distance to the *Greens Farms* district, 0.6., where there are many spacious estates. The many windmills here were, at one time, used to pump sea water into the pans and evaporation tanks of an early salt works. Here just beyond the railroad station on a triangle of the old Green, stands the *Machamux Boulder* with a tablet that records important events in the history of the early settlement which was called Machamux by the Indians.

The highway parallels the shore for a short distance, affording a splendid view of Long Island Sound. Beside the road, at *Frost Point*, is a towering elm, with a circumference of 25 feet, three feet above the ground. On the left are the beautiful landscaped gardens and extensive greenhouses on the *Estate* (*open, free*), *of the late E. T. Bedford*, oil magnate. The Bedford residence and those of Laurence Craufurd and Johannes Schiott, surrounded by spacious lawns, stretch along the water front (R).

East of Sasco Creek is a junction with West Way Rd. (R). Across the street (L) from the junction is the *Pequot Library* (*open weekdays* 9–5), containing one of the most complete American genealogical collections in the United States.

At the junction, this route, leaving State 136, turns right on West Way Rd. to SOUTHPORT (Town of Fairfield), 16.2 *m.*, at the mouth of Mill River. After the burning of Fairfield, Southport became the business center of the town. Most of the influential citizens lived here and erected the many dignified substantial homes bordering its hilly, elm-shaded streets.

The historian Barber, writing in 1836, said, 'More shipping is owned here in proportion to the size of the place than in any other port between Boston and New York.' The 19th-century 'Pedlar' ships, which carried on a lively trade with both those cities, and the marine shops that once lined the water front have given way to the moorings of the large yachting

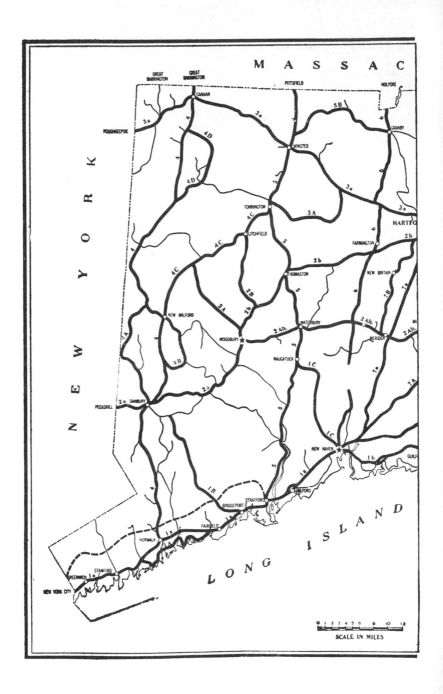

SCALE IN MILES

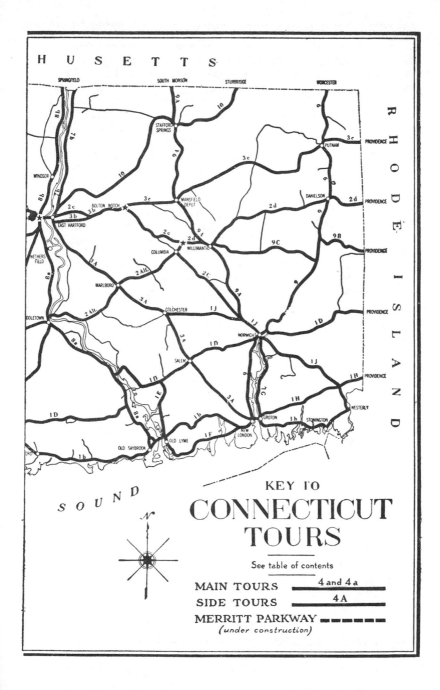

KEY TO
CONNECTICUT
TOURS

See table of contents

MAIN TOURS ———— 4 and 4a
SIDE TOURS ———— 4 A
MERRITT PARKWAY ▬ ▬ ▬ ▬
(under construction)

fleet and clubhouse of the Pequot Yacht Club. Here in Revolutionary days, many crews were organized for the unofficial whaleboat warfare carried on in retaliation for the numerous Tory depredations suffered by settlements along the Sound. One such expedition, commanded by Captain Amos Perry, sailed in the sloop 'Racer' one stormy night. At dawn it was sighted by the British fleet, apparently drifting helplessly. The commander of a Tory sloop came alongside, boarded the 'Racer' and demanded surrender. Captain Perry stamped his foot and immediately his crew swarmed up through the hatches, surrounded the boarding party, and captured the British vessel and its cargo.

Near the southwest corner of West Way Rd. and Harbor Rd. is the *William Bulkley House* which was spared by the British invaders in 1779. Close by the end of the bridge over Horse Tavern Creek is the *Old Store*, built in 1765, which served Bulkley as store and warehouse. At the northwest corner of Old South and Willow Sts. is the *Sheffield House*, the birthplace (1793) of Joseph Earle Sheffield, founder of the Sheffield Scientific School of Yale University.

The *Perry Houses* (1845 and 1850) (L), are imposing examples of the Classical Revival period.

Bearing right on East Harbor Rd., this route parallels old Southport Harbor, and passes at 16.8 *m.*, the *Tide Mill Tavern*, which was operated as a mill until 1915 and stands on the site of a succession of early gristmills. Some of the mill structure has been retained, although extensively remodeled. Beyond the tavern the road leads across a bridge over Mill River and turns left to rejoin US 1 (*see Tour* 1) at Fairfield (*see FAIRFIELD*), 17 *m.*

T O U R   1 B :   *From* BRIDGEPORT *to* JUNCTION WITH US 202, 18.1 *m.*, State 58.

Via Easton.

Macadamized roadbed.

Tourist accommodations at intervals.

STATE 58 branches northeast from US 1 at Bridgeport (*see Tour* 1) and runs through a shady countryside.

Passing the *Samp Mortar Reservoir*, the highway meets a side road at 2.8 *m.*

> Left on this road is *Samp Mortar Rock*, 0.4 *m.*, a natural formation scooped out by glacial movements, which was used by the Indians to grind their corn. The great stone pestle, fashioned by the local tribe for use with the mortar, has been removed

to the Peabody Museum in New Haven for preservation. From the summit of this hill are splendid views of the surrounding countryside.

This unusually attractive route passes *Hemlock Reservoir*, its banks thickly planted with evergreens.

At 9.9 *m.* is the junction with State 106.

Right on State 106 is EASTON CENTER (alt. 360, town pop. 1013), 1 *m.* Here set high above the road in traditional New England manner, is the *Congregational Church* (1817), its flat façade surmounted by a steeple of two octagonal stages, crowned with a short, conical spire. In an appropriate setting of old trees and with an adjacent wellhouse is the *Parsonage* (before 1800) with a square pillared portico and an unusual hall which passes through the chimney.

On the right stands the *Staples Academy* (1797), one of the first free secondary schools in the country, founded in 1781, and now used as a community center.

Left of State 58 in the underbrush, at 11.2 *m.*, are *Primitive Ruins*, locally known as 'crows' nests.' Not yet classified by antiquarians, they are believed to be foundations of the first homes built by settlers in this district.

At 14.4 *m.* is the junction with a side road.

Right on this road which leads, 0.6 *m.*, to a crossroad, a right turn crosses a little wooden bridge spanning an impressive 50-foot cascade. At this point the Aspetuck River is confined between the walls of a rock gorge, called the Devil's Mouth. The road continues for 1 mile along the Aspetuck Valley.

Ascending a long hill, State 58 enters REDDING RIDGE (alt. 705, Town of Redding, pop. 1599), 14.8 *m.*, from which a wide view extends eastward. The present *Episcopal Church* is the successor to that which during the Revolution was under the rule of the Loyalist, the Rev. John Beach, whose pastorate endured 50 years. On the west gable of the church structure is the damaged weathercock from which the legs were shot by one of Tryon's men as his force marched through this district en route to Danbury. Next door to the Episcopal Church was the home of Squire Heron, who pretended that he was a Tory in order to spy upon the British for the Continental Army.

Passing several old houses in a thickly wooded district, State 58 reaches *Israel Putnam Memorial Camp Grounds* (L), 16.9 *m.*, Connecticut's 'Valley Forge,' where General Israel Putnam's troops, the 'right wing' of the Continental Army, endured the rigors of the bitter winter of 1778–79, when they camped here in order to be in a strategic position to march to the defense of West Point or the towns on Long Island Sound.

Guarding either side of the entrance are reproductions of Revolutionary block-houses. Within the park are several attractive drives leading past the granite obelisk commemorating General Putnam's impassioned speech to the poorly clothed and scantily fed soldiers who threatened to desert and had already formed in line to march to Hartford to demand redress.

Right on 'Company Street' are tumble-down stone piles, the remains of chimneys of the soldiers' huts, lying exactly as they fell when the troops burned the cabins after they evacuated them in May, 1779.

A short distance farther on (R) to the *Colonial Museum* (*open from Decoration Day to the end of Sept.*, 1–5), which includes in its collection many Revolutionary relics found on the grounds.

The main driveway leads past *Philip's Cave*, about which many legends have been told, to a reproduction of one of the army cabins, and beyond to a little circular driveway (L), the site of the camp fire, where Joel Barlow, one of the celebrated 'Hartford Wits,' entertained the soldiers. Down the hill is the old camp oven.

At 18.1 *m*. is the junction with US 202 (*see Side Trip off Tour 2, sec. a*), 3.3 miles east of Danbury.

T O U R   1 C :   *From* NEW HAVEN *to* NAUGATUCK, 16.5 *m*., State 67 and State 63.

Via Bethany.

Macadam and concrete surfaced highway.

Limited accommodations.

LEAVING New Haven (*see NEW HAVEN and Tour* 1), on Whalley Ave. (State 67), this route passes through the Westville district of New Haven, at 1.3 *m*.

Beside the road at 4.9 *m*. (L), is one of the few stone tanbark mills, powered by oxen, ever used in New England. The great circular crushing stone, rigged with an ox yoke and pole, stands as though ready for work on the stone trough in which the bark was laid. This mill, used before 1720 in a swamp near Foxon (town of East Haven), is of the type commonly used in the arid districts of Asia. On such a mill Samson ground corn for the Philistines.

At 5.9 *m*. is the junction with State 63 (R) which this route follows to Naugatuck.

BETHANY (alt. 520, pop. 480), 10 *m*., is a hamlet on a hilltop. Originally the site of numerous small mills, the town is now devoted to dairying and agriculture. The *Congregational Church* (L), built in 1832 and extensively altered in 1851 and 1866, was designed by Ira Atwater. The *Episcopal Church* (R), with arched gallery windows, reminiscent of New England Georgian, was designed by David Hoadley and built in 1809.

Eastward, steep fields slope down to Lake Bethany; to the south, the valley merges into the foothills of the West Rock range. Roadside pastureland is fragrant with sweet fern, juniper, and bayberry.

At 10.2 *m*. stands the *Darius Beecher House* (R), built by David Hoadley in 1807, with a delicate Palladian window and a hooded porch sheltering a finely designed doorway. The interior includes a ballroom with a spring floor, and a wide hall spanned by two arches.

An *Aviation Field* (L), at 11 *m.*, maintains planes for brief sightseeing trips. At 11.3 *m.* is (L) a mink farm.

Descending a long hill, brook waters splash over a small stone dam (L) at 11.8 *m.*, though the mill for which it supplied power has long since crumbled.

At 13.2 *m.* the highway passes below scrub-grown *Beacon Hill* (L). On the summit an air beacon flashes through the night, and a huge boulder 40 feet in circumference and 20 feet in height is a vantage-point from which the church spires of several Naugatuck Valley towns are visible.

Beyond the ravine of *Cotton Hollow Brook*, at 13.5 *m.*, in the little community of STRAITSVILLE, 13.7 *m.*, the long *Collins Tavern* (1811), with a two-story colonnade across the front, stands, like a roadside Mount Vernon, close to the road (R). The symmetry of its lines supports the tradition that it was designed by David Hoadley, Connecticut's most versatile early architect.

Across the road are the *Laurel Lodge Trout Pools* (L), operated by a private club. An old shear-shop formerly stood beside the stream.

At 14.7 *m.* State 63 passes the deserted track of the *Beacon Valley Fair Grounds*, site of former country fairs and previously the home site of Chief Two Moons, Indian medicine man, who amassed a fortune bottling questionable cures for gullible white men in the days of torchlight salesmen. State 63 continues past the factory-lined Naugatuck River to NAUGATUCK, 16.5 *m.* (*see Tour 5*).

T O U R   1 D :   *From* NEW HAVEN *to* RHODE ISLAND LINE (*Providence*), 76.2 *m.*, State 15, 80, 9, 82, 165, and 138.

Via North Branford, Deep River, East Haddam, Norwich, Preston City, Voluntown.

Macadam-surfaced highway.

Limited accommodations.

A MORE direct route between New Haven and Providence than US 1, this route travels an excellent highway through a sparsely populated inland area with many unexpected and delightful vistas, abounding in lakes and ponds, entering dense stretches of upland forests, and opening suddenly upon well-cultivated fields separated by sturdy stone walls. It is a less-traveled highway, free from the annoyance of interstate and local busses and trucks with their attendant roadside stations. As the highway was not completed until 1936, few gasoline and service stations have been erected, and they are often many miles apart.

State 15 leaves US 1 at New Haven on State St. and at 2 *m.* turns sharp right, following the car tracks over a bridge and crossing the Quinnipiac River at 2.6 *m.* At a double underpass, 2.8 *m.*, this route turns right from State 15 (*see Tour 7A*) onto State 80.

State 80 now passes through a flat and colorless countryside which offers little indication of the general beauty of the miles ahead. Many small truck gardens in this district have wayside stands for the sale of produce.

Beyond, at 8 *m.*, the Totoket Mountain trap-rock quarry lifts its steep bare walls high above the roadway.

NORTH BRANFORD (alt. 100, town pop. 1329), 13.2 *m.*, is hardly more than an old-fashioned New England crossroads where (R) the *Zion Episcopal Church* (1819), and (L) a white *Congregational Church* (1908) stand primly along the wayside.

At 11.7 *m.* is the junction with State 77.

> Left on State 77 to a sign 'To the Churches,' which directs the traveler to the hamlet of NORTH GUILFORD. Many of the old roads are closed, houses are deserted, or only the cellars remain. Two churches, however, are well preserved and furnish an interesting comparison, for they were built within a year or two of each other. Both show early Greek Revival influence, but the *Episcopal Church* (1815) shows its allegiance by pointed Gothic windows. The steeple of the *Congregational Church* (1813) rises in two stages, a square belfry with Doric entablature, surmounted by a circular lantern. Between the churches is the Congregational parsonage (1821), Doric in detail, with a fine doorway and porch of slender free-standing columns.

State 80 leads by *Shelley Lakes*, 15.4 *m.*, in the forested hill country which distinguishes this route.

At the rotary intersection with State 79, 17.5 *m.*, is North Madison's little *Congregational Church* (1837), notable for its beautiful fluted Doric columns.

At 18.9 *m.*, State 80 crosses a high cement bridge over the narrow gorge of *Nineveh Falls*, in the Hammonasset River, banked with a heavy growth of hemlocks and laurel.

As the new highway bridge passes directly over the falls, the best view is obtained by following the foot path (R) down the stream a few yards.

Just across the bridge is the junction with a country road.

> Right on this road, which parallels State 80 and rejoins that route at the Killingworth crossroads, 3.4 *m.*, to the *Killingworth Images* on the bank of a stream. This collection of hand-carved and painted figurines, which once performed amusing antics actuated by power from a water wheel, continues to attract hundreds of tourists although the bright colors are faded and the water wheel has long since been carried away by spring freshets.

East of the falls, State 80 cuts through sheer rock formations and wild forest growth to the junction with Kelsey Drive, 20.3 *m.*, a dirt road.

> Left on Kelsey Drive to *Camp Roosevelt*, a former Civilian Conservation Corps camp in the Killingworth section of the *Cockaponset State Forest* where pleasing

drives and picnic grounds have been provided. Kelsey Drive joins Chatfield Hollow Rd. at a bridge which spans a new dam, constructed by the Civilian Conservation Corps at *Shroeder Pond*, an artificial body of water surrounded by pine trees. Along the shores, beaches have been created, and a roped-off cove provides a safe bathing place for children.

North of Camp Roosevelt, in the Pine Orchard section of the town, is *Sackett's Cave*, 1 *m.*, long a haunt of archaeologists and collectors who have unearthed many valuable Indian relics, some of which are preserved at the Peabody Museum, New Haven. Unfortunately, dynamiting has blocked part of the main entrance to the cave.

At 21.7 *m.* is a rotary intersection with State 81.

Left on State 81 to the rural center of KILLINGWORTH (alt. 425, town pop. 482), 0.3 *m.*, named for Kenilworth, Warwickshire, England, in 1667. Local misspelling and mispronunciation have resulted in the present corrupted form.

Amid rocky meadows overgrown with huckleberry bushes and patches of thick forest watered by cool narrow streams, Killingworth, chiefly devoted to dairying and poultry-raising, lies serene and undisturbed by the turmoil of modern industry. Despite its isolation, the community has twice been the center of wide interest. First, in pre-Revolutionary days, Abel Buell (1742–1822), a silversmith engraver and one of the most inventive geniuses of his time, who engraved the first map of America made in this country after the Peace of 1783, was detected altering five-pound notes. Buell was imprisoned, cropped and branded, but because of his youth and previous exemplary reputation, suffered what the stern justice of those times regarded as light punishment. Only a small piece was cut from one ear, and that he was permitted to keep warm on his tongue so that it might be replaced. The brand 'F' (forger), held on his forehead until he could say 'God Save the King,' was placed high so that it might be covered by his hair. While in prison, Buell invented the first lapidary machine ever made in this country and secured commutation of his sentence when he presented a handsome gem-studded ring to the King's Attorney.

Years later, wide attention was again concentrated on this village when the poet, Longfellow, after a visit at the *Ely House* (*private*), 0.2 *m.*, built in 1782, wrote his poem, 'The Birds of Killingworth,' in protest against the local practice of organized shooting of birds by the farmers who considered them pests.

On State 81, at 0.5 *m.*, set back (R) from the highway on a slight incline, behind large trees, is the *Killingworth Congregational Church* (1817), whose graceful tower and domed belfry are admired from hilltops many miles around. It owes something, obviously, to Hoadley's United Church in New Haven. As in the best period of early church architecture, the tower rises on the front axis of the church with a projecting pediment below, repeating the lines of the gable.

The red *Josiah Parmalee House* (*private*) of 1752, a notably good example of mid-eighteenth-century construction, stands (R), at 2 *m.*

Left here on a macadamized road, 1.5 *m.*, is an old gristmill, still in operation.

At 24.6 *m.* is one of the most beautiful of all Connecticut's roadside parks (L), in a landscaped clearing opposite *Lake Menunketesuck* (R).

In densely wooded country, is the tiny settlement of *Winthrop* (Town of Saybrook), at 25.6 *m.* Passing ponds and falls (R), at 28.9 *m.*, the highway crosses and recrosses the sinuous course of the narrow black stream for which the village of DEEP RIVER (Town of Saybrook) (*see Tour 8*), 29.5 *m.*, is named.

Left at Deep River on State 9 (*see Tour 8*) to CHESTER (*see Tour 8*), at 31.2 *m.*

Right at Chester on an oiled dirt road to the Chester–Hadlyme *Ferry Dock*, 0.6 *m.* (*ferry operates only between* 7 *and* 7; 25¢ *for car and driver;* 5¢ *each additional passenger*). From the boat can be seen the quietly flowing river, the wooded shore line, and, on the Hadlyme side, one of the steel trestles of a miniature railway spanning a rock fault. This railway was built by the late William Gillette, noted actor, on the estate where he spent his declining years. At the ferry landing on the E. bank is a small settlement of well-kept houses clustered on elm-shaded lawns along the river bank. A colonial *Shipyard Office* (R), and the *Mansion* (*private*), built about 1805, on the river's bank, once owned by Captain Henry T. Comstock, shipbuilder, stand by the remains of his old dock, from which hogsheads were easily rolled into the capacious cellar of his house.

At 0.8 *m.* is the entrance to a private highway (L) which ascends to *Gillette Castle* (*private*), Mr. Gillette's former home. The building is perched atop a high cliff like the medieval strongholds which inspired its design. Mr. Gillette, who died in 1937, specified in his will that he hoped the executors would see that the property did not get into 'the possession of some blithering saphead who has no conception of where he is or with what surrounded.'

The road nearly parallels the course of Whalebone Creek and leads east through the old shipbuilding village of HADLYME (Town of Lyme), 1.7 *m.* This road, following an old route once worn by laden ox-carts, winds through a Colonial district little changed since that bygone era, to Brockway's Corners, where it rejoins State 82, at 2.2 *m.*

At 35.5 *m.* is the community of TYLERVILLE (Town of Haddam), where a large turkey farm (R) at the road junction caters to a select clientèle. At the turkey farm, State 9 (*see Tour* 8) continues north. At this point is the junction with State 82 on which this route crosses the East Haddam bridge over the Connecticut River, at 35 *m.*, from which the view up and down the stream is exceptionally beautiful. The bridge terminates in the town of East Haddam.

EAST HADDAM (alt. 20, town pop. 2114), 35.2 *m.*, established as a trading post, became a bustling center of fisheries, shipping, and the manufacture of marine hardware and muskets. Today it is an old-fashioned river town. In the tower of *St. Stephen's Episcopal Church* hangs an ancient bell, inscribed 'Corrales me heso ... 815 A.D.,' that was brought to this country from Spain, where it was salvaged from a monastery destroyed during the Napoleonic Wars. On a knoll overlooking the river, in the cemetery, stands the little red *Schoolhouse*, where Nathan Hale taught in 1773–74.

Still standing beside the river bank are the great rambling hotels that served the river-boat passengers, who, before the construction of the shore railroad, here made connections with Sound steamers to New York.

At 36.6 *m.* is the junction with a dirt road (marked) to the East Haddam Fire Tower.

Left on this road to the *East Haddam Fire Tower*, 2.3 *m.*, from which there are excellent views of the river valley.

At Brockway's Corners, 40.4 *m.*, is the junction with the 'alternate ferry route' (*see above*). Left at Brockway's Corners, State 82 skirts along the northern boundary of the town of Lyme, passing 'Roaring Brook,' a roadside picnic park (R), 41 *m.*, and intersecting with State 86 at 42.5 *m.* (*see Tour* 1E).

At 43.8 *m.*, State 82 passes through the district of NORTH PLAINS (Town of East Haddam) in its rustic setting of wooded hills and ravines.

Left from North Plains, a gravel road leads to the *Devil's Hopyard*, 3 *m.*, a State park of 860 acres on the Eight Mile River. Here are *Chapman's Falls*, in one of the loveliest gorges in the State (*picnic grounds with tables and fireplaces*). On a rock at the top of the falls, the Devil is said to have sat, playing his violin as he directed the East Haddam witches who brewed black magic potions in the potholes beside the tumbling waters. Above the northern end of the Hopyard is MILLINGTON GREEN (Town of East Haddam), once a thriving lumber town.

East of North Plains, at 46.4 *m.*, near a pond surrounded by weeping willows, is the *Trowbridge Homestead* (*private*), home of a grandfather of Donald G. Mitchell (1822–1908), a Connecticut author who wrote under the *nom-de-plume* of 'Ik Marvel' (*see Literature*). A dirt driveway (L), 46.7 *m.*, leads to the *Old Bailey House* (*private*), built about 1790, a small gambrel-roofed house where Ik Marvel wrote his fantasy 'Dream Life,' and south of the highway, at 47.3 *m.*, can be seen the red *Mumford House* of 1769 (*private*), owned by another grandfather of Mitchell, and often referred to in his 'Reveries of a Bachelor.'

At 48.7 *m.* is the junction with State 85 (*see Tour 3A*) at Salem Four Corners.

At 49.4 *m.* (R) stands the *Dolbeare Tavern* (*private*), built about 1780, a gaunt, plain relic of the past.

State 82 now passes through forested country interspersed with wide valleys and rocky ridges.

At 51.4 *m.* is the gambrel-roofed *Bland Tavern* of about 1820 (*private*), encircled by two-story piazzas.

At 51.5 *m.* is the intersection with a dirt road.

Left on this road to *Gardner's Lake*, 0.1 *m.*, not visible from the road. *Minnie Island*, a pine-grown knoll rising from the lake's depths, the State's smallest park (1 acre), is accessible by boats for hire here.

At 54.5 *m.* is the roadside picnic area *By the Brook* (R).

Passing through the outskirts of Norwich, the highway crosses (R) the Yantic River to Norwich.

NORWICH (alt. 100, town pop. 32,438) (*see NORWICH*), 59.5 *m.*, an industrial city.

At Norwich is the junction with State 12 (*see Tours 9 and 1G*), State 32 (*see Tours 9A and 9*), State 2 (*see Tour 1J*), and State 87 (*see Tour 2C*).

Leaving Norwich on State 165, this route, paralleling the Shetucket River, proceeds through the village of Long Society.

LONG SOCIETY (Town of Norwich), 60.7 *m.*, has a name that is descriptive of the physical character of the land apportioned to the early ecclesiastical society. Here lived many of the earliest settlers of the town of Norwich. The plain white *Long Society Congregational Church* (L), originally built in 1726, is the most primitive religious structure in Connecticut. In 1817, the building was moved a few feet forward and repaired. It might easily escape attention, for it is boarded up and looks today like a modern dwelling-house, but inside it has the old box pews of Colonial days.

The small brick structure with stone trim (E), across the road, is reputed to be the *Oldest Brick Building* in Connecticut. The exact date of construction is unknown, but records show the building was standing in 1744. According to tradition, the bricks were supplied by one of the three brickyards which were in operation in the vicinity in the early days. The building, 14 × 20 feet, to which a white wooden ell has been added, once contained a large fireplace which was uncovered when repairs were made. The *Old Yellow Building* (R) was once a toll house in the early turnpike days.

PRESTON CITY (alt. 180, town pop. 3928), 64.5 *m.*, is a village with a misleading name. The 'city' is but a small hamlet, consisting of the *Baptist Church* (1815, 1832), and a group of neat white houses amid the rolling fertile fields and upland pastures of an agricultural district; the scattered settlement is scarcely noticed by the hurried tourist. On the east corner stands the *Treat Tavern* of 1730 (*private*), and on the southeast corner, surrounded by a high picket fence the *Calvin Barstow Homestead* (*private*), built in 1785, with a projecting front pediment frequently found in the eastern part of the State.

Bay Mountain (alt. 560 feet), 69.6 *m.* (R), is one of the highest points in this southeastern Connecticut lowland. Eastward, the road crosses the southern end of the main expanse of *Pachaug Pond*, a sizable body of clear water.

At 70.3 *m.* is the intersection with a tarred road.

Left on this road a very short distance, to the unkempt village of GLASGO (Town of Griswold), named for Isaac Glasko, of mixed Indian and Negro blood, who developed an extensive business in marine hardware (1806) and furnished whaling implements to all New England ports.

State 165 crosses an arm of Pachaug Pond and enters the village of Voluntown.

VOLUNTOWN (alt. 260, town pop. 651), 72.4 *m.*, is in an area originally divided into homesteads for volunteers of King Philip's War; it later became active in the manufacture of cotton thread. With the decline of the textile industry in New England, only one small silk braid factory has survived, and the village has become an isolated countryside community.

At 72.9 *m.* is the junction with State 95 (*see Tour 9B*).

Here (L) at the junction stands the *Robbins Tavern* (*open*), where Washington stopped. The old ballroom, along with much of the interior, is now despoiled of its paneling.

From Voluntown this route continues east on State 138 and passes through the timber and brook region of the *Pachaug State Forest*, the largest area in the State now undergoing reforestation. Excellent trout brooks run through this district. The highway crosses the Rhode Island Line at 76.2 *m.*, at the southern end of *Beach Pond* (L), 32.7 miles southwest of Providence, R.I.

T O U R   1 E :   *From* JUNCTION WITH US 1 *to* JUNCTION WITH STATE 82, 8.5 *m.*, State 86.

Via Hamburg, North Lyme.
Macadam-surfaced highway.
Usual accommodations.

STATE 86, branching north from a junction with US 1 (*see Tour 1*) at Old Saybrook, traverses a rugged area in the town of Lyme, where much of the tranquil life of the past has been preserved, where noted artists sketch beside the country roads, and writers rejoice in place names such as Blood Street, Tantomorantum Brook, Whalebone Creek, and Cape Horn. Many tidal inlets indent the bank of the Connecticut River to the west, furnishing anchorage for pleasure craft and fishing boats in season. Along the old landings, nets are often hung to dry during the shad run. A dealer in raw furs hangs his shingle beside the road. Duck guns boom in the marshes when frost comes to the lowlands and the pungent odor of wood smoke hangs in the air.

At 3.4 *m.*, is the junction with an oiled gravel road.

1. Right on this road to BILL HILL, 0.7 *m.*, where many old houses have been carefully restored by new owners, who include Dr. Frank Schlesinger, Director of Yale Observatory, Frank Bell, lecturer of the Christian Science Church, and Henry Hull, stage and screen star.

The road leads to *Rogers Lake*, 2.2 *m.*, where numbers of summer cottages have been built along the pleasant shore.

2. Left at the junction, 0.2 *m.*, to (R) the *Deacon Richard Ely House* (*private*), built in 1710, of simple construction with the exception of a fluted pilastered doorway with rosettes, cross panels and elaborate mouldings, an unusual feature for a door of such age. At 0.7 *m.* is the *House of Ely's Son, Richard* (*private*), built about 1790, with an odd scroll design over the door. Just beyond is the *Samuel Ely House* (*private*), built in 1750, with a handsome leaded fan and Palladian window of later date. At 2 *m.* is *Ely's Landing*, once a busy shipping point.

State 86 climbs a northern slope of Bill Hill, where from the summit is seen a wide view of the Connecticut and Eight-Mile River valleys, with a group of hills — Grassy, Brown, and Nickerson — and Mt. Archer and Candlewood Ledge in the middle distance, and the highlands of East Haddam across the cove in the background.

HAMBURG (alt. 60, town pop. 546) (Town of Lyme), 4.7 *m.*, is a community little changed since early in the 19th century when, in this busy center of shipping and shipbuilding, 100 yoke of oxen and their sturdy carts often crowded the wharf to unload railroad ties and ships' masts cut by scores of sawmills whose shrill whir resounded over the now quiet countryside.

Overlooking the cove from the farther end of a broad spacious Green is the plain little *Congregational Church* (1814), topped with a hip-roofed cupola.

River trips in power or sail boats can be arranged here with any of a dozen boat owners, down the 9-foot channel of the Eight-Mile River past *Joshua's Rock*, scene of the Indian massacre of Captain Stone and his crew, probably the first Englishmen to sail up the Connecticut River; and beyond up the broad sweep of the Connecticut River past *Selden's Neck*, largest island in the 'Great River,' covering 122 acres. Here, extensive ledges and a heavy stand of timber reach to the water's edge; the western shore of the island, beyond which are abandoned island quarries, wide level stretches and high hills, has been purchased for development as a State park. North of the Neck is *Selden Cove*, once an active fishing center and widely known for the lotus lily, or water chinquapin, which occasionally blossoms here. South of Eight-Mile River, in the Connecticut River, beyond Lord's Cove, the State has acquired a considerable acreage of marsh land, providing excellent duck and rail shooting for the benefit of sportsmen.

> Left from Hamburg on a country road, crossing the cove on an antiquated wooden bridge that has been reproduced in the paintings of many prominent artists who have been summer residents of this district. The second house beyond the bridge is (R) the *Captain Johnson House* (*private*), built in 1790, a story-and-a-half gambrel with elaborate doorway and three dormers. Within, an arched central hall passes through the large chimney. The south room upstairs, with a vaulted ceiling, was designed as a main assembly hall for the first Masonic lodge in this region.

State 86 continues past two old houses built by the Marvin family. The plain *Captain Elisha Marvin House* (*private*) at 5.7 *m*. (R), with four windows to the left of the door and three to the right, and an off-center stone chimney, was built in 1738. At 6.1 *m*. is *Captain Timothy Marvin's House* (*private*), an even plainer but symmetrical dwelling. In the cellar is a huge fireplace with a wooden lintel about 15 feet long and 15 × 17 inches thick. The house is now occupied by the school of Guy Wiggins, the artist; during the summer, his pupils, with their easels, are often seen in neighboring fields.

State 86 continues to NORTH LYME FOUR CORNERS (Town of Lyme), 6.7 *m*., where on the northeast corner stands a tall, unrestored *Red House* (R), dating from 1770, with a double overhang. Opposite is a *Hip-roofed Dwelling* (1787) with a huge brick chimney. Near-by is a *Schoolhouse* built in 1760, once red but now painted white.

At 8.5 *m*., 1.3 miles west of North Plain, is the junction with State 82 (*see Tour 1D*).

TOUR 1 F: *From* JUNCTION WITH US 1 *to* JUNCTION WITH US 1, 15.3 *m.*, State 156.

Via Old Lyme, Niantic.

Macadam-surfaced roadbed.

Accommodations of usual kinds at short intervals.

THIS route passes through numerous coastal settlements between the Connecticut River and New London that are not visible from US 1.

At 0.5 *m.* beyond the eastern end of the Connecticut River bridge, this route turns right from US 1 (*see Tour 1*) on State 156, locally called *Rope Ferry Rd.* because it connected with John Winthrop's rope ferry at the Niantic River. Passing the *Trowbridge Estate*, one of the first in Connecticut to plant a roadside garden on the highway outside its walls, the highway crosses the *Lieutenant River*, once crowded with the towering masts of clipper ships and square riggers, and enters the village of Old Lyme.

OLD LYME (*see OLD LYME*), at 1 *m.*, an elm-shaded village steeped in the seafaring tradition, is a rendezvous of many famous artists.

East of Old Lyme, the road proceeds through an underpass at 2.1 *m.* and crosses *Black Hall River*, which takes its name from a cave on its bank occupied by a Negro servant of Matthew Griswold in 1645, and originally called Black Hole — later Black Hall.

State 156 continues through OLD LYME SHORES, where many artists have built homes along the fine sandy beaches.

At 8.6 *m.* is the intersection with a side road.

1. Right on this road is *Rocky Neck State Park Bathing Beach* (558 acres).

2. Left, this side road wends its way over and along *Bride's Brook* to the small park by the same name situated on the property of the *State Farm for Women*, a correctional institution for delinquent women. A tablet on a boulder perpetuates the traditional origin of the brook's name, commemorating a marriage ceremony performed here in the winter of 1646-47, when Governor Winthrop, who had no jurisdiction outside of New London, stood on the east bank of the swollen stream and united in marriage a couple standing on the opposite bank. The legality of the brook boundary was later questioned by the people of Lyme, and in order to save the expense of appealing to the courts in Hartford, both New London and Lyme agreed to abide by the result of a fistic combat between two representatives from each town. As Lyme's champions proved doughtier men, the boundary was moved east to the Niantic River.

Eastward, State 156 borders, then traverses Rocky Neck State Park.

At 8.9 *m.* is the weathered *Thomas Lee House* (*open Wed. and Sun. 11–6, July and August, and by appointment; adm. 25¢, children under 12, free*) (R), one of the most important 17th-century relics in the State. Among the notable early features are the projecting window frames, the cellar steps hewn from solid logs, and traces of an early casement window. Built in 1660, this staunch old house, restored and consistently furnished in keeping with its period, is now maintained by the East Lyme Historical Society. Exhibits include old china, pewterware, and kitchen utensils. Adjacent, and also maintained by the society, is the *Little Boston Schoolhouse* (1734), which was so celebrated for its high scholastic standards that it was named for the early center of culture and learning in Massachusetts.

State 156 passes a roadside picnic area (L), at 9.6 *m.*, and follows a distinctly scenic route, crossing the Pataguanset River at 11.4 *m.*

At 11.6 *m.* is the junction with Lake Avenue.

> 1. Left on Lake Avenue to *Dodge Pond*, 0.5 *m.*, habitat of a variety of aquatic plants.
>
> 2. Right at this junction on a road skirting *Crescent Beach*, admired for its very white sand. At the southern end of this beach, Black Point, 3 *m.*, the coast abruptly rises to a rocky cliff, presenting an unusual contrast. Balancing on the edge of this height is a huge rock, 17 feet long, of which the natives have for generations observed, 'A mighty no'easter would topple it into the bay.'

NIANTIC (Town of East Lyme), meaning 'point of land,' 12.1 *m.*, at the western end of a long bridge over the Niantic River, is the center of many summer colonies scattered along the beaches and banks of the river, and of an active scallop fishing industry, which, since the 17th century has been the means of livelihood for many of the townspeople. During the cold and windy winter days these hardy fishermen present a fascinating picture, dragging the bed of the estuary with their heavy nets from dawn until dusk. At low tide, sand and silt flats — excellent clam beds — are visible along the sides of the channel.

> Left at the hotel, on Oswegatchie Hill Rd., is the *State Military Camp*, 0.3 *m.*, which maintains a landing field for airplanes.

East of Niantic, State 156 passes a sheltered yachting anchorage, and crossing the Niantic River, reaches the village of Jordan at 14.8 *m.*, at the head of tide water on Jordan Creek. On the country roads south of the village are a number of 17th-century houses. In contrast is the extensive *Harkness Estate* with its famous gardens (*private*) on Great Neck Rd. State 156 rejoins US 1 (*see Tour 1*) at 15.3 *m.* (1.7 miles west of New London).

T O U R   1 G :   *From* GROTON *to* NORWICH, 14 *m.*, State 12.

Via Gales Ferry.
Macadamized highway.
Limited accommodations.

STARTING from Groton, at the junction with US 1 and State 84 (*see Tour 1; see Tour 1H*), this tour traverses the Thames River Valley from Groton to Norwich.

At 2.5 *m.* is the *U.S. Navy Atlantic Submarine Base* (*open daily; guides provided upon application to the sentry at the gate*), a Government reservation where 130 officers and 636 seamen of the Navy receive special training for submarine service. A conspicuous feature of the reservation is a 135-foot tank where submarine crews are instructed in methods of escaping from disabled submarines by the use of the mechanical 'lung,' a device which supplies air to the escaping man as he floats upward to the surface. At the base of this tank, which contains one quarter million gallons of salt water, is a compartment resembling the conning tower of a submarine from which future submarine crews make practice 'escapes' up through 100 feet of water.

From this point is an unobstructed view of the Thames River as it winds northward and widens southward to its mouth. Opposite, on the crest of the ridge on the western bank, are the granite buildings of *Connecticut College* (*see NEW LONDON*), and south of the college, the red brick buildings of the *U.S Coast Guard Academy* (*see NEW LONDON*). The annual Yale and Harvard boat races take place along this section of the river in the month of June.

Beyond the Submarine Base is Long Cove at 5 *m.* and Mill Cove at 5.1 *m.*

Left at 5.8 *m.* is a group of buildings called *Red Top*, the training quarters of the Harvard crew.

At 6.1 *m.* is the Gales Ferry crossroad.

1. Right on this road, past the Community Church (L) and around a curve (R), at 0.3 *m.*, stands (R) the *Trout Brook Cottage* (*private*), built by Jonathan Stoddard in 1796, on the slope of a high wooded hill. Up a slight rise on a driveway (R) at 0.7 *m.*, is the *Lawrence Minor House* (*private*), with unpainted shingles, lean-to and front porch, shaded by elms and a beautiful juniper. Numerous legends linger around this old dwelling, popularly known as 'Ruddy Gore.' The date of its construction — 1785 — is marked on the chimney.

Left from this Gales Ferry Rd. at 1.6 *m.*, on a macadamized road, and again left at 1.8 *m.* on a gravel road. A few feet up the gravel road a steep driveway leads up a hill. A sign directs the visitor to park his car and proceed on foot to the *Larrabee Oak*. At the end of the driveway is a large white house (*private*), *Birthplace of the Hon. William Larrabee* (1832–1912), twelfth governor of Iowa and a pioneer in railroad legislation. Through a turnstile in the yard, down a woods path, 0.3 *m.*, an enormous oak stands alone in a clearing. This giant, known as the *Larrabee Oak* and '*Friend of Lafayette*,' with a spread of 182 feet, a height of 85 feet, and a girth of 25 feet, is one of the oldest and largest oaks in Connecticut.

2. Left at the Gales Ferry Crossroads is the riverside village of GALES FERRY (Town of Ledyard), 0.1 *m.*, named for the proprietor of the first ferry across the river at this point. Neat white houses and shady lawns stretch along the embankment overlooking the Thames River. Two shipyards were located here in the 18th century, using timber from the near-by forests.

Two houses west of the railway underpass is (R) the *Ichabod Cottage*, said to have been used as a training school by Decatur when he was blockaded here in 1812. A left turn at the end of the main street leads past a long, low building (R), the

Training Quarters for the Yale University crews, who spend several weeks here each spring in preparation for the Yale–Harvard boat races which are held on the Thames River, late in June.

At 6.6 *m.*, on a sharp curve, is the junction with a steep path.

Left on this winding path to the hilltop where *Fort Decatur* stood, now marked with a stone tablet. On this site Commodore Stephen Decatur, naval hero of the war with Tripoli, built a fort (1812) to protect his blockaded ships from bombardment by the British.

Decatur and a prize ship, pursued by a British fleet, had sought refuge in New London Harbor and retired up the river for safety. Months passed, but the watchful British frigates constantly patrolling the mouth of the river seldom relaxed their vigil. Finally, after careful planning, Decatur's ships, stripped for action, were ready one dark night to steal quietly down stream on a fair wind in the hope of surprising the British. But 'anchors aweigh' had not yet been ordered when mysterious blue lights gleamed from the eastern hills and a large British fleet hastily stretched out across New London Harbor, cutting off all possibility of escape. Thereafter, 'Bluelights' became the local nickname for Tories.

At 7 *m.* is the junction with a dirt road.

Left on this road, 0.5 *m.*, on the river bank is ALLYN'S POINT (Town of Ledyard), once an important shipping center before the days of the shore line railroad, although nothing remains to indicate the fact except coal docks.

State 12 reaches a junction with a dirt road at 8.2 *m.*

Right on this road is (L) the oldest house in Ledyard, the *Avery Homestead*, 1.9 *m.*, built by Deacon Morgan (about 1700–25), a salt-box house with a rear roof so high that there is room beneath it for tiny second-story windows. The wide 18-inch cornice overhang of this dwelling is similar to that of early houses in Lebanon and New London.

At 3 *m.* is a junction at a crossroad.

1. Right from the crossroads a few yards is the hamlet of LEDYARD (alt. 190, town pop. 1144, sett. 1653, inc. 1836), named for Colonel William Ledyard, commander of Fort Griswold at Groton, who was slain by the British at the battle of Groton Heights.

On the short, almost deserted main street are the white *Congregational Church* (1843) and the *Bill Library*, which is open only one hour a week (*Sun. directly after church services*), when the townsfolk gather from their scattered farmhouses. Within the township live about 100 descendants of the original Rogerine Quakers, a group organized in 1674 under the leadership of John Rogers of New London, who established themselves in the southeastern part of Ledyard. In the early days, this group asserted violent opposition to the Congregational Church and in the 18th century were so zealous that the Congregationalists were seldom able to conduct a service without an interruption by Quaker hecklers. The Quaker men stood beneath the windows making loud noises, and the Quaker women often carried their spinning wheels into the church and proceeded to work in the midst of the service as a protest against the established sanctity of the Sabbath.

The descendants of the group still live apart from the life of the community, adhere to their own views even when they conflict with the law, and have an inherited distrust of the world and worldly things. Intermarriage has been general.

Many strange tales have come out of this region. One about Jemima Wilkinson, who founded Penn Yan, N.Y., is the most interesting. Jemima, an eccentric lady with a mind of her own, died sometime between 1770 and 1790. Her Ledyard neighbors dutifully gathered about the coffin to pay their last respects to the departed vixen. The weeping was loud and insincere, as a friend lifted the lid of the coffin to let relatives and friends gaze a last time on the face of one whom they were not sorry to see pass on to another world. Jemima, however, had other plans. As the coffin lid was raised, the slender lady arose from the pine box and announced to the startled congregation that she would do the preaching herself that day! Claiming that she had passed through the gatesʲof a better world and had been sent back to earth as a second Redeemer, the impassioned Jemima preached that the day of her resurrection was to mark the regeneration of the world.

When the news spread throughout the surrounding countryside, work was set aside; farmers hitched up their wagons and with their entire families rode into town to see for themselves the living proof of a miracle in their midst. For some time Jemima's exhortations attracted large congregations, until her neighbors began to whisper that 'Jemima always had been queer.' Then she and a few converts moved on to fresh fields in Tioga County, Pa., where an enthusiastic sect of 'Jemimakins' gathered around her standard. Impelled to spread their tenets, the entire colony later moved to New York State, carrying Jemima through the woods in a resplendent chariot drawn by her proselytes.

Settling in Yates County, they called their first community 'The City of Jerusalem.' When a post office was needed and a shorter name for it seemed desirable, they chose Penn Yan, for the two factions who made up the congregation, the Pennsylvanians and the Yankees. Thus a Connecticut woman preacher named a New York State town.

2. Left from the crossroads on a road alternately graveled and macadamized, stands a well-preserved example of an early 19th-century *Store*, 0.8 m. Across the street is the *Tavern of Henry Bill* (about 1800) whose popularity is attested by the large number of hitching-post rings in the stone wall. Beyond the store, a lane at 1 m. leads (L) through an old stone wall to a cellar that marks the *Birthplace of the Rev. Samuel Seabury* (1729–96), first Episcopal bishop in America. The future bishop graduated from Yale in 1748, was admitted to orders by the Bishop of London in 1753, and was the first minister at St. James Episcopal Church, New London, where he is buried. Like most of the Episcopal clergy, he was a Tory and at the outbreak of the Revolution, became a British army chaplain. At the close of the war, his fellow clerics asked to have him consecrated as bishop, but the Archbishop of Canterbury refused because of the required oath of allegiance to the King, which Mr. Seabury dared not take. He finally obtained consecration from the non-juring Bishop of Aberdeen, at Aberdeen, Scotland, November 14, 1784.

Right at the next fork on a gravel road that leads up a steep hill to the old *Grey House* (1750), 1.4 m., from the dooryard of which stretches one of the finest views in New London County. Numerous Indian graves have been found on this farm.

At 10.8 m. are the landscaped grounds of the *Norwich State Hospital* (L). Opposite is the junction with a macadam road.

Right on this road which follows the shores of Poquetanuck Cove, is the village of POQUETANUCK (Town of Preston), 1.3 m., a single street with a few old houses, which still retains the aspect of affluence inherited from the bygone days of its thriving maritime prosperity.

The large, red frame *Chapman House* (R), which has a one-story stone foundation, was an inn in Revolutionary days. In the west side of the stone basement two grated windows look out from a dungeon where indiscreet tipplers were imprisoned until able to continue their journeys.

Passing through the village of HALLSVILLE, 2.6 m., a small cluster of houses opposite the Hall Woolen Company, this road intersects with State 2 (*see Tour 1J*).

Beyond the Norwich State Hospital, this route passes the *Norwich County Home* (R) and, skirting Laurel Hill (R), crosses a bridge over the Shetucket River, near its confluence with the Thames River, to the city of NORWICH (*see NORWICH*) at 14 *m.* At Norwich are the junctions with State 165 (*see Tour 1D*), State 2 (*see Tour 1J*), State 32 (*see Tours 9 and 9A*).

T O U R   1 H : *From* JUNCTION WITH US 1 *to* RHODE ISLAND LINE, 16.6 *m.*, State 84.

Via Center Groton, Old Mystic.
Macadamized roadbed.
Accommodations limited.

THIS highway, completed in 1936, is a shorter, though less interesting, route than US 1 between Groton and the Rhode Island Line. Through a sparsely populated region thickly covered with underbrush and third-growth timber, it passes but a few isolated farmhouses and two small village centers, and enters Rhode Island, 39.1 miles southwest of Providence.

North from US 1, 0.3 *m.* east of the eastern approach to the Thames River bridge, State 84 crosses through the small rural community of CENTER GROTON, 3.4 *m.*, little more than a crossroads, with many old weather-worn houses in a distinctly Colonial atmosphere.

At the village four corners stands (L) the *Smith Tavern* (1781) with fluted pilasters and excellent raised paneling.

At 3.6 *m.* is the *Nathan Daboll Homestead*, where the famed almanacs, still printed, were first issued in 1772, and where three generations of this energetic family conducted the Daboll School of Navigation from 1805 to 1873. The one-room ell with a bay window was used as a practice pilot house.

OLD MYSTIC (Towns of Stonington and Groton), 7 *m.*, is at the head of navigation on the Mystic River. Once a busy center of trade and shipping, Old Mystic is now a serene, almost forgotten little village, with many charming old houses, the only remnants of once prosperous seafaring days.

Built against a hill, on a small triangular plot bounded by roadways, is the *Dudley Woodbridge Tavern* (1750) with a gambrel-roofed ell toward the street. In the early 19th century this building was the foremost tavern on the old New London–Providence turnpike.

At the center is an interesting group of small old houses. Across a field (L) is the stone *Hatter's Shop of Daniel Williams* (1798). Close-by is an old wooden structure once used as a tannery. Its date of erection is unknown, but the hewn timbers and hand-made nails indicate its age. Some of the crude machinery for grinding bark is in good working condition, including the great stone crusher, propelled by a long hewn beam to which oxen were yoked. Some of the planks in the flooring are over two feet wide.

Right from Old Mystic on Main St., and second right (opposite a brick factory) on a lane, to the *Christopher Leeds House*, built about 1800, with a gambrel roof and overhang. Near-by is the site of the Leeds ship-yard.

On the side streets of Old Mystic (R) are the remains of the old shipyards which flourished here, launching sloops, three masted schooners, small steam ships, and later 1500-ton vessels for European and California trade.

At 9.8 *m.* stands the *Road Congregational Church*, on a high stone foundation, with its back to the road and entrance at the pulpit end away from the road. Beside it are the old stone hitching-posts and carriage sheds. The present building, erected in 1829, replaced the original building of 1764 which, sighted by the British warships attacking Stonington in 1775, and believed to mark the center of the town, drew their fire, so that cannon balls fell in the woods beyond the village.

Cutting across the town of Stonington, State 84 follows the Pequot Indian trail.

At 13 *m.* is the junction with State 2 (*see Tour 1J*).

At 13.3 *m.*, State 84 crosses the Shunock River and traverses an agricultural region, entering Rhode Island at 16.6 *m.* 1.7 miles southwest of Hopkinton, R.I.

T O U R   1 J :   *From* PAWCATUCK *to* COLCHESTER, 33.6 *m.*, State 2.

Via Norwich.

Macadamized roadbed.

Limited accommodations.

QUARTERING northwestward from the Rhode Island Line, this route crosses stony, rolling pasture lands and brush lots, once a part of the old hunting grounds of the Pequots, and passes through Norwich at the head of navigation on the Thames River. West of Norwich, the route passes mill sites along the Yantic River and climbs out of the brush lands and stony meadows to emerge in Colchester. At Colchester is a junction with State 85, which connects with the northern section of State 2 to form 'The Governor's Road' (*see Tour 3A*).

Near the Rhode Island Line, at the western edge of Westerly, is the village of PAWCATUCK (alt. 20, village pop. 500), 0.1 *m*. Within the Connecticut township of Stonington, this village is really a suburb of Westerly, R.I., separated from the smaller State only by the slowly flowing Pawcatuck River. Its main street, a busy, thrifty thoroughfare, is a lively trading center.

STILLMANVILLE, 0.7 *m*., is a roadside hamlet of frame dwellings.

State 2 passes through open country with scrub woodland along the edge of the highway. At 1.6 *m*. the route rounds a curve where the land falls away eastward toward the Pawcatuck River. Views at this point extend over several huge sand pits, winding country roads, and the low hills of Rhode Island.

Descending a long grade, State 2 becomes a maple-shaded roadway and, beyond, threads its way through a sparsely wooded section, long ago depleted by the loggers who cut oak knees, planking, and masts of pine and spruce for the Mystic River shipyards. The countryside is unpopulated today, except for the occupants of an occasional farmhouse.

Ascending a hill by a long curve, at 3.4 *m*., the route passes the *Deacon Gershom Palmer House* (*private*), at some distance back from the road, a two-story weather-beaten structure dating from 1720, in an elm-lined garden. The elaborately molded door leads to an unusually broad hall. The double summer beams in some of the rooms, the 'tombstone' panels, and slave-dungeon show this to have been an unusual house for its day.

At 3.5 *m*. the highway passes beneath arched maples, planted in uniform, well-spaced rows, which are sometimes tapped for the sap by country children who make their quills of elder and sumach. In early spring these trees are bright with shiny tin buckets hung in soldier rows just below the quills. No commercial maple sugar output is attempted here, but every farm family has ample sweetening for buckwheat cakes throughout the year.

At a large, landscaped rotary, 3.9 *m*., is the junction with State 84 (*see Tour 1H*).

NORTH STONINGTON (alt. 140, village pop. 600), 5.6 *m*., is a cluster of houses close to the road on a series of sharp curves. Just below the center (L) is the *Wheeler House* (*private*), dating from 1820, with odd swags beneath the cornice and between the posts of the veranda. Beyond the center (L) is the white *Congregational Church* (1846), with an open portico and an unusual tower in three stages decorated with bull's-eye paneling. Adjoining the church are the *Wheeler School and Library*, two large granite buildings given to the town in 1889 by the Wheeler family.

Known as 'the town with 98 cemeteries,' largest number in the State, many of which are on the isolated farms of early settlers, North Stonington, settled in 1668, is still one of the least traveled towns in the State, and has many dirt country roads. The district is now chiefly occupied by the scattered farms of the hardy descendants of old Yankee stock.

Actually the town was named for the stony character of the hilly countryside, but an old legend regarding its name persists. Three brothers named Palmerstone, according to the story, fled to this country after the marriage of one brother to a member of the British royal family had provoked royal disapproval. Beset by the ill will that followed them, they decided to change their family name. With solemn ceremony, each of the three, in the presence of the other two, buried a stone on his home property, thus symbolizing their decision to drop the suffix 'stone' from their family name and thereafter to be known as Palmer.

Winding through farm country, the ascending highway affords an impressive view of the ridges to the north. Passing a delightful rustic spot known as *Pine Plantation* (R), 8.7 *m.*, which includes an artificial pond encircled with weeping willows, the route traverses a wooded countryside dotted by many attractive summer homes.

At 9.1 *m.* the maple-lined highway passes the *Hewitt Estate*, beautifully situated on high land surrounded by dense foliage. One house (1811) of the three on the estate, which stretches back from both sides of the highway, is still owned by descendants of the original Hewitt settlers.

At a roadside park, the *Rockery*, 11.1 *m.*, is the junction with a side road.

> Left on this road, at 1 *m.*, *Lantern Hill* (alt. 520) rears its glittering summit of quartz rock. The crystals, sparkling in the sunlight, are seen from the sea, and have been relied upon to guide sailors to ports in southeastern Connecticut. The hill's name is also derived from the fact that Sassacus, the Pequot sachem, maintained a lookout here; and in the War of 1812, a watch that manned the summit lighted barrels of tar to warn the defenders in Stonington of the approach of British vessels. The view from the summit, accessible by footpaths, overlooks Long and Lantern Hill Ponds, and extends east and south to the Atlantic Ocean. At *Long Hill*, to the south, quartz was mined in the early days.
> The winding side road leads past Lantern Hill to *Lord's Pond*, a summer resort (R). On the left is an Indian Reservation, home of eight half-breed Pequots.

At 12.5 *m.* is the *William S. Merrell Company* (L), a birch sawmill on Indiantown Brook. The highway passes an occasional farm with well-tilled fields and a sign swung from the brackets of crude posts offering 'Eggs for Sale' or 'Home Baking to Take Home.' When out of stock, these roadside merchants usually hang a burlap bag over the sign. Sweet corn and berries in season are offered for sale without even a sign to attract the passer-by. A barefoot boy sits in the shade of a giant maple with a bunch of pond lilies, hopefully awaiting a customer, or two little girls hold up a pail of huckleberries and smile at the motorist who applies brakes and backs up to price their wares.

At 13.6 *m.* is the junction with a road (L) to the Pequot Reservation, 3 *m.* (*see Indians*).

The highway passes two picnic areas; the *White Pine Grove Highway Park* (R), at 15.3 *m.*, and the *Preston Highway Park* (L), at 15.5 *m.*

At 15.6 *m.* the view of brick factory buildings housing *Hall Brothers Woolen Mills* (L), in the distance, marks the beginning of the textile area.

At 15.9 *m.* is the junction with a macadam road which branches left to connect with State 12 (*see Tour 9*).

Again passing through brush land the route enters the city of NORWICH (alt. 100, town pop. 32,438), at 18.6 *m*. (*see NORWICH: Tour* 9, *Tour* 1*D*, *Tour* 1*G*, *Tour* 9*A*).

West of Norwich, State 2 crosses the Yantic River, at 21.6 *m*., and enters the small mill village of YANTIC (alt. 120, village pop. 100), at 22.3 *m*.; here is the junction with State 32 (*see Tour* 9*A*).

At 22.7 *m*. are fine *Views of the Lebanon Hills* to the north.

FITCHVILLE (alt. 180, village pop. 200), at 24 *m*., is a neat and prosperous mill town built up around a quilt factory. This village is named for its founder, Colonel Asa Fitch, distinguished patriot of Revolutionary days and a noted philanthropist. The stone schoolhouse, still in use, was one of the Colonel's gifts to the community. In 1750, the old Huntington Iron Works were established here by Nehemiah Huntington and Captain Joshua Abell.

The highway crosses the Yantic River, at 24.1 *m*., and passes the large *Mill* of Palmer Brothers, manufacturers of quilts and comfortables. Built of native granite, shaded by large trees, these mills have an air of unusual permanence.

At 26.1 *m*., GILMAN (alt. 200, village pop. 100) is a streamside hamlet formerly known as Bozrahville where an old (1814) stone mill furnishes employment to the villagers for a part of the year. The mill workers piece out their income by working the land as part-time farmers.

The only blocking dummy made in the United States that will do a 'comeback' after being knocked down is the product of the *Marty Gilman Sporting Goods Company* of this village. A young man with considerable football ability, Gilman went to the State College and attained stardom. During the summer months he had difficulty in finding enough youngsters in the little mill town to offer him an opportunity to practice football, so he devised the first Gilman 'Pyramid,' made of leather and stuffed with shoddy and cotton waste from the Gilman mill. Coaches saw the contraption and liked it; Gilman realized the commercial possibilities, kept his eye on costs, peddled the dummy from coast to coast, played professional football to finance his one-man, backyard industry, and today serves all of the better clubs in the country. Gilman uses the tactics of the Yankee 'pedlar' in his salesmanship, the water-power and shrewd ability of the Yankee mill operator in his manufacturing, and his one-man office is in a building formerly used as a hotel by the owners of the big stone mills on the Yantic River.

At 28.5 *m*. the route passes the *Lebanon Country Club* (L), and enters a rolling upland where farms are of larger acreage and Devon cattle are often seen grazing in roadside pastures. This area is rural Connecticut unspoiled and, although buildings and fences do not show much paint, the country is pleasant and interesting.

At 30.3 *m*. the *Old Bank Highway Park* (R) offers picnic facilities and views of rugged hills at the right and left of the road.

Residents of this district often participate in barn dances, especially just before haying or after the fall harvest. Dimly lit by kerosene lanterns, the great barn floor, smoothed through the years by the thousands of shuffling feet, is alive with merry dancers doing the old-fashioned square dances. Prompters are enthroned in the loft, or stand atop an old fanning mill. Music is furnished by violins, banjos and harmonicas, and the musicians often crowd into a feed or harness room just off the main floor. The Lancers, the Quadrille, Paul Jones, Captain Jiggs, Turkey in the Straw, Pop Goes the Weasel, and many other dances, offer entertainment and pleasure for the customers as well as exercise for the leather-lunged prompter who shouts: 'Get your partners for a quadrille! Four more couples! Two more couples!' until the sets are filled. Typical calls through a number are: 'Right and left six! Salute your partners: first couple lead up to the right, swing four hands halfway around, and right, and left six with your opposite couple! Lead to the next, ladies change, up to the last couple and swing four hands halfway around, and right and left six with your opposite couple! Balance your partners and swing your corners and promenade all!' Commands are given with all the authority of a drillmaster. The prompter taps the floor with his foot and counts the beat of the music. Hayseed and very dusty cobwebs fall from the ceiling onto the perspiring couples, fair faces are flushed, slick hair becomes dark with moisture, and the males rush for the cider jug the moment the last wailing note of the fiddle dies away.

Square dancing 'comes natural' to the Connecticut Yankee. He will dance until dawn and then work in field or woods until darkness and the call to the next barn dance.

COLCHESTER (alt. 340, town pop. 2134), 33.3 m. Entering Colchester the highroad passes through the Jewish quarter of the town, a settlement that has preserved its communal life and religious unity in a way characteristic of Old-World Jewish colonies, but rare in the average American rural town.

At 33.6 m. is the junction with State 85 (see Tour 3A).

MERRITT PARKWAY

The MERRITT PARKWAY, when completed, will be an alternate route from the New York State Line to a connection with Nichols Avenue in the town of Trumbull, a distance of 38.1 m. A by-pass at this point will connect with US 1 at the Washington Street Bridge in the town of Stratford.

This extensively landscaped parkway, a continuation of the Hutchinson River Parkway in Westchester County, New York, will parallel US 1 traversing an unspoiled, rural countryside. Safeguards and restrictions have already been provided which will preserve the natural beauties along the right of way against many of the objectionable features of the Post Road (US 1).

This project is being financed by a Fairfield County Bond Issue of $15,000,000. The Parkway right-of-way now (1938) extends through the towns of Greenwich, Stamford, New Canaan, Norwalk, Westport, Fairfield, and Trumbull, with the exception of some four and a half miles not yet purchased. Grading and paving is progressing over that portion of the Parkway which has been purchased and surveyed. Of the 68 projected structures along the Parkway, such as bridges and crossing eliminations, all but twenty-five have been built, designed, or contracted for.

T O U R   2 :   *From* NEW YORK LINE (*Brewster*) *to* RHODE ISLAND LINE (*Providence*), 114.6 *m.*, US 6 and 6A.

Via (*sec. a*) Danbury, Bethel, Newtown, Southbury; (*sec. b*) Woodbury, Watertown, Thomaston, Plymouth, Bristol, Hartford; (*sec. c*) via South Manchester, Coventry, Andover; (*sec. d*) Willimantic, Brooklyn, Danielson, R.I. State Line.
Alternate sections of water-bound macadam and concrete highways.
Accommodations of all usual kinds.

Sec. a.   NEW YORK LINE to JUNCTION WITH STATE 14, 25.2 *m.*

ENTERING Connecticut from New York State 4 miles east of Brewster, New York, over US 6, this route passes through level country to Danbury, winding up hills to Newtown with its fine views over valleys and rolling hills from the hilltop main street. Passing the northern end of Lake Zoar on the Housatonic, it follows streamside to the Pomperaug and the junction with State 14.

At 1.4 *m.*, the white wooden *Mill Plain Union Church* (L) stands beside the road. An old yellow wooden railway station, of the usual American Gothic design, now serves as a filling station.

At 3.5 *m.* (R) are the *Danbury Fair Grounds* (*see DANBURY*) with yellow barns and exhibition buildings covering a green meadowland bordered by soft or swamp maples. (Fair, first week in October.)

DANBURY (alt. 375, city pop. 22,261) (*see DANBURY*), 5.6 *m.*, is a hat manufacturing center.

Beyond the *State Normal School* (L) on White St., is the junction with US 7 (*see Tour* 4) at 6.7 *m.* At Danbury is also the junction with State 37 (*see Tour 4A*).

Right from Main St., Danbury, on US 202, the winding, twisting road of alternate sections of cement and asphalt, posted at frequent intervals with *20 miles per hour* signs, enters BETHEL (alt. 400, town pop. 3886), 2.8 *m.* Named in 1759 for the Hebrew 'house of God,' and incorporated in 1855, this town had four small hat factories as early as 1793 and hat making is still the principal industry.

At 21 Grassy Plain St. the *Peter Barnum Place* (L), a pre-Revolutionary salt-box house, has been sympathetically restored and is the best preserved of the town's old houses.

As the Bethel Parish of Danbury, the village took an active part in the Revolutionary War. When Tryon's British force marched through on April 26, 1777, en route to raid the military stores at Danbury, a local patriot made a single-handed attempt to block their progress and almost succeeded in stampeding them when he fired on the advance guard and shouted orders to an imaginary force in a roadside woodlot.

The *Farnam Tavern* (1760) (*private*), high on a bank, 245 Greenwood Ave., is a rather modernized, white, two-chimneyed house in which the ballroom and fiddlers' box are still intact.

The *Bethel Library*, a simple, tall-columned Greek Revival house, at 189 Greenwood Ave. (US 202), was the birthplace of three college presidents, Julius Hawley Seelye (1824–95) (Amherst), the Rev. Laurenus Clark Seelye (1873–1910) (Smith), and Laurens P. Hickox (1798–1888) (Union). This building is locally known as the Seelye Place.

At 55 Greenwoods Ave. is the *Birthplace of Phineas T. Barnum*, premier showman of his day, who was born here July 5, 1810 (*see BRIDGEPORT*).

The small village Green has the usual soldiers' monument. Along the narrow main street many assorted shops cater to a rural trade and to the commuters who park their cars on the quiet side streets and entrain for New York every morning.

Beyond Bethel, the rolling terrain on both sides of the highway supports many upland game birds and white-tailed deer. The highway passes several typical one-room country schoolhouses, their windows usually gayly decorated according to the season, with yellow pumpkins, black witches, Christmas wreaths, or spring flowers.

Along the way are many kennels and nurseries that cater to the passing trade and to the new ruralists who have bought Connecticut homes to escape high metropolitan taxes. The toy breeds and medium-sized dogs are favored hereabouts; cocker spaniels and wire-haired fox terriers are most in demand. Nurseries grow dwarf evergreens, lawns are green blankets of velvet, houses usually have a fresh coat of paint, and the countryside is clean and free from billboards.

At 7.7 *m.* US 202 enters DODGINGTOWN, a crossroads hamlet named for the many drovers, horse-traders, and peddlers 'on the dodge,' who congregated at the crossroad taverns. Beyond, at a rotary traffic circle, 10.2 *m.*, the route turns left into Newtown and climbs the hillside main street past the *Parker House* (L), where meals are served in a low-ceilinged dining-room profusely decorated with antique glassware, harnesses, old prints, and hardware.

At 10.6 *m.* in Newtown, is the junction with US 6 (*see below*).

US 6 proceeds to the top of *Snake Hill*, with views of hills where stone walls separate upland pastures from huckleberry lots and snake fences enclose meadows. The land is not fertile, but there is some charm in its rough, bushy, stony slopes; the stone walls testify that early Yankees had to clear stone from most of these fields before even an ordinary crop of buckwheat could be raised. The usual day's work of a layer was two rods per day, the farmer furnishing a team and helper. These men never picked up a stone unless they had a place to put it; their work was usually a side line, handled after the crops were gathered or before the spring plowing.

On the hills above Newtown, plantings of evergreens (R) shield country mansions from the prevailing (NW) winds.   At 13.1 *m*. are fine views of the western hills.

At 14.1 *m*., US 6 enters NEWTOWN (alt. 560, town pop. 2635) on Main St. Purchased from the Indians in 1705, named a 'New Town,' incorporated in 1711, the area soon attracted settlers from near-by villages. Although notorious for its Tory leanings during the Revolution, Newtown entertained both Rochambeau and Lafayette.

On the rural main street lined with many sedate country homes, are several public buildings given to the town by Miss Mary Elizabeth Hawley. Among them is the *Edmond Town Hall* (1930), which includes a moving picture theater, an auditorium, a completely outfitted kitchen, a post office, a probate court, bowling alleys and a gymnasium, as well as offices for public officials.

At the Center (R) is the *Congregational Church* (1818), topped by a bullet-pierced weathercock preserved from an earlier structure. French troops who passed through the town in 1781 and 1782, used this weathercock as a target. The parish of the shapely stone *Episcopal Church* (L), was built in 1870; it is one of the earliest in this part of the State and was served by the Rev. John Beach for 50 years from 1732.

Turning sharp left at the Center, US 6 passes the country printing establishment of the *Newtown Bee*, a rural weekly that carries more advertising than any Connecticut publication in its class.

At SANDY HOOK, 15.6 *m*. is the junction with State 34 (*see Side Trip off Tour 5*).

Across the bridge at Sandy Hook, this route turns sharp left and passes through a hemlock glen at 16.8 *m*., where the Pootatuck (L) splashes over a ledge and a milldam, on its way to join the Housatonic. White cottages with blue shutters border the highway, half hidden among the hemlocks.   In this glen are many mills, some of them manufacturing fire hose, others producing molded products of phenol resin compositions.   Here Nelson Goodyear, a brother of the discoverer of the process of vulcanizing rubber (*see NAUGATUCK*), manufactured rubber coats as early as 1851.

Across a steel bridge, 17.2 *m*., which spans the waters of Lake Zoar, is the junction with an oiled dirt road (L), which within 2 miles becomes very rough and narrow.

> Left on this narrow dirt road, following the east bank of the Housatonic River, this streamside, wilderness route follows a Pootatuck Indian trail through a beautiful area seldom visited except by fishermen, hunters, and the rural mail carrier. Flint or quartz arrow-heads are often found in the freshly plowed fields or on the river bank.
>
> Over this route traveled the first white settlers who coveted the rich bottomlands and traded more or less worthless trinkets for them. Stages used this road and ox teams rolled southward over it bringing freight from the back country to tidewater.
>
> At 0.2 *m*., *Muskrat Plains*, across the river (L), fertile flats, formerly productive farmlands, are irrigated during dry weather, and during winter months produce muskrats which furnish a marketable fur crop.

At 1.1 *m.* is the junction with a foot trail.

Right on this trail to a fork, 0.5 *m.*, where a *Cellar Hole* marks the site of the first white settlement in the Pootatuck lands. Here a Mr. Mitchell built a great log house in the wilderness and traded with Indians who passed by on their way to the Pomperaug Valley. In the brush beside the trail, half hidden and elusive, is a pile of small round stones that marks the burial place of an unknown chieftain. Every warrior who passed along the trail placed a stone on the mound as a token of respect and white men have left the pile undisturbed.

At 1.2 *m.*, on a bluff (R) beside the road are the bleached limbs and trunks of a *Pootatuck Indian Orchard.* Iron chains have been effectively used to brace these dead trees against the winter winds that bluster down the valley.

At 1.5 *m.*, under a sycamore tree (L), and now partly washed away by the river, is the only known *Pootatuck Cemetery* in Connecticut. The red men picked a bend in the river for their burial place, where there are open stretches of water to the north and south. The Mitchell family, first white settlers, agreed to keep this ground inviolate, but a representative of the Peabody Museum, New Haven, discovered the cemetery and removed many valuable relics during the dark of the moon. Discovered, this gentleman refused to leave the work of excavation. The community rallied in defense of the spot, posted sentries with shotguns around the area, and finally secured a restraining order on the technical grounds that it is illegal to open a grave. The museum thereupon abandoned excavation and townsmen immediately carried in many tons of stone to protect the burial place. Only the spring freshets and ice from the river violate this ground today, but a skull or leg bone is occasionally seen when the river undercuts the bank. Probably the best collection of Indian relics in the Peabody Museum came from this spot; a skull, a stone war-club head, and a tiny stone pipe were found here after the flood of 1936.

At 1.7 *m.*, shaded by giant sugar maples are the three comfortable homes (R) of Pootatuck's present day inhabitants. The *Warren Mitchell House* (1787) (R), has been remodeled and improved until little remains of the original except the massive oak timbers and the Roxbury granite of the foundation. In front of the great house, a carefully groomed lawn extends across the road to the very river's edge. On the other side of the river, towering high above the laurel, are giant hemlocks that have probably seen many flotillas of birch-bark canoes float past, en route to the salt-water shellfisheries on Long Island Sound. Today, a snug, self-sufficient little community is surrounded by productive acres of deep, rich loam. Squire Mitchell, respected citizen and thrifty farmer, directs a State-wide milk producers' co-operative from his office in the old house.

Along this stretch of river, fishermen often net German carp, which are shipped in large tank-trucks for the Jewish trade in New York City. The carp boats are sturdy craft, propelled by oars, with big three-legged derricks at the stern to handle a large dip net.

Nate Everitt is a local trapper who carries his gear and raw pelts on his back. Nate always has time to relate tall tales of the habits of mink and otter, or he may invite the visitor to inspect the huge bullfrogs he keeps in his cellar.

Passing the Mitchell Farms, the gravel road, protected by an old rustic guard rail, enters a wooded gorge. From the river rapids and deep pools, a good string of trout may be caught in season.

LITTLE YORK, 3.9 *m.*, was the scene of considerable activity when eel racks were operating here and the mills were busy. Only one house remains, although a few woodsmen and trappers have cabins in the area.

At 4.1 *m.* the road parallels a series of great cut-stone mill-races. A rusted iron flume leads to a *Stone Dam* (R). There is no record of either the mill owner or the origin of the placename. The brook that fed the millpond is locally known as the 'Jack Smith Brook' but nobody in this neighborhood remembers Mr. Smith or any of his family.

At 4.3 *m*. is an *Old Tavern* (R), now a summer residence. Open carriage sheds stand just off the wheel track, square and ready for use.

At 4.8 *m*. the Shepaug River flows beneath a narrow iron bridge and joins the Housatonic. There are miles of State-leased trout waters on the Shepaug, where brown, rainbow, and native brook trout are plentiful. Along the river bank trailing arbutus buds beneath the snow and blooms with the first warm spring sun.

At 5.5 *m*., just across the Housatonic (L), lively *Pond Brook* splits the very center of a hemlock glen, roaring in with spray-flecked waters from Hanover Springs, and *The Dingle*, a beautiful wooded spot to the west. Trout run up this brook from the river to spawn in the quiet pools of The Dingle.

At 5.8 *m*. black-and-white signs are tacked on tree-trunks to inform the traveler that he is passing through 'Private Lands.' Masked by a grove of evergreens at the hilltop is the main house of *Three Rivers Farms* (R), a secluded retreat that produces milk for the New York market. A cable car swings over the Housatonic at this point, transporting live stock to the opposite hill pasture in a manner suggestive of the old cash-carrier systems in city stores. The car is lowered to ground level, a cow steps aboard and is fastened in, the car is then raised and pulled across the river where green pastures await. Cattle seem to enjoy the ride to the far bank, but visitors gasp as the bovine ferry is raised high and then coasted down the slack cable. Farmhands are refused transportation on the cableway, and have to travel north to cross the river at the Southville Bridge.

The valley broadens at this point and many stone walls among the second-growth timber indicate former agricultural efforts. An occasional stand of sugar maples or a lilac bush beside the road marks the site of a former farmhouse. Exploration at such points usually uncovers an old cellar hole and a neglected herb garden or berry patch. An iron kettle or even an ancient crane or huge door latch is sometimes found in the trash in the bottom of the cellar hole. Along some of the grass-grown walks are decorative borders of pure white silica or rose quartz; residents of this area once enjoyed a part-time income from the mining and grinding of silica. Perfect garnet crystals are often discovered in the wheel tracks, where refuse from an old dry garnet mill has been used to fill the chuckholes.

At 7 *m*. is SOUTHVILLE, a ghost town where hats and paper were manufactured until the late 19th century. Several rickety houses remain, tenanted by poor Negro and white families who anticipate new activity in the valley when the power company builds its Southville Reservoir. Only the foundations and the flumes remain on the millsites; quail whistle from the neglected meadows and a weatherwise groundhog fattens on wild clover.

At this point is a junction with State 25 (*see Tour 4B*). Straight ahead the rocky old Indian trail continues through an amazingly beautiful countryside to Lovers' Leap at Stillriver, but cannot be followed by a modern car. Hikers, riders, and owners of Model T Fords still travel the winding road and report good fishing and hunting to the north.

Lake Zoar stretches along the right of the highway for a mile and a half. A forested cliff across the water dips down to the shore where hemlocks rise from the water's edge. This lake is a widening of the Housatonic River made by the backing up of waters from Stevenson Dam downstream, where a hydroelectric plant produces current for the industrial area in the valley of the Naugatuck, just over the ridge to the east. There is fine fishing here in season, and cottage colonies spread along shore among the hemlocks. Boating is a popular summer pastime; many bright canoes are to be seen, and only a few noisy motors are heard.

At 19.1 *m*. is the junction with a dirt road where a sign points the way to CHURAEVKA (Russian village).

Left on this road, 0.2 *m.*, is a hillside colony of 35 landowners, who, prior to the Russian Revolution, were members of the Imperial Army. The late Count Ilya Tolstoi with Grebenshchikoff, novelist and lecturer, founded this colony about 1920.

A red-gabled building of curious construction, visible from the main highway and standing a short distance from the Russian village road, is the *Latas Printing Establishment*, headquarters for the publications written by White Russians in this country.

A small *Church*, characteristically Russian, stands among the trees almost at the top of the hill, its dome and colorful façade alien to the New England countryside. The buildings of the community are of simple construction and living conditions are extremely poor as judged by American standards. Gathering around their samovars, these people relive days of former Russian glory in their little homes on the Connecticut hillside.

At 19.9 *m.* (R), easily seen from the highway, is a large trap-rock boulder or *Glacial Erratic*, evidently brought down from the trap-rock ridge to the north during the Ice Age. On the eastern hilltop at this point, in a section known as Kettletown, the German-American Bund purchased wooded acreage in 1937, with the object of establishing a camp. The proposal created such a stir in the peaceful little community that even the newsreels took note. The town council passed an ordinance prohibiting military drilling in that section, and the camp project was abandoned.

At 20 *m.* is the junction (L) with State 172.

Left on this road is SOUTH BRITAIN, 1 *m.*, a tiny riverside community apparently without an industrial, political or economic worry. Facing a small green stands a graceful white church (1825) with a tall spire rising in three stages above a pedimented façade. The Pomperaug flows through the center of the town, the village forum meets at any one of three stores, the town preacher stands by to act as umpire over the checkerboard, and youngsters fish for trout from the bridge at the edge of the town.

At 20.8 *m.* the highway dips across Cedar Hollow with views of hemlocks and the Pomperaug River (L). Riverside cottages are clustered in an area known as *Cedarland*.

Just off the highway in a cottage (L) beside a glacial knoll, encircled with a cedar fence made without use of nail or wire, an old Indian fighter, veteran of campaigns against the Sioux and northern Cheyenne, spends his declining years. This old, one-eyed cavalryman still talks reminiscently of Tongue River Reservation and winter campaigns in the Powder River country. He has served the town well as constable, and today can cut the spot out of an ace with a service pistol at twenty-five yards.

At 21.7 *m.* is the junction with State 67, which combines with this route for 1.5 miles.

Right on State 67 past the Southbury *Town Pound* (L), 0.2 *m.*, a railed enclosure where stray livestock is impounded until bailed out by its owner. Near-by is a fine example of an undershot waterwheel (L), at 0.4 *m.*, that turns a generator for a local resident who refused to purchase electrical energy 'as long as there is water in South Bullet Hill Brook.'

The mass of *Kettletown Hill* (alt. 600), rises (R) at 0.5 *m.*, a surprisingly large hill when the purchase price — one kettle — is considered.

SOUTHFORD (alt. 490) (Town of Southbury), 3.1 *m.*, is a cluster of houses and a store, where the milk truck's arrival every morning is the event of the day.

Right from Southford, 0.5 *m.*, on State 188 to the *Southford Falls State Park* where the site of the former Diamond Match Company factory has been purchased by the State and converted into a recreational area of exceptional charm. The fire that destroyed this plant left the hamlet without a payroll.

Southward on State 188, 3 *m.*, is QUAKER FARMS (Town of Oxford), settled in 1680; here the stately *Episcopal Church* (1812) thrusts its white spire through the treetops. Its windows, including the Palladian over the entrance, are pointed in the Gothic fashion.

On the hilltop (L), from which wide views are obtained, the *Oxford Fire Tower* is seen across the fields. The highway itself, at the crest, is an excellent vantage-point. Dutch roofs are conspicuous through this locality. At 4.7 *m.* a wind-twisted, gnarled oak shades the roadside, and the very old *Tomlinson House* (R), with an exceptionally wide cornice overhang, tops the hill at road's end, 4.8 *m.*, where there are fine views north and west.

Straight ahead through Southford; State 67 passes through RED CITY, 5.2 *m.*, in which every house was formerly painted a bright red. Ambrotype and daguerreotype cases were produced here for many years.

OXFORD (alt. 360, town pop. 1141), 6.1 *m.*, is a village in an agricultural town where rough land makes farming difficult. Yankee farmers are gradually giving way to Poles who are apparently able to obtain better results from submarginal land. Woolen yarns were once manufactured here, and considerable export trade was carried on with the West Indies. A *Congregational Church* (1795) modernized about 1840, a small old *Episcopal Church*, and several early 19th-century dwellings give Oxford a sleepy, old-time atmosphere.

At 8.3 *m.*, on State 67, is the junction with Moose Hill Road.

Right on this road, 0.1 *m.*, is an old sawmill (R) that still operates in a picturesque setting on Little River.

Several old stone dams at former mill sites are along State 67 as it follows Little River into SEYMOUR, 10.2 *m.* (*see Tour* 5), at the junction with State 8 (*see Tour* 5).

SOUTHBURY (alt. 260, town pop. 1134), 22 *m.*, was settled by pioneers from Stratford, who came up the Housatonic and Pomperaug Rivers in 1673, and incorporated in May, 1787. Many of the houses built by early settlers are still in good condition. An air of quiet and comfort pervades the village. Residents sell their land only after careful consideration of the qualifications of the buyers. Having been admitted with such caution, the newcomers soon feel the community spirit and are thereupon absorbed into the local picture. The main street is simply a thoroughfare lined with homes, as there are no industries in this part of the town. The district school still functions here; there is but one physician, and one regular clergyman; the rural fire department has a pumper too large for use in the average brook in the vicinity. Devon oxen are often seen along the roads drawing loads of hay from the fields to the great barns.

The first of the group of large 18th-century Hinman houses, that line the broad Southbury street, stands behind heavy trees on the right just after making the turn. It was built about 1770 by Charles Hinman, one of four brothers who built their houses at intervals of half a mile. This is a central-hall house with double overhang and notable for its excellent paneling, a little of which can be seen in its unusual door frame.

The *Congregational Church Parsonage* (R), built about 1805 by Harry Brown, drover, has gouged flutings in the cornice that are a good example of the decoration of the period. This building and the almost identical *Timothy Hinman House*, opposite, have broad paneled open porches which are among the best of the type for which Southbury is famous.

The red-brick *Bullet Hill School House* (L), one of the oldest school buildings in continuous use in New England, was built of brick baked in a near-by meadow. A sign on the masonry is marked 1778, but local records indicate that the building was completed before the outbreak of the Revolution. Cass Gilbert, the architect, regarded the walls of this building as the finest existing example of early brick work.

Near the center of the village are the *Methodist Church* (L), a plain white building which was built in 1840, the stone *Episcopal Church* opposite (R), dating only from 1858, and (L) the *Congregational Church* (1844), with a recessed Ionic porch and floral scrolls in the pediment.

A *Field-stone Tower* (L) marks the site of the first church in this area, now known as White Oak. Across the way are the substantial homes of the Hinman family, painted chrome yellow with white trim.

Poverty Hollow (L), 23 *m.*, backed by the ridge of *Bates Rock*, offers vistas of fertile meadowlands reaching to the very edge of the Pomperaug River. Wallace Nutting, author and photographer, sketched and photographed here; the rail fences and apple trees of the district are pictured in his book, 'Connecticut Beautiful.'

At 23.2 *m.* is the junction (L) with State 67 (*see Side Trip off Tour 4B for connecting route to Roxbury*).

Opposite the junction is the *Colonel Increase Moseley House* (R), described by Cass Gilbert as the most perfect house of its period (about 1805) that he knew. Colonel Moseley, a lumber merchant of Sullivan, Maine, is said to have brought the wood from that State. The open pediment door is the most graceful feature of the house, although all of its detail shows originality.

The brick *Peter Parley House* (R), 23.4 *m.*, was built by Benjamin Hinman for his son Sherman in 1777. It takes its name from the *nom-de-plume* of Samuel G. Goodrich (1793–1860), editor and writer of juvenile literature who lived here for a time. The dwelling is a broad gam-brel-roofed structure displaying a very early Palladian window, and under it a segmental arched Dutch doorway with a circular leaded transom and sidelights. It is now a German Lutheran home for the aged.

At 23.5 *m.* is a shaded Common known as the *King's Land* (L), believed by local people to belong to the British Crown because the town failed to confiscate the property after the Revolution, as was done in other towns; no taxes are paid on this land, no title to it is found in the town records. The land is misnamed, however, because it is within the territory placed under sovereignty of the United States Government by the Peace Treaty of 1783.

Two of the houses of this section are still occupied by the Stiles family, whose ancestors built them. Their finest dwelling is the spacious and dignified *Benjamin Stiles House* (1787) on the bank opposite the King's Land (R). Its hip roof has an indefinable spirited French line, attributed by tradition to an officer of Rochambeau's army who camped near-by six years before the erection of the house and drew up the plans for the builder. It was once the home of President Ezra Stiles of Yale.

At 23.8 *m.* (R) is the large, yellow, gambrel-roofed *Nathan Curtis Tavern* (1754). The barn is one of the few octagonal structures in this area. Beside the house is a stone milldam, which, according to tradition, was in the process of construction when the men were called away to serve in the Continental Army; when the war was over the men returned to work on the massive dam.

At a triangular Green, 25.2 *m.*, is the junction with State 14 (*see Tour 2 Alternate*).

Sec. b. *JUNCTION WITH STATE* 14 *to HARTFORD*, 37.1 *m.*

Poor asphalt roadbed, except between Bristol and Hartford where the surface is of concrete. Speed limits strictly enforced.

Tour 2 Alternate, via State 14, avoiding the heavy traffic in Hartford, is recommended for a smooth, speedy, and scenic cross-State route.

US 6 passes directly through Woodbury and Watertown, two of Connecticut's proud little country communities. The terrain is rugged and rather heavily wooded over a portion of the route. Along the way are both quiet and peaceful villages and industrial communities where ball bearings, locks, and clocks are made. Some stretches of the highway are narrow and slippery in wet weather. The tour by-passes Bristol and Farmington, except for a brief turn through the very northern edge of the former, and enters Hartford over the new 'Farmington Cutoff.'

North from the junction with State 14, 4 miles north of Southbury, US 6 proceeds to the junction with an asphalt road at 0.2 *m.*

> Left on this road, which passes a native *Cranberry Bog* (R) at 0.1 *m.*, through a community of rundown mill-type houses to the *Falls of the Pomperaug*, 0.6 *m.* The wooden mill at the Falls (L) is a former pioneer silk mill converted into a rural machine shop. Beneath the stone dam, the Pomperaug plunges over a series of boulders and between laurel-clad banks into pools and eddies where giant trout lurk. A one-armed game warden keeps tally on the creel. From the hills beyond, guns boom during the upland gamebird season. Children gather baskets of trailing arbutus in the spring, and nuts in the fall, for sale to travelers.

At 0.3 *m.* stands the *Curtis House* of 1754 (L), a much enlarged hostelry of considerable local renown still operated as a hotel. The original sign swings over the walk, as it did when stage drivers pulled into the yard for a mug of flip and a change of horses.

WOODBURY (alt. 350, town pop. 1744), 0.4 *m.*, was originally settled by white men in 1672 and chartered in 1674. Chief Pomperaug was the town's first proprietor and is now believed to rest beneath a boulder on Main St., where a tablet and a 'Private Property' sign have been erected.

The quiet main street, shaded by giant maples and elms, is bordered by many beautiful houses of the Colonial period and five churches. Dairy farming today provides practically all the income enjoyed by Woodbury farmers, but the summer residents furnish part-time employment for local labor not employed in agriculture.

Woodbury contributed freely to the Revolution. Many members of Ethan Allen's force at Ticonderoga came from homes along the banks of the Pomperaug. In all, some 1500 of Woodbury's sons served with the Continental Line and great stores of rations and funds came from this valley. Two noted Civil War generals, Grant and Sherman, traced their lineage to Woodbury families.

On the Hollow Rd. (L), is the *Jabez Bacon House* (1762) with separate slave quarters at the rear. This great white gambrel-roofed mansion has been carefully restored and appears as it did when Mr. Bacon, local merchant prince, lived here and amassed a fortune of some $500,000 during the Revolutionary War. In the small red store beside the Bacon House, Daniel Curtis made German silver trinkets (1806 to 1840) that were sold by the Yankee peddlers. The same building was later used by a tinsmith and the youths of Woodbury congregated there and begged to see his 'tinker's dam.'

Beyond (L), on Hollow Rd., the *Glebe House* (*custodian in an ell at rear; open weekdays* 9.30–5.30; *winters* 9.30–4.30; *Sundays* 9.30–11, 1–5.30; *voluntary contributions*), built by Nathan Hurd in 1745–50, was the home of the Rev. John Rutgers Marshall, a Tory. In this large gambrel-roofed house Dr. Samuel Seabury (*see Tour* 1G) was elected first bishop of an Episcopal diocese in America, March 25, 1783. The Rev. Mr. Marshall, at odds with local patriots, used a secret passage opening into a tunnel that led to the hill, a feature of the Glebe House that seems to indicate that the good man was an engineer as well as a preacher.

The Glebe House, itself a house of unusual distinction, has been carefully restored and is maintained as a shrine by the Seabury Society for the Preservation of the Glebe House. Many of the original furnishings, documents, and fabrics are preserved here, including even a Colonial mousetrap in the kitchen.

At the south end of the Woodbury Green is *King Solomon's Temple*, the Woodbury Masonic Hall (R), dating from 1839. This simple wooden Greek Revival structure is impressively perched at the top of a fifty-foot ledge of traprock.

St. Paul's Episcopal Church (1785), the oldest and, unfortunately, the most remodeled of the Woodbury churches (L), shows a fruitless attempt to make it Gothic with an applied half-timber effect; incongruous stained-glass windows detract from its Colonial appearance. The large house (1771) beside the church was, after 1785, *The Rectory* of the Rev. John Rutgers Marshall. The small ell to which the Tuscan columns were later added is said to date from 1700 or earlier.

The *First Congregational Church* (1817), at the center (L), is an even finer.

simpler example than its neighbor churches. It has a closed octagonal second stage in the belfry, and a steeple instead of the shorter bell-shaped lantern. The balustrades have a lattice pattern of alternating diagonals that lend a lightness to the design. All in good scale, it is one of the best old churches of the State.

At North Woodbury, 1.6 *m.*, is the junction with State 47 (*see Tour 2A*).

North of the junction on a slight eminence the *Congregational Church* (1814) is in unspoiled condition, an excellent example of the finest period of church building. The tower, in three contrasting stages, projects half-way beyond the front wall of the church. An entrance pediment is faced with four reeded Doric pilasters. Conspicuous features of the building are triglyphs repeated in every cornice and four cylindrical reeds with flutes between, in a style frequently found throughout Woodbury. The interior is rich and unspoiled.

> Left from Woodbury Green with its cannon and Soldiers' Monument, on an improved road to *Orenaug Park*, 0.4 *m.*, a wooded traprock ridge donated by a former resident as a town park. A steel tower, rising 60 feet, provides a view of six townships. *Bethel Rock*, a natural stone pulpit on the east side of the park, was the worshiping place of Woodbury's first settlers before they erected a church.

At 5.6 *m.* is the junction with State 61. US 6 turns sharp right, leaving the valley of the Nonewaug River.

> Left on State 61 to BETHLEHEM (alt. 880, town pop. 544), 4.1 *m.* Known as North Purchase when it was bought from the Indians in 1710, the territory was settled in 1734. This typical Connecticut hill town, sequestered from the rush of modern traffic, retains much of its old-time charm. On the Green (L) stands the *Brick Church* (1829) opposite the *Isaac Hill House* (1759), an old post tavern. Here on the Green, one of the first theological seminaries in the country was established by the Rev. Joseph Bellamy in 1750. The Rev. Bellamy (1719-90), born in Cheshire, was pastor of the Congregational Church (Bethlehem) from 1740 to 1790. He wrote many books and was surpassed in influence only by Jonathan Edwards.

At 6.4 *m.* is a large *Cut-Stone House* (L), with a queer observatory atop the hipped roof. Set in a hollow, this house has no view to any point of the compass and the observation tower seems to have been added merely to satisfy the whim of some country squire.

WATERTOWN (alt. 600, town pop. 8175), 8.7 *m.*, dating from a 1780 incorporation, is another one of Connecticut's 'parlor towns.' On Watertown's rolling uplands General David Humphreys (*see Tour 5, ANSONIA*) grazed a part of his flock of imported merino sheep. The strain that he developed came to be regarded as superior, in some respects, to the original stock. Connecticut Red draft cattle, bred in Watertown, found a ready market in other communities. A Watertown factory that grew up in answer to local needs still produces bull rings of superior strength and quality.

John DeForest manufactured palm-leaf hats here in 1825 and, until a few years ago, Watertown Wool Dusters flaunted their varicolored plumes in many New England general stores. Stephen Bucknall began producing hand-made locks in 1840, and the Wheeler and Wilson Sewing Machine

Company, which later moved to Bridgeport to serve world markets from the seaboard, was organized here in 1851.

The Watertown terrain does not lend itself readily to the developing of a long elm-shaded main street as does that of near-by towns, but her citizens have carefully improved the natural advantages. Grouped around the central Green are several interesting houses of the period from 1772 to 1800, some of soft gray Roxbury granite, others of white clapboards with green shutters, each set in landscaped grounds.

At Watertown is the junction with State 63 (see Tour 2B).

> Left from Watertown on Echo Lake Rd. is the *Bishop Tavern* (1800), 0.5 *m.*, now remodeled and distinguished by two rows of dormer windows. This famous old tavern, which formerly stood at the foot of Academy Hill on the Litchfield–New Haven turnpike, was conducted by the spectacular James Bishop, whose activities were once discussed at every fireside in New England. Among his hobbies was the cutting of his 50-acre meadow in one day. Runners were sent throughout the county to notify farmers of the date for the mowing, and few men or boys failed to be on hand. When the sun rose over the eastern hills, long lines of mowers, scythes in hand, stood ready for the rousing blast of the horn. The tedders followed the mowers, with the rakers fast on their heels. By sunset, the field of waving grass was smooth stubble, dotted with great rounded hay cocks. Five meals were served during the day, and plenty of cider, switchel, and New England rum.
>
> Bishop, who also owned a tavern in New Haven, determined one year to cart all of the hay from that meadow in one load to New Haven. An enormous wagon was built for the purpose, bridges along the route were repaired, trees were cut down, and one small building was moved to widen the highway. Twelve yoke of oxen, their yokes decorated with scarlet streamers, pulled the load, on top of which sat a band that played enlivening tunes. Preceded by outriders, and Bishop himself in a shining barouche drawn by a pair of beautiful grays, the cavalcade was greeted by admiring crowds whose accounts of the event have been handed down for generations.

US 6 passes the buildings and campus of the *Taft School for Boys* (L). The original grounds are protected by strong fences and stone walls, but the newer buildings and the golf course are separated from the road only by carefully trimmed hedges.

From Watertown US 6 is a narrow, asphalt highway that twists through mixed hardwood forests following the route of an Indian trail. Grades are gentle and there are frequent curves.

Black Rock State Park (excellent bathing facilities), at 12.3 *m.*, has many fine woodland trails leading through carefully patrolled acres of forest.

THOMASTON, 13.3 *m.* (see Tour 5), is at the junction with State 8 (see Tour 5). From this point US 6 joins with State 8 for 1.2 miles.

At 14.5 *m.* US 6 turns right, leaving State 8, and ascends the sharp grade of Plymouth Hill which requires cautious driving, but a roughened concrete surface partly eliminates the hazard.

PLYMOUTH (alt. 700, town pop. 6070), 15.4 *m.*, is a quiet village at the top of Plymouth Hill. Its streams once turned mill wheels in early clock factories.

Plymouth was first settled as Northbury in 1728, incorporated in 1795, and named for Plymouth, Mass., probably because the first settler, Henry Cook, was a great-grandson of one of the Pilgrim fathers.

Facing the triangle at Main and Maple Sts. is a brick house (1817), once a blacksmith shop that was the original *Blakeslee Ives Toy Factory*, forerunner of the present-day producers of toy electric trains.

Clustered around the Green (L) are: the *Congregational Church* (1838), a rather heavy Ionic building, which contains an original Eli Terry clock whose wooden works often swell and stop after a driving rainstorm; the *Soldiers' Monument*; the *Town Signpost*; the old white clapboarded *Academy* (1820) with an open octagonal belfry; the *District Schoolhouse*; and a new stone *Episcopal Church* (1915).

TERRYVILLE (alt. 700) (Town of Plymouth), 17.7 *m.*, is a manufacturing village where Eagle locks are made. The wooden wheels of an original Eli Terry clock still tick off the minutes in the gable end of the *Congregational Church* (1838) on the left.

The second house west of the church was the *Home of Eli Terry, Sr.*, inventor of the shelf clock (*see Industry, and Tour 5, THOMASTON*), a frame building with exterior walls of vertical smooth sheathing. It is an early attempt to express the Gothic style in wood, an effort that seems artificial today. Here in Terryville, Eli Terry, Jr., for whom the village was named, engaged in the manufacture of clocks (1824). His son, James, developed the first cabinet lock in America, and the Eagle Lock Company, formed by him, long held a monopoly on the product. Another son, a pioneer in the manufacture of malleable iron, organized the Andrew Terry Foundry. These two firms, still in operation, are the main industries of the village.

> Right from Terryville on South St. and left on Tolles Rd. to a junction with Wolcott Rd., 2.5 *m.*; left on Wolcott Rd. to the first intersection and left on that road, 4.1 *m.* Here, to the right of the road in the region known as *Indian Heaven*, is *Jack's Cave*, once inhabited by three old Indians who lived here as late as 1830. The cave, named for the leader of the group, has an entrance corridor 20 feet wide and 10 feet long that leads into a rock chamber used by the Indians as sleeping quarters. Near-by is *Jack's East Cave*, used by the same group of Indians.

At 18.8 *m.* is the junction with the combined US 6A and US 202, which this route travels; it is the better road.

In *Baldwin Park* (L), at the junction, is a memorial to Dorence Atwater, who, taken prisoner during the Civil War and assigned to work in a Confederate hospital, compiled a secret record of 13,000 dead Union soldiers that proved of great value to the War Department for identification purposes.

At 19.6 *m.* is the junction with an improved road.

> Left on this road, 0.8 *m.*, to the extensive plant of the *Bristol Nursery Company*, where an annual chrysanthemum show is held in early October; the nursery gardens blossoming in great blocks of brilliant color are visible from many vantage points on the neighboring hills.

US 6A climbs and descends *Chippens Hill*, the secret gathering-place of Tories in Revolutionary days and scene of the book 'Tories of Chippenny Hill,' by Leroy B. Pond.

BRISTOL (alt. 240, town pop. 28,451, sett. 1727), 20.2 *m*., now an industrial city, early made history with its clock production. As early as 1790, Gideon Roberts was making clocks here and peddling them on horseback. Jerome, Rich, and Ingraham were other early Bristol clock manufacturers, and Joseph Ives, in 1832, produced an eight-day clock with rolled brass works. Jerome's clock shop was the largest in the country and, in 1842, he exported his wares to England. The E. Ingraham Company clock manufactory is conducted by grandsons of the founder, and the Sessions Clock Company is an outgrowth of a business started here by J. C. Brown in 1833. Bristol early expanded as a manufacturing village; clock springs, saws, fishing rods, ball bearings, bells, coaster brakes, silverware, castings, and heavy machinery were soon produced for world trade. At one time a Bristol plant manufactured a very high-priced, high-grade automobile, the Hupp-Rockwell. In the back-country, inaccessible by road, about four miles to the north, a copper mine produced some $200,000 worth of ore between 1847 and 1854.

Moses Dunbar, a Tory resident who provoked local animosities and was charged with high treason, was tried at Hartford and found guilty on January 23, 1777; he was hanged near the spot where Trinity College stands.

At the *Forge Plant* of the New Departure Manufacturing Company (L), developers of the coaster brake and now a division of General Motors, cherry-red bars of high-carbon, high-chrome steel are fabricated into bearings for automobiles.

The *Congregational Church* (1832), on Maple St., opposite Prospect Place, is a combination of Greek Revival and slightly gothicized elements, such as the finials on the square tower. The two-chimneyed *Miles Lewis House* (1801), at 100 Maple St., and the *Hooker House* (about 1815), on Hooker Court, off Riverside Ave., are the best remaining early houses in the center.

At 10 King St. is the *Ebenezer Barnes House* (1728), a former tavern. It is an inconspicuous but interesting house with early side-lights and, within, some rooms with feather edge boarding on walls and ceiling. The original stone-chimneyed house was enlarged by salt-box additions at both ends, and became the Pierce Tavern, an important stop on the Hartford–Litchfield Rd.

Right from Bristol on West St. (State 69), along which are views of the industrial sky line of chimney tops surrounded by a circle of wooded hills. The highest of these hills is *Johnny Cake Mountain*, so named because, according to tradition, residents there lived on 'johnny cake.' At the top of Fall Mountain lies *Cedar Lake* (R), 3 *m*., noted for its fishing. From this point, hunters, working to the east, sometimes stumble onto the lost *Pike's Hill Cemetery* where early settlers from Wolcott were buried. Nothing remains of the cemetery now except a few leaning headstones, overgrown by underbrush, in the dense woods.

At 5.7 *m*., at the top of a hill, is an excellent vantage point for a view of the Mad River Valley and distant hills to the west.

Traversing heavily wooded, rolling country, this route reaches a country crossroads, at 6.6 *m*. Here, screening the *Mad River Falls* from the highway, is the *Pritchard Sawmill* (1748) on a site that might have become a busy industrial center had the conservative town fathers not looked with disfavor upon the plans of a native son, Seth Thomas, to establish a clock factory here. Thomas' petition for water rights was refused and this pioneer in the use of brass instead of wooden clockworks moved to a near-by town where he established a factory which became the largest clock industry in America (*see Tour 5, THOMASTON*).

> 1. Left at the crossroads, 1.2 *m.*, to WOLCOTT (alt. 860, town pop. 972), a secluded village clustered about a hilltop Green. On the Green, the thirsty passer-by can refresh himself with the clear, cold water of a well, dug and stoned up in 1773 by Abraham Wooster.

> 2. Right at the crossroads, 1.5 *m.*, on a winding country road to the *Site of the Birthplace of Amos Bronson Alcott* (1799–1888), who went to Virginia as a 'Yankee Pedlar' with a tin trunk upon his back, but who, because of his dislike for trade, sold his pack at Norfolk for five dollars and established a school. Later he moved to Concord, Massachusetts, where he became a member of the Transcendentalist group and eventually founded the Concord School of Philosophy.

South of the crossroads, State 69 passes through many acres of submarginal farmlands to the junction with a dirt road at 8.3 *m.*

> Left on this road to the *Woodtick Schoolhouse* (*open during summer months, free; key may be obtained from Claude Badger who lives next door*), 0.7 *m.*, built in 1825. This district schoolhouse built of stone has been restored and equipped with old desks, benches, and an antique stove, and is maintained by the Mattatuck Historical Society of Waterbury for occasional exhibits.

At 10.6 *m.* (R), built into the hill beside the road, is *Welton's Stone Wagon Shed*, a great shed of native stone, long a landmark. The face of the shed is a graceful arch, carefully laid without cement or mortar. The Yankee mason hand-dressed the stone and, at the very top of the arch, sculptured a dove, fruit, and other devices.

At 11.2 *m.* is WATERBURY (*see WATERBURY*), in which State 69 follows Wolcott St., and connects with State 14 (*see Tour 2 Alt.*).

At 25.3 *m.* the combined US 6A and US 202 pass the entrance (L) to the *Shade Swamp Game Sanctuary* (*open in daylight hours*), where are many kinds of wild life living in natural cover under natural conditions.

At 26.3 *m.* is a junction, 1.8 miles south of Farmington, with the combined US 6 and State 10 (*see Tour 6*).

> Left on the combined routes with which US 6 unites for 1.8 *m.* to FARMINGTON (*see FARMINGTON*), the home of Miss Porter's School and a residential community.

At Farmington US 6 turns right, leaving State 10 (*see Tour 6*) and US 202.

> At 5.3 *m.* on US 6 (L) is the *Reservoir* of the Hartford Municipal Water Department.

> At 7.3 *m.* the highway passes through wide-awake, residential WEST HARTFORD (*see Tour 3*).

> The highway here becomes a city street, lined with apartment houses and cluttered with traffic lights to slow up the streaming flow of motors to and from Hartford (*see HARTFORD*), at 10.4 *m.*

From the junction at 26.3 *m.*, US 6A, the recommended road, follows what is locally known as the Farmington Cutoff. This straight, well-kept, two-lane concrete highway offers a quick express route, avoiding the heaviest traffic in Farmington and Hartford.

At 33.4 *m.* is residential ELMWOOD, a Hartford suburb.

Traversing New Britain Ave. and Washington St., US 6A enters HART-
FORD (see HARTFORD) at 37.1 m. At Hartford is the junction with
US 44 (see Tour 3), State 175 (see Tour 7B), US 5 (see Tour 7), State 9
and US 5A (see Tour 8).

Sec c. HARTFORD to JUNCTION WITH STATE 14, 23.7 m.

Leaving Hartford with its serrated skyline, US 6 crosses the Connecticut River and the tobacco-fields beside the river to enter the textile
area of eastern Connecticut. Alternately rising to skyline ridges, or
dipping into narrow valleys where lively streams furnish water-power
for rural mills in a verdant setting, the route enters the rougher, less
interesting portion of the Eastern Highlands.

Leaving Hartford on a nine-arched stone bridge over the Connecticut
River, US 6 enters EAST HARTFORD at 1.2 m. (See Tours 3, 3A, 7,
and 10).

Left, or northward, on Main St. at 1.2 m., US 6 proceeds over a wide,
heavily traveled street to a complicated traffic signal at 1.7 m.

Right, at 1.7 m. US 6 traverses narrow streets and passes poorer houses
to a junction with State 83 (L), at 6 m.

US 6 is the right fork at this junction.

At SOUTH MANCHESTER (see Tour 3), 7.4 m., is a junction with
US 44 with which US 6 unites for 8.9 m. (For tour description to Bolton
Notch and junction with US 6A; also for tour description to Coventry,
see Tour 3.)

At 12.7 m. at Bolton Notch, is the junction with US 6A (R) (the newly
constructed section which has replaced the older, rougher, obsolete US 6 and
is now the main highway).

Straight ahead from Bolton Notch, 3.6 m., US 6 proceeds to COVENTRY (alt.
600, town pop. 1554), 4 m., in a rolling, hilly countryside, chiefly noted as the birthplace of Captain Nathan Hale (1755–76), the American patriot whom history
credits with the regret that he 'had but one life to give for his country.' With an
abundance of water-power, Coventry early turned to manufacturing. Today, fish-
lines, throwing silks, thread, and bookbindings are produced by country mills in
a verdant setting.

At Coventry US 44 (see Tour 3) proceeds straight ahead, leaving US 6 which turns
right.

At 7.3 m. on US 6, near the summit of a hill (R), is the Jesse Root House (1736), a
gambrel-roofed dwelling, with a central chimney and a Dutch door. The lower
half has the cross-panels which were popular in Coventry, and the upper has five
lights in the door itself. The year it was built, this house was the birthplace of
Chief Justice Root of the Connecticut Courts.

Diagonally across the street is the Ripley House (1792), a large, central-hall type
of dwelling, with end chimneys and a well-designed door. The rooms are richly
paneled.

At 8.6 m. US 6 enters the village of SOUTH COVENTRY (Town of Coventry),
a prosperous little community of neat homes, substantial public buildings and
thriving small industries. The Booth-Dimock Library stands (L) on a small eminence across from both Methodist and Congregational Churches. Also on Main St.
(L) is the Bidwell House, a hostelry built in 1822. About 1840, horse-breeders here

developed a high-class pacer of medium size and great endurance that could travel to Boston (72 miles) and return in two days with an ordinary road rig.

Right, at a junction with a macadam road beside the Union Hardware Company plant, 0.2 *m.*, up a small but very steep hill, is the *Nathan Hale Cemetery* (R), with an imposing granite obelisk, 45 feet in height, erected in honor of the noted patriot. In the cemetery is the Hale family plot and the grave of Asher Wright, Hale's orderly.

Here, this road skirts the south shore of *Lake Wamgumbaug*, passing a *Nathan Hale Salvation Army Camp* maintained for poor children of the State. The village Green on *Monument Hill*, at 0.3 *m.*, was used as a training ground by two military companies organized here in 1728, and by Coventry soldiers during the Colonial wars, the Revolution, War of 1812 and the Civil War. Near the flagpole in the center is a six-inch gun, 1890 model, presented to the town by President Calvin Coolidge in 1928.

Left from the Green on a side road to a junction, at 1 *m.* Here (L), at the junction stands the *Huntington House* (1763), where Nathan Hale was prepared for Yale College by the Rev. Joseph Huntington, the local minister.

Right at the Huntington House to a junction with a bituminous-macadam road, and right on this road to *Gerald Park*, 1.9 *m.*, a 400-acre expanse bordering the shore of Lake Wamgumbaug where many prominent radio and vaudeville actors have established summer homes. A large sign (L) contains the names of the resident celebrities.

Following the shore northward, this road passes the colorful bungalows of the summer colony, including the *Bolton Stone Home of Joe Germini*, noted European vaudeville performer.

At 2.4 *m.* is the junction with another side road. Left on this road to the *Birthplace of Nathan Hale* (R), 1.1 *m.*, a large, central-hall type of structure with a long ell, erected in 1776 by Deacon Hale, Nathan's father. According to records, Nathan was born in the ell which is part of the earlier house (about 1746). The present building contains much of the woodwork and furnishings of the original birthplace, most of which was demolished in 1776. The house, carefully restored, is now owned by George Dudley Seymour, antiquarian, who has collected many historical relics connected with Hale's life. (*The house is open to visitors on Sunday afternoon only; appointments must be made in advance.*)

A short distance east of the house is the replica of the *Bela Lyon Pratt Statue of Nathan Hale*, at Yale University; near-by is a pear tree which was planted by Nathan Hale's father, Deacon Richard Hale.

A small, red *Salt-Box House* (*shown at the convenience of the owner, Mr. Seymour*), 2.6 *m.*, with copious barns and outbuildings, some of early date, is an earlier and very unusual house. Unlike most Connecticut salt-box dwellings it has two end chimneys. The southern and earliest section (about 1715–20) which appears to have been a two-story, end-chimney house, was enlarged in an unusual way, with a central hall joining the old and new sections. The paneling is elaborate.

At 10.6 *m.* is a junction with the combined US 6 and State 32 (*see Tour 9A*).

Right on the combined routes is a junction with State 14 at 14.5 *m.*

At 16.3 *m.* is the junction with a country road.

Left on this road to the *Hendee House* (1760) (L), 0.3 *m.*, the oldest house in Andover. Within are mysterious secret closets and a tunnel from the cellar to a thicket, 100 feet from the house, a relic of 'Underground Railway' days when colored slaves were assisted along the route in their escape to freedom in Canada.

ANDOVER (alt. 380, town pop. 430), 18.2 *m.* Settled in 1718, this pastoral community was organized as a parish in 1747, incorporated as a town in 1848, and named for Andover in Massachusetts. Daniel Burnap, born here in 1759, became a famous early clock-maker. After his apprenticeship to Thomas Harland of Norwich, Burnap opened a clock shop in East Windsor in 1780 where he carried on an active business, employing Eli Terry (inventor of the shelf clock), as one of his first apprentices. Returning to Andover in 1800, Burnap became a watch repairman and silversmith. Houses typical of Andover have large chimneys and steep-pitched roofs. Agriculture is the chief activity in the town, and the single small factory produces wooden heels for women's shoes.

> Right from Andover on the Gilead Road, is a solitary upright *Slab*, 1.7 *m*. (R), marking the grave of Captain Simon Smith and his horse. According to tradition, Smith, en route to his home in New London from a campaign of the French and Indian War, became ill with fever and fell from his horse at this spot. Soon afterward, he died of smallpox. Fearing contagion, the residents buried his horse and equipment with him and erected a large headstone on which the now almost illegible inscription reads in part — 'Loved, yet unattended. All alone. Sweetly repose beneath this humble stone ye last remains.'

At 23.7 *m*. is the junction with State 14 (*see Tour 2 Alt.*), a broad, smooth, and interesting route to western Connecticut.

Sec. d. From JUNCTION WITH STATE 14 to RHODE ISLAND STATE LINE (Providence), 28.6 m.

This route crosses the rougher portion of the Eastern Highlands where the Resettlement Administration has purchased lands and retired them from agriculture. Between the hills in narrow valleys lie many textile mills, some of them now dormant, beside the swift streams where the pioneer manufacturers first built their crude waterwheels. Skyline crests, wooded side hills, pleasant glades in the timberland: all these can be found along the winding, rolling highway of this route.

From Katzman's Corner, 2.8 miles west of Willimantic, at the junction with State 14 (*see Tour 2*), US 6A follows a series of winding curves, one of which, 0.7 *m*., is banked the wrong way, creating a hazard for motorists.

Spanning the Willimantic River, on a cement bridge at 2 *m*., and crossing two unprotected grade crossings at 2.1 *m*. and 2.3 *m*., this route reaches a junction with the combined State 32 (*see Tour 9A*) and US 6 (*see above, Side Trip from Tour 2*), at 2.7 *m*.

WILLIMANTIC (alt. 260, city pop. 12,102) (Town of Windham), 2.8 *m*., at the junction of the Willimantic and Natchaug Rivers which converge to form the headwaters of the Shetucket, is known as the 'Thread City' for its production of spooled thread. The streets of the outskirts, lined with modest, well-kept mill houses, lead into a main thoroughfare where numerous small shops form a trading center for the agricultural area surrounding the city. Only 39 per cent of the population is of full native parentage, and the patois of the French-Canadian is heard almost as often as English.

Life in this wholly industrial city centers largely around the massive gray granite mills (R) of the *American Thread Company* (*visitors' permits issued at the office*), 322 Main St. This company, organized as the Willimantic Thread Company in 1854, sponsored the pioneer research which developed the first cotton thread manufactured in the United States. Previously the public demanded foreign thread and refused to buy the product of American manufacturers. English and Scottish manufacturers claimed an advantage over American thread-makers because of certain atmospheric conditions, believing that the moisture content of their air enabled them to do a better job of spinning; through the use of primitive humidifiers, the necessary moisture was obtained and American Thread became standard.

At 779 Main St. the *Windham National Bank*, moved here from Windham Center in 1879, is famous for its issue of frog-adorned bank notes, celebrating the 'Battle of the Frogs' (*see SOUTH WINDHAM, Tours 9A and 9C*). Colonel Dyer was pictured at one end of the notes and Colonel Elderkin at the other with the embattled frogs portrayed in a fighting mood at the center.

At 4.3 *m.*, on the outskirts of Willimantic, US 6 turns north leaving State 14 (*see Tour 9C*), crosses the Natchaug River at 4.6 *m.*, and passes the golf links of the *Willimantic Country Club* (R), at 5 *m.*

Paralleling an area of wide, uncultivated flats that border the highway, US 6 enters the village of NORTH WINDHAM (Town of Windham), 7.5 *m.*, a rural village with small industrial plants on the Natchaug River.

Passing through a luxuriant growth of pines (L), at 8 *m.*, the highway proceeds to *Sherman's Corner* (L), 9 *m.*, the junction with State 91.

Left on State 91, a concrete highway, across a bridge to a gravel road, 0.5 *m.* Left on this road is the *Abel Ross Homestead* (1786) (R), a large central-chimney dwelling. BEDLAM CORNER, 1.2 *m.*, is a small village named for a quarrelsome family who raised 'Bedlam' in this vicinity.

Northward on State 91 which by-passes the center of CHAPLIN (alt. 380, town pop. 414), at 1.5 *m.*, a placid agricultural community, where elaborate 19th-century houses border the main street. In this former thriving industrial community, where felt hats and calfskin boots were manufactured, silkworm culture subsidized by the State reached a peak production of 1200 pounds in 1838. Chaplin was incorporated in 1822 and named for Benjamin Chaplin, land-wise surveyor and basket-maker, who purchased many acres from non-resident owners.

Left on a macadam road at the by-pass on the main street are (L) the *Congregational Church* (1814) which has a high stone basement and a pedimented front with quoins on the corners; the *Gurley Tavern* (R), built in 1822, with a recessed porch, pilasters, and a Palladian window; (L) the *Dorrance House* (1815) and *Griggs House* (1825) with corner columns and a recessed doorway, on either side of the church; and the red brick hip-roofed *Witter House* (1828). All of these houses are excellent examples of the comfortable solidity of 19th-century dwellings.

At 1.8 *m.* State 91 passes the *Natchaug State Forest Nursery* (R), a plantation of many small trees.

At 5.3 *m.* is the junction with a country road.

Right on this road through the *Natchaug State Forest* to the junction with a gravel road, at 1.4 *m.* Left on this gravel road about one hundred yards is the *Site of the Birthplace of Nathaniel Lyon*, the first Union general killed in the Civil War. Only the chimney foundation remains. The wooded area surrounding his birthplace has been converted into the *Nathaniel Lyon State Park*. Continuing north, this gravel road joins the old Phoenixville Road, at 2.4 *m*. At the junction is the, *Phoenixville Cemetery* (L), the burial place of General Lyon. A 15-foot memorial shaft and three old cannons stand on a knoll surrounded by barberry hedges. For his service in Missouri, General Lyon's memory has been honored by the city of St. Louis, Missouri, which has erected two equestrian statues and named a school in his honor. At 3.5 *m*. the gravel road rejoins State 91.

Northward from its first junction with the country road, at 5.3 *m*., State 91 continues to 7.5 *m*. where it is rejoined by the side road and at 8 *m*. intersects with US 44 (*see Tour* 3) in Phoenixville.

East of Sherman's Corner is the entrance to *Buttonball Brook State Park*, at 9.1 *m*. The highway passes *Birchbank Highway Rest* (L), at 9.5 *m*.

CLARK'S CORNER (Town of Hampton), 11.7 *m*., was formerly named Goshen.

This very small community's chief point of interest is the *Jonathan Clark House* (R), built in 1825, with a Palladian doorway inside a recessed porch, corner pilasters, and a monitor roof. The village was named for the owner who built this house for a tavern, but was slower in the construction than his brother, who built a smaller house and got the license away from him.

US 6 proceeds through an area of open fields bordering the highway, and passes a luxuriant growth of tall, stately pines (L), at 12.1 *m*.

HAMPTON (alt. 680, town pop. 511) (Town of Hampton), 13.5 *m*., is a charming village of spotless white houses on spacious lawns, shaded by old trees. About the village are the residences of many summer visitors. Hampton's most illustrious citizen was Chauncey F. Cleveland, Governor of Connecticut from 1842 to 1844.

The town of Hampton was incorporated in 1786, when it was formed from parts of Windham, Pomfret, Brooklyn, Canterbury, and Mansfield.

The Main St. (State 97) extends north and south, crossing US 6.

On the Main St., north of the crossroads is the white *Moseley Homestead* (R), built in 1786, with a very high stone foundation and a two-storied porch.

Opposite the crossroads is the *Congregational Church*, moved here in 1840, apparently a plain structure of that period, but reconstructed on the frame of a 1754 church. US 6 swings sharply right past the *Governor Chauncey F. Cleveland House* (1831), with tall Ionic porticoes similar to those of many Farmington houses.

1. North from Hampton on State 97 to '*The House the Women Built*' (R), 0.9 *m*., a hundred yards back from the road. According to tradition, this gray, wooden, two-story building, of the central-chimney type, was built in 1776 by a bride, Sally Bowers, whose husband, like all the other able-bodied men in town, had joined the Continental Army. Aided by townswomen and a one-legged carpenter, Sally Bowers erected her home.

2. South from Hampton on State 97 is the *Hampton Cemetery* (L), 1 *m.*, where Governor Chauncey F. Cleveland is buried. The *Thomas Fuller Salt-box Tavern* (R), at 1.7 *m.*, dates from 1715. It faces south and has chamfered beams inside like many Guilford houses. At 3.4 *m.* is the junction with the old Brooklyn–Windham Rd., a gravel thoroughfare.

Left on the Brooklyn–Windham Road is the abandoned *Howard Valley Baptist Church* (R), 4.3 *m.*, built in 1843, now falling into ruin. Through this entire river valley are many early 18th-century, one-and-a-half-story houses.

At 5.2 *m.* (L) is the old *Curtis Tavern*, reputedly started in 1763, but giving little evidence in its heavy Ionic pilasters and ornate carving of a date earlier than 1825. Among the several legends associated with this hostelry, is a tale of the proprietor's wife who was ordered by two inebriated young guests to prepare a doughnut a yard long, and a 'flip' (a drink made by putting a red-hot poker into a pitcher of cider). Nothing daunted, the good woman repaired to the cellar, and much to the amazement of the gentlemen, returned a little later, triumphantly bearing the drink and a yard-long doughnut. Another story accounts for the unusual name — *Man Coming Out of the Little End of the Horn* — by which the tavern was originally known. The proprietor, when building the sign for the inn, asked his wife to suggest an appropriate name. Discouraged by their economic difficulties, she promptly told him to paint on it a picture of 'a man coming out of the little end of the horn.' It is said that the creaking of this sign, swinging in the wind, echoed down the valley like a laugh of scorn. The tavern, a square building with an ell, contains 18 rooms, including one of the few extant 'spring' dance floors, this one having '16 springs to the beam.' These 'spring' dance floors were so constructed that each board had an equal amount of spring.

At 15.6 *m.* on a hilltop (R), is a rusty gasoline pump by the roadside. Across the road, a modest brick house has been built upon a ledge, where various markings are supposed to indicate the site of a fabulous treasure buried by Black Beard, the pirate.

At 18.2 *m.* is *Blackwell's View Highway Park* (L).

Eastward, at 18.8 *m.*, on *Blackwell's Brook*, are three old mills (R): the *Lawton Gristmill*, which still uses an old type waterwheel and millstones; the *Mabie, Todd and Bard Mill*, one-time manufacturers of gold pens, now a cider mill; and *Basset's Gristmill*, which, until the 1936 flood, used water-power.

BROOKLYN (alt. 280, town pop. 2250), 19.5 *m.*, incorporated May, 1786, is a quiet residential town of many substantial 18th-century houses, overlooking a Green bordered by tall elms.

Most of the land now comprising the town was obtained by Sir John Blackwell, an officer under Cromwell, as a prospective refuge for Irish dissenters, and was originally called Mortlake Manor, from Mortlake in Surrey, England. However, as the shifting fortunes of English politics changed the plans of Cromwell's supporters, the land was sold in 1713 to Governor Jonathan Belcher of Massachusetts, who divided it into two manor farms, Kingswood and Wiltshire, which were later purchased by the political enemies, Putnam and Malbone. Near-by tracts, however, were settled about 1703 as sections of Pomfret and Canterbury, between which towns they lay. In 1752, these settlements and the Mortlake claims were combined and named 'the Society of Brooklyn' (brook-line, from its eastern boundary on the Quinebaug). The village was the county seat from 1819 to 1888. At that time many factories were operated here, producing silverware, furniture, tinware, cotton and optical supplies, but with the growth of the textile city of Willimantic, local industries declined and the residents returned to agricultural pursuits.

The last public hanging in the State took place in 1835 on Prince Hill, a mile and a half east of the Green. On the fatal day, the victim, a man named Watkins, peering through the iron bars of his cell, and seeing the townfolk scurrying to the place of execution, is said to have remarked, 'Why is everyone running? Nothing can happen until I get there.'

On the northwest side of the Green are the *Captain Eleazer Mather Tavern* (1783) and the *Francis Clark House* (L), built in the late 18th century.

The *Town Hall* (L), conspicuously high, with a bell cupola, was built in 1820. Behind it is the long *Burdick Tavern* (about 1800).

On the Green (R) is a *Rustic Town Well* with a pump. The only building on the Green is the *Unitarian Church*, the first in Connecticut, erected by the Congregational Society in 1771, but lost to that church during the Unitarian controversy in 1819. In the belfry is a *Paul Revere Bell*. The interior is disappointing, but the exterior, with its lofty walls, double tiers of pedimented windows, and straight tall tower with five stories of windows and open belfry, is an excellent example of 18th-century church architecture. Opposite the church is a bronze plaque marking the *Site of the General Wolfe Tavern* (R), of which only the ell remains. General Putnam moved to this inn from his farmhouse on his return from the French and Indian War, when his wife suggested that the erection of a hostelry would permit him, without seeming indelicate, to charge his many visiting friends for the expense to which they put him. The place was, according to local tradition, the scene of Putnam's precipitous departure on receipt of the news from Lexington and Concord, when he abandoned his plow in the field and, without changing his clothes, sped on horseback to Cambridge, where he became one of the commanding officers at Bunker Hill.

The second building to the south (R), is the present *Congregational Church* (1832) with a Doric portico.

Close-by is a large bronze *Equestrian Statue of General Putnam* on a massive stone pedestal beneath which General Putnam is buried.

South of the statue stands *Mortlake House* (R), a three-story hip-roofed dwelling, built by the Tylers, probably for a tavern, in 1767, and now owned by Mrs. Theodore Roosevelt, Sr.

At Brooklyn is the junction with State 93.

1. Left from the Green on State 93, past the *House of Samuel J. May* (L), 0.3 *m.*, uncle of Louisa May Alcott, prominent Unitarian minister, abolitionist, and close friend of William Lloyd Garrison. According to local tradition, this house was the first in town to be built without the use of liquor at the 'raising.'

At 2.4 *m.* is the junction with a gravel road. Right on this road is the brown, shingled, two-story farmhouse, 2.8 *m.*, where General Putnam lived. The eastern end was built by Putnam in 1765, and given to his son in 1770 when he moved into town.

2. Right from the Green on State 93, bearing left at all forks to the summit of *Tatnic Hill* (alt. 525), 1.2 *m.*, which affords a complete view in all directions over the valley of Blackwell Brook, east, and Tatnic Brook, west. On the hilltop stands the *Litchfield House* (1747), the oldest dwelling in town. On the eastern slopes of the hill are rocky caverns about which numerous legends are told, including the tale of Lyon's Den, in which a resident, named Lyon, hid to escape being drafted in Revolutionary service.

US 6 now follows a fairly straight course to *Creamery Brook*, at 20.3 *m.*, and traverses an area where a colony of Finnish immigrants have established thrifty farms. *Finnish Hall* (L), at 20.6 *m.*, is headquarters for their social activities as well as for a branch of the United Farmers' Co-operative Association, an organization of Finnish farmers with headquarters at Fitchburg, Mass., that has carried on the co-operative systems developed in their native land.

At 20.8 *m.* is a junction with a bituminous-macadam side road, Church St.

Left on this road is the *Malbone Episcopal Church* (R), 0.2 *m.*, Windham County's oldest Episcopal church, erected in 1771 by Godfrey Malbone, a Tory sympathizer, whose quarrels with Israel Putnam precipitated many stirring incidents in the town's history. When the Congregationalists, under Putnam's leadership, prepared to build a church, Malbone, rather than have his church tax devoted to the construction of a church he would not attend, erected this Episcopal church.

Malbone, who had moved here from Newport with his southern bride and her retinue of sixty slaves, was rumored to have privately equipped and drilled the Negroes for the defense of the King. Terror of an uprising spread among the inhabitants of the town, but proved unfounded.

The Malbone Church, used only on All Saint's Day (November 1), has a hip roof and pedimented doorway, and is still in good repair. The interior has the original beautiful walnut paneling, considered the finest in the State. Not a box-pew nor a post has been changed. Alone in its cedar grove, it remains a haven of peace in a troubled world.

Putnam Elms, 0.9 *m.* (L), is the original Malbone manor farm, which was united with the Putnam farm upon the marriage of the doughty General's son, Daniel, to Malbone's daughter. The house was built in three units. The gambrel portion dates back to 1750, the central unit to about 1782, and the southern ell, to about 1900.

The highway descends a steep hill and crosses *Long Brook*, at 21.4 *m.*

EAST BROOKLYN (Town of Brooklyn), 22.8 *m.*, is the home of mill workers employed in the near-by Quinebaug Company plant in Danielson, across the Quinebaug River. A row of two-story, four-family, company houses lines the highway. Maple trees set on neat, well-kept lawns, afford a broad belt of shade.

US 6 continues across the bridge over the Quinebaug River to the village of Danielson.

DANIELSON (alt. 260, borough pop. 4210) (Town of Killingly), 23.6 *m.*, a bustling manufacturing borough, the largest center of cotton manufacturing in the State, is at the junction of the Assawaga (or Five Mile) and Quinebaug Rivers. The present borough was formed in 1854 by the union of the villages of Danielson, Westfield and Tiffany. Here in 1807, a cotton mill was established by the Tiffanys, the family which later founded the New York jewelry firm of the same name.

The *William Danielson House* (L), on Maple St., is a large dwelling with a beautiful interior, dating from 1786. Raised paneling is used in the window blinds, fire boards, cupboards and doors, and featheredged paneling covers one wall of the dining-room.

At Danielson is the junction with State 12 (*see Tour 9*), which unites with US 6 for 0.5 mile.

Past the junction with State 12, the highway penetrates a densely wooded area and crosses *Fall Brook*, at 24.8 *m.*

Snake Brook, at 25.9 *m.*, runs parallel to a hiking trail that crosses the highway here in a southerly direction.

At the top of a steep incline is the village of SOUTH KILLINGLY (alt. 560) (Town of Killingly), 26.5 *m.*, a small hilltop community, the birthplace of Dr. William Gaston, former Governor of Massachusetts, and Mary Kies, who, for her straw and silk weaving machine, received the first patent ever granted to a woman in the United States, in May, 1809. On the northeast corner at the village center is the *Dr. Alexander Gaston House*, a large red house with two center chimneys, built about 1775. West of it stands the *Congregational Church* (1837).

Descending a steady grade from South Killingly, the highway passes through a valley, dotted with pleasant farms, passes the *Dark Lantern Highway Rest* (R), descends a rather steep incline to *Quaduck Brook*, 28.2 *m.*, and crosses the Rhode Island Line at 28.6 *m.*, 22 miles west of Providence.

T O U R   2   A L T E R N A T E :   *From* JUNCTION WITH US 6 *to* JUNCTION WITH US 6A, 59 *m.*, State 14.

Via Waterbury, Meriden, Middletown, East Hampton.
Alternate stretches of concrete and macadam highway.
Usual accommodations.

THIS alternate route is actually the main route across the center of the State. It avoids the dense traffic of Hartford and the older, rough and narrow US 6. Signs at either end of State 14 advise the tourist that this route is the shortest, quickest, and best.

Climbing from the Pomperaug Valley, dipping into the Naugatuck Valley, climbing again to the top of Southington Mountain, with broad views of the old course of the Connecticut River, finally crossing the Connecticut and topping skyline ridges to the east of the Long River, this route rejoins US 6, 2.8 miles west of Willimantic.

At a triangular Green, 4 miles north of Southbury, State 14 branches right from US 6, rising steeply to the top of *Ben Sherman Hill*, at 2 *m.*, with views of the Pomperaug Valley and the Roxbury Hills (L).

State 14 crosses maple-covered swamplands, passing patches of pines, to *Lake Quassapaug*, at 4.1 *m.* The lake has been stocked with bass; summer homes are confined to one end of the lake and the opposite shore is in its natural state. At the southern end of this lake, were formerly satinet mills and the pioneer factories of the Diamond Match Company.

At 4.7 *m.* lies a *Pond* (R) that furnishes the water supply for Westover School (*see below*); the shore line is fringed by plantings of white and red pines for which the township of Middlebury is famous; these are carefully identified by signs giving the variety and age.

At 5.6 *m.* is the junction with a side road.

> Sharp right on this side road is MIDDLEBURY (alt. 700, town pop. 1499, inc. 1807), 0.4 *m.* Named for its position midway between Woodbury and Waterbury, this village is situated on a plateau from which there are excellent views of the surrounding industrial area to the east. Dairying and the raising of saddle horses are the chief occupations, although there was once considerable manufacturing in small back-yard factories. There are many fine estates in the town of Middlebury; acres of riding country are a maze of bridle paths. A country blacksmith still operates a smithy behind the general store.

> Around the beautiful Middlebury Green are the new *Congregational Church*, a restoration of the original Greek Revival building (1839), and the modern *Town Hall*, designed with taste and restraint, which replace those destroyed by fire in 1935, and the campus and chapel of the *Westover School for Girls*. The architecture of the school buildings is a good, modern adaptation of the Colonial, designed by Theodate Pope.

> In Revolutionary days, Middlebury was the scene of an event which has inspired numerous stories and poems. A youth, Chauncey Judd, on his way home one night from courting a young lady in a near-by town, met a band of Tories who were escaping after plundering the home of a patriotic resident. Judd recognized some of the men and was taken prisoner. The chief of the band threatened to kill him, but finally relented. Soon a posse was in hot pursuit. While attempting to reach Long Island, the Tories, as they crossed the Sound, were finally sighted by an eagle-eyed mariner who watched them from a church steeple in Stratford, and directed thirty patriots from Derby, who, heavily armed, took up the pursuit in two whale-boats. The mariner wig-wagged the necessary directions and the Derby patriots bent to the oars. Out across Long Island Sound rowed the pursued and the pursuers, but the Tory craft arrived at its destination. Exhausted, they pulled their boat on shore and fell asleep. Stealthily, the patriots crept up on the sleeping men, captured all but one, released the frightened boy, and dragged off the captives to jail. The kidnapers were variously dealt with: the leader was executed and the others sentenced to Newgate Prison. The poor young man, who had been crippled, thereafter stayed at home nights; from an undisclosed source he received $4000 for his injuries. Several authors have written books about the incident.

> South from Middlebury on South St., at 2 *m.*, is (R) the *Pope House* where Judd was kept prisoner by the Tories. The building has been completely remodeled.

At 9.3 *m.* State 14 passes over *Town Plot Hill*, where a bronze tablet on a boulder (L) records the names of the early settlers and the history of the original Colony at Waterbury.

WATERBURY (alt. 300, town pop. 99,902) (*see WATERBURY*), 10.3 *m.*, known as the 'brass center of the world,' is one of the chief industrial cities in the State.

At Waterbury is the junction with State 69 (*see Side Trip off Tour 2, at Bristol*).

At 10.4 *m.* is a junction with State 8 (*see Tour 5*).

East of Waterbury State 14 crosses the tiny *Mad River*, at 13.6 *m.*, a stream that once furnished power for mills and tanneries, but now serves only as a mill-race from the reservoirs to the brass mills in Waterbury. The highway passes through *Fort Swamp*, where, according to legend, there was an Indian stronghold on an island in the center of the deep swamp. The highway rises from the Waterbury suburbs where dairy farmers operate on the edge of the industrial area, to *Gate House Hill*, at 16 *m.*

At 16.3 *m. Hitchcock Lake* (L), a summer resort and amusement park, is seen through the trees. In the field opposite, stands a *Glacial Erratic* left by the melting ice-sheets of another age.

At the top of *Southington Mountain* (alt. 720), 16.8 *m.*, the route passes through a rock cut. There are traces of an old trolley roadbed along the ridge where the King's Highway once crossed. An early settler on this hilltop recorded that each night his family had to 'run their hands about under the blankets to see if any of the great snakes had crawled into the beds during the day.'

At a highway rest area, 16.9 *m.* (R), are excellent views of the valley toward the east. The gravelly hillsides are ideal orchard lands; apple trees stretch along the mountain on both sides of the road. Eastward, the route descends the long grade of Southington Mountain.

In MARION (alt. 160, Town of Southington), 17.5 *m.*, bolt-threading machinery was invented in 1840 by two blacksmiths, Barnes and Rugg. They produced the first machine-made bolts manufactured in America, eliminating the laborious hand threading process. Their invention unpatented until 1840, resulted in the establishment of several carriage-bolt factories in Plantsville and other villages in the vicinity. Industry has long since moved from the quiet village at the foot of the hills.

MILLDALE (Town of Southington), at 18.8 *m.* is a small bolt-making center with pleasant homes along a straight highway.

At 19.5 *m.* is a junction with State 10 (*see Tour 6*).

On a brook at 20.7 *m.* a commercial trout hatchery (L) once did a thriving business, but now only the pools and the dams remain. Children of the neighborhood occasionally catch a giant rainbow in one of the pools and swim in the deep holes with almost as much dexterity as the trout themselves.

Beyond, the road climbs a grade that gives an impression of being even longer and steeper than it really is. Apple orchards, at 21.1 *m.*, cover the side hills on both sides of the highway.

At 23.1 *m.* is the entrance to *Hubbard Park* (L).

Left into Hubbard Park through shady drives around beautiful *Lake Merimere*, climbing in and out among rocky eminences to the summit of *West Peak*, 3.5 *m.*

Other plainly marked drives lead to *Castle Craig*, the middle peak. Nature trails, camping facilities, tennis courts, a winter skating rink, are among the park's attractions.

According to legend, West Peak is haunted by a black dog of whom it is told, 'if a man shall meet the Black Dog once it shall be for joy; and if twice, it shall be for sorrow; and the third time he shall die.' More than six mysterious deaths, all of which occurred after the victims are said to have seen the black dog thrice, have confirmed local belief in the weird tales of this strange dog who is said to leave no footprints behind him either in the snow of winter or the dust of summer, and who has been seen barking although no sound is ever heard.

State 14 winds under the shadow of the *Hanging Hills*, the highest point within 25 miles of the coast south of Maine. This range is composed of two lava flows in three distinct and separate hills, the most westerly of which, West Peak (*see above*), rises to 1007 feet and offers a panoramic view of all central Connecticut.

At 24.2 *m.* is the junction with State 71 (*see Tour 7B*).

MERIDEN (alt. 250, city pop. 38,481) (*see MERIDEN*), 24.9 *m.*, the 'Silver City.'

At Meriden is the junction with US 5 (*see Tour 7*).

From Meriden State 14 climbs a grade over a rough brick pavement to the junction with US 5A (*see Tour 7*), at 25.5 *m.*

At 27.4 *m.* are the *Ruins of the old Parker Manufacturing Company's Factory* (L), where the famous Parker Gun was once made and silver spoons were blanked out for the early 'pedlar' trade. A spring beside the road furnishes water for thirsty passers-by, and a one-room school across the road indicates that the gun factory once formed the center of a lively community.

The route proceeds to *Black Pond* (R), 28.2 *m.*, in *Black Pond State Park*, which offers black bass fishing unsurpassed in Connecticut waters. The park includes an attractive picnic ground, below the jagged rock cliffs rising precipitously on the eastern shore of the Pond.

State 14 continuing, crosses through a wide gap, a notch in the mountain range, separating Mt. Higby, the northern peak, from Mt. Beseck, the southern peak.

At 29 *m.* is the junction with State 147.

Right on State 147 is *Beseck Lake*, 1 *m.* (R), a summer resort.

At 1.8 *m.* is the junction with Powder Hill Rd. on which is the *Elias Coe Homestead* (1720), 0.7 *m.* (R), an integral salt-box house with a double overhang and an unusually large central chimney. It contrasts with the Coe House of a century later, which stands just beyond. On Powder Hill Rd. at 0.9 *m.*, in the fields (R), about 100 feet back from the road is an abandoned sandstone quarry where are *Dinosaur Tracks*, made by the gigantic prehistoric reptiles that roamed the Connecticut Valley. Presented to Yale University by Professor Wesley R. Coe, this quarry is now maintained by the Peabody Museum as an outdoor exhibit.

State 147 turns sharp right up the hill, at 2 *m.*, and passes the plant of the *Lyman Gun Sight Corporation* (L), at 2.1 *m.* Riflemen from all over the world come here to have their special rifles fitted with ivory and gold bead sights. The company encourages youngsters to form junior rifle clubs; senior clubs sponsored by the company participate in national and international competitions.

At 2.4 *m.* is the junction with a dirt road. Right on this dirt road, 2.6 *m.*, are the *Lyman Farms* (L), where a mammoth cold-storage plant refrigerates a variety of fruits, and exports shipments to England. Along this road stretch the orchards that are featured every year in May during the Apple Blossom Festivals for which Middlefield is noted. The Governor and his staff attend the festivities, which include crowning the Apple Blossom Queen, music, and feasting.

Between 29.5 *m.* and 29.9 *m.* the highway passes along a causeway across Mt. Higby Reservoir, a part of Middletown's municipal water supply. During the summer, pure white herons are often seen fishing in the shallow water (R).

A pine planting along the highway, at 30.1 *m.*, is especially attractive and the view of the *Mt. Higby Reservoir* from the hill is excellent.

At 31.7 *m.* just off the road (R) is a reproduction of a *Spanish Hacienda* with a mission bell, commanding an excellent view of the hills behind Middletown.

At 31.7 *m.* (L), on a shady stone terrace, facing Middletown, is the *Judge Seth Wetmore House* (1746). Though its dormers, broken pediment doorway, and fan-light windows in the gable are modern, it is one of the best 18th-century houses in the State, and has an elaborately turned stairway of a type that simple Connecticut houses seldom saw. Two long service ells extend to the rear.

At 32.2 *m.* (R), is the *Southmayd House* (1737), a salt-box dwelling with a sign advising passers-by that the owner 'resilvers mirrors.'

State 14 passes through a narrow underpass at 32.8 *m.* and over a very slippery stretch of asphalt to Middletown.

MIDDLETOWN (alt. 50, town pop. 24,554) (*see MIDDLETOWN*), 33.7 *m.*, an industrial city, seat of Wesleyan University.

At Middletown is the junction with State 9 (*see Tour* 8) and State 15 (*see Tour* 7A).

State 14 crosses the Connecticut River at Middletown.

PORTLAND (alt. 220, town pop. 3930), 34.7 *m.* Originally East Middletown, this area surrounding the village has rich sandstone quarries which attracted settlers as early as 1690. Incorporated as a part of Chatham in 1767, and as a separate town in 1841, Portland was named for Portland, England, a town noted for its quarries. With tobacco plantations extending along the river banks, and with the development of shipbuilding after 1741, the town reached the peak of prosperity during the early part of the 20th century. In recent years the quarries have ceased operations and the shipyard has closed, leaving but a few small factories in operation.

On Main St. is the *Portland High School* (L), a handsome building of Tudor type. Opposite is the *Samuel Warner House* built before 1732. Main St., lined with maples and elms, runs north through a residential section.

Left from Main St. on Silver St., 0.1 *m.*, toward the Connecticut River. Approaching the extensive diggings of the *Brainerd, Shaler & Hall Quarries*, at 0.2 *m.*, the road passes along a narrow ridge between two great quarry pits, now partially filled with water. Rock walls (L) sheer perpendicularly to the water.

On the right is the pit of the old Town Quarry, now called the *Middle Quarry*, once the property of the town of Portland, which, by offering this rock for building purposes, induced Wesleyan University to establish itself in Middletown. Water has now filled in the quarries to a depth of from 25 to 50 feet.

During the long period when the brownstone industry flourished, stone from these quarries was transported to many cities in the United States, especially New York City, where many late 19th-century buildings are constructed of brownstone. For the past ten years the quarries have been idle. Dinosaur tracks are frequently found at certain levels in the brownstone, and some tracks may be found on the various broken pieces of stone on the quarry dumps. In an old office building (L), now used by an oil company, a fireplace has been constructed entirely of slabs which bear dinosaur tracks.

At Portland is the junction with State 15 (*see Side Trip off Tour 3A*).

From Portland, State 14 veers right and eastward to the Portland R.R. Station (R), and a grade crossing of the Airline Division of the N.Y., N.H. & H. R.R. (A new straight road to replace this section is under construction, 1938.)

The road passes Pacaussett Pond, a river cove (R). High on the forested slopes of the opposite bank of the Connecticut shine large outcroppings of mica. The highway, winding north around several sharp curves, ascends *Sand Hill*, 36.5 *m.* From the top of Sand Hill, the dome of the State Capitol and the Travelers' Tower in Hartford are visible (L) on clear days. At this point is the junction with State 15 A.

Left on State 15A, through an underpass at 0.1 *m.*, to a junction with an improved road, 1.1 *m.*; right on this road to another junction, at 1.3 *m.*; right again on a poor gravel thoroughfare is *Strickland Quarry* (L), 2.2 *m.* Containing the greatest variety of minerals to be found in any one place in Connecticut, this great quarry pit has for years been a mecca for mineralogists who find beryl, garnets, quartz and many other mineral specimens. Mining was started by Deacon Ralph Pelton in 1877 and has continued ever since. Today, mica and felspar are the chief products.

At 37.7 *m.* is the junction with a private road to *Job's Pond*, known as Mystery Lake (L), in a glacial kettle not visible from the road. Uninfluenced by rainfall and with no apparent outlet, the water level varies as much as 15 feet. Often the highest level is reached during a dry season and the lowest during a wet season. Observers state that the water rises regularly for six or even twelve months, then falls during a period of equal length.

Beyond, State 14 turns in a southerly direction, rounding a gradual curve with rock ledges banking the road to a point, 38.4 *m.*, where the land sheers abruptly down to the Connecticut River. From a high rock (R), there is an imposing vista of winding river and forested hills on the opposite shore. At the base of the rock is a parking area.

COBALT (Town of East Hampton), 39.3 *m.*, is an agricultural and residential village of scattered homes dating from 1762, when a cobalt mine was operated at the foot of Great Hill. Exploitation of the mine failed when it was found impossible to separate the cobalt from the arsenic and nickel in the ore.

1. Left from Cobalt on a dirt road, uphill to a junction with another dirt road, 0.7 *m.*

Right on that road to a path among the trees (R), 0.4 *m.* This path leads down a ravine to Mine Brook and a *Narrow Tunnel* in the hillside, where cobalt was discovered in 1661 by Governor John Winthrop, who, according to local legend, spent weeks in the woods assaying metals and casting gold rings, thus giving rise to the name 'Governor's Ring' which was applied to the area.

In 1762, Dr. John Sebastian Stephanney, a German, reopened the cobalt mine and manufactured a deep blue paint. Twenty tons of cobalt ore were shipped to China for use in glazing chinaware. One thousand tons were shipped to England, where it was discovered that the ore contained a large percentage of nickel.

Farther on this side road, at 0.7 *m.*, another path (R) leads to the ruins of furnaces where nickel was smelted in 1844. On the mine dumps may be found a number of minerals including the rare erythrite and a variety of cloanthite, containing a large percentage of iron, which has been named chathamite, for Chatham, the original name of the township. Garnet crystals are plentiful in the mica schist.

Northward from the junction at 0.7 *m.* (*see above*) is *Great Hill Pond* (L), 1.2 *m.* Along the shore, public picnic facilities are provided. Right, rises the towering forested *Great Hill* (alt. 720).

2. Right from Cobalt on State 151, past the *Union Hill Cemetery*, 0.4 *m.* (R), dating from 1782, is

MIDDLE HADDAM, 0.6 *m.*, a quiet, rural village on the slope of the Connecticut River Valley. Now composed of farms and modest residences, this settlement was once noted for shipbuilding and shipping activities. Serving as a water gateway to the towns farther east, the community prospered until lack of timber and the opening of other river ports to the north caused the village to decline into a small agricultural center.

Christ Church (L), built in 1786, has a projecting tower which indicates its 18th-century origin, despite the stained-glass windows added later. At the west corner, an old store, now a library, is interesting for its upper story corbeled out on ships' knees.

The *Hurd House* (L) (about 1795) is one of the finest early stone houses in the State. According to tradition, stone from every State in the Union was used in the construction.

Right from Middle Haddam, past an old bulletin-board (L), on a winding drive down to the east bank of the Connecticut River, where is the *Site of the Old Ship-yard* (R), 0.2 *m.* Here, Thomas Child, noted shipbuilder, constructed and launched 237 vessels. The first Connecticut ships for the China tea trade were built here, as well as several of the first London packets, some with elaborate interiors of mahogany, rosewood, black walnut, and other fine woods brought to port by West Indian traders.

South from Middle Haddam, on State 151, along the Connecticut River to *Hurd State Park* (R), 2.3 *m.*, a recreational area of 548 acres, equipped with picnic areas. Along scenic paths at the northern end, the land sheers abruptly into a shaded gorge revealing strata of granite and schist. At the western side, which borders the river bank, is a boat landing, and a large breakwater built of stone quarried in Portland.

At 3.8 *m.* is the junction with an asphalt road.

Right, 0.4 *m.*, on this side road to HADDAM NECK, a remote old hamlet nestling among riverside hills, seldom visited except during the annual Haddam Neck Fair, each fall, usually the day after Labor Day.

Here lived an extraordinary Negro, Venture Smith, whose autobiography, when published, ran into several editions. Born in Dukandara in Guinea in

1728, the son of Saungm Furro, King of the Guinea tribes, Broteer, who later became Venture Smith, was captured by enemy tribes and sold into slavery. Bought by a sea captain, he was later given his freedom and settled here. Many tales are told of the remarkable physical prowess of Smith, who was more than six feet tall and so broad that he had to turn sidewise to enter the average doorway. It is said that he could carry a barrel of molasses on each shoulder, and that once he cut 400 cords of wood within a few weeks. Carefully saving his wages, he gradually acquired a hundred acres of land, three houses and twenty sailing vessels engaged in river trade. His grave in the cemetery at the Congregational Church is marked with a stone inscribed:

> Sacred to the Memory of Venture Smith,
> African, though the Son of a King, he
> was kidnapped and sold as a slave, but
> by his industry, he acquired money to
> purchase his freedom, who died Sept. 19,
> 1805, in ye 77th year of his age.

South of the junction with the Haddam Neck Road is the junction with State 149, at 8.1 m. Left on State 149 to MOODUS (Town of East Haddam), 1.2 m. Here, early mills produced sail cloth, and twine has been manufactured for over a century. The *Julius Chapman House*, built in 1816 (R), at the center, is an untouched example of the residence of a country gentleman of the early 19th century.

Right on State 149 to a sharp left turn, at 8.6 m. At this point is an excellent view of *Mt. Tom*, center of the mysterious subterranean rumblings and explosions, known as the 'Moodus Noises.' The terrifying noises, long interpreted by the Indians as threats of evil spirits, and sometimes still heard here, sound like the rumble of boulders, tumbling down yawning abysses, striking crags as they plunge downward. The early white settlers soon discovered that the noises were caused by encounters within the mountain, between the Haddam witches, who practiced black magic, and the East Haddam witches, who practiced white magic. Within a subterranean cave, lighted by the blinding glare of a great carbuncle, Machimoodus watched from a sapphire throne. When the fights were too prolonged, he waved his wand; the mountains trembled with his wrath, the light of the carbuncle went out, and the witches were blown from the cave by a mighty draft.

Some skeptics, who doubted that explanation, were delighted in 1765 when the mystery was satisfactorily solved by 'Dr. Steele from Great Britain,' a very old man who was locally accepted as a savant of great learning. After spending considerable time excavating and exploring in the vicinity, Dr. Steele built a strange house on the mountain-side, stuffed the keyhole to shut out prying eyes and secretly worked at his anvil and forge. One dark night, preceded by a weird white light which led him to the Rocky Moodus Cave, he pried away a great stone from the entrance. A blood-red light streamed forth, staining the very stars a crimson hue. The next day, Dr. Steele had vanished, but he had left word that he had discovered the cause of the subterranean cannonading and had taken it away with him. As proof, he announced that he had found two pearls which had caused the disturbances. He warned the residents, however, that he had found others in miniature, which, when developed, would produce similar noises in later years.

The 'Moodus Noises' did not recur for more than 25 years, confirming the Englishman's theory. However, his supporters' equanimity was violently shaken on May 16, 1791, when ominous explosions like artillery fire beneath their feet were followed by two violent shocks which toppled chimneys and opened crevices in the earth. Throughout that day and night the village trembled with more than 100 shocks. The quake was felt from Boston to New York. According to the report of an eye-witness 'the concussion of the earth and roaring of the atmosphere was most tremendous.' Many terrorized people believed that 'the town would sooner or later be sunk.'

According to modern scientific opinion, Mt. Tom is located at the intersection of lines of fracture within the earth's crust and stands over the corners of these fissures. At any point along such a fracture, there is possibility of an earthquake, but the danger is always greatest where the fissures intersect. The subterranean rumblings, when unaccompanied by quakes, are believed to be frictional vibrations caused by sliding portions of earth blocks, which are of insufficient capacity to disturb the surface of the ground.

Southward on State 149, 12.4 *m.* is the junction with State 82 (*see Tour 1D*) in the village of East Haddam (*see Tour 1D*).

EAST HAMPTON (alt. 500, town pop. 2616), 42.4 *m.*, today known as 'the Bell Town,' has been the site of numerous bell factories since 1808 when sleigh and hand bells were first manufactured here by horse-power. Many similar shops, seven of which still operate, began to produce bells — such as cow bells, house bells, and church bells. In 1872, Barton invented the first wheeled bell chimes made in America, a revolving chime toy, which in modernized form still finds a wide market. Here also was made the novelty 'Chestnut Bell' which enjoyed unusual popularity during the gay nineties when every dandy jauntily wore one of the tiny bells on the lapel of his coat, and rang it whenever a story-teller offered a 'chestnut.' Other East Hampton factories today make thread and fish lines, and a distillery produces witch-hazel and oil of birch.

Joel West Smith (1837–1924), a native son, modified and recast the whole Braille system along scientific lines. Among his inventions was the 'unigraph,' a typewriter for the Braille system.

Old Home Day, celebrated annually at a three-day festival, attracts many former residents and hundreds of visitors to East Hampton on the first Friday in August and the two following days. A feature of the occasion is a. historical pageant, depicting important incidents in the town's history; band concerts, speeches and a midway furnish entertainment. More than 25 local societies sponsor booths and a large part of the proceeds is donated to the American Legion.

Left from East Hampton to *Sears Park* (R), 0.6 *m.*, a pine-shaded grove on Lake Pocotopaug, with facilities for picnicking, boating and swimming.

Passing many cottages and a summer hotel and rounding a turn, the highway passes the entrance to the public bathing beach (L) at *Lake Pocotopaug,* 42.6 *m.* According to an Indian legend, the Indians of this region, frightened by the many drownings in the lake, appealed to the Great Spirit, who demanded the sacrifice of the Chief's beautiful young daughter. While the old man sat silently over the campfire, hesitating between love for his child and duty to his tribe, the young girl, who had overheard the message of the Great Spirit, jumped into the lake, preferring to sacrifice herself that others might live. Thereafter, not until the present century was anyone drowned in Lake Pocotopaug. Opposite the lake is the entrance to the town *Cemetery* (R), containing many old graves.

At 43.6 *m.* is the peak-roofed *Nathaniel Markham House* (L) (1786), one of the many taverns where Washington is believed to have spent the night. Northward, the highway descends a hill, crosses Fawn Hill Brook in a wooded valley and climbs the summit of another hill, 46.3 *m.*

MARLBORO (alt. 540, town pop. 319), 46.8 *m.*, is a roadside hamlet which remains, as it was in Colonial days, a crossroad. The area was settled in 1715 and named for the Duke of Marlborough. Here in this thickly wooded, sparsely settled district were born a number of zealous Connecticut pioneer inventors, whose devices gave impetus to early manufacturing and established the reputation of 'Yankee ingenuity.' Among them were Henry Dickenson, who invented a washing machine; Joseph Carter, who devised a bread knife; Charles Hall, who secured a patent for a wagon seat, and Jonathan Kilbourn (*see COLCHESTER and Tour 3A*), who made the first large screw and boxes (weight 200 pounds) ever made in Connecticut by machinery, and invented many small mechanical appliances.

At the crossroads (R) the *Marlboro Tavern*, built by Elisha Buell in 1740, a famous stop on the old Hartford–New London turnpike, has been reopened as a tavern, by the Colonial Dames. This gambrel-roofed building has unusual doors of crested paneling. Beside the tavern is a barn in which central Connecticut artists hold an exhibition each summer.

South of the crossroads is the white *Congregational Church* (1841), with a conspicuous gilt dome.

At Marlboro is the junction with State 2 (*see Tour 3A*).

Descending a long steep hill, State 14 passes the *Marlboro Highway Rest* (L), at 48.9 *m.*, and follows a winding course through heavily wooded country past many small farms. Shagbark hickory trees offer shade for the passer-by and food for squirrels' caches in stone walls and hollow trees.

At 52.1 *m.* the highway crosses *Salmon River*, on which is the *Ruin of Porter's Grist Mill* (R). The water wheel has disappeared; only parts of the big wooden flume remain intact. Inside the ruin, amid a jumble of beams, parts of the grinding devices polished by countless streams of grain appear as new as in former years. There are two sets of millstones: one a burr stone of volcanic composition, used in the milling of fine flour; the other, of granite, used for grinding grain.

HEBRON (alt. 600, town pop. 879), 52.4 *m.* Incorporated in 1708, the town of Hebron is an agricultural area. The Rev. Samuel Peters, an ardent Tory resident, incurred such resentment through his pro-British propaganda that the local Sons of Liberty forced him to confess his transgressions before an assemblage of townsfolk on the Green. Mr. Peters fled to England, where he anonymously published 'The General History of Connecticut; Including a Description of the Country and Many Curious and Interesting Anecdotes,' which contained a spurious description of the Connecticut Blue Laws in which he charged that the settlers here 'out-pop'd the Pope and out-king'd the King.' More burlesque than satire, this publication is generally credited with being the cause of later ridicule against New England's strait-laced statutes.

A short distance south is *St. Peter's Church* (R), erected 1825–26. Its ivy-covered tower projects from the far end of the building. A graveyard at the rear reminds one of an English churchyard. Beside the church is a *Brick Mansion* (1806) with a graceful porch, the former home of the clergyman's nephew, John S. Peters, who was Governor of the State, 1831-33.

1. Right from Hebron on State 85 which traverses high, gently rolling country to the village of AMSTON (Town of Hebron), 1.8 *m.*, another typical country hamlet. Originally a mill village known as Palmertown, Amston now has only a small distillery.

Left from Amston, 2.3 *m.*, on an improved country road is *Amston Lake* (L), an artificial lake built as a reservoir, but now a summer resort.

2. Left from Hebron on State 85 which is bordered by high stone walls and comfortable small farms. Trees and thick shrubbery line the highway which climbs gradually.

GILEAD (Town of Hebron), 2.8 *m.*, is a little village with a single street bordered by old houses, some of them peculiar in shape and structure. Tall, well-trimmed maple trees line the highway, which traverses a ridge with a fine view to the west. The soil is of a reddish texture, typical of the red clay found in the Connecticut Valley. On Bolton Rd. was the home and church of the Rev. Samuel Peters.

Rounding a sharp curve the highway climbs to the top of *Post Hill* (alt. 800), 54.1 *m.* Here a panoramic view stretches over an expanse of valleys toward low, flat hills. On clear days Mt. Tom in Holyoke, nearly a hundred miles distant, is visible. Here (L) is an old well which in Revolutionary days stood beside a toll gate on the old Middletown Road. The highway proceeds through rough, sparsely populated country to the junction with West St., a country road, 54.9 *m.*

1. Left on West St. is the *Nathaniel White House* (L), 0.6 *m.*, built in 1700, the oldest dwelling in Columbia. This salt-box house is in good repair and preserves many of its original features of construction — narrow, hand-riven clapboards on the north side, central chimney, and twin Dutch ovens.

2. Right on West St. to a junction, at 0.5 *m.* Left on a dirt road to a second junction at 0.7 *m.*, and right at that junction, 0.9 *m.*, to the deserted village of WELLS WOODS settled early in the town's history, where more than a dozen old houses crumble on foundations of huge, hand-cut granite stones, which weigh two or three tons each. Some of these blocks are 12 to 15 feet long, two-and-a-half feet wide, and eight inches thick. Many old houses of the settlement have been destroyed by fire — their charred, caved-in timbers lie heaped in vine-grown cellars. Behind one old foundation is a private burial plot, containing four gravestones of the Root family.

Eastward, the top of the hill, at 55.9 *m.*, is a vantage-point for views of distant blue hills. Passing through an open stretch dotted with small farms fenced by crumbling stone walls, and traversing thickly wooded areas, State 14 descends a steady incline.

COLUMBIA (alt. 500, town pop. 648), 57 *m.*, is a rural town of substantial old houses and comfortable residences about a hedge-bordered village Green. Originally a part of Lebanon, the town of Columbia was set apart and incorporated in 1804.

The *Wheelock House* (L), an 18th-century structure, was once the home of Eleazer Wheelock's Indian School, 1735-70 (known as Moor's Charity School). Here, Samson Occum, Mohegan Indian, converted during the Great Awakening, studied with other Indian youths whom Mr. Wheelock invited to come to his house for instruction. Encouraged by the response, Dr. Wheelock determined to establish a free school. Joshua Moor donated a house and two acres of land. Within a few years, more than twenty Indians from three tribes were enrolled as pupils. Occum became the first Indian minister ordained (1759) in New England, and served as a missionary to his own people and to the Oneidas. In 1766 he was sent to England to raise funds for the education of 'ye native savages of North America.' As a result of his sensational tour and impassioned appeals, he returned with a fund of $50,000, a large amount of which was subscribed by the Earl of Dartmouth. Four years later, Governor Winthrop's offer of land on the Connecticut River was accepted and the school was moved to Hanover, New Hampshire, where it became the nucleus of Dartmouth College. Dr. Wheelock, the first president, spent the remaining years of his life there.

According to tradition, had it not been for the attitude of the early residents, the college would have been established in this town. Local prosperity, however, was dependent upon the fruit and cider industry, and fearing that the proverbial weakness of all boys for good apples would lead to continual raids on the surrounding orchards, the residents urged the removal of the school.

Opposite, on the northwest corner of the junction of State 14 and State 87 (the Jonathan Trumbull Highway), is the *Old Inn* (L), built about 1750, and once used as a stop for stagecoaches on the Hartford–New London Turnpike. It has an interesting ballroom on the second floor, with arched ceiling and a spring floor.

On the Main St., north of the crossroads, is the *Congregational Church* (R), beside which stands a white *Schoolhouse*. This school was constructed with timbers taken from a building which housed Wheelock's original Indian school; for, in accordance with the original deed, the land can be used for school purposes only as long as the original schoolhouse is used. Opposite the church is the *Saxton B. Little Library* (L), which contains a collection of historical data, including old sermons and books, and a portrait of Samson Occum, Wheelock's Indian pupil.

At Columbia is the junction with State 87 (*see Tour 2C*).

Left from Columbia on State 87 which is bordered by comfortable homes and follows a level but winding course to a junction with an improved road, 0.9 *m.*

Left on this road are a public bathing beach (R), and summer colony and *Columbia Lake* (alt. 700), 0.3 *m.*, an artificial lake, covering 375 acres, created by the Willimantic Linen Company in 1865. Originally a reservoir, Columbia Lake is now owned by the town, and annually attracts thousands of devotees of fishing, hunting, swimming, ice-boating and skating.

State 87 skirts the edge of the lake in a series of winding curves, which become more abrupt as the highway mounts the summit of Woodward Hill to the *Lyman-Little House* (L), at 2.1 *m.*, an added lean-to house, built about 1790. The top of Woodward Hill, 2.4 *m.*, is a vantage-point for good views of the lake to the south, and of Andover to the north. Summer cottages line both sides of the highway.

At 59 *m.* is a junction with US 6A (*see Tour 2*), which is 2.8 miles west of Willimantic.

Via Washington, Washington Depot.
Macadamized highway.
Limited accommodations.

LEAVING North Woodbury, State 47 climbs steadily to hilltop Washington and its sheltered, shaded Green. Dipping sharply to the Shepaug Valley, then twisting through the Bee Brook vale, the highway bends around the hills and finally approaches the more heavily traveled State 25 with which it intersects just east of New Preston (*see Tour 4C*).

The highway passes between trim country homes each with generous lawns and fronted by a shaded gravel walk, and enters the valley of HOTCHKISSVILLE, 1.4 *m.*, where an old knife shop still stands (R). Houses of mill workers, along with old stores, now either vacant or hopefully hanging on for the scant summer trade, line the highway.

At Hotchkissville is the junction with an asphalt-surfaced road.

> Right on this road, passing a number of scattered farmhouses and former mill sites, the highway approaches the valley of the *Weekeepeemee River* which broadens out in fertile meadow land encircled by ever-rising hills.
>
> At the foot of *Carmel Hill* (alt. 1000), 2.5 *m.*, are views of sky-line ridges ahead topped by steel towers carrying high-tension feeder lines from the Housatonic Valley hydro-electric plants to the industrial centers eastward.
>
> On *Todd Hill* (alt. 1020), just north of the cemetery, stands the early 19th-century *Welles House*, a weathered dooryard red-brick structure; a loom, built into the attic, is anchored to the oak rafters. Isolated and peaceful, this house enjoys the distinction of crossroads location at the lonely end of nowhere. The area abounds in brushy pasture-lands, the woodland is thin and wind-twisted, and the outcropping ledges at this point give agriculture insurmountable handicaps. Only on the hilltops to the south and in the brook valleys is there soil of a character to promise a return for labor.
>
> The traveling blacksmith and the rolling store are often seen in this back-country, catering to the needs of the farm folk who, facing starvation, still cling to rough hilltop acreage, hopefully awaiting a chance to sell-out to a city purchaser who will value the land for other than its soil.

At 2.2 *m.* (R), an old, white double overhang, stone-chimneyed *Salt-box House* (*private*) bearing a 1744 date, looks down on the road from a sloping lot where many vari-sized hencoops offer typical evidence of a city man's disgust with his lot in town and his determination to achieve independence on these submarginal acres.

At 3.6 *m.* is the junction with a dirt road.

> Left on this road, as it climbs ever-rising hills topped by the *Good Hill* and *Painter Ridge* masses (alt. 1005), are many 18th-century houses that have been purchased by city people who occupy them during the summer and autumn months. Artists discovered this section some years ago, brought their easels to the road's end,

painted the old farms that they eventually bought, and now work in almost ideal surroundings in a community of their own.

Legend has it that the original settlers of Woodbury, after a long trek up the Shepaug Valley from the Housatonic, climbed these hilltops and, glimpsing the beautiful valley of the Pomperaug stretching out below them, fell on their knees in prayer and, ever after, spoke of the ridge as 'Good Hill.'

At 4.5 *m.* is another junction with a dirt road, which is the most direct, though not recommended, route to Washington.

Right on this road, proudly marked 'Ye Old Albany Turnpike,' the course of Sprain Brook is followed as it winds through a narrow but fertile valley. The brook waters poultry farms, fills many swimming pools made by summer residents, and forms mirrored pools of beauty beside the road. Side trails bear such names as 'Honeysuckle Lane' and 'Hazel Valley Road.' Hay is stacked here in the meadows because the barns are small, and, off in the lot to the east, stands one of the few six-sided houses in this part of the State.

Dust sometimes detracts somewhat from the full enjoyment of the journey, but the beauty of the roadside is such that fast driving is not desirable. Laurel blooms in June, azalea even earlier; and great patches of tiger lilies and lilac hedges grow in old cellar holes.

At 2.8 *m.* is WASHINGTON (*see below*). The last mile of the road is uphill and rough, and is not recommended for motor travel.

At 8.8 *m.* State 47 climbs to WASHINGTON (alt. 720, town pop. 1775), a hilltop residential village settled about 1734 and incorporated January, 1779.

Facing the hilltop Green is the *Congregational Church* (1801), an odd little church with a simple belfry over the square tower, beneath which is a fine Palladian window.

On tablets at either side of the church doors are recorded historical events of importance in the annals of the church.

The *Gunn Memorial Library* and *Museum* (*open Tues., Thurs., Sat.,* 2–5), at the southeast corner of the Green, contains a large collection of Indian relics.

Across the Green (R) is a white building known as the *Red House* (*private*), where, during Revolutionary days, a Tory, Joel Stone, and his Whig brother, Leman, lived, quarreled, and separated. Joel finally joined the British army and his half of the house was promptly confiscated. One of the rooms in Leman's section was later decorated by a local 19th-century artist known as Stimp, in a stenciled design of fauns and satyrs topped by a vine pattern twined about alternate deer and eagles. Each eagle's head is surmounted by 13 stars surrounded by the words 'Federal Union.'

The highway dips sharply to cross the *Shepaug River*.

WASHINGTON DEPOT (alt. 480), 9.6 *m.*, the railroad and commercial center of the town of Washington, is a village of slight interest crowded into the narrow river valley. The *Bryant Memorial Town Hall*, a modern Colonial brick structure with white trim, has been tucked away in a corner just across the railroad tracks.

At the Town Hall is the intersection with a narrow dirt road.

Left on this dirt road along the Shepaug River to *Steep Rock*, 3.1 *m.*, a 600-acre game preserve, presented to the town by E. K. Rossiter, a resident. The park is named for a sheer cliff, a feature uncommon along the lively little Shepaug River, adept as it is at dodging hills and finding the easiest route through a rough countryside.

Farther along, this road enters the preserves and rolling acreage of the so-called *Judd's Bridge Farms*, extensive holdings of a landowner who believes that Connecticut farmland is the most effective hedge against inflation.

The route passes from the Shepaug Valley into the valley of the crooked little *Bee Brook*, a tiny stream that chatters and twists through dells and dingles.

At 12.8 *m.* is the junction with State 25 (*see Tour 4C*).

TOUR   2 B :   *From*   WATERTOWN   *to*   LITCHFIELD, 11.1 *m.*, State 63 and State 61.

Via East Morris.

Macadamized highway.

No accommodations.

THIS connecting route crosses the rolling hill country of lower Litchfield County where dairying is the chief industry and where out-of-State investors have recently purchased acreage and remodeled their farms for beauty as well as profit. Red barns with white trim, white houses with green shutters, and paddock fences of wood instead of wire, proclaim the coming of 'city money' to the Yankee hills.

Leaving Watertown on State 63 the route crosses Steele Brook, 0.9 *m.*

At 3.9 *m.* is a narrow vista of distant blue hills some 20 miles to the south.

At 4.4 *m.*, a sign (L) marks the *Site of the Straits Turnpike Toll Gate* (1797).

Crossing East Morris Brook, 6.8 *m.*, the highway enters the village of East Morris.

EAST MORRIS (alt. 940, village pop. 75) (Town of Morris), is a crossroads settlement with a gasoline station and several substantial dwellings grouped about the road intersection. The meadows and barns of a modern dairy occupy the southwest corner of this junction.

At East Morris is the junction with State 109.

Left on State 109 to MORRIS (alt. 1120, town pop. 450), 1.2 *m.*, a summer residential town where 68 per cent of the taxes is paid by non-residents. Here Columbia University maintains a summer school of surveying and drafting. Near the modern brick school (R) is the *Site of the James Morris Academy* (1790), where were educated many boys who later became nationally distinguished.

Climbing from the shallow valley of East Morris, State 63 passes the *Litchfield County Air Service*, 7.4 *m*. (R), a tiny hangar on a small flying field. Privately owned, it is operated for the benefit of student pilots and an occasional passenger.

State 63 begins a winding, gradual descent through a thickly forested region and, at 8.1 *m*., intersects with State 61 which this route now follows to Litchfield.

Northward, the road passes through the *Litchfield Morris Game Sanctuary*, also known as *White's Woods*, a large tract of forest land donated by Alain C. White. The area, maintained by the White Memorial Foundation, contains many walks and bridle paths.

State 61 traverses a pleasant district dotted with scattered farms and paddocks, then crosses the *Bantam River*, at 9.9 *m*.

LITCHFIELD, 11.1 *m*. (*see LITCHFIELD and Tour 4C*).

T O U R   2 C :   *From* COLUMBIA   *to*   JUNCTION   WITH STATE 32, 14.8 *m*., State 87.

Via Lebanon.
Asphalt roadbed.

TRAVERSING a thinly settled area this route leads to historic Lebanon with its long village Green and Old War Office, and connects with State 32 (*see Tour 9A*).

State 87 branches south from State 14 (*see Tour 2 Alt.*) at Columbia, descending past *Balanced Rock* (R), 0.3 *m*., a slab resting T-fashion on an upright boulder in a rock-strewn gulley. Crossing Gifford's Brook, at the bottom of the hill, 0.6 *m*., and ascending another steeper hill, the highway passes the *Collins House* (R), 0.8 *m*., a central-chimney, 18th-century, salt-box dwelling.

Attaining a summit, State 87 traverses a high ridge with a northeastern view that extends over distant blue hills to the far horizon.

CHESTNUT HILL (alt. 400, Town of Columbia), 1.8 *m*., is a tiny settlement. An old store (L), across the railway tracks, has a fine assortment of very old rifles and other relics. The visitor is never asked to buy, and the elderly proprietor, a former Saranac Lake merchant, has many interesting stories to tell.

Southward, State 87 ascends another steep hill along a curving route overlooking distant countryside, and passes *Lebanon Highway Rest* (R) at 3.2 *m*., opposite a now idle, paving-stone quarry.

LIBERTY HILL (alt. 480, Town of Lebanon), 3.5 *m*., originally called Paunch Hill, but renamed in 1831 when a liberty pole was raised here, is a small cluster of tree-shaded dwellings on a hilltop. Of interest is the old public signpost (R).

Descending a steep hill, State 87 passes *Liberty Hill Cemetery* (L), 3.7 *m*., burial place of Captain S. L. Gray, whaling skipper who died when his ship was shelled off the island of Guam by the Confederate raider 'Shenandoah,' and whose body, preserved in a cask of spirits, was brought home by his wife and interred, still in the cask. After this encounter the 'Shenandoah' went to the Bering Sea where it engaged with the northern sealing and whaling fleet in the last battle of the Civil War.

Along another hilly stretch, at 5 *m*., the fields beside the highway recede into thickly wooded areas.

At 5.8 *m*. State 87 enters the main street of Lebanon, along the eastern side of the 100-acre Lebanon Common.

LEBANON (alt. 480, town pop. 1436), 6.6 *m*., incorporated in 1700 and named for the Biblical Lebanon, is an uninvaded rural center of old dwellings shaded by towering elms. The spacious lawns and Common have been little changed since the momentous days when they were the setting for the brilliant uniforms of parading Hussars.

Headquarters of the Trumbull family and their extensive West Indian trade with branches in Norwich, Wethersfield, and East Haddam, the village of Lebanon also became a cultural center of some importance. Nathan Tisdale's Academy (1743), now gone, attracted students from other colonies and the West Indies. As early as April 9, 1770, Lebanon freemen, incited by the Boston Massacre, met and drafted a declaration of rights and liberties that preceded the Declaration of Independence by more than six years. The document was drafted by William Williams who was later a signer of the Declaration of Independence. Enforcement of the Stamp Act (1770) cut Lebanon's trade, bankrupted the Trumbull family, and created a still more hostile attitude toward the Crown. Lebanon thus early became a key town in Colonial military activity, with Jonathan Trumbull, the town's foremost citizen, counselor to Washington, and the only Colonial governor to espouse the revolutionary cause. When facing a financial or commissary crisis, Washington so frequently said 'Let's see what Brother Jonathan can do,' that the appellation came to be synonymous with the present term, 'Uncle Sam.'

During the winter of 1780–81, the mile-long Common was used as a parade ground for 200 Hussars under the Duc de Lauzun, who were quartered here. Later that winter Rochambeau arrived with five regiments that camped in Lebanon until June 23, 1781, when the French troops left to join the Continental troops at Yorktown.

At the head of the Common is the *Dr. William Beaumont Memorial* (R), a boulder bearing an inscribed bronze tablet. Dr. Beaumont (1785–1853), who was born in Lebanon, became world-famous as a result of his reports (1833) on the case of Alexis St. Martin whose recovery from a gunshot wound in the abdomen left him with a hole in the stomach and abdominal walls through which the digestive processes could be studied. Dr. Beaumont's work laid the foundation of present scientific knowledge of the physiology of digestion.

Just north of the center of the village is the *Jonathan Trumbull 2d House* (L), built in 1769, home of the son of the first Governor Trumbull, who was himself Governor from 1797 to 1809. It might not be recognized as an old house now except for its well-designed front door.

Diagonally opposite, on the Common, is a tablet marking the *Site of the French Bake Oven*, used by the French cantonment during the winter of 1780–81.

Across the Common (R) is the *War Office (open Sat. free; other days 25¢; key from custodian)* (1727), now a museum. Under Trumbull's direction this building served as the northern business headquarters of the Continental forces and supplied from Connecticut more men and money than were furnished by any other Colony, with the exception of Massachusetts. No call for aid ever lacked response during the entire war. In 1780, when Washington, scarcely daring to hope for further aid for his starving troops, sent to Trumbull for food and the Connecticut Governor replied with a train of ox-sleds laden with 1500 barrels of beef and 3000 barrels of pork, Washington wrote in his diary, 'No other man than Trumbull would have procured them and no other state could have furnished them.' Washington once said that 'except for Jonathan Trumbull, the war could not have been carried to a successful termination.' Here, in the War Office, the Council of Safety of Connecticut held 1200 meetings; plans were made for outfitting privateers; troop levies were issued; and conferences were held with Washington, Lafayette, Rochambeau, de Lauzun, Adams, Jay, Benjamin Franklin, and his son William, former Tory Governor of New Jersey, who was held prisoner in Lebanon. This red, one-story, two-room gambrel-roofed building contains many mementoes of Revolutionary days. Of especial interest is a stone sink and a connecting trough that runs through the clapboards to the outside of the house. The original iron bars still bolt the shutters.

Next but one to the War Office, the *Governor Trumbull House* (1740), a white clapboarded house built by the War Governor and later moved to its present site, is an historical museum *(open Thurs. and Sat., adm. free)*. Both front door and ground-floor windows have pediments with moldings broken on the slope; and both casements and cornice project heavily, as they do in early buildings in this region. The most unusual feature of the house is the chimney, which unites as one central chimney in the attic the flues of three stacks down below. This permits a central hall and stairway. At the head of the stairs is the small room which served as a secret office when the British Government put a price on the Governor's head. The only window is a small shuttered opening, 27 inches square, placed above the head level of a seated person as a precaution against stray bullets. Outside the office door is the Sentinel's Box, in which a guard was always stationed. The house contains many relics of the Revolutionary period including a Trumbull chair, a 300-year-old sampler, an engraving, a self-portrait by John Trumbull (*see Notes on Connecticut Art*), and innumerable relics of the War of Independence.

A *Stone and Tablet*, NW. cor. State 87 and Colchester Rd., mark the original site of the War Office. On the opposite corner (R) is *Redwoods* (*private*), built in 1704, the earliest of the Trumbull houses and the birthplace of Governor Jonathan Trumbull, Sr. It has the appearance of being the latest, however, having been remodeled by David Trumbull in 1797, when he inherited the management of the family estates. It then became a hip-roofed house, its overhang covered by a small applied cornice and its large lower windows and corner boards quoined to imitate stone. The second-story windows, however, are smaller, and original. Of special interest is a set of unusual black and white tile blocks around the fireplace, depicting Aesop's fables. David Trumbull became the father of the third Governor Trumbull, Joseph (1849–50). During the winter of 1780–81, the house became the headquarters of de Lauzun and some of his officers.

The *Congregational Church* (1807), opposite, is the center of architectural interest in Lebanon. It is notable, not merely because it was designed by John Trumbull, the artist, but because it is of brick and was the first of the churches in this section of the State to have the recessed porch which became so popular in the area. The four engaged columns across the front are of brick, painted white. A wooden spire of three stages, two of them octagonal, seems not overlarge for so solid an edifice.

Set back from the road at the triangular southern end of the Common (R) is the *Welles House* (*private*), of 1712, now somewhat remodeled. It was the birthplace of William Williams, a signer of the Declaration of Independence. Opposite are two *Buckingham Houses* (*private*), one (1804) the birthplace of William Buckingham, the Civil War Governor of Connecticut (*see NORWICH*); the other, the original homestead (about 1735). The next house to the north is the *Home of William Williams* (*private*), corner of State 202, where Squire Williams entertained both Washington and Lafayette. He added the corner pilasters and door to a house of 1712. The *Thomas Hunt House* (before 1720), the last house in the village, going toward Norwich on State 87, and the *Clark Homestead* (1708), half a mile down Goshen Rd. from the Hunt House, are other early buildings.

At LEBANON CENTER, 6.6 *m.*, is the junction with State 207 (L) and the Colchester Rd. (R).

   1. Right from Lebanon Center on the Colchester Rd., crossing the brow of a hill, past an old cemetery (R), 0.4 *m.*, and across Pease Brook. Slightly beyond the base of the next hill is the *French Deserter's Grave*, 0.6 *m.* (R), marked by a cairn of stones on the sloping bank of a field beside the road. Many legends have been told concerning the death of this young soldier, who was supposed to have been a nobleman serving as a private. The foraging of hussars among neighboring farms led to the issuance of a regulation making absence from camp between sunset and sunrise equivalent to desertion. Stealing from camp to meet a village maiden, Prudence Strong, this young man was caught, tried and sentenced to death. On hearing of the impending execution Mistress Strong hastened to Lauzun and

pleaded for her lover's life. A messenger was dispatched with a reprieve but failed to arrive before the soldier had been shot in the presence of the entire legion.

2. Left from Lebanon Center on State 207. Descending a slight slope in the road, and crossing Susquetonscut Brook, the highway passes an old burial ground, 0.9 *m.* (R), the resting place of Governor Jonathan Trumbull, Sr.; Governor Jonathan Trumbull, Jr.; Governor Joseph Trumbull; William Williams; and many Revolutionary War veterans.

State 207 winds cross country through rough, rolling, bushy, eastern Connecticut uplands where the most optimistic farmer is soon forced to admit the hopelessness of trying to wrest a living from the barren soil, sells out to a newcomer, and moves to a more fertile district, or gets a job in town.

At the hamlet of NORTH FRANKLIN, 3.1 *m.*, is the junction with State 32 (*see Tour 9A*). The back roads of Franklin contain a number of simple 17th-century houses.

South from Lebanon, State 87 passes through a sparsely populated area to the junction with State 32 at 14.8 *m.* (*see Tour 9A*), 2.8 miles northeast of Norwich.

T O U R   3 :   *From* NEW YORK LINE (*Poughkeepsie*) *to* RHODE ISLAND LINE (*Providence*), 105.5 *m.*, US 44.

Via (*sec. a*) Salisbury, Canaan, Norfolk, Winsted, Avon, Hartford; (*sec. b*) South Manchester; (*sec. c*) Mansfield, Pomfret, Putnam.

Macadam and cement surfaced highway.

Excellent accommodations.

Sec. a. NEW YORK LINE to HARTFORD, 53.7 m.

US 44 enters Connecticut at Salisbury in the loftiest corner of the State and traverses a section unusually rich in natural beauty. As the journey begins, the Taconic Hills roll away to the north, Lake Wononscopomuc offers lake trout fishing in season, and Twin Lakes glitter in the sunlight just off the road. The route continues through Salisbury with its beautiful hills, contented North Canaan, and sedate Norfolk, and after passing through Winchester township, leaves the western highlands and dips down to the valley of the Farmington River. Through Satan's Kingdom, which intrigues the traveler with its queer place names, and the Farmington valley where the 1936 floods have left their mark, the road climbs Avon Mountain and descends to the valley of the Connecticut.

Throughout the entire first half of the route are wide fields where in winter ski trails zigzag across clean snow far from the factory smoke of industrial Connecticut. Organized winter sports are conducted at

Salisbury, Norfolk, and Winsted, and there are ski jumps at each of these points. Music-lovers look forward to the annual musical events in Norfolk, and artists sketch in Salisbury and the surrounding country. Mystery and romance linger along the first half of the route. Tales of the unreal, the unexplainable, come out of Winsted, where the town's greatest liar has been honored by an inscription on the bridge over Sucker Brook, financed by the Works Progress Administration. The Satan's Kingdom country abounds in tall tales of extreme heat and frigid cold. Ice worms are reported from the Kingdom, moose have been seen in the woods above Winsted, and the Greenwoods country is a laurel-clad, scented paradise when Connecticut's State flower blooms in late spring. The taverns along the western portion of the route offer excellent food, served without haste by country waitresses. Indian legends are told of many places along the way. Stories of the Barkhamsted Light-house and the two Indian maidens for whom Twin Lakes are named, and tales of the mountaineers who live miserably on the slopes of Mt. Riga are many. The iron country of Connecticut, centering about Ore Hill in Salisbury, is at the extreme western end of this road, and much industrial history is connected with the woodland forges and now crumbling furnaces where guns were cast during the infancy of these United States.

US 44 enters Connecticut from Millerton, N.Y. At 0.6 *m.* is the junction with a dirt road.

> Left on this road 0.3 *m.* to the *Shagroy Turkey Farms* where 25,000 birds were raised in 1936. Viewed from the highway this farm resembles a resort hotel. In the marketing season the birds are handled with the dispatch of western slaughter houses. Killed by being pierced through the brain, chained to a conveyor that moves through a shower of hot water, then a cooling spray, and immersed in hot wax before further cooling, the birds are picked clean by the removal of the wax that carries away even the tenacious pin feathers.

Climbing toward the east, the highway passes a pond at 1.4 *m.*, which covers the spot where *Ore Hill* once produced iron ore of the finest quality. Around the pits are clustered the weather-beaten cabins of former miners and the ruins of an old tavern that boasted 'the longest bar east of Albany.' Above the sagging porch hangs a frieze of the vine-and-leaf design, typical of Salisbury. The hill has been dug away. About the time the Bessemer process made the use of poorer iron ores profitable, the pumps failed to keep ahead of the water. The flooded Ore Hill pit closed down in 1923 and was abandoned.

Beyond Ore Hill many country estates border the highway. Freshly painted paddock fences enclose fields where blooded saddle stock graze in grass to the hocks. This end of the township seems to have gained more than it lost from the failure of the iron business. Summer residents have managed to cover most of the slag and cinder dumps with land-scaped grounds and gay gardens.

LAKEVILLE (alt. 800, Town of Salisbury), 3.1 *m.*, trading center of the town, is at the junction with State 41, where US 44 turns sharply left. Few of the old houses in Lakeville remain, but many of the dwellings are distinguished by a jigsawed frieze of grapevines cut in the center of wide pine boards by some local builder.

At the junction stand the red-brick buildings of the *Holley Manufacturing Company Plant* (R), the first factory to produce pocket cutlery in this country, on the site of the Ethan Allen Forge (1763). Here that lusty Revolutionary soldier cast cannon for the Continental Army and 'put iron in the blood to whet resolve.' His historic manifesto referred to the ardent band of Salisbury patriots of whom he wrote: 'We can muster as good a regiment of marksmen and scalpers as America can afford.' The guns of the U.S.S. 'Constellation' were forged here, and Salisbury raised and equipped Colonel Sheldon's troop of horse and sent 121 men to the Continental Army.

Right from Lakeville on State 41, the highway passes the sparkling waters of *Lake Wononscopomuc* (R), 0.6 *m.*, and climbs the hill to the campus of the *Hotchkiss School*, 1.7 *m.*, a preparatory school for boys, with faculty houses, golf course (L), and tennis courts (R). The main buildings of the school, of brick, in a modernized form of Georgian, stand at the hilltop (R).

At 4.2 *m.* is the junction with a side road.

Left on this road, 0.3 *m.*, to the *Old Stone House* (R) that was built by a Gay in 1765. It is a gambrel-roofed dwelling, one-and-a-half stories high except at the rear where the ground falls away to terraced gardens. During the Revolution, this house was used as a prison; both slaves and ammunition were hidden here.

On State 41 at 8.2 *m.* is SHARON (alt. 800, town pop. 1703, inc. 1739). Acreage in this town was sold at auction in New Haven. A forge was established in 1743 and in 1825 a blast furnace supplied several small foundries. The Burnham stove, currycombs, round shot, lumber, ox-bows, rakes, hardware, tools, duck for sails, barrels, cigars, shoes, clothing, and even wooden mousetraps were once manufactured in Sharon, but there is no longer any industry in the town. White mulberry trees along Main St. date back to an early attempt to introduce silkworm culture here.

Sharon was the home of Benjamin Berkley Hotchkiss (1826–85), inventor of the Hotchkiss explosive shell for rifled guns. The Hotchkiss munitions business reached its peak during the Civil War and was removed to Bridgeport.

An early Sharon patriot, one Adonijah Maxam, was captured by the British and taken to England to be exhibited as a specimen of the boorish race of Yankees, or Yahoos, who had rebelled against the mother country; but not many years later, the town produced enough wealth and culture to import masons from Italy to construct stone mansions for early industrialists.

Sharon is the center of an increasing summer population. The surrounding hills offer ideal sites for numerous cabins and studios that are gay with varicolored awnings during the season when the forest background is of the brightest green. Shutters and trim of the brick and stone houses of this area are varying shades of blues and red; the familiar Connecticut color scheme of white with green trim is seldom seen.

Entering Sharon the highway passes three or four of the town's many brick houses. One of the most pleasing, at the head of the broad main street, is the *George King House*, which is usually dated 1790, the year it was completed. The oldest part, the ell, was built by John Penoyer about 1769 and the low, gambrel-roofed main section with dormers was started by King about 1790. The wide, open portico, five dainty dormers (the middle one with a Palladian window), the leaded sunburst fan-light, and the quoins give the house an air of elegance. The comparison of these open coved porticoes and Palladian windows will prove interesting, since in them, the usual Connecticut portico reached a peak of originality and variety after 1800. Earlier houses, like the *Colonel Fisher Gay House*, built in 1775, south of the Library on the east side of the street, have the simpler, more common kind.

Across from the Gay House, the *Congregational Church* (1824), though modernized, has a tall steeple and a trio of doorways that are original. Beyond an intersection, also on the west side, is the little old brick *Episcopal Church* (1813).

In the next block is the *Clock Tower* (L), built in 1885 of gray granite with red sandstone trim. South of it towers the *Sterling Elm*, planted in 1757 and now 18 feet, 9 inches in girth.

At some distance down Main St. are Sharon's most notable houses. *John Penoyer's Brick House* (1757) close to the street on the east side, has a curiously inscribed doorway. It is distinctly Dutch, foreign to the Connecticut scene. Re-roofing and remodeling have robbed the house of much of its original appearance.

The great stone *Smith House*, which is just south, is comparable to the Van Cortlandt Mansion in New York (1748), or to a Philadelphia or southern mansion. Dr. Simeon Smith built it over a period of years from 1757 to 1775. The main hip-roofed section, with three handsome fronts, dates from 1775. It has a broken pediment window with a wheel window above, gray and blue stonework, a flaring roof and odd railing of Chippendale line. John Cotton Smith, Governor of the State from 1812–17, made this house his home.

A kinsman of the Governor, Apollos Smith, built a central-chimney *Brick House* in 1776, located farther to the south facing up Main St. This house, of light-colored, large-sized Dutch brick has an imposing new doorway. It carries the Dutch-Indian name, Kesuckwand, meaning Sunshine.

At Sharon this route turns southwest onto State 343.

At **9.7 m.** State 343 crosses the New York Line, 3.6 miles east of Amenia.

At **3.6 m.** is the junction with a dirt road.

Left on the road to LINCOLN CITY, 0.8 *m.*, a tiny group of houses scattered along the southwestern slopes of Mt. Riga in the shadow of *Bear Mountain*, Connecticut's highest peak (alt. 2355). On these slopes during the winter the Salisbury Ski Runners hold many meets in which local runners, trained in the sport by their Norwegian fathers who once worked in the iron foundries, take many of the prizes. Salisbury placed two men on the 1936 Olympic team and her colors have been seen against the hard-packed snow of the best ski jumps in the world.

At **3.8 m.**, (L) behind a garage, general store, and filling station, and flanked by 'No Trespassing' signs are the *Davis Ore Beds*. The tawny yellow banks of an open excavation show signs of past activity when Salisbury notes were paid in iron rather than money.

SALISBURY (alt. 690, town pop. 2767), 4.7 *m.* The discovery of iron here in 1732 brought about a State-wide stampede, which rapidly gathered the fervor of a gold rush. The especially fine quality and great tensile strength of the iron led local enthusiasts to anticipate that Salisbury would become the 'Birmingham of America.' During the Revolutionary War the iron works were taken over by the Government, and General Knox was stationed here in charge of casting cannon. Only after 1800, with the growth of the western mines, did the Salisbury output dwindle in significance.

The first settlers, including William White and Abraham Vandusen from Livingston Manor, N.Y., migrated here in 1719, followed the next year by the Dyckman, Dutcher, and Knickerbocker families. A combination meeting-house and dwelling was built with its walls enclosing a stake which was the exact center of the township. The town was incorporated in 1741.

Salisbury today is a proud little hill town, stretching along an especially neat main street bordered with old homes and shaded by great elms and maples.

The *Stiles House* (1772) (L) is a large two-and-one-half-story, peak-roofed house, standing back from the road amid beautifully landscaped grounds.

Behind a neat white paneled and picket fence stands (L) the *Bushnell Tavern* (*private*), dated 1800, but appearing to be of much earlier construction, with a two-story porch across the entire front, supported by square columns.

The *Scoville Library* (R), the first tax-supported library in the United States (organized 1803), is housed in a modern building (1894) of cool gray, native granite, with a great square tower from which melodious chimes sound the hour. Above the fireplace is a bas-relief from Salisbury Cathedral in England. This piece of stone may have been a part of Hungerford Chapel, for it is carved with a chained raven, a lion rampant, and three fleurs-de-lis — the coat of arms of a family which intermarried with the Hungerfords. The inscription states that it was 'carved in the XV century.' The books of Salibury's first library association, formed November 18, 1771, are preserved in the library, together with an exhibit of many articles of historical interest.

The stately Salisbury *Town Hall*, directly across the street, was built from a portion of a church that was raised on November 25, 1749, with the help of '16 gals. rhum, half one hundred weight of shuger and two pounds of all-spice,' as well as 'eight bushels of wheat' made into cake for the occasion. Beside the Town Hall stands a 'kettle' fountain, originally a Salisbury iron kettle, but now a rounded cement bowl, in which runs spring water from the heights of Mt. Riga. According to legend, the visitor who drinks of this spring will surely return.

Behind the Town Hall is the old cemetery with the little brick *Town Jail* just over the fence. The town drunkard was once allowed to make this building his home.

The *Congregational Church* (1798) has much of the stately dignity that characterized Salisbury architecture. The tower, topped by an open belfry, has a series of Palladian windows on each side.

Left from Salisbury at the Town Hall, a dirt road climbs 2.2 *m.* to the top of *Mt. Riga* (alt. 2000). Here Swiss and Russian workmen once labored at the forges. Historians differ as to which group gave the mountain its name, some believing that it was derived from the Swiss 'Righi,' others, from the former Russian 'Riga.'

Iron ore was carried over this road in saddle-bags and by ox-team. A thriving village grew up on the shores of *Forge Pond*, a lonely lake at the mountain-top, whose waters, day and night, reflected the glare of blast furnaces. Commerce soon followed the industrial activity. The Salisbury women who wanted silk for a dress had to journey to this village on the mountain, where a thriving department store kept four clerks to serve the flourishing trade and supplied a variety of merchandise not obtainable in near-by towns. Here was forged the great anchor for the 'Constitution' which was drawn by six yoke of oxen to the Hudson River for shipment. Naval officers stationed at Riga to inspect anchors and chains of Salisbury iron added gaiety to the weekly dances and balls. In this region, Katherine Sedgwick found inspiration for her story 'The Boy of Mount Righi.'

The last forge cooled at Mt. Riga in 1847, houses tumbled to ruins, laborers went down the hill to work at forges ,nearer the railroad, and Nature reclaimed the mountain-top for her own. Three of the original houses remain, one with a great loom in the front room and another with a flower bed in the dooryard that adds a touch of color to the weathered grays of rotting fencerows and bleached clapboard siding. Away in the woods is a lonely graveyard.

Along the lower slopes of Mt. Riga, tucked away in shallow mountain coves, are the cabins of 'The Raggies,' a 'lost' people about whom little is known. The ancestry of the Raggies may possibly be traced to Hessian deserters who worked the woodland forges at the top of Mt. Riga, or to the early woodsmen, who, when there was no longer use for charcoal, still stayed on, knowing no trade and having no means to move from the area. They live in squalor, intermarry, and twelve or fourteen are often crowded together in a two-room shack. Sanitation is entirely inadequate: sink drains flow into springs of drinking water unrestrained.

Canned woodchuck is a favorite dish along the lower slopes of Mt. Riga. A local woman has taught the people to 'put up' the meat of Johnny Chuck, to can brook suckers and preserve the berries that grow on the rocky slopes.

Ghosts are said to enjoy the moonlight with great freedom. Tales of their wandering have been numerous since November, 1802, when for several days and nights three houses in Sage's Ravine were bombarded with pieces of mortar and stones of a variety not found in this region. Fifty window panes were shattered by the missiles which, strangely, did not hurtle into the rooms but were carefully deposited on the window sills as though placed by an unseen hand. A vigilant watch was set and although the stones continued to fly, no tangible assailants could be discovered. Surely, say the natives, here was evidence of black magic such as the 'Raggies' believe in today.

At Salisbury is the junction with State 41.

Left on State 41, locally known as 'The Undermountain Road,' in the shadow of the western ridges, offering pleasant views to the eastward. At 0.8 m. is an excellent view of distant hills and the white buildings of Salisbury School against the forest green.

The highway passes a golf course, terraced pastures fragrant with sweet fern and juniper, narrow stretches of farmland, and several weather-worn houses backed against the mountain for protection. Early sunsets cast long shadows here while the opposite hills are still aglow.

At 4.9 m. a bridge crosses the brook flowing from *Sage's Ravine* (*private*), a hemlock-shaded glen. The route enters Massachusetts at 5 m., 6 miles south of South Egremont, Mass.

At 8.5 m., is *Dutcher's Bridge* over the Housatonic. Here during the early 18th century, Ruluff Dutcher carried passengers across the river in a canoe ferry. A modern poultry farm (L), which uses the most advanced scientific methods and equipment, stands at the bridge, with headquarters in an old farmhouse painted white with black trim.

At Dutcher's Bridge is the junction with an oiled dirt road.

Left on the oiled road to *Twin Lakes*, 1.1 m., a summer resort. Known as Washining and Washinee ('Laughing Water' and 'Smiling Water'), the lakes, according to local legend, were named for two daughters of an Indian chief who ruled over the tribes between the Housatonic and the Hudson. Suitors traveled far to seek the maidens' favor, but all were rejected. During a tribal war, a young Indian was captured and brought to the shores of the lake to be tortured. The sisters befriended him, loved him, and endeavored to secure his release from their father. Their efforts were unsuccessful, and on the evening preceding the day set for his torture, both sisters embarked on the waters of the twin lakes and never were seen again. Today it is said that when the moon is full, an empty canoe is seen on the lake, drifting down the shimmering path of reflected moonlight, slipping noiselessly over the waves.

Many other legends are woven about the natural phenomena of this area and the eccentric recluses and half-breeds who lead strange lives in huts half hidden among the undergrowth of the back country. On private property south of Lake Washinee are the *Moving Stones*. These boulders on a hillside have pushed up mounds of sand before them and left paths behind, as though tossed like dice from the hilltop, although other near-by rocks have been unmoved by the same force which must have shaken the great rocks loose.

Northward, beyond Twin Lakes, the oiled road leads to the junction with another country road at 1.4 *m.*

Left on this road, 0.7 *m.*, to TACONIC (alt. 740, Town of Salisbury), where the ancestral estates of Robert and Herbert Scoville, descendants of an early ironmaster, cover 2500 acres. Their gray stone houses, roofed with red tile, set amid copper beeches and ornamental shrubs behind thick stone walls create an almost feudal impression of wealth and power.

US 44 turns sharp left at 8.9 *m.*, and at 11.3 *m.*, passes through Canaan (*see Tour* 4) at the junction with US 7 (*see Tour* 4).

The route, southeast, passes many antique shops which sell fine old glass and occasionally offer a good piece of furniture or a well-made clock.

At 13.8 *m.* is the hamlet of EAST CANAAN, with its modest, fine old *Congregational Church* (1822). Early limekiln fires have long since cooled and the furnaces fallen to ruins. Near a disused rickety railroad station, which seems to wait for passengers to board a phantom train on the rusty rails, outcroppings of lime and several rusty stacks mark the location of the old kilns.

At the center is the junction with the *Lower Road* (*see Tour* 4) which leads past the ruins of crumbling iron furnaces.

At 16.3 *m.*, attractively set on landscaped grounds, is the *Captain Titus Ives House* (1785) (L), a large salt-box dwelling with a pair of handsome front doors.

Across the field (R), at 16.7 *m.*, can be seen the *Norfolk Ski Jump*, center of many meets in which the best ski runners in the East compete.

US 44 continues down grade to the level of the Blackberry River and follows the valley to the southeast. On the right, a range of hills in varied shadings of green, offers a changing skyline. An occasional paper birch stands like a white knight among the evergreens at the end of an abandoned log road leading into the Green Woods. Off to the north a power line crosses the mountains, cutting a gash in the timber at the crest where the trees have been cut away to guard against fire. Here and there a mountain brook tumbles down a slope to plunge over a ledge in an unnamed waterfall, as beautiful as anything to be found in more widely publicized areas. The bottomlands on the river are divided into neat meadows, often with a row of trees at the fence lines and a giant elm or maple left mid-field as shade for man or beast. During the winter months these fields are crossed by a network of ski trails, and in sheltered spots groups of gayly clad youngsters gather close around the warmth of a fire, preparing their lunch after a frosty morning in the open. Blue woodsmoke rises from every farmhouse chimney along the route, for here men still use wood for fuel, scorning the smudge of coal or the odor of oil.

At 18.3 *m.* is the junction with a side road.

> Left on this road is *Haystack Mountain State Park*, 0.7 *m.* At the top of the mountain (alt. 1680), a stone *Tower*, erected by Mrs. Carl Stoeckel in 1929 in memory of her father, Robbins Battell, rises 36 feet, affording an excellent view of the surrounding countryside and the rising foothills of the mountains to the north.

NORFOLK (alt. 1260, town pop. 1298), 18.7 *m.*, named for the English county, incorporated in 1758, is now the center of an exclusive summer colony and attracts devotees of winter sports to its excellent ski trails in winter. The Litchfield County Choral Union and the Norfolk Music Festival, established by Mr. and Mrs. Carl Stoeckel in 1899, were internationally known for their annual concerts until 1925, when they were discontinued after the death of Mr. Stoeckel. Many famous composers were commissioned to write the music presented, and internationally known operatic stars participated in the concerts. Among composers who conducted presentations of their own work were Coleridge Taylor, Sibelius, Horatio Parker, and Henry Hadley. Now, under the patronage of Mrs. Stoeckel, an annual concert is held by the Choral Union of 700 voices, each June. The program is usually broadcast, but admission to the Music Shed is by invitation only.

Norfolk was one of the Connecticut towns which owed its rapid early growth to the enterprise of a single citizen. Joseph Battell, proprietor of the local store, by his native commercial ability, made the town the trading center for the surrounding countryside and a far more influential factor in the county than its industrial progress warranted. Late in the 19th century, prominent industrialists, financiers, scientists and men of letters, attracted by the seclusion of the forest-clad mountain slopes and sparkling lakes, began to build summer homes here. Today their landscaped estates merge with the rugged wilderness which still echoes with the scream of the wildcat and the bay lynx, when these husky warriors take their toll of the upland game birds.

Norfolk is surrounded by many beautiful hills, including *Ball Mt.* (alt. 1760) and *Haystack Mountain* (alt. 1680). During the winter months, snow trains bring hundreds of enthusiasts every week-end from the larger centers of population to ski runs and meets. In the summer, many visitors seek the numerous bridle paths and the side roads leading past large estates in the sheltered valleys well off the heavily traveled paved roads. Blackberry River once turned many millwheels in the town, and now furnishes excellent trout fishing in clean, State-stocked, fast flowing waters. The stream is crowded with anglers during April, May, and June.

Norfolk is the birthplace of Dr. William Henry Welch (1850–1934), famous pathologist, whose 80th birthday was celebrated in fifty of the world's largest cities. Dr. F. S. Dennis, distinguished surgeon, pioneer in the field of anaesthesia, Robbins Battell, and Sterling W. Childs are among the patrons of art, music and science, who have made their homes here.

At the southern corner of the Green is the *Joseph Battell Memorial Fountain*, designed by Saint-Gaudens and executed by Stanford White.

On the western knoll (R) overlooking the Green is the *Congregational Church* (1813), with a well-designed tower and spire. Both entrance portico and interior have been remodeled, however, and only the fluted columns remain within.

The three-story *Battell Homestead* (R), which was originally built in 1800, and locally known as the *White House*, stands at the northwest corner of the Green. At the rear of the house is the *Music Shed*, seating some 2000 people, where annual concerts are presented. At the northwest corner of the Green, the *Ariel Lawrence Tavern* (*private*), built in 1797, was remodeled when opened as a tavern in 1820. At the northeast corner, is the earlier *Giles Pettibone Jr. Tavern* (*private*) of 1794, with a curious chimney in front of the ridge. On the east side is a versatile building erected for an academy, and then used successively as town hall and jail before it became a house.

At 19.5 *m*. (L) is the 1775 *Tavern* built by Joel Phelps.

Southward, US 44 enters WINSTED (alt. 765, city pop. 7,883), 28.6 *m*., principal community of the town of Winchester. Here in the center is the junction with State 8 (*see Tour 5*).

Winchester, a wilderness camp site beside a bridle path, was laid out in 1758 and distributed by lottery. Incorporated in 1771, the township saw Winsted, its principal village, become a city in 1917. The city lies in a well-watered valley below rounded ridges covered with a dense growth of evergreens and mountain laurel. Long Pond, now known as Highland Lake, spilled its surplus water down a narrow stream with a 150-foot fall to furnish power for five early forges, four large scythe shops, assorted mills and an axe shop. The Hoadley brothers and Riley Whiting made clocks in 1807, 'with cog wheels of cherry, pinions of ivy (laurel), and faces of whitewood.' From this humble beginning rose the William L. Gilbert Clock Company whose founder financed the William L. Gilbert Home for Dependent Children, with an initial bequest of some $400,000. The Litchfield County Hospital owes its beginning to small contributions dropped into a box beside the bed of Miss Adelyn Howard, an invalid gentlewoman. The hospital was finally dedicated in 1902.

Winsted has always been a 'never-never-land' where the unusual is expected to happen and usually does. Tales of 5-legged cows, talking owls, tame trout and even a wild man are flashed over the wires from this area. Irving Manchester wrote a story of 'The Winsted Wild Man,' and a local woman exhibited photographs of moose snapped in the yard of her cabin in the Green Woods. The family of Caleb Beach started the first wild tale from these hillsides. Seated at dinner one evening, they heard the sounds of weaving from the loom room, investigated and found only a wide-open door with fresh tracks of a cloven hoof in the snow outside and 'a slight mark as if a forked tail had been drawn across the powdery surface.' Later, a member of the parish was whipped for witchcraft.

Present-day Winsted clings to its tales of the unusual, holds an annual Laurel Festival, strings its buildings along a seemingly endless main street, and fosters small industry. Twelve million pins are manufactured daily; knit goods, clocks, scythes, coffin fittings, hatter's fur, small hardware, edge tools, fishing tackle, wire goods, and electrical goods bear Winsted trademarks. Varied building lines, alternate rows of one-story shops or modern brick business buildings, 'Sucker Brook' flowing behind the tenements on the main street, and French-Canadian mill-hands gossiping at the doorways of the many taverns — all are typical of this city at the edge of the Green Woods.

At the corner of Lake and Prospect Sts. stands the *Solomon Rockwell House* (*open, free*), built in 1813 by an early ironmaster for his bride; it is now occupied by a rural museum in charge of the Winsted Historical Society. The house, a Greek Revival mansion with pillared ell and out-buildings, is almost southern in appearance and interesting for its delicate interior detail. Splinters from a wrecked plane that crashed in Winsted in 1917 share a case with a petrified potato from Arizona, but there are also many relics and specimens of real interest rather carelessly arranged.

Mrs. Rose Terry Cooke, writer of New England stories, lived in Winsted in a house of 1795, at 320 N. Main St.; the structure is replete with corner quoins and heavy caps on the windows.

At 33.1 *m.* is the junction with State 181. US 44 turns sharp right.

> Left on State 181, a macadam road, is the hamlet of PLEASANT VALLEY (Town of Barkhamsted), 0.8 *m.*, one of Connecticut's sleepy streamside settlements, where an occasional tourist stops for gasoline. Here hikers pause to rest beside the Farmington River, or woodsmen drop in at the Post Office for mail and fresh chewing tobacco.
>
> At 0.9 *m.* is the junction with a dirt road.
>
>> Straight ahead on the dirt road is the *American Legion State Forest*, an area of 549 acres purchased and given to the State by this organization.
>
> State 181, at 0.9 *m.*, turns right across the bridge to the junction with a dirt road at the eastern end of the bridge.
>
>> Left on this dirt road, along which laurel grows in profusion, through the *People's State Forest*, 1861 acres of woodland. At 2.3 *m.*, a bronze tablet (L) marks the site of an old dwelling known as the *Barkhamsted Lighthouse*. To the hillside, many years ago, trekked Molly Barber, of Wethersfield, and an

Indian named Chaugham. Defying her family, they eloped, built a crude cabin here, and lived happily the rest of their lives.

Unlike ordinary Indian cabins, Chaugham's home was always well lighted and served as a landmark for stage-drivers urging tired horses along the rough road. Sleepy passengers were aroused to attention by the booming voice of the driver as he shouted, 'Thar's Barkhamsted Lighthouse, only five miles to port.'

Within the forest, near the site of the lighthouse, are the graves of Chaugham and about 40 other Indian men.

This forest, which lies between Pleasant Valley and Riverton, with elevations ranging from 500 to 1120 feet, was the gift of citizens of Connecticut, purchased from contributions of individuals and organizations to the Connecticut Forest and Park Association. Within the forest are two study plots, one of pine, the other of hardwoods, and a nature trail of unusual interest and beauty. When the Frenchman, de Chastellux, visited this region in 1782 he wrote: 'Here the trees are superb; they are firs but so strong, so straight and lofty, that I doubt whether there are any like them in North America.'

Eastward on State 181 to BARKHAMSTED (alt. 480, town pop. 697), 3.8 *m.*, a town that will eventually be partly submerged in the new reservoir of the Hartford municipal water supply. Of this once lively little village, named for Barkhamsted, England, in May, 1732, and incorporated October, 1779, nothing now remains at the Green but one house and a Congregational church built in 1846. Here the Masons held secret meetings during the agitation against them in the 1840's, while 'Little Johnny' Merrill was stationed outside, armed with a drum to sound the alarm when anti-Masonic mobs arrived to break up the meetings.

A Barkhamsted woman, Esther Alford Loomis, was active in securing equal rights for women in school matters and the ownership of property in Connecticut.

US 44 passes *Greenwood Pond*, at 34.4 *m.*, which, since the breaking of the dam, is little more than a swampy basin crossed by a stream that trickles over an old wooden dam, built long ago across the center of the reservoir, but submerged for so many years that its existence was forgotten until revealed by the subsiding flood waters. On the eastern bank are the remains of several old mills.

At 34.8 *m.* US 44 passes through NEW HARTFORD (alt. 360, town pop. 1834), where the breaking of the Greenwood Dam caused considerable damage during the spring flood of 1936. Settled and named in 1733 by Hartford proprietors, the town was incorporated in 1738. The brick *Congregational Church* (1828) and the *Academy* (1838), now its parish house, stand a little back from the center, behind an avenue of trees. In the northwestern section of the town a growing summer community of artists includes, as its most prominent resident, Alma Gluck.

At CHERRY BROOK, 38.8 *m.*, the oldest house in Canton can be seen across the Farmington River — the red salt-box *House of Ezra Wilcox* built in 1740.

The Cherry Brook Rd. leads north to CANTON CENTER, 1.3 *m.*, with a Gothicized *Congregational Church* (1814), and to NORTH CANTON, a remote crossroads settlement that a full century seems to have passed by. The *Adams Houses* all date from around 1800.

CANTON, 41.2 *m.*, is a village in the township of the same name, which has been superseded in importance by the manufacturing center of

Collinsville. Formerly a part of Simsbury, Canton was originally named 'Suffrage' because of the severe suffering of the first settlers in 1740.

Early Canton was noted for its production of ships' stores, resin, pitch, and turpentine. The pioneers were hard drinkers: early records state that in a 'cider house,' across the way from the church, a barrel of cider was kept for the use of church goers. Early preachers established wide reputations by their unceasing war against the cider brandy stills maintained by every farmer.

One starless night during the Revolution, a French paymaster stopped here at Canton Tavern on his way from Hartford to Saratoga with saddlebags containing gold to pay the French officers. When he failed to reach Saratoga, investigators could trace him no further than the Inn. The innkeeper swore that his guest had left the tavern in good health, but years later when the hostelry burned to the ground, the discovery of a whitened skeleton confirmed the suspicions of earlier days. Today, so some say, out of the mists of the valley, rides a lone horseman, who, from afar, seems to be headless. Horses bolt, so the story goes, as the specter gallops by, and headlight beams shine straight through both horse and rider.

Right from Canton on Canton St. and left on Maple St. to COLLINSVILLE (alt. 400, town pop. 2397), 2 *m.*, where are produced axes, machetes, and edged tools known wherever men struggle with nature.

Here in 1826 Samuel and David Collins and their cousin, William Wells, established the first axe factory in the world. Previously axes were made to order by blacksmiths, and the purchaser ground his own blade. From this factory, John Brown, a native of Torrington, obtained pikes for his insurrection at Harpers' Ferry.

Modern axes bear a strange assortment of names, usually descriptive of their use or of the section of the country in which they are most favored. Colors, too, vary with the markets; a red-headed axe is demanded in the north woods because it is easily found in the snow. Many a Collins Charcoal Tempered Axe has been passed down from father to son, used until 'the bit was as round as an apple,' stoned and whetted to a razor edge.

At 41.5 *m.* is the junction with State 177. The *Isaac Mills House*, built in 1799, just west of this corner on the south side, has a delicate cornice and leader heads.

Right a few yards beyond the junction, stands the 1776 house erected by Jared Mills in that year. This old salt-box dwelling, now a tea house, still displays its original tavern sign — 'Food for Man and Beast.'

South at the junction with the first road (L) to the big-stone *Case* or *Mather House* 0.3 *m.* (L). Built in 1786, it is a gambrel-roofed dwelling with a crude stone belt course extending across the front at the first floor window caps, and three original dormers. The gable ends are clapboarded, and the doorsills are of red Simsbury stone. Within are preserved many of the original features including a stone sink, a built-in kettle, and a long attic with a fireplace at each end. Masonic meetings were once held in this room.

At 41.9 *m.* (R), is the *Canton Public Golf Course* (9 holes) where an entire day of golfing costs only 50¢ (*Sundays* 75¢).

Eastward, the highway traverses an area grown with mixed pine and birch trees and crosses *Nod Brook* at 44.4 *m.*

At AVON (*see Tour* 6), 44.8 *m.*, is the junction with State 10 with which US 44 unites for 0.8 *m.*

At 45.6 *m.* State 10 (*see Tour* 6) leaves US 44 and turns south.

The route passes a *Monument* (R), 46.5 *m.*, in memory of James H. Mc-Donald, State Highway Commissioner, a pioneer in the construction of modern trunklines through the State. The road climbs the steep slope to the top of *Avon Mountain*, where there is an impressive view of Talcott Mountain with the pinnacle of Heublein Tower on its summit.

At 49.8 *m.* is the junction with a paved highway.

> Right on this highway is WEST HARTFORD (alt. 100, town pop. 24,941), 1.5 *m.*, a residential suburb of Hartford. Settled in 1679 but not organized as a separate town until 1854, it is now under a commission form of government. The growth of this community is evidenced by the figures of the grand tax list. In 1919, taxable property was listed as worth $19,369,385; in 1934 the value had increased to $69,225,000. The Hartford municipal reservoir and watershed occupies much of the area of the town. The residential sections are protected by a strict zoning ordinance, so that there are no unsightly buildings in the area.
>
> Quakers came to this district in 1780 and lived here for fifty years, giving their name to Quaker Lane. From West Hartford, Moses Goodman rode to Valley Forge in 1777 with $30,000 in his saddlebags contributed by Hartford residents for the Continental Army.
>
> At 139 N. Main St. is the *American School for the Deaf*, the first permanent institution of its kind in the United States. Founded in Hartford in 1817, by the Rev. Thomas H. Gallaudet, this school now accepts deaf mutes from four New England States for training and rehabilitation.
>
> At 227 S. Main St. is the *Birthplace of Noah Webster* (1758–1843), renowned American lexicographer. It is an added lean-to, salt-box house of 1676. The ell and the paneling, some of which is very good, date from the 18th century. The rear wall represents some of the earliest New England brick work.

Crossing the northern end of the town of West Hartford on Albany Ave., the old Albany Post Rd., US 44 passes the *Children's Village*, 51.8 *m.*, a Hartford orphanage, in a setting comparable to the farm of a country gentleman.

US 44 enters Hartford, 53.7 *m.*, on Albany Ave. (*see HARTFORD*). At Hartford are the junctions with US 6 (*see Tour* 2), US 5 (*see Tour* 7), US 5A and State 9 (*see Tour* 8), State 175 (*see Tour* 7B).

Sec. b. HARTFORD to BOLTON NOTCH, 13.2 *m.*

After passing through metropolitan Hartford, the highway is bordered by tobacco fields to Bolton.

Leaving Hartford, US 44 crosses the Connecticut River on the Bulkeley Memorial Bridge (*see HARTFORD*), to EAST HARTFORD, 1.2 *m.*

At East Hartford are the junctions with State 2 (*see Tour* 3A), State 15 (*see Tour* 10), US 5 (*see Tour* 7), and US 6 (*see Tour* 2).

At 3.7 *m.* the highway affords a good view of the gray outline of the *Travelers Tower*, rising above the Hartford skyline. At 3.9 *m.* the road passes through an area giving a view of the *Sunset Ridge Country Club*, on a high ridge to the left.

The *Samuel Olcutt Tavern* (L), at 5.4 *m.*, is an 18th-century building with a Greek Revival doorway. Just beyond is the half-gambrel *Thomas Spencer House* which was built in 1790. Eastward, the highway follows an old Podunk Indian trail, known as *Ye Olde Connecticut Path* (*roadside markers identify*), over which Thomas Hooker and his congregation trekked toward Hartford. At 6.7 *m.* is the junction with US 6 with which this route combines for 8.3 miles.

US 44 passes through an underpass of a spur track of the New York, New Haven & Hartford Railroad to the city of South Manchester.

SOUTH MANCHESTER (alt. 140, pop. 21,973, Town of Manchester), 7.6 *m.* Once known as the Five Mile Tract, settled as a part of Hartford in 1672, incorporated as a town in 1823, this lively industrial center has built its prosperity on silk, wool, and paper manufacturing. Silk has been the foundation of the larger fortunes in Manchester since the Cheney brothers discovered, in 1885, an economical method of utilizing and spinning silk waste.

Manchester's Civic Center, facing the Green, is composed of several buildings in pleasing adaptations of Colonial Georgian style. The striking *Congregational Church* (1904), the *Municipal Building* (1923), by Farley and Beers, with delicate wooden cupola, and the *Telephone Building* (1928), by Douglas Orr, form an outstanding group.

At the center of Manchester is the junction with State 83.

On Park St. is the *Plant of Cheney Brothers*, silk manufacturers. This factory has earned for Manchester the name 'Silk City.' In landscaped grounds near the plant are many fine residences of the Cheney family. US 44 passes (L) the remodeled *Timothy Cheney House* which was built about 1757, and the old *Manchester Cemetery* (R), and proceeds to the junction with Pitkin St.

West of the Green and south at 54 Pitkin St. is the *Pitkin House* (*private*), a two-and-a-half-story, shingled structure with a two-story ell dating from 1765, but entirely remodeled about 1830. On Putnam St., west of Pitkin St., are the picturesque *Ruins of the Pitkin Glass Works* to which, in 1783, the General Assembly gave a monopoly of glass-making in Connecticut. This ivy-covered building probably dates from 1783; only three of the lower story walls are standing, with arched windows and doors, and rough granite sides, like an Old-World ruin.

MANCHESTER GREEN, 10.1 *m.*, is a suburban village of dignified residences about a small maple-bordered street and Green. At the *Woodbridge Tavern* (L), a two-and-a-half-story house with an ell, now converted into tenements, George Washington was entertained in 1781.

US 44 and US 6, entering a straight stretch of highway, pass the abandoned factory of the *Glastonbury Knitting Company* (L), and skirt the base of *Turkey Hill*.

The highway ascends Turkey Hill and halfway up the incline, at 12 *m.*, is the junction with a macadamized road.

Right on this road, climbing a steep hill, is BOLTON CENTER (alt. 760, town pop. 504), 2.1 *m.*, a small village on high fertile land, about a central Green, where Rochambeau's army camped in Revolutionary days, en route from Newport to the Hudson River. The town was named for Bolton, England. The march of architectural style is illustrated in houses about the Green: notably in the little *Daniel Darte House*, built about 1725, on the south; the large *Williams House*, a dwelling of 1751–61, on the northeast; and the brick *Tavern* (1800) at the north. The pretentious *Jared Cone House*, on the west side, built in 1800, is now the post office. The architect was so anxious to use all possible embellishments that the doorway and the Palladian window are kaleidoscoped in a curious way.

Left from Bolton Center on a macadam road to a fork at 0.4 *m.*; here (L) stands the *Asa White House* which was built in 1741, now shabbily covered with tar paper. In this former meeting place of French Hussars, the walls in several rooms are scarred with saber and bullet holes.

Right at the fork, 0.2 *m.*, to the *Thomas Loomis House*, built in 1750.

Continuing the ascent of Turkey Hill, US 44 passes *Bolton Pines Highway Rest* (L), 12.3 *m.*, and skirts the south shore of Bolton Pond.

At 13 *m.* is the junction with a gravel side road.

Right on this road, over a wooden bridge, crossing a deep gorge in the rock, to a *Quarry* (R), 0.1 *m.*, where quarrying of the iridescent Bolton stone at one time furnished the town's chief industry.

At Bolton Notch, 13.2 *m.*, is the junction with US 6A (*see Tour 2*).

Sec. c. BOLTON NOTCH to RHODE ISLAND LINE, 38.6 m.

Beyond Bolton Notch, with its roadside quarries and hilltop lakes, the route enters the silk manufacturing area about Mansfield, and traverses the rather sub-marginal farm lands of the 'Father Dunn country.'

After crossing the beautifully landscaped residential areas among the Pomfret hills, the highway follows the Quinebaug Valley to Putnam, passing juniper-grown pasture land and low hills en route. Beyond Putnam, the road crosses numerous brooks and enters Rhode Island at West Gloucester.

Precipitous rock ledges tower high above the road, extending eastward through a deep pass. About thirty feet up the side of the rocky eminence (L) is *Squaw Cave*, a narrow aperture that tunnels about twelve feet into the stone. Here Wunneeneetmah, an Indian squaw, hid with her fugitive Dutch husband, outlawed for chopping wood on the Sabbath, who was finally discovered and shot while with her in the cave. The area occupied by this mountainous rock is now a State park.

COVENTRY, 3.2 *m.*, is a small roadside village, with a few scattered houses and a church overlooking open fields that slope away to the south. The *Pomeroy Tavern* (*private*), a large central-hall building (L), was erected in 1806.

At Coventry US 6 (*see Tour 2*) leaves this route, branching to the right. This route, US 44, continues easterly.

The highway descends a long slope and crosses the Skungamaug River at 4.3 *m.*

Eastward, at 6.2 *m.*, is (L) the *Brigham Tavern* (*private*), an old inn now used as a dwelling. A tablet states that George Washington once breakfasted here and mentioned the place in his diary.

US 44 continues across the Willimantic River, at 6.3 *m.*, and enters MANSFIELD DEPOT, 6.6 *m.*, a small trading center for surrounding farms about a station on the Central Vermont Railroad.

At 6.8 *m.* is the junction with State 32 (*see Tour 9A*).

At 7.1 *m.* is the *Mansfield State Training School and Hospital for Mental Defectives.* This plant has a waiting list larger than the actual number of patients. Connecticut is now planning a more modern institution to be located at South Britain. Need for improved institutional facilities has been so pressing that even this new $4,000,000 training school will not care for the waiting list. Mansfield, with a capacity of 1200, can furnish care for only the most difficult cases.

US 44 passes *Houston's Tree Nursery* (L), at 8.2 *m.*, and crosses over Cedar Swamp Brook at 8.6 *m.*

MANSFIELD (FOUR CORNERS), 9.2 *m.*, is a crossroads hamlet at the junction with State 195. *Fuller's Tavern* (L) was an 18th-century stopping-place for stage-coaches on the Boston Post Rd. This white wooden house has swinging partitions.

Right from Mansfield on State 195, winding over the top of a hill, to the *Storrs Fire Tower* (R). The lookout house of the tower is set atop one of the twin water tanks that rise 80 feet above the summit of the hill. Left is the *Connecticut State College Poultry Plant*, and immediately beyond is double-knolled, *Horsebarn Hill* (L), scene, during winter months, of college skiing and toboganing.

Connecticut State College, formerly known as Storrs Agricultural College, is open to both men and women for training in agriculture and allied professional and specialized fields. The 1710 college acres include a well-equipped campus, extensive woodlands and fields allotted to the Experiment Station, which was the first State-supported station in this country to put science to work for agriculture. This station conducts research in agriculture and such related fields as livestock and poultry-raising. Its publications have successfully promoted the conservation of land, orchards, and forests throughout the State.

Established in 1881, with gifts of 170 acres, several buildings, and a $6000 endowment fund, presented by Augustus and Charles Storrs, the college is now supported by Federal and State grants.

Descending a long grade past the college *Dairy Building* (L), 1.2 *m.*, with a well-equipped dairy barn behind it, the highway passes the *Storrs Community Church* (R), 1.4 *m.*, a noteworthy modern brick reproduction of an early American church. In an original early edifice of this style the tower would have been placed midway on the front axis and have had heavier columns than those which stand out in contrast with the variegated brick. Modern work can usually be told by its greater delicacy. The proportions of this tower are close to perfection.

At this point there is a traffic light and a three-pronged intersection.

The far branch passes the church, and the adjoining *Community House* and *Mechanics Arts Building*, which houses Radio Station WCAC. The middle road mounts a slight elevation overlooking the college campus and extends past *Beach Hall*, the administration building.

At the fork, State 195 swings sharply left passing the college grounds (R). *Holcomb*

Hall (L) is the girls' dormitory. Just beyond the dormitory a road branches right to the center of the campus.

Passing a fine growth of pines on the shore of *Swan Lake* (R), State 195 climbs a gradual slope to the junction, 2.4 *m.*, with Hanks Hill Rd., a bituminous-macadam road.

> Left on this road to a junction, 0.7 *m.*; right to HANKS HILL, 1.1 *m.*, a small farming community that grew up around the Hanks Silk Company, built in 1810. After mill operations ceased, the residents turned to agriculture. On the shore of a small pond (R), is the *Site of Hanks Mill*, now marked by a wooden sign. The mill, only about 12 feet square, which contained Horatio Hanks' invention of a double-wheel head for spinning silk, was purchased by Henry Ford and removed to his industrial museum at Dearborn, Michigan, in 1931.
>
> South of the village, at 1.7 *m.*, is the *Site of the Benjamin Hanks Foundry*, where early brass cannon were cast. Later, church bells were made here.

On State 195 is SPRING HILL (alt. 320, Mansfield town pop. 3349), 4.4 *m.*, a small hilltop village, seat of the town government.

Incorporated in 1703, Mansfield early utilized the water-power of its many streams, becoming the home of numerous small industries, some of which were the first of their kind in the State or country.

Here, in 1775, Dr. Nathaniel Aspinwall transplanted mulberry trees from his Long Island nursery, giving impetus to an active interest in the culture of silkworms. In 1793, one-half ounce of mulberry seed was sent to every town in Connecticut, and the legislature offered a bounty on mulberry trees and raw silk (*see HANKS HILL above*). The Mansfield Silk Company, established in Gurleyville (Town of Mansfield) in 1829, was the first silk mill in the United States to reel successfully from native cocoons by water-power. By 1830 the State's production of raw silk had reached 3200 pounds, and Mansfield was producing more silk than any other town in the country, laying the foundations for the State's present-day silk manufacture. Although a blight destroyed Connecticut mulberry trees in 1845, and local factories closed, the manufacture of sewing silk and twist has become an important industry in the State.

Descending the steep grade of Spring Hill, with a fine view of heavy forests to the south, the highway mounts another hill, then descends, passing PERRY'S POND (R), 5.3 *m.*, where an early circular saw factory was operated in the 18th century by Daniel Hartshorn.

The *Eleazer Williams House* (L), at 5.4 *m.*, was erected in 1720 and is the oldest building in town. Its wide door, flanked by fluted pilasters, and the pediments that can be traced over its windows are similar to those of the famous Parson Williams House (1708) in Deerfield, Mass.

MANSFIELD CENTER, 5.7 *m.*, is a little community along a maple-bordered highway. Here the town's original settlement was made and named 'Ponde-Place.' The town *Sign Post* (L) is of the original timber used generations ago as a whipping post. Beyond (L) is the old *Cemetery* where many of the first settlers and several Indians are buried.

Passing *Shady Oak Highway Rest* (L), at 10.1 *m.*, the highway crosses Fenton River, 10.5 *m.*

At 10.8 *m.* is the junction with a gravel road.

> Right on this road, descending toward the east bank of the Fenton River, to an old *Sawmill* (R), 0.2 *m.*, in which a single up-and-down saw, one of the very few left in the State, is in operation during the cutting season. These saws show the step made from a hand-operated pit-saw toward the power-driven band, or rotary rigs, of production milling. Farmers once valued these up-and-down saws highly because of their adaptability to the sawing of stone-boat planks.

Above an agricultural countryside, the gray outline of *Storrs Fire-Tower* rises to the east, with a spiral outside stairway winding upward like a giant grapevine.

At 14.3 *m.* is the junction with State 74, the 'Eliphalet Nott Highway,' a water-bound macadamized road.

> Left on State 74, up a gradual ascent to (R) the *Site of the Birthplace of the Rev. Dr. Eliphalet Nott* (1773–1866), 0.9 *m.* An eminent inventor and educator, Nott rose from comparative obscurity to serve as president of Union College for 62 years. He was largely responsible for the great advancement of the college in scholastic standing and financial security. Among his inventions was a stove for burning hard coal. The spot is marked by a boulder and tablet.

WARRENVILLE, 15.4 *m.*, is a small crossroads village notable for a group of houses erected before 1800. On the outskirts stands *St. Philip's Church* (L), a field-stone and stucco structure (1936), erected by the local farmers themselves. The *Palmer Tavern (private)*, set well back from the northeast corner, is, despite its plain exterior, one of the most interesting buildings in this part of the State. The earlier east end, probably dating from the first half of the 18th century, has its tap-room intact at the end of a 35-foot kitchen. The west end, added in 1775, contains two richly carved diagonal fireplaces and a tiny secret room. The *John Warren House*, or *Durkee House (private)*, on the opposite, southwest corner, is a much later building, despite its local reputation. Warrenville, originally Pompey Hollow, was renamed in appreciation for a gift to the town of $1000 from John Warren. The *Memorial Town Hall* (R) was donated by Charles Knowlton in honor of his ancestor, Colonel Knowlton, gallant Continental officer who fell at the battle near Harlem Heights, September 16, 1776 *(see below)*.

At Warrenville is the junction with State 89.

> Left from Warrenville on State 89, a macadamized road, ascending a low ridge with excellent views toward the west, winding through pasturelands, past small farmhouses.
>
> WESTFORD (alt. 720, Town of Ashford), 4.1 *m.*, a village high among overgrown hills, originally built up about the once nationally known glassworks of Michael Richmond, established here in 1850.
>
> At the village crossroads (R) stands the *Capt. John Dean House*, built about 1815, and known for its ornate recessed front door and Palladian window, united in one design; opposite is (L) the later and still more ornate *Michael Richmond House*, built in 1828, and now housing a general store and the post office. These recessed doors are typical of the northeastern part of the State.

Climbing a long ascent, US 44 proceeds to a junction with a gravel road, 16.5 *m.*

> Left on this road, to a *Silver Fox Farm* (R), 0.7 *m.*, one of the very few in the State. Visitors are permitted near the cages of some of the tamer animals.
>
> At 1 *m.* on this road is the *Site of the Knowlton House*, built by Colonel Thomas Knowlton, Continental officer and organizer of Knowlton's Rangers, of which Nathan Hale was a member. When the news from Lexington reached Ashford, Knowlton raised a platoon of 78 men and arrived at Boston in time to reinforce the Continental troops at Bunker Hill, where his men manned the rail fence at the hill crest.

ASHFORD CENTER (alt. 680, pop. 726), Town of Ashford, 17.6 *m.*, is a small settlement of old houses whose residents are now pioneering in the modern development of a Farmers' Co-operative Association, which buys as well as sells products for a rapidly growing membership, under the direction of a young, progressive priest, Father Dunn.

Northeastward, the highway ascends a rolling stretch of land, descends a sharp grade through dense woods and crosses Branch Brook at 18.9 *m.*

PHOENIXVILLE (Town of Eastford), 19.5 *m.*, is a small crossroads hamlet on Still River, which grew up around a twine mill (1831), now abandoned.

At Phoenixville is the junction with State 91.

Left from Phoenixville on State 91, to EASTFORD CENTER (alt. 500, town pop. 529), 1.7 *m.*, a small collection of houses on open land, extending westward toward a small hill. Visible about 0.1 *m.* up a side road (L) is the *Castle*, built in 1800 by Squire Bosworth. A monitor-shaped, upper structure on the flat-topped roof was used as a former Masonic meeting-place. Within, the benches are still in place, ranged along the fireplaces at either end. One man is reported to have worked an entire winter on the woodwork in this one room.

Passing the *Tatem Company* (R), manufacturers of wooden handles, State 91 crosses Still River at 2.4 *m.* and again at 2.8 *m.*

WOODSTOCK VALLEY (Town of Woodstock), 4.7 *m.*, is a small roadside hamlet of small farms and a few residences strung out along the highway. At Woodstock Valley is the junction with a gravel road.

Left on this narrow road, through dense timberland thickly overgrown with underbrush, to *Green's Tavern* (*private*), dating from 1780–1820, at a fork in the road, 2.1 *m.* (R), a bustling hostelry in the early 19th century.

Right at Green's Tavern to *Session's Tavern* (*private*) (L), 2.8 *m.*, built in 1820, a freakish structure with elaborate porches and odd-shaped windows, which seem the more fantastic for being in so isolated a location.

Eastward, on State 91, beyond closely grouped farmhouses is WEST WOODSTOCK (Town of Woodstock), 6.4 *m.*, a rural community group of houses on a crossroads of the old King's Highway. They include the conspicuous old *Tavern* (*private*), and half hidden behind trees, the *House of the Squire* (*private*), with his midget office building beside it.

At 7.1 *m.*, and well back from the road, is (R), the *Birthplace of Colonel Joshua Chandler, Jr.*, a confirmed Tory, who, with his son and daughter, fled from the town during the Revolution, and was shipwrecked near St. John, Newfoundland. All on board were lost, and superstitious Newfoundland fishermen, believing that the father and his children haunt that section of the coast, have named the reef on which the boat foundered, Chandler Rock.

At 8.1 *m.*, off to the left 0.3 mile, on a gravel road and visible from the main highway, is (L), the *Site of the Birthplace of the Rev. Jedediah Morse* (1761–1826), noted author of school geographies and father of Samuel F. B. Morse, inventor of the telegraph. After a series of winding turns, State 91 continues through overgrown country and at 9.2 *m.*, skirts *Fort Hill* (L), a steep, forested bluff. Atop this hill, in the days of the early settlements, stood a fort which served as a refuge for women and children during Indian raids. Today, a wooden sign marks the spot. State 91 crosses a stream at 9.4 *m.*, and *Mascraft Brook* at 9.7 *m.* At 10.1 *m.* is the junction with a gravel road.

Left on this gravel road along an open ridge, a magnificent view, 0.5 *m.*, extends to the south and as far east as the city of Putnam. Descending steadily and turning north through wild forest land the road proceeds to *Eliot Rock* (R),

0.9 *m.*, a granite boulder roughly square in shape, approached by steps leading from the road through a small gate. The rock served as a boulder-pulpit in 1674 for John Eliot, noted missionary to the Indians, who came south with the Woodstock settlers from Roxbury, Mass., and preached to the native Wabbaquassetts.

At 1 *m.* is a fork in the road. Left at the fork to the historic *Pulpit Rock*, 0.1 *m.* (R), an oblong, flat-topped boulder bearing the inscription 'Pulpit Rock, Sacred Forevermore, 1686–1886.' Here, in 1686, the first religious services in the town were held when a minister, using the rock as a pulpit, preached to a congregation of settlers seated on the hillside.

At 1.3 *m.* is the junction with State 93, in the village of WOODSTOCK HILL (alt. 600, town pop. 1712), 1.7 *m.*, the site of the town's first settlement, and the present political center of the township, formerly known as Plaine Hill, an elm-shaded village of comfortable white homes among wide lawns, grouped about the spreading, informal Green, and along the single, wide village street.

At the northern end of the Green (R) stands the *Bowen Tavern* (*private*) erected by Asa Bishop in 1782. The wooden main unit contained a vaulted ballroom running the entire length of the second floor. The more southerly brick extension was built in 1809 as Grange hall, post office, and store. Dr. Hamilton Holt, President of Rollins College in Florida, spends his summers in this ancestral home. Beyond it, at the northeast corner of the Green, are the buildings of *Woodstock Academy*, founded in 1802, now a semi-private school. South of this, across the wide *Burial Ground* (1689), commanding a blue misty view of the Thompson Hills, the white spire of the *Congregational Church* (1821) reaches above the tree-tops. It is a perfectly proportioned building with three round-topped doors and an open steeple.

On the opposite, west side of the Green, is '*Roseland*,' the Tudor residence of Henry C. Bowen, an influential publisher of the 19th century, who in 1848 established *The Independent*, of which Henry Ward Beecher and Theodore Tilton were successively editors. At this house were received and entertained, for the annual Fourth of July celebrations, all the Presidents from Grant to McKinley.

At 2.5 *m.* is South Woodstock at the junction with State 91, which combines with State 93 for 0.4 *m.*

From the junction with the gravel road, at 10.1 *m.*, State 91 leads east to South Woodstock.

SOUTH WOODSTOCK (Town of Woodstock), 11.8 *m.*, is a peaceful hamlet of old houses overlooking a well-kept Green. Facing the Green on the north is the *Arnold Inn* with a long ell and rambling carriage sheds, built by General Samuel McClellan in 1769. General McClellan, a veteran of the Indian Wars, purchased the land for his homestead from Dr. David Holmes, grandfather of Oliver Wendell Holmes. Three large elms on the Green, opposite the house, are said to have been planted by the General's wife immediately after the battle of Lexington. Diagonally across the street (SW. corner) is General McClellan's store.

Left from South Woodstock on a bituminous-macadam road to the junction with a gravel road, 0.7 *m.* Right on the gravel road to *Roseland Park*, 0.8 *m.*, a large, well-kept park on the north shore of the lake, with pleasant drives winding past green lawns, shaded by many elms and maples. Here in the 19th century were held the Woodstock Fourth of July celebrations, which attained national importance because of the prominence of the speakers.

Beyond South Woodstock the road crosses Saw Mill Brook and, at 12.1 *m.*, State 91 branches left. Traversing a section lined with blue spruce (R), State 93 proceeds to the junction with the main tour, 14.7 *m.*, at Pomfret.

The highway crosses Still River at 19.6 *m.*, and following an undulating course, passes *Frog Rock Highway Rest* (L), named for a painted profile of a frog on the outcropping rock at the roadside, 21.6 *m.*

At 21.8 *m.*, is the junction with Fire Tower Rd.

> Left on this road to the *Pomfret Fire Tower*, 1.2 *m.*, a steel structure rising 75 feet above the hilltop (alt. 822). From the tower is visible an imposing panorama of forested hills and valleys, grassy clearings and cultivated fields.

US 44 passes through a desolate wooded area 22.3 *m.*, once ravaged by fire, where a stand of gaunt bare trunks rises starkly above green underbrush. Descending an incline, the road crosses *Lyon Brook*, at 22.5 *m.* Climbing a long hill beyond the brook, the highway reaches the summit at 23.3 *m.*, where a fine eastern view extends across the valley and the white steeple of Abington Church pierces the tree-tops. Descending a steep grade, US 44 passes the long, elm-encircled *Samuel Sumner Tavern* (L), 23.6 *m.*, built in 1796, still in good condition, and crosses Abington Brook at 23.9 *m.*

ABINGTON (Town of Pomfret), 24.1 *m.*, a tiny village of old houses grouped about a crossroad, is at the junction with State 97.

A short distance south of the crossroads is the *Abington Library* (L), a wooden building housing the original collection of a proprietary library formed here in 1793, and the books of the Ladies' Library, organized in 1813.

South on the crossroads is a group of weathered old structures. The white, gable-roofed *Congregational Church* (L), built in 1751, is the second oldest church in the State, and still in use, although successive renovations have preserved only the frame of the original structure.

Descending a steep hill US 44 passes through a wooded area dotted with small farms to a railroad overpass at 24.2 *m.*

At 24.9 *m.* is the junction with a gravel side road.

> Right on this road, through an opening in a stone wall enclosure, 1.8 *m.*, to a picnic area, 1.9 *m.* At this point, conspicuous signs indicate a trail that slopes into a rockbound ravine, leading to *Israel Putnam's Wolf Den.*
>
> Into this ravine, Israel Putnam and five of his neighbors pursued a she-wolf who had continually ravaged sheep-folds of the countryside. When the animal disappeared into her den, the hunters hesitated to follow. Angered by the cowardice of his fellows, Putnam fastened a rope to his waist and crawled into the cavern. Growls, shouts, and frantic jerks on the rope warned the hunting party that Putnam had found the beast. Fearing for his life, they dragged him back to safety so rapidly that his shirt was pulled up over his head and his skin cut on the jagged rocks. A second and a third time Putnam rallied to the attack, urged on by the plaudits of his fellow huntsmen. As he fired his trusty smoothbore, the hills seemed to shake. Buckshot seared its way to the brain of the she-wolf. Dazed, half-suffocated by gun smoke, and exhausted from the struggle, Putnam grasped the wolf firmly by the ears and was hauled to the surface. In the fissured granite walls, the Daughters of the American Revolution have erected a tablet in honor of the exploit.

Winding through an area where patches of forest mingle with cultivated fields, the highway leads to the junction with a gravel side road at 25.2 *m.*

> Right on this road to *Mashamoquet State Park*, 0.2 *m.*, a picnic area equipped with benches, fireplaces, and tables, in a rustic setting beside Mashamoquet Brook which has been dammed to form a swimming pool.

Winding along an S-curve, US 44 proceeds to the junction with State 93 in POMFRET STATION, 26.7 *m.*, a group of houses clustered about a small station of the New York, New Haven & Hartford Railroad.

Here route US 44 crosses *Wappoquia Brook*, and passes the *Pomfret Golf Club* (R), at 27.5 *m.*

POMFRET (alt. 580, town pop. 1617), 27.9 *m.*, a residential town of substantial homes in a setting of landscaped lawns and gardens, was named and incorporated in May, 1713. Major James Fitch secured in 1684 a tract of the Wabbaquasset country which some authorities say included almost all of the present Windham County. On May 1, 1686, Fitch sold rights to a party of twelve. Pomfret was settled by Fitch's party from Roxbury, Mass., who had originally purchased 15,100 acres. A sale of 5750 acres to a Captain (sometimes known as 'Sir') John Blackwell, Puritan member of Parliament and leader of a group of fugitive English and Irish Dissenters, was confirmed by the General Court of Connecticut and this portion of the tract was named Mortlake, for a village in Surrey, England (*see Tour 2, BROOKLYN*). Mortlake was considered a feudal holding 'above the law,' but a survey of March 20, 1714, placed 'Mortlake Manor' within the limits of Pomfret. Blackwell returned to England with the accession of William and Mary and the holdings reverted to Major Fitch as a part of the Wabbaquasset country. Captain John Sabin, purchaser of 100 acres for £9, settler in 1691, master of a fortified house, and friend to the Indians, is frequently mentioned in Pomfret history. Until 1698 he is believed to have been the only settler. In that year Benjamin Sitton bought 50 acres of wilderness and became Sabin's neighbor 'at a place called Mashamoquet.' South of the Mashamoquet River, the Mortlake patent, although in the limits of Pomfret, remained entirely outside its jurisdiction until 1713, and even then was only partially controlled by the parent settlement. This was actually a feudal holding, free from the responsibilities and privileges of suffrage, paying no taxes, recording no deeds, and furnishing no recruits for Colonial military service. Tales of extreme hardship and lawlessness abound. Mashamoquet Plantation was no place for weaklings; these pioneers held their lands by superior marksmanship and intestinal fortitude. Deeds, when they existed, were sketchy affairs that cause confusion even in present-day land records. Schools were not built until 1723; a ravaging wolf slaughtered livestock in 1740; Mortlake outlaws created difficulties even as late as 1750, when that district was finally made a parish. But Pomfret had a library in 1739, and during the Great Revival of 1741, the church secured 106 converts from wicked Mortlake.

Through the development of many small water-power factories, Pomfret rapidly became one of the important towns in Windham County. Following the panic of 1837, the town's industry rapidly declined, but the rolling hills and natural scenic advantages soon attracted many newcomers who have established substantial summer homes among landscaped gardens, overlooking valley pasturelands and wooded western hills.

On the western brow of Pomfret Hill are the ivy-covered, modern Colonial brick buildings of *Pomfret School* (1894), a preparatory school for boys (L). Between them and the road is the *Norman Chapel*, a remarkably impressive version of an early English church, and the tall *Sun Dial*, copied from the famous one at Corpus Christi College, Oxford. On the right is the large white *Congregational Church*, with elaborate Ionic columns, erected in 1832. Adjoining is the long, columned porch of the *Ben Grosvenor Inn* (R), built around a nucleus of 1738 and enlarged for an inn toward the close of that century. Rows of cedar line the walk leading to the doorway.

North of Pomfret St. (US 44), a shaded thoroughfare, lined with dignified mansions and well-kept estates, past the *Colonel Grosvenor House* (L), erected in 1792, and now much remodeled for the *Rectory School* for boys. The grounds, hidden from the street by a long row of pines, extend along the highway for 0.2 mile. Facing down Pomfret St. is the impressive *Overlock House* (*private*), its two-storied porches reflecting the full glory of the Greek Revival. Four chimneys protrude incongruously above the porches, flanking the gable. The *Small House* (*private*), next west of it (L), also has two-story porches, which cannot be original, for it was a plain country store when Washington, who recorded it in his diary, bought here some 'bad tobacco.'

East of Pomfret, at 28.9 *m.*, US 44 turns abruptly right and State 93 swings off to the left.

The highway, passing a *State Pine Plantation* (L) at 29.5 *m.*, crosses Bark Meadow Brook at 29.7 *m.*

US 44 pursues an undulating course eastward, through wide, rolling meadowland, 29.8 *m.*, to the summit of a hill at 30.7 *m.*, which affords a twenty-five mile *View* over scrub woodlands to the south.

Descending the hill and not far from the summit, the highway passes (L) the old *Perrin House*, which was built in 1766, a central chimney dwelling of simple, solid construction, typical of the 18th century. Curving sharply to the left the route passes the *Day-Kimball Hospital* (R), one of the two public hospitals in Windham County.

Continuing eastward, the highway crosses the Quinebaug River, 32.3 *m.*, with a view of the series of low cascades known as *Cargill Falls* (L).

PUTNAM, 32.4 *m.* (*see Tour* 9), is the leading industrial center of northeastern Connecticut. Here is the junction with State 12 (*see Tour* 9), which combines with US 44 for 0.7 mile.

At 33.1 *m.*, State 12 (*see Tour* 9) swings off to the left.

At 33.5 *m.* is the junction with a country road.

> Right on this road, 0.3 *m.*, is a house of about 1795, the *Home of Armand Denys* (*private*), the African explorer, and his wife. Some good paneling, with unusual motifs and courses of reeding, has been preserved.

The highway passes the *Putnam Roadside Highway Rest*, at 33.8 *m.*, and crosses *Little Dam Tavern Brook* which loops around and flows under another bridge at 34.1 *m.*

US 44 proceeds to the top of a low hill at 34.8 *m.*, which affords a fine view of the rolling land to the south and west. Beyond, the road descends through a heavily wooded section and at 36.6 *m.* curves sharply left, proceeding through rough, hilly country where thick growths of pine border the hillside pastures.

EAST PUTNAM, at 37.5 *m.*, a former mill settlement, is now little more than a few scattered houses along the road.

Beyond East Putnam the highway traverses an area distinctive for its abundant natural growths of pine and proceeds to the Rhode Island State Line, at 38.6 *m.* US 44 enters Rhode Island at West Gloucester.

T O U R   3 A :   *From* EAST HARTFORD *to* NEW LONDON, 42.6 *m.*, State 2 and 85.

Via Glastonbury, Marlboro, Colchester, Salem.
Concrete roadbed resurfaced with asphalt; tourist accommodations.

THIS route, following the old Hartford turnpike known as The Governor's Road, passes through rural territory where villages on the former stage-coach line between the affluent whaling port of New London and the State Capital have for years been sequestered. Local representatives in the legislature long opposed the construction of a new road and the deep ruts and sandy hollows in the old turnpike discouraged visitors. In 1921 the cement highway was laid. Since then, many summer residents have purchased and remodeled weathered old houses among the rolling hills.

South of the junction with US 6 in EAST HARTFORD (alt. 40, town pop. 17,125), 0.0 *m.*, State 2 passes a small Green (L), 0.1 *m.*, with a monument to World War Soldiers, and the newly built brick *Courthouse* in Colonial style with a cupola, 0.2 *m.*

At 0.4 *m.* is the old *Meeting-House Green* (R), where a memorial boulder marks the *Site of the First Two Meeting-Houses* in the town; the second was used as a hospital for the French army in 1781–82.

Right at East Hartford on Pitkin St., at the Green, is the old *Elisha Pitkin House (private)* of 1740, 0.1 *m.* (L), a large, unpainted gambrel-roofed dwelling with a Dutch-roofed ell. Once a pretentious Colonial mansion, this old house still contains some of the fine original paneling. Rochambeau was a guest here twice, en route to Hartford for conferences with Washington.

At 0.7 *m.* is the junction with Silver Lane.

> Left on Silver Lane past several interesting old houses to a small Green (R), 0.4 *m.*, where stands the *Rochambeau Boulder*, commemorating the camp made here by Rochambeau's army on the way to join Washington and again on its return from Yorktown. The silver in which the soldiers were paid was so rare in this country that the side road on which the army camped has ever since been known as Silver Lane.

> At 1.8 *m.* is the *Silver Lane Pickle Company Plant* (R), established in 1880. At 2.9 *m.*, the route turns sharply left, traversing a district dotted with old houses. The *James Forbes House* constructed in 1765, where money used to pay the French soldiers was stored, stands (L) at 3.6 *m.*; and the *Silas Eaton House* (1693), located at 135 Forbes St., 3.7 *m.* (L), is a large primitive building with very early paneling. The *George Risley House*, at 52 High St., is dated in about the same period; it is a salt-box house with a six-inch hewn overhang at the front, and one in the gable ends.

Southward State 2 passes the *Mutual Aircraft Club*, 1 *m.*, and, crossing Willow Brook, at 1.3 *m.*, traverses an extensive market gardening section, where the intensively cultivated area incongruously echoes from dawn to dusk with the roar of airplane propellers.

At 1.4 *m.* is the junction with Willow St.

> Left on Willow St. is the entrance to *Rentschler Field*, owned and operated by the United Aircraft Corp. From this well-equipped 157-acre field the American Airlines maintain a regular service to Boston and New York. Excellent facilities are provided for aviation instruction, air taxi sight-seeing service, and aerial photography. Planes manufactured in adjacent factories are tested at this field.

At 1.5 *m.* (L) are the *Pratt & Whitney Aircraft Works* where are made Wasp and Hornet engines, which power more than 75 per cent of all airmail planes flying in the United States and foreign countries (1936). These engines hold twelve world records, have been used by Byrd and Lindbergh, and girdled the earth in Wiley Post's 'Winnie May.' Just beyond are the *Factories of the Chance Voight Corporation* which produce Corsair airplanes used extensively by the United States Navy and Marine Corps, as well as the air forces of China and many Central and South American countries.

Adjacent is the *Plant of the Hamilton Standard Propeller Company*, whose significant achievements in the propeller field include the development of the controllable pitch mechanism for which the company was awarded the Collier Trophy. Notable among the foreign airlines using Pratt and Whitney engines and Hamilton Standard Propellers, is K.L.M., the Royal Dutch Airlines, which operate the longest single airline in the world (9000 miles) between Holland and the Dutch colony of Java. In the thirty test houses beside the factory, engines are given a ten-hour test, and on re-assembly are again tested for three hours, with one hour at full throttle.

Near-by are the administrative *Offices of the Sikorsky Aircraft Corporation* which manufactures the trans-oceanic 'Clipper' amphibians at its plant in Stratford (*see Tour* 1) and installs the engines here.

At 2.2 *m.* is the northern end of the *Brewer Tobacco Plantation* (R), which stretches along the road for more than a mile. The original

Brewer House, a dwelling of about 1800, stands on the left of the high-way at 254 Main St., flanked by modern homes.

HOCKANUM, 2.5 *m.*, a residential community, is hardly distinguishable from the thickly settled outskirts of East Hartford.

At WELLES CORNER, 4.5 *m.*, at the junction with State 15 on the outskirts of Glastonbury, stands the *Welles Tavern* (1776), established by an ancestor of this well-known family. Opposite, just behind a red-brick structure, stands the *Samuel Welles House*, a large building erected in 1780 that retains few old features; it was occupied (1862–78) by Gideon Welles, Secretary of the Navy in Lincoln's cabinet, whose memoirs have furnished interesting details of the problems that confronted President Lincoln. His birthplace was the large house on State 94, moved from its original site now occupied by the Post Office.

Right from State 2 on State 15 is GLASTONBURY (alt. 50, town pop. 5783), a dignified, prosperous community, which because of its convenient commuting distance from Hartford has become a residential suburb of that city. The village with its tree-shaded streets, wide lawns and attractive homes, also derives much of its affluence from the cultivation of the farmlands and tobacco fields surrounding the community. Named for Glastonbury in Somerset, England, this town was settled as a part of Wethersfield in 1650, and incorporated as a separate town in 1690. In April, 1777, when the food shortage became acute in New Haven, the junior class of Yale College was moved to Glastonbury, where the students were boarded at the house of William Welles, a tutor at Yale. Two large industries are here; the J. B. Williams Company, manufacturers of soap, and the Williams Brothers Company, manufacturers of silverware.

The *Daniel Wright House* (1740), located on State 15 just south of State 2, two-storied with a portico, stands opposite an older *Daniel Wright Residence* built in 1720. Beyond, 0.2 *m.*, are (R) two *Benton Houses*; the first of which dates from 1735 and the second from 1740. Both have been remarkably preserved, though the fan-light and portico on the second are later additions. Just beyond is the *Congregational Church* (1867) with stained-glass windows.

Farther south, a succession of early dwellings lines the highway. The *Deacon Ebenezer Plummer House* (L), of 1760, was the home of the Deacon who kept a store at which he sold rum; the slave quarters of his estate are at the rear of the house. Next stands the gambrel-roofed *Wickham House* (R) of 1735, and (R) the happily proportioned *William Miller House*, a small gambrel which has charm, even if it cannot justify so early a date as that ascribed to it, 1693.

North of the village Green, at 0.8 *m.*, is the *Oldest Cemetery* in town. Here, three table gravestones mark the graves of the first minister, the Rev. Timothy Stevens, and his two wives. South of the Green (R) is the *Samuel Smith House*, built in 1709.

Traversing extensive tobacco fields, the highway passes (L) the *Jonathan Hale House*, which was built in 1750, and (R) the *Kimberly House*, standing at 1.6 *m.* Built before 1740, this house, which has passed back into the hands of the Kimberly family, was occupied in the 19th century by a Sandemanian minister, Zephaniah Smith, whose five eccentric and learned daughters — Hancy Zephina, Cyrinthia Sacretia, Laurilla Aleroyla, Julia Evelina, and Abby Hadassah — attained national prominence by their militant championship of the abolitionist cause and later, of equal suffrage. Local historians claim that the first petition against slavery circulated in this country was drawn up by Mrs. Hannah Smith and her five daughters and was signed by forty Glastonbury women. This petition was presented to Congress by John Quincy Adams. After the Civil War, the sisters became active in the equal suffrage movement. Their refusal to pay taxes on the ground that they were not allowed to vote and the consequent seizure and auction of their cows provoked widespread publicity that gave great impetus to their cause. Year after year, many of their possessions were sold by a stubborn town government, but their allegiance never wavered. The townsfolk still tell many stories of Mrs. Smith, an assiduous reader of foreign books, who had a glass cage constructed in which she might read undisturbed, warmed by the sun's rays; and of the daughters, who owned the first piano in Glastonbury and learned to play it before its arrival by practicing on blocks of wood. Laurilla Aleroyla was a painter and Julia Evelina made five translations of the Bible, one from Latin, two from Greek, and two from Hebrew.

Southward, old central-chimneyed houses line both sides of the road. Among the best is (L) the *Welles Shipman House* (1743) at 3.1 *m.* Some of the exterior trim, as the cornices over the window heads and the dignified doorway, with its full quota of triglyphs, guttae, and modillions, use detail which one would not expect to find ante-dating the Revolution.

SOUTH GLASTONBURY (Town of Glastonbury), 3.2 *m.* Beautifully situated in a hill-encircled valley, this former rural manufacturing settlement has preserved a number of old houses. The dark-red *Welles House* standing at the center is said to have been built in 1736 and retains many old features. At the northeast corner of Hopewell Rd. is a charming house of nearly a century later, the *Pratt House*, in the Greek Revival style often erroneously called 'Colonial.'

South Glastonbury is the home of the much publicized *Rattlesnake Hunt Club*, whose expeditions in Meshomasic State Forest and annual capture of numerous rattlers have attracted wide attention. The return of one member with a bag of seven rattlers to a New York hotel, the story of their escape, and the huntsman's subsequent single-handed recapture of the reptiles, has become a local legend.

At 3.4 *m.* is the junction with Tryon St.

> Right on Tryon St., crossing a brook, at 0.2 *m.*, past the oldest house (R) in Glastonbury, the *John Hollister House* (*private*) of 1675. Although modern fenestration, new clapboards and chimney have marred its 17th-century appearance, it retains the 'hewn overhang,' the carved heads of the posts showing out through the clapboards. The chimney is back of the ridge. When this district was inundated by the spring flood of 1936, the old house was partly submerged in five feet of water. At 0.4 *m.* is the red *Amos Hollister House* (1695) with a suspended porch roof in the Dutch fashion. By the roadside, directly opposite, stands a great oak, nearly 20 feet in circumference, with a height and spread of 50 feet.

At 3.5 *m.* is the junction with a dirt road.

> Left on this road, which follows the banks of *Roaring Brook* through a deep gorge (R), with the steep wooded face of *Forge Hill* rising sharply left, to the ghost town of COTTON HOLLOW. This district, years ago, resounded with the hum of industry, but has now reverted to wilderness.
>
> At 0.3 *m.*, a mass of ruined masonry in the underbrush (L) is the remains of a powder factory that supplied powder to the Continental army in 1776 and was ruined by an explosion in 1779. Near-by crumbles the imposing wreck of a large stone cotton mill, established in the early 19th century. Beyond, a row of uninhabited mill houses is falling into ruin.

On State 15 at 4 *m.* left of the highway, the extensive orchards established by J. H. Hale, known as the 'peach king,' stretch for acres. Here, on barren upland farmlands, Hale proved that peaches of a superior flavor could be produced in Connecticut, and became a widely known lecturer and authority on peach culture.

GILDERSLEEVE (alt. 60, Town of Portland), 9 *m.*, is a beautiful shaded village at the top of a small hill near a bend in the Connecticut River. Residences border the main street and small farms fringe the outskirts. The village grew up around the Gildersleeve shipyard, which ceased operations in 1930 after almost a century of existence. During the peak of its prosperity, these shipyards launched packets for the New York to Charleston Line (1836-47). Starting in October, 1741, with a schooner of 90 tons, the yards swung into speedy production and during the Revolution and War of 1812, launched the 'Trumbull' of 700 tons and 40 guns, and several privateers and merchantmen. The only industry here today is the Charles Jarvis Company, makers of tapping devices.

The *Congregational Church* (1850), at 9.1 *m.* (L), was organized in 1721. In this vicinity some of the few remaining yokes of oxen in the State may be seen plodding along the roads or in the fields.

At 9.5 *m.*, at the top of a slight rise, a fine view stretches to the west over acres of shade-grown tobacco sloping down to the river bank.

At 11 *m.* is the junction with State 14 (*see Tour 2 Alt.*) at PORTLAND (*see Tour 2 Alt.*).

Southeast of Welles Corner in Glastonbury, State 2 passes the *J. B. Williams Company Plant*, manufacturers of soap, 5.7 *m.* Beyond Hubbard Brook is the *Herman Roser Company Plant* (L), 6 *m.*, manufacturers of pigskin leather products, an industry established here in 1700.

Gradually climbing from the central lowlands, the highway begins the long ascent of *Eight Mile Hill*, reaching the summit (alt. 700), at 8 *m.* Here, *Lane's Tower* (L) offers a complete panorama. In clear weather there are distinct views of Mt. Tom in Massachusetts and Mt. Monadnock in New Hampshire.

At 9 *m.* stands the *Joseph Hill House*, built in 1720, a white, peak-roofed cottage commanding a fine view of hills (R).

Southeast of *Roaring Brook*, 9.3 *m.*, past a row of magnificent maples, is a great *White Oak* (L), 9.4 *m.*, by the roadside. This familiar landmark, about 300 years old, has a circumference of 18 feet. Directly across the road stands the *Israel Hollister House*, of 1780, with its overhanging eaves.

At 9.5 *m.* is the junction with State 83, a paved highway.

Left on State 83, stands the *Samuel Talcott House* (*private*) (1756), 0.3 *m.*, with a double overhang and lean-to. Here was born Mary Talcott, grandmother of Admiral Dewey. Through a region of farmlands, the winding road climbs steadily to the crest of a high ridge, paralleling Roaring Brook, which flows through a deep gorge (R).

EAST GLASTONBURY, 0.9 *m.*, right of the highway, is clustered about the *Mills of the Angus Park Company*, manufacturers of woolen goods.

Skirting Roaring Brook Ravine, the highway climbs a steep hill past a fine grove of oak and pine (L), ascending to a hilltop, 2.3 *m.*, that affords an extensive view of distant ridges (R), and then descends into a thickly wooded valley.

BUCKINGHAM, 3.3 *m.*, on a slight elevation, is a roadside hamlet of neat white houses gleaming through the trees.

Right from State 83 at the triangle, onto the road marked 'Gilead and Hebron,' is a route commanding a superb view across the deep valley, encircled by wooded hills, and tortuously ascending to the summit of Mt. John Tom.

At 0.8 *m.* (L) the *John Goslee House* stands, a weathered salt-box dwelling of 1720, with a five-window front that still retains most of its original features, including the sash. The ceilings are 6 feet 6 inches high. At 1 *m.* (L) is the *Asa Goslee House*, which was built in 1760, with a gambrel roof, distinguished by a long flare in the rear slope. Along this road are numerous stone dwellings of native granite, erected between 1830 and 1860, but built of huge blocks of stone in the manner of earlier structures.

At 1.2 *m.* is the *James Goslee House*, built in 1760, (R), an unpainted wooden dwelling which has weathered to a soft gray through the lifetime of many generations. Farther up the steep ascent, commanding a remarkable view is (L) the *Elizur Hale Jr. House*, which dates from 1774, with an excellent paneled doorway and one interior panel of record size, 54 × 66 inches.

At 2.6 *m.* (L), the imposing two-and-a-half story, white *Jared Hills House* (1774), stands almost at the summit of *Mt. John Tom* (alt. 920), which is reached at 6.1 *m.* Here a magnificent panorama of the countryside stretches out to the encircling hills on the horizon.

Winding down the long descent, the highway passes a large peach orchard (L), and the *John Tom Community House*, at 6.5 *m.* Just east of this point is the junction with a dirt road. Right on the dirt road 0.8 *m.*, to *Diamond Lake.* This small body of water, in a deep depression in the hills, has become a popular vacation resort, and is fringed with summer cottages.

At 8.3 *m.* on State 83 is the junction with US 44 (*see Tour* 3) and US 6 (*see Tour* 2).

At 9.5 *m.* directly opposite the *Elisha Hollister Homestead (private)*, built in 1760, is a road (R) leading to the *Meshomasic State Forest* (*see Tour* 2), a tract of 5492 acres, where the following of hiking trails should not be attempted without stout, high boots because of the prevalence of rattlesnakes.

This sparsely populated district is plentifully supplied with a variety of game, including pheasants, partridge, quail, rabbits, and raccoon. At 12.6 *m.* on State 2 is the *East Glastonbury Fish and Game Club* (L), and at 13.2 *m.* a roadside park, *By-the-Brook.* Skirting the shore of *Lake Terramuggus*, a long lake well stocked with pickerel, yellow perch, and bullheads, and fed by streams where trout and black bass abound, the highway reaches Marlboro.

MARLBORO (alt. 570, town pop. 319) (*see Tour* 2 *Alt.*), 14.1 *m.*, at the junction with State 14 (*see Tour* 2 *Alt.*).

Passing a highway park called *Turnpike Green* (R), at 16.6 *m.*, and *Marlborough Gardens*, an attractive landscaped area (L), at 16.8 *m.*, the road descends into a forest glade and crosses the Blackledge River at 17.4 *m.* East of Fawn Brook, at 17.8 *m.*, the road climbs to a hilltop, 19.1 *m.*, from which there is a fine view of the hills and valleys to the south.

COLCHESTER (alt. 425, town pop. 2134), 22.5 *m.*, named for Colchester in Essex, England, is a semi-rural community with wide, tree-lined streets and white Colonial houses that reflect the early industrial prosperity of the town. Here, Nathaniel Hayward, who was associated with Charles Goodyear in perfecting the process of vulcanizing rubber, established (1847) a large rubber factory which later produced more than a million dollars' worth of merchandise annually. In 1893, the plant was sold to the United States Rubber Company but 15 years later was destroyed by fire and never rebuilt.

At the north end of the Green, stands (R) the imposing hip-roofed *Deming House* (1771), a former stage-coach tavern notable for the fact that here was organized the first Masonic Order of Knights Templar in the United States. Diagonally opposite (L) is the gambrel-roofed *Hayward House* (1776). Both houses contain exceptionally fine paneling.

The *Congregational Church* (1847) many years ago was presided over by the Rev. John Bulkley, who was so widely famous for his wisdom that his advice was frequently sought by distant persons and communities in critical times. The membership of one church, disrupted by differences of opinion and threatened with disorganization, appealed to him. When Mr. Bulkley replied, he also wrote a letter to a tenant of his on a distant farm. The reply received by the church was read aloud: 'You will see to the fences, that they be high and strong, and you will take especial care of the old black bull.' A puzzled silence followed the reading, and then an old member of the congregation arose and said, 'Brethren, this is just what we need. We have neglected our fences too long; all sorts of strange cattle have come in among us and with the rest that old black bull, the Devil, who has made us all this trouble! Let us repair our fences and drive him out.' Again reunited in spirit, the church prospered from that time on. No record exists of the benefits which the tenant derived from his letter.

The *Bacon Academy* (R), at the center, was founded in 1803 by a bequest of Pierpont Bacon and once ranked with Phillips Exeter in New Hampshire as a preparatory school, attracting students from many parts of the country and abroad. John Adams, who became principal of Phillips Andover, was the first preceptor. Today the Academy is a public high school. At the rear of the Academy is the *Old Colchester Cemetery*. Among the many gravestones of early settlers is that of Jonathan Kilbourn, inventor of many mechanical appliances. His epitaph reads:

> He was a man of invention great
> Above all that lived nigh;
> But he could not invent to live
> When God called him to die.

On the knolls, a short distance north, is the *Site of the Encampment of Rochambeau's Army* in 1781.

On the south side of the Green is the tiny one-room gambrel-roofed *Foote House* (1702) moved from its original foundation, restored, and now maintained as a museum by the Daughters of the American Revolution (*admittance on application to custodian*).

At Colchester the Governor's Road, this route, continues on State 85. State 2 (*see Tour 1J*) turns east.

> Right from Colchester, State 16, a macadamized highway crosses several brooks and descends a steep hill through a grove of beech trees to a crossroad, 4.6 m. Back from the crossroad stands the red *Michael Taintor House*, a dwelling built in 1761, which has remained in the family of the original builder. The materials for this house were brought by ox-cart from Norwich, a distance of 22 miles. It contains the exceptional paneling characteristic of some forgotten Colchester carpenter before the Revolution.
>
> Right at the four corners, 0.2 m., to WESTCHESTER GREEN. Here, facing a spacious plot of ground, shaded by old trees, stand two 18th-century houses. The gambrel-roofed *Mansion of Colonel Henry Champion* (R), a commissary officer in the Revolutionary army, was built in 1790. With its two gambreled ells, its fine detail, and its entrance porch, it is an outstanding house, excep-

tionally well preserved. With Peter Colt, Champion bought and delivered $200,000 worth of live cattle to Washington's army at Valley Forge. Facing the Green on the east is the *Loomis House*, a more orthodox dwelling, with 24-pane windows, a small fan-window and original oak clapboards. The house, built as an inn in 1800 and still in possession of the same family, is surrounded by an extensive yard shaded by splendid maples.

West of the crossroad, State 16 climbs to the crest of a hill and on the long and steep descent, at 5.9 *m.* affords an excellent view of distant wooded hills. The highway crosses Salmon Brook at 7 *m.* Here, downstream (L) stands *Comstock Bridge*, one of the few remaining covered bridges in the State, now closed to traffic but preserved for its historic interest.

At 9.6 *m.* is the junction with State 196. Right on State 196 at 10.8 *m.* to EAST HAMPTON (*see Tour 2 Alt.*) at the junction with State 14.

The *Breed Tavern* (*private*), at 23 *m.* (R), said to have been built in 1710, has an early ballroom with a vaulted ceiling.

South of Colchester, on State 85, at 24 *m.*, is the junction with an improved country road.

Right on this road to *Lake Hayward*, 2.6 *m.*, formerly called Shaw Lake, where is a summer cottage colony with facilities for bathing. At 4 *m.* is the intersection with a dirt road. Sharp right here and sharp left at 4.5 *m.* to the State park known as the *Devil's Hopyard* (*see Tour 1D*).

At 27.2 *m.* stands the gambrel-roofed *Joseph Smith Homestead*, built in 1785, and notable for its happy proportions and attractive setting. The *Strickland Tavern* (*private*), at 29.2 *m.* (L), built about 1785–99, was originally a tinshop and later a tavern on the New London–Hartford stage-coach line. At 29.4 *m.* is the old *Toll Gate House* (R), now remodeled.

SALEM (alt. 362, town pop. 403), 29.5 *m.*, a hamlet, was originally purchased from the Indians by Colonel Samuel Brown of Salem, Mass., who settled here about 1700 with his household, including 60 families of slaves. For generations, the scattered farmhouses of Salem have quietly dozed on its rolling wooded hillsides content to dream of bygone days when the royal blue Music Vale Seminary coaches lumbered over the dirt roads bringing important personages from many cities to the elaborate musicales and operas presented here by Oramel Whittlesey and his pupils. Sequestered from tourist traffic for many years, because of its poor roads, Salem has, since the paving of the old Hartford turnpike, begun to attract summer residents.

Beyond the white *Congregational Church* (1840) and the schoolhouse, stands the *Town Hall* (1830) which was built from the timbers of the old Episcopal Church in Norwich (1749). Aside from a little paneling which has survived in the gallery, all that the traveler sees dates from the time of its reconstruction in Salem. The Doric portico, resting on granite blocks, and the fine arched windows are typical 19th-century work.

At 29.7 *m.* (L) stands the *Red Cottage*, built in 1728, the home of the Rev. John Whittlesey and his bride of Saybrook, who settled in Salem bringing with them the spinet presented to a Whittlesey ancestor by Lady Fenwick. Here Lorenzo Dow (born Coventry, 1777), the fiery

Methodist exhorter, notorious for his violent gestures and ironical repartee, was married. After unsuccessfully courting the lovely Sally for many months, late one evening he finally obtained her consent. Jumping upon his horse and swinging the lady to the saddle, he sped to the Red Cottage and aroused the sleeping Mr. Whittlesey. Just as the ceremony was to be performed Sally changed her mind again but finally yielded to Dow's importunities, with the vow that she would 'be a thorn in his flesh and a sword in his side' all the days of his life. However, Sally evidently changed her mind again for she was a constant companion on his continual wanderings, listened to his sermons which often lasted five hours, and proved to be his one faithful friend. In the Red Cottage was born Oramel Whittlesey, founder of Music Vale Seminary (1835).

At the foot of the hill is the *Site of the Music Vale Seminary.* A flight of stone steps (R) at 30 *m.* leads to the cellar where the famous seminary stood before it was destroyed by fire in 1869, rebuilt, and again burned down in 1890. This first normal school of music in the United States authorized to confer academic degrees, brought national fame and recognition to its founder and for 41 years attracted students from all parts of the United States, Canada and the West Indies.

At 30.6 *m.* is the junction with State 82 (*see Tour 1D*).

At 31.8 *m.* State 85 skirts Mountain Lake (R) passing *Lovers Leap* (R), where tradition says an Indian girl and her white lover, pursued by her father, an Indian Chief, spurred the white horse on which they were escaping, over the ledge into the lake beneath. On moonlight nights, old women say, the white mane of the horse may be seen floating on the lake just as it was seen by the bereaved chieftain as he reached the cliff.

CHESTERFIELD, 34.6 *m.*, is a roadside hamlet consisting of a few country stores and dwellings in the district colonized by Jewish immigrants under a foundation established (1892) by Baron de Hirsch, and named in honor of Lord Chesterfield.

Lake Konomoc, at 36.4 *m.* (L), is the New London reservoir, over two miles in length, surrounded by wooded hills. Off to the southeast is *Konomoc Hill,* where the old Holt estate, known as the C. Y. Horse Ranch, is now a breeding and training farm for rodeo horses.

Traversing a section of rock-strewn fields State 85 forms a junction with US 1 (*see Tour 1*) in NEW LONDON (*see NEW LONDON*), 42.6 *m.*

At New London is also the junction with State 32 (*see Tour 9*).

T O U R 4 : *From* NORWALK *to* MASSACHUSETTS LINE (*Sheffield*), 76.8 *m.*, US 7.

Via Danbury, New Milford, Canaan.
N.Y., N.H. & H. R.R. parallels the route.
Alternate stretches of asphalt and concrete.
All types of accommodations.

US 7 is known as the Ethan Allen Highway, because it was the route taken by the eager-eyed recruits from Connecticut who hurried north to join the Green Mountain Boys.

Between Norwalk and Danbury the highway follows the path of the retreat of the British raiders under Tryon after the burning of Danbury, and northward to New Milford traverses fertile farmland.

Side trips to quiet Lake Waramaug and lively Lake Candlewood present varying attractions that range from camping and boating in summer to fishing and ice boating in the winter. The nature-lover will find peace and solitude under the stately arches of Cathedral Pines, and the stockman will discover fine sires and dams at any one of a score of stock farms in the region.

Orderly villages along the route are characterized by the independent reserve, typical of rural Connecticut. The city people, who come to rest for a summer or two, often become attached to the country and purchase homes here. Cornwall and Kent have their art colonies; music-lovers gather at Music Mountain; artists exhibit annually in Kent; and sturdy fellows with gunnysacks and forked sticks chase the elusive rattlesnakes along the slopes of Schaghticoke Mountain. Kent Falls, Macedonia Brook, Dark Entry Trail, the Sharon and Cornwall Hills offer attractions for hikers who care to venture just off the beaten path.

The northern half of the route follows the valley of the Housatonic, overshadowed by the rugged hills of the western highlands. Mixed growths of pine, hemlock, paper-birch, and hardwood cover the hills. Countless spring-fed brooks spill their waters down the abrupt slopes into the winding river. Here the thinner and more acid soils are thick with mountain laurel, dagger ferns, arbutus, and running pine. Along streamsides, gallant violets bloom beneath wild blue-flag. Black bass abound in the river and in dozens of lakes just off the route; trout fishing is good along most of the streams. Shooting is fair, improving each year as cover is extended with the retirement of poor land on non-productive upland farms. Winter sport facilities, too, are increasing with the growing interest in skiing.

Approaching the Massachusetts Line, US 7 follows a valley rich in limestone, crossed by schist and quartzite ridges. The lime deposits supplied North Canaan's first industry, when early settlers burned the lime and

SCENIC AND MARINE

FROM the thickly settled, indented shore line of Long Island Sound Connecticut gradually rises to the rolling uplands of the northern boundary where lakes and woods offer scenic variety and recreational opportunities. From salt marsh and sandy beach to the bracing air of the hills is less than an hour's drive. There are clear and lively brooks, and woodlands stony and rough in their natural beauty. Meadowlands stretch away from the highway's edge to the pasture fences, sometimes of weathered wooden rails, but more frequently of stone; and pastures merge with the forest.

Along the Connecticut shore, numerous excellent harbors furnish protective anchorage for yacht club fleets and visiting pleasure craft. The Coast Guard Academy and Coast Guard Base 4 are at New London, the Atlantic Base for submarines of the United States Navy is across the Thames River in Groton, and the Bureau of Fisheries maintains an experimental laboratory at Milford. Though coast-wise passenger boats have ceased operations, freight still uses the water haul.

Swordfish and scallops are important items in the income from the sea. Lobsters and oysters are highly favored and profitable Yankee delicacies. Connecticut maintains a lobster hatchery at Noank, and her seed-oyster harvest is impressive in dollar value. Commercial fisheries are small, but there is a considerable yield from the renting of boats and gear to sportsmen who go out in pursuit of salt-water game and pan fish.

HOUSATONIC GORGE

KENT FALLS

CATHEDRAL PINES, CORNWALL

PASTORAL, HAMDEN

FENCES, BETHANY

BRIDGEWATER HILL

COAST GUARD PATROL BOATS, NEW LONDON

SUBMARINE IN NEW LONDON HARBOR

OYSTER DOCKS, MILFORD

OYSTER BOATS, CITY POINT, NEW HAVEN

LIGHTHOUSE POINT, NEW HAVEN

carried it in saddle-bags to Hartford. Later, in the early 18th century, after the discovery of iron in Salisbury, the lime was used in the many blast furnaces that sprang up along the brooksides, where iron masters, whose fame spread throughout the country, forged ships' guns, anchors and chains, accumulating fortunes.

North from US 1 at NORWALK (*see NORWALK, see Tour* 1), US 7 proceeds to a junction with a macadamized road at 1 *m.*

> Left on this road, which follows the winding course of Silvermine Creek, is the artists' colony of SILVERMINE, 2.2 *m.* At the village crossroads is the exhibition room (L) where the many artists who make their summer homes in this district hold an art exhibit through July and August (*adm. free*).
>
> Right at the crossroads, 3.4 *m.*, is the *Buttery Sawmill*, which has been in operation since 1688, the oldest sawmill in the United States in point of service.

At 3.9 *m.*, in an old red wooden building (L), a country blacksmith shapes hand-forged fire sets, hinges and sconces, while school-children stop at the doorway to watch him working with cherry-red iron.

At 5.2 *m.* State 33 joins US 7 from the right and combines with it for 1.7 *m.* On a triangle at the intersection stands the lilac-hidden *Homestead* built in 1725 by David Lambert, who migrated from Wilton, England, and was made local 'towne taverner.' Beneath the gambrel roof are the remains of a secret stairway that leads from the attic to a dark cellar, where it connects with a tunnel to a near-by salt-box house, a reminder of the Abolitionist societies and the Underground Railway operatives who secreted escaped slaves *en route* to Canada. The woodwork in this house, especially that in the State Chamber on the second floor where Lafayette slept, is of exceptionally fine quality.

US 7 here crosses a pastoral countryside and is lined with fine shade trees and weeping willows. In occasional kennels and antique shops along the highway, barking puppies and displays of old glass share the attention of tourists.

At 5.8 *m.* the modern *Wilton Town Hall* (R), set back from the highway, is a well-designed, red-brick building with white columns.

At 6.9 *m.* State 33 turns left and US 7 turns right.

> Left on State 33 is WILTON, 0.4 *m.*, a community where life is still unhurried as it was during Colonial days. Settled in 1701, this town, which sent 300 sons to the Continental Army, is now the home of many artists, authors, and musicians.
>
> On the northeast corner of Lovers' Lane and State 33 is the tree-shadowed *Congregational Church* (1790) with double tiers of windows. The simplicity of the old interior, with box pews and white woodwork, has been well preserved.
>
> Opposite is the *Wilton Academy Building*, erected by Professor Hawley Olmstead in 1828 and later used as a town hall. The building has recently been restored and is now used by the local Garden Club.
>
> Right, a short distance on Lovers' Lane, are the *Ruins of an Old Mill* (1748) beside a 30-foot waterfall.

At 7.4 *m.* is an old *District School*, topped with an unusual, crude belfry, the work of a local craftsman.

At 7.7 *m.* is a beautifully landscaped *Highway Park* (L).

At 8.2 *m*. (R) is the collection of houses known as CANNONDALE (town of Wilton). At *Sharps Hill Burying Ground* (R), many of Wilton's Revolutionary veterans have been buried, including Captain Azur Belden, who fought throughout the war from Bunker Hill to Yorktown.

At 8.3 *m*., back from the road (R) is a large, three-story *Mill* of cut stone, slowly crumbling beside the river.

At 10.4 *m*. is the junction with a dirt road.

Left on this road is a settlement of Finnish factory workers, 0.5 *m*. Behind their homes are bathhouses, tiny, stone-paved shacks that are filled with steam from water heated in large corner fireplaces.

At 10.5 *m*. is the junction with State 53.

Right on State 53, a winding road, is GEORGETOWN, 0.3 *m*. (alt. 308), a small village with a large number of Finnish residents, many of whom are employed in the community's only industry, a wire-screen factory.

Turning sharply left at 0.6 *m*., State 53 runs past the *Gilbert Farms Experimental Station* of Connecticut State College, which is stocked with milking short-horn cattle.

At 3.3 *m*. iron gates at a private driveway (L), mark the entrance to *Stormfield*, formerly the estate of Mark Twain. His hilltop home, which later burned to the ground, commanded a magnificent view of the surrounding valleys.

At 3.5 *m*. beside the road, but easily missed by the hurrying motorist, is the deep gorge of *Knob Crook Brook*, where the narrow stream tumbles down a ravine thickly grown with hemlock and beech trees. Mark Twain believed this to be one of the loveliest spots in America and spent many hours here.

Rounding a curve, the highway dips downhill, affording a splendid view of the valley, and at 3.7 *m*. curves through a tilted rock formation of sandstone, of interest to geologists.

At 4 *m*. is the junction with State 107.

Straight ahead on State 107, at 0.6 *m*., is the junction with a dirt road. On this road is the *Aaron Sanford House* (1753), on which a tablet marks the structure as 'the Cradle of Methodism' in Connecticut. Here Jesse Lee, the itinerant Methodist preacher, converted Aaron Sanford in 1789.

State 107, passing a *Pheasant Farm* (L), at 0.8 *m*., climbs the hill to REDDING, 1.2 *m*. (alt. 685, town pop. 1599).

The little white *Town House* (L) facing the Green was built in 1834, on the same plan as the earlier one of 1798. The house immediately north is on the *Site of the Deacon Stephen Burr House*, where Colonel Aaron Burr often visited his uncle, of whom he wrote in his diary, 'My uncle Stephen lived on milk and punch and at the age of 86 mounted by stirrup a very gay horse and galloped off with me, twelve miles without stopping, and was, I thought, less fatigued than I.'

The *Salt-Box House* (R) was built in 1753 by the Reverend Nathaniel Bartlett, who was pastor of the Congregational Church here for over fifty years.

Left on State 53, at the junction with State 107, at 4.5 *m*. (L) is the *Mark Twain Library* established by the author in 1909 and containing his personal library.

At 6.7 *m*. (R) stands the *David Barlow House* (about 1724–44), a long salt-box with two stone chimneys, that retains some of the original shingles at the top of the north peak. Here, Joel Barlow, one of the 'Hartford Wits,' spent the winter of 1777 and wrote a part of his 'Columbiad' (1807).

BRANCHVILLE (alt. 347) (Town of Redding), 11.1 *m*., is a scattered settlement about an old depot, a few stores, and garages.

At the depot is a junction with a tar road.

Right on the tar road, across the railroad tracks to the junction with another side road, 0.1 *m.* Left on this, at 0.3 *m.*, is the *Branchville Quarry.* More than 31 kinds of minerals have been found here, and many fine specimens can still be picked up in the old dumps.

Traversing rugged, wooded country, US 7 reaches the junction with State 35, at 15.5 *m.*

Left on State 35, the road leads through the *Outpost Nurseries*, past a lake, 1.8 *m.*, where weeping willows bend their graceful branches over the water's edge and white swans paddle beneath a rustic bridge that leads to a tiny island.

RIDGEFIELD (alt. 760, town pop. 3580), 3 *m.*, is a residential town of many landscaped estates and summer residences. The principal thoroughfare, bordered by handsome shade trees and sweeping lawns, is one of America's most beautiful rural streets.

Purchased from the Indians in 1708 and surveyed the following year with a 'six-rod road' running across the ridge, this community was settled by twenty-five men from Norwalk and Milford, who chose their home sites by lottery. Here, on April 27, 1777, was fought the stirring battle of Ridgefield, in which the militia, reinforced by farmers of the neighborhood, attempted to halt Tryon's retreating British troops after their raid on Danbury.

On Main St., a tablet (L) in the wall indicates the site of the barricade hastily erected by the 500 men under General Benedict Arnold. Here General Wooster received a mortal wound and was carried back to Danbury where he died. Just beyond, another tablet, commemorating the battle reads in part:

In Defense of American Independence
At the Battle of Ridgefield
April 27, 1777
Died
Eight Patriots

Who were laid in this ground
Companioned by
Sixteen British Soldiers
Living, their enemies, Dying, their guests,
In honor of service and sacrifice
This Memorial is Placed
For the Strengthening of Hearts.

On Main St., at the northeast corner of the junction of State 35 and State 102, stands the 1713, one-and-one-half-story, gambrel-roofed *House of the Reverend Thomas Hawley*, with a wide Dutch stoop under a curving roof whose lines flow out of the lower slope of the gambrel; an old box-garden, adjoining, dates from 1800.

Embedded in the walls of the *Timothy Keeler Tavern* (L), 25 Main St., is a round shot, fired during the battle of Ridgefield. This old dwelling (1760), with a broad gambrel roof and wide overhang, was owned and occupied by Cass Gilbert, the architect, until his death in 1934.

Following the narrow stream of the Norwalk River, the winding highway continues through partly wooded terrain.

Wooster Mountain, to the left of the highway, is crossed by numerous hiking trails. Major General Wooster, the first officer to command the entire militia of the State, led his men over this mountain in their attempt to cut off the retreat of General Tryon's forces after the British raid on the military stores at Danbury.

On both sides of the highway, at 16.5 *m.*, are the cultivated acres of the *Outpost Nurseries*, covering over two square miles. Practically every known species of northern evergreen is grown here, and ornamental shrubs and perennials perfume the air during the spring and summer months.

High ridges pinch the narrow valley almost to the highway's edge to *Wooster State Park*, 17.9 *m.* (R and L). Driveways (R) through the park lead to shady picnic areas equipped with fireplaces.

At 19.5 *m.* the highway passes the *Danbury Fair Grounds* (L), where one of the few remaining old-fashioned fairs in New England annually attracts thousands of visitors during the first week in October. Exhibits include agricultural products and a cattle show; entertainment is supplied by trotting races and a midway. Several Yankee farmers have been exhibitors at this fair for over fifty years.

At Danbury is a junction with State 37 (*see Tour 4A*) and US 6 (*see Tour* 2).

DANBURY, 20.8 *m.* (alt. 375, city pop. 22,261), 'the Hat City' (*see DANBURY*).

At 24.2 *m.*, *Glacial Eskers* are on either side of the highway. Many of them have been partly cut away in highway or railroad excavations and the clean white sand, gleaming from the open banks, gives a clear view of the formation.

US 7 reaches a junction with State 133 at 26.7 *m.*

> Right on State 133 is BROOKFIELD (alt. 285), 0.4 *m.* (*see Tour 4B*), with its old mills along the banks of Still River.

US 7 passes roadside markets catering to the motorist trade, numerous pre-Revolutionary houses carefully remodeled, and an old *Lime Quarry* (L), at 29.3 *m.*

Traversing rolling, agricultural country, US 7 passes the *American Beauty House* (L), 31.2 *m.*, a brick dwelling (about 1812), with four chimneys and a stone-arched Palladian window, made famous by Edna Ferber's novel 'American Beauty' (1931). The great house is a monument to better days when the fertile fields supported country squires in style.

At 33.4 *m.* is the junction with a dirt road.

> Right on this dirt road, through a sparsely populated region where old deserted houses on land acquired by the hydraulic company are falling into ruins, across the Housatonic on an iron bridge, 1.3 *m.* On the hilltop on the west bank of the river (L), north of the bridge, was *Chief Waramaug's Palace*, recorded as the most ornate Indian dwelling in the Colony. Historians agree that the palace was a Long House about 20' × 100', made from bark that was carried for many miles on the backs of the artisans. The interior walls of the main council room were decorated in colorful paintings of the chief, members of his family, councilors, and judges. In other apartments were representations of all the four-footed beasts, birds, reptiles, and insects. Artists, lent to Waramaug from distant tribes, labored for many moons to complete this unusual work of primitive art, which, unfortunately, was not preserved.
>
> At the east end of the bridge is the junction with a dirt road; sharp right on this road up the hillside, 1.4 *m.*, to *Lovers' Leap*, a wooded crag overlooking the turbu-

lent waters. When white men first found their way to the river, the Pootatuck Indians under their chief, Waramaug, lived along the precipitous slopes above the rapids. One winter's day, according to tradition, Lillinoah, daughter of the chief, found a stricken white man, weak from exhaustion, wandering in the forest. Against the opposition of the tribe, Lillinoah nursed him back to health. By the end of the summer, Chief Waramaug had given his consent to their marriage, but the white man wished first to return to his village to tell his people of his safety, saying that he would return to claim his bride.

Through the long winter Lillinoah hoped and waited. In spring, she decked her hair with woodland blossoms and wandered down the trail in the vain hope of meeting her returning lover. When autumn came, she grew pale and listless. The worried chief suggested to Eagle Feather, his most stalwart aid, 'The girl sickens in loneliness. You shall wed her.'

Lillinoah overheard the conversation. That evening she stole down to the river and pushed a canoe out into the stream. Tossing away the paddle, she drifted swiftly toward the rapids. Suddenly, above the roaring of the waters, she heard the voice she had waited so many months to hear, joyously singing a song that she knew. The branches on the crag above her parted and for one agonized instant her lover looked down on the doomed canoe. Lillinoah raised her arms, beseeching his help. Unhesitatingly the white man leaped into the river, just as the canoe, careening in the current, capsized. On the brink of the falls, he reached her and together they were dashed on the rocks below.

On the summit of Lovers' Leap, Chief Waramaug was buried. The spot, in the *Hurd Estate* (*not open*), was formerly marked by a rough stone monument and the usual pile of stones built by passing warriors as a mark of respect, but the great house was erected, and the main fireplace now stands directly over the chief's grave.

The Cove, at the south end of the gorge just below Lovers' Leap, was once considered to be one of the best fishing places in the Colony. Shad and eels were caught here in sufficient quantity to warrant export. As early as 1642 a Mr. Goodyear of New Haven, owner of Goodyear's Island, traded with the Indians in the Cove and finally established a trading post there. In 1773 fishing rights on the Cove were leased by Benjamin Hawley for a 99-year period to thirteen men who were obligated to pay the lessee one fish for each thirteen caught. The great dam built at Derby in 1870 brought an end to fishing at the falls.

At 36.1 *m.* is the intersection with a crossroad (R) to NEW MILFORD (*see Tours 4C and 4B*).

On both sides of the highway, at 37.3 *m.*, the *Rocky River Plant* (*visitors welcome*) of the Connecticut Light and Power Company attracts attention with its 60-inch pipeline through which the waters of the Housatonic are pumped to Lake Candlewood (*see Tour 4A*), and there stored to supply power when the river is low. This plant, the first of the 'pump-plant' type in the country, and at the time of its construction in 1928, the only one in existence outside of Switzerland, pumps water from the Housatonic River up 210 feet to the Lake Candlewood reservoir, with a capacity for handling 112,500 gallons a minute.

Following a winding course to *Boardman's Bridge* (alt. 226), 38.6 *m.*, US 7 passes the extensive works of the New England Lime Company (R).

At 39.1 *m.* is the junction with State 37 (*see Tour 4A*).

At 41.4 *m.* the highway passes *Tory's Hole*, in the woods (L), a many-chambered cave of stalactites where Tories are said to have taken refuge from the tar-and-feather punishments inflicted by the Sons of Liberty.

At 42.2 *m.* is the entrance to *Straits Rock Highway Park* (R), a shady picnic area at the river's edge, where fishermen find black bass plentiful.

At 42.7 *m.* is the *Naromiyocknowhusunkatankshunk Brook.*

At GAYLORDSVILLE (alt. 314) (Town of New Milford), 43.6 *m.*, the
highway crosses the Housatonic.

BULL'S BRIDGE (alt. 300) (Town of Kent), 44.6 *m.*, is a scattered settlement, dominated by the huge stacks of the hydro-electric plant of the
Connecticut Light and Power Company on the river (R).

South of Kent, US 7 follows the east bank of the Housatonic River, passing a quiet stretch of water where Kent School crews are often seen rowing.
At a bend in the river, 47 *m.*, the Housatonic is less than a mile from the
New York State Line. Schaghticoke Mountain, across the stream at the
bend, rears its shaggy head abruptly from the river's edge. At its base
are a few weather-beaten shacks occupied by the descendants of the
Schaghticoke Indian Tribe, which in the Revolution furnished more than
100 warriors to the Continental army. These Indians acted as a liaison
unit, relaying messages from Stockbridge to Long Island Sound by means
of drumbeats and signal fires on Pickett Rock, Straits Mountain, and
Candlewood Mountain.

The *Schaghticoke Indian Reservation* consists of 400 acres of submarginal
land and a few poor dwellings. Not more than a dozen Indians of this
tribe remain, and the total value of their holdings is placed at $5000.

At 49.3 *m.* is the junction with State 341.

> 1. Left on State 341 across the Housatonic River is the campus of *Kent School,*
> a preparatory school for boys, 0.3 *m.* The school farm lands are on the right and the
> buildings on the left. Established in 1906, this Episcopal institution directed by
> the gifted Father Sill has a large waiting list, is internationally known, and fre-
> quently sends a crew to row at Henley, England.
>
> Westward, crossing State 341, is the popular *Appalachian Trail,* which skirts
> the eastern slope of Schaghticoke Mountain where hikers must be watchful if they
> are to avoid trouble with the rattlesnakes that bask in the sun on ledges. The
> snakebite hazard is serious enough for trail authorities to keep first-aid stations at
> certain points along the well-marked hiking trail (*for trail information see Appa-
> lachian Trail Publication No. 19N, Conn. Forest and Park Ass'n., 215 Church St.,
> New Haven, Conn.*)
>
> Beyond Kent School a gravel road (R), at 1.8 *m.*, enters *Macedonia Brook State
> Park,* 1920 acres of woodland traversed by hiking trails and a lively trout stream
> which flows past the crumbling ruins of many an old-time forge.
>
> 2. Right on State 341 to the junction with a macadam road, at 0.6 *m.*
>
> Right on this road past *Leonard Pond* (L), at 1.2 *m.*, and *Hatch Pond* (R), 2.6 *m.*,
> to the driveway, 3.6 *m.*, which leads to *South Kent School* for young boys, an off-
> shoot of Kent School, established in 1923. South Kent was formerly known as
> Pigtail Corners, because an angry colonist cut the tail off an enemy's pig.
>
> Beyond this junction State 341 winds through wooded country between *North
> and South Spectacle Ponds* (R and L), 4.4 *m.* Summer foliage screens the lakes so
> that they are scarcely visible from the highway. At the north end of North Spec-
> tacle Pond is a tamarack spruce bog. Ascending the long, steep grade with frequent
> vistas over neighboring hills, the road affords a magnificent view of the horizon,
> at 6.2 *m.*, and climbs to the tiny hilltop center of WARREN, 7.8 *m.* (alt. 1200,

pop. 303), almost bleak in its Puritan severity. Warren was settled in 1737 by people from the coast towns, and was first called East Greenwich. Incorporated in 1786, it was named for General Joseph Warren, hero of Bunker Hill.

On the hilltop, back from the road (R), is the *Congregational Church* (1818), with a square tower set far back from the projecting pediment and rising in a series of open stages to a spire reminiscent of a candle snuffer. Pilasters against the façade frame three arched doors. Grouped about the church are several stately 19th-century houses.

Right from the center of Warren, a dirt road leads to a junction, 8.5 *m.*; here to another junction at 9.1 *m.*; left again at 9.6 *m.* to the entrance of *Above All State Park* (alt. 1460) with woodland trails, excellent views, and a 'top-of-the-world' isolation that explains the name.

KENT (alt. 380, town pop. 1054), 49.6 *m.*, was a part of the Western Lands formerly held by Windsor and Hartford. The General Assembly appointed a committee to lay out the area in 1710, and auctioned off the land at Windsor in 1738. Purchasers from Colchester, Norwalk, and Fairfield immediately started settlement and, in 1739, the town was incorporated. The pioneers soon discovered deposits of iron ore, and by 1845 operated three blast furnaces with a peak production of some 3000 tons per year.

Kent has a large art colony; numerous summer camps are scattered through near-by valleys. The elm-and-maple-shaded main street beside the Housatonic is sheltered by imposing rounded ridges to the east and west. Winter sports are popular here; devotees of hiking, riding, hunting, and fishing find exceptional facilities for the enjoyment of their sports. Geologists discover fine specimens of limestone, marble, and schist in the neighborhood. Kent preserves numerous old houses with entrance porches of a charming, slender-columned local variety. These porches have open gables and molded cornices that often follow the entire roof lines; the details are carried out in the window caps.

On a railroad crossing the main street, frequent milk trains roll southward to New York. Lads from Kent School row on the Housatonic, and hikers come in from the hills to buy raisins, chocolate, and cool drinks before they again enter the trails. The general store displays new farm machinery, gaudy with red and blue paint, at the very edge of the cinder sidewalk.

Climbing easy grades that afford excellent views, US 7 winds northward to KENT FURNACE (Town of Kent), where both Kent and Salisbury ore was converted into iron at the Monitor Iron Works. *Seven Hearths* (1756), 51.0 *m.* (R), a large, two-chimneyed house, was an early fur-trading post. Planking around the lower walls of this house is of native pine, 36 inches wide and $2\frac{1}{2}$ inches thick. Above one of the many fireplaces is a pine panel made from one board $41\frac{1}{2}$ inches in width. The former *Parsonage* (R), 51.1 *m.*, built about 1740, with double doors, four-paneled, with a transom, is in very good original condition and has some exceptional interior paneling.

At FLANDERS (Town of Kent), 51.2 *m.*, a roadside hamlet, are two well-preserved old houses.

At 53.1 *m.* is the entrance to *Kent Falls State Park* (R), containing one of the most spectacular of Connecticut's waterfalls, where the brook, arched by hemlocks, rushes over a precipice in two cascades, down a' 200-foot drop within a quarter of a mile. The lower falls have cut their way over white marble steps and have scooped out many potholes in the ledges. The best view is obtained by following the brook a short distance on foot. Fireplaces and tables offer picnic facilities.

Across a modern cement bridge (L) spanning the Housatonic, just south of the site of a famous old covered bridge that was carried away and crashed to kindling against the new structure in the spring flood of 1936, is the settlement of CORNWALL BRIDGE (alt. 420), 57.5 *m.* (R).

At Cornwall Bridge is the junction with State 4 (*see Tour 4D*).

To the right the *Housatonic Meadows State Park*, 57.7 *m.*, along the birch-lined river bank, offers picnic spots and views of the shallow, turbulent river.

In the *Housatonic State Forest*, US 7 passes a narrow cleft in the rocks (L), 60.7 *m.*, where a mountain stream, *Pine Swamp Brook*, tumbles down a narrow hemlock glen in a series of cascades to join the river.

At 61.3 *m.* (R) is the junction with State 128 and the little village of WEST CORNWALL (alt. 520), reached by a covered bridge across the Housatonic River. An art show is on display there during the summer months, usually in the Masonic Hall. There is an excellent view of the Housatonic River gorge at 62.6 *m.* (R).

At 63.7 *m.* is the *Baer Art School*, where handicraft articles are made.

At 65.8 *m.* is the junction with State 112.

Left on State 112 is the village of LIME ROCK (alt. 600, Town of Salisbury), 1.5 *m.* The very old slag dumps and ancient iron furnaces are now overgrown with wild flowers and artists sketch along the quiet waters of Salmon Fell Kill.

Forges once lined the brookside and anvils clanged with steel on steel as iron workers forged links of the great chain which was stretched across the Hudson River at West Point to obstruct the passage of British warships. Here, Salisbury iron, famous for great tensile strength, was cast into guns for the frigate 'Constitution' and produced cannon and cannon balls for the Continental army. The first railroad that ran through this area used wooden rails shod with iron.

Lime Rock Lodge (L), at the center, stands on grounds granted to a Colonial officer for his services in the Pequot War. Crossing the Salmon Fell Kill, State 112 passes an *Old Mill*, 1.6 *m.*, which makes hand-made rag paper. The highway follows the route over which iron ore was once transported in saddle-bags from the numerous Salisbury workings to Lime Rock forges.

US 7 passes through fertile meadowland and crosses the Housatonic River, 66.1 *m.*

On US 7 at 67.7 *m.* is the junction with State 126.

Left on State 126 to a junction at 0.3 *m.*; left here to FALLS VILLAGE (alt. 580, Town of Canaan pop. 563), 0.5 *m.*, where early lumbering industry used water-power from the Great Falls of the Housatonic River. An early paper mill (1783) and a gun-barrel factory (1797) were destroyed by fire in 1800. Iron forging early became the chief industry of the town and has left its imprint in the plain, practical dwellings. The *National Iron Bank* (R) does business today under a name from the past.

The Town of Canaan was sold at auction in 1738 at New London. The rights brought the highest prices paid for Litchfield County land up to that time. Pictured as 'a land flowing with milk and honey' by the promoters, this rugged chunk of Connecticut terrain was so desirable to its enthusiastic future settlers that bids started at £60 per right and climbed rapidly. There is, in fact, fertile bottomland along both the Hollenbeck and Housatonic Rivers, but miles of rocky ridges and mountainous land are too barren to be used for any agricultural purposes.

US 7 turns left at SOUTH CANAAN (alt. 700, Town of Canaan), 69 m., where a fine old *Congregational Church* (1802) stands at the cross-roads, passing under the shadow of Canaan Mountain (R), with magnificent views of Mt. Riga, Bear and Monument Mountains (L), at 71 m.

At South Canaan is the junction with State 43 (*see Tour 4D*).

South of the *Great Swamp*, where early autumn foliage is brilliantly vivid, are the remains of an *Old Mill*, 72 m. High on the mountain above lies the milldam to which the miller climbed each time he opened or closed the gates.

At 74.3 m. on US 7 is a junction with Sand Road. Here, at the junction, near the present Knickerbocker Hotel, stood the former *Knickerbocker Tavern*, whence passengers of the Albany stagecoach line, on stopping for the night, often carried away exciting tales of turbulent scenes when the 'Red Eye Infantry,' as the men from Canaan Mountain and the Barracks were known, came to town.

    1. Hard L. on Sand Road, 0.3 m., is the *Lower Cemetery* (R), in which many Revolutionary soldiers are buried. Here beneath an insignificant stone lies Captain Gershom Hewitt, who, through a ruse, secured the plans of Fort Ticonderoga for Colonel Ethan Allen.

    2. Left at the junction on a driveway marked 'The Canaan Golf Club,' 500 feet, is the old *Douglas Tavern* (1762). According to legend, the cellar of this building was used as a prison for Hessian soldiers, captured by General Gates during the Revolution.

South of twin bridges over the Blackberry River, at 74.8 m., is the junction with an oiled dirt road, known as the Lower Road.

    Right on this road following the Blackberry River, which furnished power for many early furnaces and mills. At 1.3 m., just across an iron bridge, is (L) the *Squire Samuel Forbes House*, built about 1770 by this early iron master. Near-by stood his forge, in which Ethan Allen was a partner before he moved to Vermont and began his spectacular military career. The articles of agreement between Forbes and Allen are still preserved in the town records. Although the Forbes's forge has long since disappeared, along the road are many signs of the early iron industry. At 2 m. stands the crumbling, brush-grown ruins of an old furnace (L); and at 2.1 m. the solitary, gray-white chimney of another deserted forge is reflected in the still waters above an old milldam whose stone-work has withstood the spring freshets of passing centuries. Across the stream are the slag dumps, shining with a green, glassy brilliance after every rain. At 2.5 m. this Lower Road reaches the beautiful old *Congregational Church* (1822), with an octagonal spire and Ionic pilasters separating the three entrances, at the EAST CANAAN crossroads which mark the center of a hamlet of scattered farmhouses, and the smaller homes of former lime-kiln workers.

At 74.9 m. (L) is the *Captain Isaac Lawrence House* (1751), with a huge stone doorstep on which the Captain, who was the first settler in this region, chiseled the dates of his arrival in town, and of the building of his home, as well as the names of his children. This building, erected on the spot where Lawrence pitched his tent on his arrival from Stamford, was originally intended for a tavern and contained a ballroom, with a musicians' gallery over the fireplace, in the second and third floors of the southern end.

CANAAN (alt. 660) (Town of North Canaan, pop. 2287), 75.2 *m.*, is a snug village with a remote and self-sufficient air, the heritage of long, hard winters, before the days of modern highways when snow-drifted roads isolated the community from the outside world.

At the village crossroads is the junction with US 44 (*see Tour* 3).

The highway passes the State Line and the *Canaan Airport* (R), 76.8 *m.*, where planes can be chartered for long or short trips. Right, the blunt northern ridge of Canaan Mountain towers over the valley. Across the Massachusetts Line, at 0.5 *m.*, is Ashley Falls, Massachusetts.

T O U R   4 A :   *From* DANBURY *to* JUNCTION WITH US 7, 20 *m.*, State 37.

Via New Fairfield, Sherman.
Limited accommodations.
Macadamized highway.

STATE 37 leaves Danbury on the Padanarum Road, and 'letter-esses' over the hills to the Big Basin and the west shore of Lake Candlewood. Tapping an area that has been undiscovered until the advent of improved roads, this is still essentially a wilderness route. Among these hills and in the Big Basin now covered by Lake Candlewood, the 'pecker wood' sawmill men made their last stand. Above the waterline, slashings have been masked by a sturdy growth of hardwoods, and hemlock still grows tall in many roadside glens. Among the hills are a few cabin dwellers; the Quaker lived here for a while but has passed on, leaving only his place names. Names on rural mail-boxes are Yankee names, and traditional Yankee thrift is evident in the long stone walls, well-stocked woodsheds, in the great piles of yellow pumpkins, the stacked hay, shocked fodder, and bulging corncribs in the autumn. Although the fields are small and a farmer frequently explains that he has, 'Ten acres of tillage and the rest Creation,' the tour traverses a tranquil countryside where people seem content and unhurried.

Padanarum Road leaves Danbury (*see DANBURY*), unmarked except for frequent 'Lake Candlewood' signs, to twist through the outskirts of the city past well-painted homes of hat-shop workers. Traffic has been left behind on busy US 7.

At 4.5 *m.* (L) is *Margerie Pond,* an expanse of water that stretches for over a mile beside the highway. This new source of water supply for the city of Danbury is on a flyway of migratory waterfowl and, during flight season, squadrons of ducks are seen, riding the ripples. On the hilltop (R) stands one of the oddest structures in this section of Connecticut, a tall dwelling of pink brick and clapboard siding, with trailing ells like a Maine farmhouse. The front of the main house and larger ell is of brick with wooden pilasters; beneath an intricate dentiled and bracketed cornice are heavy caps above the many 24-light windows. Although the date of erection is unknown, the dwelling is probably the early 19th-century masterpiece of an energetic local joiner.

NEW FAIRFIELD (alt. 700, town pop. 434), 5.5 *m.,* was named for Fairfield (*see FAIRFIELD*), from whence came the first settlers. This village, incorporated in 1740, formerly a lumbering community, has experienced a drop in population from a high of 1665 in 1800 to the present figure. New Fairfield enjoyed a spirited boom in 1925 when the Big Basin was logged off just before the dams creating Lake Candlewood were erected.

Chestnut and white-oak logs were once piled high beside the road and rural constables dreaded Saturday night when loggers came to town. Paul Bunyan may have passed this way after his Onion River job, because woodsmen hereabouts still speak of 'blue oxen' and are reputed to shave with double-bitted axes.

At New Fairfield is the junction with State 39.

Right on State 39, across Short Wood Brook and past Millers Corners, at 0.8 *m.* are gentle hills. From the top of this slight ridge, *Lake Candlewood* stretches along the middle distance (R) at the foot of Green Pond Mountain. Along the lake shore are hundreds of small summer cottages.

At 2 *m.* (R) is a great *Dutch Windmill* on a hilltop. It has a wingspread too great for Connecticut breezes. A series of rock-cuts along the highway show the borderline formation between limestone and schist. Here the asphalt highway humps and dips in a manner which discourages fast driving.

At 3.9 *m. Squantz Pond State Park* merges into the *Pootatuck State Forest* at the junction with a dirt road. Left on this road, 0.1 *m.,* former farmland has been converted into grassy picnic grounds and sports fields. To the north, the eastern and western hills meet at a notch, suggestive of Franconia. Hiking trails abound. A bathing beach slopes gently into spring-fed Squantz Pond, where youngsters are safe in shallow water. On the edge of the forest is *Camp Hood,* a Civilian Conservation Corps camp whose members have provided many of the improvements and facilities in this area (1937). A causeway separates Squantz Pond from Lake Candlewood, but a fishway has been provided so that angling is equally good in either body of water.

Passing three cemeteries within a mile, the highway crosses a rough terrain where farmyard barns show marked Dutch influence in their gambrel roofs. Here small houses sit cater-cornered to the road, and great stone walls proclaim the handicap Yankee farmers have faced in their efforts to wrest a crop from submarginal land. This section had never had an erosion problem because nature has placed her own riprap where it holds the soil of hillside fields.

At 9.9 *m*. (L) peaceful valleys push back the hills from the flow of *Quaker Brook* and a few tenacious farmers still wage a losing fight with poor, stony land.

At 11 *m*. in a hemlock-grown ravine, are great piles of clamshells beside the crumbling ruins of a dance-floor. In the pasture, near-by, are five mounds of empty shotgun shells that correspond with the former location of five firing pins where trapshots used to snuggle their cheeks against the combs of their stocks and shout, 'Pull!' at Crosseyed Turner's combination pigeon-shoot-clambake-wrestling-match-square-dance gatherings. Sometimes, in the event of a tie at the shooting, the festivities ran into the second and third day. Stout fellows came here to shoot all day and dance all night. The torchlit grove echoed to the shouts of the prompter; the fiddle and banjo tunes of now forgotten men made young hearts thrill, as one of the Turner twins sprinkled wax on the dance platform under the stars. Here today, by the asphalt highway, stands a red gasoline pump and a Red Cross First Aid Station, but old men often pause as if listening for the clatter of buckboard wheels on gravel, and the gay 'Halloa' of gathering comrades.

At 12 *m*. the highway crosses Quaker Brook and a little pond fills a hollow (R). An occasional great blue heron fishes here — sober, stiff, seemingly asleep until a fish swims near.

At 12.9 *m. Greenwood Lake* glitters through trees (R), and a cabin colony hugs the shoreline and the hill to the eastward.

At 13.1 *m*. is the *Site of the Perry Boney Store* (L) (prior to 1916) locally famous as 'the smallest store in the world.' This emporium was conducted by a thin little recluse with china-blue eyes who seemed to be seeing things no other eyes could ever see. The hill youngsters said that he talked with the fairies that lived in the mist above the pools along Greenwood Brook. Perry purchased stock at the general store in Sherman, carried it to his own little establishment in a market basket and resold it at the same prices. The store was so tiny that only one customer could be served at a time. The door, swinging on leather hinges, was approached by a winding path that led up from the road between fences of peeled saplings, just wide enough for one man to pass at a time, as if the storekeeper feared dealings with more than one customer. Hunters planned on stopping there for a package of soda crackers and store cheese; and tramps who stopped to beg never went away hungry. One day Perry failed to open his store. Where he went and what happened to him is as uncertain as the will-o'-the-wisp on the mountains that he loved.

On the site of this queer store now stands a rustic Swiss chalet with half-timbered walls, built at the very edge of the road, facing the triple roll of Green Pond Mountain on the eastern shore of Lake Candlewood. This mountain, inaccessible except by private road, is named for the pure, spring-fed lake at the very top, whose deep, green waters sparkle like a jewel in the center of a wilderness. A flume was once blasted through the solid rock to furnish water-power from the lake to an old mill below.

At 13.5 *m.* a deep, hemlock-shaded glen parallels the highway; woodland stretches away in seemingly endless miles. The wood thrush greets the dawn from these dense thickets.

At 14.6 *m.* long rows of sugar maples, bordering the highway and side roads, are eagerly tapped at 'sap time' by small boys of the neighborhood who are adept in the use of auger and elder quills. The narrow highway dips and ascends like a crazy roller coaster, with all the curves banked on the wrong side. Beside most of the scattered farmhouses in this section are private burying grounds shaded by evergreens.

At 15.5 *m.* is a rare *Hardbeam Grove* (L), that was probably planted by some provident farmer to furnish whipstalks for ox whips. They have grown too large for such use now, but their gun-barrel-straight trunks show why early drovers valued them.

The highway dips here to cross a lively trout stream, *Greenwood Brook*, which has its source somewhere in the Turner Mountain region. Off in the woods, on Turner Mountain (*inaccessible to motor traffic*), Charley Light, whose hilltop home was known to the countryside as '*Sherman Lighthouse*,' was reputed to have been the originator of corn beer. Other farmers have attempted to duplicate his brew, but Charley never shared his recipe with anyone and the secret of his beverage died with him.

The Connecticut Yankee uses grapes for 'jell' and prefers the larger fruits for beverage-making because they make juice faster. Blackberry brandy is highly valued for intestinal complaints. The apple is used for cider, sweet and 'hard,' and the best barrels are saved 'to make the scythe cut better' during haying. The freezing of cider and drawing off the 'core' are usually done behind the barn, for the farm women distrust the potent applejack.

October was corn beer month in the Sherman hills. Charley brewed it in secret, but the effects of a batch furnished town gossip for many months. It inspired men to bravery extraordinary. Charley used it freely when in need of courage and it never failed him. During one hunt on Green Pond Mountain, Charley followed a wildcat into her den in the ledge. The hunting party built a fire and waited several hours. Just as they were about to leave Charley to his fate, the old warrior backed out of the hole, dragging the wildcat by her ears, his pockets full of jumping kittens. The male cat, Charley said, died of fright, so he left him in the hole.

SHERMAN (alt. 500, town pop. 391), 16.2 *m.*, is a little crossroads hamlet that basks in the secure contentment of a five-mill tax and no town debt. Named for Roger Sherman, signer of the Declaration of Independence, this unpretentious hill town is rich in native lore of old-time New England. Incorporated in 1802, Sherman had a population of 984 in 1850, but the younger folks have gradually left the farm for an easier life in town. Most of its present residents are descendants of the original settlers. A tame raccoon was once the town's mascot. No town in the State offers better hunting in season and woodchuck and raccoon suppers are still enjoyed in this hamlet. Occasionally wildcat and bay lynx are brought in from Green Pond Mountain, jack rabbits flick their ears at the best hounds and wily foxes are sure to lead the dogs a merry chase as they head for Squash Hollow. A man's word is as good as his bond in this little community where Yankee thrift is still the rule. The story of a tax collector who hung himself when town gossips falsely accused him of a shortage of funds typifies the character of these upright people. The general store in Sherman is worth a visit. Drugs, groceries, hardware, or dress-goods can be purchased under the same roof. Sherman collects taxes on land now flooded by Lake Candlewood through an agreement with the power company that controls the lake.

At 16.4 *m.* an arm of *Lake Candlewood* (R) reaches northward almost to the highway. Enterprising countrymen have erected signs to entice the tourist down a lane to a 'Boat Livery.' This lake, covering 6000 acres, 15 miles in length, one of the largest artificial bodies of water in the East, was created in 1926 as a power reservoir into which water from the Housatonic River is pumped, during off-peak hours, from the Rocky River Hydraulic Plant (*see Tour* 4). More than 100 homes were torn down or moved preparatory to flooding the valley. Well stocked with game fish, the lake attracts many sportsmen in season.

At 16.9 *m.* the road traverses a fertile valley, a checkerboard of tilled fields and pastureland.

On the slope of a hill, at 17.4 *m.*, is a State highway picnic area called *Sunset Rest.* Here (L) stands a farmstead which might have been the inspiration for Mark Twain's story of the lightning-rod salesman, for it bristles at every gable with rods of various lengths. The rolling heights of Turner Mountain, Mizzentop, and Quaker Hill rise to the west where Connecticut and New York State meet.

State 37 tops a hill at 18.4 *m.* with a view of the Housatonic Valley and the rolling hills beyond New Milford. The highway sweeps on, downgrade, in a long letter S to a junction with US 7 (*see Tour* 4) at 20 *m.*, 0.5 mile north of Boardman's Bridge.

T O U R   4 B :　*From* NEW MILFORD *to* JUNCTION WITH US 7, 11.2 *m.*, State 25 *and* 133.

Via Bridgewater, Roxbury, Brookfield Center.

Limited accommodations.

Macadam highway.

THIS route follows a meandering highway into the older hill towns of western Connecticut. It offers little except scenery and specimens for the mineral collector. The route traverses country historically famous because of the exploits of Remember Baker, Seth Warner, and Ethan Allen. This section has always bred good riflemen and, during the World War, a Roxbury youth, so his partisans claim, participated in the much-publicized Sergeant Alvin York incident. This Roxbury man, Percy Beardsley, now breeds Devon steers and enjoys a peaceful existence in the rolling hills of Ethan Allen's one-time home town. The country is primarily a dairying section and much fluid milk is produced in this area.

South of New Milford, State 25 climbs up the steep incline of *Chicken Hill*, 0.7 *m.*, named for an Indian sachem, Chief Chicken. From the crest, at 0.9 *m.*, superb views embrace the Housatonic Valley, Candlewood and Green Pond Mountains, and the southern Berkshires are enveloped in a distant blue haze.

BRIDGEWATER (alt. 580, town pop. 432), 3.9 *m.*, named 1803, incorporated 1856, is a pleasant agricultural village of considerable local wealth and a growing summer residential population. Architecturally, Bridgewater is a town of the early 19th century. The *Congregational Church* (1807), at the center, has been somewhat disguised by Greek Revival remodeling. The projecting tower, the octagonal belfry, and old sash are indicative of the earlier period. Here about seventy years ago, a native son, Charles B. Thompson, established a mail-order business, booming the village to the dignity of a first-class post office. Thompson, who particularly appreciated the value of advertising, built up a famous mail-order business, founded on the appeal of premiums. Beautiful dolls were among his most successful premiums, for little girls throughout the country, intent upon obtaining one, sold such quantities of toilet soaps and facial creams that manufacturers could not supply Thompson's orders and he established a plant of his own here in Bridgewater.

It is said that, at a time when Thompson's credit was very low, he placed orders for five carload lots of lanterns when he needed but a half carload, in the hope that some dealer would fill at least a part of the order. When the news came that all five carloads were on the rails rolling toward Bridgewater, Thompson's genius for merchandising asserted itself. Bridgewater gleamed at night like Broadway, when the glow on the horizon from the light of Thompson's lanterns attracted customers from faraway places, vastly improving the fortunes of this early opportunist who had the courage to take a chance.

Despite the fact that the postmaster's salary and percentages on stamp sales, increased by the volume of stamps bought by the mail-order house, brought him such affluence that he erected the pretentious home that is still known as 'the house that Thompson built,' he was often at odds with Thompson, and many local legends have grown up regarding their difficulties. After one quarrel, Thompson transferred all of his mailings to New Milford, leaving the enlarged force at the Bridgewater office without work until the postmaster was ready to arbitrate.

At Bridgewater is the junction with State 67.

Left on State 67, winding over the hills to the Shepaug River and ROXBURY STATION (Town of Roxbury), at 2.9 *m.*

> Left at Roxbury Station, a dirt road crosses the railroad and turns into the property known as *Mine Hill* (*private property, visitors welcome; park car and proceed on foot; care should be taken to avoid hidden mine shafts*), 0.3 *m.* The mine, which was originally opened in 1750 by prospectors who hoped to find silver, contains one of the few American deposits of siderite. The vein of spathic iron averaged about eight feet in width and was uncovered for a distance of one mile. More than a million dollars was expended in developing the mine, which for 42 years was operated by the American Smelting Company. Ten tons of pig iron was the average daily output. Now maintained for demonstration purposes by the Columbia School of Mines, Mine Hill is of especial interest, not only because its iron deposit is a fine example of an ore vein along a fault, but also for the many large and perfect pyrite crystals and other minerals in small crystals which can be found here.

North of Roxbury Station, State 67 crosses a concrete bridge and passes *Pulpit Rock* (L), 3.1 *m.*, at the river's edge, behind a barn, where John Eliot, apostle to the Indians, is believed to have preached his Gospel of Peace. State 67 swings sharp R. and combines with State 199 at 4.6 *m.*

> Left on State 199 is *Washington Green*, 4.5 *m.* (*see Tour 4C*). Traversing a region rich in old houses, fragrant with sweet rocket in season, this is a pleasant journey for any traveler with time to spare for leisurely exploration.

ROXBURY (alt. 660, town pop. 553), 5.3 *m.*, was the home of Ethan Allen, Seth Warner, and Remember Baker. The *Episcopal Rectory* (1740), at the center (R), still retains bullet holes in the ceiling as a reminder of wilder days when youthful patriots assembled to depart for the wars. Seth Warner, hero of Crown Point, is buried on the village Green at the foot of a shaft of Roxbury granite.

Christ Church, at the west end of the Green, has a pulpit and lectern of Mine Hill stone, contributed by a parishioner. A pretentious structure of about 1784 is the *Phineas Smith House* (L), standing east of the Green on State 67. This house is a sort of country cousin to the Cowles House (1780) in Farmington, and has a version of Spratt's design in the projecting pediment with a Palladian window, supported on four Ionic columns. Opposite (R) is an *Early 19th-Century Building* with fluted Doric columns, which has served in turn as Toll House, Courtroom, store, and dwelling. The *Congregational Church* (1838), a plain Greek Revival building (R), with a still heavier, plainer chapel, stands east of the Green.

> Right from Roxbury Green, State 199, an asphalt highway, passes the *General Hinman House* (L), now remodeled, and the *Asahel Bacon House* (R), built for one of the operators of Mine Hill. Both of these houses were built about 1784. A small brick 'Records Building' (1796) stands at the edge of the highway (R).

> At 2.8 *m.* is the junction with a dirt road; right on this narrow road to *Roxbury Falls*, where an old silica mill crumbles beside the rushing stream near an iron bridge. From sunny pockets among laurel-clad ledges, trailing arbutus perfumes the springtime air.

Here at Roxbury Green, State 67 swings right to the valley of *Jack's Brook*, a trout stream winding southward to the Shepaug.

At 10 *m.* is the Transylvania Crossroads, locally known as *Pine Tree*. A good example of a salt-box house (1750), painted red, stands (R) beneath the shelter of a giant pine tree.

At Transylvania is the junction with State 172.

> Right on State 172, 0.3 *m.*, under the hill at the west of the highway, is a dwelling of unusual character, probably the *Oldest Structure in South Britain Society.* The southern half of this two-story structure is of rough, native stone; the northern half, of later date, is of wood, showing early craftsmanship in both materials.

At 0.7 *m.* on State 172 is the junction with a dirt road. Right on this dirt road, 1.5 *m.*, that climbs ever higher through a sylvan paradise along the course of Flagg Swamp Brook, an ice-cold, spring-fed stream that falls over mossy ledges to drop into shady glens where the hemlock cover is so dense that sunlight never reaches the stream itself. Speckled trout grow large in this stream and show fight when hooked by barefoot boys who fish with ash pole and garden hackle. At the very end of this road, sheltered by the damp, mossy ledge to the westward, is an *Old Farmhouse*, unchanged since the first Flagg trekked in from the valley to build his mansion beside the clear streams. Fireplaces, panels, hidden closets, and low-ceilinged, poorly lighted rooms with smoke-stained walls, offer a glimpse into the pioneer past. A modern rifle is hung on deer spikes above the fireplace, antlers of a nine-point buck hang above the door, and the pelts of mink and otter are stretched in the shed beside the trail. This is Road's End, peaceful, quiet, beautiful as only the mountains can be. Nobody ever goes there, but Wallace Nutting once offered several thousand dollars for the property as an ideal site for a studio. The owner who does not see twenty dollars from one year to the next refused the offer. 'Anyway,' he said, 'what's the use of money up here in Flagg Swamp?'

At 11.7 *m.* State 67 crosses the *Pomperaug River*, with views of bottomlands and Poverty Hollow to the R. Wallace Nutting (a former resident) widely publicized this area with his tinted photographs of the scenery.

At 12.1 *m.* is the junction with US 6 (*see Tour 2*).

South from Bridgewater State 25 follows a high ridge to SOUTHVILLE (Town of Bridgewater), 8.1 *m.*, where an old iron bridge crosses the Housatonic.

At either end of the bridge (R and L) are dirt roads that follow along the river banks, offering excellent views of the lower gorge of the Housatonic.

At 8.3 *m.* is the junction with a narrow dirt road (L) that enters *The Dingle*, where cool streams flow through a verdant valley, soon to be flooded to form a new reservoir.

South of the iron bridge, State 25 makes a right turn to climb *Obtuse Hill*, where, from the crest at 8.7 *m.*, a splendid northern view of the Berkshire and Taconic Mountains rewards the visitor on a clear day.

BROOKFIELD CENTER (alt. 500, Brookfield town pop. 926), 9.7 *m.*, stands at a hilltop crossroads. Originally known as Newbury, this town was incorporated in 1788 and named Brookfield in honor of the first pastor, Thomas Brooks. In 1795, a widow, Mary Northrop, left the town an estate of 147 pounds, 4 shillings, and 6 pence to be used for an educational fund. Interest from the principal, which is still known as Molly Money, is divided among the school districts each year. Brookfield is today the center of a large summer colony, and enjoys a few brief months of activity each year during the vacation season. At Brookfield Center, State 25 turns sharp left and winds over hill and dale to the junction with US 6 (*see Tour 2*). That route is recommended only as a quick way to get out of the Brookfield section if traveling toward Bridgeport, or points south.

Brookfield's old houses are notably bare in paneling. The oldest building at the center is the *Chamberlain Inn and Store* (1740), on the east side of Main St., the third house right from State 25. Just north of it stands the well-restored *Fairfield House*, built in 1820, and beyond that, the little

Dutch roofed *Bungalow* of Daniel Holley, built in 1740. On Long Meadow Rd., which forks to the right from Main St., are a number of houses which are interesting variations of the salt-box type.

Right from Brookfield Center, on State 133, is the junction with US 7 (*see Tour* 4), at 11.2 *m.*, 6.2 miles north of Danbury.

T O U R   4 C :   *From* NEW MILFORD *to* TORRINGTON, 24.2 *m.*, State 25.

Via Litchfield.

Concrete and macadamized highway.

Limited accommodations (except at lake resorts).

THIS connecting route taps lake and hill vacation resorts. Travel is usually heavy only on week-ends and holidays. Much of the terrain is in woodland, and the rolling hills are well clad. On Sandy Plains, east of Bantam, some plantings of pine appear but the usual coverage is of mixed hardwoods. A few stone houses are found in the vicinity of New Preston but the average farm home is of wood, painted white with green shutters. The farmsteads are of sturdy construction and well fenced.

NEW MILFORD (alt. 260, town pop. 4700), 0.3 *m.*, settled in 1707, incorporated October, 1712, has the largest area (40,321 acres) of any town in the State. Here dairying and small industries appear to have struck an almost ideal economic balance. First settled by John Noble and his eight-year-old daughter, of Westfield, Massachusetts, who tramped through the wilderness in search of productive farmlands, the district slowly developed from a frontier town to a busy rural community, centering about a well-kept village Green where the town band still gives concerts on summer evenings. A pure white papier-mâché horse stands on a pedestal beside the harness store. A pottery display of many colors graces the hardware store, and Main Street is alive with farmers' cars and trucks on shopping days.

Roger Sherman, signer of the Declaration of Independence, came here from Newton, Massachusetts, at the age of 22 (1743), and opened a cobbler's shop at the corner of Main and Church Sts., where the Town Hall now stands. Sherman later became a surveyor and, after studying law, was elected to the Assembly.

Facing the Green is the white *Congregational Church* (1833) of the Greek Revival period, with a Doric portico. The *William Taylor House* (about 1820), of the same architectural type, is at the northeast corner of Main and Elm Sts., north of the Green. On the west side of the Green is the

Elijah Boardman House (1793), a hip-roofed dwelling designed by Jacob Stott, an officer of Burgoyne's army.

North of New Milford on State 25 at 7.8 *m.* is the junction with State 45.

> Left on State 45 is NEW PRESTON (alt. 600, Town of Washington), 0.1 *m.*, where the Aspetuck River turned early mills. Eli Weeks and Daniel Burnham here manufactured horse-rakes, wagons, and sleighs that were shipped to Chicago in 1850. Opposite the post office is (R) a small house (about 1785) with an original Dutch roof and a piazza under the overhang.
>
> North from New Preston Village on State 45 is *Lake Waramaug* (L), 0.6 *m.*, one of the most beautiful natural bodies of water in the State. Bordered by many summer residences, hotels of the better type, a private country club, and, at the head of the lake on the west shore, a State Park of 75 acres offering camping, bathing, fishing, and picnic facilities, this pure lake is a favorite vacation spot for New York and Connecticut people. A drive, crooked and rough in places, encircles the lake, a distance of 7.6 *m.*
>
> From the foot of the lake, State 45 continues to WARREN, at 5.6 *m.*, and to a connection with US 7 (*see Side Trip off Tour 4*).

At 8 *m.* is the junction of State 25 with an old macadamized road.

> Right on this road is the *Major William Cogswell Tavern* (1760–62), 0.2 *m.*, with a handsome pedimented doorway ornamented with carved rosettes and fluted pilasters.

State 25 passes quiet upland farms to the junction with State 47, at 8.9 *m.* (*see Tour 2A*).

At WOODVILLE, 11.3 *m.*, the Shepaug Tunnel enters the eastern hills to burrow across country under *Bantam Lake*, carrying pure mountain water into the East Branch Reservoir at East Morris for municipal use in Waterbury.

Ascending the hills toward Mt. Tom, especially good vantage-points are at 11.4 *m.*, where the highway crosses the West Branch of the Shepaug River, and at 11.8 *m.*, where, through a 'gunsight notch,' the hills rise higher and higher, merging in the distant blue haze.

Mt. Tom State Park (R), 12 *m.*, and *Mt. Tom Pond* (R), 12.1 *m.*, offer bathing and picnic areas.

BANTAM (Town of Litchfield), 15.2 *m.*, is a small manufacturing borough and trading center for the summer colony at Bantam Lake and industrial center of Litchfield township.

> Right from Bantam on State 109 is *Bantam Lake*, 1 *m.*, where a large summer cottage colony surrounds the shores of the lake which covers 1200 acres. Excellent bass fishing is enjoyed here in season.

LITCHFIELD (*see LITCHFIELD*), 18.6 *m.*

At Litchfield is the junction with State 61 (*see Tour 2B*).

Northeast of Litchfield, State 25 traverses submarginal agricultural land, following the old Indian trail which later became the first turnpike between Litchfield and Torrington.

At 23.2 *m.*, high on the hill (L), stands the *Charlotte Hungerford Hospital*.

At TORRINGTON, 24.2 *m.* (*see Tours 5 and 5A*), are the junctions with State 8 (*see Tour 5*) and State 4 (*see Tour 5A and Side Trip off 4D*).

TOUR 4 D : *From* JUNCTION WITH US 7 (*Cornwall Bridge*) *to* SOUTH CANAAN, 15.2 *m.*, State 4 and 43.

Via Cornwall.

No accommodations.

Macadamized and gravel highways.

THIS tour traverses a thoroughly wild and primitive area. Hills, rushing mountain brooks, giant pines and hemlocks, quiet wooded valleys, and little sleepy communities are features of this route.

The natives are shy and reticent, but the summer folk and week-enders add considerable life and gaiety to the region until the winter snows blanket the countryside.

Trout brooks are leased by sports clubs and patrolled by trusted local woodsmen with bright brass badges. Winter sports enjoy limited popularity but are growing in importance. Artists sketch beside the road or in roadside and streamside studios, and hiking parties or bicyclists from one of the 'cycle' trains that the railroad is now popularizing traverse these shady byways. From almost any hill crest a view of the surrounding terrain rewards the traveler. Mountain laurel, the rare 'whippoorwill-shoe' or moccasin flower, trailing arbutus, and a variety of ferns furnish coverage for the forest floor in this section.

Straight ahead on State 4 from the junction with US 7, at Cornwall Bridge, this route passes the footpath entrance (R) to Dark Entry.

> Right from State 4 is the blue-marked *Dark Entry Trail*, a route taken by hikers to the dead end and mystery of *Dark Entry*, 2 *m.*, or *Owlsbury*, a rough hillside cloaked with hemlock, pine, and laurel. No road, other than a pack-horse trail, ever penetrated this forbidding region. In 1854 there were four houses hidden among the dense thickets, but in 1871 there were none. Today the woodland shelters a variety of game and great horned owls whose prevalence gave the area its first name. Tradition tells of one man who, with his wife, built a cabin in this wilderness. After an absence of two days, in which he had tramped to a village for supplies, he returned to find his wife a raving maniac, driven mad by some terrifying experience which she was never able to relate. Somewhere in the woods are lonely graves and stories are told of occasional woodsmen who have gone 'bushed' and died of starvation or from an accident, far from the reach of aid. Hikers hurry to reach civilization before the night closes in on Dark Entry and the shrill owl's hoot shatters the gloom.

State 4 follows the valley of Furnace Brook to CORNWALL (alt. 110, town pop. 878), 3.3 *m.*, a village on a quiet elm-shaded main street.

Facing the Green, is the *Congregational Church* (1841), a simple, but effective example of the fully developed Greek Revival. Beside it is the *Rumsey School* for young boys, on the *Site of the Foreign Mission School* that was founded in 1817 following Edwin W. Dwight's discovery of 'a dusky skinned youth weeping on the steps of Yale College,' because he could not obtain an education there. Here many Hawaiians and Indians were educated as missionaries to their people, until the marriage of two Indian youths to maidens of the town in 1826 aroused such apprehension among the residents that the school was closed. Henry Obookiah, a former pagan priest of the Sandwich Islands who was converted and attended this school, died while a student and is buried in the local cemetery.

Here in Cornwall lived Matthew Lyon, soldier, editor, author, lumberman, miller, inventor, manufacturer, and Congressman, a stormy petrel of Revolutionary and early Federal days, of whom innumerable anecdotes have been told. Lyon, born near Dublin, came to this country at the age of nineteen in 1765 with one guinea in his pocket. The captain of the ship, to whom he entrusted the money, kept the guinea and sold Matt as a redemptioner to Jabez Bacon of Woodbury. A year later he was again sold in exchange for a pair of 'stags,' to Hugh Hanna of Litchfield. After buying his freedom, Lyon moved to Cornwall, subsequently fought with Ethan Allen at Ticonderoga and was a ringleader in numerous military exploits. Lyon edited a paper in Vermont, paid a $1000 fine, served four months in jail, furnishing the outstanding civil liberties case under Adam's Alien and Sedition Laws, went to Congress from Vermont and Kentucky, and contested for an election in Arkansas. Cashiered from the army and later lionized as a hero, sentenced to jail and elected to Congress while still behind the bars, this energetic opportunist furnished gossip for New England firesides during many a long winter evening.

Possibly no Connecticut town has more interesting place names than Cornwall. There are Agag, Ballyhack, Puffingham, Mast Swamp, Wildcat, Hogback, Great Hollow, Crooked Esses, and Indian Lane. All were once populated but are now deserted except for the white-tailed deer. Many settlers died during the hard winters of Cornwall's settlement (1738–40) when cattle were often kept alive only by giving them venison broth, and when children froze in their beds. This was not a kindly country, and people did not covet the lands given to Yale College in the College Street area. Only the very poor or the very brave settled here.

Bearing left at the south end of Cornwall Main St., on a dirt road, 0.5 *m.*, to the *Cathedral Pines*, a virgin stand of white pine regarded as 'the finest in the eastern States and not surpassed in the lake region' (U.S. Geological Survey). Here in the twilight hush of a primeval forest, where deep layers of pine needles cushion the tread of footsteps, the silence is unbroken, save for the lilting songs of birds. At times rare shafts of sunlight, slanting through rifts in the dense canopy overhead, suddenly strike the scarlet plumage of a red-headed woodpecker, whose energetic tap-tap echoes through the serried ranks of towering trees.

At 4.4 *m.* is a junction with State 43, on which this route continues, and State 128.

1. Left on State 128 at 0.7 *m.* is a beautiful view of distant hills stretching away on a three-quarter horizon on the left of the road.

At 0.8 *m.* CORNWALL CENTER slumbers beside the highway with more wide views, a town signpost, and little else.

Here is a junction with a dirt road (R), leading in 1.6 *m.* to NORTH CORNWALL (alt. 1140), where several old houses stand opposite the white *Congregational Church* (1826) (L). The projecting entrance pediment of the church is supported by four fluted Ionic pilasters, interspaced with the usual trio of round-topped doors. The octagonal steeple is cramped but not unpleasing. The interior, with barrel vaulting and a new Palladian window over the pulpit end, was restored in 1926.

At 2.1 *m.* is a crossroads. Left on this dirt road at 2.9 *m.* is the entrance to *Cream Hill Pond and Clubhouse*, a mountain resort patronized only by the summer folk in the vicinity.

At 3. *m.* is a sharp turn left with views of near-by hills.

Straight ahead here on a dirt road to the *Yelping Hill Reservation*, 1.5 *m.*, a summer colony.

At 3.7 *m.* is a sharp turn right on still another dirt road. At 4.1 *m.* on a high hill overlooking the valley and distant mountains, stands the old *Gold Homestead* (1770, remodeled in 1842). Here in 1845 was founded the famous *Cream Hill Agricultural School*, one of the earliest of such institutions in the country. From the porch of the great, rambling old structure, Cobble Mountain and Sharon Hill rise to the west, and the quiet waters of Cream Hill Pond reflect the fleecy white clouds which seem always to hang over Connecticut hills.

At 4.3 *m.* stands the oldest house in Cornwall, the *James Douglas House*, dating from 1750, a very large two-chimneyed, central-hall type dwelling, which, unfortunately, is no longer in good repair.

2. Eastward, State 4 climbs *Bunker Hill* to the entrance to *Mohawk Mountain State Park* (R), 1.2 *m.*, where a lookout tower (alt. 1680) affords magnificent western views. *Tyler Pond* (L), at 2.8 *m.*, covers about one square mile and offers good fishing in season. Passing a pine grove on both sides of the highway at 4 *m.*, and a tamarack swamp (R), at 4.4 *m.*, this route proceeds to the junction with State 61 at 5.3 *m.* at GOSHEN (alt. 1360, town pop. 683). Homesteads here, sold at auction in New Haven in 1737, were settled two years later, and the area soon became an important dairying community. Captain John Norton of Goshen went to Vermont when it was still a wilderness, staked off a farm, and built a distillery, and in 1798 was the first to make the Vermont pottery that is highly prized today, both in the redware and the salt glaze. The manufacture of pottery was carried on by the Norton family until 1894. A patent for pineapple cheese was secured by Lewis M. Norton in 1810 and Yankee pioneers from this hill town introduced cheese-making as far away as Wisconsin. Land, granted to Yale College at the time of the town's settlement, is leased for 999 years.

East of Goshen, on State 4, stands a central, stone-chimneyed house, a light gray salt-box (L), 5.6 *m.*, built in 1760. At 6.7 *m.* stands one of the most notable brick houses in the state, the *Birdseye Norton House* (1804–10), a red Georgian structure with marble window caps, slender porch columns and four chimneys. The beauty of the house is in the fine detail, as the front open pediment porch, and the Palladian windows over the doors and in the south gable. The flat-pitched pediment of the doorway is supported by a decorated frieze with delicate cornice, and by two fluted Ionic columns with reeds in the lower part of the flutes. The same influence is seen inside in several of the exquisitely hand-carved mantels.

At this point, 6.7 *m.*, is the intersection with Pother Rd.; left on Pother Rd., 0.8 *m.*, to the intersection with John Brown Rd.; right on John Brown Rd., at 1.1 *m.*, to the *Site of the Birthplace of John Brown* (1800–59), abolitionist, whose dramatic raid on the U.S. Arsenal at Harper's Ferry, October 16, 1859, and subsequent execution were among the stirring events of pre-Civil War days. The house, which was purchased by the John Brown Association in 1901, burned to the ground several years ago and today only the cellar hole and the well remain.

At 8 *m.*, on State 4, near the junction with Lovers' Lane, a bank overgrown with blue gentians is the *Site of an Old Indian Stockade* erected by local Indians as protection against raiding Mohawks.

At 10.1 *m.* is TORRINGTON (*see Tour* 5) at the junction with State 8 (*see Tours 5 and 5A*).

State 43 leads from the junction with State 4 and State 128 to the little hamlet of CORNWALL HOLLOW, 8.2 *m.*, which centers about an imposing memorial to a distinguished native son, Major-General John Sedgwick, Commander of the Sixth Corps, Army of the Potomac, a veteran of many campaigns in the Seminole, Mexican, and Civil Wars, who was killed at Spotsylvania, May 9, 1864.

North of Cornwall Hollow, on an excellent asphalt-surfaced macadam highway, this route proceeds through a wilderness area where most of the farms have been bought by a country club of wealthy sportsmen, now known as the *Hollenbeck Country Club.* The Hollenbeck River is probably the best trout water in Connecticut and many wardens are on patrol through this area the year round.

Tumbledown houses, sagging fence rows, barns that lean to the southward away from winter winds, are features of this preserve in which nature is reclaiming her own.

Beside the road, gleaming in the edge of a cut where the highway engineers have lowered the older road level, are glistening piles of dark green slag from the old iron furnaces that formerly lined the Hollenbeck River, working on Salisbury iron ore and fired with Cornwall charcoal.

At 13.8 *m.* is the junction with State 126 and an oiled road.

Left on the oiled road to *Music Mountain,* 2.2 *m.* On the hillside, at the end of the oiled road, the *Jacques Gordon Musical Foundation,* founded by the former conductor of the Chicago Symphony Orchestra, conducts summer concerts and provides instruction for worthy young musicians. Along the road are scores of apple trees, believed to have been planted by the peripatetic Johnny Appleseed (*see CLINTON, Tour* 1) who journeyed westward from Massachusetts by way of Connecticut, planting apple trees as he went. The Foundation property includes a concert hall, four modern colonial houses and one old colonial house.

State 43 leads in 15.2 *m.* to SOUTH CANAAN and a junction with *US* 7 (*see Tour* 4).

TOUR 5 : *From* STRATFORD *to* MASSACHUSETTS LINE (*New Boston*), 65.3 *m.*, State 8.

Via Shelton, Derby, Ansonia, Seymour, Beacon Falls, Naugatuck, Waterbury, Thomaston, Harwinton, Torrington, Winsted.
Alternate stretches of asphalt and concrete.
Usual accommodations.
N.Y., N.H. & H. R.R. parallels route.

STATE 8, one of the most heavily traveled arteries in the State, connects the Sound and the Berkshires following the Housatonic Valley and the Naugatuck Valley northward, through the region where the power of many rushing streams turned the mill wheels of early Connecticut industries. Today more than thirty per cent of the country's brass products are manufactured in this area.

The route offers many varying contrasts: compact little industrial towns along the river banks; the sheer rock walls of the river gorge rising blunt and forbidding from the highway's edge; and rolling hills and laurel-clad slopes, where the roadsides are a mass of pink and white bloom in season. The lower stretches of the river are lined with chemical, brass, and rubber factories. Further north, the smoky, acrid odors of industry give way to the piney aroma of the greenwoods, sweetened by the fragrance of laurel and azalea.

State 8 turns north from US 1 (*see Tour* 1) at Stratford and passes through Butternut Hollow, where there are no longer any butternut trees, to cross Farmill River, at 4.4 *m.* The name suggests a mill back in the woodland somewhere (L), one of those little mills on the downstream lip of an overflow from a quiet millpond. The cardinal flower blooms alongshore, and cat-tails whisper when the breeze stirs ripples on the placid surface. The kingfisher knows of this pond and may, as some woodsmen believe, bring in his own minnows to drop them into the little pond where transplanting improves the minnow race. Countrymen bring logs to this mill and the millman saws them to order. The slab pile grows near-by and a yellow cone of clean sawdust has been fashioned especially for filling for rag dolls that little country girls find in their stockings at Christmas.

Across the Housatonic (R), at 7.8 *m.*, are old docks and the new tanks of an oil company that receives its commodities direct from the tide-water. Where West Indian schooners once spread sails, an oil barge now slowly bucks the river current, assisted by a tugboat seemingly too small for the job. Oaken staves, knocked-down furniture, farm produce from the fertile upper valley, and fish from the cove in far Still River to the north, were once shipped out by this waterway.

SHELTON (alt. 120, town pop. 10,113), 8.8 *m.*, was settled, in 1697, by pioneers from Stratford, who first tilled the soil at Huntington Landing on the west bank of the Housatonic, almost opposite Derby Landing. In 1717 a separate parish called Ripton was established. Ripton was renamed Huntington and incorporated in 1789. Finally receiving a city charter in 1915, Shelton was named for Edward N. Shelton, an early industrialist. The building of the great dam on the Housatonic River in 1870 furnished power to Shelton factories; the numerous wire, hardware, and metal-working mills expanded, and textile mills were established. Tacks became an important product when, in 1849, they were actually worth their weight in gold. A pound of gold sold for $192 and was an even exchange for tacks on the Pacific Coast. The Shelton Tack Company has been in continuous operation since 1836. Today the largest factories are producers of high-grade silk dress goods, velvet and automobile plush, and the Star Pin Company manufacture pins, hair pins, hooks and eyes.

> Left from Shelton on State 108 to HUNTINGTON GREEN, 3 m., site of the early settlement of the town. The *Episcopal Church of St. Paul* (1812), on the Green, retains the double tier of windows and simple façade of the 18th century, with a doorway and Ionic octagonal belfry in the classic style that was new when it was built.
>
> On the west side of the Green is the large double-chimneyed *Neil De Forest House*, built in 1775 and somewhat remodeled; east of the Green is the *Benjamin De Forest Salt-Box* of 1772, with next door to it the country store built by De Forest in the previous year. The *Linsley House*, another type of the salt-box prevalent in the 18th century, stands north of the Green.

Passing the great plant of *Shelton Looms*, and turning right at rotary traffic, 9.3 m., in the center of Shelton, the route enters the industrial beehive that clutters the valley where the Naugatuck joins the Housatonic.

Right across a bridge over the Housatonic. At the east end of the bridge is the junction with State 34.

> Left on State 34 is a large *Electrical Generating Plant* (L), on the canal spanned by a narrow, dangerous bridge (R).
>
> The highway straightens and widens at this point and the sound of rushing waters over the dam of masonry is a reminder that the Housatonic River is a powerful, well-harnessed stream.
>
> The *Dam* at 0.7 m. (L), caused the most controversy of any hydro-engineering work in the State when it was first erected. This dam, planned by the *Ousatonic Water Company*, was finally completed in 1877 after prolonged and bitter controversies in which all the interests upstream, fearing for their livelihood, banded together to fight the power company. Shad fishermen from the Cove Fishing Company of New Milford claimed that this dam would, as it did, ruin their fisheries, and protested to the General Assembly at Hartford. The power interests finally sent to Maine for an expert to come to the General Assembly to set up and operate a working model of a fishwheel that they contended would allow the shad to reach the spawning grounds upstream despite the dam. Inland legislators were convinced, against their will, and the franchise was eventually granted, but the Cove Fishing Company disbanded, its employees deprived of their subsistence by the dam that furnished power for the factories of Derby and Shelton.
>
> At 0.9 m. (L), is the *Bob Cooke Boat House*, headquarters for the Yale crews for their early spring and autumn practice. The quiet waters of the river offer an ideal rowing course from this point for two miles upstream. The trim shells and their perspiring crews, followed by bawling coaches in motor launches, are almost daily sights along this stretch of the Housatonic. Derby Day, a series of races held late in May, prior to the Yale crews' transfer to Gales Ferry in preparation for the Yale-Harvard races, is the only contest of the season on the Housatonic.
>
> The route becomes increasingly interesting from this point northward; with alternating views of the rippling river, rapids, and quiet pools the stream winds between shaded banks where bass, brown trout, and lesser fish await the lure. The blue heron knows this country well; foraging gulls fly in from the sea but find this blue stream too pure for their scavenging. Cottagers have built their humble dwellings on the western bank and small groups of these structures are seen beneath the trees on the eastern shore, but the country has not yet been exploited by the realty salesfolk and enough large landholders retain their riverside acres to discourage the so-called 'development.'

The hills pinch in from either side of the river, forming notches through which still more distant hills show a backdrop. The Pootatuck Indians hunted and fished here. Settlers from along the shores of Long Island Sound poled their boats upstream in search of greener pastures, and even today the country upstream invites further exploration.

At 6.1 *m. Stevenson Dam* interrupts the flow of the river and forms the eight-mile stretch of deep water known as Lake Zoar. The lake has been named for the old Zoar Bridge, the red structure formerly used following the historic 'bridge battles' of the valley. Here, many bridges were built for the toll revenue; often three of them tried to do business at the same time. Shotgun guards patrolled the bridges and men held their franchises here by right of might rather than legal claim. One bridge was actually moved several times, but the river itself periodically eliminated the trouble by washing all bridges away.

Beneath the dam a *Power House* nestles close to the masonry, and great cables leading from the generators to the towers above take the current over the hills to the industrial areas beyond.

The highway crosses the top of the dam on a wide spread of concrete. Below the dam the river is swift, but the lake above is as placid as a millpond and much more beautiful. Shores are abrupt, sloping down from the surrounding hill country. No cottage developments are seen here, only the rolling hills and the few power company houses for personnel.

Crossing Stevenson Dam, the route leaves the river and proceeds through the narrow valley crossed by *Boy's Halfway River*, a tiny stream, really much less than 'halfway' a river, and rolls up hill and down dale through a sleepy hamlet known as STEVENSON. Here, a country post office was ordered moved from the feedstore to a country home. Townspeople protested so effectively that the feedstore retained the postal facility and quiet again descended on the shores of Boy's Halfway River.

The route curves and winds like a blacksnake past stately farmhouses with signs offering 'Home Baking to Take Home,' or 'Cocker Spaniels for Sale.' Red barns and silos crowd close to the houses and the pastures are usually very stony and well watered.

At 13.6 SANDY HOOK crowds close to the Pootatuck River with the commercial influence notable in 'Auction Barn' and 'Hooked Rug' signs swinging from roadside trees on the lawns of well-built houses of the Gay Nineties, sometimes heavy with jigsawed and lathe-turned ornamentation.

At Sandy Hook is the junction with US 6 and US 202 (*see Tour* 2).

DERBY (alt. 60, town pop. 10,788), 9.5 *m.*, at the junction of the Naugatuck and Housatonic Rivers, is another manufacturing town, producing, chiefly, sponge rubber and metal specialties.

In 1642, Captain John Wakeman of New Haven, established a trading post at the junction of the rivers. The region, then known as Paugasset, was purchased from the Paugasuck Indians. Wakeman was soon joined by a group of colonists from Milford, and, in 1675, the colony was made a separate township, named for Derby in England. Shipbuilding, started about 1657–60, was an important industry until 1868, when river obstructions, dams, and bridges, and the highway and railroads built through the town made water trade unprofitable. Derby sloops carried on a thriving trade with the West Indies during the 18th century, exporting fish and livestock and importing French, Dutch, and Spanish products, as well as large numbers of slaves. In 1800, the annual Negro 'election' and celebration, formerly held in Hartford, was moved to

Derby. Negroes gathered from all parts of the State to elect a 'governor,' parade, feast and dance. Mounted on the horses of their masters in the inaugural parade, they boisterously sang the improvised songs for which they were famous, and marched to the accompaniment of fiddles, fifes and drums. The 'governor,' who usually claimed direct descent from an African king, was the local authority among his people, imposing fines, punishing flagrant misconduct, and settling disputes.

A turnpike to New Haven, built in 1798 in the hope of increasing local shipping, and another to Newtown built a few years later, proved disadvantageous to Derby by deflecting commerce to seaports on Long Island Sound. In 1806, the Derby Fishing Company was organized and enjoyed an extensive trade with the northern Mediterranean. In 1836, Anson G. Phelps and Sheldon Smith set up a copper mill on the west bank of the Naugatuck and named that area Birmingham for the English industrial city. John I. Howe, inventor of the first pin-making machine (1832), moved his plant to Birmingham in 1838. The Howe enterprise successfully undersold the English product and continued operating until 1908, when it was sold to Plume and Atwood, another Connecticut concern. The great dam above Derby on the Housatonic River brought new power to the mills, but finally put an end to fishing and shipping.

Derby is the birthplace of two noted war heroes. General William Hull served with distinction during the Revolutionary War, but in the War of 1812, as Governor of Michigan territory, surrendered the fort at Detroit, sacrificing his reputation rather than expose the white residents to the ravages of the Indians who reinforced the British army. He was tried, found guilty, and sentenced to be shot, but was finally pardoned by President Madison for prior distinguished service. Commodore Isaac Hull, the General's nephew, was in command of the frigate 'Constitution' in its victorious battle with the 'Guerrière' off the coast of Nova Scotia on August 19, 1812.

Overlooking the city on Windy Hill, the *Ansonia High School* (1937), Howard Ave., by William Lescaze, is the only example in the state of the experimental style of architecture developed in Germany. It goes even beyond the 'modernistic' in the rigid suppression of ornament, relying wholly upon a relation of plain block surfaces for external effect. From a practical point of view there is much of interest in the school. Light and ventilation are provided for, as in modern factories, by turning whole walls into sheets of glass which can be opened in sections, at different angles. The auditorium, which seats 1108, is a fully equipped theater, in a segmental or 'pie-plate' design, its domed ceiling divided into thirds, the front and the rear of acoustic plaster. Radio is connected with each of the twenty-three classrooms.

At 11.8 *m.* is the junction with a macadamized road.

Right on this road, crossing a bridge over the Naugatuck, at 0.8 *m.*, and right onto the Main St. of ANSONIA (alt. 120, city pop. 19,898), at 1 *m.*

Although sparsely settled as a part of Derby in 1651, Ansonia did not become a separate community until 1845, when Anson G. Phelps, thwarted in his attempt to gain control of acreage for his copper and brass mills in Birmingham (Derby), bought land to the east and set up his industrial empire. Phelps' genius for organization and promotion brought funds to the new community and new industries grew. The borough was organized in 1864; additional land was granted the community in 1871; in 1889 Ansonia became a township, and in 1893 a city. The Farrel-Birmingham Company, Inc., is the largest specialty roll shop in America; Cuban sugar mills order their great cane rolls here.

At 1.8 *m.* is the junction with Elm St.

Left on Elm St. 0.2 *m.*, to the yellow *Humphreys House* (1698; rebuilt in 1733), the birthplace, in 1752, of General David Humphreys, who, before entering the woolen industry, was aide-de-camp to Washington, and later a Minister to Portugal and Spain. As a young man he was a member of the 'Hartford Wits' and contributed to the satiric political papers *The Anarchiad.* In 1800, the house was enlarged by the addition of the one-story structure that had formerly been the first Episcopal Church of Derby, moved from across the street where it was erected in 1740.

The old *Episcopal Burying Ground* (1737), opposite, contains a monument to the Deerfield Indians.

Elm St. curves and becomes Jewett St. At 0.5 *m.* (R) is the weathered saltbox *Richard Mansfield House* (*open, custodian in charge;* 10¢), 35 Jewett St., built in 1748 for the Rev. Mr. Mansfield, first Episcopal minister in the town, who served his parish for 72 years.

At 2 *m.* is the junction with Academy Hill Road.

Left on Academy Hill Road 0.4 *m.*, to a red salt-box (R) long known as the *Brownie Castle,* perched on the brow of the hill overlooking the city of Derby and the river valley. It is a well-preserved early house commonly dated 1686, but probably, from its rafters, which run straight through from the ridge to the first floor, it was built a quarter-century later.

At 13.9 *m.* the dead backwaters of a reservoir built by Anson G. Phelps stretch away to the right. This early promoter brought in the first Irish labor to this area to construct the dam that was to furnish power for his brass mills in the city later named for him.

A sharp turn (R) over an iron bridge, at 15.1 *m.*, passes the falls of the Naugatuck (L), where old plush mills and a copper factory still operate by water-power. On the right, the *Seymour Town Library* (1916) of Connecticut brick and Vermont marble, designed by Murphy and Dana, shares a corner location near the Seymour High School with the Congregational Church (1846).

Crossing a cement bridge at this point, State 8 by-passes Seymour.

SEYMOUR (alt. 160, town pop. 6890), 15.2 *m.*, a manufacturing town, producing hard rubber specialties, telegraph cables, stamped brass goods, German silver, brass and copper wire, and mohair plush and yarns, was settled in 1680 by colonists from Derby. Organized as a town in 1850, the community was named in honor of Thomas H. Seymour, then Governor of the State.

The settlement was originally known as Chusetown for the last sachem of the Derby Indians, who, wishing to live near the white men, built his wigwam at the falls, a few rods north of the present building of the Chaminade Velours Inc. Other Indians settled beside him and their wigwams stretched out in a row beneath a grove of great white oaks.

Chuse attempted to teach the white men to follow the Indian custom of traveling down to Long Island Sound each year to 'salt.' He and his family sailed down the river, camped on the beach at Milford for about two weeks, eating clams and oysters and drying a supply of clams to be bartered in the winter for venison from the northern Indians.

After 1802, when Colonel David Humphreys imported a flock of merino sheep and established here the first large woolen mill to be successfully operated in the United States (1806), the settlement was known as Humphreyville. Colonel Humphreys was active in securing labor legislation to provide for factory inspection and was one of the first industrialists to become vitally interested in the education of his workmen and improvement of their living conditions. One of the innovations was the establishment of a village for orphan boys whom he brought from asylums in New York and other cities to work in his factory. Competent teachers were hired to instruct them at evening and Sunday school. Organizing them as a military company, he furnished them with uniforms and drilled them himself in the manual of arms. Many of Humphreys' boys later became prominent men in the affairs of this and other States.

The mills of Seymour soon assumed importance in the manufacture of paper, mohair, tools, and brass goods. The development of the electrical business in America brought prosperity to the little riverside community.

Cable and wire mills handled contracts from all over the world and Seymour cable now is known in Cape Town and Havana. The first auger ever sold in the New York market was made in this town by Walter French who came from Mansfield in 1810, and commenced manufacturing screw augers by hand. The first mohair plush made in the U.S.A. was produced in Seymour in 1880 by John H. Tingue.

State 8 twists like a blacksnake around hillsides to a junction with State 67, at 15.3 m. (see Side Trip off Tour 2, sec. a).

At this point was (L) a large reservoir, but the river, cutting through glacial sands, has filled the basin. Beside the road, where the trolley tracks cross at an angle, an enterprising local contractor has established a business in washed sand. As a result, the road here is hazardous for unwary or careless motorists.

Traversing a narrow river plain, the highway is flanked (R) by the massive rocky ridge known as Rock Rimmon, 16.5 m. Here, at the top of the crag grew a lofty hemlock, for which, tradition says, the Indians named the district Nau-ko-tunk ('one large tree').

State 8 turns sharp right at Pines Bridge, 17.7 m., at an underpass and rounds more curves where, after a storm, the slippery pavement is a serious hazard.

Behind a house on the hillside, some 400 yards from the highway (R), at 18.4 m., a large Indian mortar stands in a hillside field, and traces of arrow-makers have been found in various chipping grounds in the area.

BEACON FALLS (alt. 200, town pop. 1693), 19.3 *m.*, was settled about 1678 by colonists from Derby. The town was cut off from Oxford, Seymour, Bethany, and Naugatuck and incorporated in 1871. Friction matches were first made here in 1834, by Thomas Sanford, who later moved to Woodbridge, became discouraged, and sold his 'recipe' for $10; the Diamond Match Company finally acquired the formula and used it to advantage. Woolen mills made capes here prior to the Civil War; styles changed, and the mills turned to mackintosh production. Finally, a very high-grade brand of rubber footwear ('Top Notch') was produced, and the village became a lively, thriving, industrial community that boasted a company hotel, a company band, a company store and theater. With the purchase of the business and trade name by the U.S. Rubber Company, the machinery was moved to Naugatuck, and Beacon Falls now slumbers, except for the hardware shop that specializes in piano hinges.

At 20.6 *m.* the asphalt twists through a scenic gorge where Sunday schools once held their annual picnics at *High Rock Grove.* Now the highway department has established a picnic area (L) with a table and parking space for those who care to halt before hastening toward clearer, cleaner atmosphere. High above the river, topping a bare rocky hill, stands a forest fire lookout tower. The *Naugatuck State Forest* of 1967 acres has been established in this area, and slow-growing hardwoods are gradually covering the hills, hopefully striving to hide the scars left by greedy wood choppers and sawmills.

In the ravine of *Cotton Hollow Brook*, at 21.2 *m.*, cotton mills once operated. An Indian medicine man, Chief Two Moons, established a reservation in the back country near an old trotting course, and real estate operators hopefully tried to boom the area. Today, this once thriving area boasts only a beer hall and a filling station. The river banks close in at this point, and highway engineers project new grades to eliminate the triple hazard of curves, bridge and underpass.

State 8 leads past a chemical works and a rubber regenerating plant to the junction with State 63 at 22.5 *m.* (*see Tour 1C*).

NAUGATUCK (alt. 200, town pop. 14,315), 22.8 *m.* Settled in 1702, and organized as the Society of Salem Bridge, the town was incorporated in 1844, and Naugatuck was chartered as a borough in 1893. Charles and Henry Goodyear established a rubber mill here in 1843 which is now the main plant of the U.S. Rubber Company's footwear and druggists' sundry divisions, employing many thousands of people and producing the largest quantity of rubber footwear of any mill in the world. Naugatuck products range from gray iron castings to motion picture cameras, from chemicals to chocolate bars.

Around the industrial borough, many steep, rocky hills offer views of the valley, but the general scenic beauty of the area is somewhat marred by smoke and chemical odors emanating from a factory producing acids and perfumes.

State 8 enters UNION CITY (Town of Naugatuck), at 23.9 *m.*, passing the dwellings and business houses of the foreign section of the town. Polish weddings are often held in this area, where gay music crashes out from a rented hall. The *Porter Tavern* (1765) a broad gambrel-roofed cottage where Washington is known to have stopped, is on the north side of Woodbine St., just off North Main.

The highway now proceeds along the east bank of the river through an uninteresting, smoky area.

WATERBURY, 26 *m.* (*see WATERBURY*), center of the brass industry.

> To avoid traffic and by-pass the city turn left at Washington Ave. traffic light; right at the railway underpass onto South Riverside St., straight ahead across Bank St. onto Riverside St.; right and over the bridge on West Main St., and a final sharp left onto Thomaston Ave., a broad, smooth, level piece of straight concrete pavement.

At Waterbury is the junction with State 14 (*see Tour 2 Alt.*) and with State 69 (*see Side Trip off Tour 2, sec. b.*).

At 31 *m.* State 8 passes through WATERVILLE (alt. 300, Town of Waterbury). The former knife and hosiery mills here have long since given way to brass shops.

Left at 31.5 *m.*, is the great brass casting shop of *Chase Metal Works*. The Naugatuck River is shunted away from its original course here, and the buildings stretch along the old river-bed. This is one of the many munitions shops along the valley that sprang up during the World War to make cartridge brass and shell cases. Across State 8, from this mill are the last of the stucco barracks where the foreign-born from all over the world, who flocked here to work at high wages, were housed during the war boom. Some were stranded here when the boom was over, and part of these provide a social and economic problem for the community.

At 31.9 *m.* is a junction with an oiled dirt road.

> Right on this road, passing the *Site of an Old Gate House* at the junction, to a turn sharp right at 1.2 *m.*, onto an unimproved dirt road that leads past an early 19th century brick house to GREYSTONE, 2.1 *m.*, an almost deserted, former manufacturing village.
>
> Hancock Brook flows through this valley and boasts several excellent trout pools where rainbow trout are taken in season. Laurel grows here in great abundance. The hardwood forests, formerly depleted by the demand for 'muffle wood' in the brass industry just over the hills in Waterbury, have made a partial recovery.
>
> A pond and a crumbling mill mark the site of the 1807 clock works where Eli Terry, Seth Thomas and Silas Hoadley started work on 4000 clocks, produced in lots of 500, from native woods. This undertaking took the pioneer industrialists three years, although they produced only the works. The cases were made by a local cabinet-maker. Many authorities credit Terry with the introduction of the system of interchangeable parts. Terry continued to devise new mechanisms and new methods up to the date of his death in 1852. Terry clocks still continue to tick off the minutes throughout New England.
>
> North along the Greystone Road to a junction at 3.3 *m.*
>
>> Left at the junction, a narrow dirt road runs 1.8 *m.* to *Mt. Tobe Airport.* Not on any commercial airline, isolated and small, this field is used only occasionally by some barnstorming flying circus that flits in like the proverbial crow, garners a few dollars from the air-minded and departs.

Long Hollow Picnic Area (L), 32.9 *m.*, on the edge of the *Mattatuck State Forest*, is well named. The forest here grows to the roadside. Within the 2583 acres of woodland is one of the Leatherman's caves, a regular stop on the route of that slightly deranged and exceedingly unsanitary wanderer, whose pilgrimages through Connecticut towns were eagerly anticipated by the small boys of every village. Eyes wide with wonder at the possible adventures of this strange man, they followed at a discreet distance and often hid in the underbrush near his caves, eavesdropping while the distraught man talked incoherently to himself of things that might have been.

Born Jules Bourglay, at Lyons, France, he emigrated to this country after the failure of his father's business, resulting from speculation in leather, prevented his marriage to the beautiful daughter of his father's partner. He became a wanderer through Connecticut and eastern New York, clothed always in a suit that he fashioned of odd pieces of leather, and living on charity, though he was never known to ask for money. On March 24, 1889, he was found dead in a cave on the farm of George Dell at Mount Pleasant (near Ossining), New York.

At 34.6 *m.* is a *Motorcycle Hill Climb* (R) on a hillside behind an inn. Here the highway becomes a twisting, winding, crooked ribbon that yearly takes as victims many careless motorists who drive too fast through this area.

At 37.4 *m.* is the junction with US 6 (*see Tour* 2), which joins this route for 1 mile.

THOMASTON (alt. 378, town pop. 4188), 37.6 *m.*, named for Seth Thomas, was incorporated in 1875. This community, formerly known as Plymouth Hollow, has been a famous clock-making center since 1803, when Eli Terry, inventor of the shelf clock, set up a factory in the township and began the production of clocks by machinery. In 1814, Terry marketed the shelf clock, an invention that revolutionized the industry by reducing the price of clocks from $25 to $5. Terry's clocks were sold in all the States and along the advancing frontiers by the famous Connecticut peddlers, who promoted sales by establishing an early 19th-century system of the installment plan.

Here, in 1812, Seth Thomas, a former partner of Terry's, opened a clock shop which developed into the largest clock factory in the world, expanding so rapidly that the community came to be known as Thomas Town. The business is still carried on under the name of the Seth Thomas Clock Company. Other industries here include the manufacture of brass goods and automatic machine parts.

South of the Green on a well-kept plot landscaped with flowers and shrubs, is the simple story-and-a-half *Marsh House*, dating from 1775. Its front porch, a modern addition, is ornamented with elaborate wood carving and jigsawed brackets.

At 38.4 *m.* is the junction with a dirt road.

Left on this road to *Crow Hill*, 3 *m.*, at the end of a very old Indian trail. A mortar under an oak tree marks the spot where dusky squaws pounded the native maize into meal.

The *Eclipse Glass Company Plant* (L), at 38.4 *m.*, has developed from a backyard industry. Working in a tiny factory during the very lowest days of the depression, the proprietor started bending crystals for clocks and instruments. Soon the business outgrew the cramped quarters, and a small factory was built; in a short time an addition was needed. Later another factory was built, and today the plant is a model of modern industrial efficiency.

At 39.5 *m.* is a junction with a new scenic highway (R) to Harwinton, 8.2 *m.* (*see Tour 5A*). Across the river (R) a full-blooded Indian squaw, about whom local children have woven many strange tales, keeps a simple home, raises goats, and hopefully fishes in the Naugatuck.

FLUTEVILLE (alt. 420, Town of Litchfield), 40.2 *m.*, was named for the applewood flutes produced here by Asa Hopkins as early as 1830. His company later merged with J. Firth and Hall Company of New York, and operated under that name until 1852, making flutes, flageolets, clarinets, fifes, guitars, drumsticks, castanets, and other wood, wind, and bone instruments.

At 41.3 *m.* (L), just upstream, a wooden mill produces various specialties from native lumber.

At 41.7 *m.* a hill farmer raises Black Angus beef cattle on river pastureland.

At 42.6 *m.* in CAMPVILLE (R), is an early 19th-century brick mansion known as *Maple Shade*, with four chimneys on the outside walls, and an air of wealth and comfort. Across the street is a real log cabin.

At 44.4 *m.* State 8 leaves the northern end of the gorge of the Naugatuck. The highway twists and curves around sheer rock walls as it follows the narrow, crooked valley.

Across the flats (L) and over the railway tracks, at 44.9 *m.*, lies the tiny group of houses known as EAST LITCHFIELD. A sharp curve at this point onto a rather narrow bridge should be taken cautiously.

At 45.4 *m.* an *Automobile Graveyard* (R) fills the field beside the road with rusted, twisted relics.

At 46.1 *m.*, across the Naugatuck River, is Torrington's new *Sewage Disposal Plant* (1937), that will eliminate stream pollution and make the lower stretches of the river more attractive. Also across the river is the *Clubhouse* of the now dormant *Torrington Trotting Association*. At the old track, admirers of the *Hambletonian* and *Messenger* once drove many dusty heats on the little 'twice around,' or half-mile. Tall, cool drinks were sipped on the clubhouse veranda by horsemen who graduated from the smaller time to the Roaring Grand Circuit tracks.

TORRINGTON (alt. 571, town pop. 26,040), 46.5 *m.*, an industrial town fringed by the Litchfield Hills, was named, May, 1738, for Torring-

ton in Devonshire, and incorpórated in May, 1740. Originally known as
New Orleans Village, or Mast Swamp because of the pine trees on the hillsides used for shipbuilding, this community early took its place among the
brass towns of the Naugatuck Valley. In 1834 Israel Coe, using the so-
called battery process, was making the first brass kettles in the country,
and as early as 1878 Torrington was shipping cartridge brass to Spain
and Russia. The manufacture of needles, another local product, dates
from the invention of a special swaging machine by O. L. Hopson in
1866. Woolens, lathes, skates, electrical goods, and hardware helped to
place Torrington in the front rank of Connecticut industrial towns.

At Torrington is the junction with State 4 (*see Tour 5A*), State 25 (*see
Tour 4C*) and State 4 (*see Tour Side Trip off 4D*).

At 50.7 *m.* the road passes a group of country filling stations where
frequent gas price 'wars' are an advantage to passing motorists. A
transient basket-maker often parks his old car here to tempt the passer-by
with offerings of split ash or woven willow receptacles, for everything
from sewing silk to potatoes.

State 8 traverses *Swampy Barrens* (R), forming a countryside not unlike
the Quebec bush, with an occasional black spruce or tamarack rising
out of the alders. Black duck nest here, and muskrats build their swamp-
grass tepees beside a pool where yellow water lilies bloom. Chain pickerel
are taken from coffee-colored swamp streams; when the bogs freeze over,
children skate and play hockey on the ice.

BURRVILLE (Town of Torrington), 52.7 *m.*, is a settlement of a few
houses around an old brick tavern (R), and a deserted foundry in which
the windows are missing and the stack rusting.

> Left from Burrville a dirt road enters the *Paugnut State Forest*, a 1450-acre tract,
> named for Chief Paugnut, the last Indian of this region. The forest contains the
> 80-acre *Burr Pond*, stocked with pickerel, improved by the Civilian Conservation
> Corps, a gem of a lake in a woodland setting, with a foot trail circling it. At 0.5 *m.*
> (L) is the *Site of Borden's Condensed Milk Factory* (1857), the first successful com-
> mercial condensed milk plant in the country, operated by Gail Borden. Condensed
> milk from this modest plant was used by the Union Army during the Civil War.
> Although the building no longer remains, and the forest has grown over the old
> Borden meadows and upland pastures, a sign marks the site of the plant.

At 53.5 *m.* an old *Waterwheel* (R) still turns in a moss-grown wheelpit,
although the mill has long since rotted away.

At 53.8 *m.* is the junction with an oiled dirt road.

> 1. Left on this road to *Highland Lake*, 1.2 *m.*, a summer resort.
>
> 2. Right on this road to *West Hill Pond*, 2.1 *m.*, on the shores of which are many
> Y.M.C.A. and Boy Scout camps.

Passing in a straight course through an area dotted with glacial eskers,
curving right over a narrow railroad overpass, and then left at the end
of a bridge, the highway approaches, at 56.3 *m.*, a *Mill* (R), surrounded
by acres of native pine and hemlock piles, which converts the lumber into
box shooks.

At 56.7 *m.* is WINSTED (*see Tour* 3) at the junction with US 44 (*see Tour* 3).

At 58.1 *m.* a *Grist Mill* (R) continues to operate on Still River, a stream that flows northward, in variance from the usual direction.

At 58.5 *m.* is the junction with State 20 (*see Tour 5B*).

Between 59 *m.* and 60 *m.* the laurel is especially sturdy, and many sugar maples have been spared to furnish a small income from the syrup and sugar. Corncribs have higher legs in this section than farther south because winter snows are deeper. Woodpiles are huge heaps of well seasoned, split timber. Houses follow the northern pattern of tailing off into a series of assorted sheds that connect with the barns, often with seven or eight different roof heights.

The highway swings (R) around the hill, and, at 62.6 *m.*, leaves the river, entering an area where a 'peckerwood' (transient) sawmill has worked in native softwoods and left the usual 'slash.'

At 63.6 *m.* State 8 turns left, crosses the river on a cement bridge and passes *Ski Hill*, where the better jumpers gather in season to compete for the honor of representing their clubs at the competitive meets farther north.

At 64.4 *m.* stands a two-story, wooden *District School* (E) with square cupola and a large, stubby flagpole, overlooking a wide view of the river and valley.

At 64.5 *m.* is a well-filled graveyard, and (L) a white wooden *Methodist Episcopal Church* (1833) is embellished with four fluted columns, and has a two-story shuttered tower. Crossing the river at this point is a cable-suspension foot-bridge, used by residents of the west bank to reach the church.

At 64.8 *m.* is the *Colebrook River Inn* (R). Next door is an old, deserted store with counter and scales in place, as if the proprietor had just stepped out. A former stage tavern stands on the corner (L), where a sign points the way to a barn dance-hall just beyond an iron bridge that crosses the river.

Four miles south of New Boston, Mass., State 8 crosses the Massachusetts Line, 65.3 *m.*, on the main street of COLEBROOK RIVER (alt. 660, Colebrook Town pop. 584), a village on the east bank of the West Branch of the Farmington River. Small industry once thrived here, but closed down many years ago. Oldsters sit beside the road on the porch of an abandoned store; a youngster fishes for trout in the clean, fast stream; and a sawmill snarls through a log of knotty native ash.

Via Harwinton, Burlington.

Macadamized highway.

No accommodations.

CLIMBING to the Harwinton hills this route passes over skyline ridges into the Farmington River Valley. The terrain traversed is of varied character, but is practically all wild woodland or upland pastures. Industry clings only to the valleys, agriculture is unprofitable, and summer residents have not yet found this area.

East from Torrington State 4 leads to a junction with State 117, an asphalt highway, at 0.7 *m.* Right on State 117, this route climbs grades to a picnic area beside *Lead Mine Brook*, at 3.1 *m.*

At 4.5 *m.* is the junction with State 116. The early settlement of Harwinton was located at these crossroads. At the southwest corner at the junction is the imposing *Catlin House* (1799), with an extra large Palladian window.

At the junction this route turns left on State 116.

HARWINTON (alt. 860, town pop. 949), 5.1 *m.*, a rustic community is the birthplace of Collis P. Huntington (1821–1900), financier of the Southern Pacific Railroad, who started his financial career as a Yankee peddler. Harwinton was settled in 1731 and named, May, 1732, by combining syllables from the names of three other Connecticut towns, Hartford, Windsor, and Farmington.

Daniel Messenger, probably of Farmington, came here in 1730, turned a furrow, planted buckwheat and corn, and decided to stay. Land hunger became a prime force in the settlement of the Connecticut hinterlands, and, by 1737, enough pioneer families had reached Harwinton to warrant its incorporation as a town. The Sons of Liberty were organized, became a scourge to Tories, and furthered the cause of independence in their unofficial way.

A legend of a vast deposit of lead persists in the town's history. Although *Lead Mine Brook*, mentioned in the town records as early as 1732, is the only tangible evidence that lead ever was found here, an old narrator tells the story of one Joseph Merriman, who took lead ore from the bed in solid ingots and melted it into bullets, but failed to locate the lode when he returned for a fresh supply. During the Revolutionary War, three clergymen organized a searching party of several hundred men and boys, but, although they hunted for three days, they were unsuccessful. Later, a Mr. Tyler, strolling through the forest, came upon 'a great lead rock.'

Determined to salvage it, he loaded it upon his shoulders and started homeward. However, he had not gone far 'when the invisible hand of an unknown enemy pounced upon him with such a blow that he fled in terror and relinquished his precious burden.' A great wind moaned in the tree-tops and the sky darkened as if from an approaching storm. When Mr. Tyler recovered from his 'corporal wound,' and gained sufficient courage to return to the woods again in search of the 'great lead stone,' it had vanished. In 1812, a Harwinton resident took samples to Yale University for analysis. In the period from 1812 to 1817 the district was visited by many scientific men who continued the search with no success.

On the hilltop at Harwinton Center stands the *Congregational Church* (L) (1806), with an elongated open belfry in place of the usual steeple. The slightly projecting portico has three doorways of equal height. Above the central door is a Palladian window, which is repeated in three sides of the tower. The main door is six feet wide and fashioned of two boards.

Near-by is the *Memorial Chapel*, the gift of Collis P. Huntington, a Gothic building in marked contrast with the simple colonial structures of the rest of the town.

At 17.1 *m.* is BURLINGTON (alt. 700, town pop. 1082). Formerly 'West Woods' or 'West Britain,' a section of Farmington, Burlington was first settled by nineteen families of the Seventh Day Baptist Church, who came from Westerly, Rhode Island, to seek asylum in the wilderness, and organized a church here, September 18, 1780. Twenty-six years later (1806) the town was organized and named for the third Earl of Burlington.

The *Congregational Church* (1804 and 1832), *Elton Tavern* (about 1800), and many houses reflect the atmosphere of the early Federal period.

Today Burlington contains the southern portion of the Nepaug State Forest, a part of Hartford's municipal water supply, and a trout hatchery conducted by the State Department of Fish and Game.

East of Burlington, at 19.3 *m.*, is a junction with State 4.

North on State 4, at 21.3 *m.*, is COLLINSVILLE (*see Tour 3*).

TOUR 5B: *From* JUNCTION WITH STATE 8 (*north of Winsted*) *to* GRANBY, 17.9 *m.*, State 20.

Via East Hartland.
Macadamized highway.
No accommodations.

STATE 20 branches east from State 8, 2.2 miles north of Winsted (*see Tour* 5), and climbs from the greenwoods section of Winsted to a 1225-foot elevation at East Hartland. The route traverses a heavily wooded, hilly country where Appalachian hardwoods merge with the evergreens of northern forests. Contrasting shades of evergreens soften the hillsides even in the winter months. Laurel, juniper and princess pine furnish dense cover for a large variety of small game and game birds. The streams are boisterous, rowdy mountain brooks stocked with native speckled and rainbow trout. Excepting the highway itself, there has been little change in this countryside or in the mode of living since the village miller led a party of 117 settlers from Hartland to the Western Reserve in 1802.

At 2.3 *m.* is the village of RIVERTON, in the northwest corner of the town of Barkhamsted (*see Tour* 3). The *Gothic Union Church* (Episcopal, 1829) at the center (L), of random, ashlar, gray granite with wood-mullioned pointed windows, has a strange white wooden tower in two stages. Wooden pinnacles on the corners of the belfry and on the shoulders of the building add to the exotic effect. The *Congregational Church* (1843), left on the Robertsville road, is an orthodox specimen of the Greek Revival. The route turns a sharp right to cross the Farmington River just in front of the old *Riverton Inn* (1800), formerly called the Ives Tavern. From the verandas, for many years guests looked across the stream and its wooden dam to the brick factory set up in 1818 by Lambert Hitchcock to produce the chairs that were famous for over 50 years. His first chair factory (1826) is now the ell of the present factory (1834). Sturdy, inexpensive, usually painted black or red with gilt stencil designs of fruit on the spreaders, these rush-seated chairs are now eagerly sought by antique dealers and collectors. Today the mill produces druggists' sundries of rubber. The brick, 18-room double *Alford House* (about 1820), across the Street, with columns of solid wood, was built by Hitchcock and his partner-brother-in-law, Arba Alford. The ell was added in 1823. The little village bore the name of Hitchcockville until 1866.

The highway rises obliquely with occasional curves from the valley of the West Branch of the Farmington River. The character of the countryside here suggests the Allegheny Mountains rather than the Berkshires. State 20 descends a steep grade to a crossroads at 5.8 *m.*

1. Right from State 20 at the crossroads, a dirt road (soon (1937) to be made a State highway) leads to the *Site of the Consider Tiffany House* (R), 1.8 *m.*, the foundations of which still remain. Tiffany was so outspoken in his Tory convictions during the Revolution that he was confined to the limits of his farm, and although the ban was lifted at the close of the war, he refused to be liberated. The *Tiffany Elm*, near-by, the fourth largest in the State (circumference 21 feet, branch spread 100 feet), was planted by him.

2. Left from State 20 at the crossroads, on a macadam road that passes the *Second Congregational Church* (1844), 0.9 *m.* (L), and enters the western division of the *Tunxis State Forest* where a *Fire Tower*, 2.1 *m.*, stands (L). From this tower, at an elevation of 1400 feet are seen extensive forest preserves in Massachusetts and Connecticut; with field-glasses it is possible to count as many as 30 (some persons have claimed as many as 57) church steeples to the north, east, and south.

State 20 descends into *Hartland Hollow*, 10.5 *m.*, a crossroads unmarked by any buildings, in the valley of the East Branch of the Farmington River. This valley, formerly supporting prosperous farms, will soon (1937) be flooded to a depth of 40 feet, becoming a part of the Hartford metropolitan water system.

Left from Hartland Hollow a narrow and stony road follows the river to the *Red Lion Inn* (1760), 3 *m.*, in NORTH HARTLAND. In the days when Blandford, Mass. (instead of Springfield), was the largest and most important town in Hampden County, this inn was the first convenient stopping-place for stage-coaches and ox-trains en route to Hartford.

Today the inn is occupied by the Old Newgate Coon Club, one of the numerous such clubs in Connecticut where coon hunting has been a traditional sport since the dog of some early settler first treed a raccoon and the farmer's son discovered the excitement of shaking the 'washing bear' to the ground.

Men, dogs, lanterns, and, invariably, a number of small boys, make up the usual Connecticut coon hunting party, which never starts until after sundown, when the raccoon leaves his den. The 'coon,' busy in some hillside cornpatch is unaware of the hunt until he hears the bark of a distant hound. Coon hounds are seldom thoroughbreds; often they are crosses of such diverse breeds as bulldog and collie, but they must be good trailers with superior intelligence.

When the first dog yelps, the little 'washing bear,' one of Nature's comedians, pricks up his pointed ears and starts to travel. Usually, he heads for a swamp, as he knows he can lengthen his lead where the pools and tiny brooks hide the scent. The huntsmen do not follow the dogs through the swamps, because a good coon dog always trees his prey on higher ground. When two dogs are running, one 'circles,' trying to pick up the freshest scent while the other follows the trail. A howl quickly advises his partner of any new scent. Men and boys follow the chase by ear or by their knowledge of the terrain. When the dogs bark 'treed' (a queer yelp on a much higher note than the howl of the trail) the huntsmen hurry across the country and circle the tree, flashing their dark lanterns or flashlights to locate the coon by the shine of his eyes. Usually he is out at the end of a branch, resembling a bunch of leaves or a great bird's nest. Once found, the coon is sometimes winged by a marksman on the ground, but usually he is shaken from his lofty perch by a daring climber, to the waiting dogs below, who worry their prey amid a din of exultant yelping, as the shouting huntsmen swing their clubs. The pelt is usually worthless, but the meat is highly prized, and after hanging for a few days, becomes the main dish at a coon supper to which all the neighbors are welcomed.

Eastward, the highway winds upward over hemlock-clad ridges. Openings in the woods, which screen the highway, offer brief vistas of distant hills enveloped in a blue haze.

State 20 ascends an extremely long grade to the village of EAST HARTLAND (alt. 1225, town pop. 296), 10 *m.*, the largest of the small communities in the town of Hartland, the only town in Connecticut in which the population has consistently decreased since the first Federal census was taken in 1790. Like many of its neighbors, Hartland is a namesake of a village in the rugged plateau region of southwestern England; its name is also a telescoped form of the 'Hart(ford) Land,' the land having been granted in 1687 to the towns of Hartford and Windsor to provide for their rapid expansion. Here on the hilltop, great woodpiles season throughout the year, storing up summer sunshine to furnish warmth and comfort as 'the days begin to lengthen and the cold begins to strengthen.'

The *East Hartland Congregational Church* (1801), at the crossroads, is a plain white structure with a severe tower. The fan-light entrance, the quoins and delicate cornice are original. On clear days points in Rhode Island, Vermont, and New York may be seen from the tower. In the adjacent, well-kept *Cemetery* are the graves of 81 Revolutionary soldiers. Six young oak trees, scions of the original Charter Oak, are planted at the entrance. In the center of the cemetery is a 'noon stone,' a crude Colonial sundial, made of an upright stone and a chiseled mark on a flat rock beneath it. When the shadow of the vertical stone 'lines up' with the straight mark, it is noon by sun time.

At *Hayes' General Store*, west of the cemetery, hangs an old army rifle, used by a discouraged Civil War veteran to end his earthly troubles. The grocer took the rifle as payment 'on account.'

> Left from East Hartland a dirt road leads into the eastern section of the *Tunxis State Forest* to *Bragg Pond*, 1.2 *m.*, where there are picnicking and bathing facilities, in addition to hiking and ski trails. This reservation is famed for its blueberries which may be picked in season. (*Fee for berry picking* 50¢).

WEST GRANBY (alt. 380), 14.9 *m.*, with its tavern surrounded by two-story verandas, its country store and little white church under the hill, is suggestive of a page out of Hawthorne's 'American Note-Books.'

At 16.6 *m.* is a junction with a country road.

> Right on this road through a scenic chasm known as the *Barn Door Hills*, 1.2 *m.*, where the hillsides, 400 to 500 feet high, were evidently split apart during a prehistoric earthquake.

At 17.9 *m.* is GRANBY, at a junction with State 10 (*see Tour 6*).

T O U R   6 :   *From* NEW HAVEN *to* MASSACHUSETTS LINE (*Northampton*), 51.6 *m.*, State 10 and 10A (College Highway).

Via Centerville, Cheshire, Southington, Plainville, Farmington, Avon, Simsbury, Granby.

N.Y., N.H., & H. R.R. parallels the route throughout. Macadamized highway with newer sections of concrete.

Accommodations of all usual kinds at short intervals.

STATE 10 and 10A, between New Haven and the Massachusetts Line, follow the broad valleys of the Mill, Quinnipiac, and Farmington Rivers; for generations this route has been known as the College Highway because it is the direct road connecting the numerous colleges and preparatory schools of the Upper Connecticut Valley with Yale University at its southern terminus. A shorter and less congested route between southern and northern New England than US 5 — The Post Road which runs parallel to the east (*see Tour* 7) — State 10 follows the old Farmington Canal built in 1828. Traces of the canal are seen along the way, passing through many small communities which experienced a brief industrial stimulation in anticipation that this water route would rival the Erie Canal as a freight carrier. When frequent landslides proved the project impractical (1838), the residents returned to tilling the fertile soil. North of New Haven extensive acreage is devoted to truck-gardening, orchards, and poultry-raising, and in all the northern towns tobacco is cultivated intensively. Wooded traprock ridges on either side of the valley are prominent features along the entire length of the route.

The College Highway leaves New Haven in two alternate routes, State 10 and State 10A, which unite at Centerville. State 10A is recommended as the better route.

North from US 1 (*see Tour* 1) at New Haven, via Winthrop and Dixwell Aves., State 10 passes from the outskirts of New Haven on a heavily traveled route.

At 3.5 *m.* is HIGHWOOD, a densely populated area into which the city of New Haven has expanded beyond its town limits.

At 5.9 *m.* is the *Bassett House* (1819) (R), now a tavern, which retains its original portico, staircase and mantels, some of the best detail work in the State.

At 6.8 *m.* is the junction with State 10A in Centerville.

Leaving the New Haven Green at 0 *m.* State 10A proceeds north on Church St. to its junction at 0.1 *m.* with Whitney Ave., a broad, heavily traveled highway lined on either side with tall arching elms, large, urban residences of the late 19th century, and modern apartment buildings.

Crossing the town line into Hamden, at 1.6 *m.* (named for John Hampden, the English patriot) State 10A leads straight ahead through the residential suburb of WHITNEYVILLE. The highway passes one of the town's most interesting architectural relics, *Eli Whitney's Model Barn* (L), 2.2 *m.*, near the corner of Whitney Ave. and Armory St., built in 1816 with arcades applied against the front.

A *Tablet* (R), 2.3 *m.*, near Mill River marks the site of Whitney's armory, one of the first arms factories in the United States. In 1798 Whitney secured a Government contract for 10,000 muskets. According to the terms of the contract Whitney gave his bond for $30,000 and was to receive $13.40 for each musket. In 1858 this factory was absorbed by the Winchester Arms Company which had its original location on this site.

At 2.5 *m.* is the intersection with Deepwood Drive.

Left on Deepwood Drive is the former *Home of Professor William Phipps Blake* (end of Drive), noted mineralogist whose survey of Alaska determined Congressional decision to purchase that territory in 1867. Many large, well-kept homes are located on pleasant, secluded drives in the Mill Rock district. From the summit of *Mill Rock* there is a fine view of the city of New Haven.

At 2.7 *m.* is the junction with Davis St.

Right on Davis St. is *East Rock Park* (R), 0.5 *m.* (*see NEW HAVEN*).

CENTERVILLE (alt. 70, town pop. 19,020) (Town of Hamden), 5.9 *m.*, the site of the first settlement in Hamden (1664) is the governmental center of the town. A residential and manufacturing suburb of New Haven, it was developed as a northern settlement of the latter city until 1786, when it was incorporated as a separate town. Although the soil has always been well suited to agriculture, many small industries developed along the bank of Mill River at an early date.

Among the town's present industries are the manufacture of car lighting equipment, insulated wire, and elastic webbing. Fruit raising and truck gardening equal the manufactured products in importance.

Beside the Hamden Town Hall (L) stands *Grace Episcopal Church* (1819), said to have been designed by David Hoadley. The detail of the original church is in excellent proportion; the over-rich cupola is modern.

At Centerville is the junction with State 10 (*see above*).

At 7.3 *m.* is MT. CARMEL CENTER. The *Rev. Nathaniel Sherman House* (L), built in 1772, has many of the most appealing features of 18th-century architecture, including an unusual transom of round-headed lights and a fine door. Beside it is the *Mt. Carmel Congregational Church* (1840), a well-designed Greek Revival structure.

At 8.5 *m.* is the junction with Mt. Carmel Ave.

> Right on Mt. Carmel Ave. is the entrance to the *Sleeping Giant State Park*, so named because the contour of five successive hills resembles that of a great prone form. The park covers 1000 acres, has fireplaces and parking facilities, and is marked with nature trails climbing the various peaks. The *Heaton Trail* climbs an easy (8 per cent grade) ascent to the 'stomach' of the giant or highest elevation (alt. 737) where there is a lookout tower.

> Near the park headquarters stands the *Jonathan Dickerman House* (1770), 0.2 *m.* Its Dutch eaves are said to have been a later addition; it is now owned by the Hamden Historical Society.

> At 0.3 *m.* is the junction with a tarred road. Right on this road along *Clark's Ponds* to a shady picnic area, 0.7 *m.*

Continuing northward State 10 leads past several interesting examples of 18th and early 19th century houses.

At 11.2 *m.* is IVES CORNER.

> Left at Ives Corner on a tarred road to the secluded community of BROOKS-VALE, 1 *m.*, at the foot of *Mt. Sanford* (alt. 938). At 1.5 *m.* is a junction with a steep, narrow road (L), rough with frequent 'thank-you-ma'ams' (*cars can be parked at the foot of the hill*); near the top of the mountain on this road is the junction, 2.4 *m.*, with the blue-blazed *Quinnipiac Trail* which leads (R), at 3.3 *m.*, to the brink of a lofty waterfall, known as *Roaring Brook*, cascading down the mountain-side in a granite spillway shaded by hemlocks. This excursion is recommended in the fall when a wide view of the countryside spreads out before the hiker as he descends into the peaceful vale dotted with cedars and clumps of fragrant bay-berry.

At 12 *m.* (White's Corner) is the junction with a dirt road.

> Right on this road to the old *Jinny Hill Barytes Mine*, 0.8 *m.*, from which perfect white crystals are taken for all large museums of the world. Many crystals can still be found in the overgrown mine dumps. Barytes, the source of barium hydroxide, is used in the refining of sugar and is also ground and used as a pigment for weighting paper and cloth.

At 12.1 *m.* (Richards' Corner) is the junction with a tarred country road.

Left on this road to a fairly accessible remnant of the old canal, 1 *m.*, a sign (L) reads 'Old Lock House and Canal.' Down a lane, 1.3 *m.*, is the original lock house (L), considerably altered, beside the scant remains of some old locks. Immediately below this point is an unusual bridge designed by a French architect to carry the railroad tracks over the waterway; the bridge is technically described as a 'multi-centered helicoidal skew arch with barrel vaults normal to the pressure lines.'

CHESHIRE (alt. 250, town pop. 3263), 13.1 *m.*, spreads along a single main street. The town was named for the county of Cheshire, England. Many residents from New Haven and Waterbury have recently established homes here.

Although the manufacture of watches once furnished employment to many of the townsfolk, the mining of copper and barytes was the most productive industry in the past century; more than 500 Cornish miners were imported to supply the large demand for skilled labor. The opening of the Farmington Canal from New Haven as far as Cheshire, in 1825, brought the community into closer contact with markets for its agricultural products, and facilitated the shipment of ores, but the subsequent discovery of rich copper lodes in western states, soon made exploitation of the Cheshire mines unprofitable. In the intensive cultivation of its land, the town of Cheshire ranks second in the State.

To the south of the Green is the *Abijah Beach Tavern* (1814) once named for Benjamin Franklin, which still has its old bar, and a ballroom on the third floor. The *Congregational Church* (1826) is fortunate in its location, a little remote from the highway, across the elm-shaded triangular Green. It is one of the series of churches of almost identical design, the first at Milford and the last in Litchfield, with a tall spire and free-standing Ionic columns. In front of the *Town Hall*, directly opposite the church, is a handsome sycamore measuring 17' 4" in circumference. Facing the Green on the north is the *Colonel Rufus Hitchcock House* (1785), little changed except for the addition of dormer windows. The molded caps over the windows and the original broad porch make it an excellent sample of its period.

The *Cheshire Academy* (R), a preparatory and tutoring school for boys, occupies the grounds and buildings of the Episcopal Academy established in 1796 which was moved to Hartford and later became Trinity College. Among the buildings of the school is the brick college (1796) of the original Episcopal Academy, a smaller edition of Connecticut Hall on the Yale Campus. Bishop Abraham Jarvis, who was instrumental in having it incorporated as a college in 1801, built the large white house with the handsome portico facing the main street (L), four houses behind St. Peter's Church, around which the road swings to the left.

At Cheshire are the junctions with State 150 and State 70.

1. Right from Cheshire on State 150 to COPPER VALLEY, 2 *m.*, once a scene of great activity when the mines were worked, but now a quiet retreat.

2. Right from Cheshire on State 70, 3 *m.*, to the junction of a tarred country road, and left on that road across a bridge to the north bank of the Quinnipiac is

CHESHIRE STREET, 3.7 *m.*, a settlement of houses now despoiled or deserted, that must once have been a delightful bit of New England. At various points along State 70 the blue mesa-like hills to the west of Meriden can be seen at their best, mysteriously 'hanging' a few miles away to the northeast.

3. Left from Cheshire on State 70 is WEST CHESHIRE, 1.5 *m.*, where, in the 'button factory' (L) hooks and eyes and other types of fasteners have been manufactured ever since the days when the itinerant 'Yankee Pedlar' was supplied with wares from this shop.

At 2.4 *m.* at a gap in the hills known as *The Notch* is a junction with State 68. Left on State 68 to the center of the once isolated town of PROSPECT (alt. 860, town pop. 531), 3.4 *m.* From the small Green is a wide view east to the Hanging Hills of Meriden and across the Quinnipiac Valley. Here are the church and tiny library, both built of round field stone, and a *Civil War Monument* erected by the State in recognition of local patriotism; more soldiers from Prospect fought in the Union armies than there were registered voters in the town.

West of the Prospect Green, 200 feet, State 68 forms a junction with State 69.

a. Right on State 69 is the stately *Hotchkiss House*, 0.6 *m.*, built in 1820. According to records preserved by the family, this house cost less than $700 to build, and the nails were the most expensive item.

b. Left from Prospect on State 69, over a plateau slightly less elevated than the crest of the western range bordering the Quinnipiac Valley, is a direct route to New Haven, 16.7 *m.* and to US 1 (*see Tour* 1). In the fall of the year, the woods, mirrored in the chain of lakes of the New Haven water supply, form a colorful tapestry of great beauty.

At 14.8 *m.* is the *Connecticut State Reformatory* (L), an institution covering 500 acres of farm land on which the prisoners raise all the produce for their use. Elementary vocational instruction and constructive employment in the machine, printing, tailor, and plumbing shops maintained within the grounds, are a part of the institution's rehabilitation program.

At the Milldale crossroads, 17.6 *m.*, is the junction with State 14 (*see Tour 2 Alt.*).

At 18.3 *m.* is the junction with Mulberry St.

Right on Mulberry St. to South End St., where at the junction, 1.3 *m.*, is the Colonial *South End Cemetery* (L), a serene old burial ground in a sylvan setting which commands a remarkable view of the *Hanging Hills* of Meriden (*see Tour 2 Alt.*). Here are many graves of early settlers and the large table-top monument of Colonel Eldad Lewis, 'Indian Fighter of Great Renown,' whose gallant career is interwoven with many local legends.

Northward on South End St., immediately before its intersection with State 120, 1.6 *m.* (R), is a black spruce and tamarack swamp known as the *Kettlebog*. This unusual botanical growth, 100 feet in diameter, includes a floating island made up of leather leaf, sheep's laurel, cotton grass, chain fern, and similar flora.

State 10 follows Main St., the old stage-coach route, opened from Hartford to New Haven in 1840, northward through PLANTSVILLE, at 19.3 *m.*, a small elm-shaded manufacturing village which, with neighboring villages, produces an appreciable percentage of the nation's supply of nuts and bolts. This industry was founded in 1840, when Rugg and Barnes, blacksmiths of near-by Marion (*see Tour 2 Alt.*), invented a machine which eliminated the tedious and laborious hand threading process.

At 697 South Main St. stands the *Nathaniel Lewis House* (R), 19.5 *m.*, with a façade which is one of the most perfect examples of early 19th-century architecture left in Connecticut.

SOUTHINGTON (alt. 154, town pop. 9237), 20.5 *m.*, in a valley between Ragged Mountain to the east and the Waterbury Hills to the west, has preserved a few old landmarks along its main thoroughfare.

At the northeast cor. of Main St. (State 10) and Meriden Ave. is the *Southington Public Library* and *Sylvia Bradley Memorial Ell* (*open daily except Sat., Sun., and holidays* 2–9) (R), 31.4 *m.*, containing a small collection of period furniture and some unusual historic relics.

Opposite the long, narrow Green, traditional center of social and civic activity since the town was incorporated in 1779, stands the large, excellently designed *Congregational Church* (1828), a fine white clapboarded structure, closely resembling its contemporary in Litchfield and the earlier churches in Milford and Cheshire. Its Ionic portico shows the transition to the Greek Revival style, as does the open belfry and tower, which carries the Ionic motif into the steeple.

Left on Center St. are the low spreading buildings of Peck, Stow and Wilcox Company, the town's most important industry, which produces general hardware and dates from 1819 when Seth Peck patented his first machine for making tinware and sheet metal.

One block north of the Green in Southington Center the highway passes the old *Jonathan Root Tavern* (L), a salt-box house with a large Dutch doorway, said to have been built in 1720.

> Right from Center St. on Mill St. to the end; right on West St. and left on the next dirt road (Jude Lane), down a steep hill. At the end of this lane a path follows *Roaring Brook* a short distance to the *Great Unconformity*. Here triassic sandstone, resting on upturned and eroded granite, which is probably the remains of a former mountain, shows the stages of a process of the formation of the earth which took place during a period of about 325,000,000 years.

At 21.2 *m.* State 10 passes (R) the *Curtis-Robinson House* (about 1766), which, because of its excellence of detail and state of preservation, is undoubtedly the finest old house in Southington. The doorway, with a broken arch pediment and rosettes over the pilasters, is one of the most beautiful in the State. Black locust trees on the grounds were brought from the Holy Land by Edward Robinson (1794–1863), distinguished Hebraic scholar and president of Union College, who was born here.

At 21.6 *m.* (at Oak Hill Cemetery), is the intersection with a tarred road.

> Right on this road are the *Rogers Orchards*, 2.9 *m.*, one of the largest fruit-growing farms in the State, with 6000 apple and 4500 peach trees. Visitors may watch fruit-picking during the late summer and autumn, and apple-packing in the cold storage plants in the winter.

At 23.4 *m.* is a junction with West Queen St.

> Left on West Queen St.; left at the end; right on the first road to *Lake Compounce*, 2.9 *m.*, a resort with facilities for bathing, boating, fishing, and picnicking as well as such amusements as a roller coaster, carrousel, etc. An abundant growth of mountain laurel and groves of fragrant pine fringe the lake shore.

Right at 24.1 *m.* is the entrance to the *Adventist Camp Grounds* where annual gatherings have been held for 40 years.

State 10 follows the new cut-off, by-passing the business section of Plainville.

At 25.2 *m.* (R) is a low sand ridge of unusual geological interest. In the pre-glacial era, the Farmington and Pequabuck Rivers flowed south into the Quinnipiac. When the ice-sheet melted, these swollen rivers piled up the barrier of sand, which, although not high, was sufficient to divert the channel so that the Farmington River now flows north through Tariffville Gorge into the Connecticut River.

PLAINVILLE (alt. 170, town pop. 6301), 26 *m.*, formerly the Great Plains of Farmington, is a small manufacturing center which produces electrical supplies and steel bearings. It is distinguished by its neat, freshly painted houses and substantial public buildings. Like neighboring towns, Plainville experienced a lively though brief industrial stimulation in the early 19th century when the Farmington Canal was opened (1828). Almost every old house now surviving was then used as a tavern, and numerous warehouses and factories were built in anticipation of the hoped-for day when Plainville might rival Hartford as a business center. The canal, however, had been dug through porous soil, and successive washouts, culminating in a disastrous one which left many canal boats high and dry, finally closed that water route to traffic.

The center of the village is left of the College Highway. In the center is the seam-faced granite *Library* (*open weekdays* 9–5) (L), Main St., where exhibits include a collection of Indian arrows, spear-heads and other relics. Most notable are an old safe constructed of wood and one of the earliest master clocks.

At the corner of Whiting and Main Sts., formerly in the old Bristol Basin, on the Farmington Canal, now filled in, are the ruins of numerous commercial buildings erected during the early days of the canal.

At Plainville are the junctions with State 72 and US 6 (*see Side Trip off Tour 2*). The latter combines with this route for 4.2 *m.*

> Right from Plainville on State 72 (New Britain Ave.) to the *John Cook Tavern*, 0.5 *m.* (L), opposite Hamlin's Pond. Built just before 1800, with its attached barns, this long rambling structure, covered with stained clapboards that give it a weathered appearance, boasts one of the largest Colonial ballrooms in New England. It is now an inn and tea house. Beyond, to the east of Cook St., stands (L) the *William Lewis House* (1780), a reputed preliminary headquarters for the Lewis and Clark expedition. This well-preserved white homestead was built over a rock cave believed to have served as the original shelter for the family before the house was erected.

> State 72 eastward follows a pre-glacial river-bed, now known as *Cook's Gap*, 1.1 *m.*

> Right from State 72 at Cook's Gap on Ledge Rd., which skirts the top of a rocky cliff, commanding impressive views of the Quinnipiac River and valley, through *Sunset State Park*, 2.6 *m.*, on the western slope of Bradley Mountain. Shaded by hardwoods and a fine stand of hemlocks, the park is a vantage point overlooking a wide view to the west, and it contains many small picnic spots commanding views over the valley.

FIELD

THE traveler through the Connecticut countryside will find frequent traces of the older industries and occupations of its inhabitants. A hundred years ago, when the railroad was in its earliest infancy, water-borne commerce on river and Sound was still supplemented by the use of the Farmington Canal, and along the streamsides were built the small factories of local industry. Dairying still contributes an important addition to the income of many a farmer, much of whose stony, hillside land is better adapted to stock-raising than to the intensive cultivation of crops.

No trip into the back country is complete without the discovery of at least one old mill. Sometimes these mills are the massive, ox-propelled stone wheels, known as the Chilean type, found where water-power was not to be had, and used to crush bark for tannery or to bruise the sorghum that furnished rather inadequate molasses. Water-driven mills are still numerous; a few still grind corn or grain; many show trim piles of native lumber beside huge cones of yellow sawdust.

CANAL PIERS, FARMINGTON

OLD CANAL, WINDSOR LOCKS

NINEVEH FALLS, KILLINGWORTH

KNIFE SHOP DAM, SOUTH MERIDEN

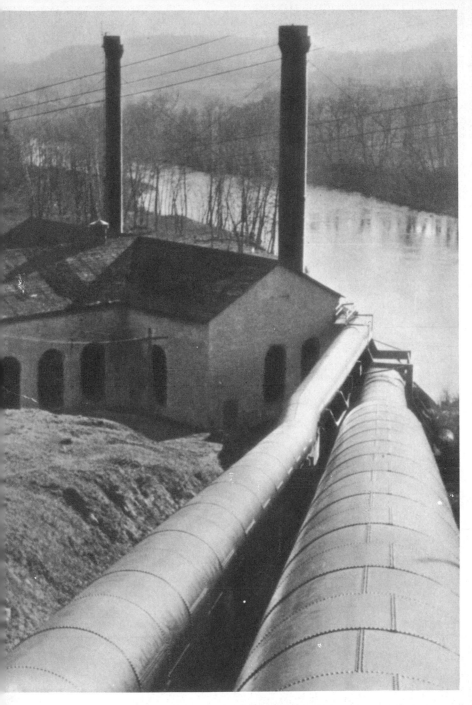

HYDROELECTRIC PLANT, BULLS BRIDGE

BUTTERY'S MILL (1688), SILVERMINE

DEVON CATTLE, OLD LYME

GOATS, AVON OLD FARMS

SHEEP, AVON OLD FARMS

SUMMER SKY, MOUNT CARMEL

HOLSTEINS, SOUTHBUR

AYING, ROXBURY

AT THE END OF THE DAY, WOODBURY

BARK MILL, BETHANY

From *Rattlesnake Mountain* (alt. 750) (R) there is a fine view to the south and east.

At 28.5 *m.* are junctions with US 6A (*see Tour* 2) and US 202, which combines with this tour to the Massachusetts border.

FARMINGTON (alt. 210, town pop. 4548) (*see FARMINGTON*), 30.2 *m.*, is a dignified elm-shaded village.

At Farmington is the junction (R) with US 6 (*see Side Trip off Tour* 2).

At 32 *m.* can be seen the ruins of an old six-pier aqueduct, 0.2 *m.* left of the highway, which was constructed to carry the canal across the river. The three remaining stone piers form a landmark.

Continuing on the Farmington River terrace, the highway now affords an excellent view of the Western Highlands.

At 33.4 *m.* is a junction with a tarred country road.

Left on this road is *Avon Old Farms*, a preparatory school for boys, 1.5 *m.* (R), and one of the most interesting modern architectural developments in Connecticut. The thirty buildings (1922–26) are arranged in an informal village, similar to the 'public schools' of England such as Winchester, and the cottages of the Cotswold. The school is intended by Theodate Pope (Mrs. John Wallace Riddle), the architect and donor, to impart a cultural education in a New England farm background. The seven dormitories, refectory, provost's house, and the rest of the school group, are of different inspirations, but all held together by a remarkable unity.

If the term 'Tudor' can be applied, the buildings are surely more truly Tudor than the larger American university groups patterned after that style, in that they are of solid masonry construction without the subterfuge of hidden steel framework. The exterior walls are of red sandstone blocks quarried on the premises and shaped by hand. Much of the timbering is of native oak. Split-oak saplings were used on the rafters, and the slates were set in cement. The irregularity of the framing, evidenced in the unevenness of the slate, softens the outlines of the roofs. With the exception of one bas-relief by Lee Lawrie, over the entrance, and a few well-placed finials and drip moulds, there is no ornamentation. The group achieves its great distinction through well-studied arrangement, fine proportions, vigorous handling of masses and its innate simplicity.

The workshops near the entrance, some distance from the main group, are dominated by a high Norman water-tower, a simple brick cylinder, unadorned and pierced by a few narrow windows. Its height is accentuated by the low stone and half-timbered smithy and carpenter shop attached to the base.

Just across the plank bridge, an oiled road winds down the hill to forest, extensive farmlands, meadows, pastures, and also stables and a polo field.

At 35.6 *m.* is the junction with US 44 (*see Tour* 3), with which State 10 joins for 0.8 mile.

At the barns of a former inn, on the southwest corner at the junction, stagecoaches of the Hartford–Albany Line changed horses. On the northeast corner, at the foot of the Talcott Mountain range, is the *Old Farms Inn* (1757), with its numerous ells.

Just beyond the junction is a newly shingled peak-roofed house (R) which was once the *Phelps Tavern* (about 1795).

AVON (alt. 210, town pop. 1738) (Town of Avon, named for the English River), 36.4 *m.*, is a peaceful agricultural community on the fertile

Farmington River plain. Little disturbed by industrial activities for over a century, it was formerly a thriving commercial center which grew so rapidly after the opening of the Farmington Canal that it was incorporated as a town in 1830. With the abandonment of the canal, Avon's manufacturing enterprises ceased. Today, only one factory, making blasting fuse, survives as a reminder of the active past.

At the center stands the *Congregational Church* (1818), designed by David Hoadley. Although the building has lost much of its appeal because of its modern windows, it is still an interesting composition. The projecting front entrance, divided by four Ionic pilasters with three doors between them, is surmounted by a three-stage tower with latticed railings and applied ornamentation on two of its stages.

Here at the village center State 10 turns sharp right leaving US 44 (*see Tour* 3).

The *Jonathan Humphreys House*, built in 1728 (L), at 37.1 *m.*, is the dwelling from which Lucius W. Bigelow, one of the 'Yankee pedlars,' set forth on his rounds. The entrance to this dwelling, decorated with pilasters surmounted by rosettes and having a door with bottom cross-panels, is typical of the Connecticut Valley. The transom is of six arched lights.

On the crest of Talcott Mountain (alt. 930) is the *Heublein Tower* (R), residence of the Heublein family. Suggestive of a Tyrolean castle, it was built by Richard M. Hoe (1812–86), manufacturer and inventor of many improvements for the printing press.

In WEATOGUE (alt. 180) (Town of Simsbury), 39.3 *m.*, which has an Indian name (*wigwam place*), on the northeast corner of the junction with State 185, stands (R) the *Pettibone Tavern* (*open*) (1801), an interesting old house with numerous extended ells.

On the Talcott Mountain cliffs to the east is *King Philip's Cave* (*reached by a private trail and inaccessible to the motorist*), traditionally known as one of the stopping-places of that sachem.

> Right from Weatogue, State 185 climbs over the Talcott Mountain range passing the gorge, 1.5 *m.* (R), still known as *Hell Hole*, in which Captain Wadsworth is said to have taken refuge after hiding the Connecticut Charter in the Charter Oak (*see History*).

SIMSBURY (alt. 180, town pop. 3625), 41.1 *m.*, like many other northern Connecticut towns, has no village Green, but spreads along wide, tree-shadowed Hopmeadow St. Broad lawns surrounding spacious, well-built houses, enriched with the delicate architectural details of the late 18th and early 19th century, are symbolic of the wealth and culture solidly founded upon successful manufacturing and agricultural enterprises, which have characterized the community since early times.

The first trail to this district was blazed in 1643 by two emissaries of the British Navy, in search of pine growths for replenishing their ships' supply of pitch and turpentine. Their reports of the abundant pasture and timber land soon stimulated the migration of settlers from Hartford and Windsor. Incorporated in 1670 and named for Simondsbury in Dorsetshire, England, Simsbury developed steadily for six years until March, 1676, when the settlers, becoming terrified by the savagery of King Philip's War, abandoned their homes and fled in precipitous haste to Hartford and Windsor. Scouts returning three days later found the village in ashes. Although many of the first settlers never returned, other pioneers soon reconstructed the village which was stimulated to bustling activity by the discovery of copper at East Granby (then part of Simsbury) in 1705. Skilled workers were imported from Hanover, Germany, to assist in the mining and smelting works established on Hopmeadow Brook. As the English law prohibited the smelting and refining of copper in the Colonies, operations had to be carried on secretly and thus at a great disadvantage.

The first copper coinage minted in the colonies was produced here by John Higley in 1737 at his furnace on Hopmeadow Brook. These pennies, known to numismatists as Higley pennies, were stamped 'I am good Copper,' and 'Value me as You Will.' In 1744, Higley manufactured the first half ton of steel produced in America, but his process proved unprofitable and its use was soon discontinued. Higley's sister, Hannah, married Joseph Trumbull and was the mother of 'Brother Jonathan,' the first Governor Trumbull (*see LEBANON*).

The landscaped industrial plant of the *Ensign Bickford Company* (R) is one of the largest and oldest safety-fuse factories in the world and the first to produce this safeguard for blasting in America. Established in Granby in 1836, this plant moved to Simsbury in 1839 and is still managed by descendants of the early American and English incorporators.

The *Congregational Church* (1830), a Greek Revival building, stands at the southern end of the street, its handsome spire rising in three stages above a projecting pediment.

North of the railway grade crossing, at 41.3 *m.*, stands *Eaglewood* (L), the 'great house' of the town, exemplifying the climax of its prosperity (1822). This broad, brick gambrel-roofed house, with side porches and arched dormer windows, has an aspect of amplitude and elegance. Here were born Gifford Pinchot (1865), ex-Governor of Pennsylvania, and some of his Eno ancestors.

At the rear of the Ellsworth House (R), just before the traffic light, is *Minister's Well*, once enclosed in the primitive stockade (1676–1720) to which the first settlers fled for protection against the Indians.

Opposite the Methodist Episcopal Church and distinguished by its graceful gambrel roof and unusual round-topped window-panes is the *Captain Elisha Phelps House* (R), built in 1771 for his son, Lieutenant David Phelps, who died in the Revolution five years later. After the War of 1812, the building became a tavern and later, as the Canal Hotel, was the scene of gala balls, official receptions, and court trials. Here, too, was organized the first local lodge of Free Masons, much to the consternation of conservative squires who feared that the mysterious rites of the members presaged a return to the hysteria of the witchcraft era.

At 41.5 m. (R) (opposite the Simsbury High School), is the white clapboard homestead built by the Rev. Benajah Root in 1762, used as a tavern during the Revolution, and later the home of Lucius I. Barber, the historian (1806-89). Adjacent is the Pent Rd., an early short-cut to the river-crossing (1668-1878) used by Revolutionary soldiers on their way to relieve Boston.

> Left from Simsbury on State 167, a paved road; (L) at 0.3 m. to the *Ethel Walker School*, 2.6 m., an exclusive finishing school for girls, moved to its present location from New Jersey in 1917.

At 41.9 m. is a junction with a country road.

> Left on this road is the *Westminster School for Boys*, 1 m., easily identified by the water-tower which marks its entrance. The school campus of more than 200 acres has 20 buildings, including a chapel, infirmary, swimming pool, dormitories and masters' cottages. Founded in 1888 at Dobbs Ferry, New York, by William Cushing, the school, which was moved to Simsbury in 1900, is operated on a non-profit basis.

State 10 now leaves the broad fertile valley of the Farmington River and enters the hillier country of Granby. Across the meadows to the right is the *Talcott Mountain Range*, a continuation of the Mt. Holyoke and Mt. Tom ranges in Massachusetts, and to the left, *West Mountain* of the Berkshire group.

At 47.1 m. is the entrance to the *McLean Game Refuge* (*closed and locked after 6; no fishing or smoking*), a tract of 2500 acres left by U.S. Senator George P. McLean as 'a place where some of the things God made may be seen by those who love them as I love them and who may find in them the peace of mind and body that I have found.' Many beautiful drives and picnic grounds have been provided.

At the *Salmon Brook Country Club* is a golf course (*open to the public; green fee $1*).

GRANBY (alt. 200, town pop. 1388), 48.1 m., a crossroads rural center of frame buildings, settled in 1664 by residents of Granby, Massachusetts, and like that town named in honor of the Marquis of Granby, has remained an agricultural district, now chiefly devoted to tobacco-growing, although during the era of the Farmington Canal (1828-38) several manufacturing plants operated briefly here.

The hardy pioneering spirit of the first settlers who, in constant peril of massacre, defended their isolated farms scattered over Indian hunting grounds, has persisted through generations. In 1762, a company of Granby men enlisted in the British expedition against Havana, which was successful in capturing that stronghold but from which only two local men returned. In 1802 Granby residents organized a migration to the Northwest Territory and founded Worthington, Ohio.

The *Bunce House* (about 1820) behind its curious fence (L) shows a very broad, hospitable open 'Connecticut' porch of the final and most elaborate type.   Just beyond it, the *Crocker House* (L), of about the same date, is also a pilastered house, one room deep, with a broad fanlight door and an interesting use of rope mouldings.

Beside a spreading elm is the home (L) of Chief Justice William Maltbie of the Connecticut Supreme Court; the nucleus of this dwelling is the oldest house in the town (1752).

At Granby are the junctions with State 20 (*see Tour 5B*), State 189, and State 9.

1. Right from Granby on State 20 a narrow tarred road to the junction with Newgate Rd., 2.8 *m.*

> Left from the junction on Newgate Rd., 0.9 *m.*   Here, above the rural country-side from the western slope of Peak Mountain, are the grim ruins, caverns, and harrowing relics of *Newgate* (*adm.* 35¢), Revolutionary and early State prison (1773), named for the notorious English Newgate which it undoubtedly surpassed in the barbarous punishments inflicted upon prisoners.
>
> Visitors descend through a trapdoor on a perpendicular ladder straight down, 50 feet, through a shaft in the rock scarcely wider than the ladder, to the mine which supplied the first copper smelted in the English Colonies (1705).   Here Tories, thieves, and debtors in iron collars, handcuffs, and leg irons, were forced to live and work.   From the foot of the ladder, a sloping horizontal tunnel twists through pools formed by seepage from the dripping rock walls, to a well shaft down which the daylight dimly filters from the prison court-yard, 70 feet above.
>
> Visitors are led into stygian caverns, now lighted by electricity that shows the circles worn in the rock floor by the pacing feet of chained prisoners; gruesome tales are told of attempted escapes and the ruthless disciplinary measures which followed.
>
> Above ground, in the museum and ruins of stone cells are numerous relics of this and other early prisons.   From the watch tower is a wide view of the valleys and hills to the southwest.

On State 20, east of the junction with Newgate Rd., is EAST GRANBY (alt. 200, town pop. 1003), 3.6 *m.*, which contains numerous old houses.   At the junction with State 187 stands the *Congregational Church* (1830), an ivy-clad structure of native traprock with a little square wooden belfry with pinnacles in the Gothic style.

> Left from East Granby on State 187, 1.7 *m.*, is the gambrel-roofed *Griffin House* (1770), a story-and-a-half brick building with a broad chimney across the rear, with string courses of black header brick between the windows.

At 4.2 *m.* is the intersection with East St.

> Left on East St. about 0.5 *m.* are several late 18th-century houses.   The most unusual house in the town is on the *Nicholson Farm*, 1.7 *m.*; it has an elaborate doorway in which the details of the pilasters combine all the Connecticut Valley motifs, flutings, and sunbursts, topped by two tiny 'tombstone' panels.   The windows contain a row of half panes in each sash, a peculiarity found elsewhere only in the Loomis House, Windsor.

2. Left from Granby Center on State 189 is NORTH GRANBY (Town of Granby), 3.7 *m.*   Here, near the village crossroads, is a simple *Congregational Church* (1834), with a rather high, two-storied tower, and the *Beecher Tavern*, which has one of the most interesting old ballrooms in the State.   Three rows of bottlenecks, used to improve the acoustics, project through the plaster dome, and the narrow gallery is protected from the eyes of youth below by 'modesty boards.'   Beyond North Granby, at 5.6 *m.*, is the old four-story *Crag Gristmill* (L), overhanging a wooded ravine.

3. Hard right from Granby on State 9, across level land where the choice Havana leaf tobacco is cultivated; occasionally the scene is varied by a passage through a notch in the hills or a sudden dip and rise out of a dingle. The highway traverses rolling hills to GRANBY STATION (Town of East Granby), 1.3 *m.*, where, a short distance south of the grade crossing, is a 40-foot arch (R), built in 1825 to carry the Farmington Canal over Salmon Brook, and now used by the railroad.

At TARIFFVILLE (Town of Simsbury), 3.5 *m.*, a small hamlet at the northern end of Talcott Mountain, the first carpet factory in Connecticut was opened in 1827, as a result of early protective tariff legislation; but since 1867 manufacturing has been replaced by the sorting and packing of tobacco as the chief industry.

At 3.6 *m.*, at the railroad trestle, is the junction with a dirt road. R. here to the hilltop (alt. 550) on which is *Bartlett Tower*, commanding magnificent views up and down the Connecticut Valley; on a clear day the summit of Mt. Monadnock, 83 miles away in New Hampshire, is seen. The tower, now in disrepair, is no longer safe for climbing.

From here, State 9 runs through the scenic *Tariffville Gorge*, cut by the Farmington River through a fault in the traprock ledge, when its pre-glacial course south to the Quinnipiac was dammed by a glacial sand ridge at Plainville.

Following the Farmington River, State 9 crosses that stream on *Spoonville Bridge*, 4.9 *m.*, so named because the first silver-plating factory in the United States was erected here on the north bank of the river in 1840 by William B. Cowles. Asa Rogers was associated with this firm in 1843 before he removed to Hartford, and with his brothers established the famous 'Rogers Brothers, 1847' trademark.

NORTH BLOOMFIELD (alt. 180), 5.7 *m.*, is a crossroads.

Right at the crossroads a surfaced road crosses a dell to *St. Andrew's Episcopal Church*, 0.8 *m.*, with its well-kept churchyard and glebe of sixty acres. Certain parts of the edifice were built here in 1740–42, moved south to the Duncaster district in 1806, and returned to the present site in 1828. Inside are a well-carved lectern and handsome paneling about the organ. The first organ used in the church is now at the Eno Memorial in Simsbury, and there is a duplicate at Harvard University. One of the present underpinnings is a wooden cider-press screw jack, expressive, perhaps, of a jest similar to those which prompted the carved grotesques in medieval cathedrals.

Wintonbury Cemetery (1739), at 9.6 *m.*, contains the graves of 528 early settlers.

BLOOMFIELD (alt. 230, town pop. 3247), 9.7 *m.*, with its attractive village Green and well-kept homes, is a residential and agricultural town devoted chiefly to tobacco-raising.

The district was settled in 1660 as a part of Windsor, organized as the parish of Wintonbury, named for Windsor, Farmington, and Simsbury in 1736, and incorporated as a town in 1835. The present descriptive name was suggested by U.S. Senator Francis Gillette, who was born here in 1807. Senator Gillette was an educator, a leader in the abolitionist and temperance movements, and chief organizer of the Republican Party in Connecticut.

Facing the *Green* (Roberts Park), at the junction of State 9 and State 184, stands the *Congregational Church* (1856). On the church lawn is an old oak tree, the last of four under which services were held while the second church edifice was being built in 1801. Opposite is the former *Methodist Church* (1830), a dignified white building now used as a recreation and community hall. To the left of the park is the handsome brick building housing both the *Town Hall* and the *Prosser Library*, which contains a collection of Indian arrow-heads.

Bloomfield has an unusual number of old houses of the plain, central-chimney, farmhouse type without overhang or exterior ornament. Some, however, have been considerably modernized.

Left from the center on Wintonbury Ave., one block, at the northeast corner of Wintonbury and Woodland Aves., is a house, now with a fan-window in each gable end, built about 1768; Oliver Ellsworth (1745–1807), later Chief Justice of the United States, had his first law office here (1772).

Right from Bloomfield center on State 184.

At 12.6 *m.* is the junction with Duncaster Rd. Right on Duncaster Rd., 12.8 *m.*, to the *Captain Joseph Goodwin Tavern* (1746), a combination of gambrel-roofed and salt-box house, with a T-shaped chimney, which has retained much of the original interior, with panels over 8 feet long.

State 9 continues south to a junction with US 44 (*see Tour 3*) at 14.7 *m.*, 2 miles west of Hartford.

Skirting *Manitook Lake* (R), at 49.1 *m.*, the route passes thrifty farm-houses on rolling hillsides and in shady valleys, and leaves the State, at 51.6 *m.*, from that curious jog of Massachusetts territory into Connecticut, 27 miles south of Northampton, Massachusetts.

Owing to an error of early surveyors, the Massachusetts boundary line ran at an angle, so that it was eight miles too far south at the Connecticut River. A struggle for jurisdiction over towns in the disputed area was temporarily settled in 1713 when an agreement was made by which Massachusetts kept the questioned territory and gave Connecticut an equal area in western Massachusetts and New Hampshire. That land was sold by Connecticut and the proceeds, £683, given to Yale College. The towns ceded to Massachusetts were dissatisfied and wished to be included in Connecticut. The indentation in Connecticut's northern boundary is the result of a survey and compromise in 1804.

T O U R   7 : *From* NEW HAVEN *to* MASSACHUSETTS LINE (*Springfield*), 59 *m.*, US 5.

Via (*sec. a*) Meriden, Berlin, Hartford; (*sec. b*) East Hartford, South Windsor, Enfield, Thompsonville.

Macadamized roadbed.

Usual accommodations.

Sec. a. NEW HAVEN to HARTFORD, 38.6 m.

US 5, traveled chiefly as a direct route between New Haven and Springfield, proceeds north from New Haven through several manufacturing towns to Hartford.

Leaving New Haven on US 5 this route proceeds northeast to the intersection with State 80 (*see Tour 1D*), 2.8 *m.*, and to the intersection with State 15 (*see Tour 7A*), at 4.5 *m.*

Left, at 5.1 *m.*, US 5 passes the *Cedar Hill Yards* of the New York, New Haven & Hartford Railroad, one of the most efficiently equipped and operated freight classification yards in the United States, with a capacity for handling 15,000 freight cars.

At 5.3 *m.* is the junction with *Cody Lane.*

Left on Cody Lane to the *Montowese Brick Yards* (*visitors welcome*) for a view of the various processes of brick manufacture.

On the northwest corner of US 5 and Cody Lane stands the dilapidated but attractive *Jedediah Button House,* built in 1759, distinguished by a long Dutch roof. The later ell to the south was added for a post office and general store.

Skirting the waving meadowlands of marsh grass that border the Quinnipiac River as it flows to the harbor at New Haven, the highway passes through a rolling countryside occupied by numerous truck gardens, and proceeds through the district known as MONTOWESE, named for the Indian Sachem whose tribe once inhabited this region.

At 7.4 *m.* is the junction with Pool Rd.

Right on Pool Rd. 0.5 *m.* Extending south from here is a bog from which the original settlers procured iron as early as 1657, and then laboriously carted it by ox-cart along the Saltonstall Ridge to an old forge in East Haven, or floated it down the Farm River to the foundry at Branford.

NORTH HAVEN (alt. 20, town pop. 3730), 8.3 *m.,* incorporated in 1786, an early shipbuilding center that launched many trim little vessels on the Quinnipiac River for coastal trade with Boston, is now a suburb of New Haven, retaining some of the tranquillity of a more leisurely day. The town divides its interests between truck-gardening and brick making. At the northwest corner of the Green is the *Timothy Andrews Tavern,* that was built in 1780, with an added lean-to. Facing the Green stands the *Dr. Foote House,* a dwelling built about 1794. Opposite, just above the hillside cemetery, stands the early brick Gothic *Church of St. John's* (1835), and three houses to the south is the *Parsonage of the Rev. Benjamin Trumbull,* who was pastor of the settlement for 60 years (1760–1820) and author of 'A History of the United States' and 'A History of Connecticut.' This well-preserved homestead, built in 1761, changed only by new shingles and a bay window on the south side, has a handsome doorway with fluted pilasters and a heavy cornice and pediment.

Beside the railroad station (L), a side road leads south a short distance to a *Clay Pit* which for generations has furnished material for brickmaking, one of the town's chief industries. When bricks are being cured here, there is an appearance of a major conflagration in the brick sheds — clouds of wood smoke roll out from beneath the eaves and through the siding, and an acrid odor fills the air for miles around.

Northward, US 5 passes *Pine Barrens* (R), about 12 acres of woodland consisting mostly of dwarf pitch pine with varieties of vegetation from prairie-like grassland to scrub hardwoods. In prehistoric times it was the bed of the Connecticut River.

At 11.2 *m.* (R) is *Wharton Brook State Park,* with a rustic pavilion at the entrance.

A dirt road right at this point leads to the *John Barker House*, built in 1756, 1.2 *m.*, one of the earliest brick houses in the State. Its gambrel roof and four chimneys are reminiscent of Connecticut Hall on the Yale campus, built four years earlier.

Across the road, a *Salt-box House*, built in 1679, with oddly spaced windows, was moved here from Groton.

US 5 skirts the western edge of Wallingford.

At 12.3 *m.* is the junction with S. Main St. which leads to Wallingford Center. S. Main St. is the east fork; US 5 the west.

WALLINGFORD (alt. 150, town pop. 14,278), including the communities of Wallingford Center and Yalesville, has been one of the foremost silverware manufacturing centers of the Nation since 1835 when Robert Wallace started the making of Britannia ware. The company, which still bears his name, is now the largest of the local firms. Of almost equal importance, the agricultural district of Wallingford produces many thousands of bushels of peaches, pears, apples and cherries annually and is noted for its vineyards and nurseries which cover many acres.

An event of major importance in the year of its occurrence was the devastating tornado remembered as the 'Wallingford Disaster' of August 9, 1878, said to be the worst in the history of New England, which left in its wake 34 dead, 100 injured, and a property damage of half a million dollars.

At 180 S. Main St. (R) is the *Samuel Parsons House* (*adm. free*) (1770), owned by the Wallingford Historical Society, which houses an interesting collection of antiques and old documents.

Right from the center on S. Main St., which becomes N. Main; right on Academy St. to its junction with Elm St.; left on Elm St. two blocks, at the junction with Christian St., is the 500-acre campus of *Choate School* for boys, an exclusive preparatory school. Among the most noteworthy school buildings are the *Andrew Mellon Library* with its valuable collections, and the *Infirmary*, designed by Ralph Adams Cram, a long, low building with a well-designed tower which stands behind the old *Caleb Atwater House*, which was built in 1774, and *Store* (1775) which are now a part of the school property. The *Chapel* (1924), also designed by Cram, is in Georgian Colonial style with an open belfry in which is a carillon.

Across the fields to the east is the *Winter Sports Building* (1932), designed by Polhemus and Coffin, a vast arena topped with a glass roof.

Left on Christian St. to N. Main St., right on N. Main St., near the corner of North St., opposite a triangular Green, stands the *Nehemiah Royce House* (L) (*adm. 25¢, open daily, summer only*), a sharp-peaked salt-box house built in 1672. Since 1924, when the house was moved from its original to its present location it has been used as a museum for a large variety of Colonial furnishings, including mouse traps. Return on Main St. to North St., right on North St. down a steep grade to the junction with US 5.

Following Old Colony Rd. through the lower and less interesting part of Wallingford, US 5 by-passes the hilltop community (R). Here an old cemetery survives in the very front yard of a brick mill, and little shops and filling stations line the road.

At 16.8 *m.* US 5 curves (L) beneath a narrow railway underpass, with a 'Prepare to Meet Thy God' sign painted by a traveling evangelist on the stone abutment, and passes through TRACY, 17.7 *m.*, a roadside hamlet.

MERIDEN (alt. 100, town pop. 37,481) (*see MERIDEN, see Tour 2 Alt. and Tour 7B*), 20.1 *m.*, the 'Silver City.'

Extending beside the road (L), are the grounds and red-brick buildings of the *Connecticut School for Boys*, a State reform school on a hill back from the highway.

At 21.3 *m.* is the junction with a side road.

> Right on this road is an old *Trap-Rock Quarry*, 2.5 *m.*, in which the pillow structure of the first lava flow is clearly indicated (*see Geology*).

The oldest house in the town limits of Meriden stands (R) at 677 Colony St., a long, low gambrel-roofed structure built by Samuel Goffe and known as the *1711 Inn*. Its gambrel roof and dormers were probably added later.

Northward US 5 traverses a woodland area bounded on the left by the *Hanging Hills* of Meriden (*see Tour* 2), and on the right by the rugged *Lamentation-Higby-Beseck Range*.

At 23.8 *m.* is *Silver Lake* (L), a beautiful expanse of water surrounded by stately pines and acres of woodland. Beyond, at 24 *m.*, the highway passes beneath the frowning precipice of *Mt. Lamentation* (R), so named because of the 'lamentable situation' in which a Mr. Chester, one of the first settlers, found himself when he was lost for two days on its thickly wooded heights. Here also, several airplanes crashed before the days of air beacons.

BERLIN (alt. 100, town pop. 4875), 26.9 *m.*, was originally known as the parish of Kensington and named in 1785 for Berlin, Prussia.

Here the Pattison brothers, Edward and William, fashioned the first tinware made in America (1740) and sold their goods by calling at each home in the neighborhood, thus becoming the first of the itinerant 'Yankee Pedlars.' As their business expanded, they employed many adventurous salesmen who, by the end of the 18th century, were covering 1500-mile routes, creating new markets for the only large-scale industry in the State. Braving the wilderness and its constant perils, these Yankees with their wares packed in trunks slung on their backs, tramped north, south, and also west, following the tide of emigration. Timothy Dwight (1752–1817) recorded in his travels that he met them on Cape Cod, on Lake Erie, in Detroit, Canada, and Kentucky, and said that they went to St. Louis and New Orleans as well. Their stocks of tinware were soon increased to include needles, pins, and buttons from the Naugatuck Valley, combs from Essex (Ivoryton), 'galluses' from Middletown, and clocks from Eli Terry's factory in Plymouth. Storage stocks were shipped to seaports in the south so that packs could be replenished far from home. The arrival of a peddler at an isolated farm was a gala event. All the family gathered around to view his glittering array as well as to hear news of their distant friends and of the outside world, with which the peddler was so adept at entertaining his customers. His reputation as a salesman, later immortalized in the stage character 'Sam Slick,' was well earned. One traveler in the early forties wrote, 'In Kentucky, Indiana, Illinois, Missouri, and here in every dell of Arkansas and in every cabin where there is not a chair to sit on, there was sure to be a Connecticut clock.' Despite the fact that after 1836 German Jews rapidly replaced these itinerant Yankees, so firmly had the Connecticut merchants established their reputation, that 'Yankee' had become almost synonymous for 'peddler.'

The early industrialist, Simeon North, who was the first man to receive a contract for making Government pistols (March 9, 1799), as well as the first to apply the principle of interchangeable parts in arms manufacture, was born in Berlin in 1765. During the War of 1812, President Madison made a special trip to North's factory to urge an increase in production. The following year North moved his factory to Middletown. Here was also manufactured the first spooled cotton thread in America at the factory of Elisha Brandegee.

The progressive character of early Berlin industries has been maintained by several present-day concerns with a large export business, which make lacquers, polishes, hardware, and industrial jewels.

Emma Hart Willard (1787–1870), pioneer in the field of higher education for women and founder of the Willard School in Troy, N.Y., was born in Berlin.

The *Fuller Tavern*, built in 1769, now marked by a tablet (L), was one of Washington's many stopping-places.

Beyond (L) is the *Elijah Loveland Tavern*, which was erected in 1797, with a double overhang and graduated clapboards.

The *Worthington Academy* (L), a brick building, built in 1831, with a wooden cupola, brownstone lintels and sills, and a recessed doorway, is now used as a private residence. Just beyond is the *World War Memorial* (L).

North of Berlin, the highway traverses acres of red clay, passing tumbledown brick sheds and great water-filled holes where brick clay has been dug in the fields just off the road.

HARTFORD (alt. 140, city pop. 164,072) (*see HARTFORD*), 38.6 *m.*, capital of the State.

Entering Hartford on Maple Ave., US 5 passes *Goodwin Park* (R), and a *Hartford Municipal Golf Course* (R), immediately after crossing the town line.

At Hartford are the junctions with US 6 and 6A (*see Tour 2*), US 44 (*see Tour 3*), US 5A (*see Tour 8*), and with State 175 (*see Tour 7B*).

Sec. b. HARTFORD to MASSACHUSETTS LINE, 20.4 m.

At Hartford this route crosses the Connecticut River and follows the east bank of the river to Massachusetts, crossing the State line at Long Meadow Station.

Along the northern section of the route, on both sides of the road are rolling fields of tobacco dotted here and there by great tobacco sheds painted the dark red shade so popular in rural Connecticut or weathered to a soft bronze-gray. After harvest time, the opened vents along the sides of the sheds, adjusted to secure circulation of air and proper humidity, stand out like the legs of a giant centipede.

Leaving Hartford the route crosses the Connecticut River on the Bulkeley Memorial Bridge (*see HARTFORD*) to the town of East Hartford.

Entering East Hartford from the bridge on Connecticut Boulevard, along which are the numerous showrooms of automobile dealers serving metropolitan Hartford, the broad main street of East Hartford is a busy center of trade. At East Hartford are junctions with US 6 (*see Tour 2*), US 44 (*see Tour 3*), State 15 (*see Tour 10*) and State 2 (*see Tour 3A*).

EAST HARTFORD (alt. 70, town pop. 17,125), 1.5 *m.*, a manufacturing suburb of Hartford, began to develop industrially soon after its incorporation as a town (1783) and is today a center of the manufacture of airplane engines. Of the early industries, papermaking, which flourished from 1783 until the later part of the 19th century, was the most important, but there were also many mills engaged in the manufacture of powder, cotton goods, watches, and hats.

Many of these early factories have been supplanted by the United Aircraft Corp. and several of its subsidiaries (*see Tour 3A*). Occupying 500,000 square feet of space and employing 2000 men, the plant in 1936 had an average output of 500 engines a month. The *Sikorsky Aircraft Corporation*, affiliated with this concern, manufactures the famous transoceanic planes in Stratford (*see Tour 1*), but has an administrative office here.

This district was formerly the home of the man who was responsible for the first English settlements in Connecticut, Wahquinnacut, Chief of the Podunk Indians, who in 1631 journeyed to Boston and Plymouth colonies to invite the white men to settle in the rich valley of the 'Broad River,' hoping that their presence would afford protection against his hereditary enemies, the Mohawk and Narragansett Indians.

The growing city of Hartford, pushing across the river, has invaded this neighboring community so that little remains of the old town, except on its neglected outskirts. On Main St. (US 5), however, a few historic landmarks and old houses have survived.

At 946 Main St., the *Center Burying Ground*, dating from 1711, contains the graves of 95 Revolutionary War soldiers. In the rear of the cemetery, near Elm St., is *Fort Hill*, the site of an old Podunk Indian stronghold. Beyond, across the street from the *Congregational Church*, a massive bold structure, erected in 1836, stands the brick *Town Hall* at 1112 Main St., originally built to house the *Academy* (1833) of Theodore Dwight, son of Timothy Dwight, president of Yale College.

North of East Hartford, at 3.7 *m.*, US 5 passes (R) a wooden *Gothic Revival Manor House*, with a great buttressed chimney. At 4.1 *m.* stands the house (R) built in 1750, with a small ell and surrounding piazzas, that was the *Home of Abner Reed*, engraver, to whom John Barber, 19th-century historian, was apprenticed.

At 4.3 *m.* is the junction with King St.

Right on King St., 0.8 *m.*, to a *Monument to John Fitch* (1743–98), inventor of the steamboat, who was born here. Half hidden in a field (L), the neglected stone slab symbolizes the fate of this early inventive genius. This vagabond clock-maker, who settled in Kentucky, succeeded in contriving a paddle-wheel mechanism propelled by steam in May, 1787, twelve years before Fulton's experiments, and spent many years in fruitless efforts to obtain public recognition of his invention. Penniless and half starved, he tramped through the wilderness from New York to Virginia, futilely petitioning the legislatures of Virginia, Pennsylvania, Maryland, Delaware, and New Jersey for financial support. His vision of the possibilities of the steam engine in opening up the West and even as a connection with Europe were regarded as the ravings of an unbalanced mind. George Washington and Patrick Henry politely listened, but shook their heads and referred him to the State legislatures or the Congress of the United States. The legislatures either refused to consider the idea or promptly voted it down without debate. After trying for two years to obtain an interview with Benjamin Franklin, who, Fitch felt certain, would use his influence with the Pennsylvania legislature, the inventor was finally admitted to Franklin's house. That great man, whom history extols for his farsighted achievements, was touched by Fitch's poverty and offered him a gift of a few dollars; but when the heartbroken inventor scorned this charity and pleaded that he sought only a chance to prove the value of his invention, the man who had baited lightning frankly stated that the idea of a steamboat was not practical and never would be.

Finally by selling stock to twenty reckless speculators, Fitch financed a boat (1790) that operated for several years, carrying passengers between Trenton and Phila-delphia on the Delaware River at the rate of 8 and later 15 miles an hour. From the profits, a large vessel was built for operation on the Ohio, but just as the boat was ready to be launched a storm dashed it to pieces and bankrupted the com-pany.

Finally a committee of interested persons raised a fund to send Fitch to France in the hope that he could obtain financial backing there, but political unrest in that country made it impossible for him to arouse the interest of French capitalists. In the hope that help might be secured in the future, he left his papers and draw-ings with Consul Henry Vail, who, several years later, showed them to Robert Fulton.

Returning to this country, Fitch built a three-foot model of his engine which he mounted on flanged wheels, and then committed suicide. Years later, when en-gineers were busily building Mississippi steamboats, they carefully inspected Fitch's model and decided that he must have intended to lay rails on the bed of a river and run his boat over the rails!

SOUTH WINDSOR (alt. 40, town pop. 2535), 5.5 *m.*, has been a tobacco-producing center since Colonial times. Originally settled as a part of East Windsor, the community was incorporated as a town in 1845. Its most important industry is the sorting and packing of tobacco leaf. Dur-ing the harvest the countryside seethes with activity, and the golden leaves, hanging in the sheds to cure, present a picture of plenty suggestive of the raiment of Ceres.

At Bus Station 48 is a good *Greek Revival House* with two wings and porches (L), and just beyond (L) is South Windsor's best old salt-box dwelling, the *Samuel Moore House*, built in 1715.

At 5.9 *m.* is the *Congregational Church* (L) (1802) which still has in its pos-session the two communion beakers presented by Governor Roger Wol-cott. Governor Wolcott (1679–1767), was born in a section of Windsor so isolated that the danger of prowling Indians made it impossible for him to attend school. Self-educated, he moved at the age of 21 to the section that is now South Windsor and ten years later was chosen representative to the General Assembly, entering on a brilliant legal, military, and political career that culminated in the governorship. His son, Oliver, who was born here but later moved to Litchfield, was one of the signers of the Declaration of Independence. At Bus Station 49 is the *Site of the Governor Roger Wolcott House.*

The *Terry House,* a small white gambrel-roofed structure (L), near Bus Station 50, was the home of Eli Terry (*see Industry and Commerce*) when he worked in the Daniel Burnap clock shop (after 1780). He operated his own shop therein in 1792–93.

At 6.9 *m.* (R) is the *Site of the Birthplace of Jonathan Edwards (see below).* A sign beside the highway designates the spot, near a large two-story brick house set back from the road.

Partly concealed by giant elms is (R) the newly shingled *Strong House,* at 7 *m.,* that was built in 1698. A modernization about 1750 added three good entrances of the rose and fluted pilaster type popular in this part of the valley.

Opposite the Strong House, at Bus Station 51, is the intersection with River Rd.

Left on River Rd. to the *Podunk Indian Burial Ground,* 0.8 *m.,* at one of the largest Indian camp sites in Connecticut. A three-minute walk through the field (L) leads to a grass-grown mound where a 'No Trespassing' sign now stands. (*Permission to enter the field may be secured from the owner*). Covered by brush and vines this burial ground is difficult to locate, especially in summer when crops in the fields hide it from view.

At Bus Station 52½ is the old *Cemetery* with graves of the Rev. Timothy Edwards (1669–1758), first pastor of the Congregational Church, who preached here for 63 years, and his wife. The memorial gateway at the entrance was erected by the Colonial Dames, in memory of the Rev. Timothy and Mrs. Edwards and their distinguished son, the Rev. Jonathan Edwards (1703–58), noted theologian and metaphysician, whose impassioned sermons, while pastor of the Northampton, Mass., Congregational Church, inspired the 'Great Awakening' of 1734–35.

At Bus Station 54 stands (L) the large white *House* that was built by Ebenezer Grant (1757), credited with having the very best doorway in the State. There is a robust, almost Jacobean flavor about it, combined with Georgian sophistication and grace. The unusual panels, the broken scroll pediment with a flame finial in the center, the latches, the elaborated window heads, all unite to give the house distinction in spite of its rather awkward lines. The door on the south side is simpler but as well designed as that on the front. The ell is 17th century.

Between Bus Stations 55 and 56 stands (R) the mellowed salt-box *Captain May House* (1780), now a workshop. The newel of its staircase is formed of four twisted columns, all carved from one piece. Next beyond

(R), is the *Barry House*, built about 1780, with a high hip roof; it has its original dormer windows. The ell of this house is one of Windsor's oldest buildings (about 1690) — a small, narrow, two-and-one-half-storied structure with a framed overhang of 17th-century construction.

At Bus Station 56 is the *Site of the Theological Institute of Connecticut* (R), later the *Hartford Seminary*. The brick chapel (1834) with a two-story portico was incorporated (1936) into a new high school building. Across the street is the *President's House* (1835), now a tea room, a dignified brick structure with a portico of fluted Doric columns supporting a huge entablature adorned with giant triglyphs.

At 8 *m.* is the village of EAST WINDSOR HILL, a community extending on one street that runs along a ridge from which broad, rolling fields stretch westward to the river's edge.

At Bus Station 59 (R), stands the village's most pretentious old mansion, the *Watson-Bancroft House*, built in 1785. This ancient imposing three-story structure represents a climax of the Colonial impulse, a type more akin to Salem and Newburyport houses than to those of Connecticut. The barn across the street and other outbuildings all are in keeping. However, the style is too formalized and is applied so evenly to residence and shed alike that it has lost its spontaneity and appeal. In the elegant detail only does the Bancroft House achieve distinction.

Crossing the Scantic River at 8.3 *m.*, US 5 proceeds through the tobacco township of East Windsor, which, in proportion to its size, has more land under cultivation than any other town in the State. Originally an Indian battlefield of the Mohawk and Podunk Wars, this region was used for pasturage and hay fields by the Windsor settlers until the end of King Philip's War (1676) made it safe for permanent settlement. At that time Windsor included the territory now occupied by the towns of Ellington, South Windsor, and East Windsor. Because of the difficulty of crossing the river, a separate parish was organized in 1695, and in 1768 East Windsor became a separate town. Many local men served in the expedition against Louisburg in 1745 and later emigrated with their families to Nova Scotia.

Since 1901, when shade-grown tobacco was introduced here, cultivating, packing, and sorting the leaf have been the town's principal industries, although some manufacturing is carried on in the small scattered communities.

Broad, level tobacco fields stretch out on either side of US 5 through a region renowned as the heart of the wrapper-leaf tobacco-producing industry. In the spring the tobacco plants are started in cold frames and brought to fair size under glass. The fields are carefully prepared, harrowed smooth as the chocolate frosting on a cake, and marked in geometric patterns so that the rows can be cultivated two ways, either lengthwise or across the field. Tobacco 'setting,' the transplanting of the plants to the fields, is done with a two-wheeled combination drill and water cart, behind which two men ride on small seats. These men, holding 'flats' or trays of plants on their knees, drop a plant every time an indicator 'ticks,' and regulate the flow of water and fertilizer into the drills. In late August and September when the rich aroma of the leaf fills the air, hundreds of men and women work swiftly, harvesting and curing the crop.

At 12.2 *m.* is the junction with State 20.

Left on State 20 to the little village of WAREHOUSE POINT (Town of East Windsor), 1.2 *m.*, named for the warehouse erected here in 1636 for the transfer of freight around the Enfield Rapids. Sailing vessels seldom attempted to navigate the river above Hartford. There the cargoes were transferred to flat boats of from 10 to 18 tons. As scows larger than 12 tons could not be poled up the rapids, their cargoes were unloaded at Warehouse Point and the freight transferred to oxcarts, hauled to Thompsonville, reloaded on flat boats and poled to Springfield.

On the main street of this tiny settlement are several buildings of the early Federal period.

At the Green is the junction with Bridge St.

Left on Bridge St. 0.2 *m.* to Water St., an attractive road that parallels the river. Here are a group of small houses reminiscent of a coastal fishing village. This drive offers a fine view of the Connecticut River. Across, on the opposite bank, are the paper and silk mills of Windsor Locks (*see Tour 8*).

At 2.7 *m.* State 20 rejoins and unites with US 5 for 3.5 miles.

US 5 follows wide Enfield St., flanked on either side by the long, narrow, elm-shaded Green of the neat and prosperous village of ENFIELD (alt. 50, town pop. 13,404), 16.8 *m.*, named for Enfield in Middlesex, England, and noted as the headquarters of the Enfield Society for the Detection of Horse Thieves and Robbers. The Society was founded 113 years ago, has a roster of 300 members, keeps $500 in the treasury at all times 'for readiness in the pursuit of thieves when called upon,' and has been a force for law and order throughout northern Connecticut. Bylaws provide that the 'pursuers' must keep a swift horse saddled and bridled, ready for immediate use in the event of an emergency. This regulation is still respected and the present emergency picket line is located in the village coal yard, where a patient beast awaits the call to action.

A memorial boulder (L) marks the *Site of the Church in which Jonathan Edwards Preached* his famous sermon 'Sinners in the Hands of an Angry God' (1741), in which he depicted God as dangling sinners over the searing flames of hell fire, and thus gave new impetus to the Great Awakening, a revival that swept from New England through Pennsylvania to the southern Colonies.

Beyond the boulder (R), is the monumental *Orrin Thompson House*, built in 1832, a dignified red-brick mansion surmounted by a balustrade and cupola, with symmetrical colonnaded wings, situated on a spacious lawn with fine trees. The estate is now a novitiate of Polish Nuns.

The old *Town Hall* (L), built in 1775 but later remodeled, with a simple Greek Revival portico, was formerly the third Congregational Church edifice, where, in the year of its building, a Sunday service was abruptly interrupted by Captain Thomas Abbey, who marched around the meeting house beating his drum to announce that a battle had been fought with the British Regulars at Lexington.

Opposite this building, in a small park fronting the lawn of the present church, is an impressive *Memorial To Captain Abbey*. On the marble seats encircling the monument is carved the genealogy of many of the first families who settled in the community. The present *Congregational Church* (1848) has been the subject of much debate. At the time it was built, the Greek Revival was copying classical forms very carefully, but spires were not a part of the original Greek concept. While the huge door and heavy columns are accurate copies, they are incongruously combined with a steeple that is absurdly out of proportion.

At 17.8 *m.* State 20 branches to the right.

At 18.4 *m.* the highway runs through the eastern outskirts of Thompsonville, to the junction with N. Main St.

Left on N. Main St. to Church St., where are the public and administrative buildings of the town.

THOMPSONVILLE (alt. 100, Town of Enfield), 0.3 *m.*, is a manufacturing village close by the river's edge. Here, before the opening of the Enfield Canal in 1829, the down-river freight was transferred to flatboats to be guided over the dangerous Enfield Rapids by experienced polemen.

Agriculture was the principal occupation of the town until 1828, when Orrin Thompson, from whom the community took its name, established a carpet factory, importing skilled workmen from Scotland. Showrooms along Main St. offer the finest domestic rugs and their windows are gay with beautiful patterns and colors. Settled under the jurisdiction of Massachusetts through the error of surveyors in 1642, Enfield was one of the 'indented' areas not annexed to Connecticut until 1749.

Passing the *Enfield Public Golf Course* (18 holes), at 19.3 *m.* (R), US 5 enters Massachusetts at 20.4 *m.*, 6 miles south of Springfield.

T O U R   7 A :   *From* NEW HAVEN *to* MIDDLETOWN, 24.6 *m.*, State 15.

Via Durham.

Cement and macadamized highway.

Limited accommodations.

CROSSING salt flats of the lower Quinnipiac River, this route traverses market-gardening acreage and sleepy little crossroads settlements where Yankees still live very much as their forefathers did. Along the way, almost hidden by streamside alderbushes, are the remains of old mills, water lily pads usurping the placid surface of their ponds. Back from the roads, natives gather brush for the rural witch-hazel distilleries; and hunters chase fox or search out the pheasant from sumach or juniper thicket. Orchards spread back over the low rolling hills. And, of course, there are the inevitable evidences of modern enterprise: the antique shop sign swinging from a maple tree in front of a red barn, and the tea room in an unmistakably old house.

Leaving the Green in New Haven on Church St., which becomes Whitney Ave., State 15 turns right on Edwards St., left on State St., and right over a bridge, at 2.1 *m.*

At 4.3 *m.* the *Sleeping Giant* — rolling hills that resemble a prostrate form — can be seen in the middle distance.

At 4.5 *m.*, in the Montowese District, US 5 branches to the left, and State 15 bears right.

At 8.5 *m.* there are excellent views (L) of the surrounding countryside, just before the highway passes between banks of red clay.

At 8.8 *m.* on a lane (R), beside the site of an old toll gate, is the *Rising Sun Tavern* (about 1760), a tea room in a well-preserved red house with end chimneys and an overhang at both stories. Its original double doors are still intact.

At 9.8 *m.* State 15 passes NORTHFORD (L), and a general store (R). Many well-kept old houses cluster about this Green, evidence of the former prosperity of this crossroads settlement. Opposite the Green (R) is the *Rev. Warham Williams House* (parish house of the Episcopal Church), a very steep-roofed and largely unspoiled 18th-century house (1750) with a doorway surmounted by a broken pediment, a rarity in Connecticut.

Left from Northford on State 168 to the crossroads hamlet of CLINTONVILLE, 2 *m.* In the back country of this area, especially in Clintonville (Northford Station), numerous backyard, or domestic factory industries were of considerable interest and economic importance. David S. Stevens, Jr., and Henry Stevens started a business card plant here in 1867, later manufacturing valentines, and then 'sparking' cards that rural swains once used in pursuit of the fair sex; finally, local talent was engaged to tint Christmas cards. The work was usually done at home and the busy little company garnered many dollars, employed many women and children, fostered no less than twenty-five similar concerns, and gained the title 'Christmas card center of America.' It failed to hold its own against the competition of greeting card manufacturers throughout the country. When the new railroad route skipped Northford entirely, the community's day in the sun was closed.

At 11.5 *m.* is the large red *Daniel Lindsley House* (R), a salt-box dwelling built in 1750. The structure has a much steeper pitch to its roof than is usual in this section. Its door is modern.

At 11.6 *m.* stands the *Linsley* or *Howd House* (1680–1700), an added lean-to salt-box house, with a deep overhang, beside a sign that reads '*Sol's Path.*' As in other early houses, the transverse girts protrude and form cornice brackets. The house and great barn are used as tea rooms. According to tradition, Solomon, a Negro with an Indian wife, one-time herder of cattle from the shore towns, passed this way as he sought pasturage inland, and established a path across the hill known as Totoket Mountain.

At 12.3 *m.* (L) are extensive apple and peach orchards.

At 17.5 *m.* flat marshy fields stretch away from the road. A witch-hazel distillery in the field (R) marks the northernmost limits of the part-time Connecticut industry that converts the brush of the swampy coastal forests into a highly prized household remedy.

DURHAM (alt. 200, town pop. 1044), 18.2 *m.*, known to the Indians as Cogingchaug, or Long Swamp, was settled in 1699, and named for Durham in England in 1704. An animated quarrel between two groups of church folk who built themselves separate churches ended dramatically. In their rivalry, each congregation endeavored to build a taller spire than the other, even borrowing money for the purpose. The South Church won; but its steeple was built to such a height that a heavy wind in 1842 toppled it. According to the story the wind raised the spire into the air, turned it upside down and dropped it point first into the roof where it remained for some time, a warning to all congregations who were inclined to pretentiousness.

A 4–H Club Fair is held in Durham every autumn.

The Durham soil is moist, and drainage is a problem; but one wealthy farmer tills more than 1000 acres, keeps a fine stable and holds fox hunts in season. A pair of Durham oxen, driven overland to Valley Forge, once furnished a meal for all the officers of the Continental Army and their servants.

Moses Austin (1761–1821), Durham miner and adventurer, obtained a grant of land in Missouri from France in 1798, and at St. Genevieve, established the first lead mine west of the Mississippi. Later he became the promoter of the American colonization of Texas. The necessary land grants were not made until 1821, the year of his death, but his plans were carried out by his son, Stephen, for whom Austin, the capital of Texas, was named.

From the shaded *Durham Green* there are fine western views of rounded wooded hills.

The *Rev. Elizur Goodrich House* (R), which was built in 1763, has an elaborately moulded door, graduated clapboards, and a double overhang, features of the better homes of the century.

The *Chauncey House* (*private*), on Fowler Ave. (R), just off the main street, was built in 1755 by the son of the Rev. Nathaniel Chauncey, the town's first minister and the first graduate of Yale College. His diploma is now in the possession of the present owner, a direct descendant. The *Town Hall* (L) and the *Methodist Church* (R), built in 1836, are separated by the long Green.

At 18.4 *m.* is an *Old Cemetery* in a picturesque setting. A mossy *Milldam* (R) forms a pond that glistens under the willows.

At 18.5 *m.* is the *Durham Public School* (R), a brick building set well back from the road.

At 18.7 *m.* a road (L) leads into the Hunt Country. 'The Watertown Hounds' run here once a year. Few wire fences are stretched through this area; stone walls and wooden rail fences offer safe hurdles for the riders.

The highway passes the unshaded *Dooley Pond* (R), at 19.6 *m.*

At 23.3 *m.* are old *Brick Mills* that once utilized the power of the Falls (L).

At 23.6 *m. Pameachea Lake* (L) stretches away at the edge of the highway, on the outskirts of Middletown.

At MIDDLETOWN, 24.6 *m.* (*see MIDDLETOWN*), is the junction with State 9 (*see Tour* 8) and State 14 (*see Tour* 2 *ALT.*).

T O U R   7 B :   *From* HARTFORD *to* MERIDEN, 19.8 *m.*, State 175 and State 71.

Via Newington, New Britain, Kensington.
Macadamized roadbed.
Limited accommodations.

THIS route passes through a pleasant countryside and several old settlements off the main highways.

State 175 branches south from Hartford, following New Britain Ave. to the *Balf Quarries* (*no admittance; dynamiting*) at 4.8 *m.* (L), which extend along the traprock ledge of Cedar Mountain.

Bearing left at 5.4 *m.*, on Main St., State 175 passes through NEWINGTON CENTER (alt. 100, town pop. 4,572), 6.4 *m.*, a residential suburb of Hartford, in an attractive, verdant setting. Settled in 1670 by residents of Wethersfield, this community, with a population of 467 in 1776, sent 100 soldiers, practically every able-bodied man, to service in the Continental Army. Captain Roger Welles, who commanded a company at the surrender of Cornwallis, was presented with a sword by Lafayette in recognition of his valor. The *Welles House* (1866), a square, brick, flat-roofed building, was the home of his descendant, Rear Admiral Roger Welles (1862–1932), who was Director of Naval Intelligence during the World War. It stands at the northwest corner of Main and Cedar Sts., facing the small Green.

Opposite this homestead is the *Church of Christ* (1797), one of the oldest Congregational structures in the State; its original lines have been considerably changed.

Opposite the church on Main St., is the *Town Hall*, housing the public library, established here in 1750, one of the first public libraries in the State.

State 175 turns abruptly right on Cedar St., passing the oldest cemetery in the town, in the rear of the Congregational Church. Here is the *Grave of Captain Martin Kellogg*, who, in his youth, was captured with the rest of his family in Deerfield, Massachusetts, and taken to Canada, where, it is said, his sister married an Indian chief. While a prisoner, Kellogg gained an intimate knowledge of tribal languages and customs that later enabled him to become an emissary of inestimable value to the Colony.

A handsome boulder of quartz and flint occupying a prominent position in the cemetery was dedicated in 1925 as a memorial to Newington veterans of all wars who rest in unmarked graves.

1. Left from the center of the village on Cedar St. is the *Newington Home for Crippled Children* (R), 0.5 *m.*, founded in 1898 by the Connecticut Children's Aid Society. The main building, erected in 1930, was dedicated by Franklin D. Roosevelt, then Governor of New York. Here, in comfortable, pleasant surroundings, crippled, deformed, and chronically ill children are cared for. Those who are able assist in the upkeep of the buildings and gardens. Classes up to and including the first year of high school are maintained.

Left from Cedar St. at the summit of the incline, on Russell Rd. to *Cedarcrest*, a State tuberculosis sanatorium, which extends over the rolling hilltop, an attractive, healthful location and a fine vantage-point for views.

2. Left on Mill St., at the triangular park, is the historic *Mill Pond*, with a natural rock dam, which was used as the main water supply of the Wangunk Indians who long continued to pitch their tents here in the midst of the colonial settlement.

3. Right on Willard St. (west side of the triangle), is the entrance to the *U.S. Veterans' Hospital*, 1.5 *m.*, which provides care and treatment for veterans from the New England states.

4. Left on Willard St. and R. on Robbins Ave. is the entrance to *Golf Club Heights*, 1.6 *m.*, occupied by the Indian Hill and Sequin Golf Clubs.

State 175 passes through the outskirts of New Britain, where there is no congestion of traffic, turning (L) onto Stanley St. (State 71), at 10.3 *m.*

Right on Stanley St.; right on Hartford Ave.; right on E. Main St., and left on Main St., to the business center of NEW BRITAIN (alt. 180, town pop. 68,128), 1.3 *m.*, an industrial center (*see NEW BRITAIN*).

On State 71 (R), at 10.9 *m.*, is the *Willow Brook Park*, a New Britain municipal park. Crossing through the section known as *Berlin Station*, 11.2 *m.*, State 71 reaches KENSINGTON (alt. 220), 11.4 *m.*, the oldest settlement in the town of Berlin (1686). At the center, on Percival Rd. (State 71), shaded by a large oak tree stands the *Congregational Church* (R), built in 1774, a good example of the New England meeting-house, though it has lost some of its character through modernization. Here the first organ in a New England church was installed to the consternation of many members who looked askance at such frivolous innovations. Nearby is a simple, dignified marble shaft, probably the first monument in the country erected as a memorial to Civil War soldiers; it was dedicated July 25, 1863, almost two years before the cessation of hostilities. Below the church (L), at 12.8 *m.*, is a salt-box house (1789), the *Home of Dr. James Percival*, the gifted and versatile poet, geologist, surgeon and linguist (1795–1856) who assisted Webster in preparing his dictionary for publication. One room retains its original open framework and unpainted 18th-century pine paneling.

Some of the earliest houses were built on the eastern side of the town in the vicinity of Christian Lane which runs north from State 71. These include the *Hannah Root Salt-Box House* (1712), and the *Jacob Deming House* (1717), with cross-panel doors, both on Christian Lane, and the brick *Rev. Samuel Clark House* (1759), on the west side of Burnham St. The Clark House, on a river bank, with its foreground of old gardens and background of towering elms, is to Connecticut what the James River plantations are to Virginia.

At 15.3 *m.* is the intersection with a dirt road.

> Left on this road to the *Berlin State Fish Hatchery* (*open 8–5; adm. free*), where trout and fresh-water fish are seen in various stages of development.

The highway, with an excellent view of *Ragged Mountain* on the western boundary between Berlin and Southington, at 16.1 *m.*, runs through the scenic *Cathole Pass*, where a cliff (L) resembled the profile of George Washington until roisterers broke off a section of rock that formed the nose.

At 17.8 *m.* (L), is *Undercliff Sanatorium*, one of the oldest institutions in the United States for the care of tubercular children.

> Right off the sanatorium driveway, a path leads to *Cold Spring* at the site chosen for his farm by Jonathan Gilbert, the town's first landowner. Up a little canyon beyond the spring (R) is a *Natural Ice House*, a small rock cavern in which ice remains most of the year.

At 19.8 *m.* is the intersection with State 14 (*see Tour 2 Alt.*) 0.7 mile west of Meriden (*see MERIDEN*), in which is the junction with US 5 (*see Tour 7*).

TOUR 8 : *From* OLD SAYBROOK *to* MASSACHUSETTS LINE (*Springfield*), 62.2 *m.*, State 9 and US 5A.

Via (*sec. a*) Essex, Haddam, Middletown, Cromwell, Rocky Hill, Hartford; (*sec. b*) Windsor, Windsor Locks, Suffield.

Local and interstate busses travel the route between Middletown and the Massachusetts Line. The N.Y., N.H., & H. R.R. parallels the route.

Concrete highway with short stretches of macadamized road.

Excellent accommodations of all types.

Sec. a.　OLD SAYBROOK to HARTFORD, 41.2 *m.*, State 9.

FROM Old Saybrook, this route traverses a wooded area to Essex.

Beyond Essex the highway, State 9, leads close to the Connecticut River past very old towns where shad fisherfolk haul their nets as they have for almost three centuries, where shipyards once launched sturdy craft of native oak that sailed for the West Indies with cargoes of onions, staves, cattle and other products from the back country. At the confluence with the Salmon River below Haddam, the Connecticut River flows from the narrows southeast of Middletown. The route follows the broad Main Street of Middletown which appears more like a mid-western town than a New England community. North of Middletown the highway enters a residential and market-gardening area, passing the largest greenhouse and cut-flower plant in central Connecticut at Cromwell. Through the peaceful countryside of Rocky Hill and Wethersfield this route proceeds over straight, good roads to Hartford.

Leaving US 1 (*see Tour 1*) at Old Saybrook this route follows State 9 to the junction with State 9A at 1.7 *m.*

Right on State 9A is the junction with a side road, 0.6 *m.*

Left on this road to an old landing, 1 *m.*, the *Site of David Bushnell's Experiments* with his invention, the first submarine torpedo boat in the world (1775).

Born in Westbrook, Mr. Bushnell first experimented with explosives under water. Filling a wooden container with gunpowder, he submerged it in a few feet of water, weighted down by a hogshead of stone. Lighting the fuse, Bushnell saw such havoc created that he was encouraged to proceed with the construction of an undersea boat for naval use. The 'American Turtle,' an oaken craft not unlike a barrel, consisting of two concave hulls joined together, was the result. This strange craft, 8 feet long and 7 feet wide, just large enough for one man, was propelled by paddle wheels operated by a treadle. The supply of air was sufficient for the one-man crew on a 30-minute voyage, but an air intake valve could be used when the decks were awash. There was, of course, no interior lighting; Benjamin Franklin suggested that Bushnell use phosphorus for illumination, quite unaware of its effect on the bones. The midget craft carried a charge of 150 pounds of gunpowder which it was hoped would blow up an enemy ship. The charge was carried in two oaken tubes on a platform aft of the rudder. The detonating mechanism was provided by two ordinary gunlocks operated by clockwork that served as a crude time fuse.

Bushnell held successful trials off Saybrook in 1775, was roundly cheered for his daring, congratulated by Government officials and offered the honor of experimenting on the British fleet then anchored in New York Harbor. After nightfall on September 6, 1776, the 'Turtle' was towed by a whaleboat crew to as near the British flagship 'Eagle' as they dared approach. The 'Turtle' was cast off and submerged to make the attack. Unfortunately, Bushnell's brother, who was to have manned the boat, was ill at the time, and a Sergeant Lee, who substituted for him, was not thoroughly familiar with its operation. He was unable to make contact with the hull of the ship, and, finally, fearing to blow himself up, cut loose the oaken tubes and paddled frantically for shore. The explosion did no damage. The trial had failed, but public attention had been awakened to the possibilities of undersea warfare.

At 2.7 *m.* (R) stands the *William Bower House* (1720). Succeeding generations of carpenters have 'improved' this dwelling until little that is typical of its age remains, with the exception of large flaring corner posts, old ovens both upstairs and down, and the unmistakable proportions of an early house.

At 3.4 *m.*, across the meadows, to the right of the highway, is *South Cove.*

At 4 *m.* is the junction with an asphalt road.

Right on this road is the *Pratt Smithy*, 0.6 *m.* (L), established in 1678, which has been handed down from father to eldest son for eight generations, and is the oldest business in the country to be continuously conducted by the same family. The ivy-clad smithy stands on the site of the early wooden structure that was torn down in the middle of the 18th century. The *Smith's House*, second to the west of it, has an ell said to have been the homestead of the founder, John Pratt (1679). As the town flourished with its Colonial shipbuilding and West Indies trade, the smithy prospered and a larger, more elaborate house was added to the older one, with handsomely paneled rooms, corner cupboards, and well-designed hinges and latches wrought by the smith himself.

Near-by lived Phineas and Abel Pratt, father and son, who invented the first successful machine for cutting comb teeth and who here produced combs in 1799.

ESSEX (alt. 40, town pop. 2777), 0.8 *m.*, a river town of old Connecticut, which reached the height of its shipbuilding prosperity about 1840, remains little changed through the years, despite the growing number of summer residents. The houses of sea captains line Main St., leading down to the landing-place. The long rope-walk, once busy outfitting the many vessels built here, has long since gone, but pleasure craft are still built at the boat yards and sail lofts are redolent with aromatic hemp.

Settled in 1690 by residents of Old Saybrook who were attracted to this area by the excellent agricultural prospects offered by the sandy river plain, Essex was incorporated in May, 1852. The 'Oliver Cromwell,' commanded by Commodore Theophilus Morgan, and mounting 24 guns, was launched here in 1775 for the Colony of Connecticut; it was soon transferred to national service. During the War of 1812, Essex's importance as a center of maritime trade marked the town for an attack by the British. Sailing up the river on April 8, 1814, the invaders raided the yards in the Middle and North Coves and burned 40 ships. Among the many ships laid down in local yards, the largest was the 'Middlesex,' 1400 tons, which was launched in 1851.

At the center is the *Osage Inn* (R), a summer hotel, named for the ship 'Osage,' which was burned to the water's edge during the British raid in 1814. For many years the charred ribs of the rotting hull lay near the shore at North Cove. Recently the chestnut timbers were salvaged by residents, who now occasionally offer for sale a chair or some other small piece of furniture made from the old ship.

Ye Old Griswold Inn (R), 48 Main St., 1 *m.*, erected in 1776, has been a tavern for more than 150 years since it was first kept by Ethan Bushnell. Diagonally across the street, surrounded by giant maples and a white picket fence, is the dignified *Captain Lewis House* (1760 or later), a large two-and-a-half-story dwelling with a well-designed entrance. Above the doorway, which is flanked by fluted pilasters and has a delicately leaded fan-light, a Palladian window carries out the lines of the door and entrance frame. In the rear of the house the old fashioned garden of the prosperous sea captain still perfumes the air with a spicy odor of mignonette, rosemary, and lemon verbena.

The last house on the right is the former *Hayden Tavern* (1766). The building, a two-story and basement, white clapboarded house with a broad porch, is now occupied by the Dauntless Club. On the door is a fine old knocker and a hand-wrought latch made many years ago at the Pratt Smithy. Uriah Hayden, original owner of the tavern, one of the leading shipbuilders and merchants of his day, was the builder of the ship 'Oliver Cromwell.' His warehouse on the river, close by, filled with sugar, molasses and tobacco brought in by the West Indian trading vessels, sent goods by river boat and overland carts to inland villages. The old tavern sign, said to have been made in England, bears a picture of a full-rigged ship and the legend '*U* and *A* 1776,' the initials standing for Uriah and Ann Hayden.

The house nearest the river on the right, locally known as *The Beehive*, was built in 1730 by Robert Lay, a prosperous West Indies merchant. The exterior of this old, peaked-roof, two-and-a-half-story house has been altered by renovations, but within are elaborately carved mantels and fine paneling.

Here, along the river front are boat docks, marine railways, and gasoline pumps. In summer, young people, gay in sport clothes, are busy with boats and fishing tackle at the landing place that once swarmed with dark-skinned men of the sea, unloading elephant tusks for the ivory shops and molasses barrels heavy with amber syrup from Cuban cane. The fumes of gasoline replace the pungent tar and the sharp odor of rum; the chug of motorboats takes the place of chanteys and the creak of gear from schooners in the West Indian trade making ready to sail.

Ely's Ferry to Hamburg (*see Tour 1E*) can be boarded at this point; excellent service is maintained by a new gleaming white craft with a tri-colored stripe at the waterline.

At 4.3 *m.* is the red *Factory of the E. E. Dickinson Company* (L), one of the world's largest distillers of witch-hazel, whose bright blue barrel heads are seen in medicinal warehouses around the globe.

At 4.8 *m.* is the junction with State 144; a *Congregational Church* of 1790 stands at the crossroads.

Left on State 144 is the village of IVORYTON (Town of Essex), 1 *m.*, a community that clusters around the former *Comstock-Cheney and Company Plant*, a piano-action concern that at one time used so much ivory that the scrap from the great mills was shipped to Japan to be carved into novelties. This concern did not survive the depression. A recent merger has been completed between this firm and the Pratt Read Company of Deep River. The summer *Repertory Theater* in Ivoryton presents plays with casts of New York professionals.

DEEP RIVER (alt. 60, town pop. 2381) (Town of Saybrook), 7.3 *m.*, was formerly in the township called Old Saybrook and was first settled by white men from the parent Colony between 1663 and 1700. Locally the town is called by the name of its center, Deep River, to avoid confusion with Old Saybrook which is usually called 'Saybrook.' The town had been known at different times as Eight-Mile Meadow and Potopaug Quarter.

In 1809, Phineas Pratt employed about 20 artisans in the production of handmade combs, and the present piano-action *Factory of the Pratt Read Company* (*open on application at office*), established in 1866, is a direct outgrowth and development of the comb shop. Ivory is imported from Kenya Colony of British East Africa, and from Zanzibar, which produces the best grades of ivory for piano keys. At the factory the ivory is cut from the tusks and is then bleached in glass-covered frames that look very much like ordinary hotbeds. The sunlight bleaching process assures a uniformity of color and texture in the finished keyboard that cannot be secured in any other way. The ivory strips are cemented into place on carefully selected and machined wood, then the completed keyboard is cut into proper shape for piano keys, and the black keys are fitted into place. During the depression this organization made small boats to keep their woodworkers busy. Alive to changes in their industry and in styles, the Pratt Read Company is now busy on the production of small piano actions.

At Deep River is the junction (L) with State 80 (*see Tour 1D*).

At 9 *m.*, high on a crag, diagonally across the river (R) is the piled-up masonry of the *William Gillette Castle* (*see Tour* 1*D*), the model of a Rhineland castle adapted to the Connecticut hills for that whimsical actor (1855–1937). The stone blends well with the browns and grays of the hilltop, and only the skyline silhouette makes the passer-by aware of the great castle standing, sentinel-like, above the waters.

At 9.2 *m.* is the junction with State 148.

1. Left on State 148 is CHESTER (alt. 80, town pop. 1463), 0.9 *m.* 'Originally the Pattaconk Quarter of Saybrook, the town of Chester was settled about 1690; the parish was named and set aside in 1740, and the town incorporated in 1836. Later a small part of the area was re-annexed to Saybrook.

Chester young people introduced a style of singing in church that is mentioned in histories as 'newfangled.' The lack of harmony between these young voices and the voices of their elders is typical of the stormy character of the entire parish.

Russell Jennings, an early preacher (1800), invented the first extension bit in America and laid the foundation for a business that still makes bits, that find a ready market anywhere in the world. Despairing of making an impression on the hardheaded, quarrelsome churchfolk of his parish, the Rev. Mr. Jennings turned inventor with more satisfactory results.

Round brushes are also made in Chester; a factory on the brook turns out tool handles of native hickory and ash, and another mill produces manicure sets of gaudy hues and odd shapes. Needles and novelties are made in the town, as are bright wire goods and many hundred gross of bits annually; nail sets and augers are forged and packed along Deep Hollow Brook that drains Hoophole Hill, Hearse House Hill, and Flute Hill.

Shipbuilding once flourished here. Governor Winthrop obtained a water-power right in the area and precipitated the first of several boundary disputes between Chester and the neighboring parishes and towns. At one time large numbers of sheep were raised here and often came during services to the square in front of the church, where they set up such a bleating that men had to drive them off.

The marshes blaze with color and resound to the boom of the duck hunter's gun; a fish peddler hawks 'Shad, fresh shad!' as a fat tomcat follows his wagon along the quiet Main Street and purrs with anticipation.

Granite was an important building stone in Chester. The most conspicuous building at the center is the *Old Stone Store* (R), built about 1809, now a beer parlor. The building has fluted stone pillars and more the appearance of a church or a bank than a tavern. The *Stone Hotel* (R) was built in the same year. Two old millstones are used as the steps of the *Chester Savings Bank* (R).

2. Right at the junction with 148 to the old *Chester Ferry* (*see Side Trip from Tour* 1*D*) which still crosses the river for customers at the signal of a motorist's horn (7 A.M. *to* 7 P.M.; 25¢ *for car and driver,* 5¢ *each additional passenger*).

From 10.6 *m.* to 11.3 *m.* the highway travels close to the river with many views of the broad stream and the rolling wooded ridges along its eastern bank.

At 11.6 *m.* is the junction with State 82 (*see Tour* 1*D*) in the tiny side-of-the-road settlement of TYLERVILLE (Town of Haddam).

At 12.6 *m.* is a junction with a dirt road.

Right on this road to the *Adventist Camp Ground,* 0.8 *m.,* a settlement of cottages grouped on the bank of the Connecticut River.

At 13 *m.* there are beautiful views across the Connecticut River (R) to the mouth of the Salmon River, which flows into the larger stream around the end of Thirty Mile Island. Shad run up Salmon River to the first dam, where they are taken with flies. Here the State maintains a hatchery.

At 14.2 *m*. State 9 passes through SHAILERVILLE, a rather drab little village, where the 'New Lights,' or 'Separatists,' as they were first termed, formed the *Baptist Church* (R) of Shailerville. This section was formerly the 'Lower Plantation' of 'The Plantation of Thirty-Mile Island,' as Haddam was known in the older records. The town mill was once operated here in a gloomy dell beside a stream.

HADDAM (alt. 200, town pop. 1755), 15.2 *m*., chief center of the only town in the State bisected by the Connecticut River, was, according to local tradition, purchased from the Indians for thirty coats. Surrounded by wooded hills, the quiet village, back from the river front, still retains an atmosphere of early fishing and seafaring days. Nets drying in the sun and signs reading, 'Shad for sale,' are reminders of the days when the village was the center of extensive salmon and shad fisheries. Shad, salted, smoked, pickled and served fresh, was a staple food in this region. Farmhands tiring of the diet, often specified in their contracts that shad was not to be served to them more than five times per week. In years when the shad run was especially large, Connecticut roads were often crowded with fish peddlers' carts, hurrying to their home towns where they made the welkin ring with blasts on their tin horns and shouts of 'Fresh shad for sale.'

Shad were often used for fertilizer; many a good crop was raised as a result of 'a fish in every hill of corn,' a practice learned from the Indians. The present-day run of shad is not very large, although limits placed on the catch may increase the future haul.

According to a legend of the local Indians the Shad Spirit yearly led the shad from the Gulf of Mexico to the Connecticut River.

The *Haddam Jail* (L) is a forbidding gray-granite building presided over by Sheriff 'Bert' Thompson, the most genial jailer in the Northeast. The handling of prisoners here has reached the psychologist's ideal. Prisoners work in the garden, cut wood in near-by timberland, enjoy freedom unusual in such institutions. Haddam was once a joint county seat, and the jail and county home are survivals of that day.

Northward is the *Congregational Church*, built in 1847, where the Rev. David Field was pastor. In this town were born United States Supreme Court Justice Stephen J. Field (1816–99), and David Dudley Field (1805–94), the eminent jurist whose reforms of the legal system of New York State were the basis of legal reform in many States and in the British Empire; Field also defended Boss Tweed at his famous trial. Near-by is the *Town Hall* (L), a large, gray-granite building, formerly the Brainerd Academy (1839). Remodeled in 1930 as a gift to the town by the Hazen Foundation, with a well-designed Doric portico, this building also houses the local Masonic Lodge. In front of it stands the big gambrel-roofed *Golden Ball Tavern*, one of the comparatively few 18th-century taverns left in Connecticut.

At 15.2 *m.* is the junction with a dirt road.

Left from Haddam village on a dirt road through the meadowland of the *Edward W. Hazen Foundation*, is a small gambrel-roofed house that now serves as an office. The Hazen Foundation, with resources of $2,000,000 ledger value, supports a varied educational program in the fields of forestry, social action, child welfare, medicine, and public health.

At 16.4 *m. Rock Landing*, across the river (R), is visible. Stone from near-by quarries, at one time much in demand for harbor improvements along the Sound, was loaded onto boats here at the ledge, which formed a natural wharf.

From 17 *m.* to 17.2 *m.* there are delightful river views (R), as the highway runs parallel to the Connecticut. Shad can still be purchased here in April, May, and June, when local fisherfolk again haul the nets and tack up cardboard signs on the great trees offering 'Buck Shad 25¢, or Roe 35¢.' Old inns beside the road offer 'Boned Shad Dinners,' quite above the average, because here country cooks know more about boning shad than in any other section of the country. Along this section of the route are broad, low, gambrel-roofed houses of the better type, built from the abundant incomes of early shipbuilding and shipping enterprises. There has been little change through the years, and though 'foreigners' occupy some of the farms, the area still retains enough of the old Yankee influence to be reminiscent of early Connecticut.

HIGGANUM (Ind.: *Higganumpus*, 'fishing place') (Town of Haddam), 18 *m.*, is a crossroads rural shopping center where the Clark Cutaway Harrow is made. A local factory operated by D. and H. Scovil Company has produced planters' hoes for the Southern trade since 1844. A fabric mill produces cords and braids, using the excellent water-power of the same stream that was utilized in operating the triphammers which forged gun-barrels for Eli Whitney, New Haven armorer (*see NEW HAVEN*). Shipbuilding was once an important industry in Higganum, and shad fisheries flourished. Opposite the *Congregational Church* (1845) is the spacious and impressive *Hubbard House* (about 1800), with an open pediment porch.

At Higganum is the junction with State 81.

Left from the village on State 81, at 1.1 *m.*, is a *Witch-Hazel Distillery* (R), where this swamp shrub is converted into a lotion. Great piles of witch-hazel brush are piled beside a red wooden building from which a plume of white steam rises against the western sky. The brush is chopped into tiny pieces, steamed, and boiled in great kettles. The liquor is then distilled. This industry is the source of income to the part-time farmers on submarginal lands in eastern and southeastern Connecticut.

Traversing a beautiful woodland area, watered by clear brooks that murmur beside the road, this highway reaches the tiny crossroad hamlet of PONSET (Town of Haddam), at 2.4 *m.* Directly opposite an old district school is the *Ponset Episcopal Church* (L), built in 1877, an outgrowth of a country Sunday school class conducted by the Rev. William C. Knowles. The Rev. Mr. Knowles, who served the pastorate without pay, built the church himself with the aid of his congregation, and branded the names of the donors of each stick of timber onto the lumber before it was put into the structure. Native mills sawed the logs, local farmers turned carpenters for the job, and a church rose in the wilderness.

Any dirt road eastward from this point leads into *Cockaponset State Forest*, 9060 acres in four sections called, respectively, the Turkey Hill, Wig Hill, Cedar Swamp, and Killingworth blocks. Here, areas of typical Connecticut hardwoods have been thinned; in one block is an exceptional stand of tulip-trees, or, incorrectly, yellow poplar. The rare wicopy, or leatherwood bush, is found in this forest in Compartment 13. This bush was used by the settlers for thongs or ropes to lash various articles together as the twigs are limber and able to stand considerable twisting and tying before showing any signs of breaking.

At 19.5 *m.*, in the *Seven Falls State Highway Park* (R), a crystal-clear brook beside the road tumbles down a boulder-strewn course in a series of small cascades. Fireplaces for the preparation of outdoor meals and seats beside the brook provide facilities for picnicking in a delightful spot.

At 19.6 *m.*, just off the road, is *Bible Rock* (L), three slabs of stone that stand on edge like an open book. Directly across the road, also in the woods, is a great flat boulder known as *Shopboard Rock* (R), where, according to tradition, an early tailor cut the cloth for a suit of clothes, using the top of the rock for a table.

At 21.8 *m.* are *Mica Mines* (R) in a ledge outcropping beside the highway. At this point is the junction with a dirt road.

Right on this road, across a brook, at 1.3 *m.* Here at the brookside lead was mined in Revolutionary times. Beyond a turn by the river is an old *Quarry* (R), 2 *m.*, where many varieties of minerals have been found, and, at various times, used commercially. This road offers excellent views of the winding river, which flows at the foot of the bluff through a wild region. This route connects with State 9 in the village of Higganum, 6.5 *m.*

At 23 *m.* are delightful valley and hill views (L).

Southeast of Middletown, over a new concrete road, built to avoid the spring floods that recurred along the old highway, State 9 dips and rises across uninteresting territory.

MIDDLETOWN (alt. 50, town pop. 24,554) (*see MIDDLETOWN*), 25.6 *m.*, seat of Wesleyan University.

At Middletown are the junctions with State 15 (*see Tour 7A*) and State 14 (*see Tour 2A*).

Closely following the Connecticut River northward, the highway passes, at 27 *m.*, *Wilcox Island*, a long wooded island near the shore.

CROMWELL (alt. 40, town pop. 2814), 27.7 *m.*, on the north bank of the Mattabesset and the west bank of the Connecticut Rivers, is an agricultural and flower-growing center largely populated by Swedish farmers who have settled near the Pierson Nurseries. The early history of Cromwell is closely linked with that of Middletown, as the two settlements were made at about the same time, probably in 1650. Originally known as Upper Middletown, the town was incorporated under its present name in May, 1851. Shipbuilding was the chief early industry. William C. Redfield constructed one of the first river steamboats, the 'Oliver Cromwell,' here in 1823. A brownstone quarry in the central part of the township was once worked extensively during the late 19th century, when brownstone was in demand in New York City. Today, the J. and E. Stevens Company specializes in the manufacture of iron toys, especially pistols, for young Americans.

At the northeast corner of South and Pleasant Sts. is one of the most attractive houses of the town, a *Salt-Box* with a double overhang; various other features indicate a probable date of about 1760.

On Pleasant St. are two houses (1800) typical of Cromwell — *Half Houses*, with a pedimented door in one corner. In the second house on the north, local craftsmen have ornamented the stairs, as elsewhere in Cromwell, with almost frolicsome carvings representing dolphins.

The gambrel-roofed *Captain John Stocking House* (1743–46) stands on the west side of Pleasant St., the sixth structure south of Wall St. The stately *Manse* opposite was built by the town in 1717 for the Rev. Joseph Smith, the first local minister.

At 85 Main St. is the little low *House of Isaac Gridley*, Yale roommate of Nathan Hale; and next to it, at No. 87, is the *Spencer House*, the girlhood home of the mother of J. P. Morgan.

Right at Cromwell Center is the junction with South St. Left on South St., which ends at the banks of the river, to an old river landing used by General Lafayette on his trip from Hartford to Middletown.

At 28.3 *m.* is the main plant and offices of the *Pierson Nurseries* (L), founded in 1871 by A. N. Pierson, a Swedish immigrant. This nursery covers 300 acres of land and about 30 acres are under glass. The annual output of roses runs close to the 10-million mark; various other cut flowers are grown here for the New York market.

At 29 *m.* is the junction with Evergreen Rd.

Left on Evergreen Rd. to *Wolf Pit Hill*, 0.5 *m.*, topped by an air beacon that guides transport and mail planes.

At 30.5 *m.* stands the Samuel Wright House, later the *Toll Gate House* (R), an early gambrel-roofed dwelling which has been given a variety of dates by differing authorities and was probably built in the 18th century. The vigilant toll-man watched the approaching vehicles from the basement window, but, according to tradition, many travelers discovered that they could avoid paying toll by detouring through Cromwell Avenue which consequently became known as 'Shun Pike.'

ROCKY HILL (alt. 100, town pop. 2021), 32.7 *m.* Settled about 1650 as the 'Lower Community' of Wethersfield, this younger colony constructed its first meeting-house in 1722 and formed a separate parish known as 'Stepney Parish,' which was incorporated as the town of Rocky Hill in 1843. As a result of the subsequent change in the course of the Connecticut River, Rocky Hill became the chief port of the town of Wethersfield and the center of a flourishing river traffic and inland trade. Shipbuilding was its first important industry.

For many years the town was noted for its taverns and many a gourmet made the journey to Aunt Betsey's Kitchen, Granny Griswold's Place, Long Tavern, Shipman's Tavern, and the numerous other hostelries. Present-day Rocky Hill has lost its river traffic, but still has a large agricultural output, an iron foundry, a rayon plant, and a quarry.

Fossils are often found embedded on the slate rock strata along the river in this area, and the fossil footprints of prehistoric animals have been found in the deposits of red sandstone. Valuable Indian relics now on exhibition in the Peabody Museum, Yale University, have also been found in Rocky Hill.

At the center of Rocky Hill is the *Congregational Church* (L), erected in 1805, the pride of the community, one of the best examples of the golden age of Post-Colonial church architecture to be found in Connecticut. Its interior is excellent, but the tower is a later addition.

At the corner of Main and Ferry Sts. is the *Thomas Danforth House* (R), built in 1783 by Thomas Danforth, a native son, who was the first man in this country to organize a chain-store system. His enterprise extended to Philadelphia, Atlanta, and Savannah, before 1818. Danforth was a well-known early pewterer and his well-stocked village store supplied peddlers who went far afield.

The next corner east of the church (R) is Washington St., where practically every house is called a 'Captain Riley House,' from an early and prominent seafaring family. One captain built for his sons the several small, odd houses from the corner down Washington St. At 12 Washington St. (L) is the *James Stanley House*, one of the most distinguished houses in Rocky Hill, built in 1808. Its flat roof, odd jointed columns, and the unique groined ceiling in the front hall show how travel and originality were beginning to influence architecture.

North of these are the Robbins houses. The one at 147 Main St., built by Jason Robbins, often known as the *Talcott Arnold House* (R) (1754), is of a type that is seldom found in this vicinity — the salt-box. A pane of glass in the front window, which was removed from Shipman's Tavern in Rocky Hill, bears a record scratched with a diamond by an epicure, 'In July, 1871, woodcock, Second of May 1871, shad and spring chicken.' The *Duke of Cumberland Inn*, built by John Robbins in 1767 at 69 Main St. (R), is one of the best brick houses of that period standing in the State. The Palladian window above the door, circular windows in the gables, and stone window caps give it a Georgian sophistication such as had not previously been attempted. Like many other houses of the Rocky Hill section this dwelling has a handsome interior.

    1. Left from Rocky Hill on West St. is the *Veterans' Home*, 1.4 *m.*, a State institution for the care and shelter of veterans of all wars who enlisted from Connecticut.

    2. Left from Rocky Hill on Elm St. to the junction with Cromwell Rd., 2.7 *m.* Here, almost directly across from the old West School House, is a government *Marker* indicating the exact center of the State of Connecticut.

State 9 continues through the old onion fields where former agriculturists were so successful with their crops that one historian was surprised to find farm women working in the fields clad in silks.

At 38.2 *m.* is the junction with Hartford Avenue.

    Right on this road is WETHERSFIELD (*see WETHERSFIELD*), 2.2 *m.*, a Colonial town with many points of historic interest.

HARTFORD (*see HARTFORD*), 41.2 *m.*, the capital of the State, where the central offices of many of the largest insurance companies in the country are concentrated.

At Hartford are the junctions with US 6A (*see Tour* 2), US 44 (*see Tour* 3), US 5 (*see Tour* 7), US 5A and State 9 (*see Tour* 8), State 175 (*see Tour* 7*B*).

Sec. b. HARTFORD to MASSACHUSETTS LINE, 21.8 m., US 5A.

Passing through busy, modern Hartford, the route proceeds on a heavily traveled concrete highway, US 5A, through an area of flat tobacco fields that stretch away for miles to the distant western hills. At the outskirts of Hartford and near Windsor, the dwellings are large and include many substantial brick houses. Farms are prosperous but have limited shade, small yards, and often unfenced acreage, because there is little livestock in this area. Piles of tobacco stalks, stakes for the headnets used in the shade-grown tobacco fields, tools, and equipment are often scattered in the farm yards. Farther north the tobacco sheds are seldom painted; farmhouses are of the older, Colonial type. The varied greens of ripening tobacco flank the highway, covering the 'good earth.' Roadside markets offer a variety of fresh produce in season. The route enters Massachusetts at Agawam, south of West Springfield.

US 5A leaves Hartford on Windsor Avenue, a smooth, fairly broad concrete highway.

WILSON, at 2.7 *m.*, is a small roadside cluster of dwellings and stores. In the *Elijah Barber House* (L), built in 1790, the historian John W. Barber was born on February 2, 1798. Originally a two-story building, this white house has been remodeled into a three-story structure.

WINDSOR (alt. 60, town pop. 8290) (*see WINDSOR*), 6.1 *m.*, is one of the first three towns settled in Connecticut.

At Windsor is the junction with State 75.

Left on State 75 through mile after mile of tobacco fields to SUFFIELD (alt. 160, town pop. 4346), 10.2 *m.*, a shaded, cool oasis in the midst of wide stretches of reddish, fertile loams. Bordering a long, narrow Green, the elm-shaded main street of this sedate little town is fringed by the lawns of many substantial homesteads, some from the late 18th century, which show traces of Massachusetts influence. Little traffic passes through to disturb the quiet of the village.

Settled in 1670 by John Pynchon, who purchased 200 acres from the Indians and obtained a grant from Massachusetts, which at that time included this area, the town of Suffield was finally annexed to Connecticut in May, 1749. The dispute over the boundary was not settled, however, until 1803.

Tobacco-growing, learned from the Indians, has been the principal occupation since the town was first settled; as early as 1727 tobacco was legal tender here. The chief present-day industry is the growing and packing of tobacco. Cigar-making was introduced in Suffield in 1810 when 'genuine Spanish cigars' were made by Simeon Viets who hired a Cuban derelict to teach the local women to roll the mild wrapper leaf of the Connecticut Valley. The first crude product was sold by peddlers. Since the introduction of shade-grown leaf, the countryside about Suffield, spread with miles of cotton netting, appears like a gigantic circus ground under a huge 'big top.'

Entering Suffield the tour passes the *David Tod House* (L), built in 1773–95, a fine old, hip-roofed house set well back from the road.

The first house (L) south of the Green is the town's most famous house, the broad gambrel-roofed *Abraham Burbank House* (1736), with wings on both sides. Probably only the south wing with a Dutch roof dates from that period. The carriage sheds to the rear are typical of a pretentious tendency, evidenced toward 1800, that treated all buildings alike, whatever their use, and applied arches and elliptical windows for the fun of the thing. The *Alexander King House* (1746) stands at 98 South Main St.; with its paired windows and cross-panel doors, it is a dignified salt-box house of the middle of the century.

Northward is the *Harvey Bissell Homestead* (R), built in 1815, with its two-story porch complete with all the embellishments of that sophisticated period.

The highway passes the ivy-covered buildings of *Suffield School* (L), a preparatory school for boys on an extensive landscaped campus with excellent athletic fields. Founded in 1833 as the Connecticut Baptist Literary Institution, the school adopted its present name in 1912. The Rev. Dr. Brownell Gage, headmaster, was a founder of the college of Yali at Changsha, China.

Directly opposite the Suffield Campus, north of the *Second Baptist Church* (1840) is (R) the town's most attractive old house, known as the *Old Manse of the Rev. Ebenezer Gay* (1742). It was built for Captain Joseph Winchell. This weathered, gambrel-roofed dwelling, with narrow clapboards and old sash, has the feature, uncommon in Connecticut, of a broken scroll doorway flanked by fluted pilasters and enclosing cross-panel doors. This treatment was a feature of the very height of 18th-century decoration, but was seldom attempted outside the Connecticut Valley.

Adjoining Suffield School is the *Kent Memorial Library* (*open weekdays* 9–5) (L), which contains the Sheldon collection of rare books on the history of Suffield and New England, and a genealogical register of great value.

North of the School, the highway passes the *Josiah King Mansion* (L), a large, central-chimney house with fluted pilasters built in 1762. Opposite is the *Gay Mansion* (R) built by Ebenezer King in 1795, a square house with a flat hip roof broken by a pediment. The pilaster-framed Palladian window just above the entrance is copied in a tiny Palladian window in the pediment. The house has two beautiful doorways with porticos flanked by Ionic columns, and topped with leaded fan-lights.

State 75 rejoins the main tour at the junction with US 5A, at 13.7 *m.*

At 9.2 *m.* is the old road to *Bissell's Ferry* (R), established in 1648 by the General Court of Connecticut, and operated until 1917.

At 9.4 *m.* is the *Thomas Hinsdale House* (L), built in 1747, and occupied as a church by the North Windsor Congregational Society from 1762 to 1793. Diagonally opposite is the *Site of the Stone Fort* (R), erected in 1633 and razed in 1809. Built of logs and stone, it had a massive oaken door, cumbersome and spike-studded, which bore the scars inflicted by numerous Indian tomahawks.

HAYDEN'S STATION (Town of Windsor) 10 *m.*, is a rural crossroad settlement with a combination country store and post office.

Left on Pink Street.

At 130 Pink St., attractively set among elms, is the *Captain Nathaniel Hayden House* (1763), 0.4 *m.*, a large, gambrel-roofed dwelling with end chimneys and string courses. A smaller, squat, brick gambrel-roofed office beside it is almost a replica.

Northward from Hayden's Station the highway skirts the river and crosses an overpass of the N.Y., N.H. & H. R.R. at 12.3 *m.*

WINDSOR LOCKS (alt. 80, town pop. 4073), 13.7 *m.*, is a bustling industrial community bearing many evidences of its manufacturing activities, principally the production of paper, machinery, cotton warp, knit goods, and lathe chucks. Tobacco sorting and packing is also an important industry in the area.

Formerly known as Enfield Falls, the town, which was named in 1833 for the canal locks completed at this point on the Connecticut River in 1829, was incorporated in May, 1854, and owed its early development to the river traffic and the work contingent on navigating the rapids at this point, first by flat boats and later by canal. The six miles of portage around the rapids were eliminated in 1829, when the canal was built.

A cable ferry, chartered in 1783, operated across the stream here at one time. Grist (1781), carding, saw (1742), and fulling mills were erected, and a gin distillery established in 1811 was popular with the farmers because it created a steady demand for grain. The paper mill, still operating, dates from 1767. By 1865, it was the largest then running in the country.

At Windsor Locks the road passes the *C. H. Dexter and Sons Paper Mill* (R).

Eastward across the railroad tracks are the hand-operated locks of the canal. Pleasure craft use these locks, which are operated by two men grown old in the service, who push the gates open and close them, using a great pole as a lever.

On the left of the main street is the *Factory of the Montgomery Company*, makers of cotton and novelty yarns, and tinsel products.

At Windsor Locks is the junction with State 20 (*see Tour 6*).

The highway passes the '*Mansion House*' (R) at 14.8 *m.*, a weather-beaten, salt-box dwelling, built by Edmund Marshall in 1718. At 15.6 *m.* the highway crosses a concrete bridge, high above Stony Brook.

At 15.6 *m.* is the *Anthony Austin, Jr., House*, a brown-shingled gambrel-roofed cottage with an added lean-to, built about 1691. It has huge splayed corner posts and a stone chimney 16 feet square. Feather bins in the attic are an unusual feature. The highway passes the *Horace King House* (R), 16.8 *m.*, a white gambrel-roofed dwelling erected in 1794.

Past a small concrete bridge at 18 *m.*, the *Bigelow-Sanford Carpet Mill* (R), a long, rambling, brick structure, is visible across the river; it occupies the site of the first carpet mill in America. Flat tobacco fields dotted with the gray, weathered tobacco sheds stretch away on either side.

The route proceeds through low, rolling country which parallels the Connecticut River. In this section the river is quite shallow except during the spring freshet season when it sometimes rises high enough to flood the highway. US 5A enters Massachusetts at Agawam, 21 *m.*

TOUR 9 : *From* NEW LONDON *to* MASSACHUSETTS LINE (*Worcester*), 56.2 *m.*, State 32 and State 12.

Via Norwich, Jewett City, Plainfield, Danielson, Putnam, Thompson.
Macadam and cement surfaced highway.
Railway parallels the route.
Usual accommodations.

THE southern portion of this route traverses historic Norwich and the old hunting grounds of the Mohegan Indians. The area is rich in Indian lore and legend, scenic in the rougher manner of eastern Connecticut, and not heavily traveled.

The northern two-thirds of the route passes through the textile towns and villages of Connecticut where frequent mill failures have altered at least temporarily the socio-economic pattern. The land utilization section of the Resettlement Administration is now making limited purchases of submarginal lands and adding to State park and forest preserves in this region.

Northward from New London, State 32 travels the same route as an old Turnpike, the first to be completed in America. This highway, developed to facilitate the transportation of cattle and produce to the deep-water wharves at New London, was surveyed in 1670 by Joshua Raymond. In May, 1792, the General Assembly authorized a toll gate and this road became the second toll road authorized in America. The first, the Philadelphia-Lancaster Turnpike Company, had been incorporated a month or two earlier, but the Norwich Turnpike was the first to be completed.

At 2.1 *m.* (R) is the *United States Coast Guard Academy* (*see NEW LONDON*). At 2.2 *m.* (R and L), is the 325-acre campus of Connecticut College (*see NEW LONDON*).

Crossing *Church Brook*, 3.2 *m.*, the highway passes the mid-eighteenth-century *Richards House* and *Barns* (L), descends a steep grade, and crosses *Hunters' Brook*, 3.7 *m.*, which flows into a long salt inlet from the Thames.

QUAKER HILL (alt. 20, Waterford Town pop. 4742), 4.3 *m.*, a residential section on a high bluff above the Thames, received its name from a group of Seventh Day Adventists, organized here by John and James Rogers, early settlers of Waterford who were locally referred to as 'Quakers.'

WATERFORD spreads fan-like about New London, a township without a community of the same name.

Leaving Quaker Hill, State 32 passes (R) the big *Rouse Browning House* (*private*), 4.6 *m.*, built in 1785, though later modernized, and following the

Thames River with frequent wide views, enters the village of UNCAS-VILLE (alt. 60, Montville town pop. 3970), 6.3 *m.*, named for Uncas, grand sachem of the Mohegans at the time of the early English settlements. The main portion of this neat, prosperous village lies right of the highway. Its industries include the manufacture of silk and cotton fabrics and paper goods.

Crossing a concrete bridge over *Oxoboxo Brook,* the highway passes *Uncasville Library,* 6.4 *m.,* at the junction with a footpath.

> Left on this path to the summit of *Haughton Mountain* (alt. 400), from which is an extensive view of the river valley.

At 9 *m.,* on the top of *Mohegan Hill* (alt. 340) is the village of MOHEGAN (Town of Montville), a thriving Indian community, no longer a Government reservation, but still nominally governed by a chief called 'Malagah' (Leap Dancer), who rules over the 36 remaining half-breed members of the tribe.

At the center stands *Tantaquidgeon Lodge (open to the public)* (R), a small structure of native granite erected as a museum by John Tantaquidgeon and his son, Harold, descendants of the Indian warrior, Tantaquidgeon, who, according to tradition, was the first to overtake the fleeing Miantonomo during the battle of the Great Plains, but being of lower rank waited for his chief, Uncas, to make the capture. Here is exhibited a collection of Indian woodenware, baskets of beadwork, and stone tools. In the yard are several types of Indian dwellings made of saplings.

South of the museum, about 200 yards (R) from the highway on the blue-marked Mohegan Trail, is the *Mohegan Congregational Church* erected for the remaining members of the tribe in 1831 by a public subscription conducted in Norwich, Hartford, and New London. Here a Brush Arbor Ceremony has been held annually in the latter part of August since 1860. Formerly green brush arbors were erected as temples to the gods of the harvest, and the Indians, forming a chain, danced through the temples where each paused to pay homage. Now, shorn of its tribal significance, the ceremony is chiefly the erection of a brush arbor at which Indian handicraft and native dishes such as succotash and yokeag (parched corn) are sold by the Ladies' Aid Society of the Indian church. Although the rites and the dances are no longer performed, the ancient custom of preserving twigs from the arbor as 'good luck' symbols is still observed.

The Mohegan Trail leads to *Fort Hill,* 0.3 *m.,* where only a few foundation stones mark the site of Uncas' fort. The hill commands a sweeping view of distant hills to the north, and of the Thames River southward to New London and Long Island Sound.

In a large field (R), at 9.3 *m.,* are the cellar stones of the *Birthplace of Samson Occum,* the first (1759) ordained Indian minister. This famous preacher served as missionary to the Pequots and the Oneidas and in 1766 went to England with the Rev. Eleazer Wheelock of Columbia,

Connecticut, and there helped raise a fund of $30,000 that formed the nucleus of the Dartmouth College Foundation. The *Cynthia Hoscott House* (about 1680), a tall gambrel-roofed structure now almost in ruins, near the site, is another early Indian house.

At 9.7 *m.* is the intersection with a road marked 'To Fort Shantok.'

> Right on this road is the *Site of the Old Fort and Burying Ground* (R), 1.4 *m.*, where Uncas and his warriors were besieged by the Narragansetts in 1645. With his food supply exhausted, Uncas faced surrender and inevitable death by torture. An Indian scout carried news of his plight to Saybrook. Lieut. Thomas Leffingwell, loading a canoe with supplies, paddled along the Sound and up the Thames, and under cover of darkness managed to enter the fort without detection.
>
> A rustic stairway leads to a wooden palisade within which are several ancient Indian graves marked by crude stone slabs. A boulder marks the *Grave of Fidelia Fowler* (d. 1908), the last Indian to speak the Pequot and Mohegan languages. At the eastern end of the cemetery is the *Leffingwell Monument*, a conical cairn set with two granite tablets in honor of that soldier's gallant action which won Uncas's enduring friendship for the English. Here, below a high bank overlooking the Thames River, are camp sites and picnic grounds. Signs direct to fresh-water springs and a bath-house.

The highway climbs to the top of *Trading Cove Hill*. This district, seat of the chieftain, Uncas, of the Mohegan branch of the Pequots, abounds in Indian history, legends, and memorials.

At 10.1 *m.* State 32 branches right from the old New London-Norwich Turnpike (*see above*).

> Left on the turnpike to NORWICH TOWN (*see NORWICH*), the original settlement at Norwich, 3.8 *m.*

Descending from Trading Cove Hill, the road crosses TRADING COVE, where early settlers from across the river traded with the Indians, and ascending a long hill, passes the *Norwich Inn* (L), at 11.2 *m.*, a hostelry built of brick in the Colonial style, set in spacious grounds, with a fine golf course. A dirt road (R) at 11.4 *m.*, marked by a sign, is the entrance to the *Solomon Lucas Memorial Woods*, a State reservation on an eminence overlooking the Thames River.

NORWICH (alt. 100, town pop. 32,438), 13 *m.*, a mercantile center of eastern Connecticut (*see NORWICH*).

At Norwich is the junction with State 12 which this route follows northward to the Massachusetts Line. State 12, southward (*see Tour 1G*), connects with Groton.

At Norwich are also the junctions with State 2 (*see Tour 1J*), State 82 (*see Tour 1D*), State 165 (*see Tour 1D*), and State 32 (*see Tour 9A*).

At 16.8 *m.* is the *Miantonomo Memorial*. A guidepost (R) points to the monument, a crude stone structure, erected to commemorate the great chief of the Narragansetts who was captured here by Uncas, chief of the Mohegans, and later executed and buried on the same spot. Miantonomo, long an enemy of Uncas because of that chieftain's friendship for the white man, violated his agreement with the English by raising a large army and invading Mohegan territory in an attempt to exterminate that tribe. By strategy, Uncas put the Narragansetts to flight and captured their leader. After a trial by the Colonial commissioners, Miantonomo was condemned to death and was turned over to Uncas with the provision that 'all mercy and moderation be exercised in the manner of his execution.' Miantonomo was marched back to the scene of his capture, and, as he approached the spot, one of Uncas's followers, who walked behind him, split his skull with one blow of a hatchet. The chief was buried where he fell. For many years afterward, passing Narragansetts heaped stones on his grave in tribute to his memory, until the cairn became so enormous that near-by farmers used the stones to build walls.

After crossing a concrete bridge over the Shetucket River, the route passes, at 17.6 *m.*, a State roadside park (L & R), the *Quinebaug River View.*

Following the winding course of the Quinebaug, the highway presents excellent views of the deep-cut gorge.

JEWETT CITY (alt. 120, Town of Griswold pop. 6010), 23.8 *m.*, producing rayon and cotton textiles, has been a manufacturing center since 1771. In one section the typical gray and white 'mill houses' predominate; modern, well-kept mercantile buildings and comfortable homes give the community a progressive appearance. In the business section is the Green (R). A one-legged veteran, member of the local small police force, directs traffic here during rush hours.

Descending the side of a heavily wooded hill, which rises steeply from the roadside on the left, State 12 passes *Clayville Pond* (R), at 24.9 *m.*, in swampy, stump-marred land. Fragrant pond lilies are offered for sale at roadside stands here in summer. Traversing level country the highway passes the *Tadpole Highway Park* (R) at 25.7 *m.*

At 27.6 *m.* is a large *Perkins House* (L) built in 1760 by Dr. Elisha Perkins who invented a 'tractor' of knitting needles for massaging sore muscles. The lane east from this house leads to *Dr. Dow's Salt-Box House* (c. 1720), the earliest and the most unchanged of the old houses of the town.

At 29.8 *m.* is the junction with State 14 which combines with State 12 for 2.8 miles (*see Tour 9C*).

PLAINFIELD (alt. 220, town pop. 8027), 29.9 *m.*, is a quiet and attractive community, the newer part of which was laid out as a model mill village. The older dwellings, with fine lawns, are set on well-kept streets; the white 'mill houses,' all similar in design, cluster about the large Lawton Mills, which were liquidated in 1936 and are now closed.

On the western side of the village, along State 14, are the extensive holdings of the *Lawton Mills* (L) which, prior to liquidation, was the largest textile establishment in eastern Connecticut.

Across the small Green (R) is the *Eaton Tavern* (1768). Washington and Lafayette met at this important stop on the coach line between Providence and Norwich, and Lafayette's room is still preserved. Unfortunately, the rare paneling which made this one of the most elaborate inns in the State has recently been removed.

Opposite, the granite *Congregational Church* (L), with a Doric portico (1816), was remodeled in 1851.

A short distance behind the church are the buildings of the *Plainfield Academy*, one of the earliest (1778) and long one of the most successful of such educational institutions in the State. The main building of seamed granite, designed by Ithiel Town, was erected in 1825. In 1848–52, about 20 Chickasaw Indian pupils from Texas were students here, and later came a group of South Americans.

North of the center stands an early 'integral' salt-box house (R) with long, one-piece rear rafters. It was built before 1720 by Captain Eleazar Cady. A salt-box house is a rarity in this section.

At 32.6 *m.* State 14 branches right (*see Tour 9B*).

State 12 proceeds to CENTRAL VILLAGE (Town of Plainfield), 32.9 *m.*, a group of houses about the *Wyandotte Worsted Mills* on the Moosup River.

Between a double row of maples, State 12 crosses rolling country to WAUREGAN (Town of Plainfield), 34.5 *m.*, a mill settlement on the Quinebaug River, clustered about the Wauregan cotton mill. An impressively large dam in the Quinebaug, at the village, was built in 1853 and rebuilt in 1934.

Northward, State 12 crosses through the western edge of the village of Wauregan and passes a private waterfowl sanctuary (R), at 35.9 *m.*, and a State highway park, *Under the Ash*, at 37 *m.*

At 38.9 *m.* State 12 passes the *Site of the Acquiunk Fort* (L), an Indian palisade on a ledge bluff at the junction of the Quinebaug and Assawaga Rivers. The highway rounds an S-curve and at 39 *m.* turns right at the junction with US 6 (*see Tour 2*), with which this route combines for 0.5 *m.*

DANIELSON (Town of Killingly, alt. 220, borough pop. 4210), 39.2 *m.* (*see Tour 2*), is a bustling manufacturing borough chartered in 1854.

At 39.4 *m.* US 6 (*see Tour 2*) branches right while this route proceeds on State 12 past a *State Police Barracks* (R) at 40 *m.* to the small manufacturing village of ELMVILLE (Town of Killingly), where sash cord and mill supplies are produced.

It was along this route that Nell Alexander, peddler (*see below*), returning from Providence one dark night during the Revolution, saw, arched across the sky, a brilliant line of '64 cannon shining like the aurora borealis, with their muzzels pointing south.' Shortly after his return home, news was received of the surrender of Cornwallis.

At Elmville is the junction with a side road.

Right on this road, through the valley of the *Whetstone Brook*, along which are the ruins of eight large mills, abandoned long before the depression of 1929 as a result of southern textile mill competition. Beside these ruins are groups of mill houses, most of them abandoned.

KILLINGLY CENTER (alt. 300), 0.4 *m.*, a cluster of small dwellings around the *Jeremiah Fields Tavern* (about 1800), was named for Killingly Manor in York. On Whetstone Brook near the village is the old *Aspinock Quarry*, once used by the Indians from as far west as Michigan as a source of whetstones for shaping arrowheads and utensils.

East of Killingly Center this road passes more mill ruins, some nearly obliterated by overgrowing brush, trees, and weeds.

At 1.5 *m.* the road passes through the practically abandoned village of ELLIOTVILLE.

East of Elliotville stand three more old mill ruins and at the edge of the brook at 2 *m.* is another.

This route leads to EAST KILLINGLY, at 2.5 *m.*, where it unites with State 101. At East Killingly an absorbent cotton factory is the only mill now operating regularly. From the crest of *Chestnut Hill* (alt. 740), 200 feet north of State 101 (R) in the village, is an excellent view of the rocky, wooded countryside.

Turning sharp left, State 101 leaves East Killingly and, descending a steep hill, proceeds to a junction with State 12, the main route, at 5 *m.*

At 41.5 *m.* is the junction with State 101 (*see above*).

State 12 enters the village of ATTAWAUGAN (alt. 240, Town of Killingly), 42.6 *m.*, a group of mill houses clustered about a factory, at a point where State 12 crosses to the west bank of the Five Mile River.

At Attawaugan is the junction with an improved rural road.

Left on this road, which runs through a wooded area, skirting the eastern edge of *Alexander Lake*, is *Wildwood Park* (R), 1.2 *m.* Here on the eastern shore of the lake are picnic areas, facilities for boating and swimming, and a dance hall.

This district was owned for generations by descendants of Nell Alexander, one of the 'Yankee Pedlars.' The lake, according to Indian tradition, arose from the earth, engulfing a mountain on which the Indians were holding a four-day celebration. One peak, where a good old squaw stood, remained above water and is now *Loon Island*. Old residents today say that their grandfathers remembered seeing the tops and trunks of tall pine trees through the clear waters.

Nell Alexander settled at Alexander Lake in 1720 on his arrival from Scotland. Just before he disembarked, he had picked up a gold ring from the ship's deck. Pawning the ring for his first stake he ran the proceeds into a sizable fortune, redeemed the ring, and eventually purchased a plantation of 3500 acres in Killingly. The gold ring became a talisman and was passed on to his only son Nell; then it was transferred to an only grandson Nell; and to quote the historian Barber, 'it will doubtless continue from Nell to Nell, agreeably to the request of the first Nell, until the last knell of the race is tolled.'

North of Attawaugan the highway passes through rolling country which affords fine views of farmland to the left. At 46.2 *m.*, opposite a cemetery, is the junction with Putnam Heights Rd.

Right on Putnam Heights Rd., and right on the old Killingly Gangway, an unpaved road, along a high ridge.

PUTNAM HEIGHTS (alt. 580), 1.6 *m.*, is the earliest settlement in the town of Putnam. Two rows of fine old residences line the historic old 'Gangway' which extends south to Killingly. The village was formerly a part of North Killingly and known as Killingly Hill, a flourishing trade center before the bulk of population shifted to the city of Putnam.

At 1.8 *m.* is the entrance to a private lane.

Left on this lane 0.7 *m.* is the *Site of the Birthplace of Manasseh Cutler* (1742–1823) (L), a leader in the organization and settlement of the Northwest Territory, and drafter of the Ordinance of 1787 which guaranteed the prohibition of slavery in that area. He was for 52 years pastor of a church in Ipswich, Massachusetts, as well as school teacher, merchant, lawyer, physician, botanist, and astronomer. He went to school in the odd little abandoned gambrel-roofed *Copp House* (1744), 2 miles north of the Putnam Heights Green, which served for many generations as a parsonage.

At 1.9 *m.* is the *Old Cemetery* (L), burial place of William Torrey Harris, noted educator, and at 2.3 *m.*, the *Congregational Church*, 1818 (L), designed by Elias Carter, stands on the Green, its three front entrances topped with semi-circular fan-lights. It is a pleasing composition, and is one of the few early edifices whose architect is known. Opposite the church is the *Samson Howe Tavern* (R), built in 1786, a landmark which still has its original fireplaces, mantels, and plank floors. This tavern was the meeting-place of several local business men who financed the building of the sloop 'Harmony' by local farmers. Transported in sections to Providence, the vessel engaged in the West Indian trade for many years. From the Killingly Gangway a fine view can be had of the city of Putnam and the low, rambling hills beyond.

PUTNAM (alt. 400, town pop. 8099, inc. 1855), named for Israel Putnam, Revolutionary hero (*see Tour 2, BROOKLYN*), 46.8 *m.*, is a manufacturing center composed of narrow, winding streets and low buildings, on four small hills. Originally known as *Pomfret Factory*, the city was chartered in 1895, and because of its situation at Cargill Falls on the Quinebaug, became an industrial center, attracting most of its population from Killingly Hill, now known as Putnam Heights. Having a station on the railroad connecting New York and Boston, the village became a shipping center for eastern Connecticut and at one time ranked eighth in New England in the volume of freight handled. Although it has suffered during the depression, Putnam is still a thriving little community.

Left on South Main St. to Arch St., 0.3 *m.*; right on Arch St. and left immediately beyond the railway overpass on Park St., which skirts the Quinebaug River, to the pine-fringed entrance of *Quinebaug Pines State Park*, 1.1 *m.* Close to the entrance is a parking space (R). The park, formerly called Priests' Island, because it was owned by the Catholic Church, is a thirty-six-acre islet, reached from the mainland by a suspension footbridge. Here is one of the most noteworthy stands of white pine in the State. There are facilities for boating, swimming, and picnicking.

State 12 passes the *Masonic Club* (R), occupying a building which was a station of the 'Underground Railroad' before the Civil War, when ardent Connecticut Abolitionists assisted escaping slaves to reach freedom in Canada.

At 46.9 *m.* is the intersection with Front St. where US 44 (*see Tour 3*) joins with State 12 for 0.7 mile.

Left, a short distance on Front St., which becomes Pomfret St. Beside Pomfret St. are the *Cargill Falls* (R), one of the most beautiful in eastern Connecticut. Although the falls are neither large nor high, the water, rushing over rocky ledges, breaks into numerous cascades and tumbles downward under iridescent spray.

On Providence St., left from State 12, past the Putnam State Trade School (L), which adjoins the High School, is the *Belding Heminway*

Mill (R), 0.4 *m.*, one of the largest silk thread factories in the United States.

At Putnam is the junction with State 91 (*see Side Trip off Tour 3*).

At 47.6 *m.* US 44 (*see Tour 3*) branches right and State 12 follows the Quinebaug River through valley lowlands. Just beyond the junction of the French and Quinebaug Rivers, the highway passes through ME-CHANICSVILLE (Town of Thompson), 49 *m.*, on an uneven hillside. This busy village, like others to the north, is important only for its textile mills. About the village, steep hills rise from the gorges formed by the narrow valley of the French River.

Following the east bank of the French River, State 12 proceeds to a junction with State 193 at 49.8 *m.*

Right on State 193 to a junction with a tarred road at 1.6 *m.*

Right on the tarred road, 0.5 *m.*, is the *Samuel Converse House* (1718) (R), oldest dwelling in the town of Thompson, a two-and-one-half-story, peak-roofed house, now a tearoom. Farther on is the *Russian Bear* (R), 1.6 *m.*, which retains an odd brick smokehouse and is now operated as a tearoom by a group of expatriate Russians.

THOMPSON (alt. 540, town pop. 4999), 1.9 *m.*, sometimes called Thompson Hill, named for Sir Robert Thompson, a non-resident Englishman who held the original royal patent for this district, is a quiet rural settlement of well-kept country estates and gleaming white or butter-yellow houses along shaded streets. The village contains much of scenic and historic interest. The Green at the center was a militia training ground on which eastern Connecticut troops were mustered in 1775 at the Lexington alarm. Most of the houses around the Green date from the early 19th century. In Thompson are the *Howe Marot School for Girls* (R) and the *Marianapolis Academy*, a Lithuanian seminary for boys (L). The building of the old *Thompson Bank* (R) is now used as a hall of records.

Facing the Green on the east, the long, yellow *Vernon Stiles Tavern* (1818) has been in operation since 1830. Here, Thomas Dorr, illegally elected Governor of Rhode Island, instigator of Dorr's Rebellion (1841), in which his followers attempted to seize an arsenal in their efforts to force a change in the limited suffrage qualifications, was in hiding when pursued by Government agents, and evaded capture by use of the complicated series of stairways in the old tavern. Stiles, the host and owner, was also Justice of the Peace, and his hospitality to eloping couples made the tavern their favorite goal in this district.

Right from the Thompson crossroads, on an improved country road is *Fort Hill* (L), 0.9 *m.*, formerly the stronghold of the Nipmuck Indians, fortified against attacks of the marauding Narragansetts. Hundreds of arrow-heads have been found near-by, as well as tomahawks, cooking vessels, and other Indian relics. A farmhouse (L) marks the point where cars can be parked. Behind the farmhouse is the crest of the hill (alt. 625) and the site of the stockade. From the summit a 50-mile view of wooded hills stretches away for nearly 300 degrees around the horizon.

Many years before the coming of the white men, the Nipmucks believed that the streams of this district were especially blessed by the Great Spirit and would always yield an abundance of fish. The local Indians, then friendly with the Narragansetts, once invited the Rhode Island Indians to a feast of eels. When the visiting tribes men arrived and the eels were served, the guests complained that the food had been cooked without dressing. The resulting argument led to a fight in which all the visitors were killed with the exception of two. That night ghostly blue flames hung over the Nipmuck fishing grounds. The early settlers drew their wooden shutters, bolted their doors and hugged the cheer of their hearthstones in terror, as the dull, slow beat of Indian drums and moaning dirges echoed across the hills in propitiation for the treachery of their ancestors. Although the warwhoop has long since ceased to echo through these hills, the Nipmuck 'fishing fires' are said to appear every seven years, shedding an eerie light through wooded dells. Skeptics point out that the phosphorescent glow is caused by the chemical result of rotting vegetation, but the natives are difficult to convince. Elsewhere in Connecticut, these blue lights are known as 'swamp fires.'

Farther on, this rural road passes through the village of QUADDICK, 2.9 *m.*, and turning left at the next crossroads, 3.6 *m.*, skirts *Quaddick Reservoir*, a beautiful body of water, six miles in circumference, about which an abundance of wild flowers grows. Higher up, atop the ledges, are sturdy growths of mountain laurel.

Left at Thompson, State 200, this side trip leads through a verdant hill-country past well-ordered farms.

At 4.9 *m.* is the junction with State 12 at Grosvenordale.

State 12 proceeds to the village of GROSVENORDALE (Town of Thompson), 51.7 *m.*, in the French River Valley, built along a broad thoroughfare, off which branch side streets lined with small gray tenements and mill houses. The village developed from an agricultural settlement after 1863, when Dr. William Grosvenor, industrialist, enlarged a small mill and imported modern English machinery.

At the center of Grosvenordale, on the narrow strip of land between the highway and French River, is the *Grosvenordale Company Mill* (L), manufacturing textiles.

At Grosvenordale is the junction with State 200 (*see above*).

Up the river valley, between abrupt hills on either side, the highway passes the *Tourtellotte Memorial High School* (R), 52.6 *m.*, a classic building set high on an eminence.

Skirting the eastern bank on the French River, State 12 turns left and crossing the river, swings right to the village of North Grosvenordale.

NORTH GROSVENORDALE (Town of Thompson; alt. 460), 53.3 *m.*, is a thriving industrial community of well-kept, gray and white tenements arranged uniformly along narrow streets. Its mills produce fine cotton goods. Formerly a part of Killingly, Thompson became a separate town in 1785 and includes eleven manufacturing villages.

Left on Main St., on a hillside, is the unusual stone grotto and *Shrine of St. Joseph* (R), 0.4 *m.*, a copy of the shrine of Our Lady of Lourdes in France. Erected through the efforts of the Marist Fathers, this shrine is the scene of numerous religious gatherings of the Roman Catholic Church.

On the highway (R) is the North Grosvenordale Mill.

At 54.4 *m.* on a bluff overlooking the valley, where the French River widens at the confluence of numerous small creeks, is a *State Highway Park*.

WILSONVILLE (Town of Thompson), 55.4 *m.*, is a small mill village composed mainly of old gray company houses. On the curve, where the

French River swings in sharply from the right, and the highway makes an abrupt turn (L), is the stone woolen mill (1830), furnishing the main industry of the town.

State 12 crosses the Massachusetts Line, at 56.2 *m.*, entering Massachusetts, 1.8 miles south of Webster.

T O U R   9 A :   *From* NORWICH *to* MASSACHUSETTS LINE (*South Monson*), 43.7 *m.*, State 32.

Via Yantic, North Franklin, Willimantic, Mansfield Depot, South Willington, Stafford Springs, Staffordville.

Cement and macadamized highway.

Limited accommodations except at Willimantic.

TRAVERSING the rougher, rolling foothills of the Eastern Connecticut Highlands, this route passes through brush pasture lands and a number of little crossroads hamlets that cling to the edge of scattered farmlands. Streams are pure, swift, and boisterous. Forests are second growth hardwoods. The farms are small, and herds of grade cattle are the rule. One-room schoolhouses at the crossroads, milk platforms beside the road, rural mail boxes that sometimes lean at crazy angles: all are as typical of this countryside as are the textile mills and foreign-born operatives of the cities and towns through which this route passes.

Leaving Norwich (*see NORWICH*) on a winding route, State 32 passes (L) the *Norwich Grange Hall*, at 3 *m.*, where country folk gather to discuss their problems of agricultural economy and participate in 'strawberry festivals,' chicken suppers, or merry dances.

Dipping to the valley of the Yantic River, the route passes through the village of YANTIC (alt. 140, pop. 500), 3.9 *m.*, built up around the large stone factory of *The Millbrook Woolen Company*, a textile mill to which the community owes its existence. The company houses here are kept in good repair and the lawns are green and thrifty. The large, long *Backus House* stands (L) with one end facing the road; the central section is believed to have been built about 1690. Within, the heavy framing, plentiful feather-edge sheathing, and the sub-cellar under the eastern end give evidence of an early date. The sub-cellar is a feature sometimes found in eastern Connecticut houses of about 1700. The west end of this house dates from before 1800 and contains some exceptionally ornate paneling.

At Yantic is the junction with State 2 (*see Tour 1J*).

Beside the church is the junction with a side road.

Right on this road is a *Granite Bridge* spanning the waters of the Yantic River. Guarding this bridge, like twin watch-towers at the entrance to some medieval castle, are two circular stone houses with conical roofs. What they were built for can only be surmised.

At 4.8 *m.* is a junction with State 87, the Jonathan Trumbull Highway (*see Tour 2C*). The elaborate *Wilson House*, built in 1784, stands opposite the fork (L).

At 7.6 *m.* a lane to the east (R) leads in 0.1 *m.* to the *Oldest House in Franklin*. It was built by Samuel Hyde in 1660 and enlarged to serve throughout most of the 18th century as a tavern.

At 8.1 *m.* is the village of FRANKLIN (alt. 340, pop. 611), a former center of numerous small industries. The town had a peak population of 1210 in 1800. Originally a part of Nine Mile Square, which was ceded to the first settlers by Uncas and his brothers for £70, the town was occupied by fifty families in 1710. In May, 1786, it was incorporated and named for Benjamin Franklin.

Right from Franklin on the Baltic Rd. is a junction, at 1.5 *m.* Left here and left at two forks, passing a cemetery (L), at 1.9 *m.*, to the *Ayer Farm*, 2.7 *m.*, the first house (L) beyond the cemetery, which has been held in direct line of male descent through nine generations, since 1663. The Bradstreet property in Ipswich, Mass., dating from 1635, is usually accorded the distinction of being the longest in the hands of one family, but the Ayer Farm appears to have a more valid claim, as it is still a self-supporting farm and not one of the 350 acres of the original grant has ever been sold or mortgaged. John Pendleton Ayer, the present owner, now (1937) 72 years old, is training the 15-year-old grandson to carry on the farming traditions of the family.

On this farm is a tree which bears the 'bloody apples of Franklin.' According to local legend, one evening in the early spring of 1693, the housewives of Franklin (then Nine Mile Square), eagerly gathered on the Green about a newly arrived peddler and his display of tinware and trinkets. The next morning, the peddler had disappeared, but later in the day his body was found beneath an apple tree on the farm of Micah Rood, with the head split open and the pack looted.

All the village suspected the taciturn Micah Rood, but no direct evidence of his guilt could ever be obtained. Rood kept his own counsel and became more solitary than ever. In the fall of the year, when the fruit of the 'murder tree' ripened, so the story goes, a bright red spot like a drop of blood stained the snowy pulp of each apple. Village tongues whispered that the dying peddler had uttered a curse upon the farm. Years later, Micah Rood died without making a confession, but the tree continued to bear the telltale fruit, and to this day the white petals of its blossoms bear a red stain, and a tree on the farm still bears fruit with a blood-red spot in its heart.

From Franklin the route passes through cultivated fields and orchards, winding over hills to NORTH FRANKLIN (alt. 300, pop. 140), 10.4 *m.*, a crossroads settlement composed of a roadside store, a milk loading platform, and a few scattered farms. The highway frequently crosses the Central Vermont R.R. tracks or ducks beneath an occasional overpass of the now defunct Willimantic–Norwich trolley line.

At North Franklin is the junction with State 207 (*see Side Trip from Tour 2C*).

Northward from the junction the highway is shaded. To the east the Shetucket is seen winding southward to furnish power for mills in Baltic, Occum, and Taftville where Yankee spindles weave cotton fabric.

SOUTH WINDHAM (alt. 200, pop. 400, town of Windham), 12.4 *m.*, is a small rural village. In the center (L) is the *Guilford Smith Memorial Library* and farther east are the factory buildings of the *Smith-Winchester Manufacturing Company*, successors to Stafford and Phelps, the manufacturers of the first Fourdinier paper-making machine in America, in 1829. An early wooden type machine was invented by Edwin Allen of South Windham prior to 1852. In this area the first successful American silkworm culture was practiced, and in 1773, Jedediah Elderkin planted a mulberry orchard and made a coarse silk which was used for handkerchiefs and vests.

At South Windham is the junction with State 203 (*see Tour 9C*).

Passing the *Willimantic Camp Grounds* (L), at 15.7 *m.*, State 32 descends a long hill with a bad curve and a dip beneath railroad tracks, at 16.6 *m.*

WILLIMANTIC (alt. 300, pop. 12,102) (*see WILLIMANTIC*), 16.7 *m.*, a thread manufacturing center.

In Willimantic is the junction with US 6 (*see Tour 2*). US 6 combines with State 32 for 5.3 miles.

Leaving the city, the route passes the broad gambreled, stone-chimneyed *Fitch House* (R), the oldest structure within the corporate limits of Willimantic, only slightly changed from its original state.

At 18.1 *m.* are the junctions with the combined US 6A (*see Tour 2*) and State 14 (*see Tour 2 ALT.*).

The route proceeds through open country offering a variety of fine western views, at 18.6 *m.* The houses are few along this stretch of highway. The cover is verdant, but the farms are small, tilled by part-time farmers who work in the mills for their cash income.

At 22 *m.* State 32 turns right leaving US 6 (*see Tour 2*), and twists through an area where there are no farms or house lots to break the monotony of the hardwood forests.

EAGLEVILLE (alt. 285, pop. 500, Town of Mansfield), 23.7 *m.*, a manufacturing village on the banks of the Willimantic River, has grown up around small factories that now produce fiberboard. The main village is to the left of State 32. At the junction of the road leading to the main street is *St. Joseph's Catholic Church*, a small structure of rainbow-hued Bolton stone in the Colonial style.

Directly to the north of Eagleville, at the top of a long grade, is a view of *Ball Hill* (alt. 652) (R), probably the finest example of a glacial drumlin in the vicinity.

Again, at 24.8 *m.*, the route passes a vantage-point from which sweeping vistas of ever-rolling hills to the westward extend to the horizon in wave-like ridges.

At MANSFIELD DEPOT, a crossroads, 25.7 *m.*, is the junction with the united US 44 and State 101 (*see Tour* 3).

Northward, from the junction, the route follows a course that for approximately 8 miles gives an almost continuous view of distant western hills, none of them lofty, none especially noteworthy, but all green, well-rounded lands.

At 27.3 *m.*, after a twisting, crooked descent from the higher lands, State 32 enters the area known as MERROW (alt. 345, pop. 150, Town of Mansfield), now only a group of scattered houses on the site of a formerly prosperous manufacturing community. Nature is reclaiming this rather poor land for her own; brush is pushing in from the fencerows, gray birch and cedar furnishing the first cover for the stony soil, later to be followed by hardwood seedlings. This is not a softwood or pine country, forests here run more to red oak, hickory, and white ash. Occasional woodworking plants hum at the road's edge, making lawn furniture, truck bodies, or tool handles.

At 29.3 *m.* the highway winds down a long incline and enters the trim mill village of SOUTH WILLINGTON (alt. 346, pop. 600, Town of Willington). Named Wellington, May, 1725, from the Somersetshire birthplace of Henry Wolcott, whose grandson, Roger, was chief purchaser in 1720, this town was incorporated in May, 1727, as Willington. Set in a scenic and rugged country, well-watered by the Willimantic River and tributary streams which furnished power for several industries, the community now basks contentedly, with only a few pearl button factories, a sawmill, and a large thread mill to furnish a livelihood for its inhabitants. On the right are the mills of the Gardner Hall, Jr., Manufacturing Company, and the Congregational Church. On the left are the athletic fields of the mill and the Gardner Hall Grammar School.

A glass factory was built here in 1824, the output reaching important volume; in 1843 Dale and Company erected a silk mill on Fenton River and soon afterwards another company was established for the manufacture of cotton spool thread. This cotton thread mill did not prosper and, in 1861, after the plant had been idle for a number of years, it was purchased by Gardner Hall, Jr., and the manufacture of thread was again attempted.

Jared Sparks, born May 10, 1789, was Willington's most famous son. Historian, preacher, author and educator, he is best known for 'The Writings of George Washington,' 'The Life of Gouverneur Morris,' 'The Works of Benjamin Franklin,' and 'The Library of American Biography.' In 1849, Sparks became president of Harvard University and served until 1853 in that capacity. He died March 14, 1866.

The route north of the village turns sharply left and ascends a winding incline. From the summit, 29.9 *m.*, are views of the *Willimantic River Valley* and of the hilly country to the west and south.

WEST WILLINGTON (alt. 380, pop. 250) is another crossroads settlement of a few scattered houses at the edge of the highway.

North of the village the route curves over uninteresting country and swings ever closer to the streamside with a wooded highland rising above the western shore. Sharp curves require special care in driving. At 35.7 *m.* beside the road is one of the typical Connecticut signs indicating the town line of Ellington, and in 0.9 *m.* another sign indicates the town line of Stafford. This short stretch of land less than a mile in width is indicative of the peculiarity of the State's town boundaries. Here the town of Ellington reaches a long finger eastward for about 7 miles to form a panhandle, known as 'The Equivalent' because it was given to the town in response to the demands of the settlers that the township be of equal size with neighboring towns. This land originally sold for two shillings an acre and is worth but little more today.

Through forested country the route becomes a narrow, shaded highway.

STAFFORD SPRINGS, 37.5 *m.*, is a market center for the surrounding countryside. Boomed as a health resort, exploited as a source of minerals, stripped of its marketable timber, never much of a success as an agricultural area, Stafford Springs has settled down to small industrial efforts by local manufacturers who specialize in such diverse products as pearl buttons and turbine water wheels.

In 1830, Simon Fairman from this township invented and secured a patent for a scroll lathe chuck embodying most of the principles now used in hand-operated chucks. The little backyard industrial plant gradually expanded until, in 1858, the owner was unable to finance himself further. Threatened with bankruptcy, the savings of years frozen in goods for which he could find no market, Fairman was saved by a Yankee tin-peddler who turned machinery salesman and marketed the entire output.

At Stafford Springs is the junction with State 15 (*see Tour* 10).

At 38.5 *m.* State 32 swings sharply right leaving the combined State 15 and State 20 (*see Tour* 10), and becomes a typical country, State-aid highway, winding through rolling country which is sparsely covered with scrub oak and Yankee pine of a stunted variety. Crossing Middle River, at 42.5 *m.*, the route proceeds past State Line Pond, bordering the highway (R).

At 43.7 *m.* the route crosses the Massachusetts Line, 4 miles south of South Monson, Mass.

TOUR 9 B : *From* CENTRAL VILLAGE *to* RHODE ISLAND
LINE (*Providence*), 7.1 *m.*, State 14.

Via Moosup, Voluntown.
Macadamized roadbed.
Limited accommodations.

EAST of Central Village, State 14 leads to the village of MOOSUP
(alt. 200), 1.1 *m.*, the largest community in the town of Plainfield, a
single street settlement of frame houses along the bank of the Moosup
River which furnishes power for the manufacture of fine cotton thread
and woolen goods.

> Right from Moosup at the three-pronged intersection on the dirt middle road, to
> a red painted sign, 3.4 *m.*, pointing to Moosup. Opposite is a woodland path (R)
> that leads to *Squaw's Rocks*. Here a jagged granite embankment looms 100 feet
> above a deep gorge strewn with enormous boulders that once must have come
> crashing down from the cliffs above. Among the numerous caves in the rocks, the
> most interesting is *Squaw's Kitchen*, a cave about 12 feet square, from which a
> cleft in the rocks forms a natural chimney up through the rock above. Ice which
> forms in this chimney during the winter is said to remain throughout the summer.
> Here, where the Indians are believed to have held councils, afterward lived a
> remnant of the tribe, and finally a lone old squaw, for whom the rocks were named.
> In the woodland a mile to the north, a seldom visited cliff, *Big Half Hill*, rises
> perpendicularly 180 feet.

Crossing two small concrete bridges, State 14, at 5.1 *m.*, passes the
Old Town Pound (1722), now a highway park, formerly enclosed with
stone walls for the safekeeping of stray cattle.

At 7.1 *m.*, at the Rhode Island Line, is the junction with State 211.

> Sharply right and westward on State 211 to ONECO (Ind.; Oweneco) (alt. 320,
> Town of Sterling), 1.2 *m.*, a small manufacturing community in which most of the
> houses are of simple, early 19th-century design, built of granite from the near-by
> quarry.
>
> At 1.8 *m.* is the junction with a dirt road.
>
> > Left on this road to the *Marriott Granite Quarry*, 0.4 *m.*, which has supplied
> > stone for building and paving purposes throughout the eastern states.
>
> Westward, the highway ascends to the community of *Sterling Hill* (alt. 660), 3.2 *m.*,
> site of the original town settlement. Rising above the village is (L) a white re-
> modeled *Baptist Church* (1797), with a handsome doorway, quoined corners, and
> elaborate carving under the eaves. Most notable of the old houses which line the
> single street are the *Robert Dixon Tavern* (1790), with long gabled ell rambling
> back from the main structure, and (L) the *Captain Putnam House* built in 1825.
> It has an ornate front door set between fluted pilasters and topped with an elaborate
> arched fan-light and pediment.
>
> At 3.8 *m.* is the junction with State 95. Left on State 95, traversing well-kept farm
> lands and cultivated fields, at 5.2 *m.*, is the junction with a gravel road.
>
> > Right on the gravel road, a short distance to the *Sterling Fire Tower*, a 90-foot
> > lookout visible from the highway.

At 5.6 *m.*, the highway follows a long ridge with imposing views of valleys and low hills (L) in Rhode Island.

EKONK, 6.6 *m.*, is a straggling village of a few dwellings scattered along a treeless ridge. Left is the *Line Meeting-House*, a small white structure standing on the Sterling–Voluntown town line, which is also the Windham–New London county line. Marriages performed in the church are illegal if the couple stands in the customary position facing the pulpit, as the town line runs directly down the center aisle and the bride and groom would be in different towns and counties.

State 95, as it continues south through open land dotted with occasional patches of trees, affords a wide view of the horizon.

At 9.3 *m.* is the junction with *Campbell's Mill Rd.*

Left on this gravel road which descends to Great Meadows Brook is an old *Mill Site* near a rustic bridge, 0.5 *m.*, where the stream flows over a bed of solid rock.

At 9.6 *m.* State 95 enters a section of the *Pachaug State Forest* that includes hunting grounds maintained by the State. The highway leaves the forest at 10.1 *m.* and re-enters it at 10.6 *m.*

At 10.6 *m.* is the junction with a gravel road.

Right on this shady road, passing the *Forest Rangers Headquarters* (R), at 0.1 *m.*, and winding through well-kept forest areas and attractive picnic grounds to Civilian Conservation Corps *Camp Lonergan*, at 0.6 *m.*, and to scenic drives beyond.

South of Great Meadow Brook, at 11.1 *m.*, is a junction with State 138 (*see Tour 1D*), at the village of VOLUNTOWN, 11.7 *m.*

T O U R   9 C : *From* PLAINFIELD *to* WILLIMANTIC, 17.6 *m.*, State 14.

Via Canterbury, Scotland, Windham Center.

Macadam and concrete highway.

Limited accommodations.

THIS route passes upland farms and pasture lands at the edge of the textile producing area, climbs the central portion of the Eastern Highlands, and levels out onto the plain, watered by streams which furnish power for the mills of Willimantic. The land is rough and stony, farm buildings are well-weathered, the many stone walls along the roadside are of native granite, and the foundations of the dwellings are usually of the same stone. Woodland is, for the most part, second growth hardwood, croplands are in small fields irregular in shape; every farm has its flower and vegetable garden and high woodpiles typical of a countryside where oil and coal are too expensive for fuel and where wood is plentiful. The lover of rural scenes will find much of interest by the way.

Leaving State 12 at Plainfield, this route turns west on State 14. At 0.3 *m*. are the extensive former holdings of the *Lawton Mills* (L) which, until liquidated, was the largest textile establishment in eastern Connecticut. CANTERBURY (alt. 240, town pop. 942, inc. 1703), 4.7 *m*., is a residential town of old houses with trim green lawns enclosed with neat white picket fences, amid an agricultural area. Early industries, such as the manufacture of rope yarns, cloth and hats, now long discontinued because of lack of transportation facilities (no railroad or bus connections), once attracted many Finnish workers who have turned to small farming. In a backyard factory, a father and son now make hoops for sailing-ship masts and yokes for Indian water buffalo. A Finnish educational society, politically allied with the Socialist Party, annually holds a two-day reunion in midsummer. Calisthenic drills, folk dances in native costume, and speeches are features of the occasion. Residents still tell of a hailstorm which, on July 3, 1788, left nineteen inches of ice on Canterbury fields.

A native, Moses Cleveland (1754–1806), lawyer, soldier, politician, and pioneer, surveyed and planned the settlement of the Western Reserve as agent of the Connecticut Land Company. In October, 1796, he laid out Cleveland, Ohio.

Jonathan Carver, author of one of the first tourists' guides of North America, who was born here in 1732, commanded a company of provincials during the French War and upon his return decided to explore the remote parts of North America, in the belief that the French had deliberately kept the world in ignorance of the wealth of the interior. Sailing from Boston in 1766 he arrived at Michilimacknac, the interiormost English post, and pushed on to the Falls of St. Anthony on the Mississippi. After exploring the Lake Superior country he returned to Boston in 1768, having covered 7000 miles. A description of his trip in eight volumes, 'New Universal Traveler,' was published in London in 1779.

Left at the village crossroads (SW. corner) stands the pretentious, well-preserved, hip-roofed *Elisha Payne House* (1815) with a flat projecting central pediment containing a triple arched Palladian window and fanlight door. It was made famous by the Quakeress, Prudence Crandall, who in 1832 precipitated a national controversy when she admitted a Negro girl to her 'select' school, and upon the hasty withdrawal of the white pupils, proceeded to enroll 'young ladies and little misses of color.' Local resentment became so bitter that in 1833 a 'Black Law' was enacted by the State Assembly prohibiting the instruction of out-of-State Negroes in any but free public schools, without town permission. When Mistress Crandall refused to comply, her house was surrounded, the windows stoned, and doors broken open. The school-mistress abandoned her home and fled to safety. Fifty years later the State legislature voted her a pension of $400.

Diagonally south on State 93, set impressively back from the highway, is the *Congregational Church* (1805), a fine old edifice distinguished from the main current of architectural tradition by its recessed portico and independently developed 18th-century detail, free from any admixture of the Greek Revival. This church has in its possession a silver beaker inscribed 'The Gift of Barnstable Church in 1716.'·

Right from Canterbury on State 93, to the *Center Cemetery*, 0.3 *m.*, a small burial plot (L), containing the graves of Moses Cleveland and the town's first settler, Major James Fitch, an influential resident of New London, who migrated into the wilderness with his nine sons and daughters in 1697 and established a trading post which became an important rendezvous for traders, Indians, and civil and military officers. The settlement which grew up about his home was for many years the only one between Norwich and Woodstock. Fitch was 'boss' of the Mohegans; called his Peagscomsuck Farm by the English name of Kent, and really maintained a 'capital of Eastern Connecticut.' The name, Fitch, is still a name to conjure with in the rough, stony, wild country of this area.

Up the slope of a high hill, past *Finnish Hall* (L), the social center of the scattered colony of Finnish immigrants, is an excellent view of the Quinebaug (R). From North Hill, at 1.6 *m.*, is a 40-mile view toward the east and into Rhode Island.

At 2 *m.* is the *Site of the Birthplace of Moses Cleveland*, marked by a wooden sign (R).

Almost anywhere in this area, right and left of the surfaced highway, may be found the ruins, abandoned cellar holes, lilac hedges, and tiger lilies that mark the site of once thrifty manufactories.

West of Canterbury, State 14 winds over steep short hills between poultry farms and scattered dwellings, to the hamlet of CANTERBURY PLAIN, 6.2 *m.*, site of the first settlement of the town in 1690.

At 7.9 *m.* the highway climbs to Mullen Hill, where it crosses through the western edge of the community of WESTMINSTER (Town of Canterbury), a village of scattered farms. At one time, four small foundries were operated here.

On the hilltop is the *Westminster Congregational Church* (1769), one of the oldest ecclesiastical structures still in use in the State. It was rebuilt, with a plain Doric portico about 1840, and is now practically a building of that date.

Passing through an area of dense young timber, the highway descends a steep hill and crosses the Little River at 9.8 *m.*

At 10.7 *m.* is the junction with the *Nipmuck Trail*, an old Indian path which branches off to the right, now maintained by the Connecticut Forest and Park Association as a hiking trail.

SCOTLAND (alt. 240, town pop. 402), 11.3 *m.*, settled in 1700 by Isaac Magoon, a Scotsman, and named for his native land, was organized as a church parish in 1732, but remained a part of Windham until organized as a separate town in 1857. Manufacturing began in 1706 when Josiah Palmer was given a water right on Wolf Pit Brook to 'set up a mill — he, building the same within three years and ditching and damming there as he thinks needful on the Commons, not to damnify particular men's rights.'

The rural placidity of Scotland's rolling hills seems to have been undisturbed since that one eventful evening in 1781 when Rochambeau's army encamped here for the night. Agriculture, dairying, and poultry-raising are still the principal occupations.

Scotland was the birthplace of the Rev. Daniel Waldo, chaplain of the United States Congress (1855-59); and Samuel Waldo (b. 1783), artist and critic.

Left from Scotland on Scotland Station Rd., is the double-chimney *Rev. Ebenezer Devotion House*, 0.2 *m.*, of the post-Revolutionary period, with a recessed door which is typical of this region.

At 3.5 *m.*, east of Scotland Station, is the gambrel-roofed *Edward Waldo House* (L), built in 1715, still in the family's possession and in good condition.

West of Scotland, State 14 crosses Merrick Brook and at 11.5 *m.* passes the *Huntington House*, built in 1700; it was the birthplace of Samuel Huntington (1731-96), a signer of the Declaration of Independence, and Governor of Connecticut from 1786 to 1796. In its heavy stone chimney, steep roof, and deep projecting window frames, it has preserved many of the characteristic features of its period.

At 12.8 *m.* is *Hickory Grove* (R), a roadside park.

Crossing Beaver Brook, the highway ascends a steep hill, at the summit of which, at 13.2 *m.*, stands the *Cary House*, built in 1776. In the house are still preserved the slides which used to hold shutters drawn over the windows for protection against intruders.

At 13.6 *m.*, in an open lot (R), are fourteen *Wells*, dug in 1781 to provide water for Rochambeau's troops during their encampment here.

At 14.3 *m.*, the *Frog Pond* (R) was the scene, in 1758, of Windham's famous Battle of the Frogs. A *Tablet* marks the site of the incident, which has served as the theme of many ballads and stories. According to one version, the inhabitants of Windham were aroused one night in the summer of 1758, during the French and Indian Wars, by a terrific din. Believing that the town was about to be attacked by an army of French and Indians, the men hastily armed themselves and rushed from their homes to defend the settlement. The weird clamor, which seemed to be coming from the eastern hill, steadily increased. Above the shouts and blood-curdling war-whoops, the terrified settlers heard one persistent cry which they finally interpreted as repeated demands for the surrender of their two prominent lawyers — 'Colonel Dyer and Elderkin, too.' All night they stood armed, waiting for the attack. In the morning, scouts discovered thousands of dead frogs in a small pond near-by. A drought had reduced the pond to a narrow rill, and the frogs had engaged in a terrific battle in their efforts to reach the last remaining drops of water.

WINDHAM (alt. 300), 14.7 *m.*, formerly the county seat, is now a quiet settlement of old houses grouped about a village Green.

Facing the Green from the west, the *Webb House*, which was built about 1750, attracts the eye with its high Doric porch, a later addition (about

1790), approached by a long flight of steps. The north ell is probably the original structure. The building has been deeded to the Windham Free Library for preservation.

On the little lanes which run off the Green are some charming old houses. On the Weir estate at the end of the lane (R), nearest the southern end of the Green, is a long low *House* (1710) which, before being altered, was one of the one-story, two-room houses first built by the settlers. On the west side of this lane is the *Higgs House*, built in 1800, with an 18th-century gambrel-roofed house added as an ell.

South of the Green stands the remodeled *David Young House*, built in 1765. Behind this house is a tall, narrow, gambrel-roofed *Hunt Building* of only one room and an attic (1790), used by Dr. Hunt (1789–1869) as a medical office. A Palladian window over the door is framed by two fluted columns reaching from the eaves to the ground. Next door stands an old remodeled *Pre-Revolutionary Inn*, built in 1760. Opposite is an odd *18th-Century Store*, now a dwelling, of one-and-a-half stories, with a deep cornice overhang.

The old brick *Windham Bank Building* (1832), now the *Windham Free Library (open 9–5 weekdays)*, west of the Green, houses a collection of antiques. One of the exhibits is the famous wooden 'Statue of Bacchus,' carved here by British prisoners captured with the British ship 'Bombrig' on Long Island Sound, June, 1776, who were confined in Windham jail. The *Old Jail* itself (about 1725), stands a little distance south on Scotland Rd.

At the junction with State 203 is (R) the conspicuous old *Windham Inn (open)*, a brick structure with a sign bearing the date 1783. It was originally a three-story structure, an ambitious project for a country town.

> Left from Windham on State 203, is the *Old Burial Ground* (R), 0.8 *m.*, which contains the grave of John Cates, the first resident, a man of mysterious origin, who is believed to have been an officer under Oliver Cromwell. One old gravestone bears the letters RSVP, instead of the customary RIP.

At Windham Center, State 14 intersects and joins with State 203. Beyond, on the combined routes, rising to a high ridge which overlooks the city of Willimantic, the highway descends a steep curve along the Natchaug River, and intersects with US 6 (*see Tour 2*) on the outskirts of WILLIMANTIC (*see Tour 2*), at 17.6 *m.*

T O U R   1 0 :   *From* EAST HARTFORD *to* MASSACHUSETTS
LINE (*Worcester*), 40.7 *m.*, State 15.

Via Vernon and Stafford Springs.
Macadamized roadbed.
Limited accommodations.

NORTHEAST from East Hartford this route veers through the tobacco
fields of South Windsor to Talcottville, and beyond Talcottville passes
several villages that were once active textile centers. Little tobacco is
now raised in this area, but sweet potatoes, Irish potatoes, and sweet
corn are profitable crops on the former tobacco soils. The land rolls
slightly and occasional dense woods offer some variety. The highway
continues through the wool manufacturing section around Vernon, and
beyond, passes through the area formerly inhabited by the Nipmuck
Indians.

In this area began the Connecticut venture in sweet potato cultivation.
On old tobacco fields, long since fallowed because the market for leaf
became oversupplied, progressive farmers have planted yellow tubers
from the South, of which the soil now yields as many as 500 bushels an
acre. The quality is good, the soil is free from non-favorable micro-organ-
isms and elements, and the venturesome farmers are given considerable
encouragement by State experiment stations.

At 1.6 *m.* US 5 branches left (*see Tour* 7); this route turns right. Rising
from the plain, at 3.1 *m.* (L), is a *Sand Dune*, with a plume of windblown
sand at its crest. Northward are intensively cultivated farm and tobacco lands.

At 6 *m.* (L) is the long *Shem Stoughton House*, characterized by a steep
peaked roof, which appears today, except for the windows, much as it
did when it was erected in 1782.

At 6.2 *m.* (L) stands the brick *Hardin Stoughton Inn and Store*, a four-
chimneyed relic of stagecoach days, which once was the center of a
community.

At WAPPING (Town of South Windsor), 7 *m.*, a peaceful village, stands
(L) the severely plain *Federated Church*, formerly Congregational, erected
in 1829.

At 9.4 *m.* is the junction with State 83, which combines with this route
for 1.5 miles.

State 15 passes through TALCOTTVILLE (alt. 220), 10.5 *m.*, a textile
manufacturing community in the town of Vernon, where John Brown
of Harper's Ferry fame was once purchasing agent for the woolen mills.
In a wooded hollow, at the curve where the highway crosses a branch of

the Hockanum River, is (L) the *Four Corner Chimney House* (*private*), which has, at the southeast corner, a Dutch oven accessible from both the interior and exterior. This whitewashed brick building was built in 1800 by John Warburton, early textile manufacturer. Mr. Warburton was a generous host and kept a hogshead of Jamaica rum on tap in an open shed by the roadside, offering free drinks to all comers.

At the traffic rotary stands (L) the *Green Circle Inn*; it is a three-story wooden Colonial structure with 16 rooms, erected in 1800 by Smith Talcott.

VERNON (alt. 290), at 11.9 *m.*, formerly North Bolton, was incorporated in 1808 and named for Mt. Vernon. Here, satinet was devised by Peter Dobson and first manufactured by Delano Abbott in 1808.

At VERNON CENTER GREEN (alt. 420), 13.3 *m.* (L), the *Congregational Church* (1826), is unlike any other in the State. Its heavy Ionic portico is crowned by a square tower with bull's eyes in each side of the base. Above a round stage is an extremely thin, tapering spire.

At 15.7 *m.* are the red-brick buildings of the *Vernon Town Farm* (L), formerly the King's Stage House, a tavern of 1820. This building with three end chimneys became famous because of the visit of General Lafayette in 1824. Directly opposite the Town Farm, on the west corner of Grove and South Sts., stands the building once known as the *Waffle Inn* (about 1700), now a residence, formerly known among stage-coach patrons for the excellence of its waffles.

At 17.2 *m.* is the junction with State 74.

Left on State 74 to ROCKVILLE (alt. 450, pop. 7445), 2.4 *m.*, a textile city (inc. 1889) in the Town of Vernon, producing fine wool fabrics and silk fishlines. The U.S. Envelope Company operates a mill here, dating from 1856, where Milton G. Puffer is reported to have perfected a machine that counted, as well as folded, envelopes. In 1802 one of the country's earliest wool carding mills opened here. The original owners of the Rock Mills would not employ a man unless he was a Congregationalist; in each workman's bobbin box was placed a Bible to be read during dull moments.

The business center of the town has a well-paved main street, excellent municipal buildings of red brick, department stores, and business houses.

State 15 continues through a rolling countryside dotted with prosperous farmlands and comfortable homes.

Crystal Spring Rest (R), at 19.8 *m.*, is a State maintained picnic area; near-by is a tract of evergreens.

Crystal Lake, at 22.7 *m.* (R), is a beautiful sheet of water, stretching away to the south, with bathing facilities on the eastern shore, where there is a large summer cottage colony. On the south side, in a large grove of pine and hemlock, another colony is being developed.

Ice fishing is a popular sport here. When the first ice is four or five inches thick, men and boys gather to discuss the prospects of catching perch and pickerel. They assemble their gear, test their lines, spend many hours honing ice chisels to a razor edge and putting new red flannel rags on the 'tip-ups' or 'type.'

The next step is securing a supply of shiners or live bait. A hole is cut in the ice of a pond that is known to be the habitat of the tiny gleaming bait fish, and large dip nets are used. These little fish are delicate and great care must be taken not to injure them before the fishing day.

The fisherfolk then await a day with a 'scud of rain in the air,' a rise in temperature that signals a coming thaw, or a south wind. A 'norther' is sure to be non-productive.

Near dawn, holes about a foot in diameter with fairly smooth edges are cut in the ice. A great reservoir for the fish after they are caught is chiseled out of the ice, with just a tiny hole at one end to let in a water supply. The depth of the pond is plumbed with a lead weight at the end of the line, and a loop is made in the line to keep the bait fish off the bottom. The tiny fish is then attached by slipping a hook through behind the dorsal fin; the little fellow is guided toward the depths so that he swims well down, in a wide radius about the hole. The tip-up is set with the flag down.

After breathless waiting, a red flag bobs up and the fishermen run to that' hole to be sure that the line is free. Playing the fish calls for an entirely different technique than that employed by either bait or fly casters. This job calls for patience and a light sensitive touch on the line. A sudden jerk or a quick haul means a lost fish; the experienced fisherman always seems careful and slow.

At 23.7 m. is the junction with a dirt road.

> Left here through the pines to a portion of the *Shenipsit State Forest*, an area of 3236 acres about *Soapstone Mountain* (alt. 1067). A fire tower at the mountain-top, reached only by foot trails, offers views of Mt. Monadnock in New Hampshire, Mt. Greylock in Massachusetts, and the Sleeping Giant (Mt. Carmel) in Connecticut.

State 15 passes *Square Pond* (R), where fishing is excellent. (*Privately owned, but permission to fish is secured at gasoline station left of State* 15.)

WEST STAFFORD (alt. 640), 24.9 m., is a village that has grown up around several pearl button and turbine factories. At the center stands the simple white *Congregational Church* (L), erected about 1840. East of the church is an 18th-century *Country Store*. The small ell with a summer beam was a stone-walled wine cellar. A later section, built on at right angles at the east end, served as an inn.

> Left from West Stafford on Myron Kemp Rd. to a site, 0.3 m., in the Shenipsit State Forest (*see above*), where evidence of an Extinct Volcano has been found. Staurolite crystals are found here.

At West Stafford is the junction with State 20.

> Left on State 20 at 4.5 m. is SOMERS (alt. 280, town pop. 1917); named, July, 1734; and annexed to Connecticut from Massachusetts. Originally part of Enfield this community was first incorporated as a town by Massachusetts in 1734 and given its name by the founder, one John Somers, a British lord chancellor. Within the bounds of the territory included under the Connecticut Charter, the town joined the secession movement from her parent Colony and was formally accepted by the Connecticut General Assembly in May, 1749.

A main street town, Somers slumbers peacefully beside the road with little or no signs of life, except when the dairy truck calls to collect the milk from the surrounding farms. The eastern portion of the township is poor, rough, rolling land, sometimes rising to heights of nearly 1300 feet. Here the farmer has hard work, but on the western edge of the township are fertile lands where almost any crop can be grown.

The *Old Homestead Inn*, at the center of the village, was built in 1804 and still caters to passing travelers as it did when the first stage-coach from Boston to Hartford stopped here to rest the horses and 'bait' the passengers. The large ballroom was the scene of the celebration of Gideon Granger's appointment as Postmaster General of the United States by Thomas Jefferson.

Eighty young ministers were trained in Somers by the Rev. Chas. Backus, pastor of the church from 1774 to 1803 and conductor of a theological seminary. The village was once a mecca for eloping couples. One justice of the peace in the village performed 100 ceremonies during his term of office, but the new State laws discourage hasty marriages.

At 6.5 *m.* the route passes through the mill village of SOMERSVILLE (Town of Somers), where the plant of the Somersville Manufacturing Company stretches along the highway. Manufacturing fine coatings, this woolen mill has floor space of 250,000 square feet and furnishes employment for several hundred workers.

At 8.2 *m.* is the junction with a dirt road.

Right on this road 2 *m.* is SHAKERS SETTLEMENT, established in 1780 by Joseph Meacham, and now used by the *Osborn State Prison Farm* for the rehabilitation of 'trusty' prisoners.

The Shakers, so called because of their spiritual dances, described as 'the involuntary result of the exhilarating and overpowering delight received through the outpouring of Divine Grace,' believed in a dual God (male and female), and the segregation of men and women. The community here gradually died out and in 1915 the remaining members moved to Pittsfield, Mass., and New Lebanon, N.Y.

Their communistic settlement produced an excellent quality of handicraft articles, and the members were widely respected for their integrity and the honesty of their business dealings, in a day when most merchants drove sharp bargains with impunity. Living in an era when many forests were wastefully burned down in order to clear farmlands, the Shakers were pioneers in the conservation of natural resources. One of their number, Elder Omar Pease, planted the first forest sown in this country in 1866. This society was also the first in this country to package garden seeds, in 1802.

Meacham House, now used as an office by the administrative board of the prison farm, is preserved in its original state, severely plain and neat like all the other buildings. The *Old Meeting-House*, opposite the Meacham House, is also devoid of ornamentation and is a well-preserved relic of Shaker days. On the hill (R), 0.2 *m.*, stands a monolith made from the united gravestones of former members of the society.

From this point are magnificent views of the surrounding countryside stretching across the cultivated fields of the prison farm to the Berkshires in the far distance.

In the immediate foreground the 'trusties' are busily engaged in agricultural pursuits, while the guards amble about, free from the need for the tense watchfulness which prevails about ordinary prisons.

At 9.5 *m.* is the village of HAZARDVILLE, a village crossroads where old mills show signs of past industrial activity.

Left from Hazardville Center, a choice of two dirt roads leads into *Powder Hollow*, 5 *m.*, on the Scantic River, where many attractive drives wind through a district of formerly active powder mills. From 1835 to 1913 these mills supplied quarries throughout the State, usually delivering with horse-drawn carts (which were given more than half of the country roads by other travelers). These powder wagons, painted red, usually driven by men who were crippled from explosions in the mills, were regular visitors to towns where quarrying or mining was carried on. Frequently, their overnight camp was made in the church sheds and nervous old ladies spent the night apprehensively awaiting the crash of a violent explosion followed by the toppling of the church spire against a flame-flecked sky.

At 12.2 *m.* is the junction with US 5 (*see Tour 7*).

At West Stafford State 15 turns sharp right.

At 25.4 *m.* beside the West Stafford schoolhouse, is the junction with a sandy dirt road.

Left on this road, which is in poor condition but passable, to *Diamond Ledge*, 0.5 *m.* Here a vein of crystal quartz runs through a granite ledge on the bank of a picturesque ravine shaded by a fine stand of pine. Along the banks of the rapidly flowing stream, fireplaces and benches for picnic purposes have been provided by the State.

STAFFORD SPRINGS (alt. 600, Stafford Town pop. 5949), 28.6 *m.*, is a textile manufacturing community, producing woolen and cotton goods. It was named for Staffordshire, England, and for the mineral springs that were in the early 19th century the center of a flourishing health resort.

Chartered as a borough in 1873, Strafford Springs is the seat of the town government. The land, set off by the General Assembly in May, 1718, was sold by the colony in 1719 to raise funds for Yale College. The town was settled and incorporated in the same year. Iron ore deposits were discovered soon after the settlement and, in 1734, an iron works was erected.

The Stafford flood of March 28, 1877, is remembered by the oldest inhabitants as a major disaster. A horseman, Edwin C. Pinney, rode ahead of the wall of water warning the residents to flee for their lives. The only two men killed went to their doom in the wreckage of the church where they had sought refuge. Freight cars were lifted from their tracks to the roofs of factories, and the property damage was heavy.

Right on Spring St. is the entrance (R) of *Hyde Park*. Here, at the rear of the library, is the *Iron Spring*, enclosed in a small wooden wellhouse. Close by, in the park, is the *Sulphur Spring* from which the community derived its name. Formerly used by the Indians, these two springs became a resort center after the Revolution, and attracted visitors from many States. Two Presidents came here to drink the waters. Hyde Park, covering 85 acres, offers bathing facilities, baseball and tennis fields, and attractive drives.

The narrow, winding streets of the trading center are lined with red brick mercantile establishments. On a small triangle at the center stands an unusual *Civil War Memorial*, a bronze statue of 'Remembrance,' rather than the customary figure of a Union Soldier in cape and fatigue cap.

At the rear of the railroad station (R) is the *Stafford Springs Hotel*, a four-story gray building, perched on a hilltop, built in anticipation of increasing spa patronage that failed to develop.

At 29 *m.* is the junction with State 19 (East St.)

Left on State 19, which winds over a rolling countryside, past dignified old houses.

STAFFORD (alt. 600), 2.2 *m.*, is a plain little village with many white Colonial buildings and an air of industrial activity blended with pastoral calm. An early industry, the manufacture of woolen goods is still carried on in two local mills.

Left from Stafford, at the post office, on Stafford Hollow Rd. (L), 0.3 *m.*, is the *Phelps House* (about 1760), the oldest dwelling in town, now painted a pea green and topped with a red roof, an unusual color scheme in this land of white houses with green blinds.

State 19 continues northeast of Stafford, past the *Swift River* (L), at 2.3 *m.*, which furnished water-power for near-by woolen mills of the Parks Company and the Swift River Company. At 3.8 *m.* a bridge spans *Furnace Brook*, named for the iron furnace near-by; opened in 1734, it was still in operation during the Revolution. Bog ore was mined here, castings for ironware, cannon and round shot were produced, but the industry died when both the ore and the wood for charcoal were exhausted.

STAFFORDVILLE (alt. 700), at 4.1 *m.*, is a community that has grown up around a pearl-button factory. White Colonial style churches, public buildings and dwellings stand amid the tranquillity of an early 19th-century village, remote from 20th-century progress.

At 29.2 *m.* banks of vari-colored flowers in the greenhouse of the *Stafford Conservatories* attract the eye.

At 29.6 *m.* is the junction with Stafford St.

Left on Stafford St., in an area settled by ancestors of General Ulysses S. Grant, is (L) the flat, hip-roofed *Minor Grant House* (1838), at 1 *m.*, with a delicate fanlight and a Palladian window. Beyond (L), the *Clark Grant House* (1810), of the central-hall type, repeats the same motifs. A small gambrel-roofed building, now altered, was formerly a store operated by the family.

After passing *Towne Grove* (R), 31.6 *m.*, a State picnic ground, State 15 traverses a wild, sparsely settled countryside, used chiefly for forestry conservation purposes.

At 34.9 *m.* is the junction with a dirt road.

Left on this road, up a steep rocky incline, too rough for motor travel, is *Union Tower*, 0.5 *m.*, maintained by the State, at the top of *Mt. Ochepetuck* (alt. 1286). On clear days an excellent view of the country for 200 miles around is obtained from this lookout tower on the highest point of land in the State east of the Connecticut River.

At 35 *m.* is a junction with another dirt road.

Right on this road to *Morey Pond*, 0.4 *m.* Numerous picnic sites are maintained here by the State. Bath houses, swimming and boating facilities are available. Fishing is permitted.

At 35.3 *m.* is the junction with still another dirt road.

Left on this road to a section of the *Nipmuck State Forest*, 2.5 *m.* This area, known by the Indians as Wabbaquasset, meaning 'mat producing country,' was formerly inhabited by the Nipmucks, one of the five great agricultural tribes of the Algonquin nation. Picnic grounds and good trout fishing along the brook can be enjoyed here.

At 35.3 is the *Site of Camp Graves*, a former Civilian Conservation Corps camp with wooden buildings spaced in orderly rows. North of the camp, the highway proceeds over roller-coaster hills, affording wide views of the surrounding country.

At 37 *m.* is the junction with a dirt road.

Left here to another section of the 2755 acre *Nipmuck State Forest.* These four blocks of woodland, scattered over twelve miles of terrain which includes Stickney, Hedgehog, and Snow Hills, are crossed by many nature trails. Here is evidence of cumulative results of twenty years' work in practical forestry, supplemented by the recent program of the Civilian Conservation Corps. Demonstration plots have been laid out, and the Blue Ribbon or best trees are marked with a blue band. Signs give information on forest management, showing how woodland can be intelligently handled to insure a profit.

At 37.2 *m.* is the junction with a dirt road.

Right here to a *Demonstration Forest* of the Yale School of Forestry (*visited by appointment only*).

UNION (alt. 980, town pop. 196), 37.5 *m.*, where lumbering has long been the only industry, is a town with the smallest population of any in the State, and the only town without electrical service. Settled in 1727 as the 'Union Lands,' a combination of East Stafford and State lands, the town was named in 1732 and incorporated in 1734. On a hill beside the highway, at the center, are a tiny, modern library, a mid-nineteenth-century schoolhouse with a Civil War cannon aimed at it, and (L) the *Congregational Church* (1834) with a little Gothic window in the gable end.

At 37.9 *m.* State 15 passes *Tom's Place* (L), a large turkey farm.

Bordered on both sides by giant pines, the highway passes a *State Roadside Park* (L), at 38.1 *m.*, with picnic benches and fireplaces. From this point is an excellent view of the countryside.

State 15 skirts *Mashapaug Pond* (R), 39.3 *m.*, a long body of water covering 800 acres, fringed by a colony of scattered summer cottages, and proceeds to the small village of MASHAPAUG, 40.4 *m.*

Beyond Mashapaug, State 15 crosses the Massachusetts Line, 40.7 *m.*, 28.2 miles south of Worcester.

CHRONOLOGY

1614 Adriaen Block sails from Manhattan Island along present coast line of Connecticut and up Connecticut River as far as Enfield Rapids, trading with the Indians en route. His explorations became basis of Dutch claim to Connecticut.

1632 Edward Winslow, governor of Plymouth, visits Connecticut Valley to investigate Indians' reports of its fertility and possibilities as a trading center.
March 19. Lord Say and Sele, Lord Brooke, and 11 others secure grant from Earl of Warwick to all land west from Narragansett River (now Bay) 'to the South Sea' (Pacific Ocean).
Governor Van Twiller of New Netherland, hearing of Winslow's trip, purchases land at mouth of the Connecticut River from Indians and nails Dutch coat of arms to a tree on the point later called Saybrook by the English.

1633 June 6. The Dutch erect fort and establish trading post on present site of Hartford, purchasing the land from Pequot Indians.
July 12. Representatives of Plymouth propose to Massachusetts Bay Colony that they establish joint trading post on Connecticut River.
John Oldham expedition from Watertown, Mass., explores and trades with Indians along Connecticut River.
Sept. 26. William Holmes and small company of men representing Plymouth Colony sail up Connecticut River and erect fortified house as trading post on site of present town of Windsor.

1634 John Oldham and colonists from Watertown settle Wethersfield.

1635 John Steel and 60 persons from New Town (Cambridge), Mass., settle Hartford in October, followed by Thomas Hooker and his congregation in spring of 1636.
English settlers under John Winthrop, Jr., erect fort at Saybrook.

1636 April 26. First General Court held in Connecticut, at Hartford.

1637 April. Massacre of Wethersfield colonists by Pequot Indians.
War declared on Pequots.
May 11. General Court votes to raise levy of 90 men for Pequot War.
May 26. Capt. John Mason destroys Pequot fort at Mystic.
July 13. Great Swamp Fight ends Pequot War.

1638 April. Theophilus Eaton, Edward Hopkins, the Rev. John Davenport, and about 250 men, women, and children arrive at Quinnipiac (New Haven).
June. Earthquake shakes southern Connecticut.

1639 January 14. Fundamental Orders of Connecticut, 'the first written constitution,' adopted by representatives of Hartford, Windsor, and Wethersfield.
John Haynes elected first governor of colony.

1640 New Haven purchases Southold on Long Island from Indians. In following years additional Long Island purchases are made.
Edward Hopkins elected governor.

1643 May 10. 'The United Colonies of New England' are formed by Colonies of Massachusetts Bay, Plymouth, Connecticut, and New Haven.

1650 Peter Stuyvesant journeys to Hartford to place his claim to Connecticut. Arbitration results in agreement that Connecticut may retain most of Long Island and that western boundary shall not extend more than twenty miles east of Hudson River.

1054 At request of England, Connecticut seizes Dutch trading post and fort at Hartford.

1655 New Haven code of laws revised by Governor Eaton.

1657 John Winthrop, Jr., elected governor.
Shipbuilding begun at Derby, on Housatonic River.

1660 Uncas is besieged by Narragansetts and relieved by Leffingwell.

1662 April 23. Charles II signs charter of Connecticut, fixing boundaries to include strip of land as wide as present State, extending from Narragansett River (now Bay) to 'the South Sea' (Pacific Ocean).

1664 Dec. 13. New Haven, which had lost its entity as a separate colony with signing of Charter, formally joins Connecticut Colony.
Connecticut releases her claim to Long Island to Duke of York in return for canceling his claim to western Connecticut.
Shipbuilding begun at New London.

1666 County governments set up.

1674 Duke of York takes out new charter for New York which includes western Connecticut, disregarding boundaries defined in Connecticut's charter.

1675 July 11. Major Edmund Andros, governor of New York, demands surrender of fort at Saybrook but, as English flag flies from ramparts, dares not fire upon it and departs.

1675–76 King Philip's War.

1679 Roger Wolcott born.

1687 Oct. 31. Sir Edmund Andros, having been appointed Governor-in-Chief of all New England, arrives at Hartford and demands surrender of charter; the document is hidden in Charter Oak.

1689 Feb. 13. William and Mary proclaimed King and Queen of England.
April 18. Andros imprisoned.
June 13. Connecticut resumes government under her charter and re-elects Robert Treat governor.

1700 Inhabitants of Rye and Bedford obliged to submit to jurisdiction of New York, in accordance with terms of 'an agreement' made with Duke of York in 1683.

1701 Collegiate School (later Yale University) founded at Killingworth (now Clinton).

1702 Collegiate School opened at Saybrook.

1703 Jonathan Edwards born at South Windsor.

1708 Adoption of the Saybrook Platform.

1711 Eleazer Wheelock, first president of Dartmouth College, born at Windham.

1717 Collegiate School moved to New Haven and received grant for buildings.
1718 Collegiate School renamed Yale College.
1727 Oct. 27. The great earthquake.
1729 Samuel Seabury, first American Episcopal bishop, born at Groton.
1740 Tinware manufactured at Berlin (first in America).
1744 Beginning of King George's War; Connecticut raises quota of 1100 men.
1745 Louisburg captured; Roger Wolcott of Connecticut second in command of the expedition and leader of Connecticut contingent.
1748 End of King George's War.
1755 The *Connecticut Gazette*, first Connecticut newspaper, printed in New Haven.
1756 Population, 130,612.
1758 Noah Webster, lexicographer, born at West Hartford.
1763 First settlement of Wyoming Valley, Pennsylvania, by Connecticut settlers from Windham County.
1764 The *Connecticut Courant* (now *Hartford Courant*), oldest paper continuously published in the United States, established.
1774 Population, 197,910.
1775 Ticonderoga expedition planned at Hartford and Wethersfield.
Outbreak of Revolutionary War. Connecticut fits out more than 200 privateers, and eventually contributes 31,939 men to Continental forces.
April 20. Israel Putnam, of Pomfret, and militia ordered by Governor Trumbull to join American forces at Boston.
June 17. Battle of Bunker Hill, in which Putnam is ranking officer on field.
May 10. Ethan Allen, a native of Litchfield, captures Fort Ticonderoga.
Aug 30. British raid on Stonington.
Sept.–Dec. Benedict Arnold of Norwich heads American forces in long march through Maine wilderness and disastrous attack on Quebec.
1776 Wyoming settlement named Westmoreland and declared a county of Connecticut.
Sept. 22. Nathan Hale of Coventry executed as spy by British on Long Island.
Connecticut Committee of Safety appoints Seth Harding of Norwich captain of brig 'Defense,' then only ship of Connecticut navy.
1777 British force under General Tryon raids military stores at Danbury.
1778 Wyoming settlement attacked by British and Indian reinforcements.
General Putnam's troops establish winter quarters at Redding, Connecticut's 'Valley Forge.'
1779 July. Tryon's forces raid New Haven, burn Fairfield and Norwalk.
1780 May 19. The 'Dark Day.' Candles are lighted, fowls go to roost, birds are silent, and colonists consider Day of Judgment at hand.
1781 Sept. 6. Benedict Arnold of Norwich leads British attack on New London and Groton, and burns New London.
End of Revolutionary War.
1782 Population, 208,850.
1784 Slavery abolished in Connecticut.
First cities incorporated (New Haven, New London, Hartford, Middletown, and Norwich).

1786 Connecticut cedes her western lands, with exception of Western Reserve, to United States.

1788 First woolen mill in New England established at Hartford.

1790 Newgate, at East Granby copper mine, made a State prison.
Population, 237,946.

1792 First toll-gate turnpike, New London to Norwich, incorporated.
First bank in Connecticut, Union Bank of New London, opened. Union Bank in Hartford opened later in year.

1795 Connecticut Western Reserve lands sold, and proceeds of $1,200,000 devoted to establishment of State School Fund.
First insurance company, Mutual Assurance Company of the City of Norwich, organized.

1799 Amos Bronson Alcott born at Wolcott.

1800 Population, 251,062.
John Brown born at Wolcottville (now Torrington).

1801 First borough, Stonington, incorporated.

1808 Building of Enfield Bridge, first to span Connecticut River.

1810 Population, 261,942.
P. T. Barnum born at Bethel.

1811 Elihu Burritt, 'the Learned Blacksmith,' born at New Britain.
Oldest surviving Hartford insurance company, The Hartford Fire Insurance Company, established.

1812 Harriet Beecher Stowe, author of 'Uncle Tom's Cabin,' born at Litchfield.

1812–14 Second War with Great Britain; 3000 men called into State service.

1813 Henry Ward Beecher, noted clergyman and orator, born at Litchfield.

1818 New State constitution ratified.

1820 Population, 275,248.

1821 Collis P. Huntington, railway empire builder, born at Harwinton.

1823 Washington College (renamed Trinity College in 1845) organized at Hartford.

1825 July 4. Farmington Canal begun.

1826 Boundary dispute between Massachusetts and Connecticut, dating from 1662, finally settled.

1828 Canal built around Enfield rapids in Connecticut River. Farmington Canal opened.

1830 Population, 297,675.
First industrial union in this country, 'The New England Association of Farmers, Mechanics, and other workingmen,' organized at Lyme.

1831 Wesleyan University, Middletown, organized.

1832 Connecticut's first railroad, the Boston, Norwich, and Worcester, incorporated.

1833 Hartford and New Haven Railroad incorporated.

1837 Train run on first railroad to operate in Connecticut, between Stonington and Providence, R.I.
John Pierpont Morgan, financier, born at Hartford.
Laurenus Clark Seelye, first president of Smith College, born at Bethel.

1840 Population, 309,978.
1844 New York and New Haven Railroad chartered.
1848 Dec. 29. First railroad cars run from New York to New Haven.
1849 Teachers' College of Connecticut established at New Britain.
1850 Population, 370,792.
      William H. Welch, eminent pathologist, born at Norfolk.
1860 Population, 460,147.
1861–65 Civil War. State furnishes 30 regiments and 3 batteries, total of
      57,379 men; sustained 20,000 casualties.
1870 Population, 537,454.
1871 Samuel L. Clemens (Mark Twain) makes Hartford his home.
1872 New York, New Haven and Hartford Railroad organized, by consolida-
      tion of Hartford and New Haven, and New York and New Haven Rail-
      roads.
1878 Jan. 28. First commercial telephone exchange in world established in
      New Haven.
      First local assembly of Knights of Labor organized at New Britain.
      Aug. 9. Wallingford hurricane.
1880 Population, 622,700.
1881 Connecticut State College organized at Storrs.
1882 National organization of Knights of Columbus founded at New Haven.
1887 State Federation of Labor organized at Hartford.
1888 March 12–14. Great blizzard.
1890 Population, 746,258.
1900 Population, 908,420.
1910 Population, 1,114,756.
      Coast Guard Academy moved to New London from Arundel Cove, Md.
1915 Connecticut College for Women opened at New London.
      Supreme Court decision in famous 'Danbury Hatters' case.'
1916 German submarine 'Deutschland' docks at New London.
1917 United States Submarine Base established at Groton.
      United States enters World War. State becomes munitions supply
      center, and contributes 60,000 men.
1920 Population, 1,380,631.
1930 Population, 1,606,903.
1933 Bridgeport elects Socialist Mayor and Aldermanic Board, first in State.
1934 Feb. 19–20. Disastrous blizzard.
1935 Tercentenary Celebration throughout State.
1936 March 18–25. Disastrous floods.
1937 Merit system inaugurated in State departments. Flood control compact
      signed with other New England States.

SELECTED READING LIST

(The titles followed by asterisks are pamphlets in the series published by the Yale University Press in commemoration of the New Haven, Connecticut, Tercentenary of 1935.)

GENERAL HISTORY

Barber, John Warner. *Connecticut Historical Collections.* New Haven, 1836.

Clark, George L. *History of Connecticut, Its People and Institutions.* New York, 1914.

Crofut, Florence S. M. *Guide to the History and Historic Sites of Connecticut,* 1937.

Johnston, Alexander. *Connecticut: A Study of a Commonwealth-Democracy.* New edition. Boston, 1903.

Mills, Lewis Sprague. *The Story of Connecticut.* New York, 1932.

Morgan, Forrest, editor. *Connecticut as a Colony and as a State.* In 4 volumes. Hartford, 1904.

Osborn, Norris Galpin, editor. *History of Connecticut in Monographic Form.* In 5 volumes. New York, 1925.

Sanford, Elias B. *A History of Connecticut.* Revised edition. Hartford, 1922.

PERIOD HISTORY

Andrews, Charles McLean. *The Beginnings of Connecticut, 1632-1662.** New Haven, 1934.

Middlebrook, Louis Frank. *History of Maritime Connecticut during the American Revolution, 1775-1783.* In 2 volumes. Salem, Mass., 1925.

Morse, Jarvis M. *A Neglected Period of Connecticut History: 1818-50.* New Haven, 1933.

Peck, Epaphroditus. *The Loyalists of Connecticut.** New Haven, 1934.

Perry, C. E., editor. *Founders and Leaders of Connecticut, 1633-1783.* Boston, 1934.

Peters, Rev. Samuel Andrew. *General History of Connecticut.* (First published in London in 1781.) New York, 1877. (Excellent but biased social history of Connecticut prior to the Revolution, written by a Tory malcontent.)

Purcell, Richard Joseph. *Connecticut in Transition, 1775-1818.* Washington, 1918.

Rosenberry, Lois K. M. *Migrations from Connecticut Prior to 1800.** New Haven, 1934.

Rosenberry, Lois K. M. *Migrations from Connecticut after 1800.** New Haven, 1934.

Trumbull, Rev. Benjamin. *A Complete History of Connecticut, Civil and Ecclesiastical, from 1630-1764.* In 2 volumes. New Haven, 1818. (Written to refute some of Peters's conclusions on early Connecticut history.)

SECTIONAL HISTORY

Andrews, Charles M. *The Rise and Fall of the New Haven Colony.** New Haven, 1936.

Barber, John Warner. *History and Antiquities of New Haven.* New Haven, 1831.

Calder, Isabel MacBeath. *The New Haven Colony.* New Haven, 1934.

Deming, Dorothy. *Settlement of Connecticut Towns.** New Haven, 1933.

Harwood, Pliny Leroy. *History of Eastern Connecticut, Embracing the Counties of Tolland, Windham, Middlesex, and New London.* In 3 volumes. Chicago and New Haven, 1931–32.

CONSTITUTIONAL HISTORY

Bates, Albert Carlos. *The Charter of Connecticut.* Hartford, 1932.

Bronson, Henry. *Chapters on the Early Government of Connecticut: with Critical and Explanatory Remarks on the Constitution of 1639.* New Haven, 1888.

Trumbull, J. Hammond. *Historical Notes on the Constitutions of Connecticut, 1639–1818.* Hartford, 1873. (Deals particularly with the origin and progress of the movement which resulted in the convention of 1818.)

SOCIAL HISTORY

Abbott, Katharine M. *Old Paths and Legends of the New England Border.* New York, 1907.

Bessie; or, Reminiscences of a Daughter of a New England Clergyman of the 18th Century. Simple Facts, Simply Told, by a Grandmother. New Haven, 1861.

Breckenridge, Frances A. *Recollections of a New England Town.* Meriden, 1899.

Child, Frank Samuel. *The Colonial Parson of New England.* New York, 1896.

Crawford, Mary Caroline. *Social Life in Old New England.* Boston, 1914.

Earle, Alice Morse. *Customs and Fashions in Old New England.* New York, 1893.

Goodrich, S. G. *Recollections of a Lifetime; or, Men and Things I Have Seen.* In 2 volumes. New York, 1856.

Ives, Franklin Titus. *Yankee Jumbles; or, Chimney Corner Tales of 19th Century Events, Comprising Subjects of Fact, Fun, and Fiction.* New York, 1903.

Shelton, Jane DeForest. *The Salt-Box House: Eighteenth Century Life in a New England Hill Town* (Derby, Conn.). New York, 1929.

Sigourney, Lydia Howard. *Sketch of Connecticut Forty Years Since.* Hartford, 1824.

Todd, Charles Burr. *In Olde Connecticut: Being a Record of Quaint, Curious and Romantic Happenings There in Colonial Times and Later.* New York, 1906.

INDUSTRY AND COMMERCE

Day, Clive. *The Rise of Manufacturing in Connecticut.** New Haven, 1935.

Fuller, Grace Pierpont. *An Introduction to the History of Connecticut as a Manufacturing State.* Northampton, Mass., 1915.

Hooker, Roland Mather. *The Colonial Trade of Connecticut.** New Haven, 1936.

Lathrop, William Gilbert. *The Development of the Brass Industry in Connecticut.** New Haven, 1936.

Parsons, Francis. *A History of Banking in Connecticut.** New Haven, 1935.
Weeden, William Babcock. *Economic and Social History of New England, 1620–1789.* In 2 volumes. Boston, 1891.

RELIGION

Barber, John Warner. *New England Scenes; or, A Selection of Important and Interesting Events Which Have Taken Place since the First Settlement of New England: Principally of a Religious Nature.* New Haven, 1833.
Beardsley, Eben Edwards. *The History of the Episcopal Church in Connecticut.* In 2 volumes. New York, 1866–88.
Duggan, Thomas Stephen. *The Catholic Church in Connecticut.* New York, 1930.
Jarvis, Lucy C., editor. *Sketches of Church Life in Connecticut.* New Haven, 1902. (Early beginnings of the Protestant Episcopal Church.)
Mitchell, Mary H. *The Great Awakening and Other Revivals in the Religious Life of Connecticut.** New Haven, 1934.

THE INDIANS

DeForest, John William. *History of the Indians of Connecticut from the Earlier and Known Period to 1850.* Hartford, 1853. (Best account of the Indians of Connecticut.)
Speck, Frank G. *Notes on the Mohegan and Niantic Indians.* New York, 1909.

GEOLOGY AND NATURAL RESOURCES

Cook, Thomas A. *Geology of Connecticut.* Hartford, 1933.
Longwell, Chester Ray, and Dana, Edward S. *Walks and Rides in Central Connecticut and Massachusetts.* New Haven, 1932.

FAUNA

Goodwin, George Gilbert. *The Mammals of Connecticut.* Hartford, 1935.
Sage, John Hall; Bishop, Louis Bennett; and Bliss, Walter Parks. *The Birds of Connecticut.* Hartford, 1913.

AGRICULTURE

Davis, I. G., and Hendrickson, C. I. *A Description of Connecticut Agriculture.* Storrs, 1924.
Jenkins, E. H. *A History of Connecticut Agriculture.* New Haven, 1926.
Olson, Albert Laverne. *Agricultural Economy and the Population in Eighteenth Century Connecticut.** New Haven, 1935.
Ramsay, Elizabeth. *History of Tobacco Production in the Connecticut Valley.* Northampton, Mass., 1930.

THE NEGRO

Weld, Ralph Foster. *Slavery in Connecticut.** New Haven, 1935.

ARCHITECTURE

Isham, Norman Morrison. *Early Connecticut Houses: A Historical and Architectural Study.* Providence, R.I., 1900.

Kelly, J. F. *Early Domestic Architecture of Connecticut.* New Haven, 1924.
Porter, Noah. *The New England Meeting House.** New Haven, 1933.
Trowbridge, B. C. *Old Houses of Connecticut.* New Haven, 1923.

CRAFTS

Curtis, George Munson. *Early Silver of Connecticut and Its Makers.* Meriden, 1913.
Hoopes, Penrose R. *Connecticut Clockmakers of the 18th Century.* New York, 1930.
Tercentenary Commission. *Three Centuries of Connecticut Furniture, 1635–1935.* Hartford, 1935.

COLLEGES AND UNIVERSITIES

Deming, Clarence. *Yale Yesterdays.* New Haven, 1915.
Fisher, Samuel Herbert. *The Litchfield Law School, 1775–1833.* New Haven, 1933.
French, Robert Dudley. *The Memorial Quadrangle: A Book about Yale.* New Haven, 1929.
Oviatt, Edwin. *The Beginnings of Yale (1701–1726).* New Haven, 1916.
Price, Carl Fowler. *Wesleyan's First Century.* Middletown, 1932.

GENERAL INDEX

For Old and Historic Houses in Connecticut see Index of Old and Historic Houses

Avery House (Old Lyme), 286
Avery Memorial Art Museum (Hartford) (see Museums)
Aviation, 53 (see also Airports)
Avon, 495–96
Avon Old Farms (Avon), 495

Bachus, Isaac, Rev., 104
Backus, Charles, Rev., 552
Backus, Elijah, 273
Bacon Academy (Colchester), 77, 445
Baer Art School (West Cornwall), 456
Bailey, Anna Warner, 158
Balanced Rock (Columbia), 412
Baldwin, Abraham, 160, 334
Balf Quarries (Newington), 514
Bank Building (Litchfield), 197
Bantam, 194, 467
Baptists (see Religion)
Barber, John Warner, 97–98
Barkhamsted, 425–26
Barkhamsted Lighthouse (Barkhamsted), 425–26
Barlow, Joel, 105, 139, 450
Barn dances, 373
Barn Door Hills, 488
Barnard, Henry, 220
Barnum Institute of Science and History (Bridgeport), 125–26
Barnum, Phineas T., 121, 124, 125–26; birthplace of (Bethel), 375; statue of (Bridgeport), 127
Barnum Place (Bethel), 375
Bartlett, Paul Wayland, 98
Bartlett Tower (Simsbury), 500
Barytes Mine (Cheshire), 490
Bassett House (New Haven), 489
Batchelder, Evelyn Beatrice Longman, Mrs., studio of (Windsor), 323
Battell, Joseph, 423
Battell Memorial (Norfolk), 424
'Battle of the Frogs,' 392, 547
Beach Tavern (Cheshire), 491
Beaches
Compo, 349; Crescent, 364; Fairfield, 144; Grove, 343; Momauguin, 338; Ocean, 264; Rocky Neck State Park, 363; Roton Point, 348; Short, 338
Beacon Falls, 478
Beacon Hill, 355
Beacon Valley Fair Grounds, 355
Beaumont, William, Dr., 413–14; memorial to (Lebanon), 413
'Beckwith Almanac,' 104
Beckwith House (East Lyme), 345
Bedford, E. T., estate of (Westport), 349
Bedford High School (Westport), 333
Bedlam Corner, 392
Bedrock (see Geology)
Beecher, Henry Ward, 108, 198
Beecher Homestead, site of (Litchfield), 198
Beecher House (Bethany), 354–55
Beecher, Lyman, 108, 198
Beehive, the (Essex), 519
Belcher, Jonathan, Gov., 394
Belcher, Samuel, 284
Bellamy, Joseph, Rev., 384
Ben Sherman Hill (Woodbury), 398
Benét, Stephen Vincent, 110

Berkeley Divinity School (New Haven), 79
Berlin, 504–05
Berlin State Fish Hatchery, 516
Bethany, 354–55
Bethel, 374–75
Bethel Rock (Woodbury), 384
Bethlehem, 384
Bible Rock (Haddam), 523
Bigelow-Sanford Carpet Mill (Windsor Locks), 528
Bill, Henry, Tavern of (Ledyard), 367
Bill Hill, 361
Birchbank Highway Rest (Chaplin), 393
Bird Life, 15–16 (see also Animal Life)
'Birds of Killingworth, The' (poem), 357
Birdsey House (Meriden), 202
Bishop, James, 385
Bissell, Daniel, Sergeant, 320
Bissell's Ferry, 527
Black Hall (see Old Lyme)
'Black Law' of 1833, 545
Blackstone Rocks (Branford), 339
Blackwell, John, Capt., 394, 437
Blackwell's Brook Mills (Brooklyn), 394
Blake, Eli Whitney, 49, 235
Blake, William Phipps, home of (Hamden), 489
Block, Adriaen, 319
Bloomfield, 500–01
'Blue Laws,' 28
Bolles Wood (New London), 261
Bolton Center, 430
Bolton Pines Highway Rest (Bolton), 430
Boney, Perry, 460; store of (Sherman), 460
Borden's Condensed Milk Factory, site of (Torrington), 482
Bosworth Castle (Eastford Center), 434
'Bourbon' (ship), 56
Bourglay, Jules, 480
Bowen, Henry C., 435
Boxwood (Greenwich), 330
Boxwood Manor (Old Lyme), 285
Boy of Mount Righi (book), 421
Brainard Collection (Hartford) (see Avery Memorial Art Museum)
Brainard, John G. C., 107
Brainerd, Shaler and Hall Quarries (Portland), 401–02
Branch, Anna Hempstead, 109
Branchville, 450–51
Branchville Quarry (Branchville), 451
Brand, Christopher C., 273
Branford, 339–40
Branford Academy (Branford), 339
Branford Green (Branford), 339
Brass industry (see Industry)
Brewer Tobacco Plantation (East Hartford), 440
Brewster, Jonathan, 155–56
Bride's Brook, 363
Bridge Farms (Washington), 411
Bridgeport, 119–31, 335
Bridgeport Brass Company (Bridgeport), 129–30
Bridgeport City Hall (Bridgeport), 125
Bridgeport Farmer (newspaper), 125
Bridgewater, 463, 465
Bristol, 386
Bristol Nursery Company (Bristol), 386
Britannia ware, 201

Broad Street Green (Wethersfield), 313
Broad Street Memorial Boulevard (Meriden), 202
Brockway's Corners, 358
Brookfield, 452
Brookfield Center, 465–66
Brooklyn, 394–96
Brooklyn Town Hall (Brooklyn), 395
Brooks, Jonathan, 159
Brooksvale, 490
Brown, John, birthplace site (Goshen), 470
Brownell, Henry Howard, 107
Brownie Castle (Ansonia), 476
Bruce Museum (see Museums)
Brush Arbor Ceremony, 530
Bryant Electric Company (Bridgeport), 130
Buck Place, Titus (Wethersfield), 316
Buckingham, 443–44
Buckingham Memorial (Norwich), 274–75
Buckingham, William A., 274–75
Buddington, James M., Capt., 156
Buell, Abel, 357
Bulfinch, Charles, 184
Bulkeley Memorial Bridge (Hartford), 190
Bulkeley, Morgan G., 190
Bulkley, John, Rev., 445
Bull, Marcus, 172
Bull, Thomas, Capt., 289
Bullard Company, (Bridgeport), 131
Bullard, E. P., 131
Bullet Hill School House (Southbury), 381
Bull's Bridge, 454
Bunce, William Gedney, 100
Burial Grounds — Indian
   Barkhamsted, 426; Farmington, 148; Mansfield Center, 432; Mohegan, 531; Norwich, 278; South Windsor, 508; Southbury, 377; Wethersfield, 312
Burial Grounds — White
   Ansonia, Episcopal, 476; Bloomfield, Wintonbury, 500; Bridgeport, Mountain Grove, 124; Canterbury, Center, 546; Colchester, Old, 445; Danbury, Old Town, 136, Wooster, 133; East Hampton, Town, 405; Union Hill, 403; East Hartford, Center, 506; EastHartland,488; Fairfield, Old, 142, Old Greenfield, 334; Farmington, Old, 148, Riverside, 148; Glastonbury, Oldest, 441; Hampton, 394; Hartford, Oldest, 181; Lebanon, Liberty Hill, 413, Old, 416; Manchester, 429; Mansfield Center, 432; Middletown, Riverside, 210; Milford, Old, 215; Milldale, South End, 492; New Britain, Fairview, 220; New Haven, Grove St., 237–38; New London, Gardiner's, 264; Norwich, Old, 281, Post Gager, 282–83; Old Lyme, Duck River, 285; Old Saybrook, Cypress, 291–92; Putnam, Old Cemetery, 535; South Canaan, Lower, 457; South Coventry, Nathan Hale, 390; Stratford, Oldest Episcopal, 335; Wethersfield, 312; Wilton, Sharps Hill, 450; Windham, Old, 548; Windsor, Palisado, 324; Woodstock Hill, 435
Burial Mound (Greenwich), 330
Buried Treasure (see Folklore)
Burlington, 485
Burnap, Daniel, 59–60, 391
Burr, Aaron, 142, 194

Burr House, site of (Redding), 450
Burritt, Elihu, 221
Burrows, Ambrose H., Capt., 156
Burrville, 482
Bus Lines, xxv, 53
Bushnell, Cornelius Scranton, 341; monument to (New Haven), 251
Bushnell, David, 60, 343–44, 517; house of (Westbrook), 343–44
Bushnell, Horace, Dr., 178, 179
Bushnell Memorial Hall (Hartford), 179–80
Bushnell Park (see Parks)
Buttery Sawmill (Norwalk), 449
By the Brook (picnic area), 359

Caledonia Insurance Company Building (Hartford), 186
Calf Pasture Point (Norwalk), 269, 348
Camp Graves, site of (Union), 555
Camp Hood (New Fairfield), 459
Camp Roosevelt (Killingworth), 356–57
Campbell, William, monument to (Orange), 337
Campville, 481
Canaan, 456–58
Canals, 52
Cannondale, 450
Canonchet, 299
Canterbury, 545–46
Canterbury Plain, 546
Canton, 426–27
Canton Center, 426
Canton Public Golf Course (Canton), 427
'Cape Cod' cottages, 83
Capitol Dome (see State Capitol)
Cargill Falls (Putnam), 535
Carmel Hill (Woodbury), 409
Carter, Joseph, 406
Carver, Jonathan, 545
Cathole Pass, 516
Cattle and sheep raising (see Industry)
Cedar Hammock Island, 269
Cedar Hill Yards (New Haven), 501–02
Cedarcrest (Newington Center), 515
Cedarland (South Britain), 379
Cemeteries (see Burial Grounds)
Center Groton, 368
Centerville, 490
Central Village, 533
Chaffee School (see Loomis Institute)
Champion, Henry, Col., 445–46
Chandler, Joshua, Jr., birthplace of (West Woodstock), 434
Chanicsville, 536
Chapel of the Perfect Friendship (see Trinity College Chapel)
Chaplin, 392–93
Chapman House (Moodus), 404
Chapman's Falls (East Haddam), 359
'Charter Oak,' 170
Charter Oak Memorial (Hartford), 181
Chase Brass and Copper Company Office Building (Waterbury), 308
Chase Metal Works (Waterville), 479
Chelsea Parade (Norwich), 277
Cheney, Benjamin, 59
Cheney Brothers Plant (Manchester), 429
Cherry Brook, 426
Cheshire, 491
Cheshire Academy (Cheshire), 77, 491

INDEX OF OLD AND HISTORIC HOUSES

Old Brookfield Inn (Danbury), 136
Old Curiosity Shop (1781) (Litchfield), 197
Old Farms Inn (1757) (Farmington), 495
Old General Store (1737) (Noroton), 332
Old Homestead Inn (1804) (Somers), 552
Old Inn (c. 1750) (Columbia), 408
Old Jail (c. 1725) (Windham), 548
Old Meeting House (Shakers Settlement, Somers), 552
Old Powder House (1775) (New London), 264
Old Red School House (1700?) (Norwalk), 267
Old Saybrook Inn (1800) (Old Saybrook), 290
Old State House (1796) (Hartford), 184
Old Stone Customhouse (1823) (Stonington), 302
Old Stone House (1767) (New Haven), 337
Old Stone House (1765) (Sharon), 418
Old Stone Store (c. 1809) (Chester), 520
Old Store (1765) (Southport), 352
Old Town Mill (1650, 1742) (New London), 257–60
Oldest Brick Building (Preston), 360
Oldgate (see Cowles House, Samuel)
Osage Inn (Essex), 518
Osgood House (1780, 1812) (New Britain), 221
Overlock House (Pomfret), 438

Palmer House, Amos (1787) (Stonington), 302
Palmer House, Dudley (1765) (Stonington), 300
Palmer House, Gershom (1720) (Stonington), 370
Palmer Tavern (1700–50? 1775) (Warrenville), 433
Parker House (Newtown), 375
Parley House (1777) (Southbury), 381
Parmalee House (1752) (Killingworth), 357
Parsonage (c. 1800) (Easton Center), 353
Parsonage (c. 1740) (Kent), 455
Parsons House (1770) (Wallingford), 503
Payne House (1815) (Canterbury), 545
Pease House (1817) (Middletown), 209
Peck Homestead (1703) (Old Greenwich), 331
Peck Tavern (c. 1675) (Old Lyme), 286
Pennoyer's Brick House (1757) (Sharon), 419
Percival Home (1789) (Kensington), 515–16
Perkins House (1760) (Griswold), 532
Perrin House (1766) (Pomfret), 438
Perry Houses (1845, 1850) (Southport), 352
Pettibone Tavern (1801) (Weatogue), 496
Pettibone Tavern, Giles (1794) (Norfolk), 424
Phelps House (c. 1760) (Stafford), 554
Phelps House, Elisha (1771) (Simsbury), 497
Phelps Tavern (1787) (Litchfield), 197
Pierpont House (1767) (New Haven), 234–35
Pitkin House (1740) (East Hartford), 439
Pixlee Tavern (1700) (Bridgeport), 121
Plumb House (c. 1733) (Meriden), 204
Plummer House (1760) (Glastonbury), 441
Pomeroy House (1757) (Greenfield Hill), 334
Pomeroy Tavern (1806) (Coventry), 430
Pope House (Middlebury), 398
Porter Home, Noah (1826) (New Haven), 237
Porter House, Noah, Rev. (1808) (Farmington), 148
Porter Tavern (1765) (Union City), 479
Pratt House (c. 1836) (South Glastonbury), 442

Pratt Smithy (1678) (Essex), 518
Pratt Tavern (1785) (Old Saybrook), 290
Pre-Revolutionary Inn (1760) (Windham), 548
President's House (1835) (South Windsor), 509
President's House of Yale University (New Haven), 237
Punderson Homestead (1787) (New Haven), 250
Putnam Cottage (1731) (Greenwich), 152
Putnam Elms (1750, c. 1782, c. 1900) (Brooklyn), 396
Putnam House (1825) (Sterling), 543
Putnam House, Israel (1765) (Brooklyn), 395

Quincy Memorial (1904) (Litchfield), 198
Quintard House (c. 1700) (Greenwich), 331

'Records Building' (1796) (Roxbury), 464
Red Cottage (1728) (Salem), 446
Red House (1770) (Lyme), 362
Red House (Washington), 410
Red Lion Inn (1760) (North Hartland), 487
Redwoods (1704) (Lebanon), 415
Reed Home (1750) (South Windsor), 506
Reeve House (1773) (Litchfield), 199
Reynolds House (1659) (Norwich), 278
Richards House (1737) (Norwich), 281–82
Richmond House (1828) (Westford), 433
Ripley House (1792) (Coventry), 389
Rising Sun Tavern (c. 1760) (North Haven), 512
Risley House (c. 1693) (East Hartford), 440
Riverton Inn (1800) (Riverton), 486
Robbins Tavern (Voluntown), 360
Rockwell House, Alfred (1814) (Norwich), 276
Rockwell House, Solomon (1813) (Winsted), 425
Root House, Jesse (1736) (Coventry), 389
Root Salt-Box House, Hannah (1712) (Kensington), 516
Root Tavern, Jonathan (1720?) (Southington), 493
'Roseland' (Woodstock), 435
Ross Homestead (1786) (Chaplin), 392
Rowland House (c. 1769) (Fairfield), 142–43
Royce House (1672) (Wallingford), 503
Russell House (1828) (Middletown), 206–08
Russell House, William (1753) (Windsor), 80–81, 325

Sabbath Day House (1730) (Guilford), 165
Sachem's Wood (1829) (New Haven), 237
Sanford House (1753) (Georgetown), 450
Schoolhouse (Columbia), 408
Schoolhouse (1760) (Lyme), 362
Scoville Library (1894) (Salisbury), 420
Session's Tavern (1820) (Woodstock), 434
Settlers Village (1935) (Waterbury), 308–10
Seven Hearths (1756) (Kent), 455
1711 Inn (Meriden), 504
Seymour Salt-Box House (c. 1715–20) (Coventry), 390
Shaw Mansion (1756) (New London), 263
Sheffield House (Southport), 352
Sheffield House, Amos (c. 1783) (Stonington), 303–04
Sheldon's Tavern (1760) (Litchfield), 198
Shelley House (1730) (Madison), 341